I0885711

A Bag Worth a Pony

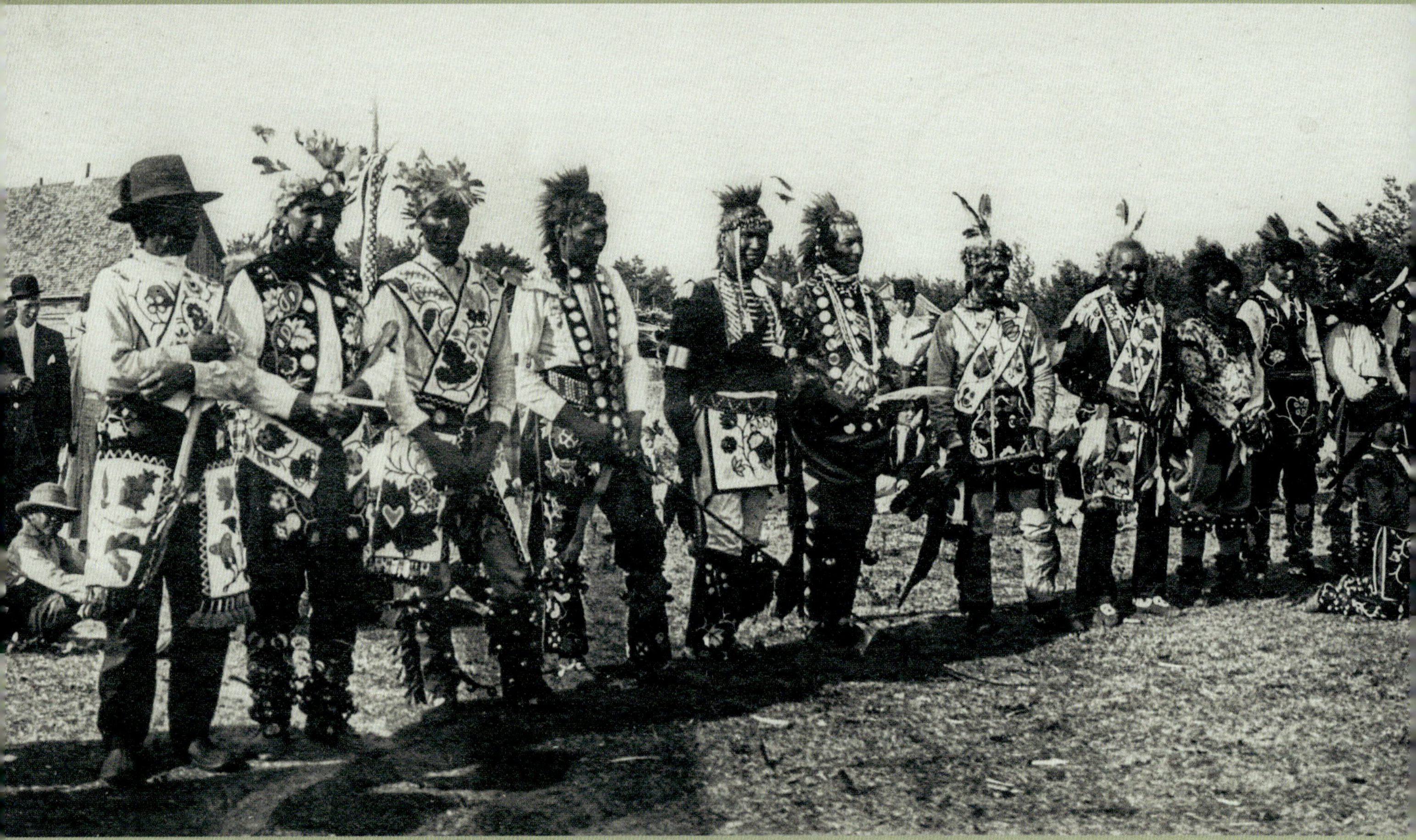

MINNESOTA
HISTORICAL
SOCIETY PRESS

A Bag Worth a Pony

The Art of the Ojibwe Bandolier Bag

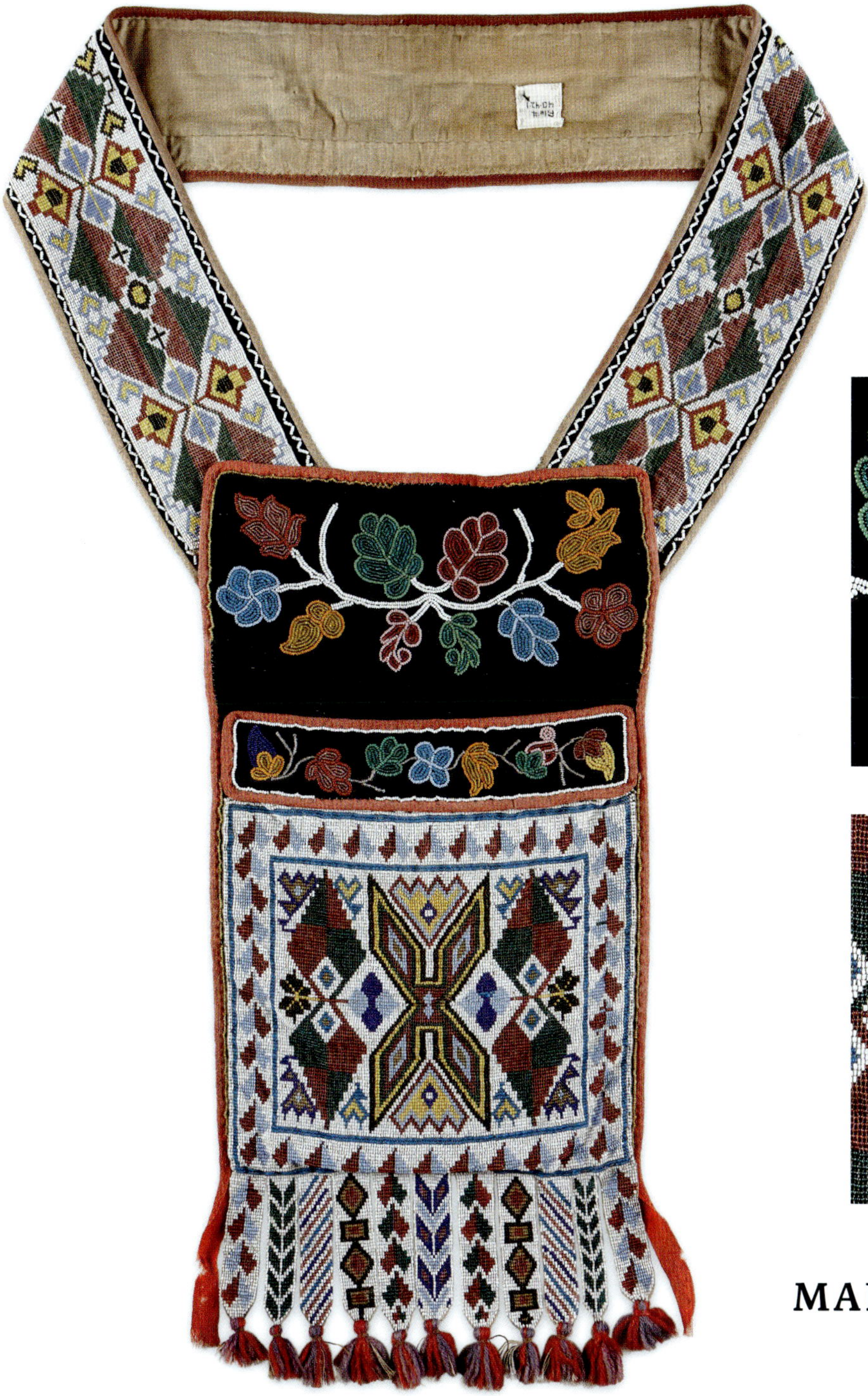

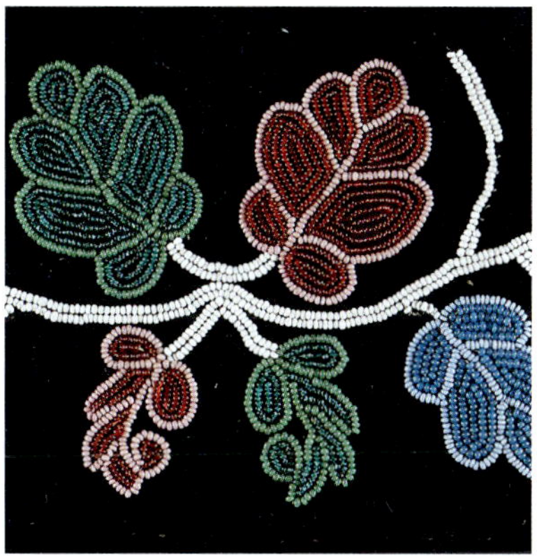

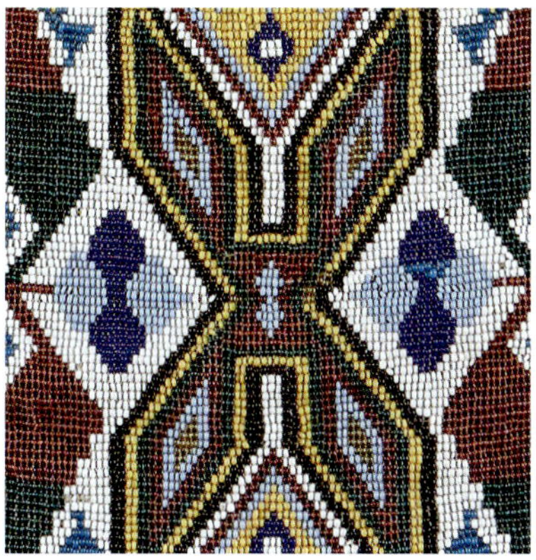

MARCIA G. ANDERSON

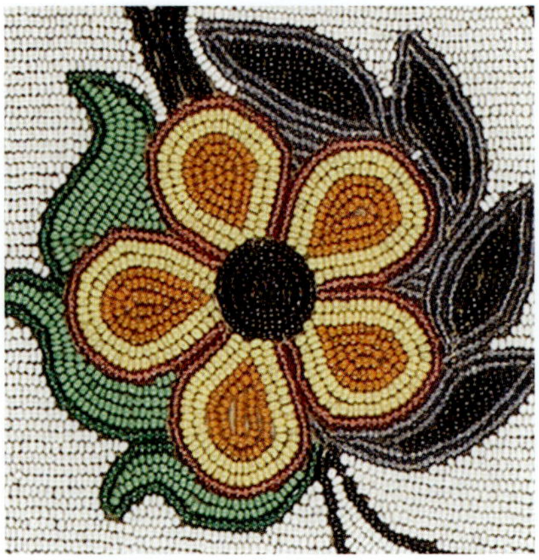

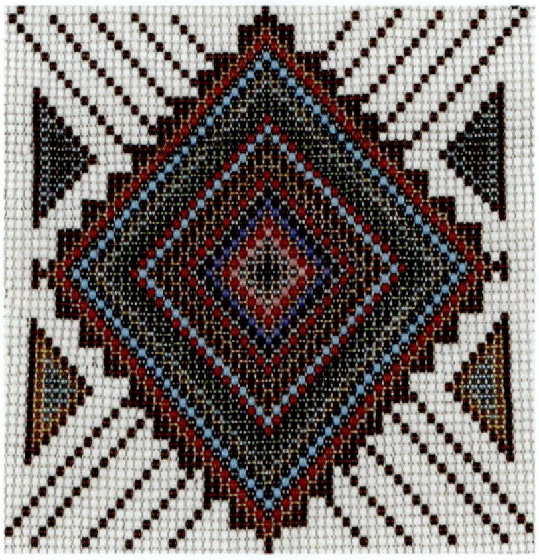

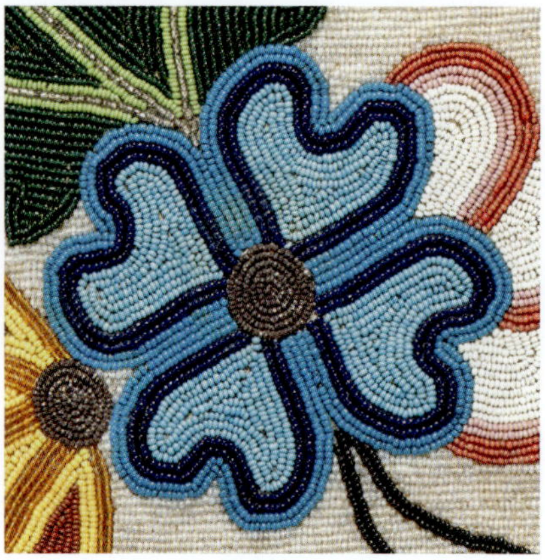

The publication of this book was supported, in part, by generous contributions from Annette Atkins and Tom Joyce and from Debbie Miller and BJ Lovegren. Additional funding was provided by Minnesota's Arts and Cultural Heritage Fund, created through the vote of Minnesotans on November 4, 2008. The author's research was supported by the Ken and Nina Rothchild Fund for Business History and Women's History and the Charles E. Flandrau Research Fund, both at the Minnesota Historical Society, as well as by a Minnesota Humanities Center Works in Progress Grant.

CLEAN WATER LAND & LEGACY AMENDMENT

Text copyright © 2017 by Marcia G. Anderson. Other materials copyright © 2017 by the Minnesota Historical Society. All rights reserved. No part of this book may be used or reproduced in any manner whatsoever without written permission except in the case of brief quotations embodied in critical articles and reviews. For information, write to the Minnesota Historical Society Press, 345 Kellogg Blvd. West, St. Paul, MN 55102-1906.

"Mary Remembering, on a July Afternoon," p. 100, was published in *The Sky Watched: Poems of Ojibwe Lives* (Santa Fe, NM: Red Mountain Press, 2016). Copyright © 2016 by Linda LeGarde Grover. Used with permission.

"Anishinaabe Beadwork," p. 122–26, copyright © 2000 by Marcie McIntyre. Used with permission.

www.mnhspress.org

The Minnesota Historical Society Press is a member of the Association of American University Presses.

Manufactured in the United States of America

10 9 8 7 6 5 4 3

♾ The paper used in this publication meets the minimum requirements of the American National Standard for Information Sciences—Permanence for Printed Library Materials, ANSI Z39.48-1984.

International Standard Book Number
ISBN: 978-1-68134-029-6 (paper)

Library of Congress Cataloging-in-Publication Data

Names: Anderson, Marcia G. (Marcia Gail), 1949– author.
Title: A bag worth a pony : the art of the Ojibwe bandolier bag / Marcia G. Anderson.
Other titles: Art of the Ojibwe bandolier bag
Description: Saint Paul, MN : Minnesota Historical Society Press, [2017] | Includes bibliographical references and index.
Identifiers: LCCN 2016047354 | ISBN 9781681340296 (pbk. : alk. paper)
Subjects: LCSH: Ojibwa Indians—Material culture. | Bandolier bags. | Indian beadwork.
Classification: LCC E99.C6 A446 2017 | DDC 977.004/97333—dc23
LC record available at https://lccn.loc.gov/2016047354

Contents

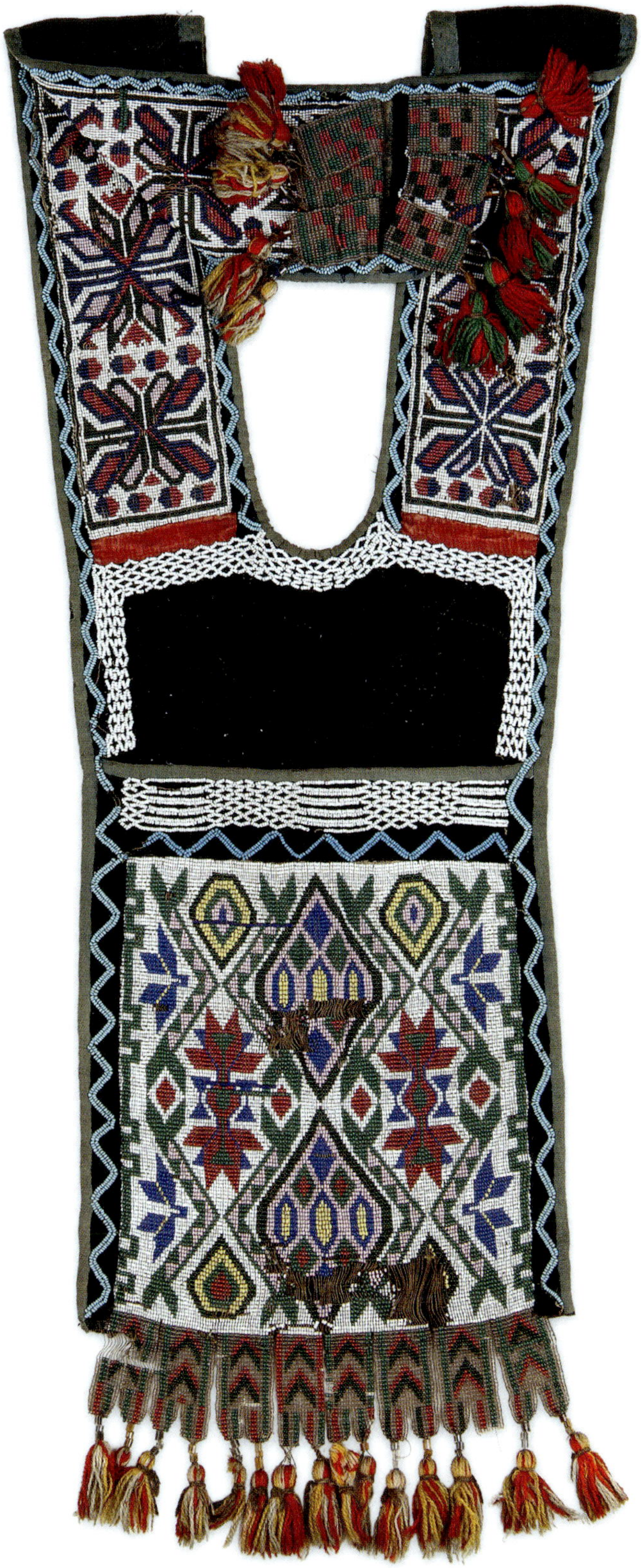

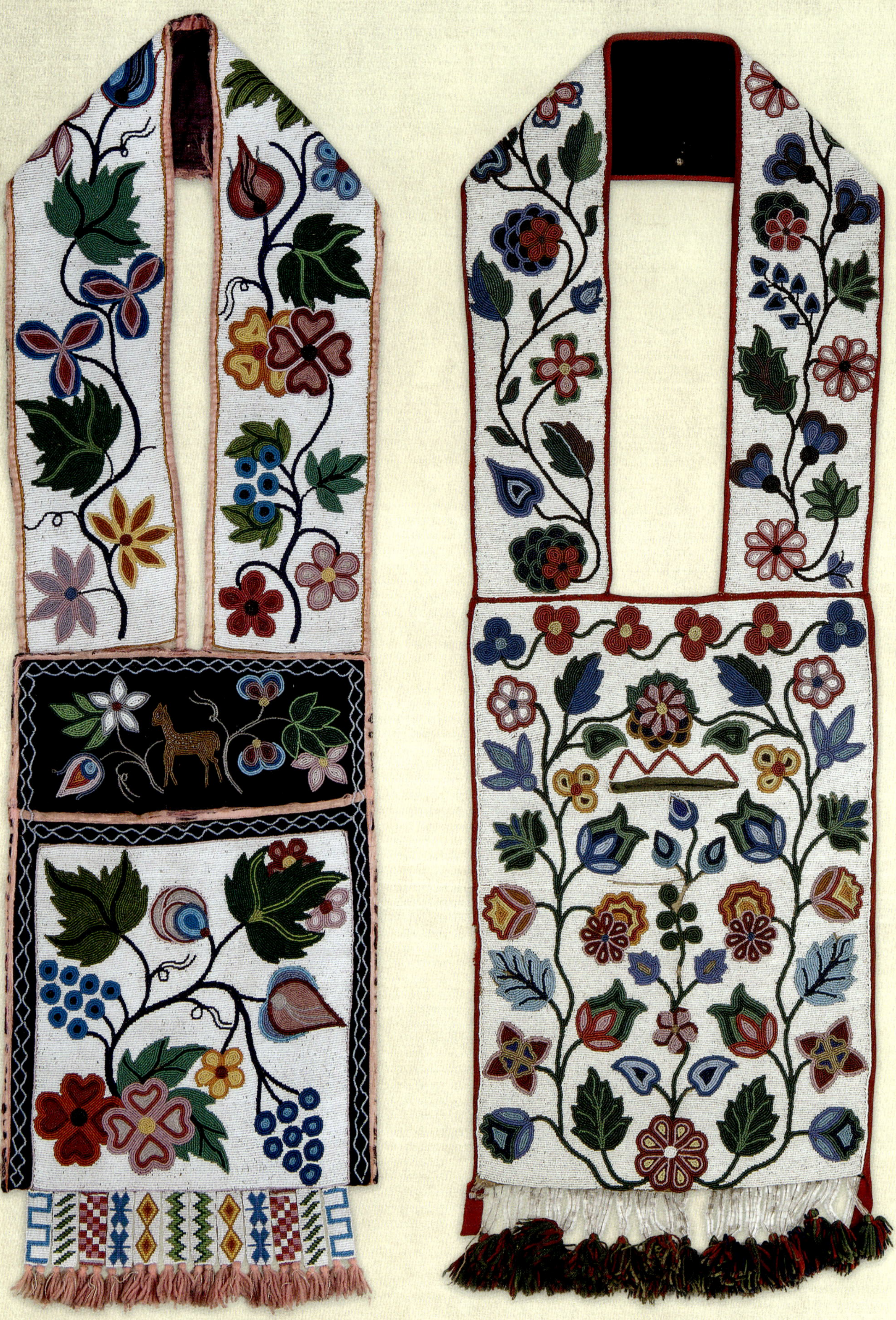

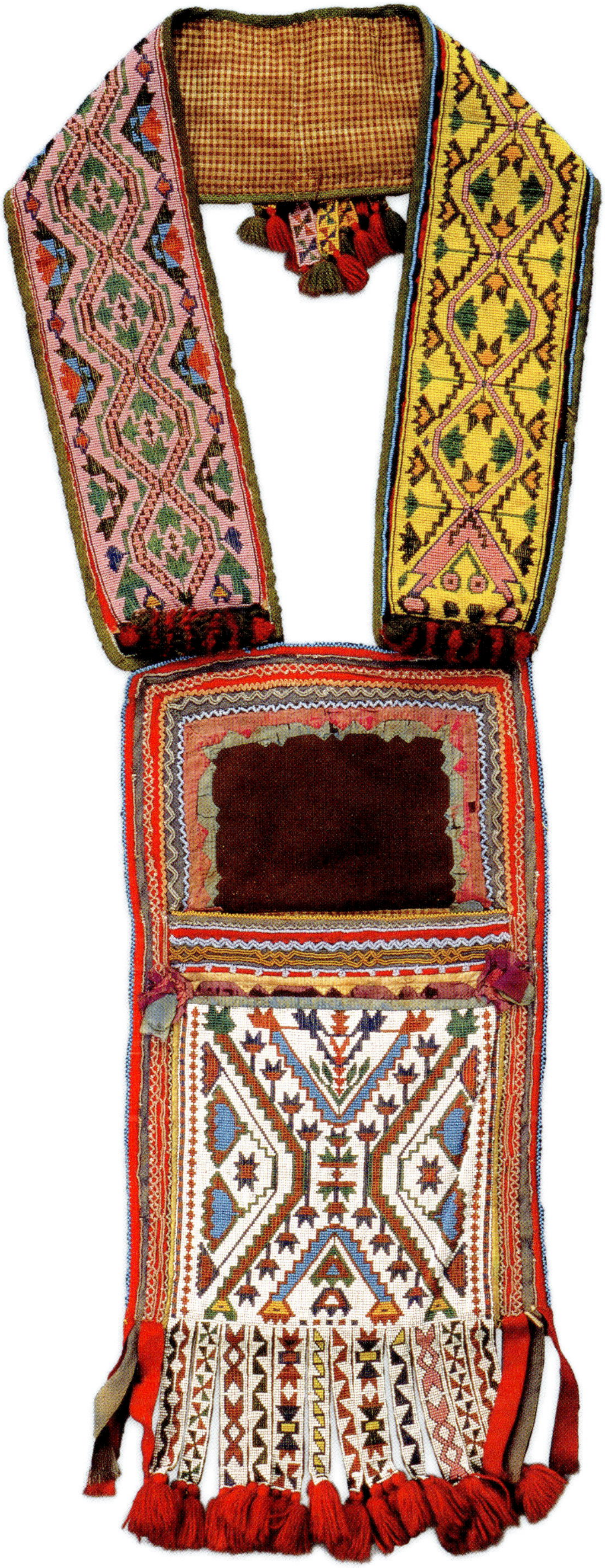

A Bag Worth a Pony

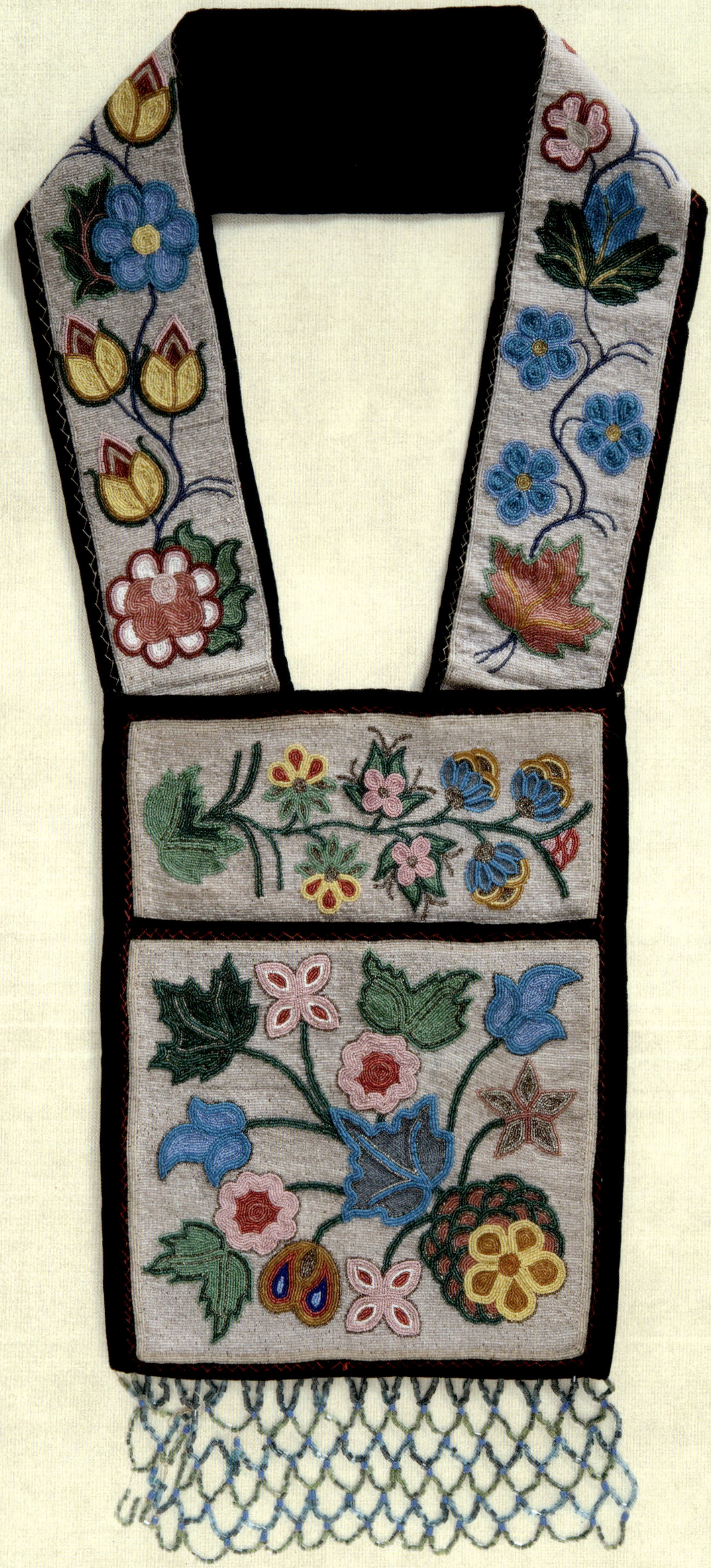

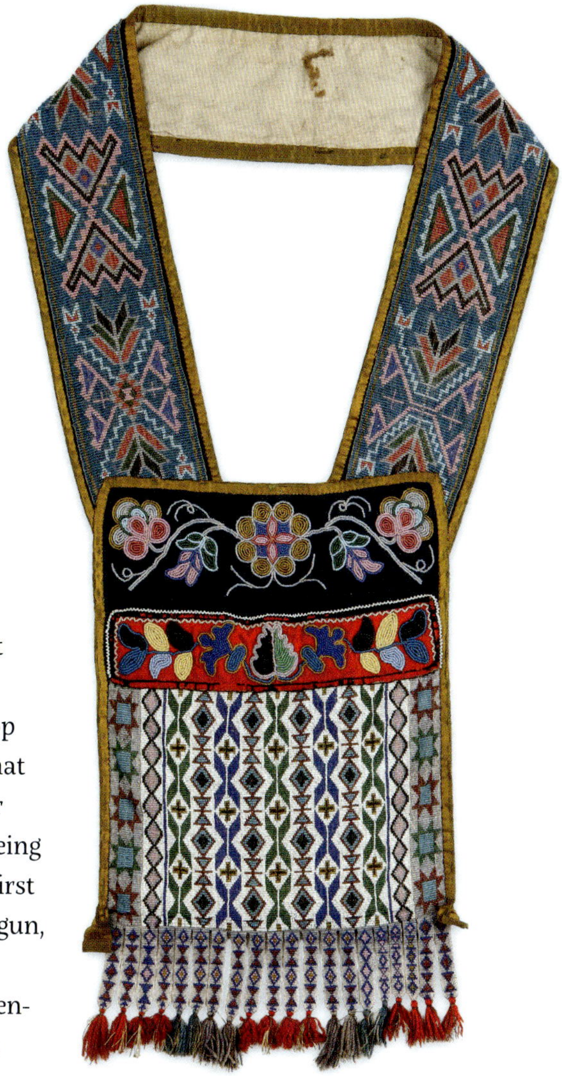

Preface

In 1981, in my early months as the newly hired collections curator at the Minnesota Historical Society, I opened a square storage box to find several beautiful beaded bags, folded and piled haphazardly on top of each other. I was conducting an inventory of the collections, and what I found was not a good situation for long-term care. Surprised by their heft—each one weighed between 1 and 3.65 pounds, with older ones being lighter and smaller—I was drawn to their sheer beauty. This was my first encounter with a bandolier bag, or *gashkibidaagan* (gahsh-kibi-DAAH-gun, gəsh-ki-bi-da:-gən).[1]

As more and more of these bandolier bags surfaced during the inventory—*gashkibidaaganag* is the plural—I began to feel an affinity with them. Made by Ojibwe (Chippewa, Anishinaabe) people, the bags comprised a small group compared to the roughly 250,000 historical objects in the collection, and yet for a single type of object their numbers were substantial. They spoke to me. I am by training a material culture specialist, drawn to fabric, crafts, and women's work, and these objects appealed to all my interests, and more. The mass, visual beauty, and composition of the bags, as well as their desperate need for improved preservation, seduced me.[2]

As I learned more about gashkibidaaganag, the questions came quickly: Who were the inventive women who created these bags? Where did the concept of the gashkibidaagan come from? How did its status and popularity grow so quickly within the Ojibwe community? How did recognition and appreciation come so swiftly in white society? Why have so many survived? Why are their origins shrouded in relative mystery?

The result has been a three-decades-long love affair with gashkibidaaganag. I have scoured archives, museums, and other sources to learn about their origins and makers; I have met, learned from, and become friends with many contemporary Ojibwe bead artists, tribal government representatives, and keepers of the history of these communities. I am particularly grateful for the time, knowledge, family histories, and companionship they have so generously shared with me. As a consequence, I felt compelled to find a way to share the story of gashkibidaaganag with individuals descended from the bags' makers, with scholars of ethnographic material culture, and with those who simply take pleasure in the beauty of extraordinary objects.

I wondered, as I began this work, how so many bags had made their way into the Minnesota Historical Society's collections. In fact, the society was the only Minnesota institution with such a large collection. For the most part, the bags were not proactively acquired by the society or collected intentionally as part of a specific category focus, such as women's bead artistry. Instead, they arrived with unsolicited donations of materials related to American Indians. Thus their existence in unusually large numbers suggested to me, as a newcomer to the history of the Upper Midwest, that they were significant for the first nations of the area, were produced in quantity, and survived in large part because of their quality and unique physical presence. My research would reveal not only that those assumptions were valid, but also that there is much more to the bags' story and their position in Ojibwe and non-Indian societies that contributed to their endurance both as objects and as cultural icons.

I regularly attended powwows in Minnesota, but it wasn't until June 2002 at the 142nd Annual White Earth Reservation Celebration and Pow Wow that I saw a gashkibidaagan being danced for the first time. Studying gashkibidaaganag up close, as material culture objects, is one thing, but seeing one in use, swinging with the motion of the dancer and completely transforming the wearer's appearance, was a revelation. On that hot summer day, Harry Ailport danced a bag made by his wife, Ivy, that commemorated those lost in the attacks of September 11, 2001, and it gave me additional respect for all the Ojibwe who wore one or more of these heavy bags over the decades with great effort and pride.

Private collections and museums are filled with examples of magnificent indigenous artistry with little or no documentation. Early collectors often acquired American Indian–made items like gashkibidaaganag for their beauty, only occasionally ascertaining their cultural or tribal antecedents. Even less frequently did collectors ask the name of the maker or user, unless an object was associated with a significant well-known individual like Sitting Bull or Hole in the Day. Sometimes objects were gifts from an individual tribal member well known to the recipient, so it didn't occur to the owner or collector to record a name or tribal association. Because many collectors were not interested in provenance, we often don't know the date of manufacture, the maker's name, or the tribal designation of many of the surviving bags.

Some bags are in poor condition, having been hung from nails, neglected in attics, or exposed to the elements. Usually little attention was paid to their preservation. Bandolier bags have suffered both from poor documentation and from the inherent vices that come with objects created from fabrics, threads, and glass: fading, stress, and brittleness. And yet, as survivors, the bags intrigue us with their visual appeal and challenge us to discover and record their voices.

Historical records have their own problems. Gashkibidaaganag have been described or identified over time by many terms, thereby obscuring historical references to them. A few contemporary observations made by non-Indians who were living among the Ojibwe, or regularly interacting with them, record the wonder and admiration that these beautiful artifacts elicited within and outside the Ojibwe community. But those records don't tell us much about these bags, their daily use, and their origins. The quality of the information varies widely, and the language used by members of the dominant culture, usually Euro-Americans, frequently demonstrates their presumption of cultural superiority. The resources created by that dominant culture include multiple spellings of the same name and generally ignore women's names, making it difficult to do genealogical research on individual Ojibwe people; understandably, the knowledge held by members of the community is not readily shared with those outside the culture.

Other accounts provided by white ethnographers may be more or less accurate, depending on the interests, approach, and experience of the observer. Many of the earliest American ethnographers were men who showed limited interest in studying the roles of women in indigenous society and their contributions to the decorative arts. The classic ethnographic literature produced by scholars in the late nineteenth and early twentieth centuries emphasized the material culture of warfare, "hunter-gatherer" activities, and religious practices, not everyday life and products. Descriptions of beadwork made by the Ojibwe between the 1850s and 1940s are typically broadly generic, and the bandolier bags generally receive only token mentions.

Fortunately, the artists themselves eventually had the opportunity to speak about their gashkibidaaganag through the efforts of a handful of female ethnographers. Frances Densmore, Carrie Lyford, Sister Bernard Coleman, and Sister Inez Hilger were primarily active in the last decade of the nineteenth century into the mid-twentieth century, and they are well known for their extensive work among the Ojibwe of Minnesota. As female observers, they paid more attention to the daily work of women and their forms of personal expression.

Other direct testimony can be found in oral histories, in manuscript collections, and in interviews with contemporary bead artists and gashkibidaagan makers. Another form of historical documentation, photography, shows some types and uses of gashkibidaaganag through the years. Whenever possible, I have included photographs of Ojibwe women, sometimes nameless, who may be the artists of related objects discussed in a photograph. My greatest research successes came when I was able to identify women bead artists.

This in-depth research on gashkibidaaganag has only been possible because of the extraordinary collection of these bags and related historical images held by the Minnesota Historical Society. Because the society's extensive collection of bags and bag components, 145 in all, comes primarily from northern Minnesota and the Great Lakes region, it is possible to analyze and compare the physical bags within a specific regional context. Furthermore, there is an unusual amount of historical documentation associated with the collection. Both the National Museum of the American Indian and the National Museum of Natural History have a comparable number of bags in each of their collections, but with a much broader cultural focus and a less specific provenance overall.

In studying gashkibidaaganag for over thirty years, I have developed an understanding of these objects and what they are. While this allows me to guess about a bag's likely date of creation or its probable place of origin, it doesn't necessarily mean that I can point to a single source or reason for an insight; an educated guess can depend on subtle comparisons or the interplay of several factors. What's more, the old truism is indeed *true*: the more you learn, the more you realize how little you know. This larger story of all North American gashkibidaaganag is too great for one person to unravel in a lifetime. Luckily, the Minnesota Historical Society's considerable and relatively well-documented collection has functioned as a laboratory for my study of Minnesota Ojibwe bags and has facilitated my efforts to place their account within a grander continental narrative.

Part 1 of this book introduces gashkibidaaganag, discussing the origins, structure, materials, types of bags, design influences, motifs, and ways that photographs and commercial records inform us about the history of bandolier bags. Part 2 discusses specific gashkibidaaganag and their wearers from each of Minnesota's seven Ojibwe reservations and illuminates the stories of Ojibwe bead artists who have for generations made extraordinary contributions in the face of cultural, economic, and other complex challenges.

Throughout the book, photographs show gashkibidaaganag, detail shots of gashkibidaaganag, and people wearing gashkibidaaganag. If a bag appears in more than one place, the caption tells readers where to find those other images; the bag's estimated dates of construction appear in the caption for the full image of the bag.

I have interviewed six Minnesota Ojibwe women and one man who are extraordinary bead artists and who have made gashkibidaaganag during the last forty years. Their voices are the anchor for this book, and they open a window onto aspects of gashkibidaaganag in the Ojibwe culture of this region. Like many creative indigenous people of North America, the bead artists I learned from were and are simply living their lives. Even when prodded with questions, they rarely reflect on what their choices might mean in the larger scheme of things; rather, they made choices based on their individual desire to learn, to excel at a skill, to accomplish something personally rewarding, or to share expertise while meeting the needs of their families and their communities.

Maude Kegg (1902–96) and **Batiste Sam** (1914–98) were Mille Lacs Band elders who shared their deep cultural knowledge with and about the Mille Lacs community in the last half of the twentieth century. These women became masters of Ojibwe cultural arts in many mediums, from birch bark to beadwork, and each made a gashkibidaagan near the end of her life. Many years before their passing, Maude and Batiste generously shared their thoughts on Ojibwe arts with me.

Ellen Bushman Olson (1929–) and her daughter **Marcie McIntire** (1951–) represent the second and third generations of gashkibidaagan makers on the Grand Portage Reservation, each enhancing in her own way the skills passed to her from Ellen's foster mother, Mary Posey (1880–1964).

Ivy Ailport (1938–2012) was a grandmother, foster parent, tribal council member, bead artist, and dance regalia and gashkibidaagan maker from the White Earth Reservation.

Cheryl Minnema (1973–) is a member of the Mille Lacs Band of Chippewa, a children's book author, and a mother of two young boys. She is descended from three generations of bead artists.

Melvin Losh (1946–) is a highly regarded quill and bead artist. He developed his skills as he learned from the women in his family and their broader community network of bead artists. Mel also does quillwork, harvesting much of the natural materials he uses.

The work of each of these individuals is singular, and yet all their bags carry elements or qualities that identify them as Ojibwe. The women I interviewed graciously allowed me to include Mel, since this formerly traditional work of women is now engaged in by both sexes.

I am grateful to each of these indigenous artists for their willingness to share their personal stories, their culture, and their passion for gashkibidaaganag. This book is dedicated to them and all the bead artists who preceded and will follow them.

Miigwechiwendam—I am thankful and grateful.

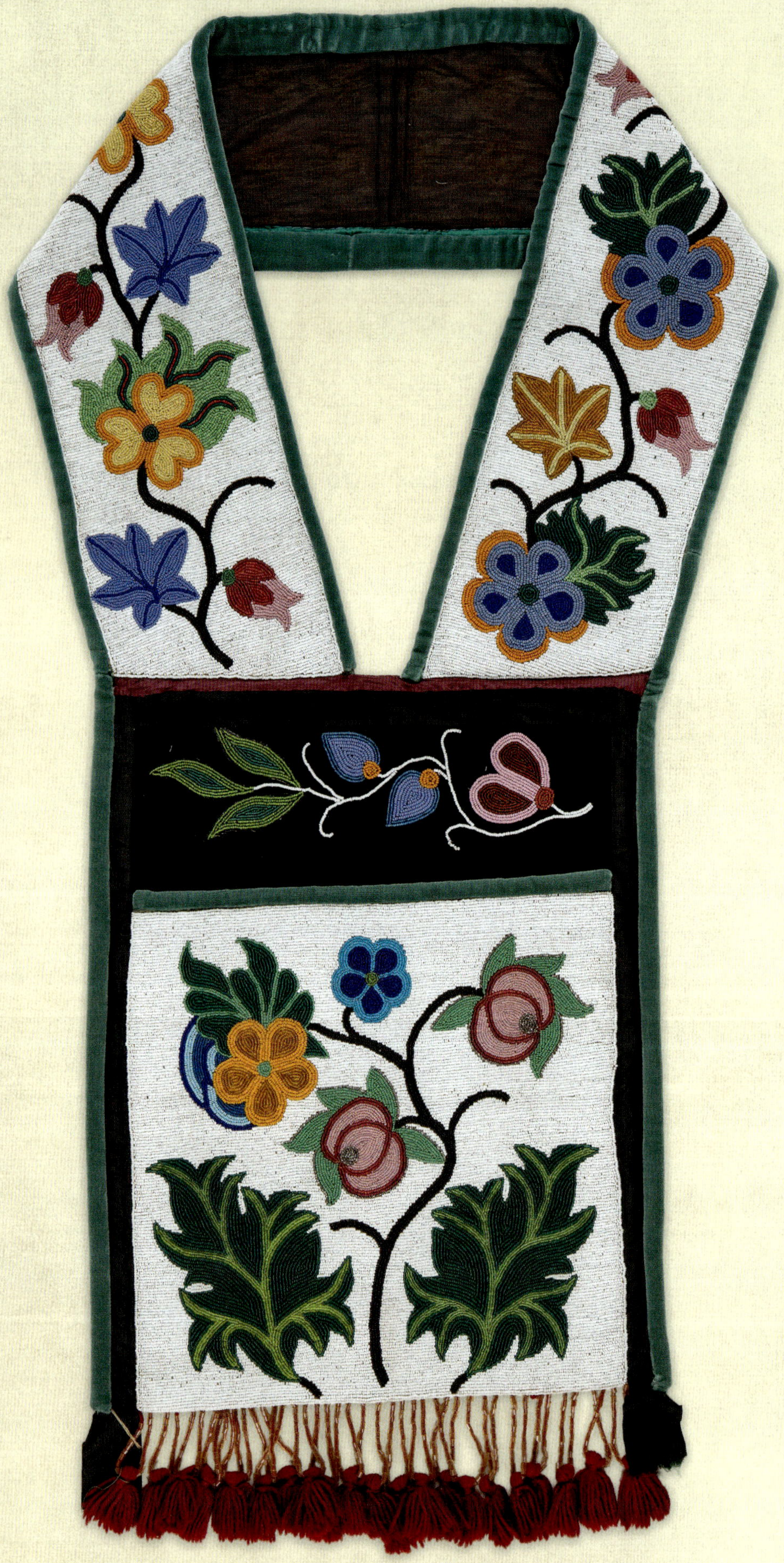

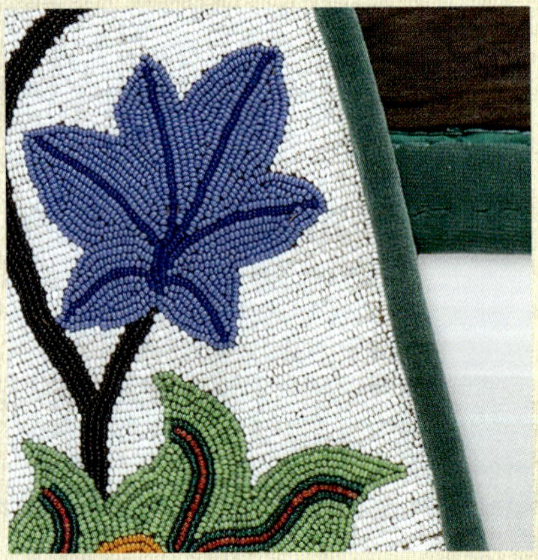

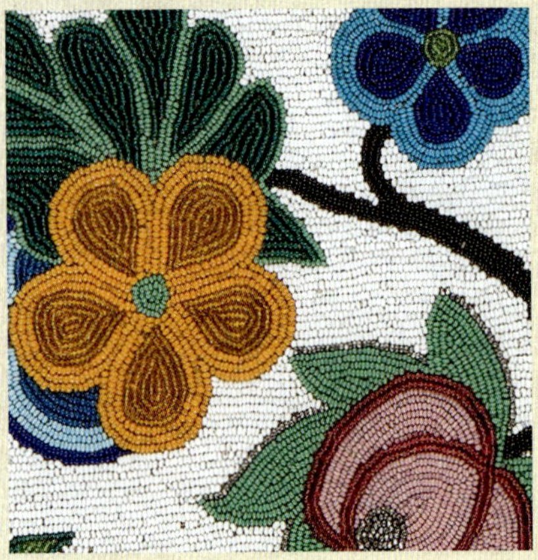

Part 1

A Bag Worth a Pony

The first part of this book focuses on the history, uses, structure, design, and motifs of *gashkibidaaganag,* or bandolier bags. The visual qualities of the gashkibidaaganag are evident to all who see them in person, or even in print. But the sensual quality of a bag in motion is harder to imagine. The bag seemingly comes to life, dancing along with its partner. Stella Stocker's photograph, taken in 1916, gives us some idea of the experience enjoyed by those who danced the bags in the nineteenth and early twentieth centuries.

A rare photo captures the movement of the dancer and his gashkibidaagan at the Annual White Earth Reservation Celebration, June 14, 1916. *Photo by Stella Stocker, KAMLASC 241568*

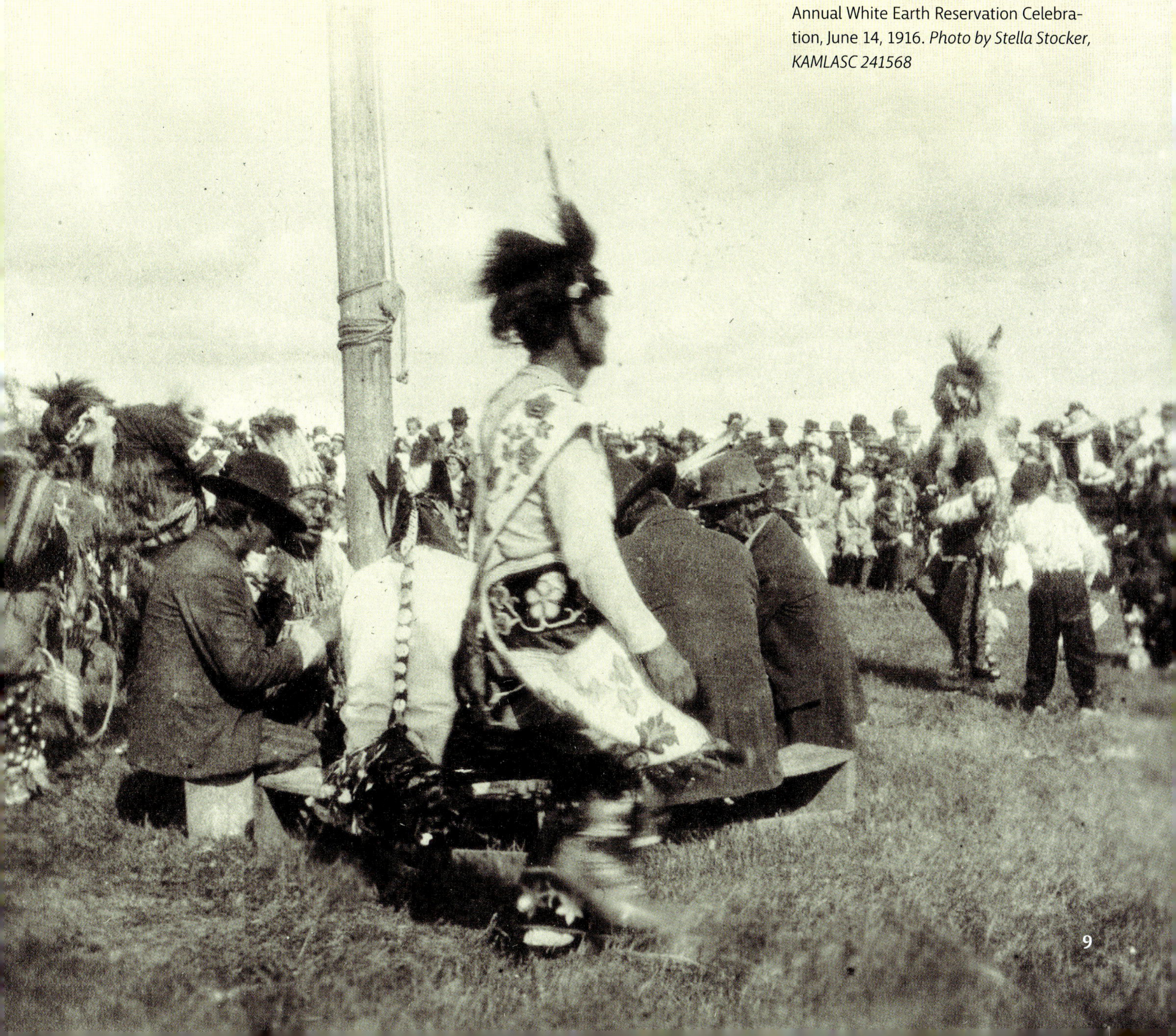

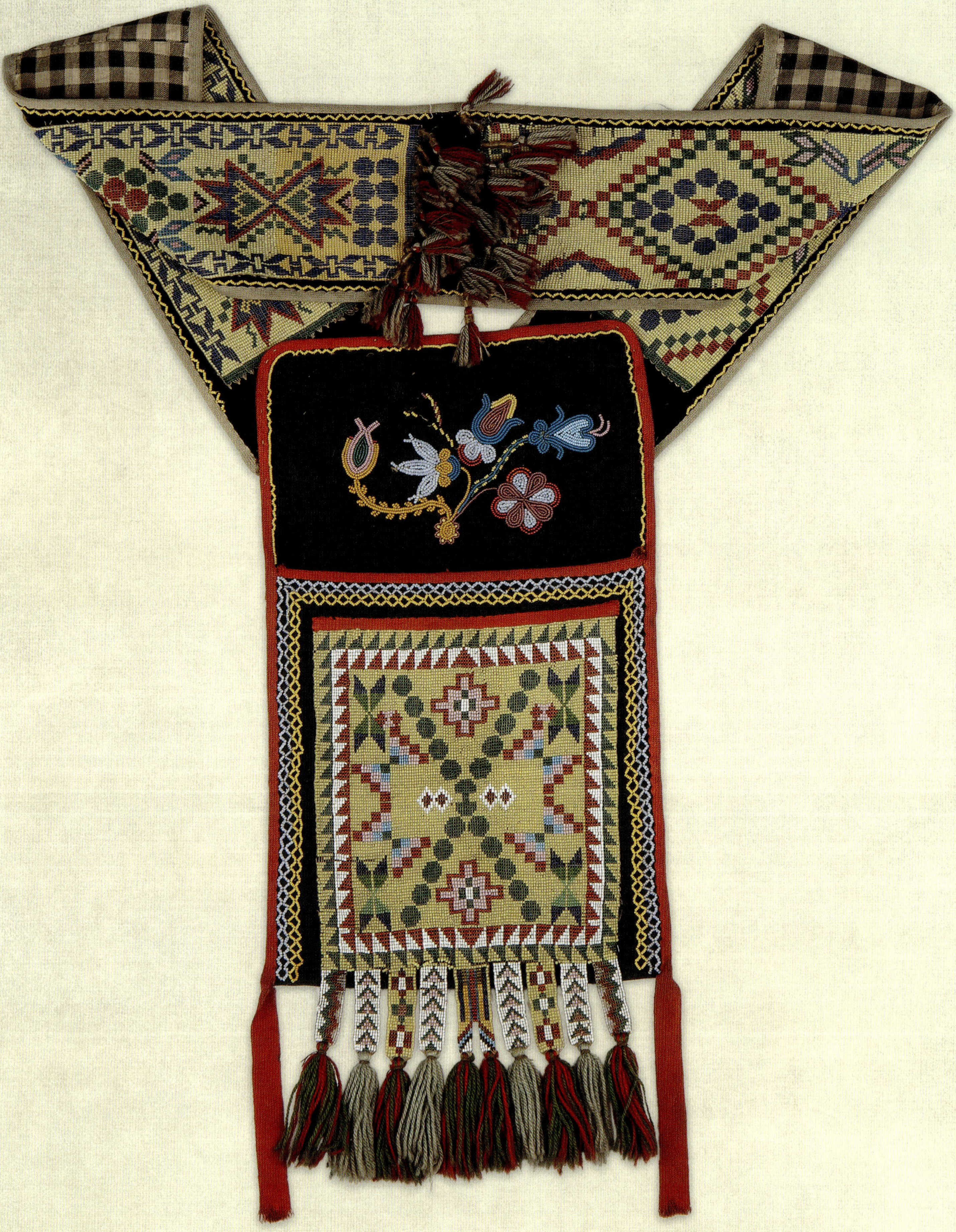

Chapter 1

Gashkibidaagan

An Introduction

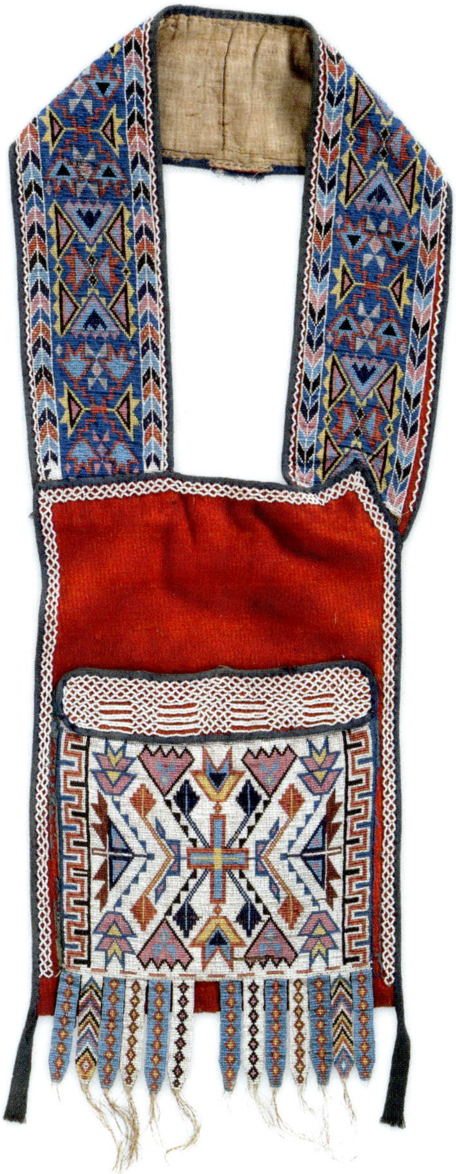

One of the bead-work pouches is the great ornament of an Ojibway, and any person wearing it is considered to be in full dress; it is worth a pony among the Sioux. Thus the stock of horses is every summer replenished.
—JOSEPH A. GILFILLAN, MISSIONARY, 1879

A *gashkibidaagan* is a large, heavily beaded shoulder bag made by the Ojibwe women of Minnesota (Figures 1.01 and 1.02). Also known as bandolier bags, similar bags are made and worn by several North American Indian tribes. They are treasured cultural icons among the Ojibwe—also known as Anishinaabe, Chippewa, Ojibwa, and other variants. The gashkibidaagan served as a valuable form of exchange and represented leadership and status within the community.

While the gashkibidaagan has existed in various culturally distinctive forms among many indigenous nations across North America, it has been most prevalent in the Midwest, and primarily among the Algonquian-speaking tribes of the Great Lakes (or Woodlands), including the Ojibwe, Menominee, Potawatomi, Ottawa (Odawa), and Mesquakie. The ancestors of these groups had migrated west together, splitting directions in 1660 when they reached the Straits of Mackinac; the Ojibwe, Potawatomi, and Ottawa are known collectively as the Three Fires. In addition, a Siouan-speaking tribe, the Ho-Chunk, also were regional makers and wearers of gashkibidaaganag.

The territory now known as Minnesota is home to what were once many independent bands, now subsumed into seven Ojibwe Indian reservations. Six of them—Bois Forte, Fond du Lac, Grand Portage, Leech Lake, Mille Lacs, and White Earth—are included under the federal tribal government umbrella known as the Minnesota Chippewa Tribe, established in 1934. Red Lake remained unaffiliated with the Minnesota Chippewa

1.01 *(right)* Earlier gashkibidaaganag featured woven beadwork, created as strips and a panel that were stitched to the straps and pocket of a cloth bag. This bag was probably made in the last third of the nineteenth century. *MNHS 9120.2*

1.02 *(far right)* By the 1890s, many beadworkers were stitching beads directly onto the bag's cloth pocket. This spot-stitch appliqué gashkibidaagan from the late nineteenth or turn of the twentieth century, acquired by Bishop Benjamin Whipple before 1901, may have been made by Sophia Smith of White Earth (see page 203); it carries its original price tag of $40. *MNHS 1831*

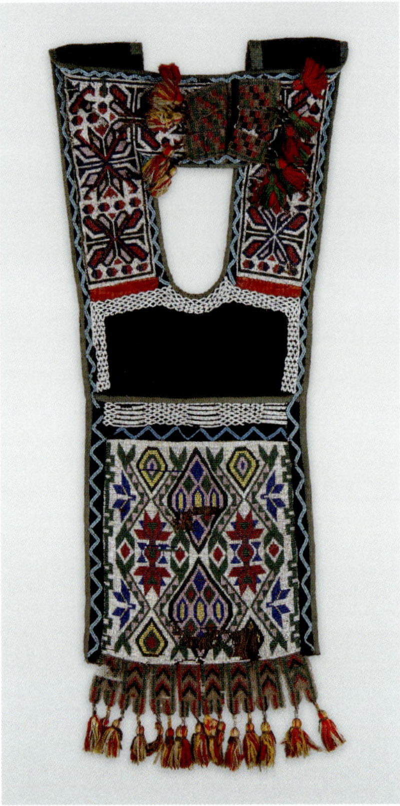

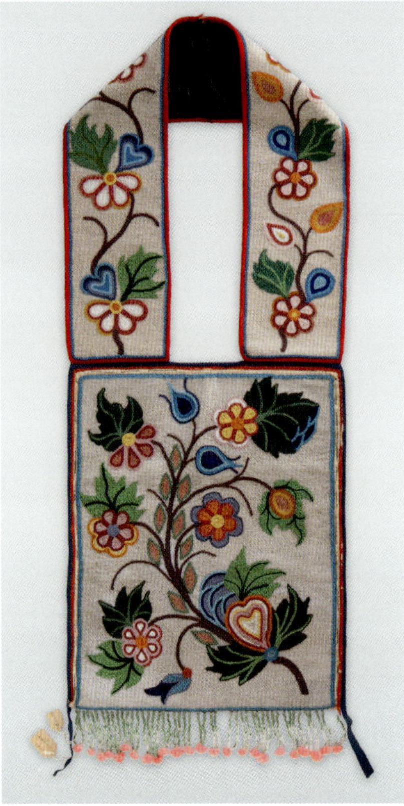

Tribe and consistently resisted allotment of its lands, instead maintaining communal possession and self-governance. Ojibwe people also live on reservations or reserves in Michigan, Montana, North Dakota, Wisconsin, Manitoba, Ontario, Alberta, and Saskatchewan—and in non-reservation communities around the world.

When the form defined as a gashkibidaagan first emerged in the mid-nineteenth century and perhaps earlier, it was, I would maintain, the Ojibwe of Minnesota who gained the distinction of being the most accomplished practitioners of this art and the greatest enthusiasts of the gashkibidaagan as a cultural icon. Gashkibidaaganag (the plural form of gashkibidaagan) have been the singular and most visually significant art and craft of the Ojibwe.

The Ojibwe name comes from word parts *gashk-*, meaning "enclosed, attached together," and *-bid*, "tie it." The English word *bandolier,* defined as a "broad band, belt, or scarf worn over one shoulder and under the other," comes from the French word *bandouliere*, meaning "shoulder belt," and traces back to the Spanish *bandolera,* the diminutive of *banda,* "sash." A bandolier was a broad belt that had loops to hold powder charges or cartridges; European infantry soldiers wore them across the chest as early as the sixteenth century. Non-Indians probably began using this term because gashkibidaaganag are worn in a similar fashion: across the chest, with the strap over one shoulder and the pocket resting on the opposite hip. These bags were only occasionally worn with the strap around the neck and the pocket on the chest, which no doubt explains one of many terms non-Indians used to describe them: apron. Unlike bandoliers, gashkibidaaganag have no association with weapons.[1]

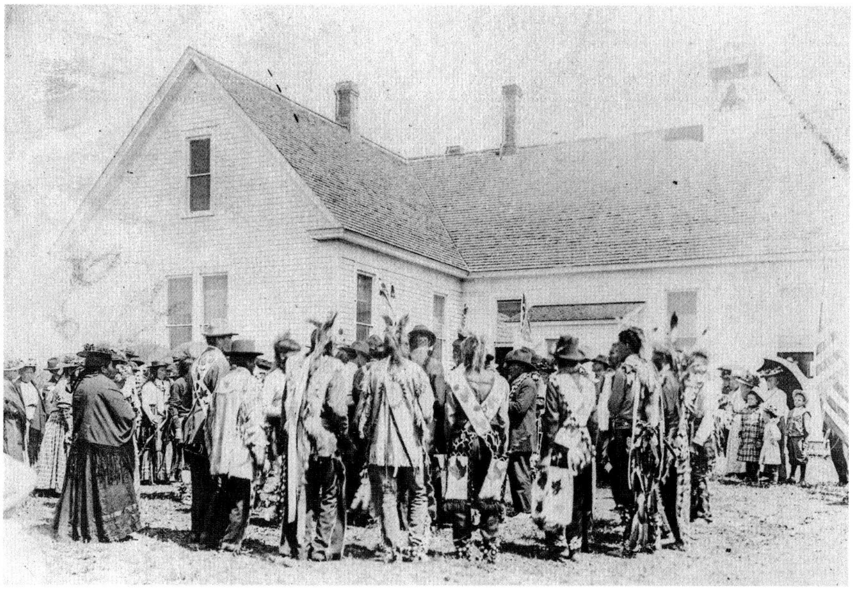

A gift of a gashkibidaagan was a significant display of gratitude and respect to friends, family, other tribes, and government officials. Gashkibidaaganag were also presented to signify respect for another individual's accomplishments or contributions. By the 1870s and 1880s, the bags were in use as a form of currency, exchanged with the Dakota and other Plains nations for a pony. While the bags no longer served this particular form of exchange by the early twentieth century, their symbolic embodiment of status, gratitude, respect, and leadership remained.

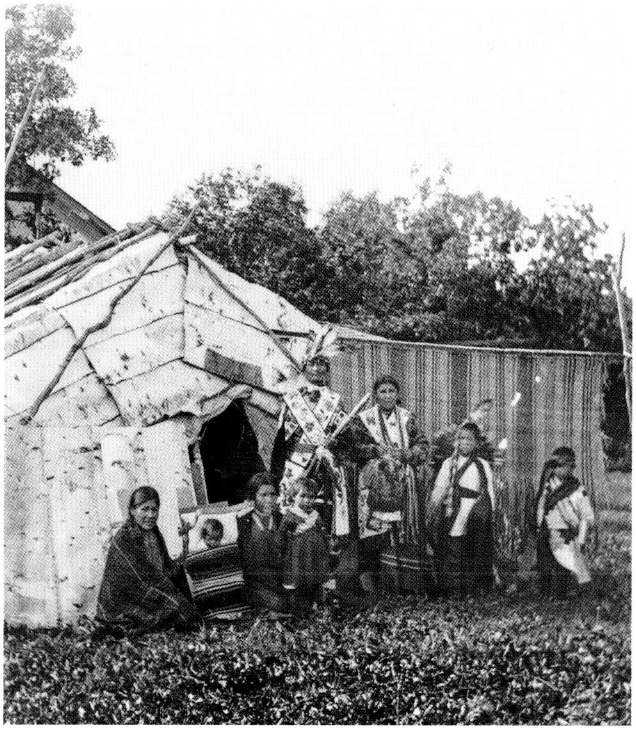

Like most functional objects, gashkibidaaganag have been documented in various uses, roles, and settings. In their earliest use, they were worn primarily by men at community events, dances, visits by notables, presentations, and formal portraits. In recent decades, the bags have also appeared at holiday programs, historical commemorative events, tourist pageants, and parades and in instructional settings. They can be worn by adults of both genders and by children. The gashkibidaagan's long-term primary role has been as a symbol of prestige, power, rank, and wealth, and also as an emblem of respect and community cohesion—and sometimes of friendship with white allies.

Photographs help to identify the roles of gashkibidaaganag in Ojibwe society. In Figure 1.03, White Earth participants and visitors gather in front of the Indian agent's home in 1915, during the Annual White Earth Reservation Celebration, held every June. Three men with their backs to the camera each wear two spot-stitch appliqué bags in the traditional manner. In Figure 1.04, William Hanks and his wife (likely the maker of the four spot-stitch appliqué gashkibidaaganag the two of them are wearing) pose in front of their birchbark wigwam at White Earth in 1915. Just as early white settlers posed with favorite possessions in front of their log cabins, the Hankses show off three generations of their family and display, with pride, the beaded shoulder bags, cradleboard bands (*dikinaagan*), and a woven mat

1.03 *(top)* A scene outside the Indian agent's office at the Annual White Earth Reservation Celebration, 1915. *MNHS Collection I.364.23*

1.04 *(above)* William Hanks and family, White Earth Reservation, 1915. *MNHS E97.31 r134*

(*anaakan*), no doubt made by the women in their family. The photographer, Robert G. Beaulieu, may have asked the Hanks family to wear these garments and pose in this manner, but as a man of Ojibwe and French heritage, Beaulieu was likely to have had the same agenda as the Hanks family: to record pride in family and culture.

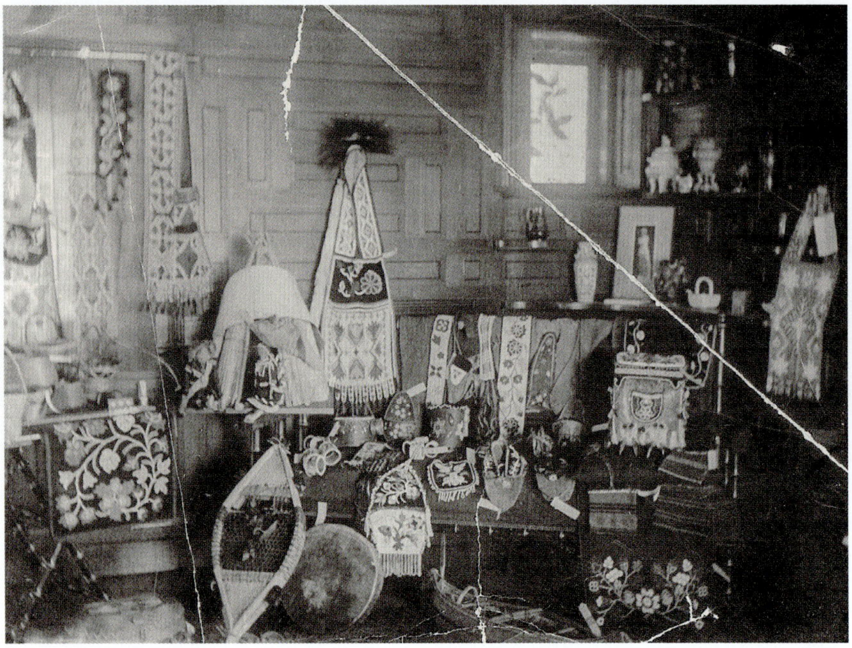

1.05 Jessie Campbell West's private Indian collection, before 1893. For the bag at far left, see Figure 12.08. BCHS *4969*

Because outsiders recognized the cultural significance of gashkibidaaganag and were impressed by their striking visual appeal and sophistication, non-Indian collectors, ethnographers, auction houses, casual tourists, and others readily bought the bags and distributed them around the country and the world. For example, Mrs. Jessie C. West of Detroit, Minnesota, acquired a variety of bags and other Indian objects, which appear to be displayed in a residence, likely her own (Figure 1.05). When she died in 1903, her husband, John K. West, gave her collection to the Berkshire Museum in Pittsfield, Massachusetts. Certainly, Ojibwe people gave away bags in formal presentations or as gifts, but in too many other instances, the bags were sold to provide subsistence for the makers' families. Whatever the reasons, too few remain in the hands of the descendants of the Ojibwe bead artists themselves, or in their communities.[2]

The bead artists

For millennia women have shared their talents and passions with the world as artists and decorators of everyday material culture. But oral histories and written records of women and their contributions to culture are often elusive or altogether absent. Women's societal roles have frequently assigned them to artistic anonymity, and their work has not been accorded significant commercial value. This anonymous status applies in particular to women embellishing everyday material culture in mediums outside those prescribed as fine art.

In other words, historically women's work was not well documented or recognized. A number of factors contributed to this deficit among the Ojibwe. For example, women traditionally do not put themselves or their work forward; Ojibwe cultural behaviors did not include self-aggrandizement. Ojibwe oral history focuses on creation stories and music, rather than on people. And Ojibwe women's accomplishments also slipped into anonymity when white record-keepers entered poor phonetic interpretations of indigenous names and ignored women's surnames after marriage.

In addition, many of the nineteenth-century treatises on cultures of North American Indians that are cited as primary ethnographic documents were written by American male ethnographers and collectors who focused heavily on material culture related to indigenous religions and to warfare and hunting. These biases influenced the early pupils of these ethnographers as well, which perpetuated the inadequate documentation of women's activities during a prime period for the study of and acquisition of material culture objects.

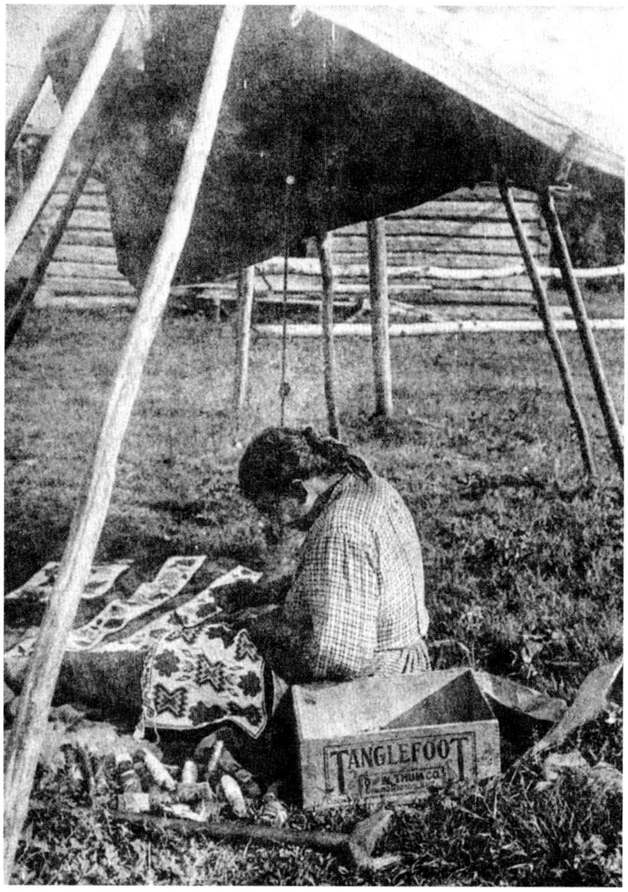

1.06 A Red Lake bead artist at work, c. 1890s. *Mittelholtz and Graves, Historical Review, 48–49*

Ojibwe women used beadwork to decorate surfaces such as animal hides, birch bark, wool cloth, velvet, and velveteen. In the Minnesota Historical Society's American Indian–related collections, bead embellishment is found on numerous objects, including gashkibidaaganag, leggings, dance aprons (also known as breechcloths, or loincloths), wrist cuffs, armbands, moccasins, belts, sashes, dresses, shirts, pipe bags, vests, shirt-yoke panels, drum bands, cradleboard bands, dolls, quivers, knife and awl cases, arm and leg garters, napkin rings, pincushions, pillows, watch fobs, bracelets, necklaces, small bags, and even birchbark containers. Of all these garments and objects, none was or is more admired—by Ojibwe bead artists, tribal governments, and non-Indian collectors alike—than the gashkibidaagan. Other beaded apparel is often lost in photographs, hidden in folds of cloth or shaded beneath a pant cuff or skirt hem. But the bag's sheer size and bold visual design immediately draw the eye, in photographs and in person.

The act of creating a gashkibidaagan is time consuming, and historically the bags also were very costly to produce. In Figure 1.06, which probably dates to the late 1880s or early 1890s, a Red Lake bead artist at work exemplifies both the simple resources used by Ojibwe women in the creation of these stunning bags and the evolving Ojibwe gashkibidaagan styles in Minnesota. She carries her beadwork and supplies in a Tanglefoot flypaper crate that dates to no earlier than 1887; the crate may also have served as her chair when she needed one. In the foreground, by her crutch, are her beads, strung on long threads that are then wound around rolled pieces of birch bark or paper for ease of use and portability. Seated on the ground under a temporary shelter, she works on both a loom-woven bag and a spot-stitch appliqué bag. The spot-stitch appliqué beaded bag parts with floral motifs are laid out off to her right, awaiting assembly, and on her lap is a loomed pocket panel with geometric motifs that she is attaching to a foundation cloth.[3]

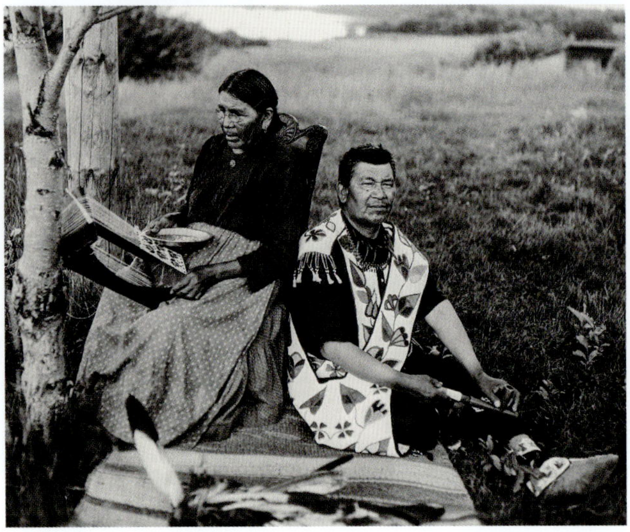

1.07 Na-wa-que-go-kwe and Juni-mii-we-gi-ji-gens (John White Feather), c. 1920s–30s. *Photo by Huron Smith, MPM 46786*

In Figure 1.07, Na-wa-que-go-kwe, from the Lac du Flambeau Reservation in Wisconsin, is working on a strap-width piece of loom work as her husband, Juni-mii-we-gi-ji-gens (John White Feather), models another gashkibidaagan and a yoke. She is likely the maker of his beadwork. We don't know exactly what Ojibwe people were thinking over a hundred years ago when they made and wore gashkibidaaganag, but we do know that the makers were aware of the bags' significance and felt great pride while making, wearing, and gifting them. Because they are so complex and take many hours to complete, few gashkibidaaganag are made today, and even fewer of these heavy beaded shoulder bags are worn at dances on warm summer days. Contemporary beadworkers interviewed between 1981 and 2016 all spoke of the bags with reverence, and many of the more advanced bead artists planned to make one. An even smaller group of Ojibwe artisans has actually completed one or more.

Since 1985, I have conducted extensive interviews with Ojibwe bag makers throughout Minnesota; their stories appear in Part 2 of this book. Ranging in age from under forty to over ninety, these artists shared nearly identical reasons for their interest in making bandolier bags and for their pride in the accomplishment. Although each of them developed an early passion for beadwork, most had never seen a gashkibidaagan in use. They knew of the bags almost entirely through stories told in the community, through the writings of ethnographers, through historical photos, and from seeing them in museums. All of these beadworkers became fascinated with the bags as beautiful objects that were important culturally, economically, and politically among the Ojibwe. Each took on the making of their first bag as a challenge to complete a large and significant object that few people were making anymore.

Origins

No one knows when American Indians, and more specifically the Ojibwe of Minnesota, first began creating gashkibidaaganag. World cultures generally do not document the evolution of traditions or cultural object forms. Such changes take place gradually, influenced by interactions within and outside the community, by the geographic location of the community, and by the simple act of people living their everyday lives.

Experts have pointed to a number of North American precursors that may have influenced the development of the bandolier bag and its parts. For eastern tribes, these earlier forms predate the arrival of Columbus in 1492; and in the Minnesota region, they predate the arrival of French traders on the Mississippi in the 1720s. Smaller related bag forms with straps, decorated originally with quillwork bands and later with glass beads, existed among the Ojibwe, Dakota, Delaware, Creek, Micmac, Meskwaki, Potawatomi, Montagnais, Seminole, and other Woodland Indian cultures. These earlier forms may have been precursors of the gashkibidaagan, and some of the bag elements may have evolved from bag forms that predate the contact period, like the early slit leather pouches that were tucked into waistbands.

The woven tab fringe on the strap ends of an early gashkibidaagan (Figure 1.08) may represent animal symbolism, echoing the pendant tail and paws elements of smaller bags made from otter skin that were used in ceremonies related to the *Midewiwin,* the Grand Medicine Society. Other precursors included similar tabbed leather straps that suspended powder horns. Slit pouches or bags in use in the first half of the nineteenth century in Minnesota incorporated quilled elements and metal cone fringe. The bag in Figure 1.09 has lost its tinkler cone fringe, but the leather thongs for attaching them remains.

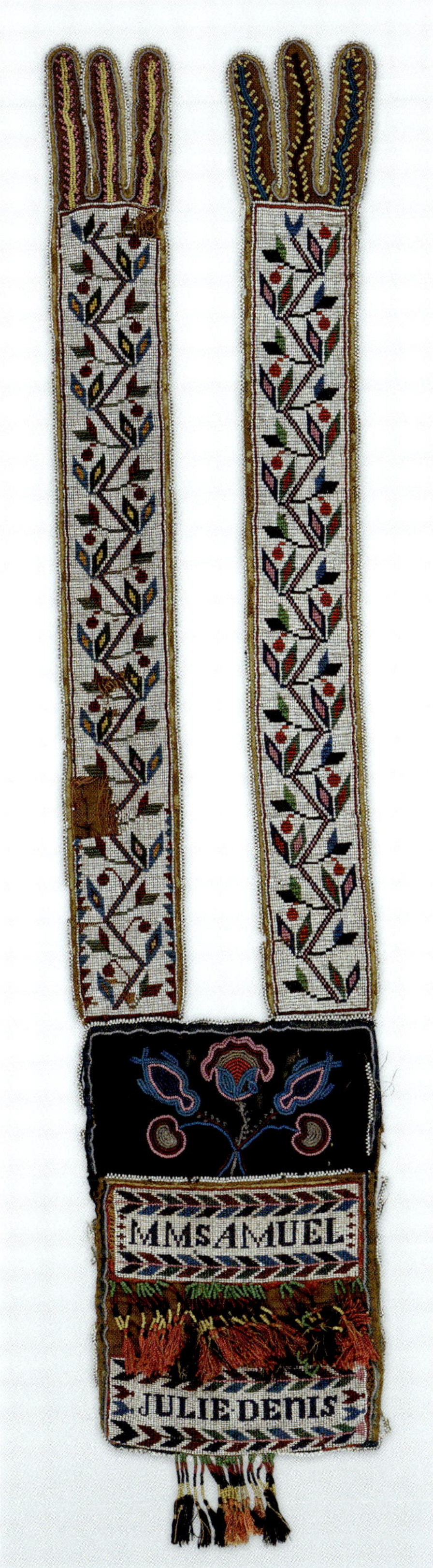

1.08 Gashkibidaagan with tabs similar to those fringe elements also seen on otter skin tail and paw pendants or tabbed leather powder horn straps, c. 1850s. *WHS 126682*

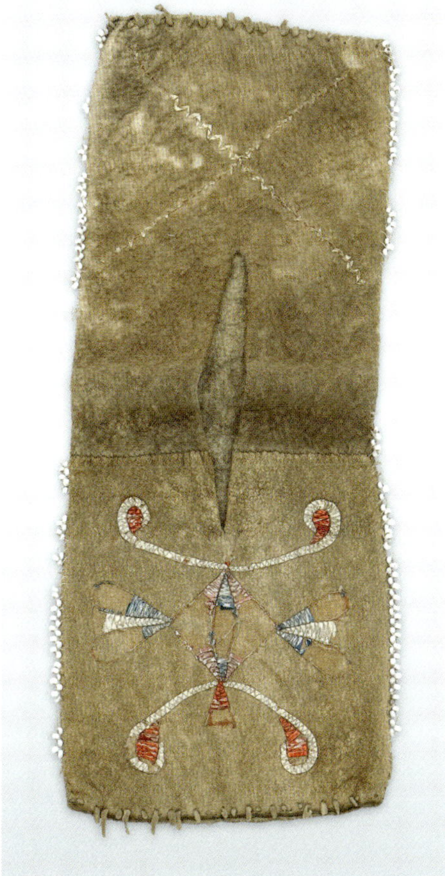

1.09 A bag made by a Dakota quillworker, c. 1840. *MNHS 6167.6*

There are several small shoulder bags or precursors of the gashkibidaaganag documented in the Minnesota region. In Figure 1.10, Joseph Rolette, a fur trader and territorial-era politician, wears a small bag with a beaded panel applied to it (known at the time as a panel bag; the term should not be confused with the later gashkibidaagan style characterized as "full panel bag," explained on page 53). Ethnographer Henry Rowe Schoolcraft's 1820 journal (Figure 1.11) includes a shot pouch, also decorated with a band of quillwork, among his Great Lakes "Indian

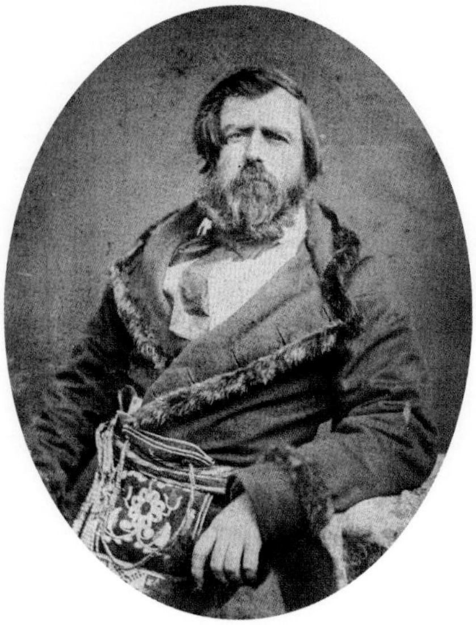

1.10 *(above)* Joseph Rolette wearing a bag decorated with a beaded panel, c. 1860. His bag is similar to leather bag styles of the period decorated with panels of quillwork or beadwork. *MNHS por 15345 p1*

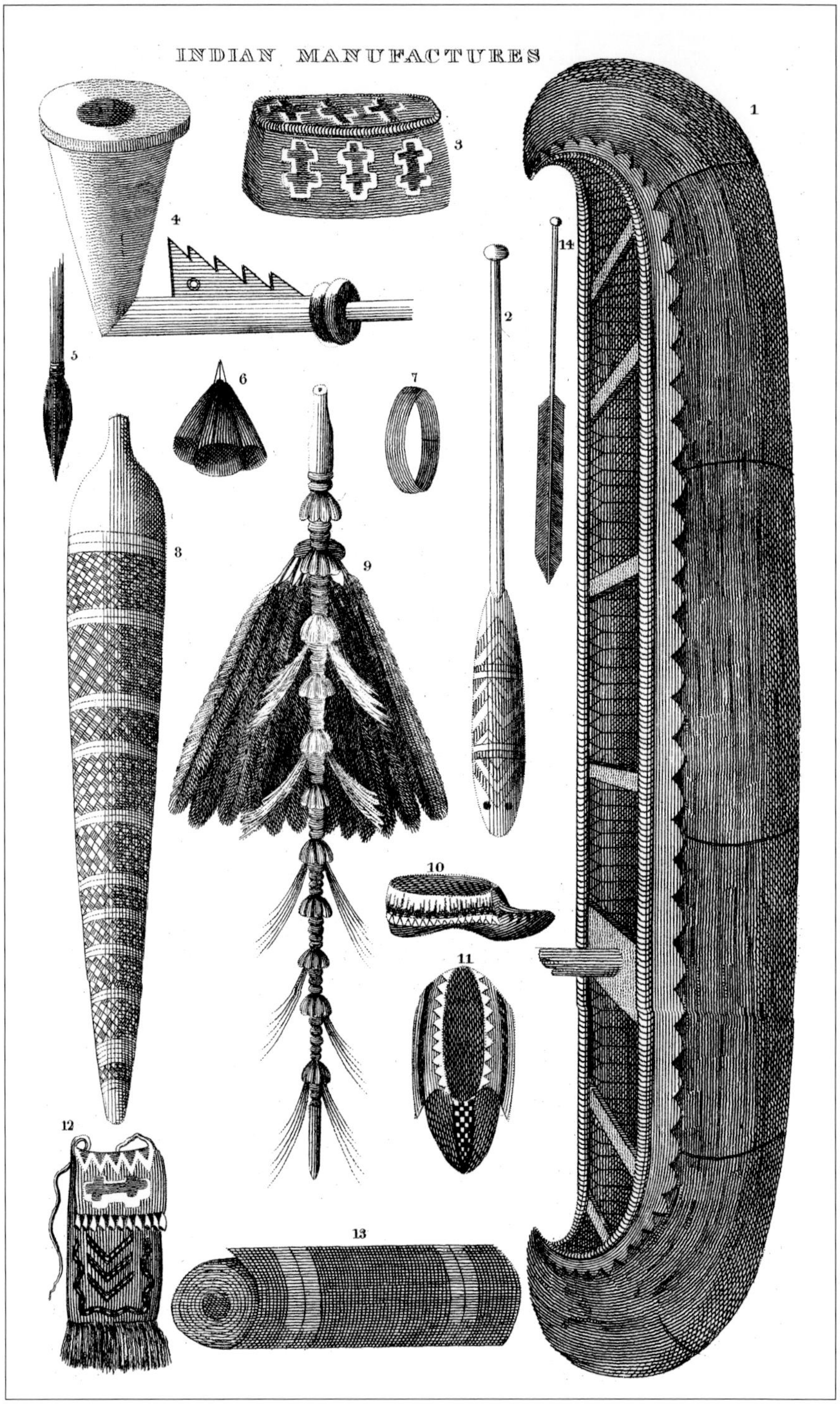

1.11 *(right)* A page from Henry Rowe Schoolcraft's 1820 journal. *Schoolcraft 1821, Pl. II*

Manufactures." A small Ojibwe or Ottawa quilled buckskin pouch (Figure 1.12) was acquired in 1820 by Captain David Bates Douglas while he served as surveyor for the Lewis Cass expedition to the Mississippi River headwaters. The two parallel patterned bands of quillwork on this pouch represent a bag component that was likely carried over into the gashkibidaagan, emerging in early bandolier bags as the area above the pocket opening and sometimes as a strip of beadwork attached to the top edge of the pocket panel as well. Bag types referred to as ear pouches and panel bags, possibly of Dakota manufacture, preceded the gashkibidaagan in the Minnesota area.[4]

This handful of precursor examples represents some of the varied bag styles in use simultaneously in the western Great Lakes region during the nineteenth century. All include one or more of the elements that eventually became essential structural components of the gashkibidaagan we know today—the pocket, strap, fringe, and an embellished horizontal band or panel. The earliest gashkibidaaganag were hybrids that incorporated the techniques and materials of precursor bag forms; some trend or inspiration caused these female artists to move toward the creation of what we have come to know as gashkibidaaganag.[5]

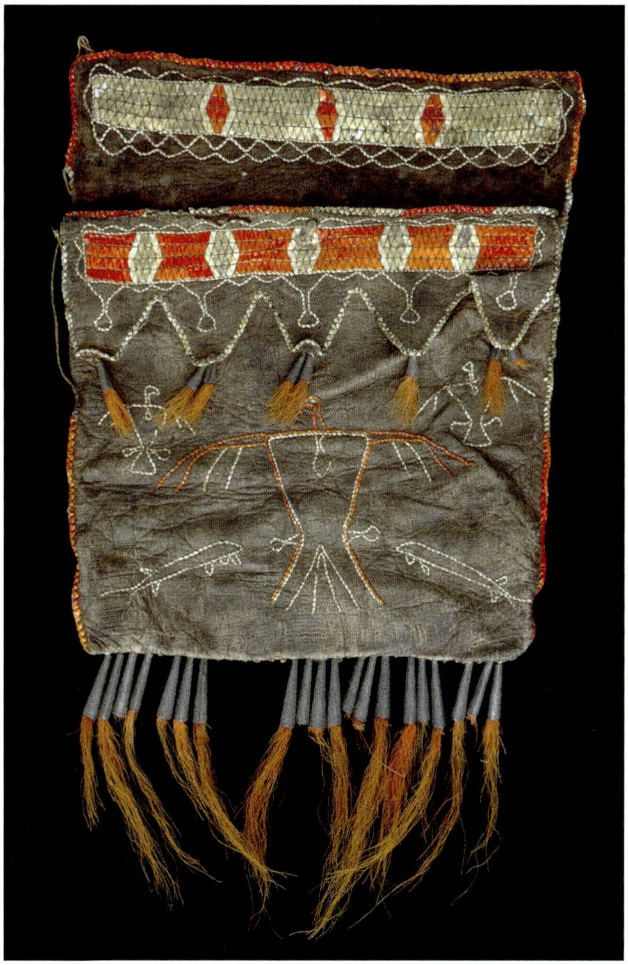

1.12 Ojibwe or Ottawa quilled buckskin pouch, before 1820; deer fur, metal, buckskin, porcupine quill; 26.67 × 17.78 cm; gift of Captain Douglas, 1822. *Photography by Mark Sexton and Jeffrey R. Dykes, © Peabody Essex Museum E6637*

By the 1870s, when the gashkibidaagan emerged as a widely used and fully developed form, the cultural traditions that birthed it had been profoundly impacted by the migrations that occurred when northeastern Algonquian peoples traveled west to the Great Lakes, plains, and prairies. This transition took place over four hundred years as the tribes moved and interacted with many landscapes and other indigenous nations, such as the Odawa, Iroquois, and Huron, resulting in a complex mix of continuity and innovation. The Algonquian artists who moved across the Great Lakes in the 1600s brought with them skills, talents, and existing construction techniques, as well as motif and design preferences for the decoration of their everyday objects.

Minnesota's location and the timing of mid-nineteenth century white settlement further stimulated this mixing (see map, page 20). Minnesota sits at the heart of a geographically diverse area that experienced cultural exchange and trade among many Indian nations, Métis people, and white explorers, fur traders, missionaries, and settlers. The Mississippi and Minnesota Rivers, the Pigeon River, the Rainy River along the Canadian border, Lake Superior, and the Red River oxcart trails that ran between the Métis community near Winnipeg to St. Paul all provided a network of land and water routes for travel and trade in and through the region.[6]

Network of rivers, oxcart trails, and general areas of occupancy in Minnesota in the mid-nineteenth century. *Map by Matt Kania, Map Hero, Inc.*

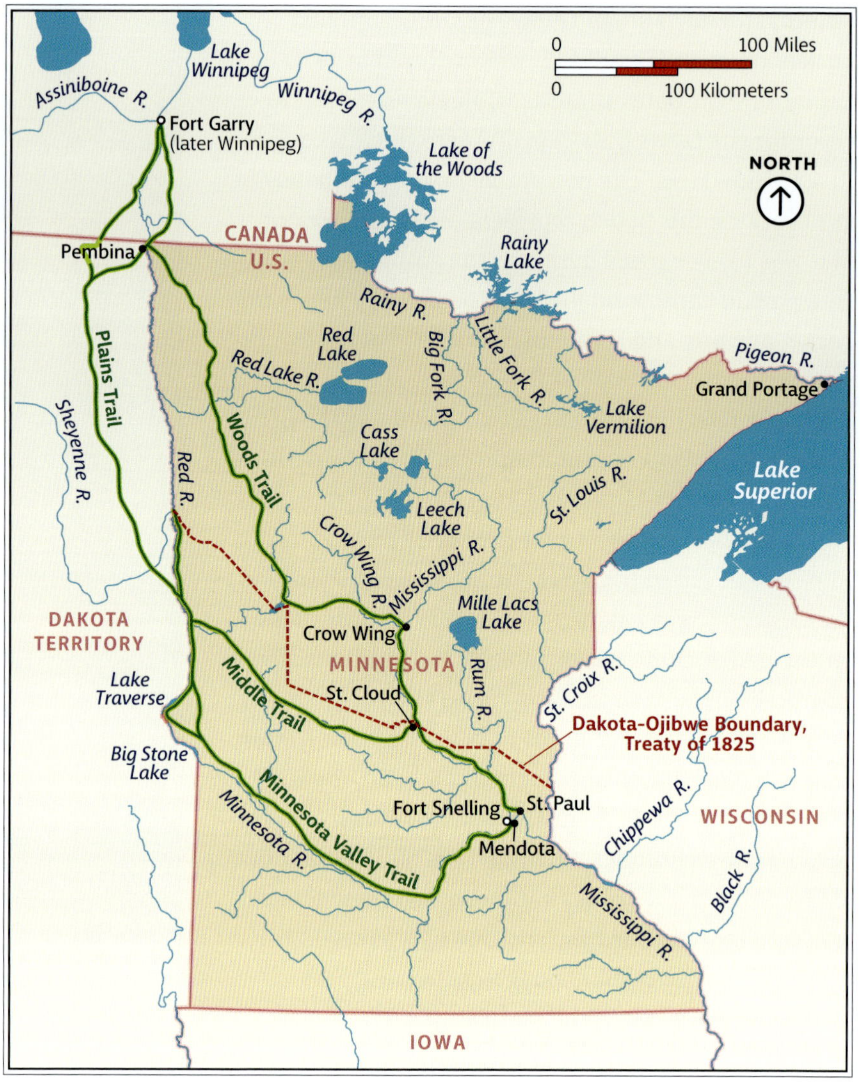

For generations, the Ojibwe of the Great Lakes moved seasonally for trapping, hunting, fishing, berry picking, wild ricing, and harvesting maple sugar. Because they lived in multiple homes in different locations through the year, the Ojibwe developed more portable household items than many other indigenous cultures of North America. They made minimal use of fragile, heavy ceramics. Bands, sashes, belts, and bags that could be rolled up for easy transport and storage were practical. Women made bags and containers from tanned leather, from birch bark, from the inner bark of basswood, and from stinging nettle fibers twined into cordage.

To decorate these objects, Ojibwe women used porcupine quills, bird quills, moose hair, shells, seeds, and other materials available in nature. Natural pigments and minerals were used initially to dye the quills and sometimes to color areas of the surface material. Eventually women adopted glass beads and other materials they acquired from traders. After Minnesota became a territory (1849) and a state (1858), the US government pushed Ojibwe people to abandon traditional lifeways and forms of cultural expression and to take up farming and Euro-American forms of housekeeping. But even into the twenty-first century, many Ojibwe families continue to follow portions of the seasonal rounds that sustain them, hunting and fishing, gathering wild rice, and working in the sugar bush, and women continue to produce beautiful beaded objects.[7]

The Ojibwes' exposure to and interaction with other cultures has facilitated the evolution of object forms and decorative motifs, as well as the introduction of new supplies used to enhance these bags and other objects. As with all artists, the Ojibwe women who made the gashkibidaaganag used what they saw and liked, whether that was a length of European printed cotton, bead types and colors available in the trader's store, a paper pattern from an auntie, or the traced outline of a thimbleberry leaf growing on the forest floor.

Cultures do not usually document their own evolving object forms, but outside observers may attempt to do so. A series of white explorers, ethnographers, and anthropologists studied aspects of Ojibwe life—some intentionally and others as a result of their travels. Early travelers kept journals on their visits to the upper Northwest, including contributors such as Henry Rowe Schoolcraft, who sought out the source of the Mississippi River in 1832. Johann Georg Kohl, a German who traveled in the Minnesota Territory in the 1850s, assessed his surroundings with his background in geography, science, and history. Newton Horace Winchell wrote numerous works between the 1870s and 1911 on the geology, natural history, and indigenous peoples of Minnesota, completing his work with *The Aborigines of Minnesota.* Their observations and those of other men were significantly augmented by the work of a number of American women who published particularly groundbreaking treatises on Ojibwe women and their culture based on the research they carried out from the late nineteenth through mid-twentieth centuries: Frances Densmore (1929), Sister Bernard Coleman (1947), Sister Inez Hilger (1936 and 1937), and Carrie Lyford (1943).

These ethnographers and contemporary Ojibwe bead artists who shared their histories and perspectives with me provide the most commonly held origin hypothesis: the entire gashkibidaagan form is an imitation of military ammunition pouches worn by the European and American military. In the 1940s, Carrie Lyford observed: "One of the most striking articles in the ceremonial costume of the Ojibwa is the ceremonial bag, a large beaded pocket with shoulder band. . . . An Ojibwa wearing a beaded pouch is considered in full dress. Two pouches were often worn, one on each shoulder. The shoulder pouch or bandolier resembled the pocket or bullet pouch decorated with a crest which was worn by the British soldier about the middle of the eighteenth century."[8]

Anthropologist Sister Bernard Coleman visited the Ojibwe reservations in Minnesota and made research notes between 1929 and 1945. In *Decorative Designs of the Ojibwa of Northern Minnesota*, she offers discerning observations on design in the material culture of the Ojibwe. She left a detailed record, alive with the voices and perspectives of the Ojibwe bead artists and elders she interviewed (whom she refers to as informants), the 900 patterns and 450 objects she studied, and the varied aspects of material culture data she collected and interpreted. Her note on the gashkibidaagan is brief: "Shoulder pouch (dashkabidagan). The original use of the buckskin shoulder pouches was for carrying articles; today, they have no practical purpose, except as ceremonial paraphernalia. Informants believe that this type of bag had its origin in the small bullet bag."[9]

It is likely, of course, that indigenous people of pre-contact North America had already adopted habits of wearing some clothing (animal skins, woven fiber) and accoutrements over one shoulder. But the manner of wearing the bags and the presence of tassels at the base of the pocket may also have been influenced by the silk sashes worn by US soldiers in the Civil War era. The sashes were commonly seen on US soldiers in full dress, tied around the waist. When serving as "officer of the day," a soldier wore the sash diagonally across the chest, similar to the gashkibidaagan strap. Some photographs show American Indians wearing these military sashes as well—across the chest, around the waist, and as a headgear element.[10]

Another origin theory is tied to the multiple definitions associated with one of the Ojibwemowin (Ojibwe language) terms used for bandolier bag, particularly tobacco bag. The term *gashkibidaagan* applies to several bag types, including a bag with a closable top, a tobacco bag, a pipe bag, and a bandolier bag. Some current bead artists have mentioned that only on occasion might a person carry charms, tobacco, and possibly a pipe, among other things, in his or her gashkibidaagan. In 1889 an Ojibwe leader at Leech Lake presented a pipe to a visiting US government official, saying, "I have heard that since coming you have been presented with a magnificent beaded sack, and a beaded sack never goes without a pipe."[11]

It is possible that one of the precursor forms that led to the gashkibidaagan was the early item described sometimes as a pouch used for tobacco and pipes. But the long, narrow pipe bag so common among the Dakota and other Plains tribes was never as popular among the Ojibwe of Minnesota. And the size and shape of early gashkibidaaganag, unlike the Dakota pipe or tobacco bag, was simply not particularly conducive to holding a long, top-heavy pipe form, or even a disassembled pipe. Both pipes and gashkibidaaganag were presented at ceremonial occasions. Non-Indians could therefore have easily assumed that the two items belonged together. A 1908 *Minneapolis Tribune* article likely describes a gashkibidaagan and accompanying pipe presented to President Theodore Roosevelt in Washington, DC, by May Zhuck-ke-ge-shig, a well-regarded Mississippi Band leader who often represented the White Earth Band in the US capitol. The journalist's account does not necessarily confirm any functional link between the two items.

> Chief May Zhuck-ke-ge-shig came to Washington from the White Earth reservation in Minnesota, to bear a message of greeting from his people to the president.
>
> He had with him an Indian pipe of exquisite workmanship; and an Indian bead bag, made by his wife, and which she sent as a gift to the nation's ruler. . . . The president was greatly interested in the Chippewa chief, and accepted his gifts of pipe and bead-bag with profuse thanks.[12]

Terminology offers other clues and challenges in determining the origin of gashkibidaaganag. Professionally trained ethnographers and common observers describe the bags in myriad ways that may focus on their visual characteristics, function, societal role, or the method in which they are worn. Terms they used include big bag, bead bag, beaded bag, bead sack, beaded pouch, beadwork pouch, beaded bag outfit, beautiful beadwork, tobacco pouch (or *kashkibitagunug*, an early representation of the term gashkibidaaganag), beaded tobacco pouch, tobacco bag, ceremonial bag, ceremonial game bag, hunting bag, ceremonial Indian beaded bag, pony bag, fire bag, dance bag, medicine bag (or *kashkibidjigan*, the term offered by Sister Bernard Coleman for medicine bag), friendship bag, shoulder bag, shoulder pouch (or *dashkabidagan*), apron, dance apron, bandouliere, bandoleer, bandoleer bag, bandolier, or bandolier bag—among others. To further the confusion, a single author may use more than one of these terms in referring to one bag.

Surprisingly, despite the status of this object in the Ojibwe culture of Minnesota, it was not identified uniquely in the Ojibwe or English language. Even the Ojibwe themselves have multiple recognized terms in Ojibwemowin that could be used to describe a bandolier bag. Gashkibidaagan is the common Mille Lacs Band term, defined as a bag with a closable top: a tobacco bag, a pipe bag, or a satchel. The term gashkibidaagan is also found in print both historically and in the present, and it is currently documented in use by Ojibwemowin speakers in other areas of Minnesota besides Mille Lacs.[13]

A second Ojibwemowin term is tied to the method of wearing the object rather than to its use or function. *Aazhooningwa'an* is a word that references wearing across the shoulder and wing, or underarm; a variation, *aazhooningwa'igan*, references bandolier bag and wing, or underarm. While this name is more uniquely descriptive, it enjoys less use among the Ojibwe of Minnesota today than the term gashkibidaagan.[14]

Importantly, the previously discussed Ojibwemowin terms clearly distinguish bandolier bags from terms used for medicine or religious *Mide* bags (*midewayaan*). Other bag terms that are not used to describe bandolier bags include *mashkimod* (bag, sack), *mashkimodegwaajigan* (pocket), and *bagiwayaaneshkimod* (cloth bag).[15]

While their origins remain obscure, gashkibidaaganag are alluded to or described in various sources, including American Indian narratives and oral histories, ethnological studies, descriptions of travelers, and among individuals who worked in contact with these isolated communities, such as missionaries, physicians, journalists, contractors, and artists. Because so few substantial historical gashkibidaagan accounts exist, the strongest evidence of the bags' use in Ojibwe life is found by studying the pictorial records left by photographers and the stories and records associated with the hundreds of extant bags themselves. That evidence is discussed in subsequent chapters.

Uses and cultural meanings

The historical and contemporary information about these bags suggests they have enjoyed multiple functions and that their earliest origins trace back to the age-old need for a simple functional bag. The specific use has evolved. My interviews with elders and bag makers indicate that while the bags could be used to carry personal items (such as tobacco, a pipe, charms, or herbs), this was not particularly important or essential to their use or function.

Perhaps their most significant original role was one recorded in many of the earliest chronicles as well as in more recent accounts. This use defines the gashkibidaagan as a means of barter or exchange: a bag was worth a pony in trade with the Dakota and Lakota (usually called Sioux in historical accounts) and other western tribes. Just as there are many terms used to describe the bag itself, the interpretations of its economic role sometimes differ in these accounts. The words used in a majority of accounts, however, betray the racial prejudices of their time.

The earliest mention I found regarding gashkibidaaganag is a commentary in Reverend Joseph A. Gilfillan's scrapbook on the agricultural fair at White Earth in 1879: "Their ponies they [the Ojibwe] got last summer, or the summer before, from the Sioux, who seem to have an inexhaustible supply of them. One otter skin and one beaded tobacco-pouch, made by a Chippewa woman, is the price they paid for each pony on the Missouri River or at Devil's Lake."[16]

In his 1896 study, *The Menomini Indians,* Walter James Hoffman discusses the extent of the Ojibwe trade in beaded crafts, by which he means gashkibidaaganag, and he offers an explanation for their occasional presence in other Native communities from Minnesota to the far west:

> So as late as 1891 a specially appointed delegation left Red Lake, Minnesota, to visit all the Ojibwa and Menomini settlements in southern Minnesota and in Wisconsin, to gather every available large specimen of beadwork for traffic with the Arikara and Hidatsa of North Dakota, from whom the northern Ojibwa obtain horses. Annual visits were made by the Ojibwa . . . [who] would, in time, procure more horses, in exchange for the beadwork[,]

from the Crows of Montana. In this manner the Ojibwa and Menomini beadwork gradually found its way as far west as the Selish [Salish] Indians, in northwestern Idaho, from whom examples have been recovered.[17]

Photographs from the 1880s document Hoffman's point. Among the numerous historic images of two famous leaders, Sitting Bull (Hunkpapa Lakota, South Dakota) and Chief Joseph (Nez Perce, Oregon), are formal portraits that were widely distributed and show each man wearing a loomed panel gashkibidaagan. In a paper presented to the Minnesota Historical Society's Executive Council in November 1897, Reverend Joseph A. Gilfillan recounted the following:

> The winter of 1896–97, on account of its deep snow, was unusually disastrous to the cattle and ponies. Some Indians had cut and stacked some hay on the meadows a few miles from where they lived, but had not hauled it home; and when the snow became deep, the ponies, being feeble, were unable to haul it, and so they nearly died. At Cass Lake there were only two or three ponies that survived; they nearly all died at Red Lake, on the White Earth reservation, everywhere. Some tried to keep them alive by feeding them branches of trees; but, as may be imagined, with poor success. One would wonder that, with the continual hard treatment every winter, and the great numbers that starve, there are any ponies left; but the explanation is that they get a fresh supply of ponies every summer from the Sioux, who abound in ponies. Most of the Ojibway men have their women make quantities of their beautiful bead-work every winter and store it up. When summer comes, the husband carries it to the Sioux country, and brings back as many ponies as he had tobacco-pouches (kashkibitagunug). One of the bead-work pouches is the great ornament of an Ojibway, and any person wearing it is considered to be in full dress; it is worth a pony among the Sioux. Thus the stock of horses is every summer replenished. The Ojibways are not horse Indians; naturally they have no horses, excepting those they get from the Sioux.[18]

A 1901 travel memoir of the White Earth area by H. E. Burleson, published in *The Young Christian Soldier*, offers the most colorful but perhaps the least culturally sensitive narrative:

> The shadows are deepening and we are far from home, so we reluctantly start on the return trip. We first peep in at the fine Government school, which is being put in readiness for the fall term, and hope to come again when the children are there to brighten the now silent halls. At the village store we see two gorgeous bead "pony-bags" and buy them to carry off as trophies. Perhaps you do not remember that a "pony bag" looks a little like an apron made of beads sewed on cloth in a pattern to resemble flowers and leaves and other similar designs. These bags, or "bead sacks" as they are

> sometimes called, are worn by the Indian braves when on "dress-parade" and in their heathen dances. The value of these sacks or bags is the same as the value of a pony, which accounts for the name "pony-bag," a bag and a pony being interchangeable without any need of United States money.[19]

In the 1940s, Carrie Lyford also remarked on the length of time involved in manufacturing a bag and suggested they had been made more than a hundred years earlier: "Since its adoption by the Ojibwa and other Woodland tribes, [the gashkibidaagan] has become more highly decorated. The Ojibwa were making the beaded pouch in the early days of the nineteenth century. It is said that at that time, when winter was over, pouches that had been beaded by the Ojibwa were carried to the Sioux country to be exchanged for ponies. Each beadwork pouch was worth a pony."[20]

Sister Inez Hilger related a role of the gashkibidaaganag in the woman's dance, "a dance still prevalent on all reservations, most especially at the time of the commercial pow-wow—an Indian dance held for tourists." Her Lac Courte Oreille informant described the dances he attended as a young man, perhaps in the early 1930s: "Women chose their partners for each occasion. If the man chosen by a woman for the first dance gave the woman a whip, he signified thereby that he would present her with a pony later. She, in turn, might then give him a beaded-bag outfit. In the dance the woman follows the man. In the old days these dances sometimes lasted 10 to 14 days but were not given very often; today they are given every Saturday night."[21]

Besides their function in trade and in dance as regalia, gashkibidaaganag also served, I would argue, as a marker of cultural identity and a form of armor-like protection of that identity. In this way, the bags were physically transformative. While the Ojibwe may have been viewed as "Christianized Indian farmers" when dressed in "citizens garb," or non-Native street clothes, wearing the bags over these clothes was symbolic of Ojibwe heritage. Whether it was a conscious or unconscious act, wearing the bags represented a code for Ojibwe culture that was acceptable to the white power structure.[22]

In her 1929 ethnography *Chippewa Customs,* Minnesota musicologist and ethnographer Frances Densmore gave only cursory coverage of the bag's role in Ojibwe society and did not include a term for it in her glossary. She did, however, include a photo of a loom-woven panel gashkibidaagan and additional sketches of design motifs used for other gashkibidaaganag, along with the observation, "Beaded bags (bandoleers) were worn on festive occasions, the broad band passing over the shoulder. Sometimes two such bags were worn."[23]

Sister Bernard Coleman observed:

> Social dances provided an opportunity for the men and women to display their elaborately decorated dresses and other paraphernalia. Women

> dancers wore the ordinary dress of the time, with the addition of extra trimmings, such as tin pendants, made from tin cans, and beaded bands. Beaded head- and neck-bands and necklaces of shells or beads were also worn, and, in later days, one feather could be worn in the hair. Formerly feathers were used only in the headdresses of men. The men displayed much more decoration in their clothing and headgear than did the women. They wore gaudy sashes, belts, knife sheaths, *shoulder pouches* [italics added], bands, and decorated vests, coats, leggings, and gauntlets.[24]

Ethnographers often imposed their personal experiences with formalized religion and the accompanying regalia onto the cultures they observed. Since gashkibidaaganag were sometimes worn by spiritual leaders during ceremonies, observers often misidentified them as medicine bags because of their quality, elaborate decorative treatment, and status within the community. Walter J. Hoffman, author of "The Mide'wiwin or 'Grand Medicine Society' of the Ojibwa" (1891), noted the presence of bandolier bags at ceremonies: "Ojibwa Mide' priests, take particular pride in their appearance when attending ceremonies of the Mide' Society. . . . Bags made of cloth, beautifully ornamented or entirely covered with beads, are worn, supported at the side by means of a broad band or baldric passing over the opposite shoulder."[25]

Albert B. Reagan worked with the US Indian Service as superintendant of the Nett Lake (Bois Forte) Chippewa Indian Agency from 1909 to 1914. In this capacity, he accumulated a large collection of Ojibwe material culture, particularly Midewiwin objects. Reagan's remarks show that gashkibidaaganag were worn by individuals who happened to be Mide practitioners, rather than having a sacred role in a Midewiwin setting: "These fire bags might be termed 'dance bags.' They are ornamented and worn chiefly by the well-to-do Indians at the dance. They seem to be worn only by the medicine men at the medicine dances. A medicine man considers himself fortunate if he owns one of them. Usually when worn, two are worn at a time, one on the left side and one on the right, though the writer has seen medicine men with but one sack. . . . It was not learned that these bags have any medicine value."[26]

Records of gashkibidaaganag being given as gifts show the status conferred in the exchange. Nathan Richardson was a member of a Morrison County committee that was established to defend the rights of the Mille Lacs Band. His many respectful interactions with the Mille Lacs Band caused several band leaders to meet with him and other Morrison County residents in 1880 regarding a threatened takeover of Mille Lacs land for timber. Richardson worked with the band on these and other issues relating to annuity payments that had been withheld. He wrote letters to the editor of the local paper, pointing out the wrong and shameful treatment of the Mille Lacs Band by those who wanted its members to remove to the White Earth Reservation, over 120 miles away. After this endeavor,

Richardson was rewarded in 1884 with a bag (Figure 1.13) presented to him with great respect by Mille Lacs chief Sha-bosh-kung. "It consisted of a large pocket or pouch, nearly a foot square," noted the *Little Falls Transcript* on December 19, 1884, "and a wide band to pass over the shoulder to support the pouch, all covered with peculiar designs in beadwork." This is one of the first published and descriptively useful accounts of a specific gashkibidaagan.[27]

Sometime between 1882 and 1887, six powerful members of the Mille Lacs community (Ma-zu-nea-ni, Ba-gru-na-pu, Cha-ba-e-kum, Mar-hi-gar, Wa-wi-eck-ko-nuk, and Ka-gna-dn-sa) presented a gashkibidaagan (Figure 1.14) to Minnesota governor Lucius F. Hubbard in recognition of his status in the state government.

In June 1920, members of the White Earth Band presented a bag (Figure 1.15) and other articles to Minnesotan Herbert S. McDuffee, a veteran of World War I, to recognize him as a comrade in arms during their Annual Celebration. McDuffee described the event:

> After indulging in a long and lively dance, a speaker steps forward and informs us that as their young braves had fought side by side with us in the Great War we were bound together by a strong bond, and that they were now going to have a dance for the returned warriors. During this dance, we that took part in the Great War are in the center of the ring. Just how long this dance lasts we cannot say but to us it seemed more than an hour.

1.13 *(below left)* Bag presented by Mille Lacs chief Sha-bosh-kung, 1884. *Morrison County Historical Society*

1.14 *(below center)* Bag presented by six Mille Lacs leaders, mid-1880s. *MNHS 64.155.29; see also Figure 3.10*

1.15 *(below right)* Bag presented by members of the White Earth Band in 1920. *MNHS 1990.506.5.A,B; see also Figure 2.12*

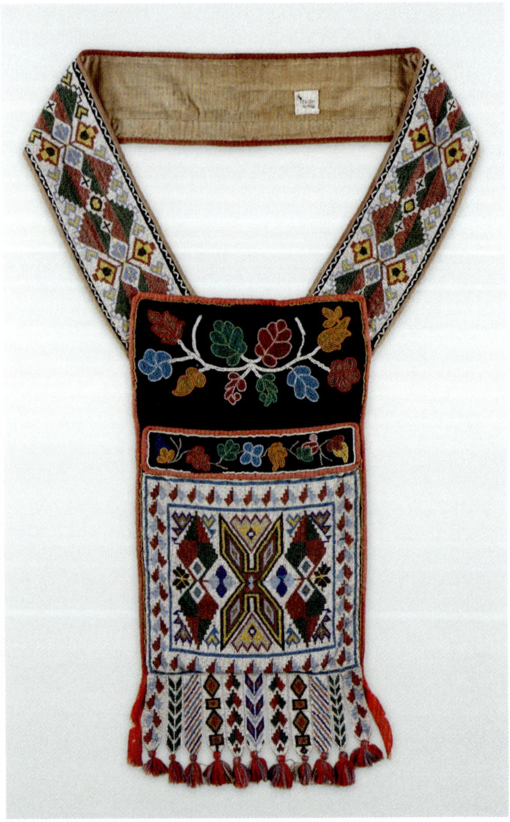

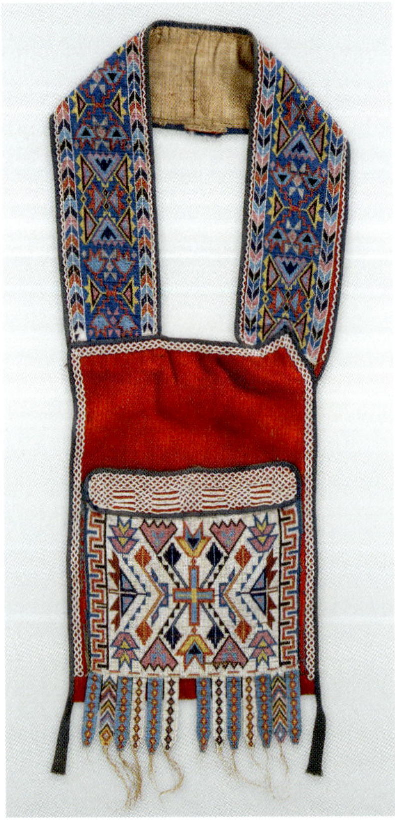

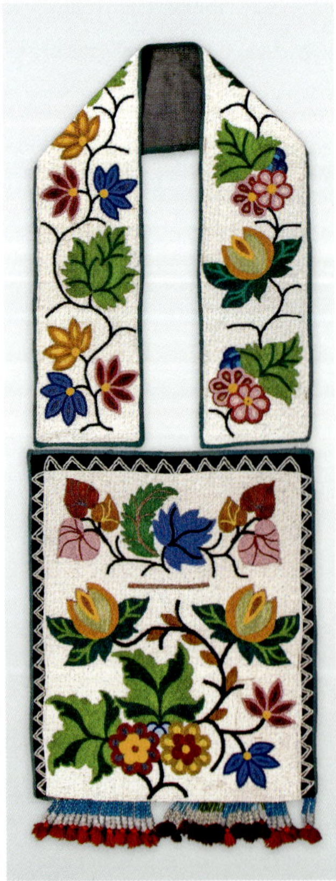

This is a long time for the un-initiated to dance but it can be done. After the dance is over, an old chief comes out with some beautiful beadwork in his arms. With very few words he presents this in token of his brotherly love for one that fought by the side of one of his braves.[28]

It was unusual for a man to own more than one shoulder pouch, but if he did, it was indicative of wealth and social position. The wearing of multiple layers of gashkibidaaganag was often documented, especially in posed settings. Albert Reagan, who had seen one person wearing four or five bags at once, noted, "It is also reported that one chief recently wore as high as a dozen at one of the social dances."[29]

The wearing of the bags during dances had diminished by the 1950s, perhaps because of postwar financial pressures; assimilation efforts, including the forced removal of Ojibwe children to boarding schools, had also damaged the transmission of culture. Older Ojibwe advisers noted there just weren't many dances until a resurgence in the 1970s. Minnesota collector Fred Blessing, who married an Ojibwe woman and was adopted into the Red Lake and Leech Lake Bands, recorded his own experience of the shift in the 1950s. He wrote frequently on American Indian subjects, making elaborate observations that were influenced by his personal interests and experiences. Blessing describes, in great detail, clothing worn at a Red Lake dance in 1956, but only mentions gashkibidaaganag at the end of his account: "A Turtle Mountain Chippewa visiting at Red Lake on July 4th, 1956, had a pink and white shell on his forehead, it being fastened to his roache [*sic*] band. He was richly attired in beadwork rarely seen today. Two bandoleer bags were crossed over his shoulders and his cheeks were painted with vermillion. . . . The sight of this elderly but erect old timer in his old time costume was particularly rewarding."[30]

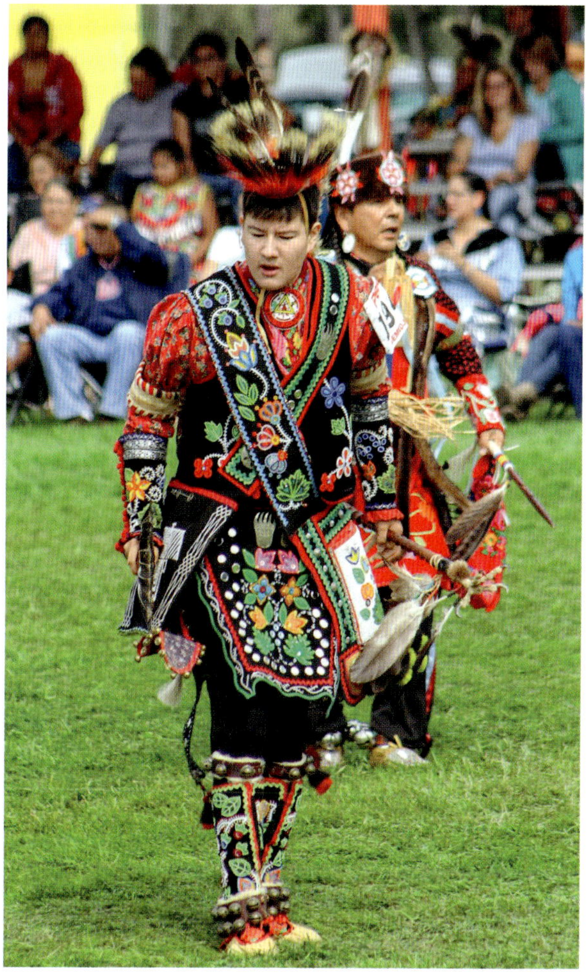

1.16 On his left hip, Ningozis White dances a bag made by his mother, Delina White, at Cass Lake, 2014. *Courtesy Delina White*

While the bags are today still valued culturally, as well as economically, the status surrounding gashkibidaaganag has shifted greatly to the bead artists themselves, who also make them for a sense of personal accomplishment, often to be retained as a family treasure. In Figure 1.16, Ningozis White dances a gashkibidaagan made by his mother, Delina White of Leech Lake. More recently, gashkibidaaganag are seeing renewed popularity. Special community-based programs to make the bags have received grant funding, websites offer encouragement and resources, and classrooms across Minnesota use an Ojibwe shoulder bag kit to teach children about bandolier bags. Pictures of new gashkibidaaganag appear on social media (Figure 1.17). In 2011 Douglas K. Limon organized a community art project in which he created

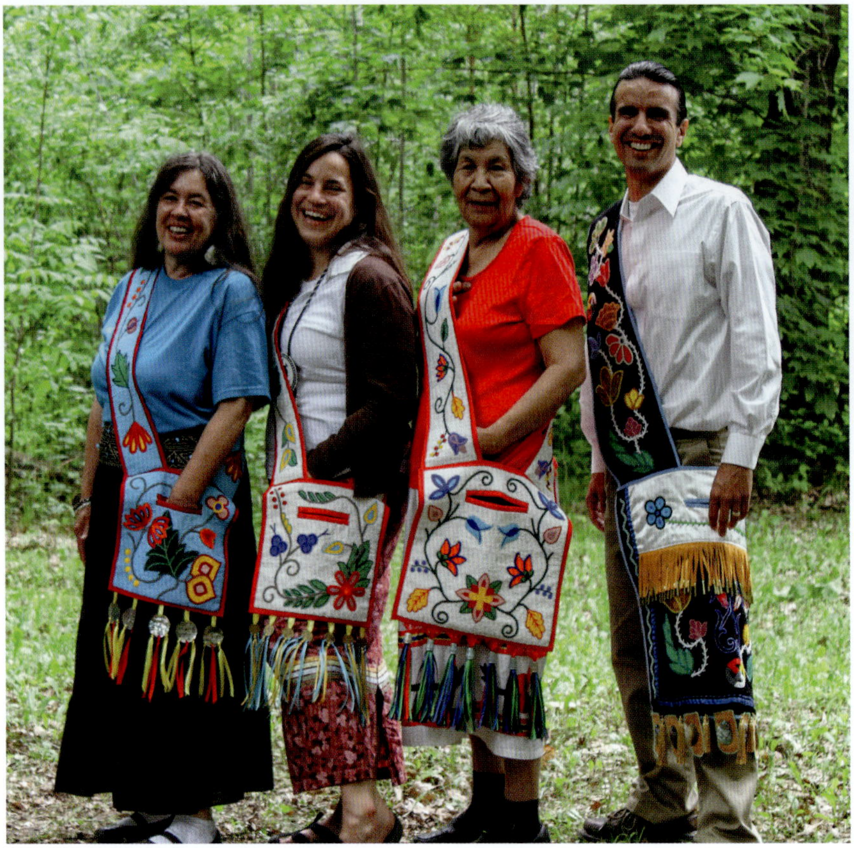

1.17 Babette Sandman, Monique Paulson, and Dora Ammann *(left to right)*, each wear a bag made by Travis DeBungee of Ponemah, Minnesota; Anton Treuer *(right)* wears one made by Connie Rivard of St. Croix, Wisconsin. From a 2014 Facebook post. *Courtesy Madeline Treuer*

a gashkibidaagan, and more than four hundred participants at fourteen venues—including reservations, powwows, museums, and art shows—stitched beads on a second bag, accepting his invitation to "Bead a part of history."[31]

During the late nineteenth and early twentieth centuries, when gashkibidaaganag were most popular, they likely conveyed different things to different individuals. In that era, a person wearing a gashkibidaagan may not have replied to questions such as "Why do you wear this bag?" and "What does it mean to you?" with anything more than a quizzical look. But Ojibwe people participating in their own culture and living their lives in the late nineteenth and early twentieth centuries must have felt a sense of pride both in the bag as a cultural icon and in its workmanship—pride generated by the imagery and artistry of each bag's grand visual statement.

Perhaps we'll never know the true source of these extraordinary objects, or even their original function, but we can continue the search and celebrate the value of gashkibidaaganag as cultural objects, as visual messages worn proudly across one's chest, and as a means for unifying a community and a culture.

Chapter 2

Forms, Construction, and Styles

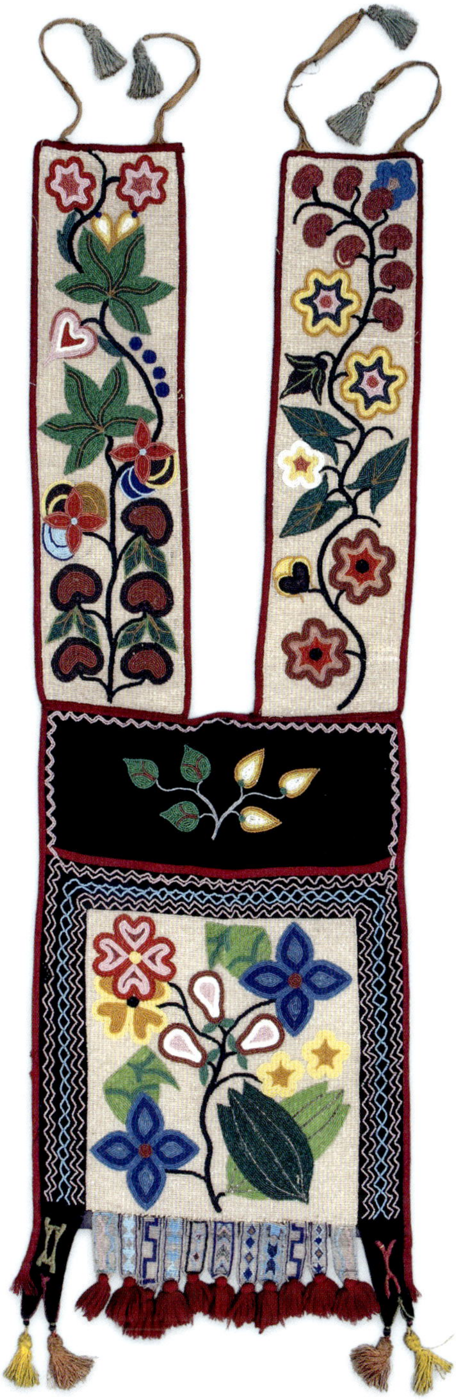

The complexity of the gashkibidaagan is not limited to its many names, uncertain origins, or multiple functions. Its physical composition changed over time, as different techniques, alterations in size and materials, and new types of bags evolved. Some bandolier bags were fully functioning objects used for carrying things; others were merely decorative beaded panels. All these changes overlapped as bead artists found new ways to express themselves.

Before considering these changes, it is important to understand the two common beadworking techniques used by Ojibwe women to decorate gashkibidaaganag. In earlier years, from the 1850s to the 1880s, women primarily created beaded panels on wooden looms, stringing single beads on the weft thread to create designs, and then attaching the panels of loom-woven beadwork to a cloth bag. In later years, artists used spot-stitch appliqué techniques: a thread strung with beads is laid in place on the cloth and then stitched or tacked in place, usually at every second or third bead; the entire surface is covered in beads, with white beads often filling the background. Bags with loom-woven panels are more symmetrical, due to the constraint of the warp and weft, with both geometric and organic motifs (Figure 2.01). The bags made with spot-stitch appliqué appear more free form, with curved lines that incorporate a greater number of organic motifs (Figure 2.02).

Earlier bags with loom-woven panels and later spot-stitch appliqué bags were probably being made simultaneously between 1880 and 1899. Examples of gashkibidaaganag beadwork are not common in photographs taken before 1890, but a few visual records exist from the 1870s to 1893; these show that floral motifs were being used on other beaded garments such as dance aprons, leggings, and belts or girdles. A 1903 Minneapolis newspaper article describes two gashkibidaaganag, each representing one of these bag forms, that were displayed with other beaded objects rather than worn in the customary across-the-chest manner: "There are two handsome specimens of medicine bags, one of woven beadwork and [the] other [of] sewed beads. The bands going around the shoulders are four or five inches wide and each bag covers the front of the wearer's person like a shield."[1]

Forty years later a similar observation of the two bag forms was made by ethnographer Carrie Lyford: "The pouch consists of a large square case or bag about 18 inches by 18 inches, with a broad band or baldric long enough to go around the neck so that the pouch hangs almost to the knees. Both the pouch and the band are highly decorated [with] bead weaving or [with bead] embroidery. Sometimes the woven square and band are all in one piece, with designs that harmonize."[2]

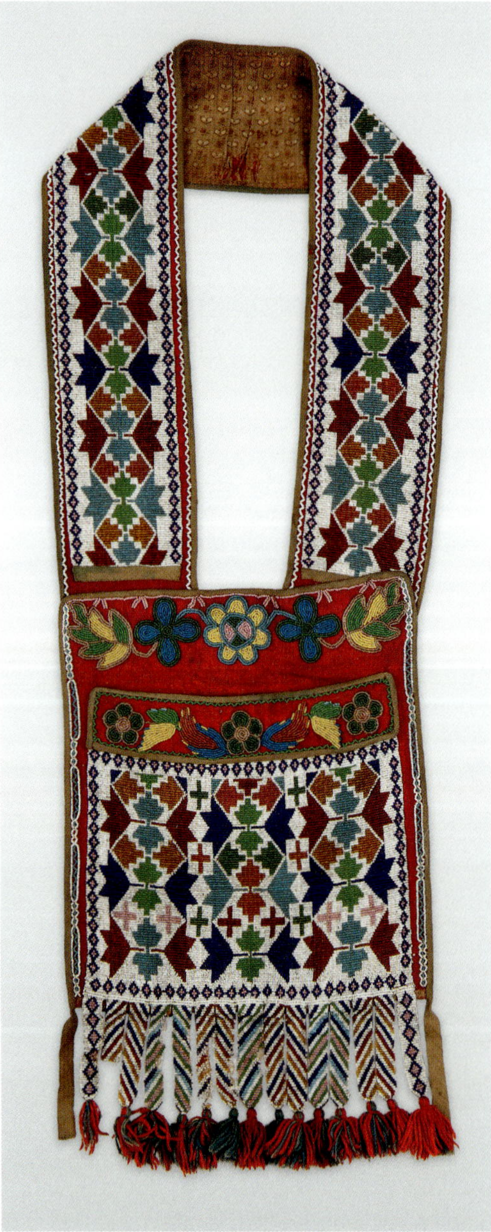

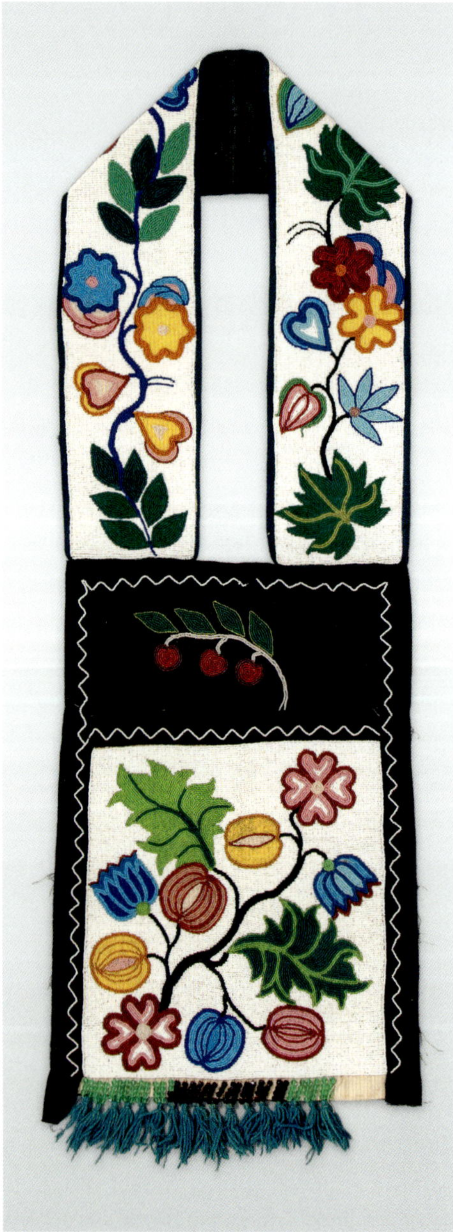

2.01 *(right)* Bag decorated with a loom-woven beaded panel, probably last third of the nineteenth century. *MNHS 6507.12; see also Figure 3.28*

2.02 *(far right)* Bag decorated with spot-stitch appliqué, probably 1890s to 1920s. *MNHS 2011.208.148; see also Figure 3.95*

Structure

The elements of gashkibidaaganag changed over time, but the basic parts of the bag have mostly remained the same. The core structural elements are its six bag components, shown in bold-face type in Figure 2.03.

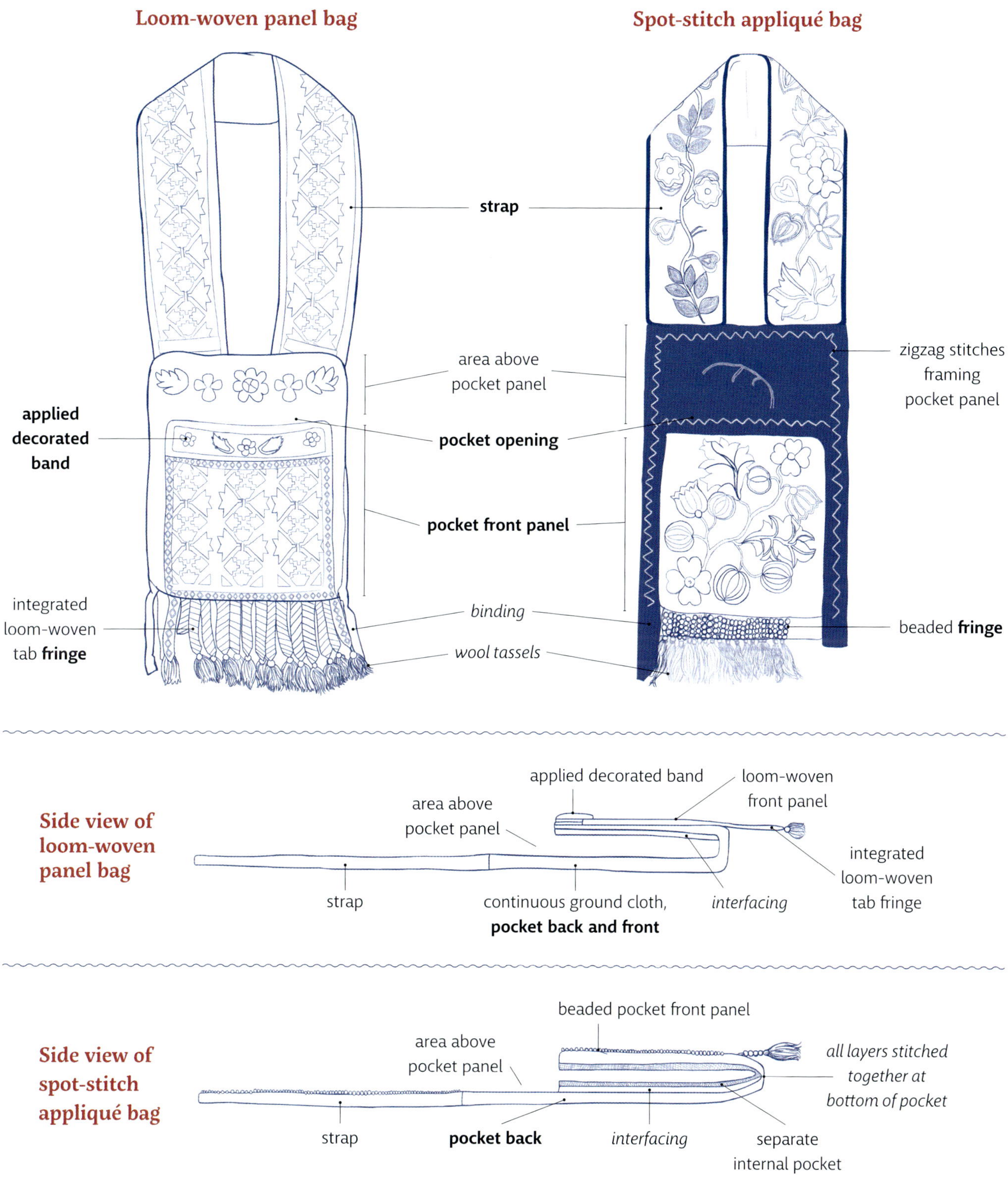

2.03 The parts of a gashkibidaagan. While there are many variations, these sketches illustrate common elements of a bag's structure. The labels in italics identify a few decorative elements and materials, which are discussed later in this chapter. *Illustration by Hannah Boehme*

Pocket back

The pocket portion of a bandolier bag is like a paper envelope with a flap that does not close. The back, or cloth ground, provides support for the beaded pocket panel on the front side of the bag. Because the pocket back is longer than the front, a portion of the back extends—and is visible—above the pocket opening on the front side. Sometimes the back is made from a separate layer of cloth—actually one of two to five pieces of fabric that are stitched together in the same manner as the pieces of a quilt to strengthen the support provided. In other cases, the back is simply the end of a continuous piece of ground cloth, beginning with the front panel and wrapping around to create a closed pocket bottom. As beadworkers developed their craft, spot-stitch appliqué decorative elements began to appear on the area above the pocket opening (Figures 2.04 and 2.05).

Pocket front panel

The decorated front panel, either loom woven or spot stitched, creates a visual and often real functioning pocket when attached to the pocket back (Figure 2.06). The pocket portion of the bag may also contain a separate bag lining, attached internally, or simply make use of the pocket back foundation cloth for that purpose.

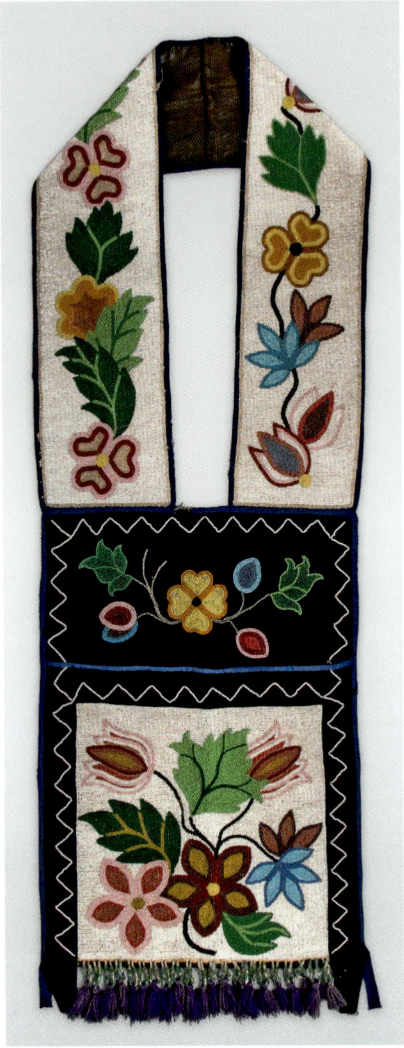

2.04 Spot-stitch appliqué bag from White Earth, owned by Paul Wage between 1900 and 1950. *MNHS 1993.260.10*

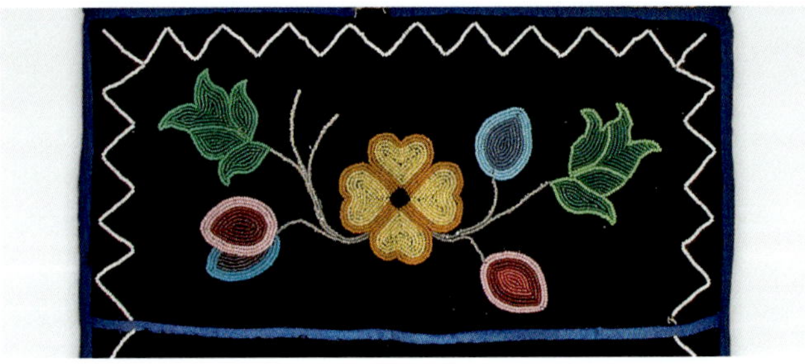

2.05 Detail of Figure 2.04 showing the floral motifs that are spot stitched onto velvet in the area above the pocket opening.

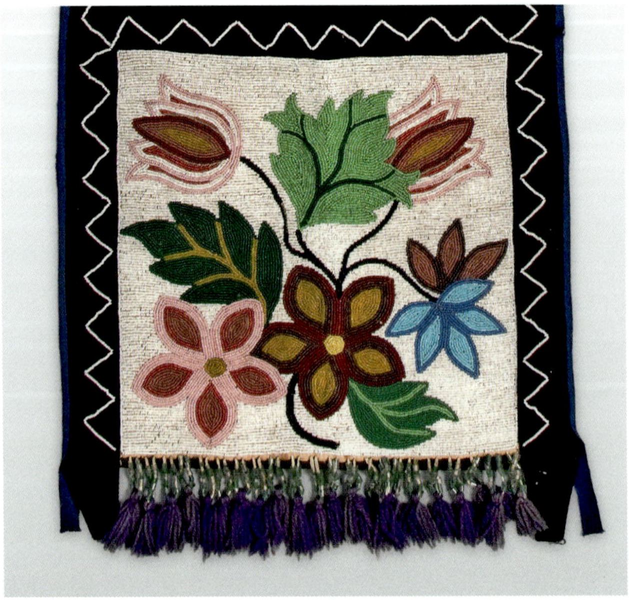

2.06 Pocket panel detail of Figure 2.04 showing the front panel of the pocket.

Applied decorated band

In early bag examples, from the 1850s to the 1870s, a separate and additional narrow strip of cloth decorated with spot-stitch appliqué is applied, sewn along the top edge of the pocket front panel (Figure 2.07). In early bags that have a loom-woven panel, this appliquéd strip of beadwork often outlines a floral motif, which may or may not be filled in with beadwork; this latter style is not typical of Minnesota Ojibwe beadwork. Sometimes the area above the pocket opening that is the visible portion of the back panel carries a running-flower, chainlike motif resembling these early bands. Sometimes this motif appears both above the pocket opening and on the band attached to the top edge of the pocket panel, as shown in Figure 2.01.

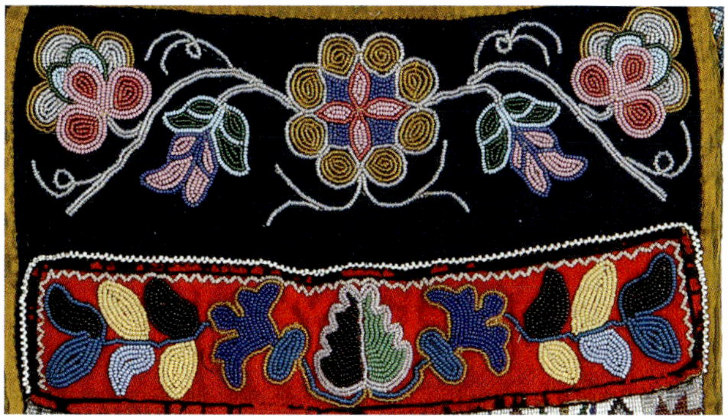

2.07 Applied decorated band attached to the top edge of the pocket opening on a bag probably from White Earth, collected by Darwin Hall c. 1891–1914. *MNHS 268. E64; see also Figure 12.18*

Strap

The strap generally consists of a rectangular length of cloth composed of either two separate pieces (Figure 2.08) or one continuous piece (Figure 2.09). Possible variations in strap construction include:

- beadwork, either loom woven or spot stitched, that has been attached to or sewn onto two separate strips of cloth but not joined physically at center top;
- two loom-woven strips of beadwork sewn onto a single strip of cloth;
- one applied continuous loom-woven strip of beadwork (usually
  attached to a single strip of cloth) or one continuous strip of spot-stitch appliqué beadwork;
- spot-stitch appliqué worked on a single length of cloth to visually appear as two separate strips, with in-filled background;
- spot-stitch appliqué bead motifs sewn on a cloth ground, without in-filled background.

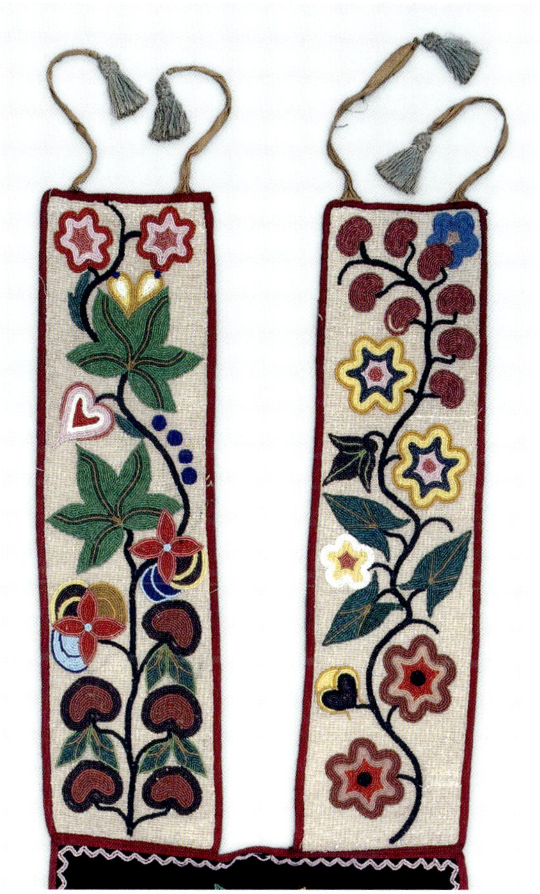

2.08 Spot-stitched strap made with two separate strips of cloth to be tied together. *MNHS 2011.208.145; see also Figure 9.09*

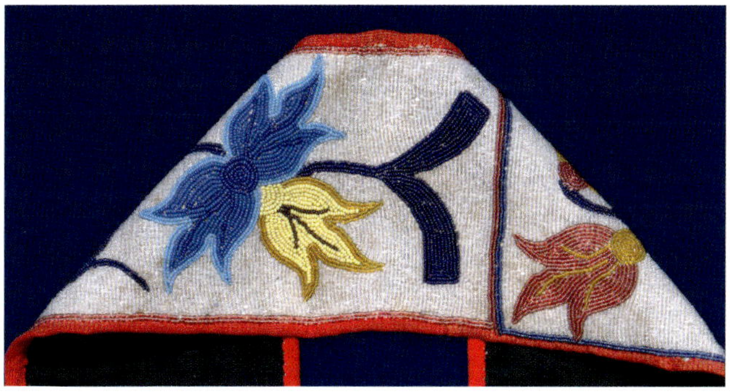

2.09 Strap made from a single strip that is spot stitched to mimic two separate pieces. *MNHS 10000.610; see also Figure 10.21*

The strap is frequently attached to the pocket with loose basting stitches (Figure 2.10), so the strap can be removed for other uses. In rarer cases, the pocket and its strap may be one continuous piece of beadwork mounted on a single piece of cloth backing.

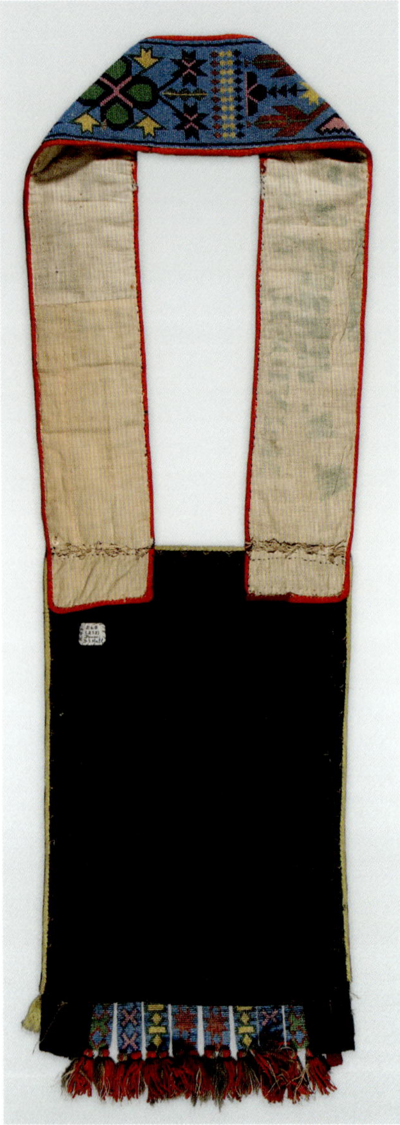

2.10 Finished ends of strap basted to the top edge of the pocket on the back side. *MNHS 272.E68; see also Figure 12.17*

Pocket openings

Gashkibidaaganag may have a full- or partial-width pocket opening; a small slit opening; a faux, or nonfunctional, pocket opening; a pocket opening on the back side and not visible from the front; or no real or suggested pocket opening at all.

The majority of nineteenth-century Minnesota Ojibwe gashkibidaaganag had full-width pocket openings. In the twentieth century, larger bags were constructed. Perhaps because the weight of a large bag would cause the pocket to gape open, distracting from a bag's beauty, the slit opening became more common. It was generally too narrow for a hand to be inserted, which made the pocket less functional (Figure 2.11). Then the slit was replaced by a bead representation about four rows in width and a few inches long, usually rendered in black or another dark color (Figure 2.12). Eventually, the pocket portion of the bag was replaced by a rectangular beaded panel; in effect, it no longer was a bag. While some artists held onto earlier bag components by beadworking motifs above and below an imagined pocket opening, even this homage to earlier bag forms mostly disappeared. With no pocket, the gashkibidaagan, now known as a full panel bag, simply has a strap and a beaded panel.

2.11 Slit opening in a bag probably made in the first third of the twentieth century. *MNHS 10000.714; see also Figures 3.80 and 3.96*

2.12 Beaded false opening. *MNHS 1990.506.5; see also Figure 1.15*

Fringe

When fringe is present, it is generally found at the bottom edge of the pocket. Fringe often terminates in wool yarn tassels, but it can also be finished with thread tassels, ribbon tassels, thimbles, bells, or tinkler cones. Loom-woven tab fringe can be *integrated* (woven as part of the pocket front panel) or *attached* as a series of separate tabs sewn to the bottom edge of the bag (Figures 2.13 and 2.14).

Fringe types most common on spot-stitch appliqué bags consist of threaded bugle beads. Variations include individual strings that are attached in a series of loops (Figure 2.15); a single long string festooned along the bottom; single strings of beads terminated with tassels; and several long strings strung together to form a netting (Figure 2.16).

On earlier bags, the straps also sometimes feature fringe, either loom-woven tabs or strings of threaded beads (Figures 2.17 and 2.18).

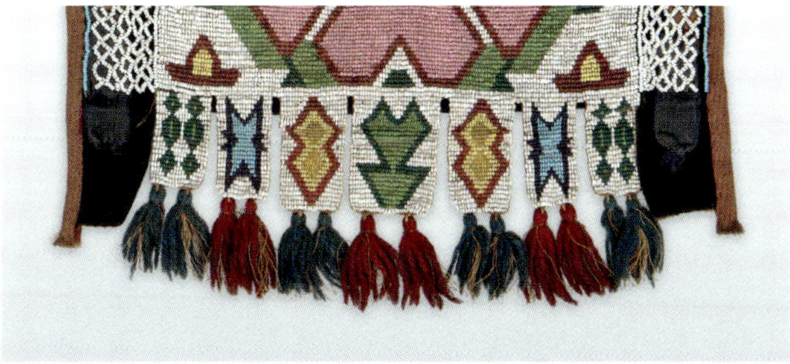

2.13 Integrated loom-woven tab fringe. *MNHS 2008.9.1; see also Figures 2.42 and 3.53*

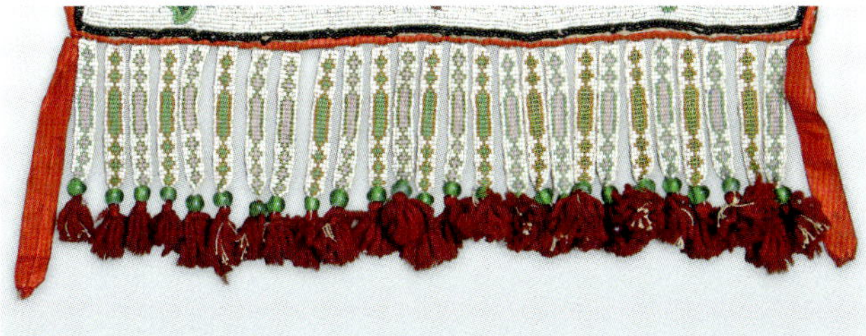

2.14 Attached loom-woven tab fringe on a bag purchased at the Hage Store in Deerwood, Minnesota, circa 1905. *MNHS 1994.19.7*

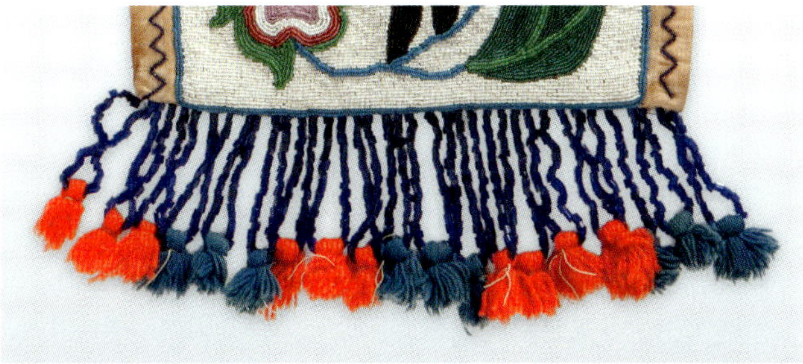

2.15 Fringe with bugle bead loops, c. 1860–1901. *MNHS 1496; see also Figure 3.65*

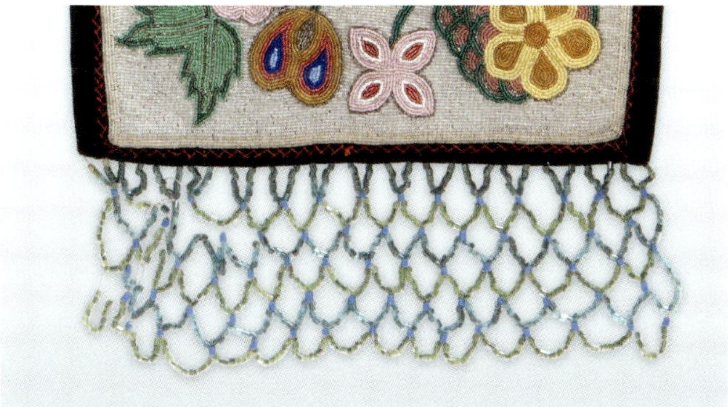

2.16 Fringe with bugle bead netting on a bag from the Bishop Whipple collection, c. 1860–1901. *MNHS 1978*

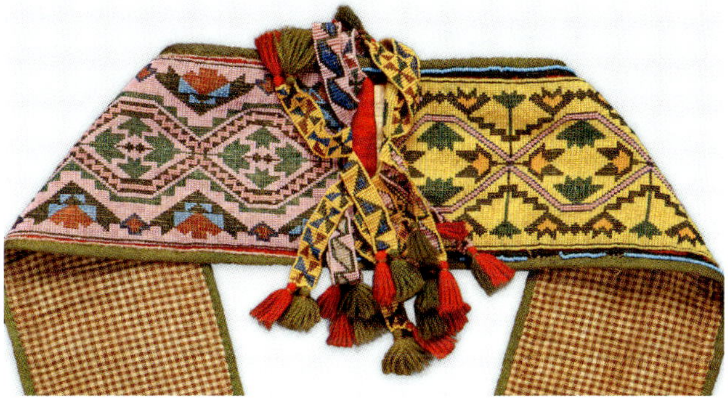

2.17 Integrated loom-woven tab fringe on strap. *MNHS 6020.9; see also Figures 3.03 and 3.21*

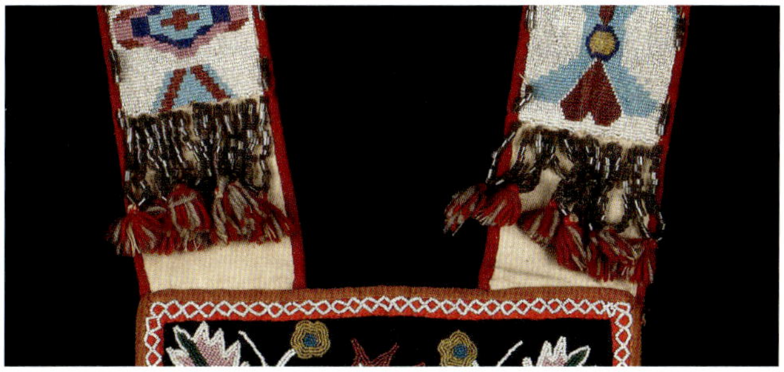

2.18 Fringe with bugle bead loops on strap. *MNHS 532.E157; see also Figure 12.08*

The beadworker's choices

How does a bead artist create a successful gashkibidaagan? An artist must address two main aspects of the form: how the bag works *physically,* for the wearer, and how it works *visually,* for those viewing the bag as it is danced. Her tools include structure, materials, technique, color palette, motifs, and other factors discussed in this book. The indefinable aspect, though, is her skill in harmonizing the disparate elements of the bag.

A bag's physical qualities are determined by the scale, or size, of the bag overall; the strap size, width, and length; and the materials used. The sizes of gashkibidaaganag have changed over the years, and each bag is unique, but the average dimensions of the bags at the Minnesota Historical Society are telling (Table 2.1). While some elements change more than others as the bags evolve over time, one element that does not change much is the length of the bag strap, which is nearly always between forty and fifty inches, particularly during the period from 1880 to 1910; the drop from the shoulder to the bag is thus shorter than twenty to twenty-five inches. (There are a few bags in the society's collections that are significantly smaller than others made in the same time period, but the examples are so infrequent that it is difficult to generalize about them.) The strap standard contributes to the overall bag length, which is also generally, during this same period, in the forty-to-fifty-inch range. This variation in overall bag length is likely a result of the maker's need to address the wearer's trunk length, rather than being determined by a formula for length in comparison to the other dimensions of the bag's components. Before bead artists began making the full panel bags, they generally created pocket panels that are roughly square in appearance, whatever their size. The greatest variations occur in the width of the strap, in the types and related lengths of fringe, in the size of the pocket, in the height of the area above the pocket opening, and in the width of the pocket edgings that frame the pocket panel. In the twentieth century, the introduction of panel bags—bags with no pockets—results in a major shift in size.[3]

The bead artist's second challenge, visual impact, is answered primarily through the color palette, the selection and arrangements of motifs on the pocket panel, and the framing of the strap and pocket panel. A bag's palette reflects the most individual of the artist's choices, perhaps revealing the artist's personality and freedom of expression. The rest of this chapter and the next address other visual aspects of gashkibidaaganag.

A few words are in order, however, on a specific question. Some ethnographers assert that the difference in color or motif on each half of the strap was caused by an inadequate supply of beads. It is clear, though, that the difference is intentional. If these bead artists wanted the strap to be one continuous strip in form, color, and motif, they were more than capable of making it so—and some did. But that was not their preference.

Table 2.1 Average dimensions of bag parts, rounded to the nearest inch

Date	*Strap dimensions (inches)*	*Pocket panel dimensions (inches)*	*Fringe length (inches)*
Pre-1890 bags, primarily loom woven	3 and wider	8 by 10 up to 12 by 14	4 to 6
Post-1890 bags, mostly floral spot stitched	4 to over 6	13 by 16 (or greater)	2 to more than 4, either short tabs or longer beaded thread loops
Later twentieth-century bags, primarily spot stitched	as wide as 6 to 8	15 by 19; later, 18 by greater than 19	3 to more than 4
Panel bags, primarily spot stitched	6 to 8	18 by greater than 21	3 to more than 4

Minnesota bead artists treated most bandolier bags, both loom woven and spot stitched, as objects with four distinct decorative components: two sides of the strap, the pocket panel, and the area above the pocket. The decoration of the strap is compatible with the asymmetrical approach of the pocket panels. Many times, the differing designs on either side of the strap are executed in the exact same palette of beads as the rest of the bag, just interpreted differently. And elsewhere in this book, in examples such as Figures 2.31, 3.03, 3.39, and 3.41, it is clear that the artists intentionally created two separate loom strips in order to adhere to some traditional meaning or to simply display two different interpretations of the palette or motifs. In spot-stitched examples, the strap was beaded in two separate sections, and a center line is evident where the two motifs meet. They are not joined as a single cohesive design element. Even in some spot-stitch appliqué bags with a beaded outline strap, that line is continued to the center of the strap and worked to represent a center seam—suggesting that the strap, in spirit, consists of two separate elements.[4]

Materials

Makers of gashkibidaaganag showed particular resourcefulness and creativity in the ways they used new and old materials in construction. Recycling cast-off cloth, finding innovative ways to apply both unusual and familiar scraps, and selecting the types and sizes of beads, the artists orchestrated beautiful bags from very little.

Fabrics

The foundation for the pocket and strap may include up to three layers: backing, interfacing, and lining. A myriad of materials are used for these layers. While their precursors were generally made of leather or hide, gashkibidaaganag are extraordinary pastiches of used, new, and repurposed materials.

Unbleached cotton shirting or muslin is the most common backing fabric, followed by polished cotton and other plain-weave fabrics, which were often used to line the interior of women's dress bodices in the nineteenth century. Frequently the sizing is still evident, and the unwashed glazed surface retains its shine more than a hundred years later.

In older or unusually large bags, recycled fabrics are found in the backing: plain weaves, twill weaves (cassimere from men's suits), coarse woolens, and wool blanket cloth are all common. The blanket fragments are readily identifiable when a blanket's bound edge is visible. Recycled newspaper, osnaburg (coarse, heavy linen or cotton), and newly purchased or used oilcloth were used as interfacing.

Other bags are backed with any manner of scrap or available cloth: glazed plain-weave cottons, printed cottons, woven dress goods, bandanas, and flour and feed sacks. Wools, cotton velveteen, and velvet (silk or rayon) helped provide support or served as a decorative surface element.

Generally, beadworkers also used scraps of available material to line the pocket panel and provide stiffening to support the weight of the beads on the outer layer. Favored fabrics for linings include new and recycled printed cottons, unbleached cotton shirting or muslin, and bed ticking.

Women at Mille Lacs could buy fabrics at the Mille Lacs Indian Trading Post. Sally Mitchell, who was born in 1910, worked there almost continuously from 1927 until 1950. In a 1991 interview she commented that in the store, behind the counter, "was where they displayed the dress goods, quilting scrap bundles, stockings, and things of that sort. There was dress material, not a lot of them, but enough so that if someone were in need they could get a length of it. Then the other material, the quilting material, was in little bundles. It seems to me like they were supposed to be ten yards in a bundle, but if they were, they were very much compacted. It was scraps really. Some were fairly good-sized, but mostly it was scrap material."[5]

Bindings

The majority of Minnesota Ojibwe bags were bound along the edges with a bias tape made of worsted wool. A bias cut, with its diagonal alignment of the grain, gives a woven fabric some stretch. Strips of woven fabric cut and folded along the bias create a tape that can follow curves and corners without puckering. This provides a smooth, clean look that was prized by the women who made gashkibidaaganag. The wool tape was of sturdy material and manufacture, making it ideal for encasing the outside edges of a gashkibidaagan to protect them from abrasion during powwow activity, rolled storage, and transport. Other, less common bindings included silk ribbon, commercial cotton bias tape, and scrap fabric. Some bags were self-bound by wrapping the edges of the backing fabric around to the front, turning them under, and stitching them down.[6]

Beads

Perhaps the most significant component of the bags is the beadwork that adorns their surfaces. By the twentieth century, beadwork instruction was readily available in person or in printed form through a variety of sources, including bead distributors and hobby magazines. The Ojibwe word for bead, *manidoominens*, means "little seed that's a gift of the spirit," and indeed, so-called seed beads made from glass are the most commonly used. While some bags display additional bead types, as well as sequins, buttons, and other embellishments preferred by individual bead artists, the most prevalent beads are discussed here.[7]

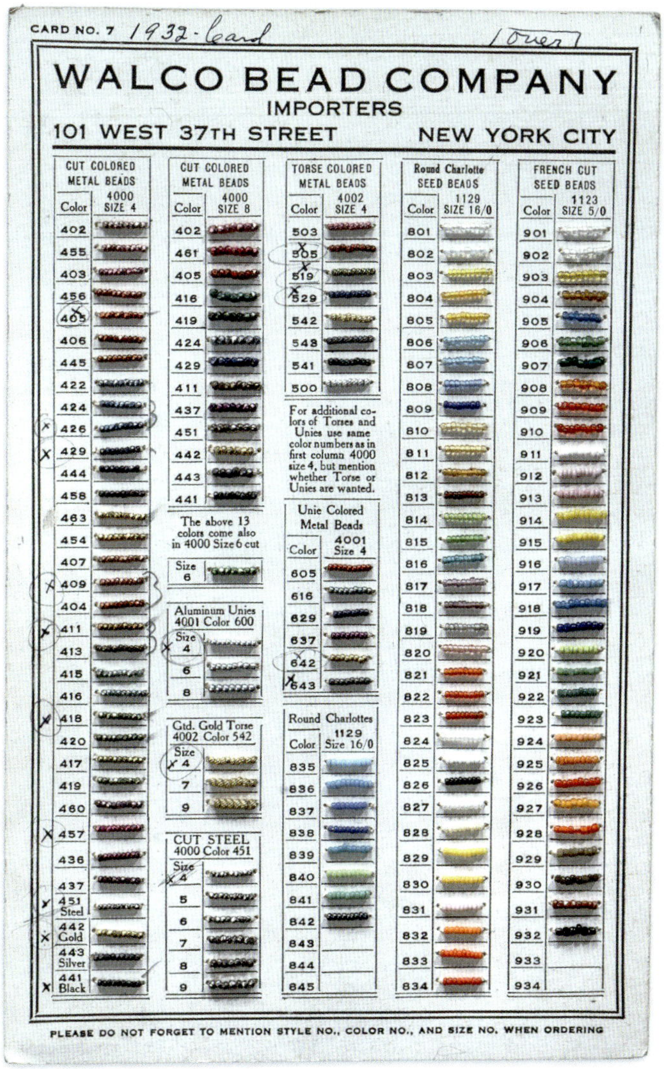

2.19 A 1932 bead sample card from the Mille Lacs trading post, marked to indicate the bead types and colors ordered. *MNHS 10000.833*

The most commonly used beads are glass. In the Great Lakes region from the 1850s to the 1940s, seed beads were primarily Czech (Bohemian), although some Italian beads were used as well. Seed beads were acquired by traders through importers from coast to coast. In early years, French, British, and American fur traders traveled into the area to exchange goods, including beads, for pelts. Later, the government issued licenses for trade on reservations.

In about 1918, Jeanette and Harry Ayer operated a trading post at Mille Lacs that functioned as a general store; by that date, their beading customers were primarily doing spot-stitch appliqué work. Surviving correspondence and bead sample cards tell us that the Ayers purchased their beads primarily from firms in New York and San Francisco. Some cards were actually dated and marked, recording what bead types and colors were ordered at that time (Figure 2.19). Others were marked, but undated. We will probably never know definitively whether the decisions about bead color, size, and type were made entirely by traders such as the Ayers or whether the bead artists had an influence on what was ordered. The evidence in the surviving bags suggests the beadworkers had a voice in color selections.[8]

Certain bead colors found in the Minnesota Historical Society's collection of gashkibidaaganag are more prevalent than others. White, red, black, green, and blue are common, while yellow and pink are also popular. Although pink is not always a prominent color, it is rarely absent. The most popular bead colors for the background of the spot-stitch appliqué bags were shades of white, including crystal white, opal white, and chalk white, which are all opaque matte, and a glossy opaque white. Records of comments from bead artists who visited the Mille Lacs trading post make it clear that they demanded a good stock and selection of the white beads, but sometimes the artists had to go to another trader when the Ayers ran out. The predominant size for the glass seed beads used in spot-stitch appliqué is usually what is today known as size 11 (roughly 21 beads per inch).

Various other beads are also found on gashkibidaaganag, as follows:

- Cylindrical glass bugle beads, cut in irregular lengths, used primarily for bag fringe. They were available in clear, naturally colored glass, and clear glass with pigments added on the inside of the bead. The latter version have shown considerable color loss over the years due to flaking paint.
- Faceted metal beads, in similar sizes, were used in tandem with glass seed beads. Bags in the Minnesota Historical Society's collection incorporate metal beads for a relatively brief period, between the late nineteenth and early twentieth centuries. Maude Kegg, a Mille Lacs artist born in 1902, said she didn't use them because they cut the threads. Several examples using faceted metal beads show evidence of rust.[9]
- Pound or pony beads, much larger, usually opaque white or blue glass. Not seen often on gashkibidaaganag, these beads were used on finger-woven sashes and other objects from the early nineteenth century, when they were preferred by the Indians of the Great Lakes and the Upper Missouri. They are shaped and used like seed beads, though they are larger; the largest have a diameter of one-quarter inch. The name is said to derive either from the use of horses to transport them or from their use in horse regalia. The white and blue colors were eventually augmented by other colors and smaller beads, but both colors have remained essential to the color palette of the gashkibidaaganag made by the Ojibwe of Minnesota.[10]
- Large faceted spherical or plain glass or metal beads. These are sometimes used for thread-strung fringe or to top off a yarn tassel, but they are not used as often as bugle beads.

Types of gashkibidaaganag

As gashkibidaagan styles evolved over time, individual bags often incorporated multiple techniques. Through the late nineteenth century, the styles shifted from predominantly weaving to predominantly spot-stitch appliqué; in the twentieth century spot-stitch appliqué took over almost completely. The history of the gashkibidaagan as an emergent form includes five slightly different construction methods:

- Rare early bags that incorporate panels of finger-woven sashes that were embellished with glass beads
- Bags with loom-woven bead panels

- Bags combining loom-woven panels and spot-stitch appliqué work
- Bags decorated entirely with spot-stitch appliqué
- Full panel bags, which are spot-stitch appliqué bags without a functioning pocket

This study focuses mainly on loom-woven and spot-stitch appliqué bags, which make up the majority of the surviving bags at the Minnesota Historical Society, but a consideration of all the forms is important for context.

Finger-woven gashkibidaaganag

The Ojibwe women of the mid-nineteenth century who made the earliest form of gashkibidaaganag, probably in the 1840s and 1850s, practiced a technique known as finger weaving to make sashes from colorful wool yarns. Once thought to be of European manufacture, these and some other finger-woven sashes found in North America are generally recognized to be of American Indian origin. Ojibwe women embellished these sashes by interlacing glass beads in an oblique pattern and by finishing the ends with lengthy braided and beaded fringes (Figures 2.20 and 2.21). The oblique interlacing of beads sets these sashes apart from the *ceinture fléchée*, or "arrowed sash," commonly seen on French Canadian fur traders of the same era.

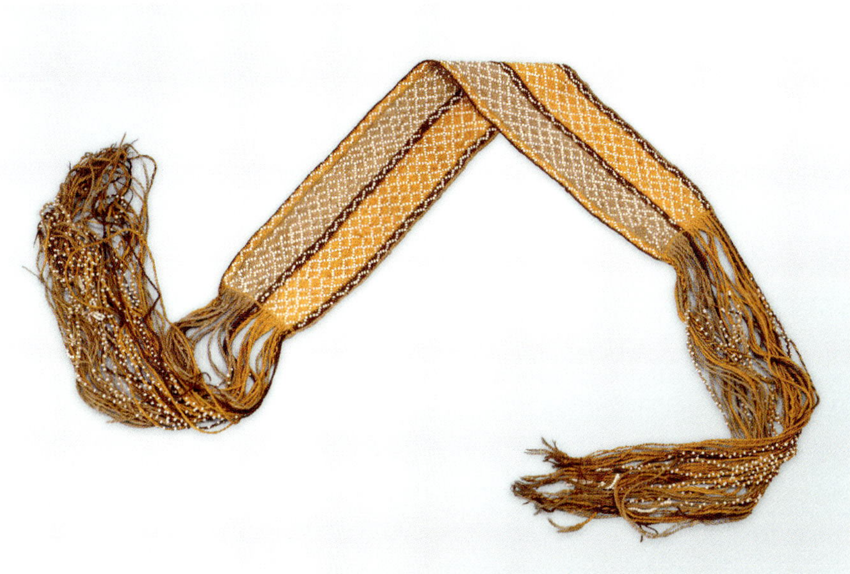

2.20 Mid-nineteenth-century finger-woven sash with oblique interlaced beads. *MNHS 10000.173*

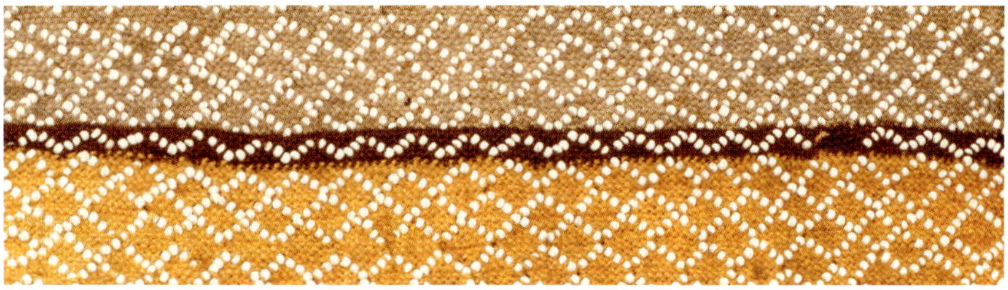

2.21 Detail of Figure 2.20 showing the interlaced beads. *MNHS 10000.173*

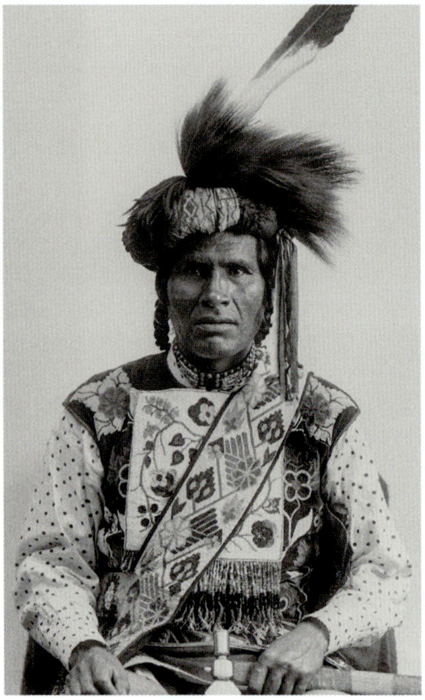 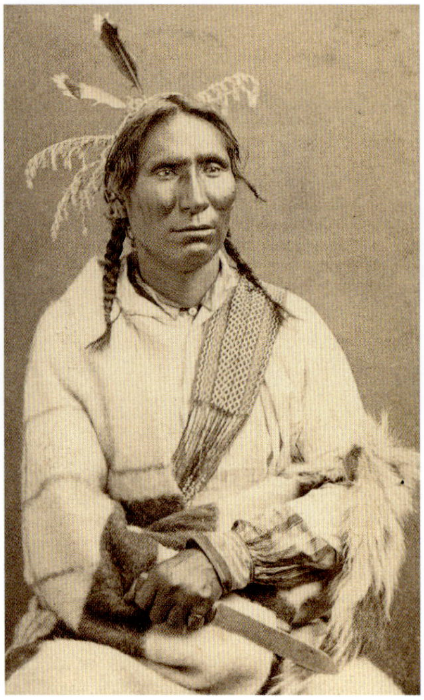 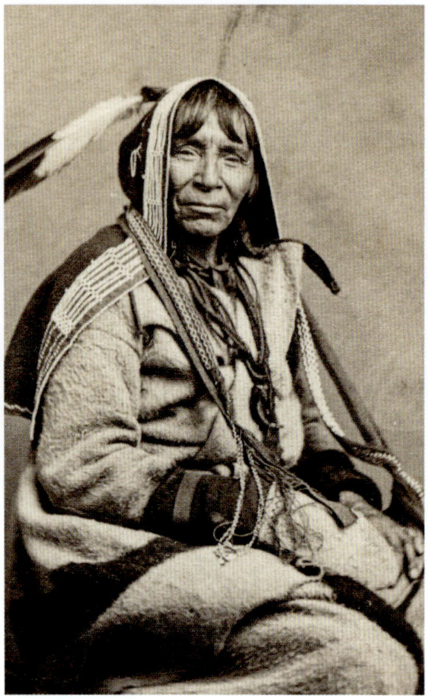

2.22 *(above left)* Midwewinind (May-dway-we-nind, or One Called from a Distance), from White Earth Reservation, wears turban-like headwear incorporating a loom-woven bead garter or band wrapped around an unknown padding material. He also wears two gashkibidaaganag: a loom-woven decorated one across his shoulder and a spot-stitch appliqué one resting on his chest with the strap folded back underneath. No doubt this wealth of beadwork was piled on at the suggestion of the photographer who took this portrait for the Bureau of American Ethnology in 1894, while Midwewinind was part of a visiting delegation to Washington, DC. *NAA-SI BAE GN 00517A 06141000*

2.23 *(above center)* O-kun-de-kun (To Keep the Net Up), warrior of the Leech Lake Band of Chippewa, wears a finger-woven sash diagonally across his chest, c. 1880. *MNHS E97.10 r17*

2.24 *(above right)* Nah-bon-a-aush (One Sided Winner), a leader of the Leech Lake Band, wears a finger-woven sash or garter draped casually around his neck over a heavily beaded wool hood, or capote. He was photographed at Whitney's Gallery in St. Paul, c. 1865. *MNHS E97.1N r25*

The Ojibwe finger-woven sash with oblique interlacing is recorded in portraits from the territory and state of Minnesota from the 1850s and into the fourth quarter of the nineteenth century (Figures 2.22, 2.23, and 2.24). Believed to be in use as early as the late eighteenth century in the Great Lakes region, the sashes were meant to be tied at the waist, but they were also frequently seen in nineteenth-century Minnesota as a component in headgear worn by Ojibwe and some Dakota male civil leaders. For this purpose, the sashes were wrapped around a roll of cloth or a fur strip and positioned on a man's head in a twisted ring. Ceinture-fléchée sashes, calico yardage, silk military sashes, and loom-woven garters or bands were also used to create this headwear. Various sash types were also worn on their own as simple headbands.[11]

These finger-woven sashes were also sometimes attached to bags as a strap. Identifying precursor bags with finger-woven sashes in photographs is tricky. The sash dimensions are similar to those of bag straps, and photographs do not always reveal whether the sash is tied to the pocket portion of a bag. Many of the early bag straps were loom woven, and they were simply basted onto the bag pocket or tied in place, so they could be removed if needed for storage, transport, or reuse in other settings. But small numbers of gashkibidaaganag with finger-woven sashes are visible in historical images. Furthermore, while most of these bags appear to be constructed of yardage intentionally woven into a pocket-width strip before assembly, other bag pockets were made from sections of sashes assembled into a bag form.

One bag, pictured in five St. Paul studio images taken between 1854 and 1865 (three are shown in Figures 2.25, 2.26, and 2.27), has a sophisticated oblique interlacing woven pocket panel and long fringe with both

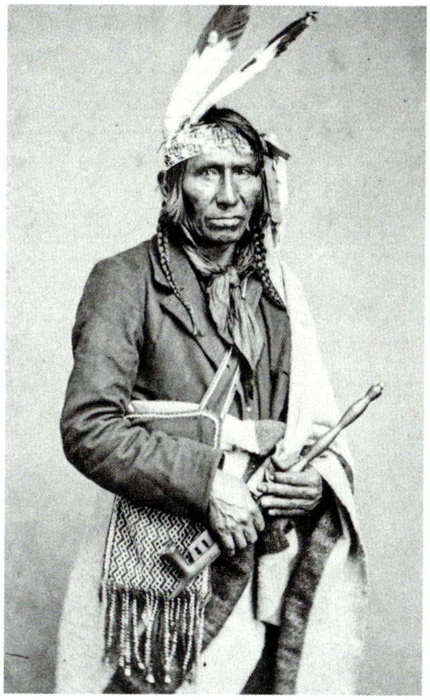

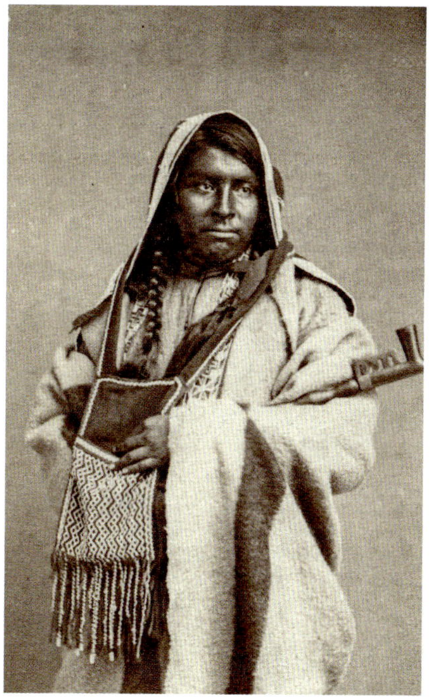

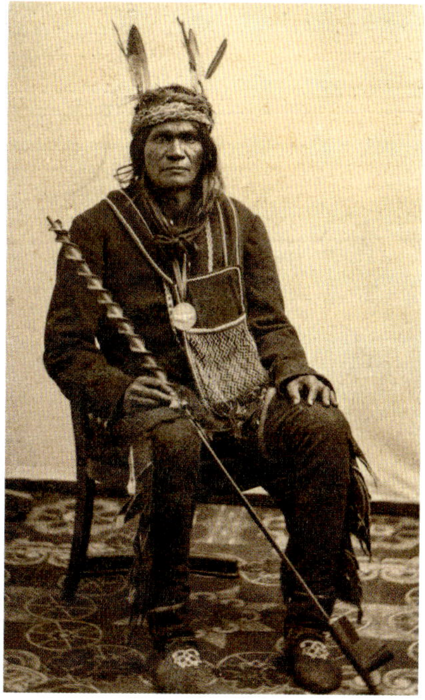

braiding and beading. The border treatment in the area above the pocket panel and on the edges of the strap appears to be simple commercial rick-rack stitched in place. The men in Figures 2.26 and 2.27 wear the bag in the "apron" manner, no doubt at the photographer's request to best feature the object. Although the appearance of the same bag in the photographs produced by different studios suggests that it was a shared prop, these images document the use of finger-woven sashes and finger-woven sash bags at specific dates and locales and among specific cultural groups.[12]

A precious record of the transitional form of the gashkibidaagan appears in Figure 2.28, a portrait of Souligny, an important Menominee chief in Wisconsin, painted in February 1858 in Keshena, Wisconsin, by Samuel Marsden Brookes. Souligny's small hybrid bag has a pocket panel made of finger-woven yarn and beads. The strip attached to the top of the pocket opening and the area above it are both decorated in the spot-stitch appliqué, outline-filled technique found in many examples of early bags with loom-woven panels. The strap is a strip of loom-woven beadwork done in a variation of the otter-track motif. The size of the bag is closer to that of precursor bags, most not quite grown to the dimensions associated with gashkibidaaganag.[13]

2.25 *(above left)* Ah-ah-shaw-we-ke-shick (Crossing Sky), chief of the Rabbit Lake Ojibwe (a sub-band of the Mississippi Band), c. 1863. *MNHS E97.1A r11*

2.26 *(above center)* Leech Lake Chippewa chief Ke-bay-nah-kay (Best Gambler), c. 1860. *MNHS E97.1k r6*

2.27 *(above right)* Aw-ke-wen-zee (Old Man), a head chief of the Lac Courte Oreilles Ojibwe, 1854. *MNHS E97.1A r17*

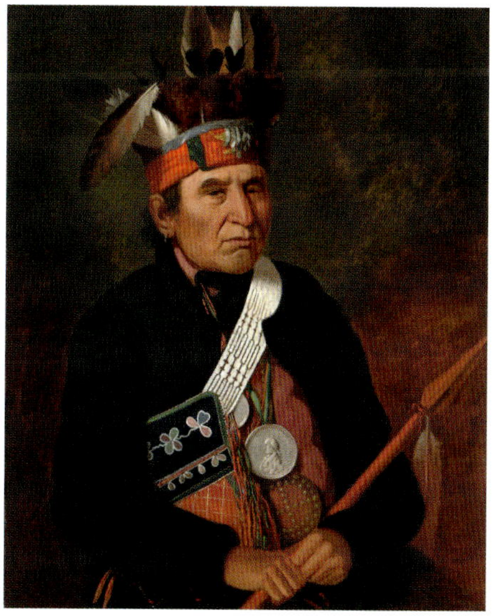

2.28 Souligny, Menominee leader, 1858. *WHS 1868*

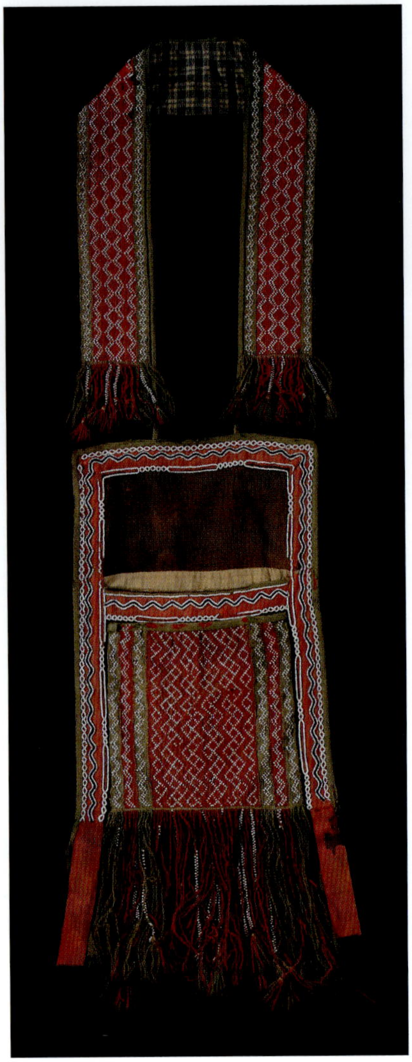

2.29 Finger-woven gashkibidaagan, c. 1830–50; cotton, wool, beads; 113.67 × 28.42 cm; Robert J. Ulrich Works of Art Purchase Fund. *MIA 2003.32*

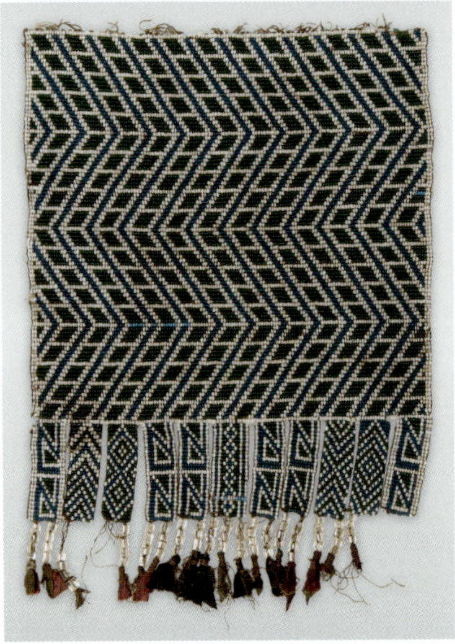

2.30 Loom-woven bag panel that imitates the bead pattern on a finger-woven gashkibidaagan, c. last half of the nineteenth century. *MNHS 7373.1*

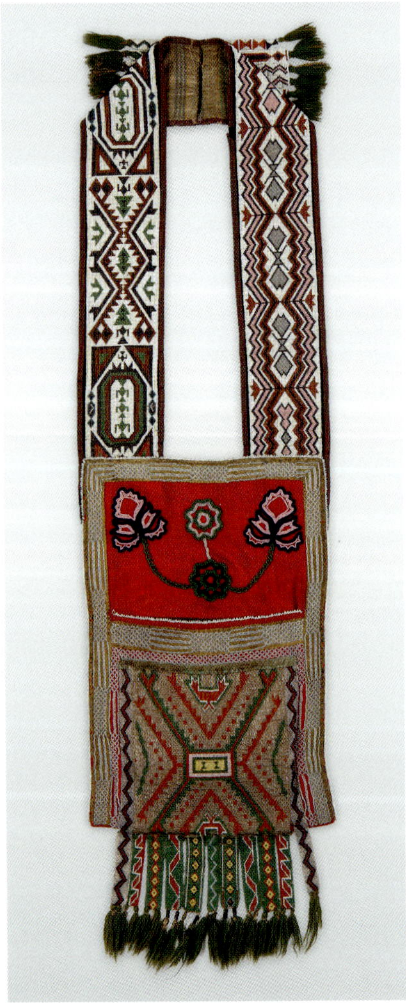

2.31 Bag with loom-woven panel, about 1870–90. Note thunderbird motifs on the left strap (in green and black). *MNHS 6020.8; see also Figure 11.03*

Only a small number of finger-woven sash gashkibidaaganag are known to survive in museum collections worldwide, and most demonstrate how the form was changing. A bag at the Minneapolis Institute of Art (Figure 2.29) incorporates different widths of finger-woven yardage in the pocket panel and strap. A loom-woven pocket panel (Figure 2.30) celebrates the effect that new materials can have on old designs.[14]

Loom-woven gashkibidaaganag

Bead artists wove rectangular and square bead panels of varying widths to decorate the straps and pockets on gashkibidaaganag (Figures 2.31 and 2.32). On rare occasions, a single piece of beadwork was woven to cover the entire bag. Women generally worked on a loom without referring to a pattern. The loom-woven bead panels were then sewn to the bag's cloth ground—the pocket back—using a needle and thread. Women used simple, sturdy looms that could be carried easily on the seasonal rounds (Figure 2.33). The process of weaving beadwork on looms was ultimately faster than the later method of spot-stitch appliqué.

The majority of bags decorated with loom-woven panels held in the Minnesota Historical Society collections are constructed using a technique described as the square weave. In this technique a single weft thread crosses the warps by passing through the bead twice, once from each direction, as shown in Figure 2.34.[15]

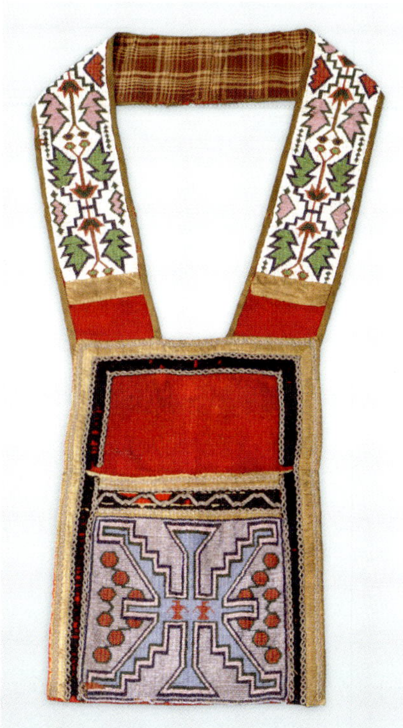

2.32 Bag with loom-woven panel, last half of nineteenth century. Note thunderbird motif at center of the pocket panel. *MNHS 10000.152; see also Figure 3.25.*

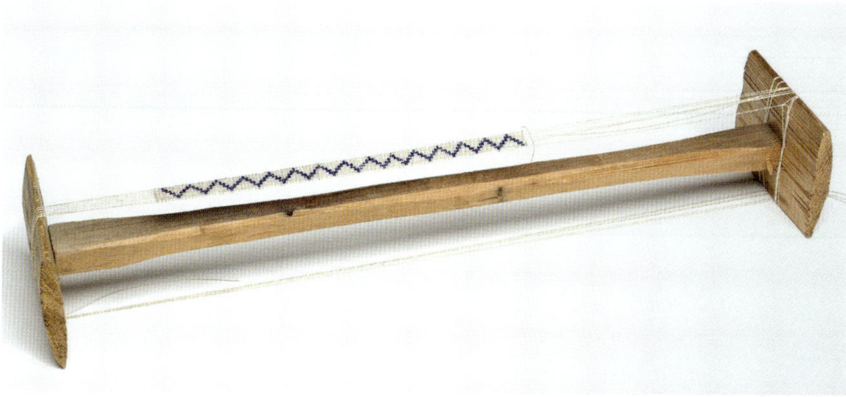

2.33 *(above)* Loom collected at Grand Portage by Frances Densmore, 1930. *MNHS 6935.32.R*

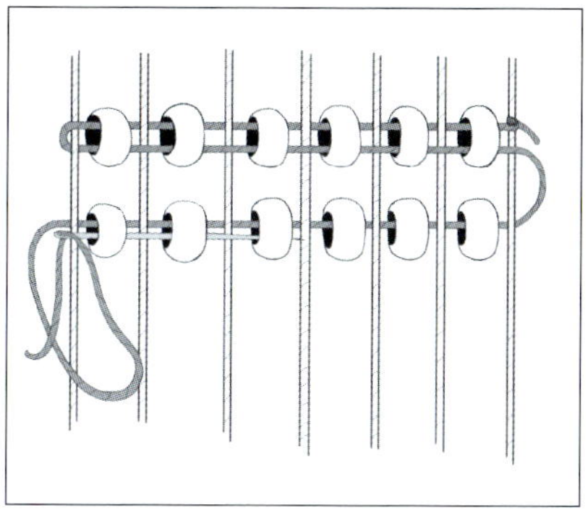

2.34 *(right)* The square-weave technique used to make loom-woven bead panels. *Illustration by Hannah Boehme*

Historical photographs can help date early loom-woven bags. In about 1865 a photographer created a large composite image of eighty-five cartes de visite from which the two portraits in Figures 2.35 and 2.36 are taken. The loom-woven bags in these portraits are probably studio props. The strap on the portrait of Noon Day shows variations of the exploding X motif; the area above the pocket opening in Plenty Hail's portrait clearly shows outline-filled spot-stitch appliqué work. The man on the far right in Figure 2.37 wears a bag with a loom-woven pocket panel with integrated tab fringe. In the area above the pocket opening, the bead artist rendered floral images in spot-stitch appliqué, possibly with filled-in outlines.[16]

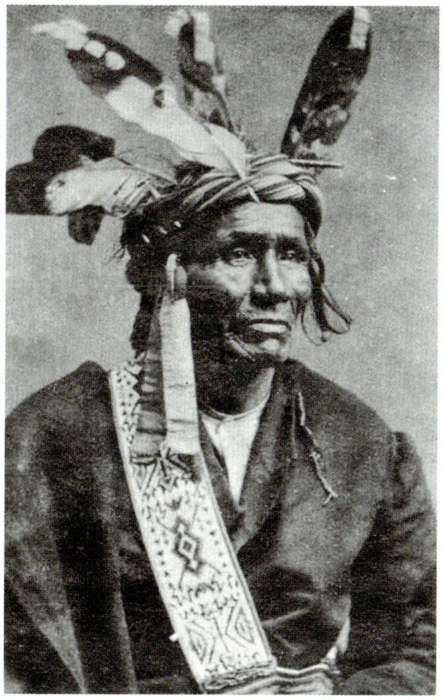

2.35 Noon Day (Now-we-ke-shick, or Now-we-ge-shick), Ojibwe leader, c. 1865. *MNHS E97.1 h1, detail*

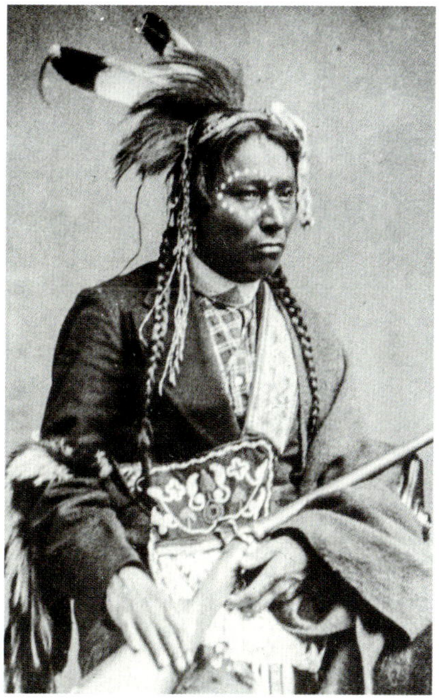

2.36 Plenty Hail (His Hail or Many Hailstones; Ta-wa-su-o-ta), Dakota leader, c. 1865. *MNHS E97.1 h1, detail*

2.37 Members of the Ottertail Band, a sub-group of the Pillagers, at an Ojibwe reservation, c. 1875. *MNHS E97.1 r135*

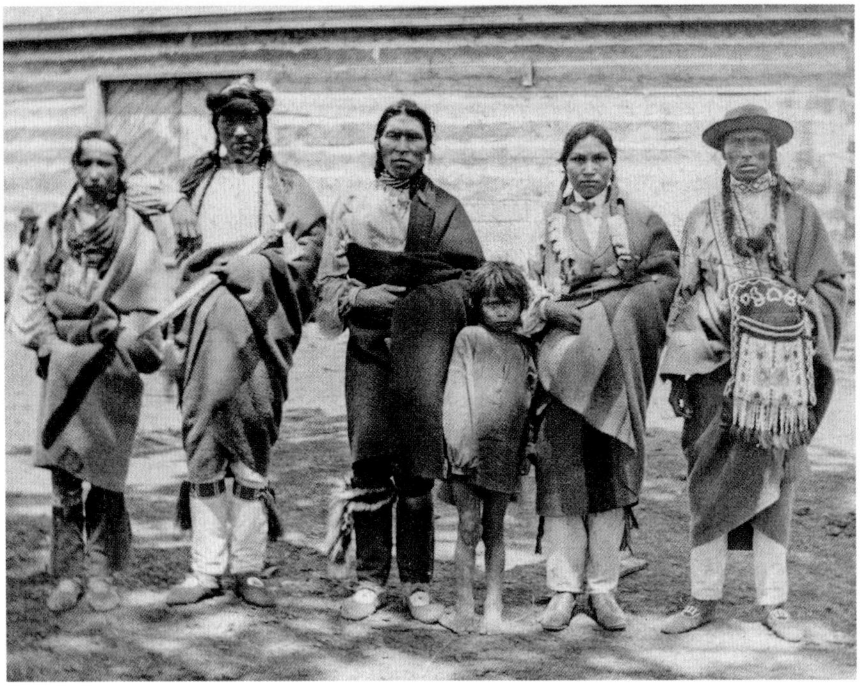

Two Wisconsin Ojibwe men wear early loom-woven panel bags in Figure 2.38, an 1880 studio shot. Edawigijig (Edawi-giizhig, or Both Sides of the Sky), from Bad River, who was a chief and a signer of the Treaty of 1854, which ceded most of northeastern Minnesota, is seated on the far left wearing a bag with an undecorated area above the pocket opening, with varied X motifs on the strap, and with repeated smaller X images on the pocket panel. Next to Edawigijig is Kis-ki-ta-wag (Giishkitawag, or Cut Ear), an important warrior associated with the Ontonagon and Bad River Bands and another of the treaty's signers. Kis-ki-ta-wag wears a bag with an undecorated area above the pocket opening, integrated loom-woven tab fringe on the strap, multiple parallel rows of zigzags with simple lozenge motifs on the strap, and repeated small X images on the pocket panel (see also Figure 3.23).

2.38 Some members of the 1880 Anishinaabe delegation to Washington, DC, wear loom-woven gashkibidaaganag. *Photo by Charles Milton Bell, NMAI P03428*

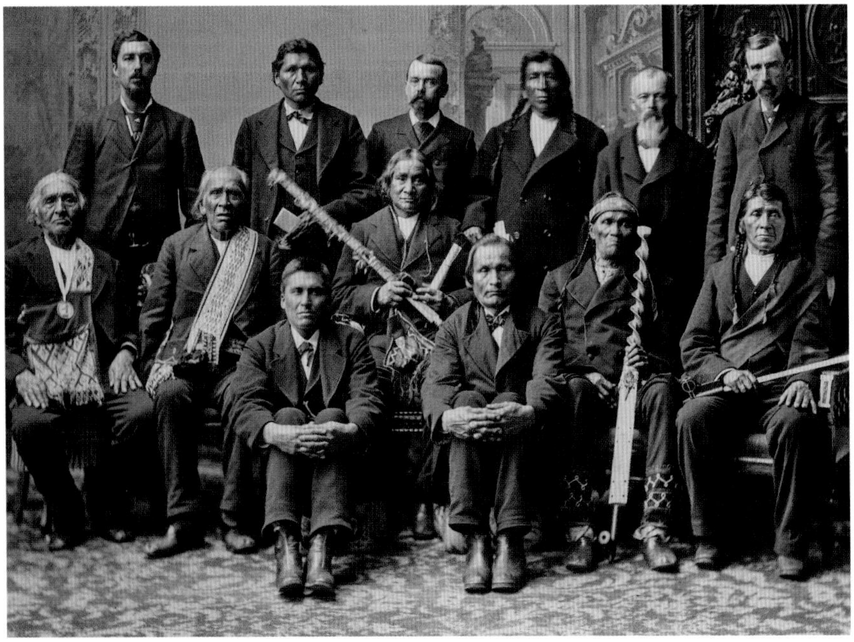

In Figure 2.39, about half the men wear floral spot-stitch appliqué dance aprons and leggings; six loom-woven gashkibidaaganag are visible; all visible moccasins are Minnesota-Wisconsin floral-decorated Ojibwe style. Most of the men are wearing a sash, all with similar spot-stitch imagery, including Christian crosses, human or angel-like figures, and a

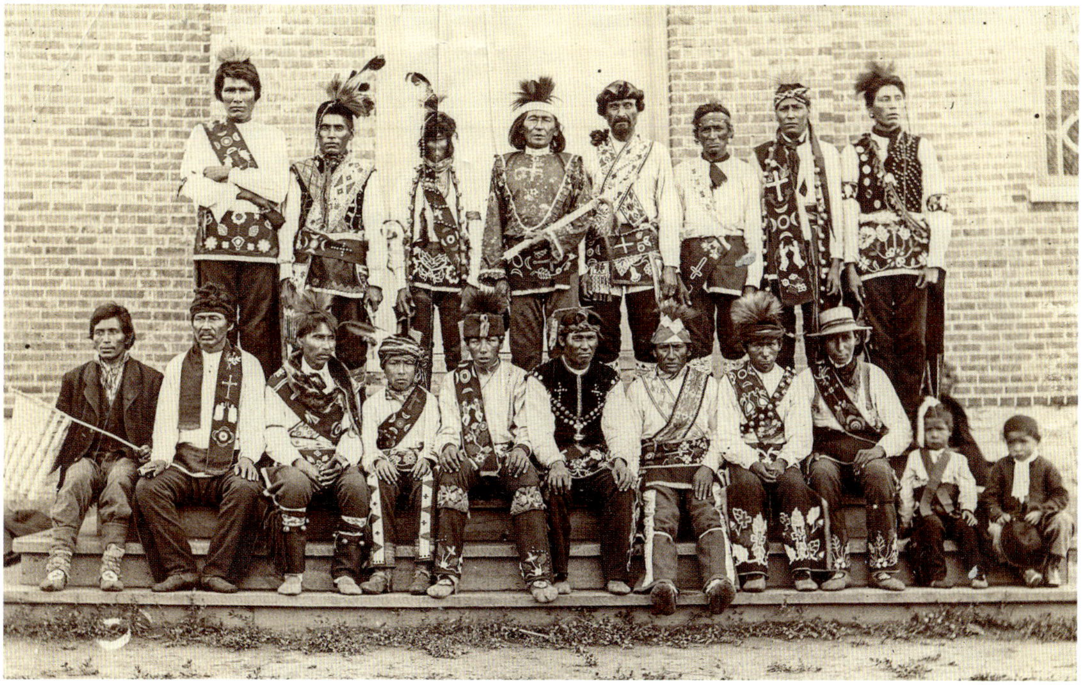

circle-centered motif. The meaning of the sash is not known, but perhaps it represents some sort of religious group like the Faw-Faw movement of the Oto and Potawatomi that flourished during the 1890s, in which members rejected European practices for more traditional ones. In Figure 2.40, Red Lake Ojibwe men are posing with a man wearing a biretta and cassock, evidently a Catholic priest.[17]

2.39 Chippewa Indians at White Earth Reservation in gala attire, 1886. *St. John's Abbey Archives, Collegeville*

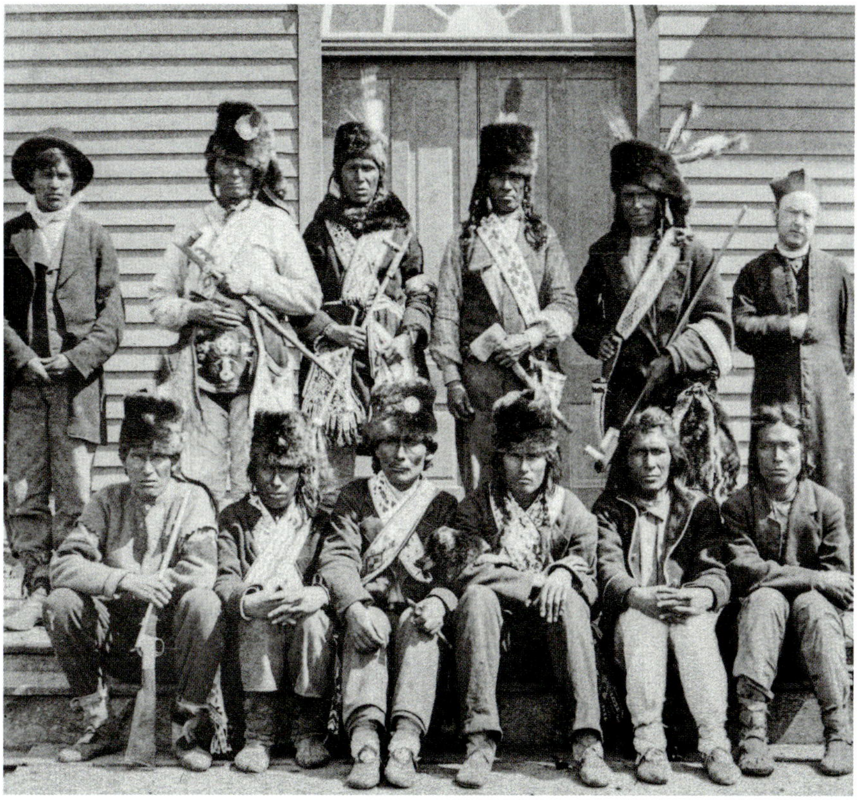

2.40 Red Lake Ojibwe men in a photograph by F. Jay Haynes, c. 1890. *MNHS E97.1 r203*

Transitional form, loom and spot-stitch appliqué combined

Women bead artists were somewhat isolated, and perhaps because of this, many versions or interpretations of gashkibidaaganag developed at the same time in different parts of the state. One outcome is bags that incorporate two or more techniques. Some of these examples may also be the result of marrying two different pieces of beadwork for convenience. In Figure 2.41, Chief White Cloud's spot-stitch appliqué bag has a loom-woven strap; in Figure 2.42, the bag has a loom-woven panel and a spot-stitch appliqué strap. Examples of earlier finger-woven bags can be found with loom-woven portions.[18]

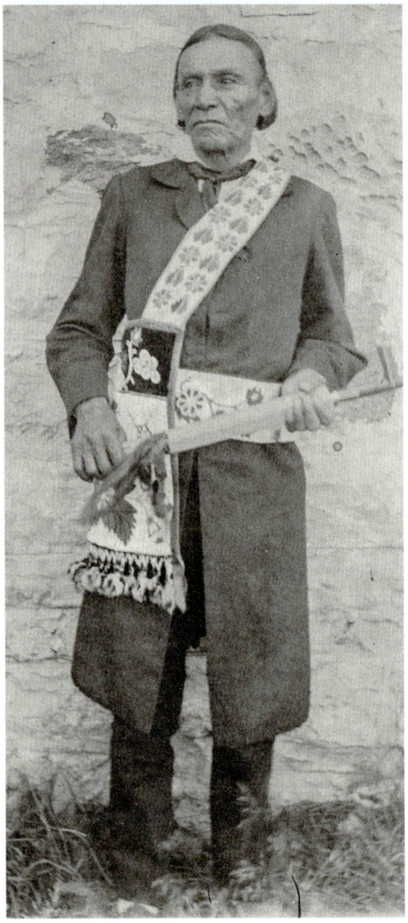

2.41 Chief White Cloud (Wa-bon-o-quot, or Wa-bon-o-quad) of the Gull Lake Ojibwe wears a bag with a spot-stitch appliqué pocket and a loom-woven strap, c. 1895. *MNHS E97.1W r19*

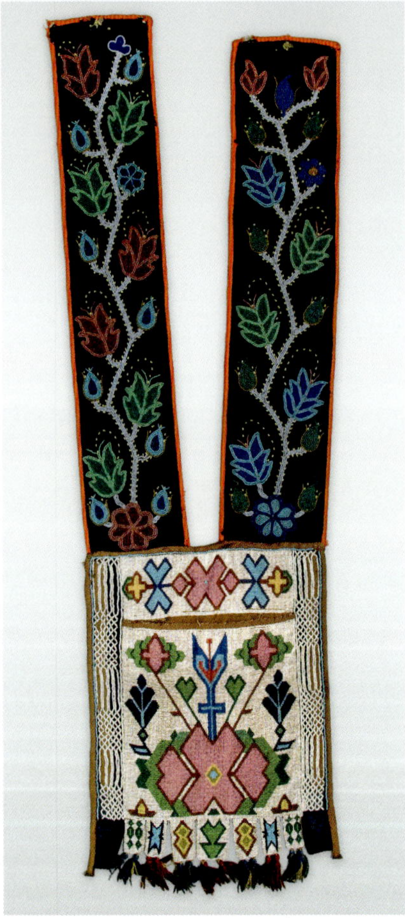

2.42 Loom-woven bag with spot-stitch appliqué strap, from the last third of nineteenth century. *MNHS 2008.9.1; see also Figures 2.13 and 3.53*

Spot-stitch appliqué gashkibidaaganag

In time, women began decorating some gashkibidaaganag entirely with the more intricate and ornate spot-stitch appliqué, which became the predominant method of adornment in the twentieth century and into the twenty-first. The spot-stitch appliqué technique, also known as overlay, overlaid, or couching, required both more time and more beads to decorate the surface. The Ojibwe women in Minnesota have created these beaded floral designs using either a single- or double-needle method of the overlaid, or spot, stitch (Figure 2.43). In the double-needle method, which is more common, beadworkers generally secure beads to the surface every two to three beads

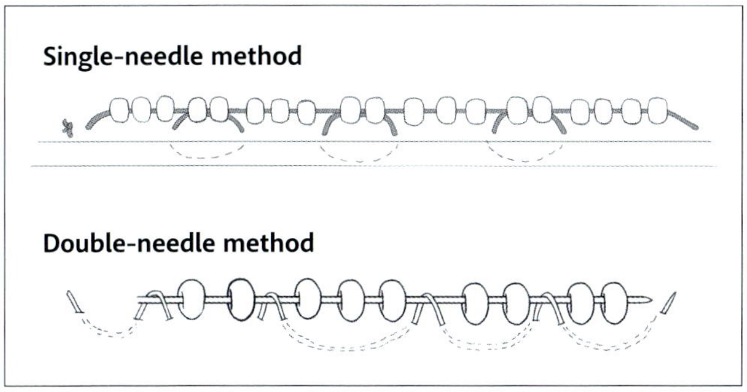

2.43 Spot-stitch techniques used to secure appliqué beadwork. *Illustration by Hannah Boehme*

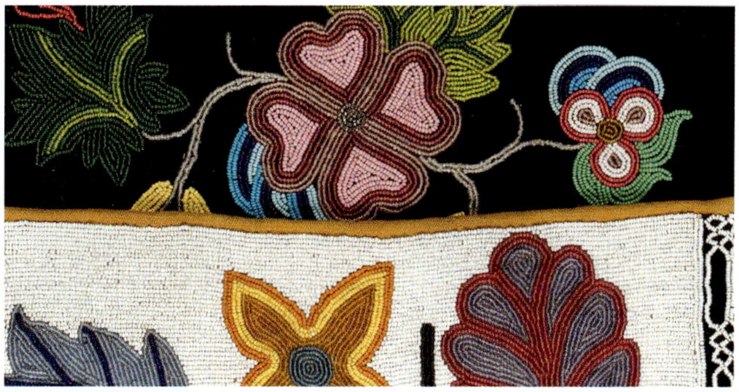

2.44 Spot-stitch appliqué detail of Figure 2.45.

in order to achieve a smooth finished surface. Figure 2.44 shows a detail of the finished surface, and Figure 2.45 shows a complete bag.[19]

Gashkibidaaganag existed with other significant floral beaded garments, including collars, yokes, vests (gibide'ebizonan), dance aprons (aanziyaan, a breech clout, breech cloth, or loincloth, a man's apron), belts (gijipizon, a belt), and leggings (aas, a legging). In early 1893, when the Women's Auxiliary Board of the Minnesota World's Columbian Exposition Commission was acquiring a number of beaded objects for display at the exposition in Chicago, the members collected fully developed versions of floral spot-stitch appliqué as well as loom-woven bags. By 1895, spot-stitch appliqué bags were predominant in photographs.[20]

Both beadwork techniques—loom weaving and spot-stitch appliqué—were highly portable and effective as surface decoration on bags, dance aprons, leggings, and belts. So why did the Ojibwe bead artists of the Great Lakes region shift from loom-woven to spot-stitch techniques in their beadwork on gashkibidaaganag?

The evolving motif imagery in loom-woven bags strongly suggests that the artists sought more freedom in rendering the kind and quality of the images they chose. While the grid restrictions imposed by the warp and weft of the looms worked well for the earlier geometric motifs, it limited the bead artists' design creativity. Their efforts to incorporate floral motifs into woven work were a preview of the spot-stitch appliqué floral masterpieces to come.

Examples of early spot-stitch appliqué floral beadwork can be glimpsed in a number of historical images. The woman in Figure 2.46, a photograph taken in about 1870, wears a floral beaded collar. In Figure 2.47, the man in the lower right foreground is wearing a gashkibidaagan that has a loom-woven strap with flower and leaf motifs, spot-stitch appliqué above the pocket opening, and what appears to be the top edge of a spot-stitch floral pocket panel. The women's fitted bodices and hats help date this image between 1888 and 1890. And in Figure 2.48, one of three taken of groups of Ojibwe at Hallock, Minnesota, on the same date in 1893, ten floral spot-stitch appliqué bags are visible.

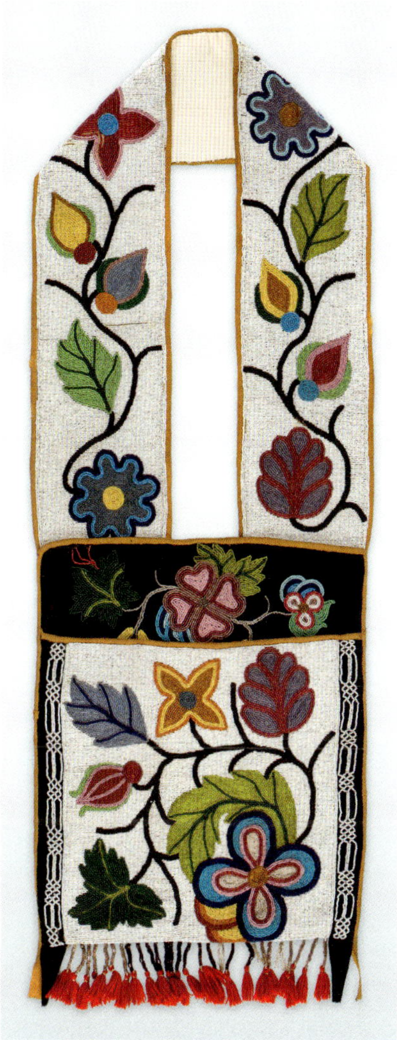

2.45 Spot-stitch appliqué bag given to Charles Lindbergh, Sr., probably 1900 to no later than 1925. *MNHS 1984.6.1*

2.46 *(top right)* Chippewa Indian woman and child in front of wigwam, White Earth Reservation, c. 1870. *MNHS E97.31 r75*

2.47 *(center right)* Chippewa Indians at White Earth Reservation, 1888–90. *MNHS E97.1 r127*

2.48 *(below right)* Ojibwe Indians at Hallock, Minnesota, 1893. *MNHS E97.31 r137*

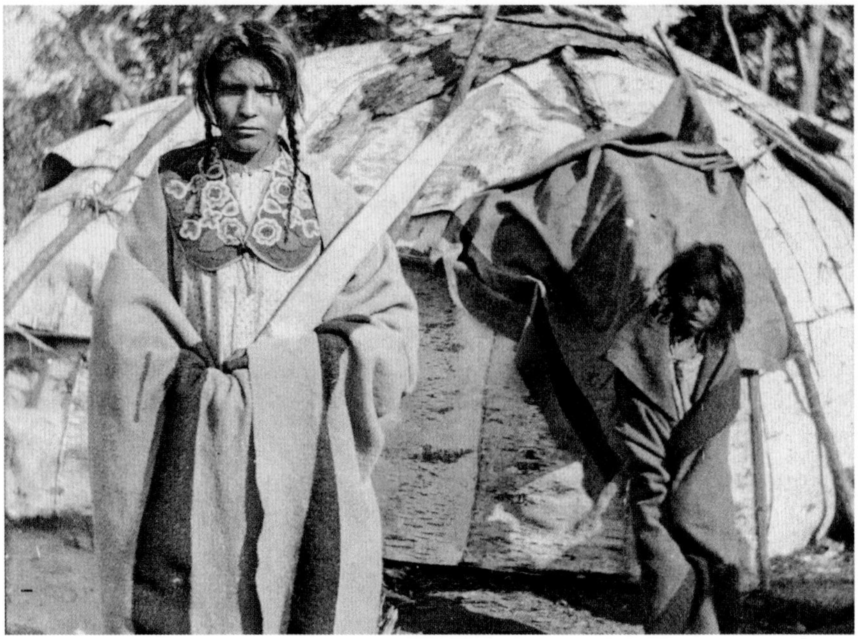

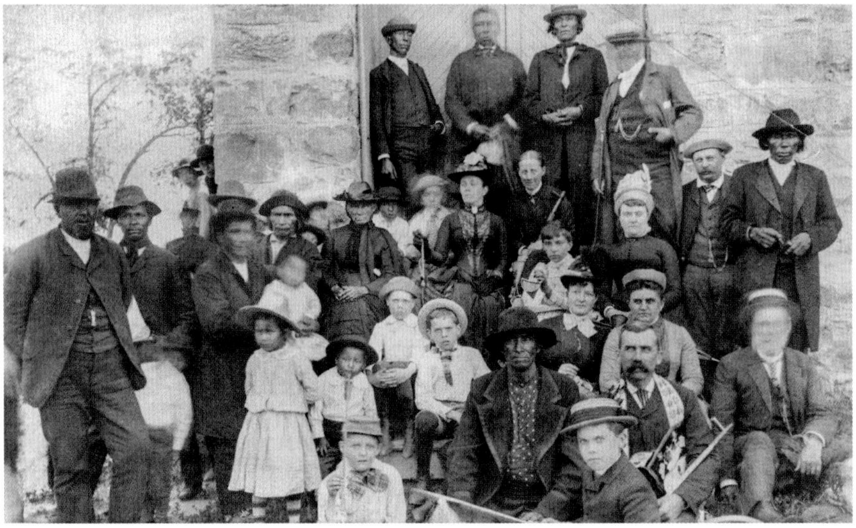

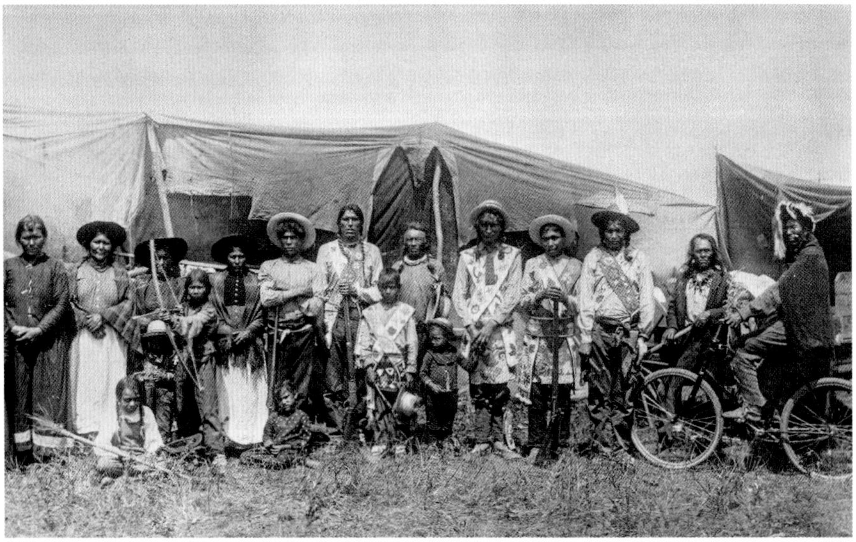

Full panel gashkibidaaganag

By the 1910s and 1920s, a significant number of bead artists were making larger gashkibidaaganag, while diminishing or eliminating the pocket element altogether. The pocket first became nonfunctional because of its diminishing opening size, and then it disappeared entirely. This form includes bags with small central openings, too narrow for hand access (Figure 2.49); bags with small central faux openings represented by rows of beads in a color that contrasts with the color of the ground (Figure 2.50);

2.49 *(far left)* Bag with a four-inch pocket opening, presented to Reverend William Denley by an Ojibwe chief of Cass Lake, no later than 1888. *MNHS 70.90*

2.50 *(left)* Bag with a narrow faux pocket opening from Red Lake or White Earth, given to Elizabeth Peake, the grandmother of donor Emily Peake, no later than 1930. *MNHS 1995.95.2*

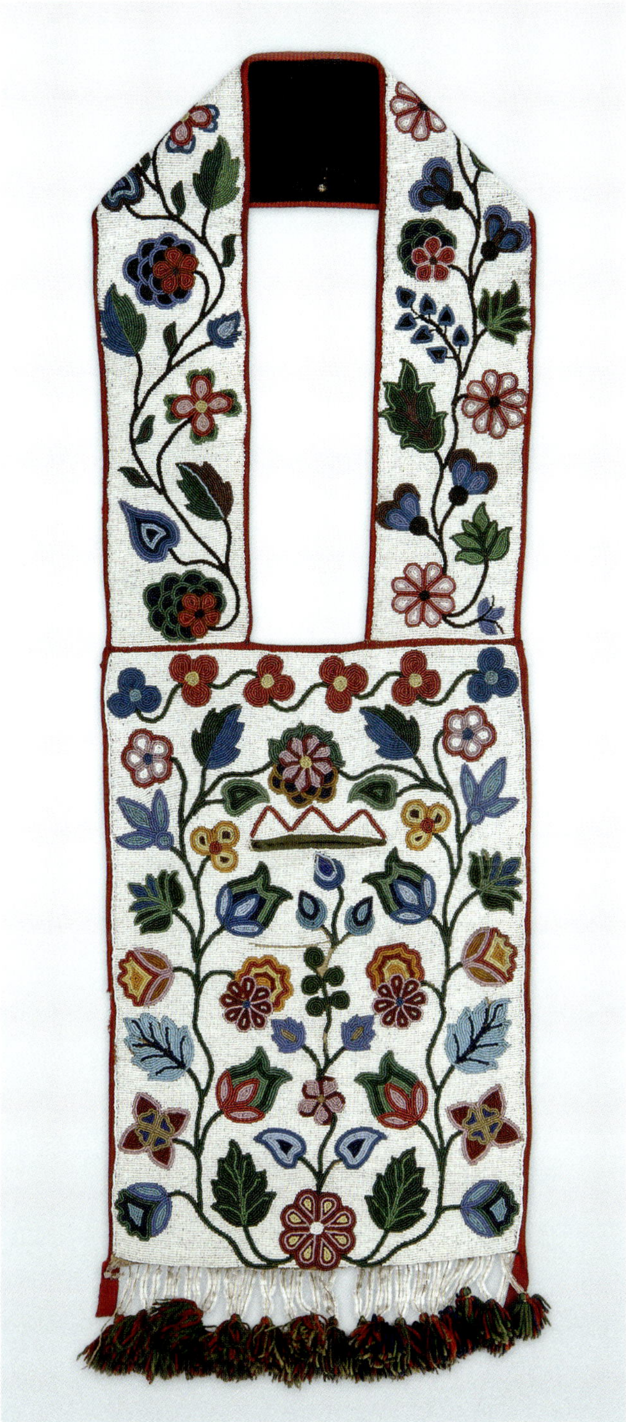

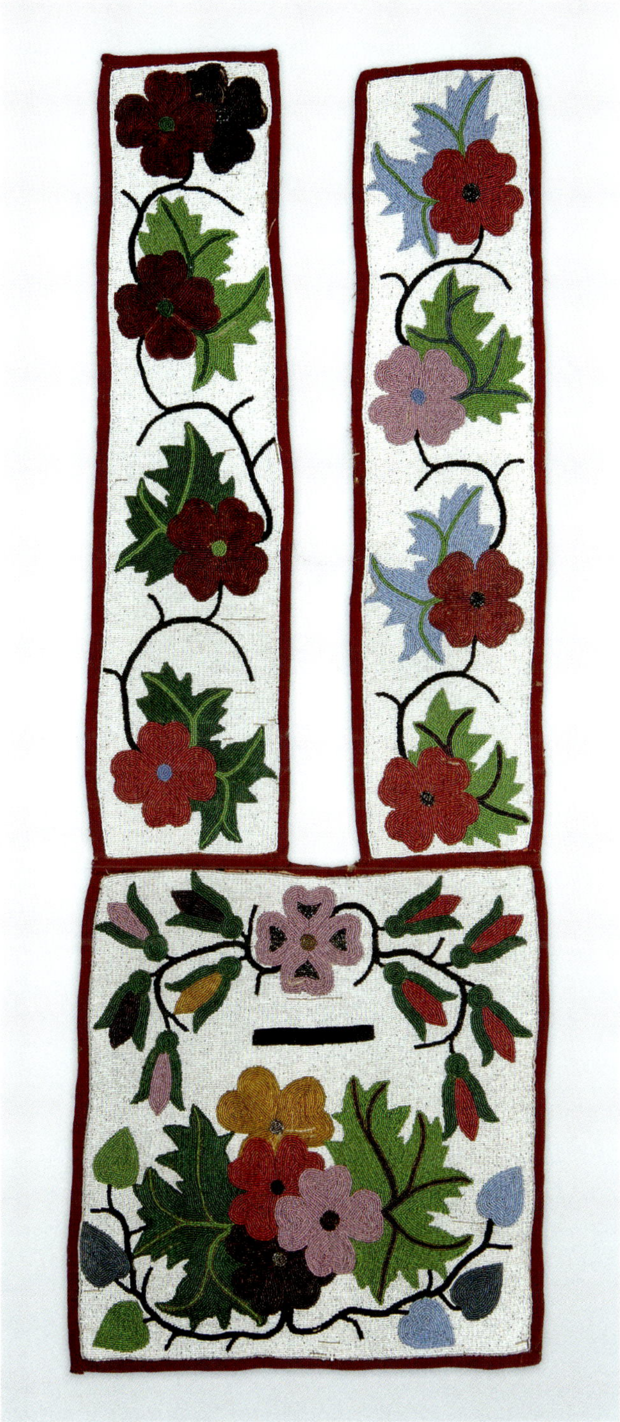

bags with no opening that feature a panel of beadwork designed to reference the two separate components that previously existed above and below a pocket opening (Figure 2.51); and finally, a beaded panel functioning simply as a blank rectangular surface for bead artistry and motif arrangements without any reference to a pocket opening or separate components (Figure 2.52).[21]

THIS ACCOUNT OF CHANGING gashkibidaaganag structures, materials, and types provides historical context for the design influences and motifs that bead artists chose. With the evolution of the bags in mind, careful study can provide clues to how ideas were adapted between loom-woven and spot-stitch appliqué bags and to how beaded designs may have spread. The next chapter examines these questions.

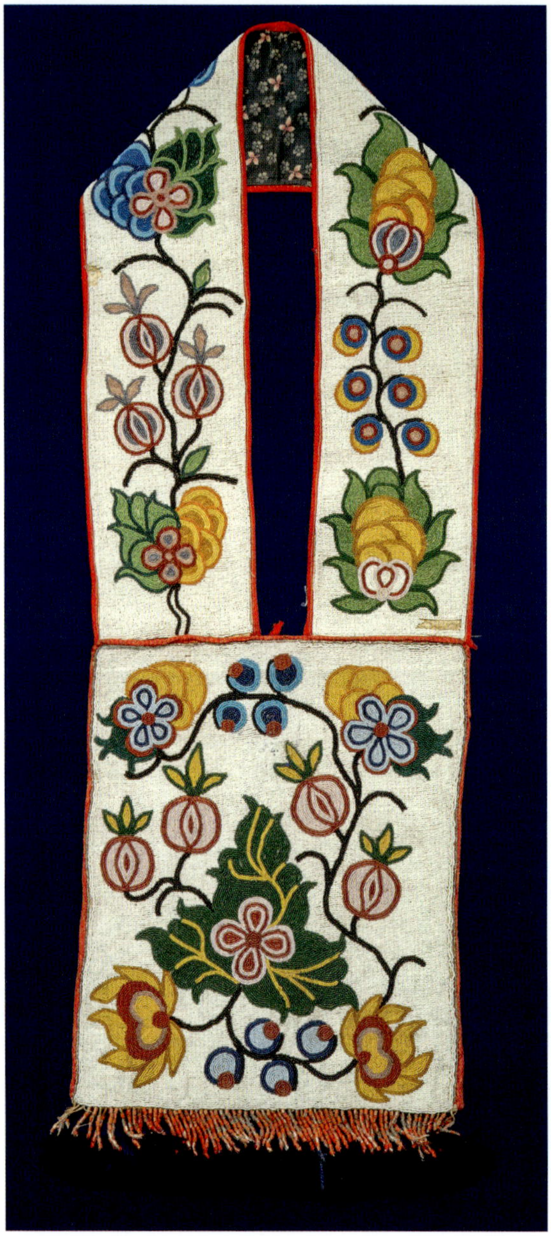

2.51 *(right)* Bag without a pocket, but with a vague reference to one. The arch of the vine up and across the top of the panel suggests what previously had been a separate area decorated with spot-stitch embroidery above the pocket opening, probably first third of the twentieth century. *MNHS 10000.159*

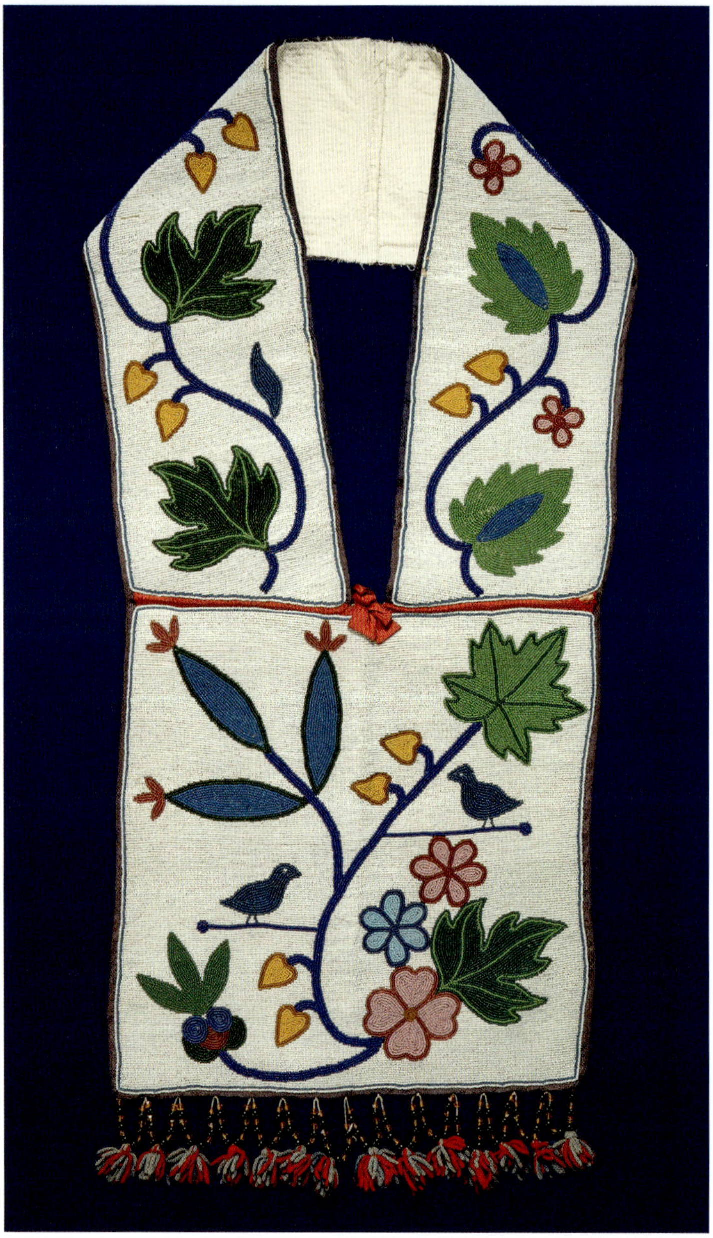

2.52 *(far right)* A panel bag created before 1925 and collected by Harry and Jeanette Ayer. *MNHS 10000.157*

Chapter 3

Design Influences and Motifs

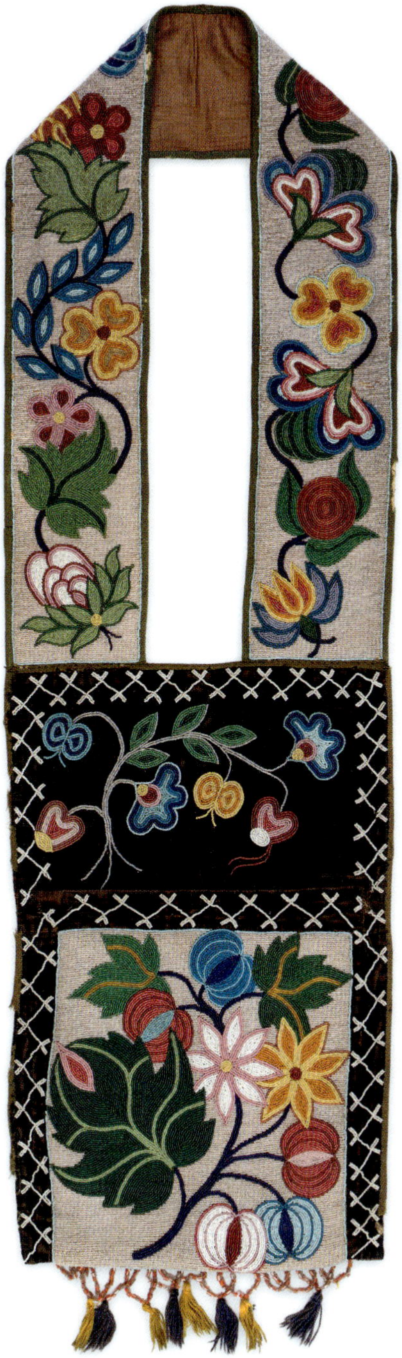

The beauty of gashkibidaaganag comes from their intricate, imaginative, colorful designs. Ojibwe bead artists speak with many visual voices, and they have found inspiration in various sources through the years, creating bags that display both traditional and new motifs. The spark of the maker's individual creativity is evident in each bag. And like all artists, each woman borrowed what appealed to her from the products and influences of other cultures (Figure 3.01). She took into account, too, the tastes of those who would be using the bags or receiving them as gifts. Most importantly, she developed her bag style by integrating old and new, familiar and exotic, envisioning and creating an object that simultaneously represented status, honor, respect, and beauty within her culture—and also provided a source of income. And she did all this, with the simplest of resources, while struggling with political oppression that amounted to cultural genocide—forced assimilation, outlawing of traditional religious practices, forced removal of children to boarding schools—and, often, severe poverty. The bags in Figures 3.02–6 are a sampler, illustrating the evolution of the gashkibidaagan from the 1850s to the 1940s, as bags decorated with loom-woven bead panels changed (Figures 3.02, 3.03, and 3.04), the spot-stitch appliqué technique became popular (Figure 3.05), and functioning pockets disappeared from bags (Figure 3.06).

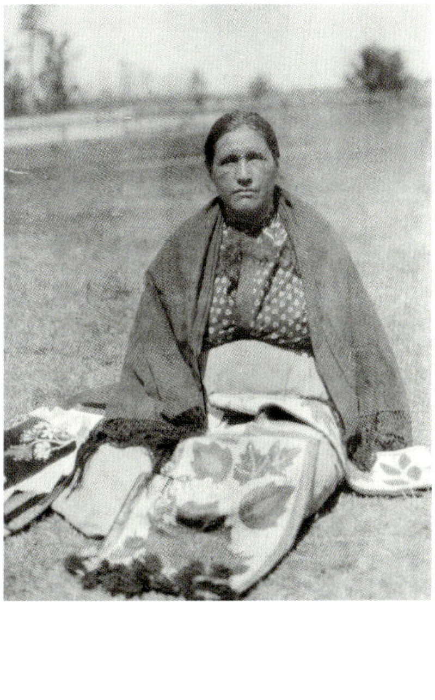

3.01 A Pine Point, White Earth, woman known as Pah-oom-bah-ig-oke (Pah-oom-bah-cumig-oke) at work on a gashkibidaagan, 1917. It appears to be a full panel style with an oversized single leaf motif in the bottom section. The tassels have been added but the strap is unattached, draped across her lap. More beadwork lies on the ground to her right. *Photo by Aleš Hrdlička, NAA-SI 4877 #121-146, 00277700*

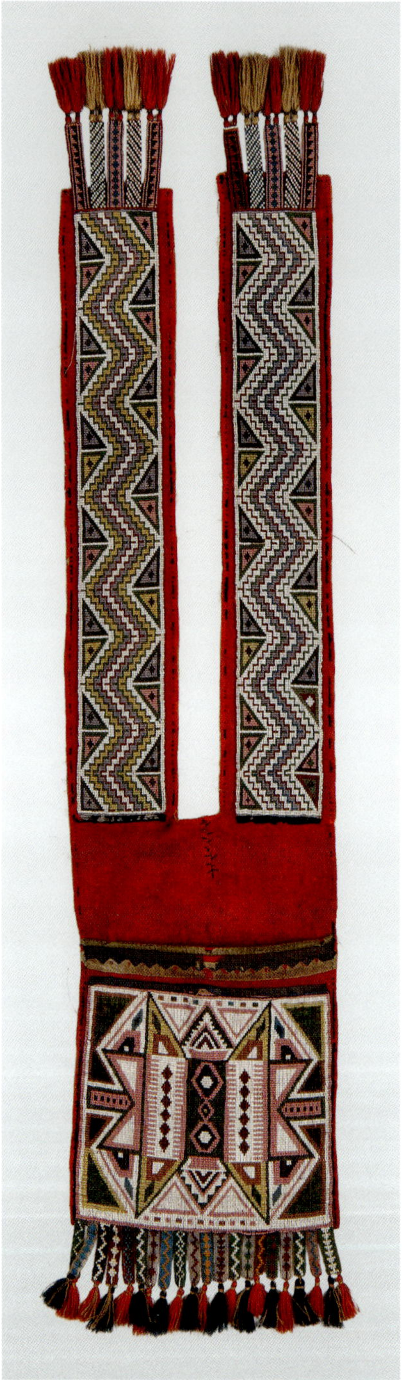

3.02 Bag with loom-woven bead panels, minimal borders, and no decoration above the pocket opening, probably dating between 1877 and 1886. *MNHS 1982.67.1*

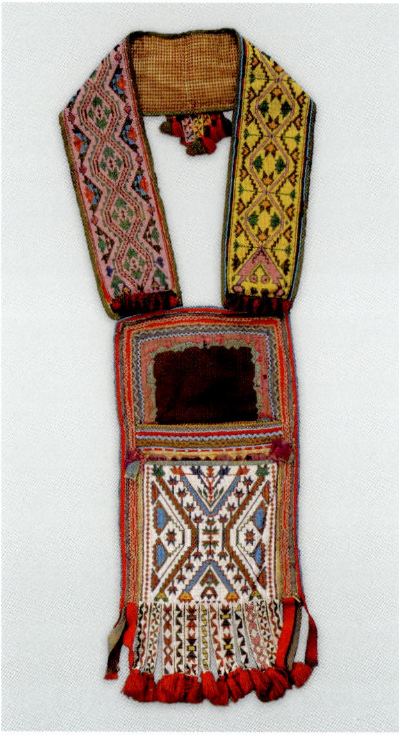

3.03 Bag with loom-woven panels and wide border trim, c. 1860s–1880s. *MNHS 6020.9; see also Figures 2.17 and 3.21*

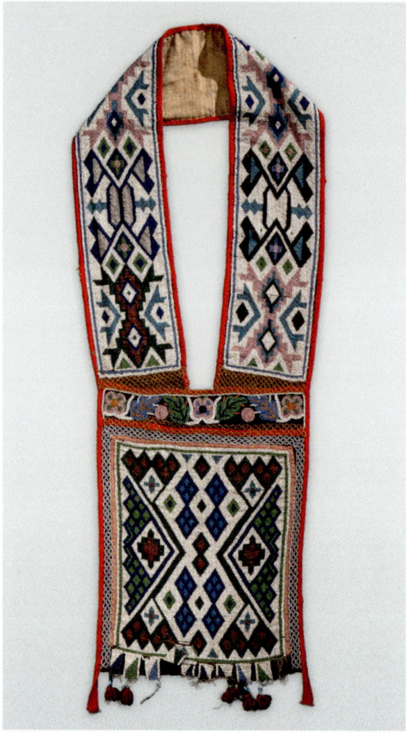

3.04 Bag with loom-woven panels in larger-scale motifs with spot-stitch appliqué above the pocket opening, late nineteenth century. *MNHS 10000.151*

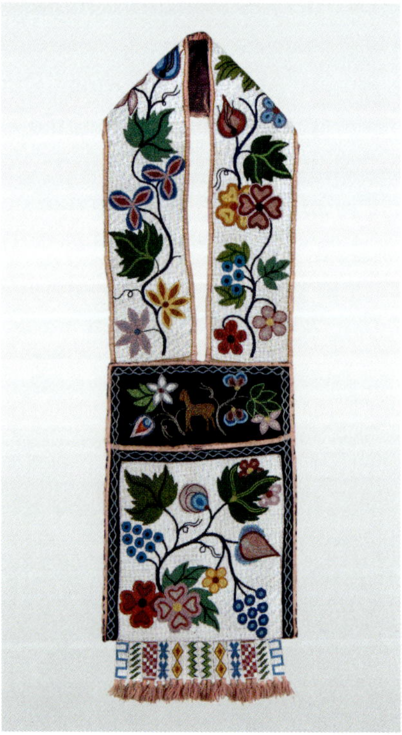

3.05 Spot-stitch appliqué bag with a functioning pocket, probably 1890s. *MNHS 8701.1*

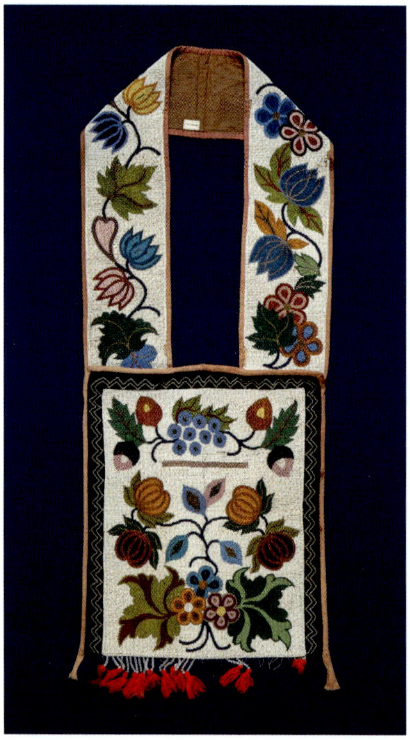

3.06 Spot-stitch appliqué bag with no pocket, first third of the twentieth century. *MNHS 10000.158*

A major influence from other cultures, of course, came from Euro-American styles, which Minnesota Ojibwe bead artists were exposed to through a number of sources, including missionaries, boarding schools, and print fabrics. No doubt these influences provided many ideas and much inspiration, but scholars frequently give too much credit to these influences alone. Ojibwe bag makers, like all artists, responded to their surroundings—the other indigenous nations around them and the plants, foods, and animals that they encountered daily. Most importantly, the bead artists made their own choices about their designs, and they deserve credit for their invention and creativity. While it may be possible to see aspects of some or all of these influences in their designs and their celebrated gashkibidaaganag, it underestimates the artists to view their work as derivative.[1]

Furthermore, while every bag is unique, bags with both loom-woven and spot-stitched designs show specific *Ojibwe* cultural patterns. Unlike many of the bags with loom-woven panels made by beadworkers from other indigenous nations in the Great Lakes region, the Ojibwe bags documented in Minnesota and parts of Wisconsin feature an interest in asymmetry, use of contrast rather than coordination of motifs, and the creative use of unmatched motifs. Bags with loom-woven decorations that are documented as Menominee, Potawatomi, or Ho-Chunk (Figures 3.07 and 3.08) appear to emphasize more repetitive use of single motifs and a more structured use of space between motifs.

Inspired by the canopy and understory of the forests, the Ojibwe spot-stitch appliqué artists incorporated decorative motifs into their bags that reflect their love of the beauty that surrounds them. The floral-based motifs are artistically successful because they create a symphony of space and movement between a cacophony of leaves, stems, vines, fruits, and flowers. Both the loom-woven beadwork and the spot-stitch appliqué represent rhythmic, flowing, eclectic, asymmetrical designs from the natural world. Because of these distinctive characteristics, many otherwise unidentified bandolier bags can be stylistically attributed to the Ojibwe.

The following discussion of design influences and motifs is organized chronologically, focusing on three general phases: early bags, bags with loom-woven panels, and spot-stitch appliqué bags. While some patterns and motifs are more common in one type of bag than another, the influences overlap. For instance, the border patterns introduced in the earliest bags have continued to the present, and motifs potentially influenced by quilt patterns appear in both loom-woven and spot-stitched beadwork.

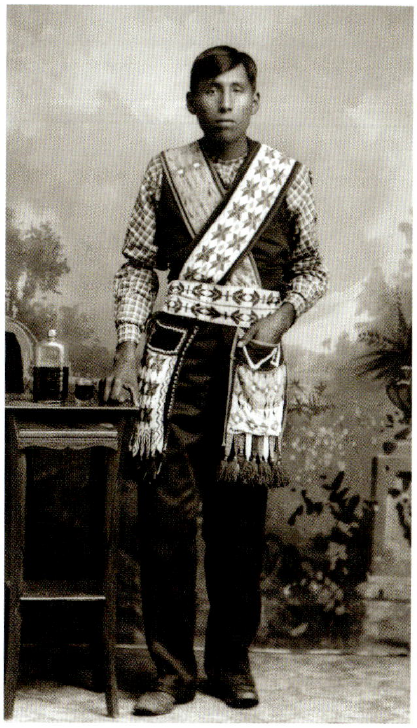

3.07 John Littlewalker, a Ho-Chunk man from Nebraska, wearing two Ho-Chunk bags, c. 1890. *WHS 62078*

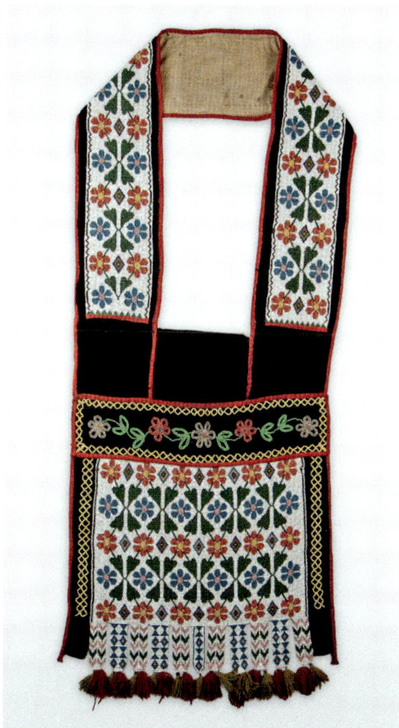

3.08 A loomed bag purchased in March 1906 from Tshi-kua-set (The Sound of Thunder) on the Menominee Indian Reservation, Wisconsin. *LMA 30664*

Simple line-stitch beadwork and edging

The earliest design influences for gashkibidaaganag decorated with loom-woven bead panels may include the simple motifs on wampum belts, the quillwork bands on small decorated pouches or loom-woven leg and arm garters, and the finger-woven sashes of the early nineteenth century.

Some of the first beaded design elements or motifs can be traced back to patterns realized using sinew, leather, quills, and other natural materials to create simple lines in otter track, zigzag, and other repeating forms. What Frances Densmore defines as "line" patterns for beadwork are the descendants of those early elements and are key to gashkibidaaganag design (Figure 3.09). These motifs were used primarily to outline larger pieces of work and as traditional border treatments (Figure 3.10).[2]

e
c
f
b

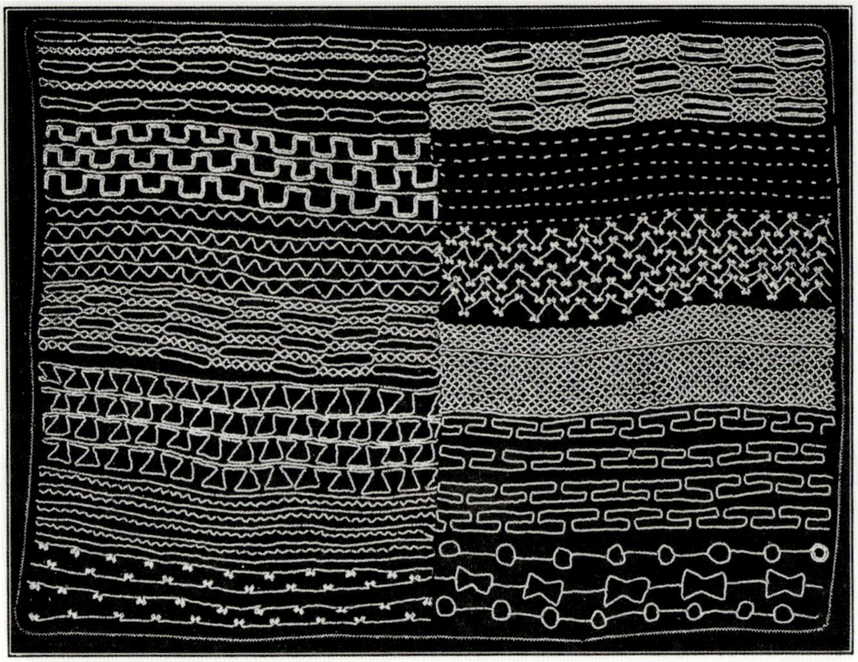

g
a
d

3.09 Nawajibigokwe (Central Rock Woman, or Mrs. Wawweyaycumig) of White Earth made this sampler of traditional line stitches for Frances Densmore. They include: a, jumping pattern; b and c, block pattern, or fret; d, diamonds; e, f, and g, versions of otter track. Densmore does not name the other stitches. *Densmore, Plate 79, Chippewa Customs*

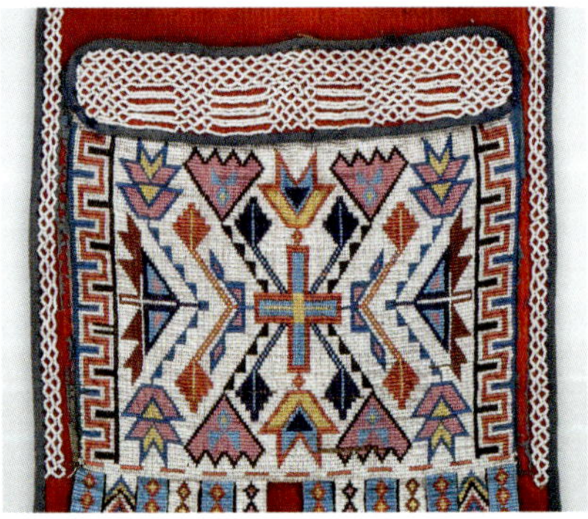

3.10 This pocket detail features diamonds, triangles, otter track, and the block, or fret, pattern in bead line border treatments. *MNHS 64.155.29; see also Figure 1.14*

Decorative borders frame the strap and pocket of almost every bandolier bag. These treatments may consist of repetitive patterns rendered in appliquéd silk ribbon or cloth strips, or in fine-line beadwork. Borders appear most often on the sides and top of the pocket panel, as well as on the outer perimeter of the smaller area above the pocket opening. Borders are also sometimes found on the strap; in spot-stitch appliqué pieces, they are usually worked as one, two, or three solid lines of beadwork in the same or contrasting colors. Within the collections at the Minnesota Historical Society, the two most predominant line motifs are otter track and variations of the zigzag.

Otter track

One of the oldest and most popular line motifs found in American Indian beadwork, the otter track has been in use for hundreds of years, especially among Algonquian speakers. A double row of zigzag lines forms a series of two, three, or four diamonds that are interrupted by elongated hexagons. Sometimes called otter trail or otter tail, it is also found in earlier object forms made with natural and other materials, including yarn, cedar,

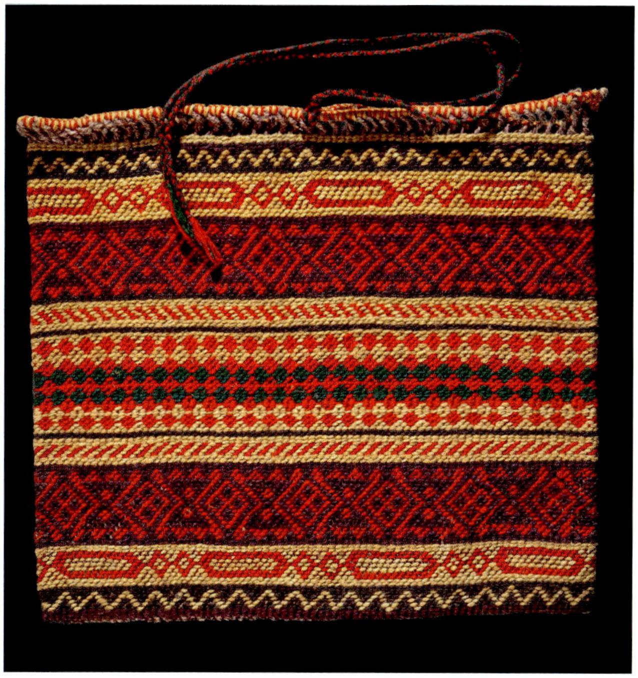

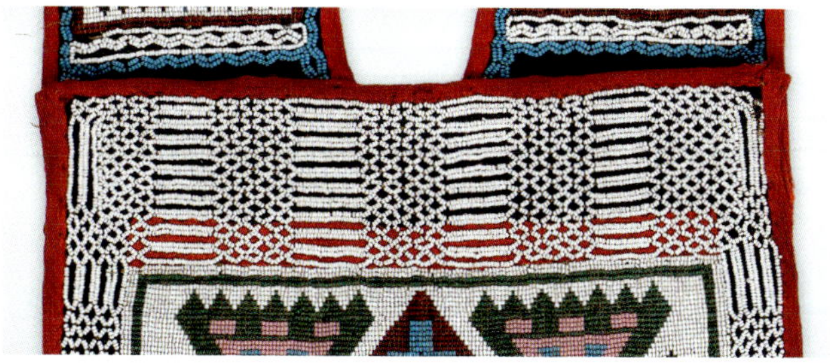

3.11 *(left)* Otter-track motif framing other line designs in a woven and twined bag made of plant fiber and wool yarns, c. 1875–1925. *MNHS 10000.224*

3.12 *(above)* Otter-track motif as integral border component of a loom-woven bag, c. 1880. *MNHS 6333.6.E; see also Figure 7.05*

bulrushes, and quills (Figure 3.11). Otter track can be rendered in single or multiple parallel rows and is nearly always made with white beads. In some loom-woven gashkibidaaganag, it consists of so many rows in width that it becomes a significant design element (Figure 3.12).

Densmore describes this common border treatment's longtime continuous use by the Ojibwe, offering one possible interpretation of its origin: "The otter tail pattern is said to have been received by the Mississippi Band of Chippewa from the Ottertail Band, but this seems conjectural, as the pattern is so clearly developed from simpler forms. It is used as a narrow border and also in various widths and combinations."[3]

This very old motif appears earlier in other regions, so restricting its origin to the Minnesota band seems misguided. The tracks of otters in winter (Figure 3.13) suggest a simpler origin as one of many possibilities.

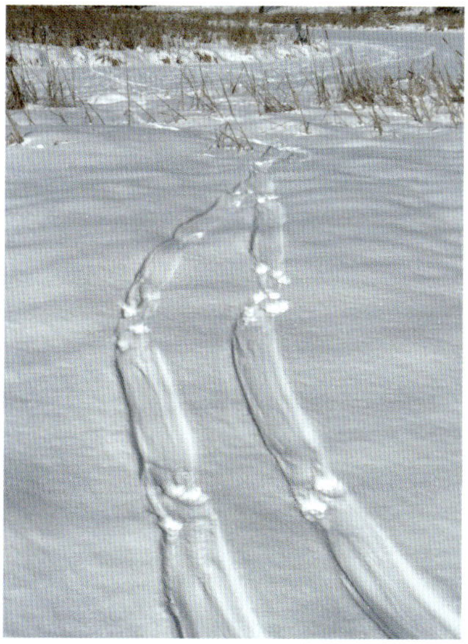

3.13 Otters' tracks in snow. *Photo by Larry Wade, oldnaturalist.com*

Zigzag

The next most popular border in Minnesota Ojibwe beadwork is a simple, and often oversized, zigzag, usually worked in white beads (Figure 3.14). It can be rendered in a single line, but it is also worked as two or more parallel or mirrored lines. Various sizes of commercial cotton rickrack were sometimes used instead of a zigzag beaded line.

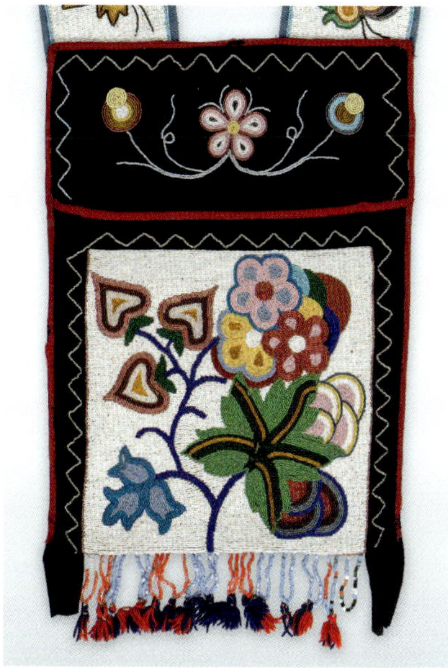

3.14 Zigzag border treatment. *MNHS 6333.6.H; see also Figure 7.09*

Beaded embroidery stitches

American women attending the popular 1876 World's Fair in Philadelphia took careful note of the Japanese design and British embroidery styles they viewed there. It was not long before crazy quilts incorporating both of these influences emerged as a full-fledged trend. These quilts, made of irregularly shaped pieces of dressier fabrics further embellished with

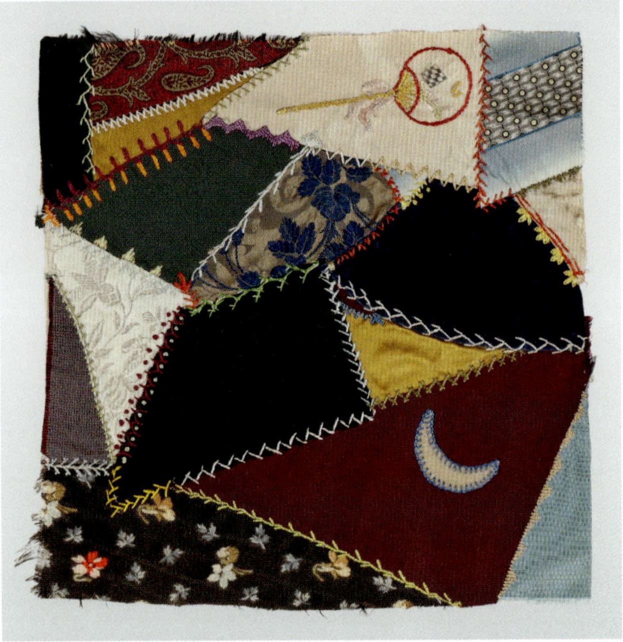

3.15 Crazy quilt embroidery. *MNHS 1982.25.15*

fancy embroidery stitches (Figure 3.15), were a significant departure from the traditional quilts assembled with cotton or wool fabrics. Rarely completed as multilayered quilts intended for warmth, the "crazies" instead served as a vehicle for women to show off their embroidery skills and decorate their parlor sofas. The stitches were used less as a functional element to hold layers of fabric together and more as an overt decorative component that outlined and drew attention to the odd-shaped pieces of cloth. The stitches were large, often done with plied silk embroidery flosses in contrasting colors that stood out against the colorful ground of the quilt top. Crazy quilts were most popular from about 1880 to 1920.[4]

At about the same time, in northwestern Minnesota, the common gashkibidaagan border decorations shifted away from embellishment featuring multiple rows of otter-track beadwork and moved toward a wider band of cloth boldly decorated with a single oversized beaded line that mimicked the embroidery stitches found on crazy quilts. Common border motifs on bags from the Cass Lake, White Earth, Leech Lake, and Red Lake reservation areas during the late nineteenth and twentieth centuries include lines that are wavy, straight, jumping (dotted), fretted, crosshatched, herringboned (Figure 3.16), zigzag, and feathered.

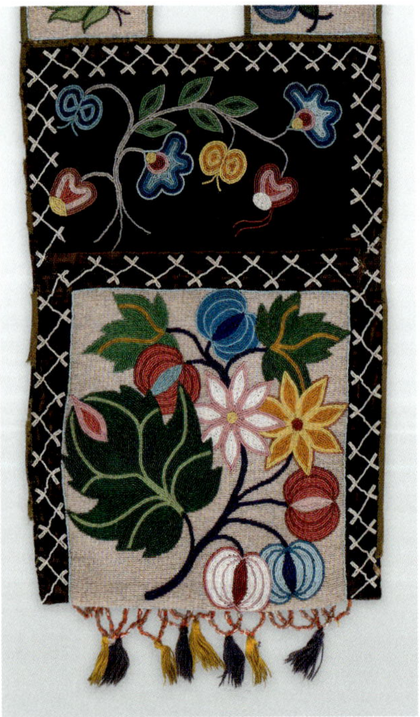

3.16 Herringboned border, c. 1880–90. *MNHS 74.32.5*

Some studies of Ojibwe beadwork suggest that this shift to oversized line borders occurred simply because they required fewer beads and less labor. But the quality of work on these later bandolier bags by Minnesota Ojibwe is undiminished, and a wider border treatment provides an effective and flattering frame for the floral "painting" on the bag's appliquéd pocket panel.

Edging choices

The bindings that provided a structural component for gashkibidaaganag (page 40) were also part of a bag's design. Usually made of worsted wool but sometimes of silk ribbon, commercial cotton, scrap fabric, or binding tape (Figure 3.17), binding was chosen in colors and widths that would complement or contrast with the beadwork.

Two-bead edging (Figure 3.18) has been used by many Northeastern Indian nations and is found on clothing and accessories as well as on many forms of small bags that preceded the gashkibidaagan. While this delicate bead edging is found in beadwork throughout the Great Lakes, it exists on only the earliest forms of the gashkibidaagan (Figure 3.19). The wool tape binding probably better fit the scale and function of a bandolier bag; the two-bead outer edging most likely would have been too vulnerable to the abrasion from wearing and dancing a gashkibidaagan.

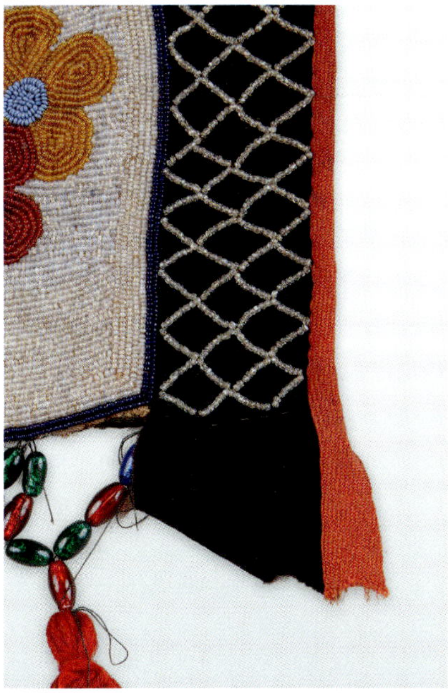

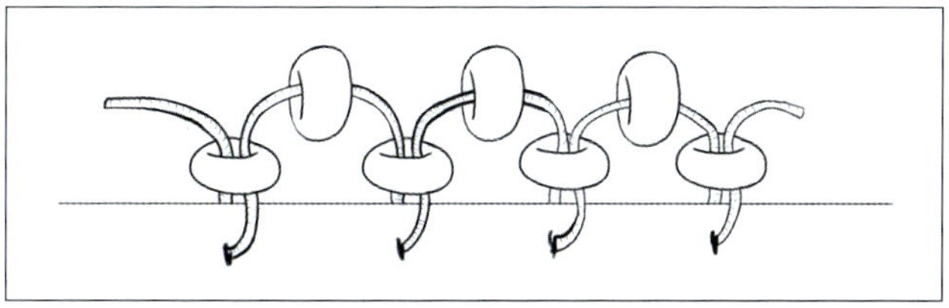

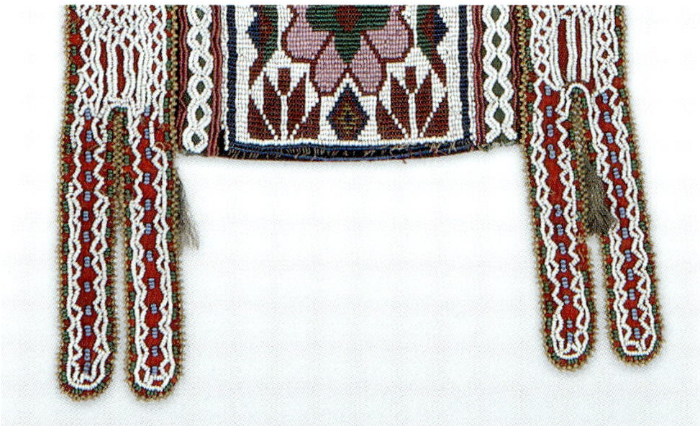

3.17 Binding, in red, made of flat wool tape, or braid—by far the most prevalent binding material used—on a bag from the first quarter of the twentieth century. *Photo by James Castle; MNHS 10000.610; see also Figure 10.21*

3.18 *(top)* Two-bead edging. *Illustration by Hannah Boehme*

3.19 *(above)* Two-bead edging in yellow, on edges of pocket framing elements and tab fringe, made before 1920. *MNHS 6037.4*

Loom-woven bags

A woman at Red Lake told Frances Densmore that bead artists of loom-woven beadwork rarely had a pattern in front of them and never completely duplicated a bag. While some bead artists used birchbark cutout patterns or bitten birchbark patterns, this particular artist said she just "had the entire design clearly in her mind" before beginning a difficult project.[5]

A number of the earliest loom-woven bags, probably produced in the 1850s and 1860s, are closer in size to the smaller precursor bags than to the gashkibidaaganag of the twentieth century. They are usually between thirty-nine and forty inches long overall. With straps under four inches in width, the pocket often rested high, above the wearer's waist and not far below the armpit. In early bags, the area above the pocket opening is nearly the same size as the pocket panel and is often undecorated. The pocket panel is roughly square; the straps are narrow. Integrated fringe is often present, on the pocket and the strap, and it is longer than the short tab fringes seen later.

This list of design influences and motifs adopted by the makers of loom-woven bags includes some patterns that appear in spot-stitch appliqué bags, as well.

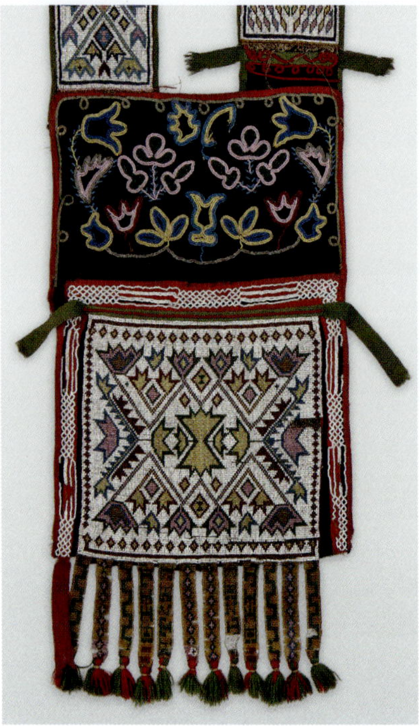

3.20 Motifs denoted with spot-stitched outlines; on this bag, c. 1880s, some outlines are also partially filled in with beads. *MNHS 8616.15*

Outline beadwork embroidery

In the area above the pocket panel on many earlier loomed bags, the foundation cloth (usually a dark color) appears as a solid dark background—part of the overall statement of the bead artist. When this component is decorated on these early bags, it often has a spot-stitched bead outline of a floral motif that is not filled in with beads (Figure 3.20). This style is atypical of the Ojibwe in Minnesota, except for beadworkers from Lake Lena (see page 151); it is similar to motifs used by the Oto, Potawatomi, Menominee, Mesquakie, or Ottawa. While no specific explanations regarding the origins of this component have been found, collector Dr. Paul Radin described it as a "leaf scroll which is unquestionably a borrowed Ojibwe old moose hair pattern."[6]

I have not been able to discover why the outline or atypical spot-stitch embroidery designs were so prevalent on the surviving examples of early bags, as if they were almost a required element. The Ojibwe in what is now Minnesota did interact a great deal with other indigenous nations in the nineteenth century, but the lack of contemporary documentation of early loom-woven bags, in written or in photographic records, does not help to resolve this mystery.[7]

Ribbon work and other border decorations

Ribbon work was used both for border decoration and, sometimes, for binding. Before the areas above the pocket opening and on both sides of the pocket panel were decorated primarily with beads, strips of plain ribbon were used side by side as patterned ribbon-work appliqué. Eventually, artists replaced ribbon with wool tape and other fabric strips to serve as an alternative ground for beaded line-border motifs.

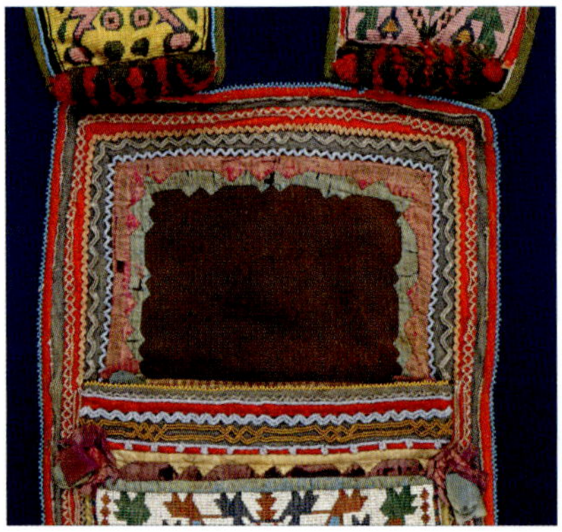

3.21 One side of an otter track rendered in cutout ribbon appliqué lines the borders above the pocket on this early bag. The motif appears twice: as an inside border along the blank wool ground in faded purple over green, and in the last horizontal band directly above the pocket opening in faded gold on top of purple ribbon. *MNHS 6020.9; see also Figures 2.17 and 3.03*

To produce ribbon-work appliqué, an artist generally used colored silk ribbons of varying widths, laying a ribbon of one color over a ribbon of another color and cutting the upper layers of ribbon in a pattern, then turning the edges under and blind-stitching them neatly in place. The usual cut pattern was either notches or diamonds, oftentimes replicating the otter-track motif. Artists sometimes used wool braid and fabric scraps (velvet, velveteen) under bead border work instead of ribbons. Other miscellaneous border trims included sequins, yarn or threads (usually wool but also silk, cotton, or linen), and soutache (a flat decorative braid).[8]

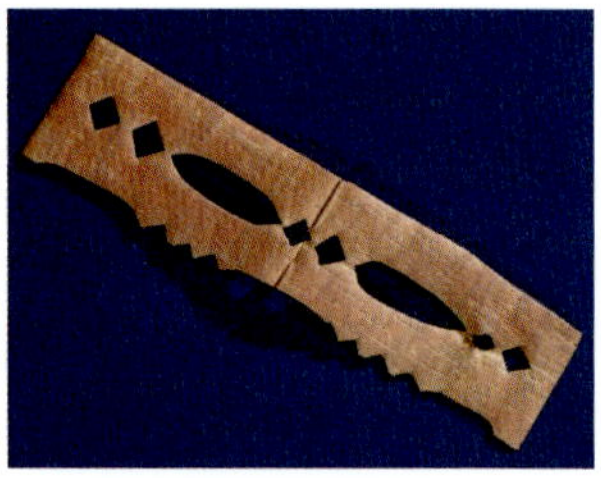

3.22 Birchbark otter-track template, c. 1918–59. When replicating just one side of the track—for example, on one side of a border—the bead artist would flip the template over to mark the other track side on the other side of the border. *MNHS 10000.1*

Ribbon work, other trims, and the fine-line beaded motifs were also often combined. The ribbon-work appliqué on the bag in Figure 3.21, for example, is one side of the otter-track motif. Figure 3.22 shows an otter-track template made from birch bark; some artists used templates to help ensure an even cutout pattern.

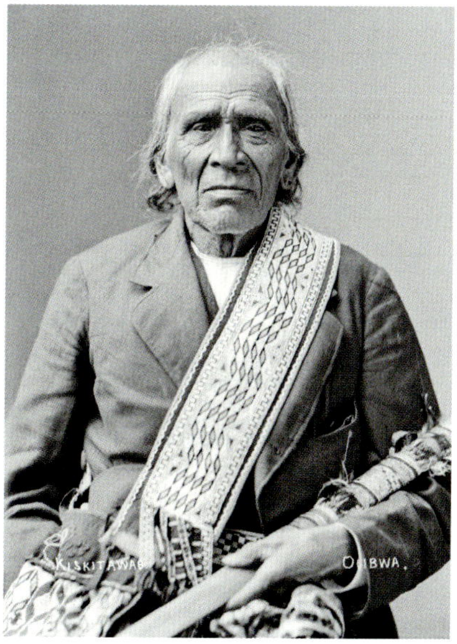

3.23 Kis-ki-ta-wag (Cut Ear), a member of an 1880 delegation, wearing a bag with lozenges, zigzags, Xs, and other line patterns. *NAA-SI BAE GN 00433B 06131502*

Geometric and Midewiwin motifs

Triangles, diamonds, lozenges, parallelograms, crosses, hexagons, octagons, dots, squares, and more are used together or in multiples across straps and panels to build complex motifs on bags—such as parallel lines of zigzags. The motifs appear in different scale when used on the strap instead of the pocket panel, but they can incorporate the same elements.

For example, in Figure 3.23 the bag worn by Kis-ki-ta-wag (a member of an 1880 delegation of Bad River, Lac Courte Oreilles, and Lac du Flambeau chiefs) has a strap decorated with zigzags represented through the use of a repeating parallelogram motif, seen often with the diamond motif in early bags. The partially visible pocket panel shows another use of the parallelogram to create rows of small Xs. The offset strap of this bag would suggest to most students of gashkibidaagan research that it was Ho-Chunk made. The birchbark patterns in Figure 3.24, which include a thunderbird, are motifs frequently seen in loom-woven beadwork, with the exception of the second from left in the bottom row.[9]

These early bags were also the ones that still carried some images associated with Midewiwin practices, power, and dreams. The images include thunderbirds (Figure 3.25) and claw designs to denote crawfish, or underwater panthers (Figures 3.26 and 3.27).

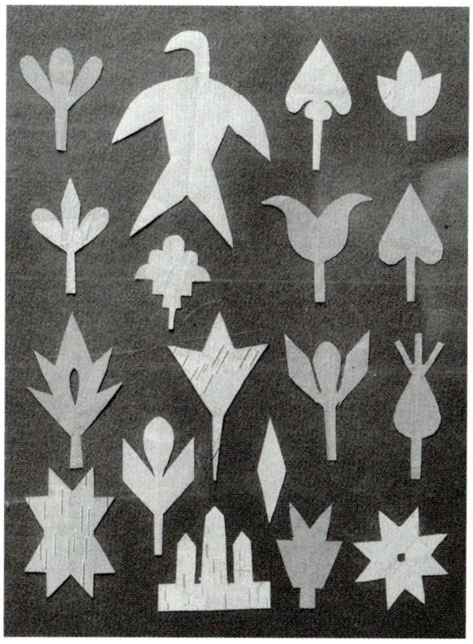

3.24 Birchbark patterns collected by Frances Densmore from Ajawac (Mrs. Louisa Martin) and by Zozed of Red Lake, before 1929. *NAA-SI Negative 596 D 124*

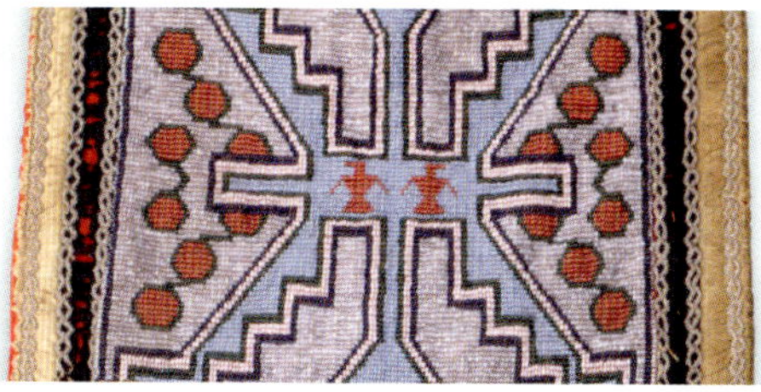

3.25 Thunderbird at pocket center. *MNHS 10000.152; see also Figure 2.32*

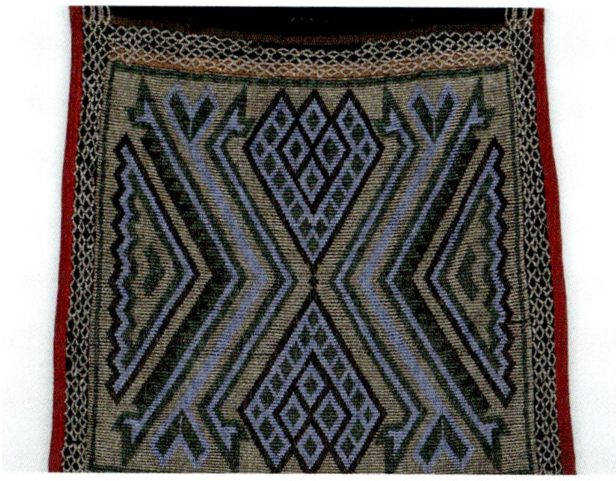

3.26 Pocket detail showing possible claw designs. *MNHS 6333.6.G; see also Figure 7.06*

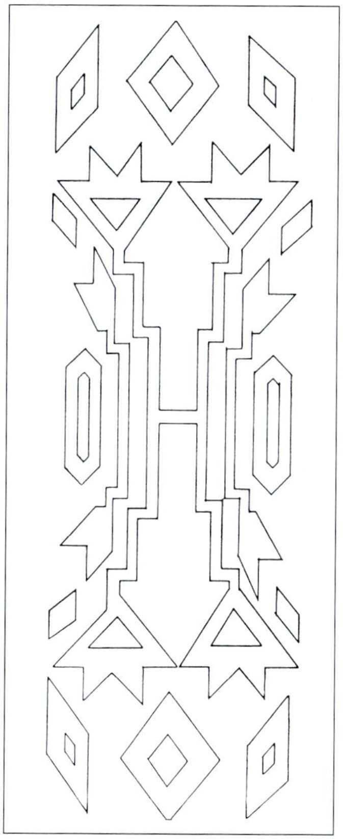

3.27 Pattern for claw (crawfish) designs, before 1943. *Lyford, Ojibwa Crafts, plate 100*

The geometric motifs on loom-woven panels were often made up of a concentration of small repeats, or echoes of portions of the major element, as in Figure 3.28.

The simple cross motif (Figure 3.29) exists historically worldwide and is easily rendered in loom work; the few examples of crosses on gashkibidaaganag in the Minnesota Historical Society's collections are found only on loomed bags. The occasional appearance of the cross in some Ojibwe beaded articles may also reflect the influence of missionary contact. While other Christian denominations sent missionaries to Minnesota, the Episcopal and Catholic churches had the most impact within the Ojibwe communities.

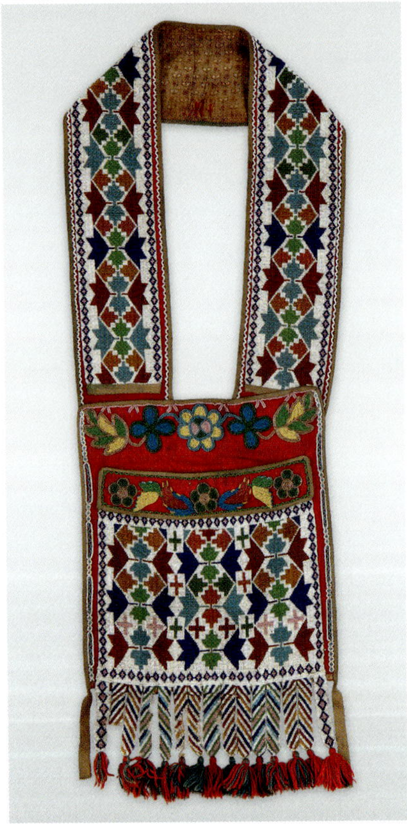

3.28 *(right)* Bag with small repeating geometric forms, last third of the nineteenth century. *MNHS 6507.12; see also Figure 2.01*

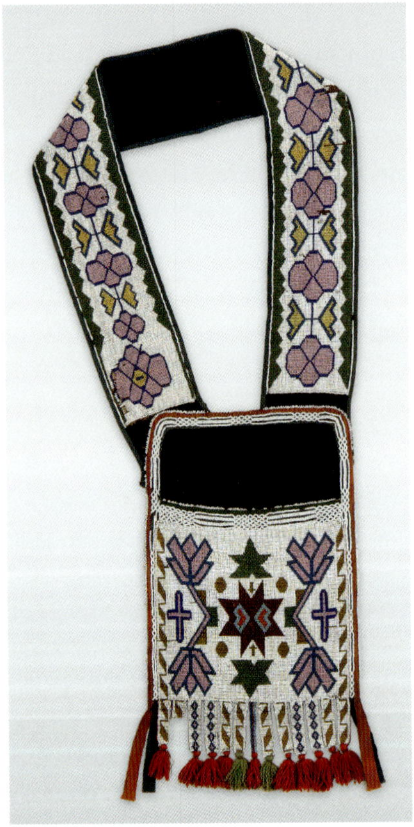

3.29 *(far right)* A loom-woven bag with cross motifs, c. 1880. *MNHS 8033.1*

Exploding X

A complex, vivid, and popular motif, which I call exploding X—with its large, embellished crossed arms—frequently fills a loom-woven pocket panel (Figures 3.30, 3.31, and 3.32). In some examples the motif is just an embellished X, but in others, its parts multiply as if they are exploding. Many scholars attribute variations on this pattern and other abstract geometric loom-woven pocket panel or strap motifs to an evolution of the underwater panther (crawfish) and other Midewiwin images found on birchbark scrolls, early woven-yarn bags, charm bags, and small quill-worked precursor bags or slit pouches. While thunderbird forms occur on some of the earliest gashkibidaaganag, none of the bead artists I spoke to believed any of the loom-woven or spot-stitched motifs had Midewiwin origins or identifiable meaning in Ojibwe cosmology. In fact, several informed me that the motifs had no special meaning. Some religious motifs, however, may have become more democratized and abstracted and prevalent in Ojibwe design over time, especially in loom-woven work. It's even possible that beadworkers may have been influenced by the designs on eighteenth-century shell wampum bead belts, the patterned ceremonial objects made by Northeastern tribes.[10]

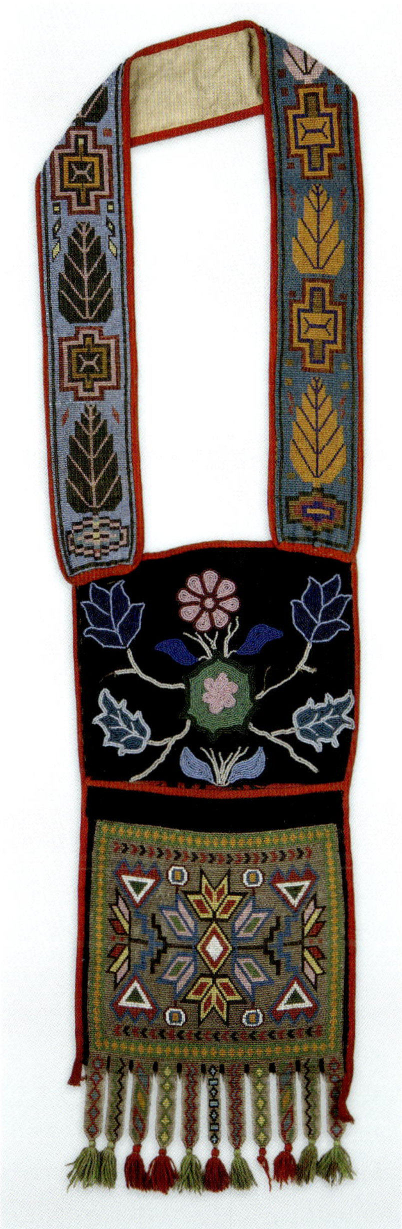

3.30 Loom-woven bag with outline and filled outline spot-stitched motifs, created about 1880. The exploding X is worked in narrow motif elements in black and blue. *MNHS 9666.7; see also Figure 3.79*

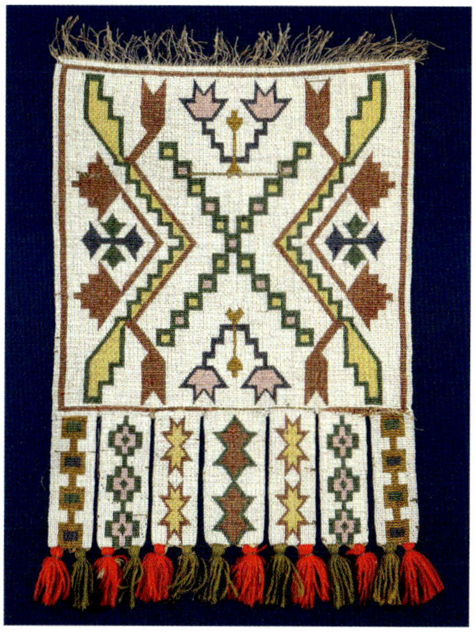

3.31 Loom-woven pocket panel collected by Harry and Jeannette Ayer, probably made between 1875 and 1900. *MNHS 10000.245*

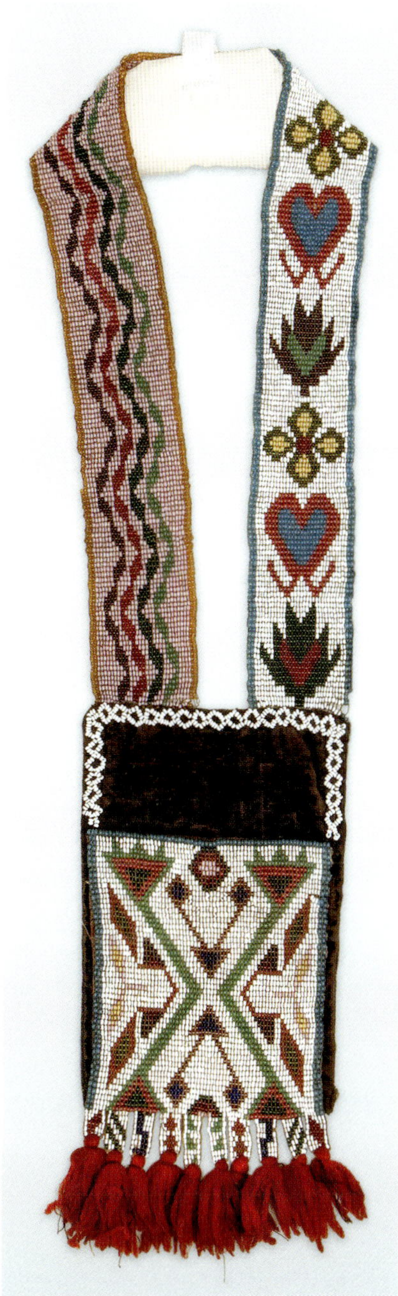

3.32 A miniature bag, made before 1947. The pocket panel is about four inches wide. *MNHS 8662.1*

Quilt influences in loom weaving

Ojibwe women used and made quilts regularly in the late nineteenth and first half of the twentieth centuries, and they have been recognized for their skills in this area. Photographs from this period show simple patchwork quilts used as door coverings on wigwams and associated with Midewiwin lodges. In some photographs, the quilts are worn blanket style, and sometimes pieces of quilts are incorporated into other garments. In most documented photographs of Ojibwe quilts, piecework was used, but appliqué patterns were employed as well. Like the early loom-woven beaded panels on gashkibidaaganag, pieced quilts were innovative arrangements of basic shapes like triangles, squares, diamonds, rectangles, and hexagons, with some shapes being combined to create eight-pointed stars, pinwheels, swastikas, and other motifs. The star quilts made by the Lakota and other Plains tribes beginning in the nineteenth century are still favored today in those communities.

The star is probably the second most common motif seen in loom-woven bags, after the exploding X. The motif likely preceded quilts: stars are found in early nineteenth-century quillwork, and later in all periods of quilt patterns. Once the spot-stitch appliqué bags appear, the star motif apparently lost its appeal, and it is much less common in floral decorated bags by the Ojibwe of Minnesota.

Quilts in the Minnesota Historical Society's collections (for the most part made by white women) demonstrate the design influences of the time. The patterns in Figures 3.33 and 3.34 appear in the bag in Figure 3.35.

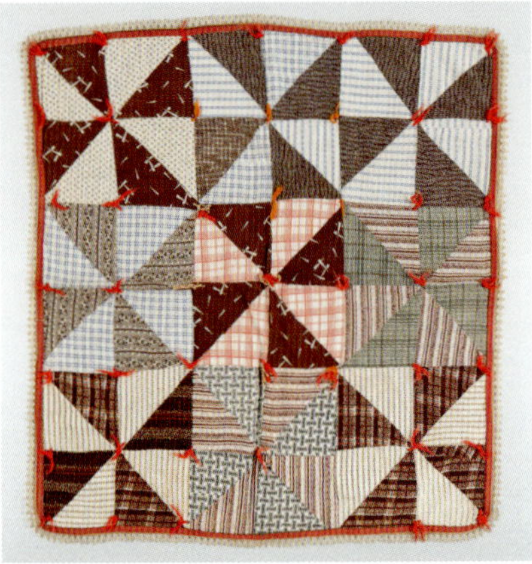

3.33 Pinwheel quilt, in which triangles form the design, c. 1900. *MNHS 67.230.315.B*

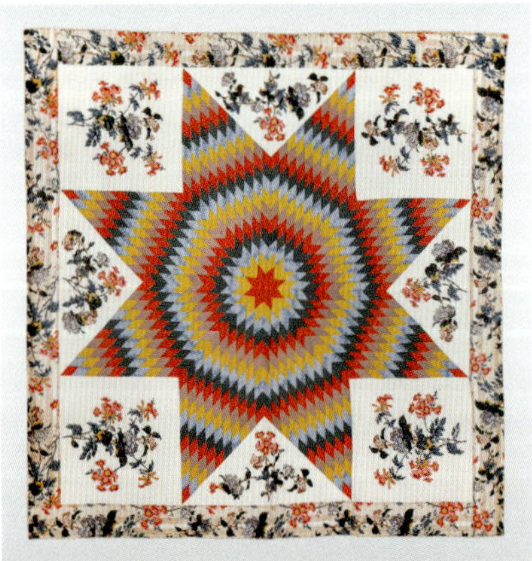

3.34 *Broderie perse* (appliqué) and eight-point star quilt, c. 1850. *MNHS 6358*

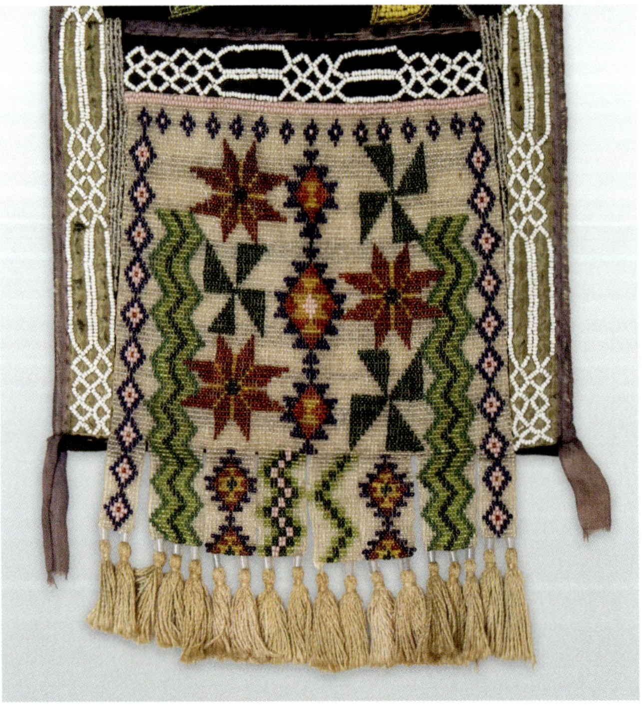

3.35 Loom-woven bag with pinwheel and eight-point star motifs, c. 1925. *MNHS 9023.2*

Figure 3.36 shows the honeycomb quilt pattern that relates to the hexagon motifs in Figures 3.37 and 3.38; the latter bag probably dates from the early to mid-twentieth century. By the time of the colonial revival trend in quilting, in the 1920s and 1930s, beadworkers may have been influenced by this same honeycomb quilt pattern, which by then was called grandmother's flower garden. Bags with this latter version of the motif have been attributed to Ojibwe, Menominee, and Potawatomi bead artists.

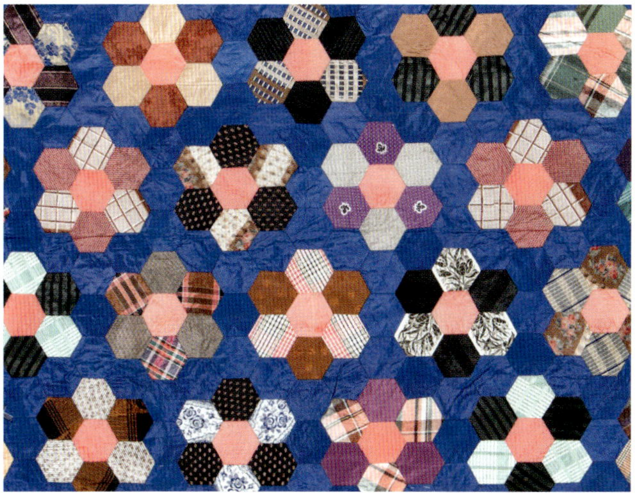

3.36 Quilt top detail, 1830–60. This silk quilt top from the LeDuc estate in Minnesota is a good example of the early appearance of the honeycomb patchwork design. *MNHS 1982.25.16.A*

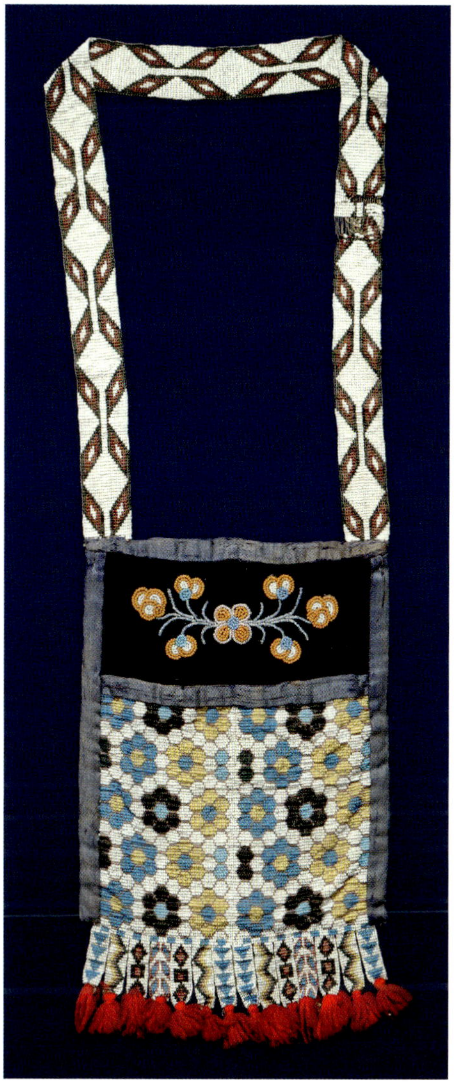

3.38 Loom-woven bag, probably early to mid-twentieth century. *MNHS 10000.148*

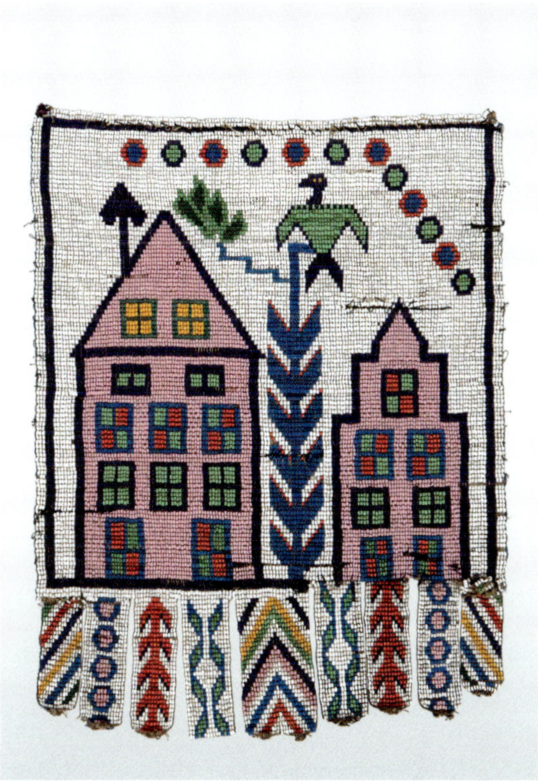

3.37 The hexagon motif, also called the dot motif, appears early in Great Lakes loom-woven beadwork. Small hexagons appear on the fringe as well as in a trail that represents chimney smoke in this pictorial pocket panel, complete with buildings, a tree, and a thunderbird, c. 1860s–80s. *MNHS 1982.67.6*

Changes in scale and the move to floral motifs

As loom-woven bag designs evolved from the 1870s to the 1890s, their dimensions changed and styles became more varied. Pocket panels grew larger, while the area above the pocket grew smaller; fringe tabs remained integrated but began to get shorter; motifs became simpler and sometimes larger in scale.

Toward the end of this period, the makers of loom-woven bags used more distinct motifs that were less connected with the rest of the bag (Figures 3.39 and 3.40). Beadworkers chose to incorporate solid-colored motif-free backgrounds as a significant part of the overall design. At the same time, bead artists were beginning to work floral motifs into the confines of the loom-woven technique (Figures 3.41 and 3.42).

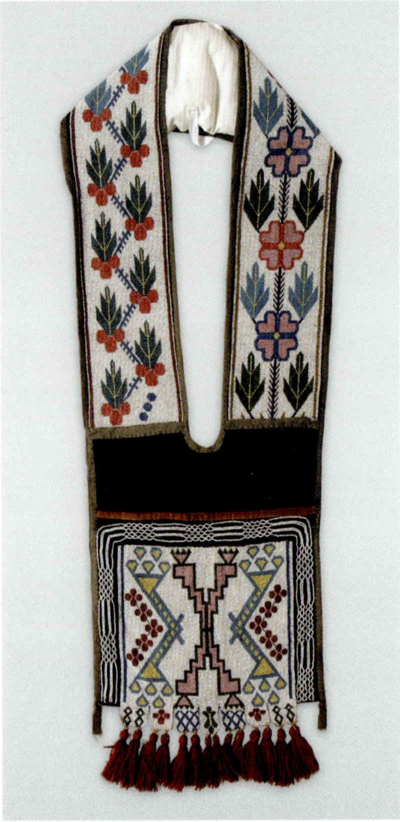

3.39 Loom-woven bag with scooped edge above pocket, made not earlier than 1891 and not later than 1914. *MNHS 285.E81; see also Figures 3.45 and 12.16*

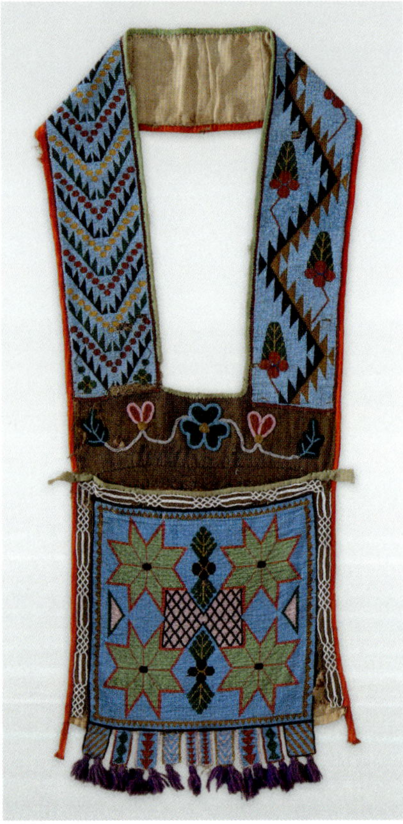

3.41 Loom-woven bag, before 1901, with floral motifs. *MNHS 7418.7*

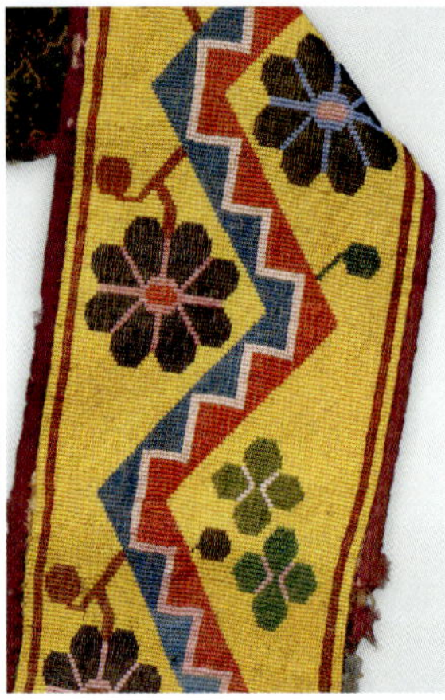

3.42 Strap detail of loom-woven bag, before 1923, with floral motifs. *MNHS 6333.6.F; see also Figure 7.07*

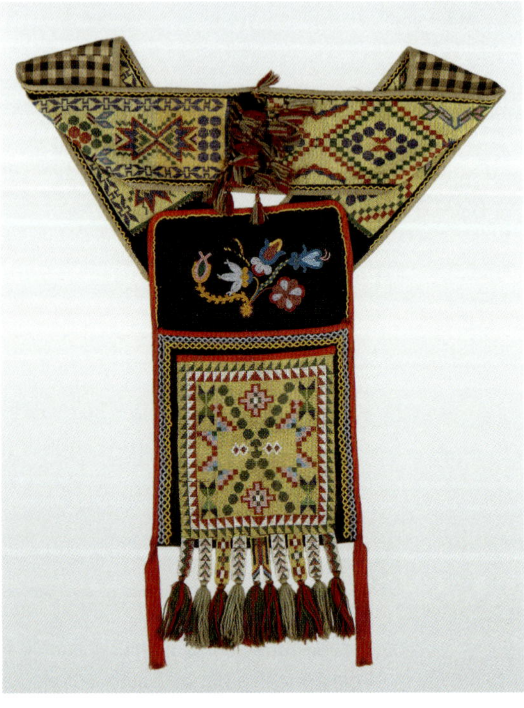

3.40 Loom-woven bag, before 1920. *MNHS 6020.10*

The classic Ojibwe motif is the rose. The pervasive wild roses native to Minnesota have five petals and all have varying degrees of indentations (Figure 3.43); beaded flowers can have from three to six petals. An "expert maker of woven work" at Red Lake told Densmore that the design in Figure 3.44 was "a conventional leaf with roses in the corners intended for the pocket of a bandoleer . . . and a smaller pattern of rose and a leaf for the shoulder band of the same article." Densmore identifies two varieties of wild rose designs: those with heart-shaped petals (which Lyford calls a conventionalized rose design) and those with simple, round petals. She even suggests that the pattern with four dot, or "round-bead," patterns arranged around a central dot is the natural development of the rose design. Realism is not required. Figure 3.45 shows a strap with loomed roses.[11]

Eventually, during this transitional period of gashkibidaagan design, some artists produced bags with one component done in loom work and another in spot stitch (Figure 3.46).

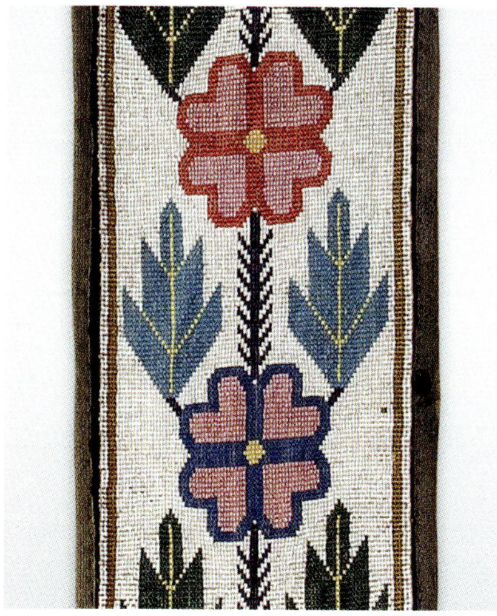

3.45 Heart-petaled flowers, loom woven. *MNHS 285.E81; see also Figures 3.39 and 12.16*

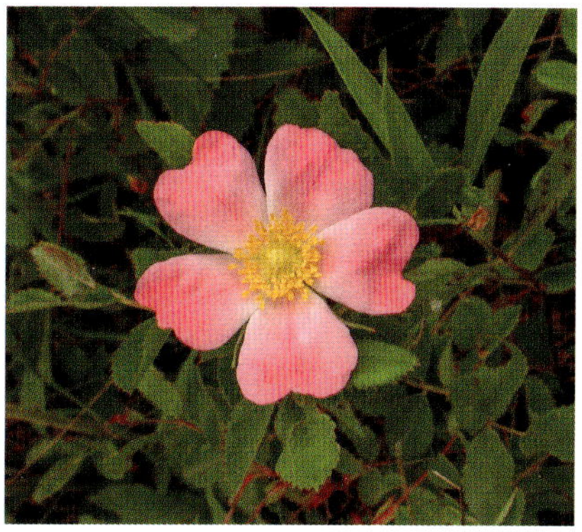

3.43 Prairie rose (*Rosa arkansana*). *Peter M. Dziuk, Minnesotawildflowers.info*

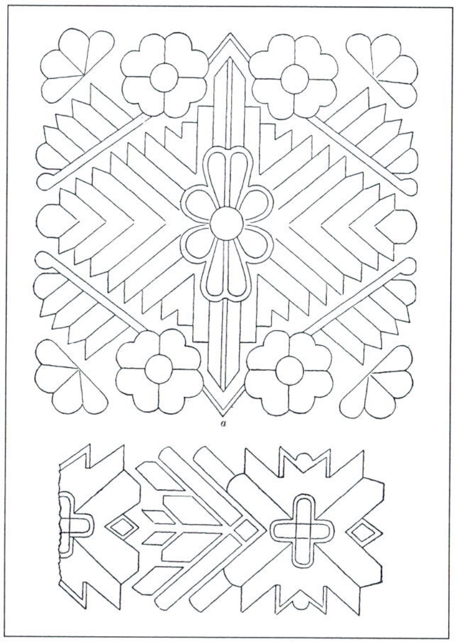

3.44 Pattern for a loomed leaf with roses collected by Frances Densmore before 1929. Heart-petaled flowers are at top and bottom center; flowers with round petals are at the corners; and a stylized rose is at center. *Densmore, Chippewa Customs, 193*

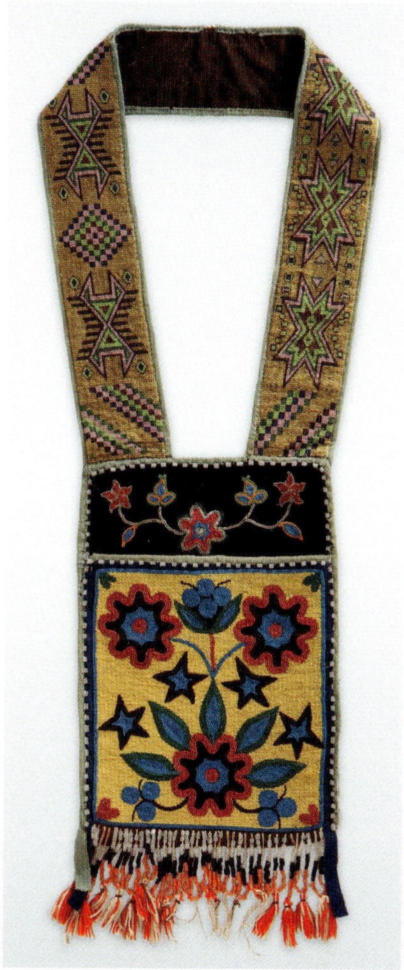

3.46 Bag with loom-woven strap and spot-stitch appliqué pocket panel, before 1901. *MNHS 1829*

Spot-stitched appliqué bags

The origins of many spot-stitched motifs—whether unusual or common—likely derive from the natural world, from other indigenous nations, and from Euro-American influences. Henry Rowe Schoolcraft, Johann Georg Kohl, Newton Horace Winchell, and other nineteenth-century travelers through the region described the plants, shrubs, and trees used by the Ojibwe of Minnesota in their everyday lives for sustenance and as a source of materials for domestic, medicinal, and transportation products. Unfortunately, these male ethnographers rarely took their study far enough to interview women, to adequately describe many of the activities of the women in a culture, or to compare aspects of native flowers, foliage, and fruits to designs evident in the craft traditions of the Minnesota Ojibwe.

The four ethnographers who did study Ojibwe women's traditions—Frances Densmore, Sister Bernard Coleman, Sister Inez Hilger, and Carrie Lyford—made their observations in the late nineteenth and first half of the twentieth centuries, and by then, many other factors had influenced the design choices made by Ojibwe beadworkers of the Great Lakes region. By the 1940s, when Sister Bernard Coleman asked the artists, they seemed to remark only on the influences from newcomers:

> Most designs were taken directly from patterns of embroidery or cross-stitch which they received in government schools. When I visited their homes, many of the women showed me these patterns which they had been keeping for years. . . . According to Mrs. Rock, the influence of the schools such as Flandreau, Pipestone, White Earth, Red Lake and St. Benedict's has been observed on the designs of the past two generations. Many women between the ages of 50 and 60 years acknowledge that they use no other design patterns except those taught them by their white teachers in classes in fancy work. Just to what extent Ojibwa women copied patterns on chintzes and calicos brought in by traders, it is difficult to determine.[12]

Regardless of where the influences came from, beadworkers needed to consider five primary elements in their spot-stitched designs:

- Arrangement of the motifs on the pocket panel
- Strap size, width, and length
- Framing of the strap and pocket panel
- Vines, or "life lines," that connect the motifs
- Stacking, or layering, of motifs

A high percentage of the bags associated with Minnesota have some form of a flower or leaf cluster that serves as the anchor or starting point for the pocket panel design. Motifs on the pocket panel might swirl (Figure

3.47) or travel diagonally out and up from the anchor, which might be in a lower left or lower right corner (Figure 3.48). They might begin at center bottom, with motifs that branch off irregularly on both sides of a roughly vertical stem or branch (Figure 3.49). Or they might reflect a roughly symmetrical placement, with vines usually starting at center bottom of the bag (Figure 3.50). Some bags feature a single large central motif (Figure 3.51).

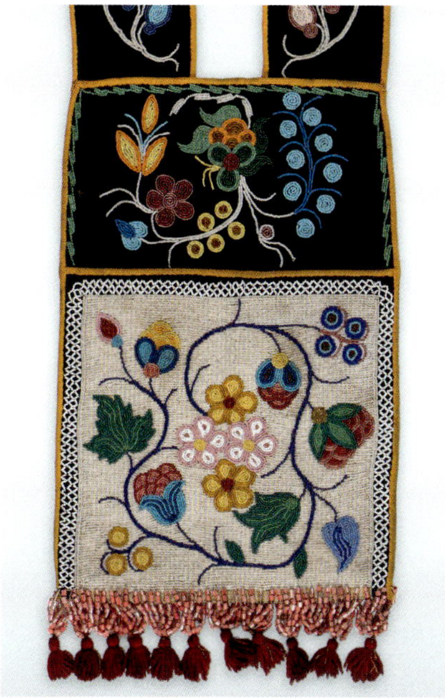

3.47 Central swirling motifs. *MNHS 9666.8; see also Figure 9.13*

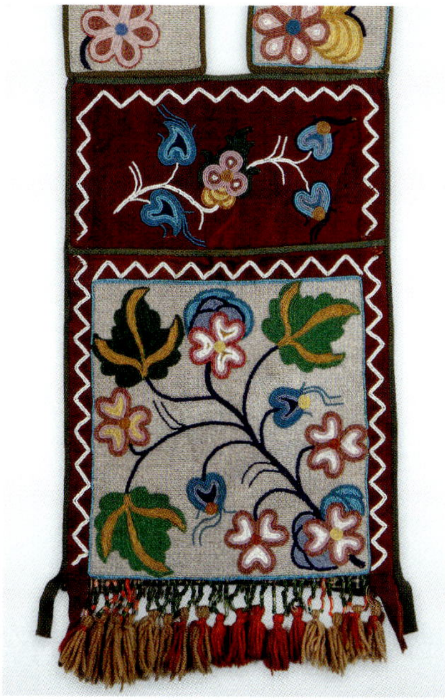

3.48 Diagonally placed motifs, c. 1890. *MNHS 6333.6.A; see also Figure 7.10*

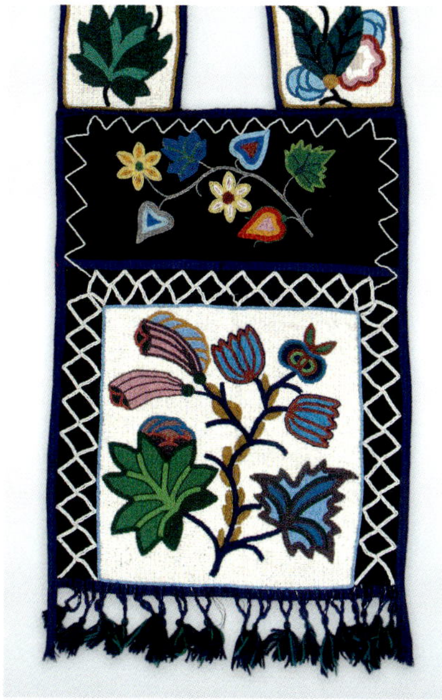

3.49 Spray, or bouquet, of motifs, first half of twentieth century. *MNHS 2011.208.159*

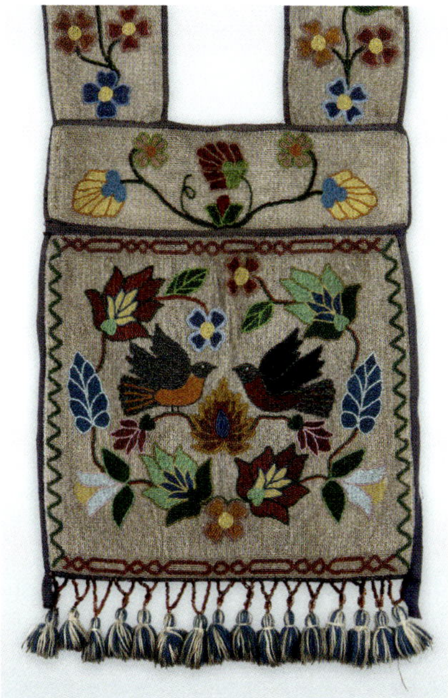

3.50 Symmetrically placed motifs, before 1923. *MNHS 6288.1*

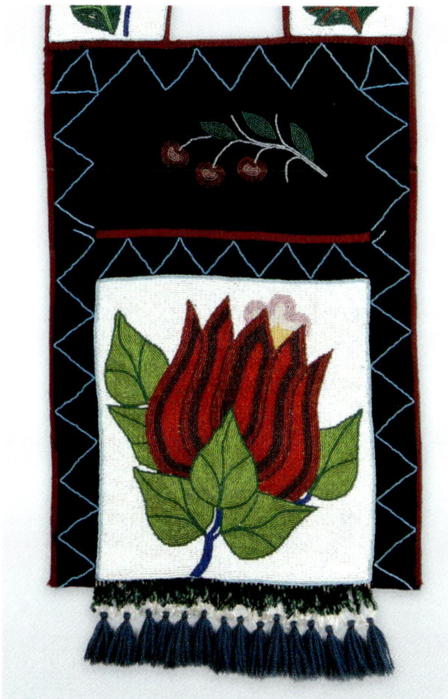

3.51 Single large central motif. *MNHS 2006.168.2; see also Figure 9.20*

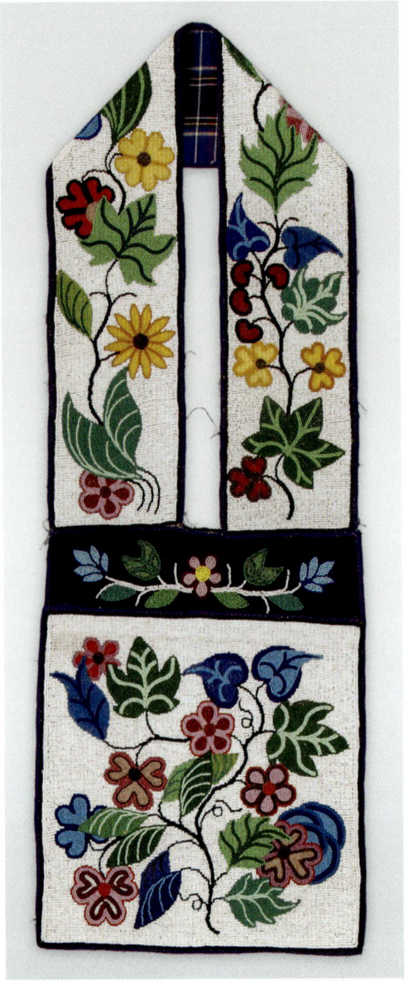

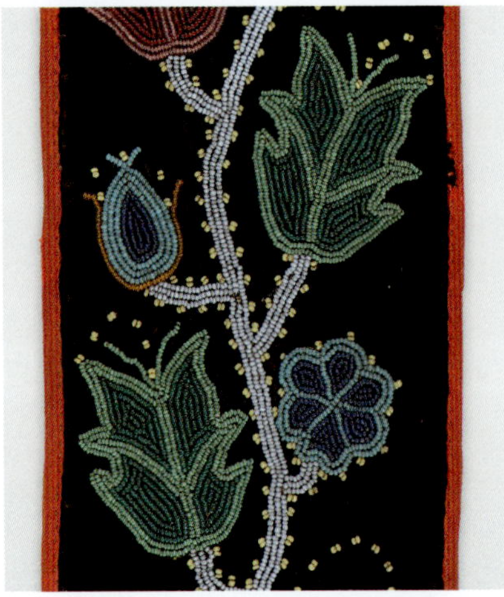

3.53 Thorns or dewdrops. *MNHS 2008.9.1; see also Figures 2.13 and 2.42*

Stems and vines connect the motifs to each other. These connecting elements, as well as tendrils, leaf veins, and borders, are generally one to four beads in width. Tendrils are rarely more than one or two beads wide. In some instances, both the vine and the tendrils are the same width throughout. In other cases, as in Figure 3.52, the bead width is reduced as the plant elements become more delicate. The yellow accents in Figure 3.53, referred to as either thorns or dewdrops, are represented by the addition of one or two beads or sometimes a sequin (Figure 3.54) placed along a stem or vine. Beadworkers have told me that, alternatively, these might not represent thorns or dewdrops and may simply be an undisclosed preference of the artist.

The actual beadwork area is usually framed by parallel rows of beads. The top part of the detail in Figure 3.55 shows the noncontrasting outline border on the strap, worked two beads wide; the bottom shows the bag's pocket panel, with a more elaborate and contrasting zigzag bead outer border on top of the silk binding plus an interior border consisting of single lines of blue beads on either side of rows of clear crystal beads.

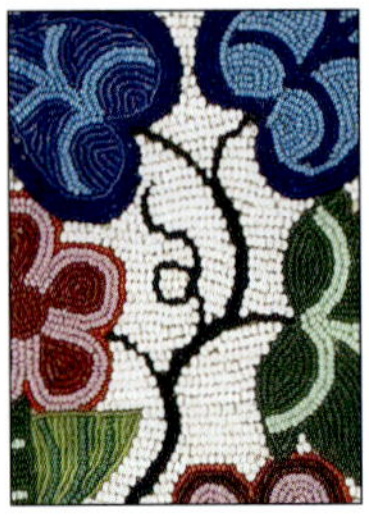

3.52 Vines and tendrils thinning out at the ends, first half of twentieth century. *MNHS 2011.208.158; see also Figure 3.73*

3.54 Sequins are often present and may have been used to represent thorns or dewdrops, c. 1875–1925. *MNHS 10000.156*

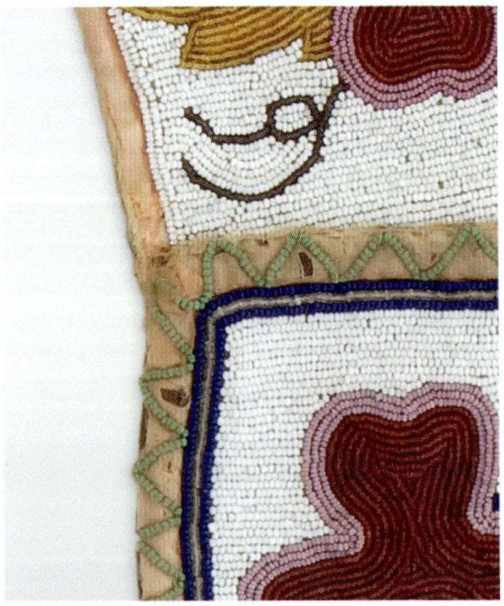

3.55 Bag detail, with two parallel rows of beads (*top left of image*) forming a narrow border on the strap in the same white as the rest of the ground. The pocket panel (*bottom of image*) has a more elaborate border. *MNHS 1826; see also Figure 3.98*

Native plant influences

Ethnographer Frances Densmore and collectors General Charles McCormick Reeve and Monroe Killy acquired motif patterns that Ojibwe women made from birch bark (Figure 3.56). Most of the bead artists I spoke with told me that those they learned from, and they themselves, collected leaves and other plant parts, tracing them to make these motif patterns for their beadwork. Twentieth-century artist Batiste Sam kept her collection of beadwork patterns, traced onto candy wrappers and other available paper, in an old cigar box. Leaf motifs are widely used in Ojibwe beadwork, but a proportionate number of bark or paper patterns have not survived. Many leaves on gashkibidaaganag are quite realistic, and artists could easily have developed them from the tracing of an actual leaf.[13]

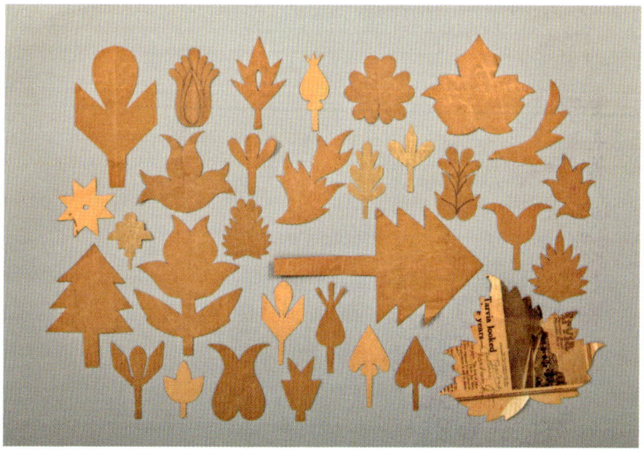

3.56 Birchbark patterns collected at White Earth Reservation by General Charles McCormick Reeve, 1918. *Southwest Museum of the American Indian Collection, Autry National Center, Los Angeles, 491.G.1462*

Plants, shrubs, and trees commonly found throughout Minnesota that can be identified in Minnesota Ojibwe beadwork include maple leaves, oak leaves, bloodroot, birch leaves, generic berries, blueberry, strawberry, bunchberry, raspberry, thimbleberry leaves, bearberry, cranberry, grapes and grape leaves, wild roses, rosebuds, rosehips, rose thorns, trillium, pinecones, acorns, waterlily, lanceolate leaves, broad-leaf arrowhead, and more. Examples of these are shown in Figures 3.57–60.

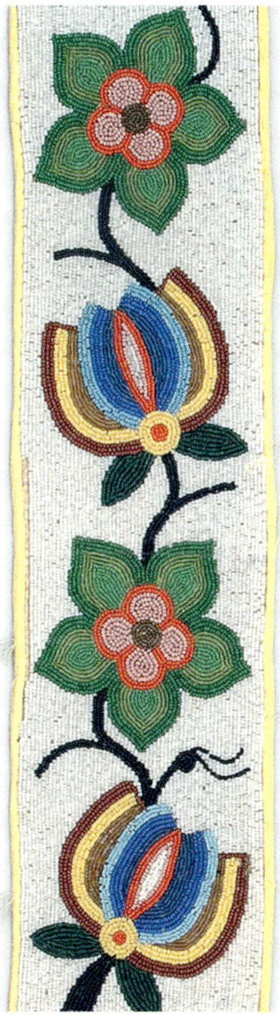

3.57 This strap alternates a bunchberry motif with a waterlily profile. *MNHS 2011.208.160; see also Figure 9.28*

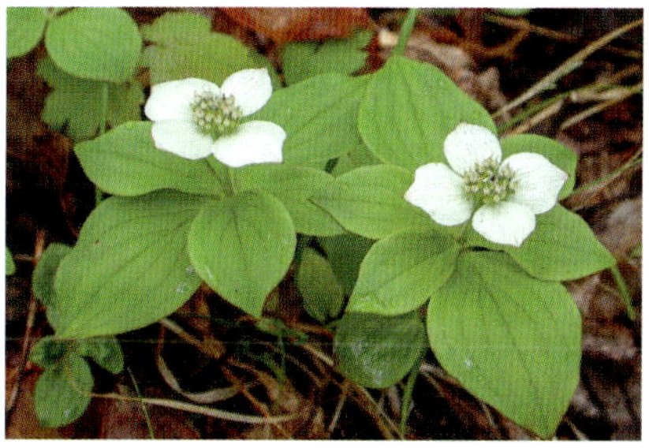

3.58 Bunchberry *(Cornus canadensis). Peter M. Dziuk, Minnesotawildflowers.info*

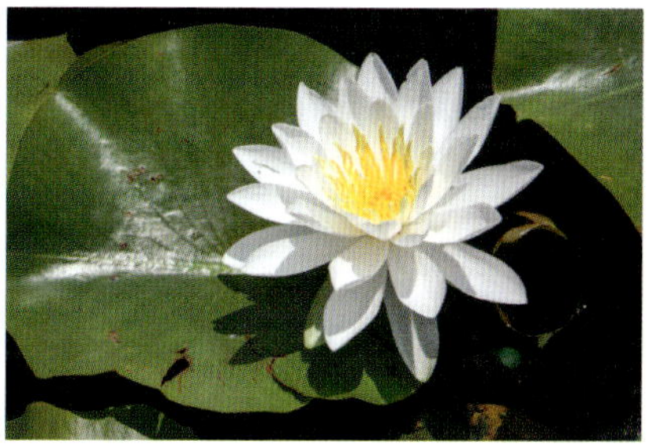

3.59 American white waterlily (*Nymphaea odorata*). *Katy Chayka, Minnesotawildflowers.info*

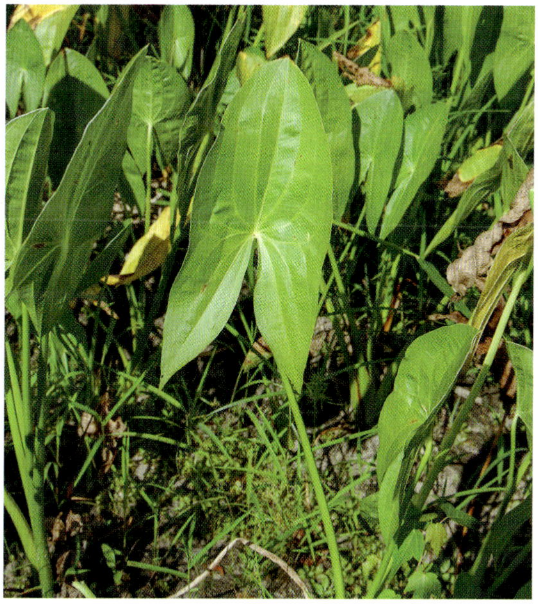

3.60 Broad-leaf arrowhead (*Sagittaria latifolia*). *Katy Chayka, Minnesotawildflowers.info*

The rose is perhaps the most pervasive of all spot-stitch appliqué motifs, featured on gashkibidaaganag throughout this volume. It can be a representation of nature (see page 69) or a quilt pattern, below. A particular refinement is what I call the gear flower, in which the separate petals disappear and the rose is simplified to a scalloped outline. The rose often has a wreathlike leaf surround (Figures 3.61 and 3.65).

Influences from Northeastern nations

Some elements common in the beadwork of many Northeastern, or Algonquian, nations also appeared in the beadwork of the Ojibwe women in Minnesota during the nineteenth and twentieth centuries. Living in a similar woodland environment, artists used similar natural motifs, including rosebuds, thorns, otter tracks, and vines as connecting elements. In addition, artists from both geographic areas used double curves and two-bead edging.

The double curve and two-bead edging apparently were not a good fit with the larger gashkibidaaganag, but artists continued to incorporate the other elements on Ojibwe spot-stitch beadwork into the twenty-first century. Both realistic and stylized rosebud designs are commonly found in spot-stitch appliqué bags, as are otter-track borders and vine motifs. If the double curve remains, it is mostly in an expanded version, as seen in the arrangement of the central motif beginning at the base of pocket panels on spot-stitch appliqué bags (see Figures 2.49, 10.31, and 12.10).

Quilt influences in spot-stitch appliqué

Ojibwe women continued to make quilts as spot-stitched beading became more prevalent, and as with loom-woven beadwork, quilting also influenced spot-stitch appliqué. Two nineteenth-century elements of quilting—pieced and appliqué patterns, and the embroidery stitches used on crazy quilts—may have had an impact on spot-stitch bag makers' floral design choices. While influences from quilt patterns based on flowers overlap with those from native plant forms, the graphic conventions of quilting can sometimes be startlingly recognizable in spot-stitch appliqué bags (Figures 3.62–73).[14]

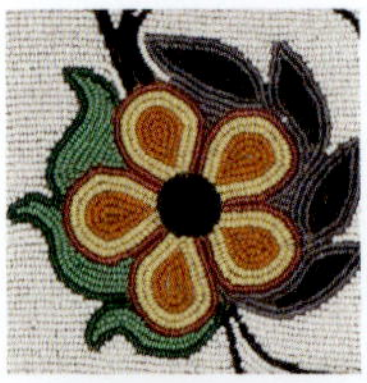

3.61 Detail of rose with surround on a strap. *MNHS 6333.6.H; see also Figure 7.09*

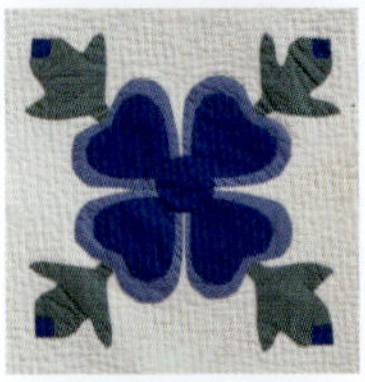

3.62 Tudor rose quilt motif. *MNHS 1984.105.2*

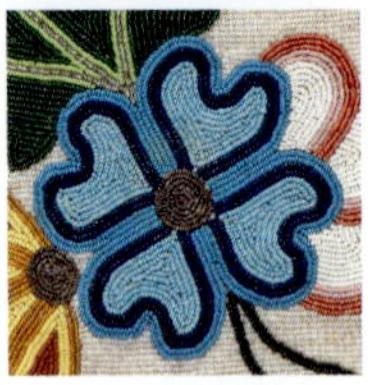

3.63 Heart-petaled flowers, spot-stitch appliqué. *MNHS 10000.153; see also Figure 10.29*

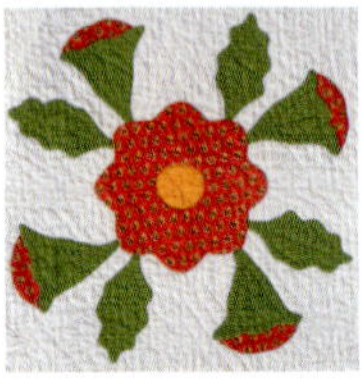

3.64 Rose quilt motif. *MNHS 8510.1*

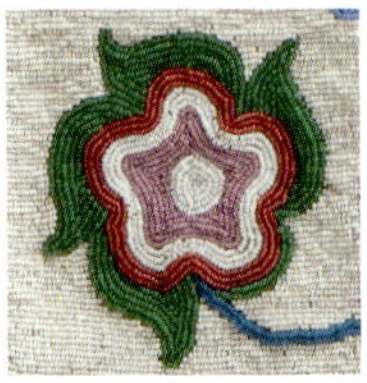

3.65 Detail of gear flower with surround on a pocket panel. *MNHS 1496; see also Figure 2.15*

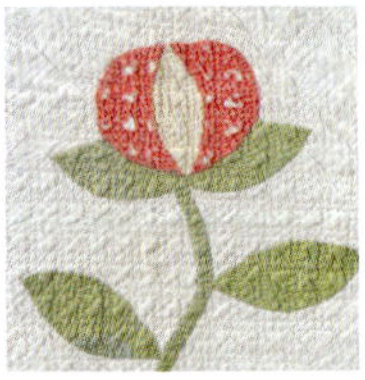

3.66 Love apple quilt motif. *MNHS 7749.4*

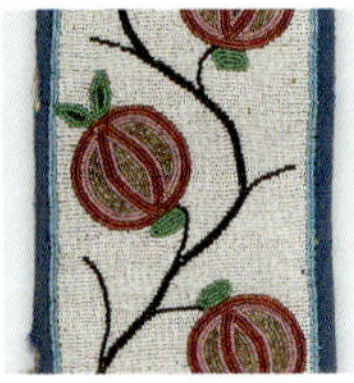

3.67 Love apple, spot-stitch appliqué. *MNHS 6333.6.H; see also Figure 7.09*

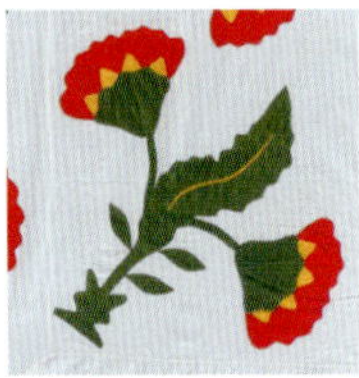

3.68 Cockscomb quilt motif. *MNHS 9224.3*

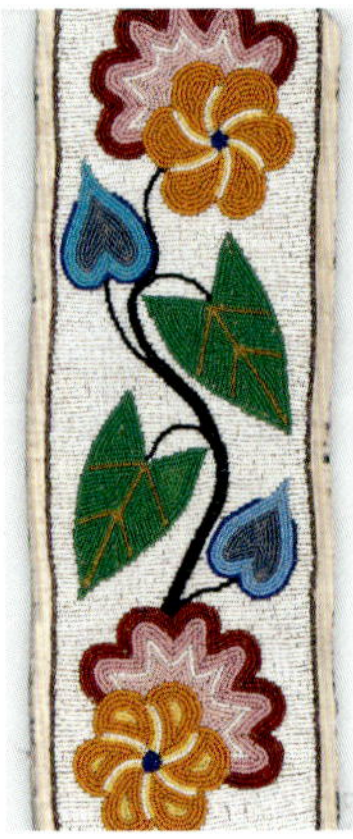

3.69 Cockscomb, spot-stitch appliqué with arrowhead leaf. *MNHS 2011.208.156*

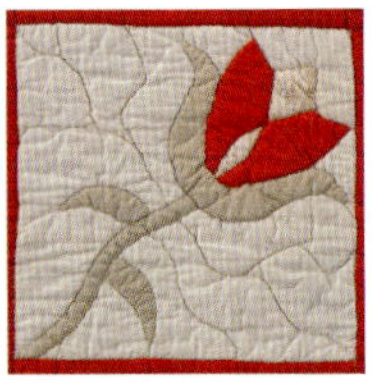

3.70 Tulip quilt square. *MNHS 69.79.20*

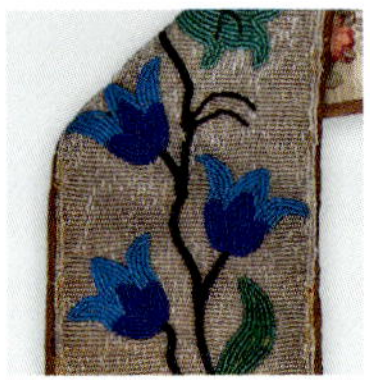

3.71 Tulip, spot-stitch appliqué. *MNHS 521.E146.2; see also Figure 12.10*

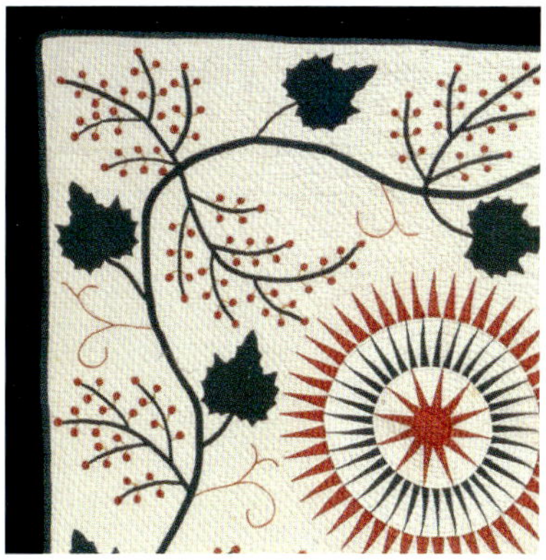

3.72 Quilt border showing vine meander with leaves, berries, and tendrils. *MNHS 67.230.132*

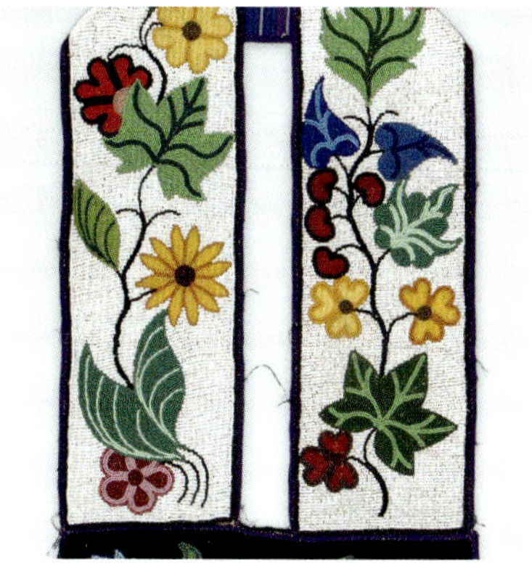

3.73 Spot-stitch appliqué strap, vine meander with leaves, berries, shamrocks, and tendrils. *MNHS 2011.208.158; see also Figure 3.52*

Lace

Missionaries, who were eager to have Ojibwe people abandon traditional ways, adopt white culture, and find westernized sources of income, introduced yet another possible influence to the bead artists. In 1884 Sybil Carter, who had been teaching school in Chicago, took a position traveling to Episcopal women's organizations to promote missionary work. She spent a year as a volunteer missionary in Japan, where she saw many women making lace. While living in Chicago, she had learned to make several styles of laces. Inspired by what she observed in Japan, she realized that lacemaking could be a source of income for Indian women. In 1886 she met with Henry Benjamin Whipple, the Episcopal bishop of Minnesota and an advocate for Native peoples, to propose that the talented Ojibwe beadworkers could be successful as lace makers, and, she hoped, "improve their station." In 1890 she spent three weeks at White Earth Reservation, teaching twelve Ojibwe women to make lace.[15]

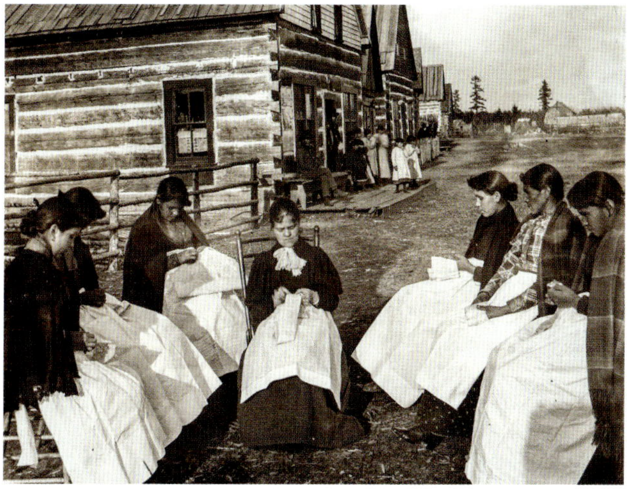

3.74 Lace makers at Leech Lake Reservation, 1906. *MNHS N4.4 p15*

The effort was judged a success, and in the next few years, at reservation schools across the nation, indigenous women learned how to make doilies and other lace pieces similar to those made at White Earth (Figure 3.74). A 1904 pamphlet reported that in Minnesota two to three hundred women were making lace at ten reservation schools, including White Earth, Leech Lake, Red Lake, and Lower Sioux. Reservation schools in Wisconsin, South Dakota, New York, Arizona, California, and Nebraska also added lacemaking instruction. The Episcopal lace program became a business; yards of lace were sold primarily to customers on the East Coast.[16]

Likely made between the late 1890s and the early twentieth century, the lace examples in Figures 3.75 and 3.76, two of a total of thirty-two that Bishop Whipple collected from Ojibwe and Dakota women, may have been influenced by the Episcopal lace program. These two pieces, however, illustrate the exceptions rather than the rule: the majority of lace examples related to the Episcopal lace program in Minnesota consist primarily of yards and yards of simple mixed-lace insertion.[17]

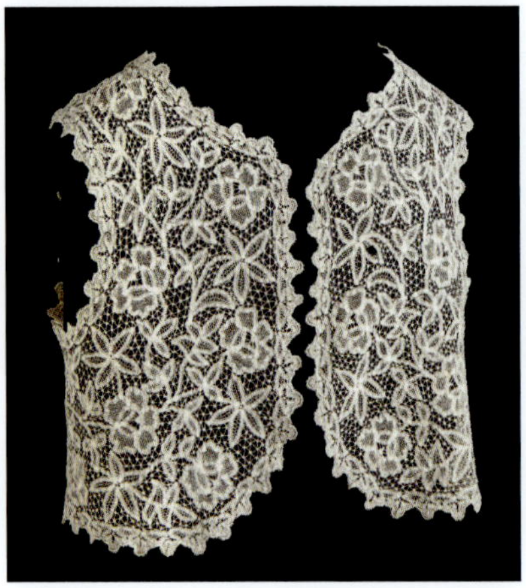

3.75 *(right)* Lace vest with floral motifs, c. 1890–1926. *MNHS 1949*

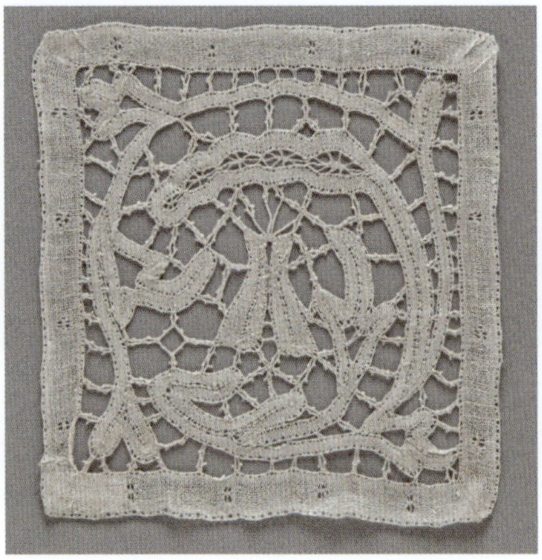

3.76 *(far right)* Lace doily with tipi motif, c. 1890–1926. *MNHS 1961*

The influence of lacemaking on floral patterns in beadwork is not clear. Photographs taken among the Ojibwe of Minnesota before 1890 document floral beadwork on dance aprons, leggings, and other items of clothing. By 1896, the fully developed and widespread floral gashkibidaagan bead tradition was well established. It seems unlikely that a relatively small number of women focused on making lace on some Ojibwe reservations would have had time to also do beadwork. Like any other potential source of design, lace patterns may or may not have influenced Ojibwe bead artists, especially considering that once the completed lace was sold it was unavailable to serve as a beadwork pattern for others. In the early twentieth century, handmade lace began to die out as machine-made lace became affordable; by the end of World War I, the lace makers were in every practical sense out of business.

Printed and embroidered textiles

Of all the possible influences cited for the spot-stitch style of Ojibwe floral beadwork, the printed chintz fabrics inspired by palampores from India and *mantons des manila* (shawls from Manila, Spain) may be the most logical (Figures 3.77 and 3.78). They offer the closest parallel to Ojibwe beadworkers' style of mixing various sizes and life phases of leaves and flowers on meandering vines without concern for realism.

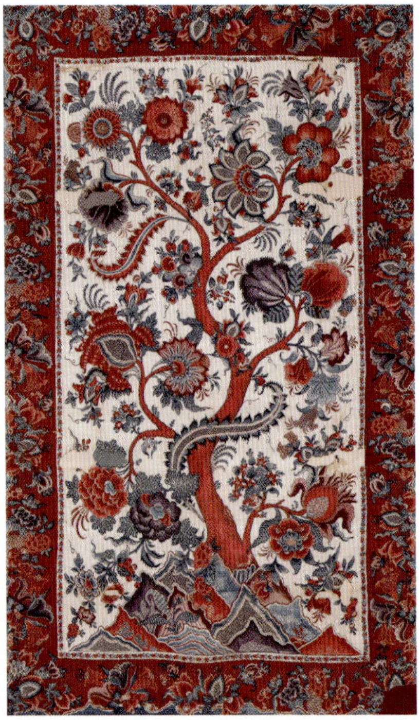

3.77 Palampore, India (Coromandel Coast), for the Sri Lankan market; first quarter of the eighteenth century. Cotton (painted resist and mordant, dyed), 113.2 × 182.9 cm. *Metropolitan Museum of Art, New York; Purchase, Fernando Family Trust Gift, in honor of Dr. Quintus and Mrs. Wimala Fernando, 2010 (2010.337); image © The Metropolitan Museum of Art, image source Art Resource, NY*

Palampores were hand-dyed and painted bedcovers and bed hangings that featured colorful and elaborate floral designs and were made for export by artists in India. British merchants brought them to Europe beginning in the 1680s, and by the eighteenth century they were traded to merchants serving the wealthy along the eastern coast of North America. Palampore designs were soon converted into much more affordable and widely available printed cottons known commonly as English chintz. The motifs incorporated elements such as the tree of life and unrealistic combinations of flowers, leaves, and other floral components that were both complex and fluid. Eventually these motifs appeared in everything from wallpaper to china to household textiles and clothing. By the nineteenth century, chintz became popular and available in the United States

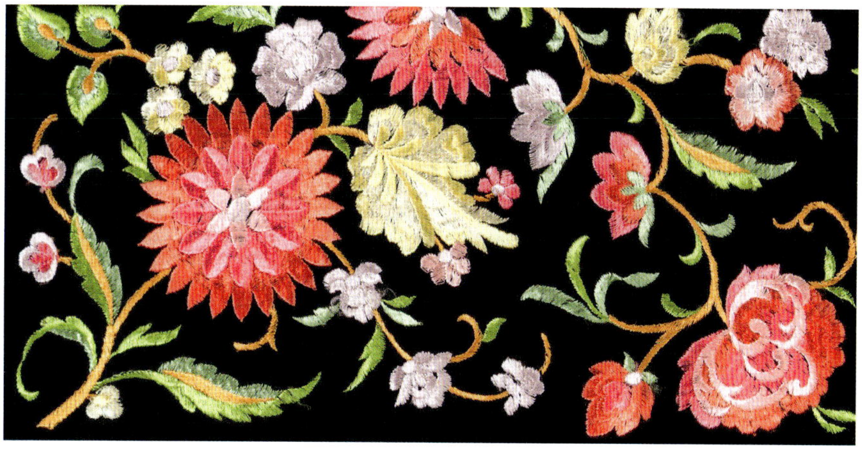

3.78 Embroidered shawl, *manton de manila,* worn to celebrate the end of World War I in 1918. *MNHS 69.115.6*

for use in appliqué quilts. Quilters could cut the clearly defined motifs from the fabric and sew them to the ground fabric, a technique known as *broderie perse.*[18]

The printed cottons that Ojibwe women used as backing material in making gashkibidaaganag were most often the brown, black, and gray drabs so popular in the mid-nineteenth century, rather than other colorful prints that were also available. On occasion, a natural muslin or dark cloth backing was replaced by various printed cottons (Figures 3.79 and 3.80) that could easily be tied to motifs seen in spot-stitch appliqué bags. Some bags used a paisley print or a "cheater cloth" (fabric printed with quilt-block patterns) of the last quarter of the nineteenth century, but most bags used plaids, shirting, or inexpensive prints common from the 1890s to the 1920s.

All manner of printed cottons and woven materials were readily available to Ojibwe women. Among the tribes of the Great Lakes, colorful printed cottons were popular for quilts and (especially among the neighboring Ho-Chunk) for colorful shirts and blouses. Some of these fabrics showed up as backing or pocket lining for gashkibidaaganag and appear to have influenced the artists.

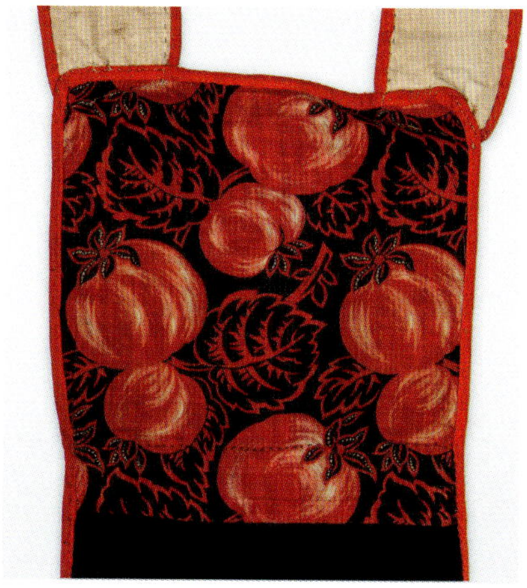

3.79 Pocket backing cloth with leaves and tomatoes. *MNHS 9666.7; see also Figure 3.30*

Bandanas and the folded leaf motif

Bandanas provide a special example of the interplay between printed fabrics and bag motifs. The handy cloths were available in the Great Lakes region at fur trading posts and other merchant locations. In both studio and snapshot images, especially those taken between 1860 and 1890, Ojibwe and Dakota men often wore bandanas knotted around the neck, as part of headgear, as a simple headband, as a prop or accent in studio portraits, and sometimes tied onto other objects for a splash of color. Little has been published on the bandana as a textile, and historical records and account books rarely mention it, yet bandanas certainly functioned as a convenient accessory to address weather and work-related issues. Photographic evidence, as seen in Figure 3.81, indicates that Minnesota Ojibwe and Dakota preferred more elaborate bandana prints.[19]

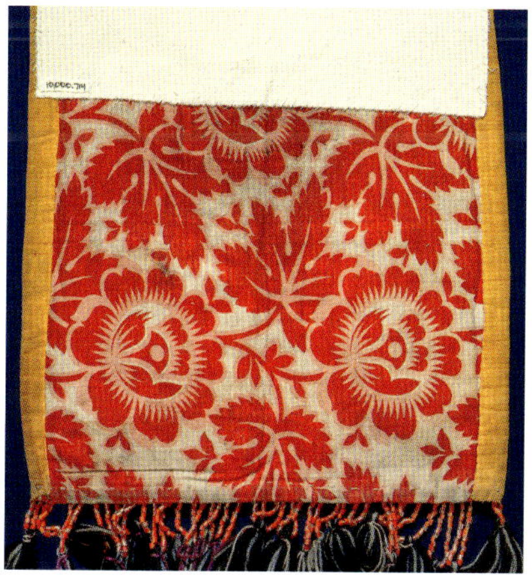

3.80 Pocket backing cloth with heavily veined leaves and heart-shaped petals. *MNHS 10000.714; see also Figures 2.11 and 3.96*

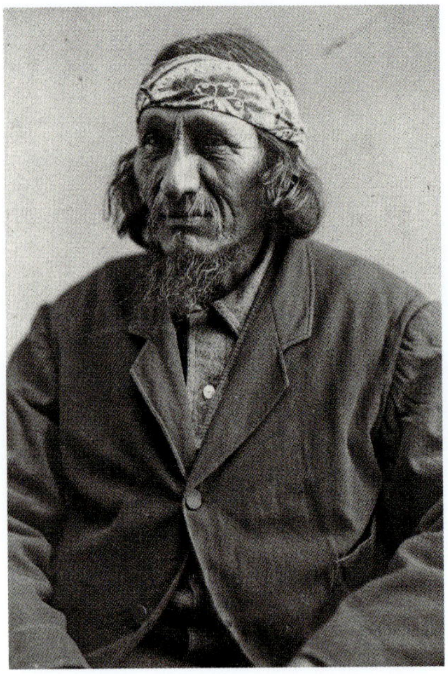

3.81 "Indian John," Dakota, c. 1880. *MNHS E91.1M p2*

A bandana seems to have been the inspiration for a specific and significant motif used in Minnesota gashkibidaagan beadwork: the folded leaf. Albert Green Heath, an amateur archaeologist and collector active in the first part of the twentieth century, acquired a bag (Figure 3.82) at an unknown date from Giwita-bines (Spotted Bird) at Red Lake. This richly beaded bag uses a near symmetrical centered floral spray for the pocket panel design and frames this motif by positioning two leaves at the top that are folded down toward the bag's fringe.[20]

Floral motifs have been common in woven and printed textiles for centuries, but I have found only a few examples of textiles with sprays, bouquets, or borders that feature a folded leaf of this style. One of them is the bandana, or kerchief, used to line the back of the Red Lake bag. It includes a border repeat containing both folded lanceolate leaves and lily pads (Figures 3.83 and 3.84).

This three-dimensional form, a folded lanceolate leaf, is one of the most distinctive Minnesota Ojibwe floral spot-stitch appliqué motifs. A gashkibidaagan strap in the Minnesota Historical Society's collections was almost certainly inspired by the same bandana print (Figure 3.85). Other examples of the folded leaf motif found in the society's collections that have clear provenance come from Ojibwe reservations in northwestern Minnesota: White Earth, Cass Lake (Leech Lake), but also Mille Lacs, with the majority associated with White Earth.[21]

It seems likely that the introduction of this bandana style in Minnesota's northwestern Ojibwe reservations inspired the adoption of a unique motif that eventually saw much use by bead artists of this region. Did the

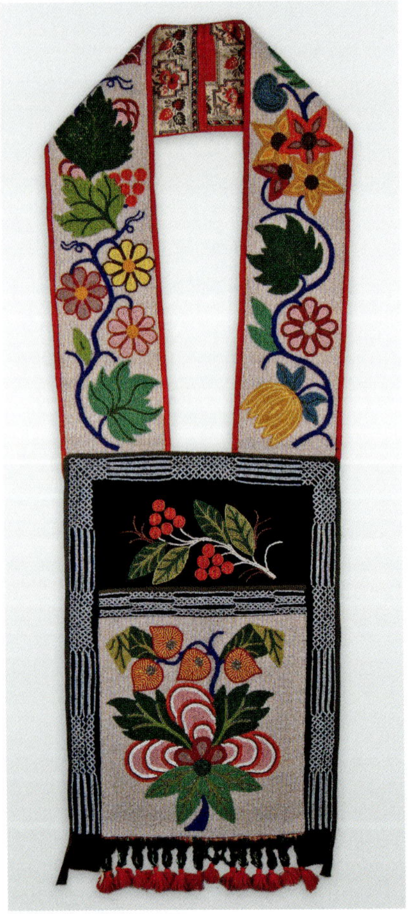

3.82 Gashkibidaagan acquired from Giwita-bines at Red Lake Reservation, before 1910. *LMA 30561*

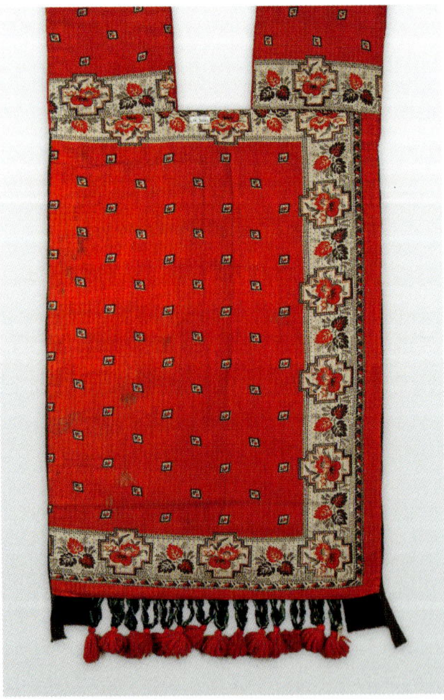

3.83 Detail of Figure 3.82 showing the Red Lake bag's back. *LMA 30561*

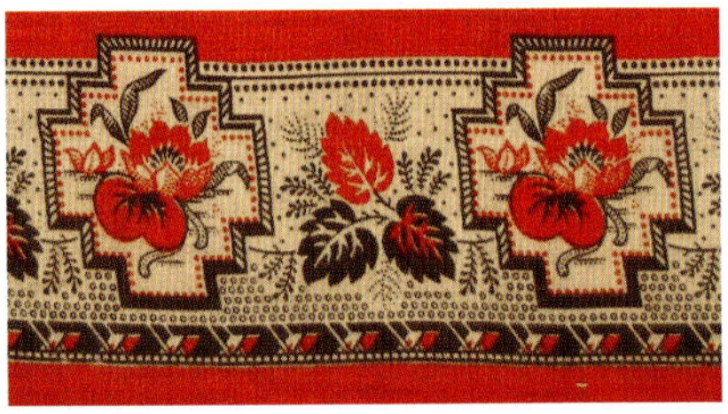

3.84 Detail of Figure 3.82 showing the bandana's border with folded leaves and lily pads. *LMA 30561*

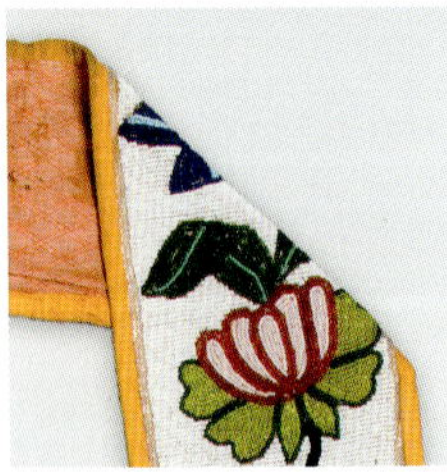

3.85 Shoulder strap detail with folded leaf motif. *MNHS 1990.502.5; see also Figure 12.12*

woman who made the bag purchased from Giwita-bines introduce this iconic Minnesota Ojibwe motif? Was shc from Red Lake? Or was this patterned bandana widely available to many who took inspiration, and this is simply the only surviving example we have found?

Euro-American symbols

Many Euro-American sources—ranging from pattern books, to church imagery, to commercially available magazines—may have influenced bead artists to add their own personally embellished interpretations. The US flag has been a popular motif in Plains beadwork. Less common but distinctive motifs that relate to other aspects of Indian-white relations and influences also appear in Minnesota Ojibwe beadwork. Cornucopias, architectural columns, shields, crosses, and human hands are found in a small group of Ojibwe gashkibidaaganag.

Inventive, daring, and talented Ojibwe bead artists at Mille Lacs sometimes used the cornucopia motif on their spot-stitch appliqué bags (Figures 3.86 and 3.87; see also page 147).

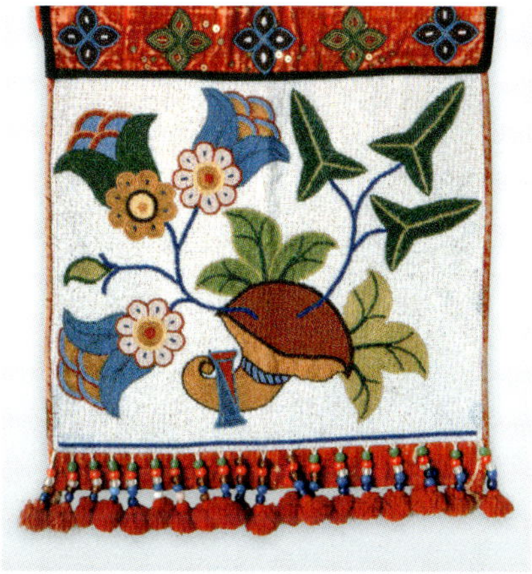

3.86 Cornucopia with a Greek column astride the horn's base, leaf clusters behind the mouth, and sprays of flowers and arrowhead leaves sprouting from the opening. *MNHS 10000.609; see also Figure 10.35*

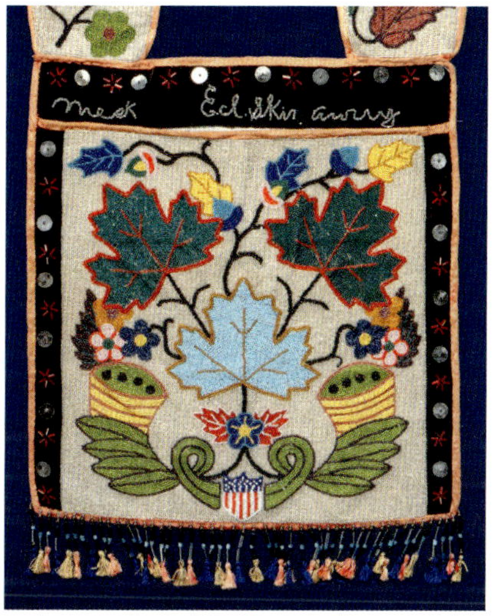

3.87 Pocket featuring the cornucopia motif with a US shield, perhaps in recognition of the military service of the bag's likely owner, Ed Skinaway. *MNHS 10000.615; see also Figure 10.32*

Distinctive bag designs

A few gashkibidaagan designs are less common but still share the origins, motifs, and overall design of other bandolier bags. These unusual bags appear to be from the eastern and northern portions of Minnesota, with a visible overlap into Wisconsin reservation communities.

One example is found in a group of bags that are tied to Grand Portage, Minnesota, that have a scoop cut out between the straps at the top of the area above the pocket opening, as shown in Figure 3.88. These bags appear in a number of historical photographs as well as in the collections at the Minnesota Historical Society and at Beloit College's Logan Museum. This scooped feature is found most often in earlier bags with all loom-woven beadwork or in bags combining the loom-woven and spot-stitch techniques. A few dancers and bag makers known to me have suggested that this particular feature allows the bag to sit well on the dancer's hip.

Another example of a distinctive form is seen in the spot-stitch appliqué bags in Figures 3.89–93, which all carry the basic structural

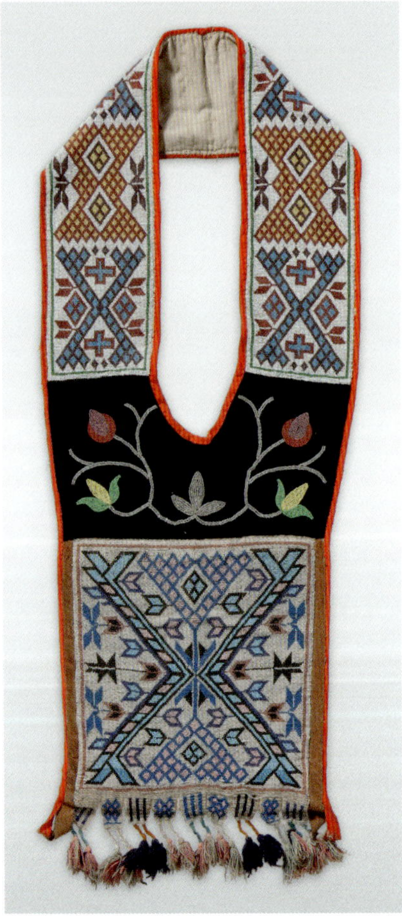

3.88 Loom-woven bag with scooped edge above pocket, c. 1875–1925. *MNHS 10000.715*

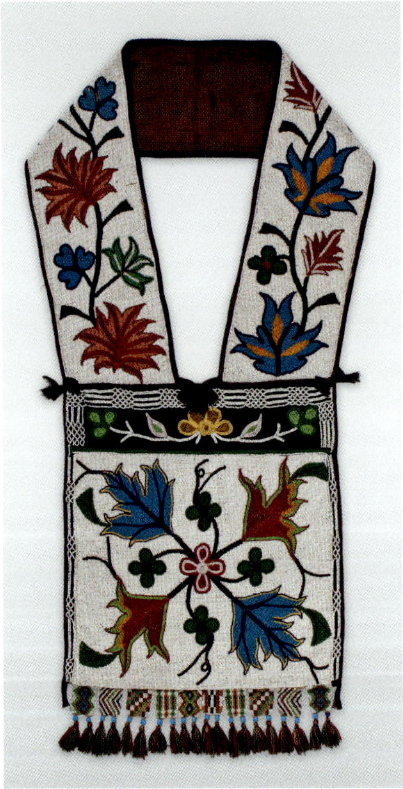

3.89 Ojibwe bandolier bag, 1880s–1890. Cloth, velvet, yarn, glass beads. Gift of Mr. H. V. Smith. *Southwest Museum of the American Indian Collection, Autry National Center, Los Angeles, 903.G.4*

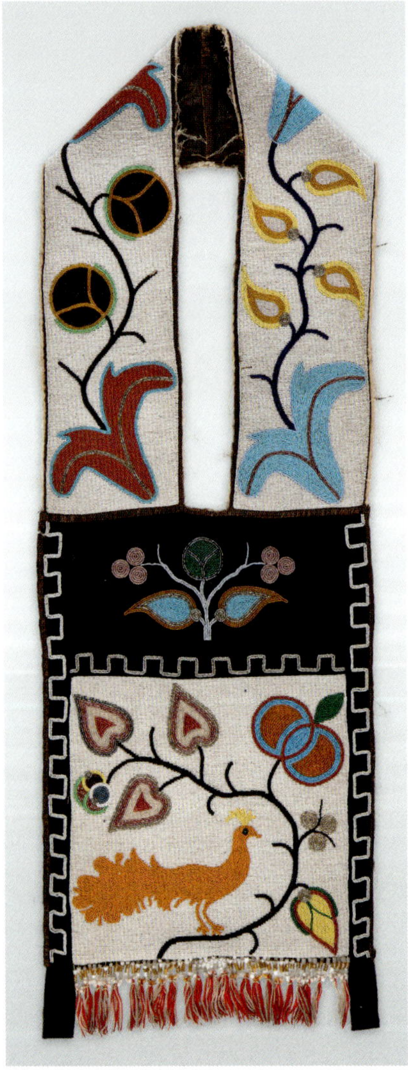

3.90 Spot-stitch appliqué bag collected at Akeley, Hubbard County, about 1900. *MNHS 69.138.5*

components discussed in chapter 2. The arrangement of motifs on the pocket panels follow those regularly seen in Minnesota Ojibwe bags. The vine meander on the straps, the border treatment on the pockets, and the floral embellishment above the pocket openings also tie these bags to Ojibwe artists. But these bags feature bolder motifs on a more expansive white background, and they are easily seen from a distance when danced at the powwow grounds. The color palettes use stronger colors, with less emphasis on pastels. More research might clarify what other indigenous nations have influenced bags in these northern areas, but both photographic and object evidence suggests a different trend from the norm. Bead artists from the northeastern part of the state may have influenced designs of others, or they may have relocated in the northwest.

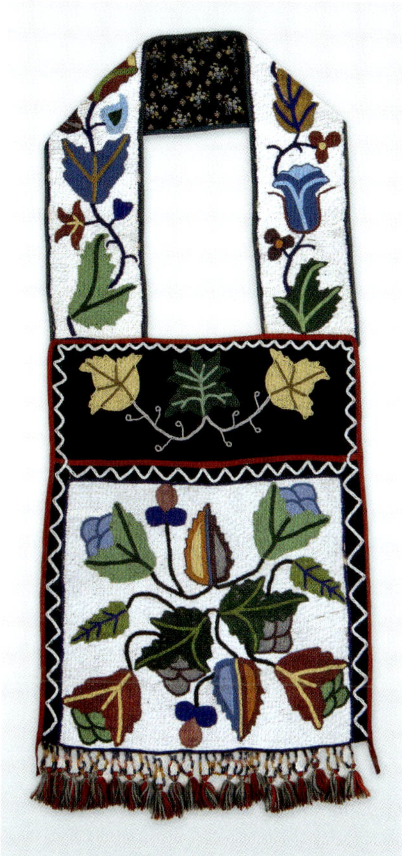

3.91 Spot-stitch appliqué bag collected before 1940. *MNHS 8034.14*

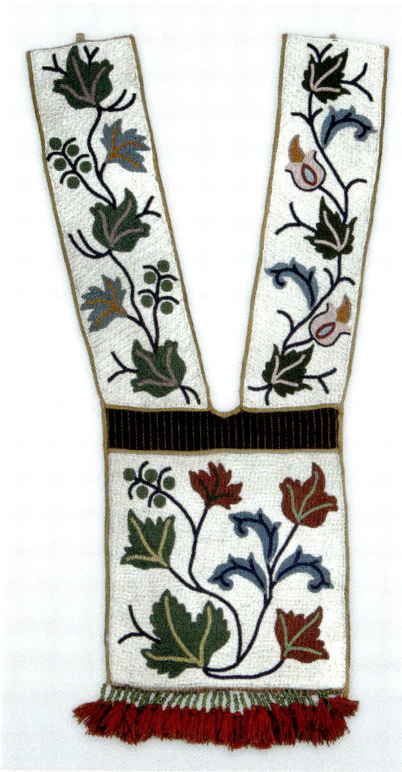

3.92 Spot-stitch appliqué bag used in Warroad, collected in 1948. *MNHS 8723.6*

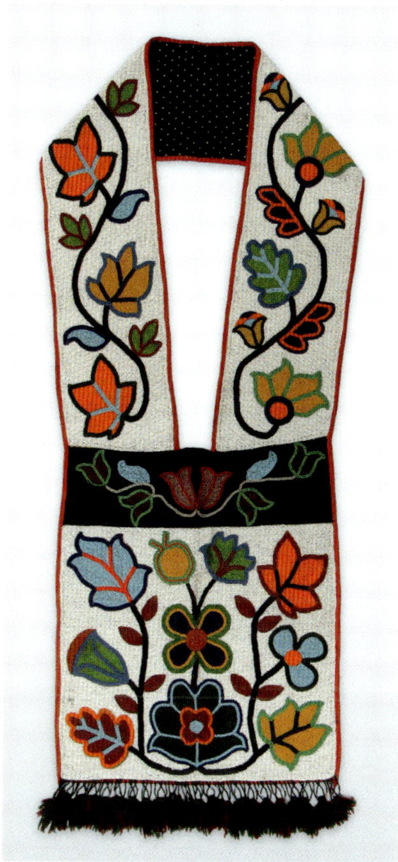

3.93 Spot-stitch appliqué bag collected in 1926 northwest of Duluth. *CVM 1348*

Using nature-based beadwork motifs

A sampler of bags associated with Minnesota Ojibwe reservations, shown in Figures 3.94–98, showcases popular motifs and illustrates the variety and freedom of expression they represent. The use of nature-based images in loom-woven bag panels is discussed above; these examples illustrate their predominance in spot-stitch appliqué bags. Here and elsewhere in this book, viewers can spot flowers formed with one or more heart petals, leaves from the broadleaf arrowhead plant (also known as common arrowhead, duck potato, Indian potato, or wapato), strawberries or cherries, folded lanceolate leaves, oak leaves, coneflowers, waterlily profiles, rosebuds, acorns, gear flowers, leaves with exaggerated veins, trillium, morning glory, bluebells, and a background form called the pinecone motif.

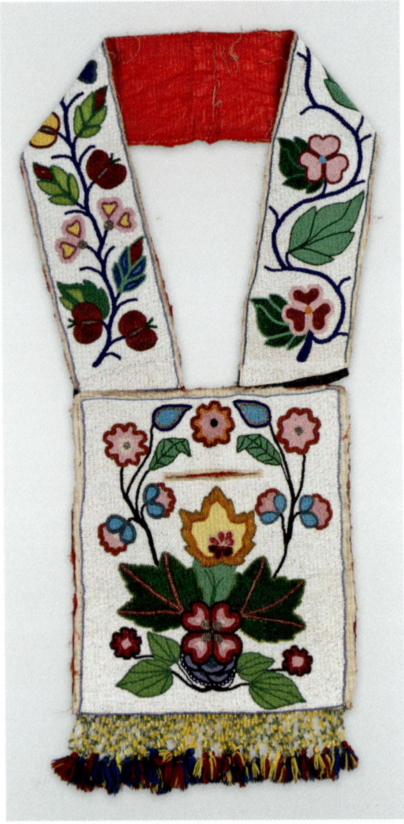

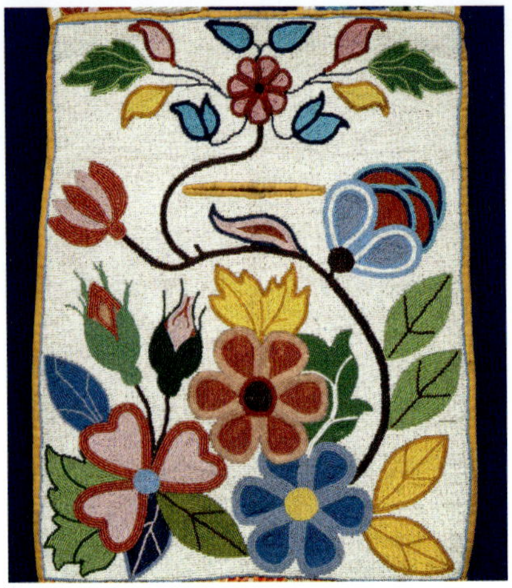

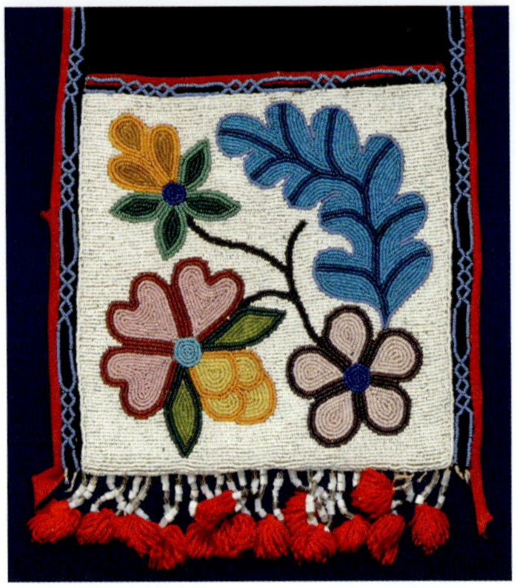

3.94 *(above)* Strap with various heart flowers and love apples; pocket with gear flowers, folded leaves, exaggerated leaf veins, and a heart-petaled flower with pinecone base, c. 1890–1917. *MNHS 1995.46.16*

3.95 *(below)* Strap with gear flowers, heart-petaled flowers, pinecones, exaggerated leaf veins. *MNHS 2011.208.148; see also Figure 2.02*

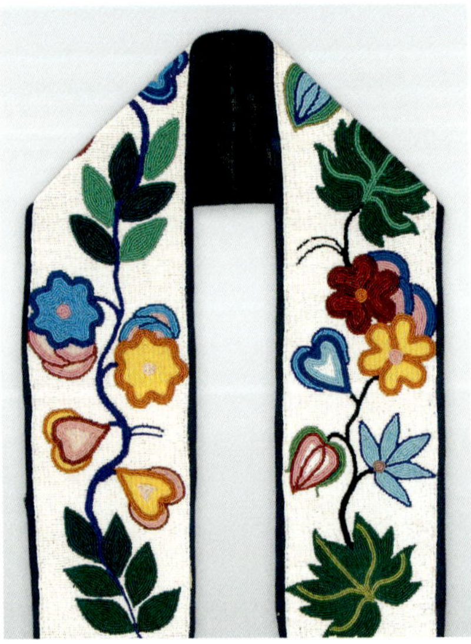

3.96 *(above)* Pocket panel with waterlily profile, realistic rosebuds, heart-petaled flowers, pinecone. *MNHS 10000.714; see also Figures 2.11 and 3.80*

3.97 *(above right)* Bag with oak leaf, heart-petaled flowers, pinecone, and composite motif. *MNHS 10000.149; see also Figure 10.27*

3.98 *(right)* Bag with stars, berries, gear flower (in blue and black), love apples, heart-petaled flowers (with three and four petals), maple or grape leaves, shamrock, and pinecones, c. 1860–1901. *MNHS 1826; see also Figure 3.55*

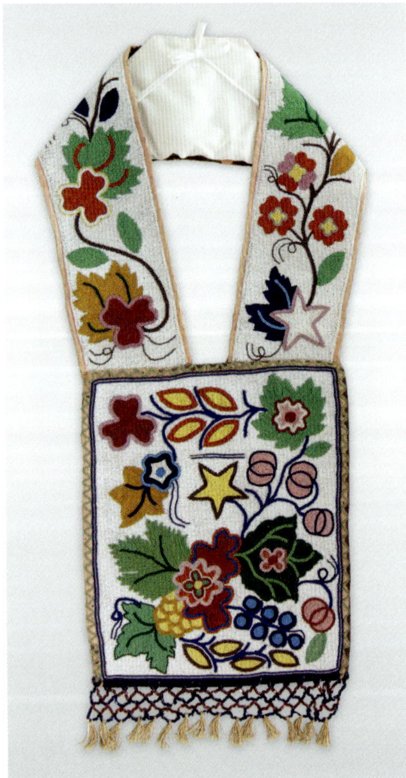

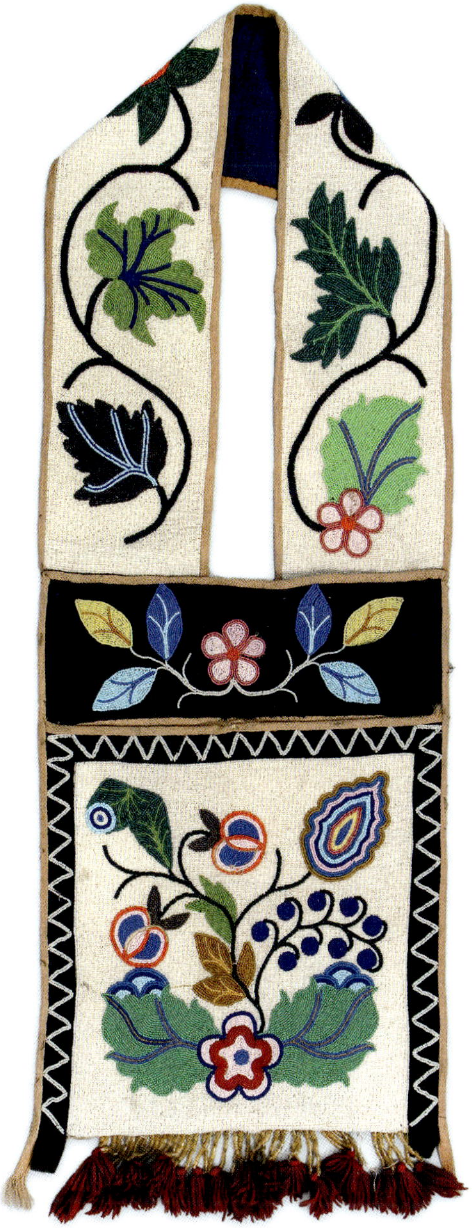

Chapter 4

Gashkibidaaganag in Photographs

Photographs can be seen as objective reflections of reality. A snapshot may be either more or less objective than a studio portrait. But in either case, both the photographers and the people captured in photographs may have made choices about how the image would appear, and the method of production also affected the appearance. Yet another important consideration of objectivity: who took the photograph? In the nineteenth and well into the twentieth centuries, the Ojibwe people themselves rarely held the cameras capturing the images.

Images representing American Indians, in Minnesota and elsewhere, are often patronizing and manipulative, created by and for members of the dominant culture. The photographer, after all, had an intended objective for the product. The subject matter, setting, and accessories may have been contrived for commercial or political purposes.[1]

While historical photographs have created and reinforced stereotypes of American Indians, they also offer clues about clothing, furniture, architecture, and other aspects of everyday life. No matter the photographer's original intent, useful data can still be garnered from the photographic record to articulate cultural preferences and regional differences; to document no longer extant locations, structures, or communities; to record contemporary material culture; and perhaps to simply provide access to the lives of individuals and personalities not otherwise available. When assessed thoughtfully, photographs can be a useful tool for the study of material culture.

Supporting data such as card mounts, postcard imprints, postmarks, studio and photographer imprints, and other clues can help provide useful information by suggesting time ranges and possible image locations. For example, the postcard in Figure 4.01 has no postmark, but the imprint on the reverse side is one that was used between 1925 and 1942. While the

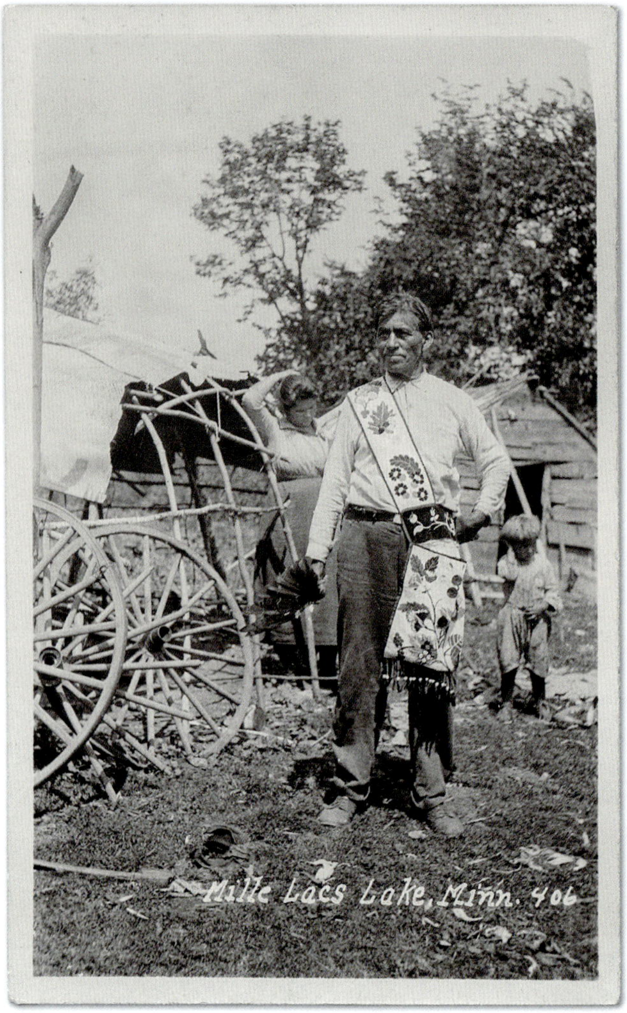

4.01 Chief Migizi wearing a large spot-stitched gashkibidaagan, Mille Lacs Reservation, probably before 1925; Janie and Mildred Mitchell in background. *MNHS E97.1M r24*

photograph may have been taken some time prior to the publication of the postcard, it might be possible to establish a more specific time range by seeking out birth and death dates for people in the photo.[2]

Even photographs showing gashkibidaaganag used as photographers' props can be of documentary value. They can establish a time period for an identifiable object and record specific examples of material culture.

Researchers and curatorial staff must use historical records of this type with specific qualifiers in mind. If the photographs used are not part of a well-documented collection, much of the significant data will not be known, which means its potential use for various applications is lost forever. In fact, what many today regard as the "historical record" remains merely a selective sampling of surviving pieces of "a story." In spite of that, much can be learned from these moments—whether spontaneous or manufactured—that have been preserved on film.

Just as photographers composed images by deciding what would be captured through the lens and therefore what moments were preserved, so too, collectors of ethnographic images made choices about what images and background information to retain. As a consequence, multiple layers of intentional or unintentional "curation" took place before the objects or photos were cataloged and became accessible to researchers through public institutions such as libraries and museums.

The Minnesota Historical Society has nearly five thousand images related to American Indians, and more than half of them have valuable documentation and deal primarily with the Ojibwe of the region. Several areas of the collection are of particular importance in the study of gashkibidaaganag.

Personal collections

Five personal collection groups at the Minnesota Historical Society are particularly significant. Made primarily between 1860 and 1980, the photographs were taken or acquired by individuals with close personal relationships or regular associations with indigenous people, and all were interested in recording and in some cases preserving cultural activities and products. These five collections sometimes intersect with each other chronologically, and in other instances they overlap. Such documentation allows for analysis and discussion of variations within a community and region. Combined, the collections recount the visual record of activity and life on one or more reservations over a period of nearly ninety years. Each includes some important images and information documenting the role of gashkibidaaganag in Ojibwe life in Minnesota and the Great Lakes region.

Bishop Henry Benjamin Whipple collection

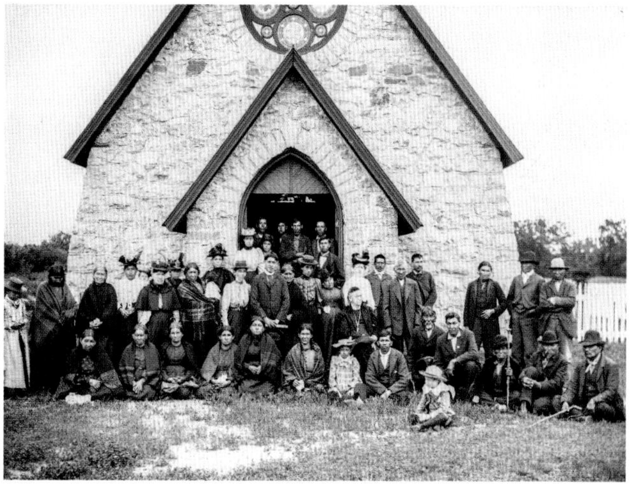

4.02 Bishop Henry Whipple and members of the congregation in front of St. Cornelia's Church in Morton, Minnesota, c. 1895. *MNHS Collection III.40.298*

Working for the Episcopal Church, Bishop Henry Benjamin Whipple (Figure 4.02; 1822–1901) and his associates accumulated and created 375 photographs that record aspects of the Episcopal ministry and other related activities among Minnesota Indians during the last half of the nineteenth century. Whipple's photographs consist primarily of mission structures, Dakota and Ojibwe Episcopal converts, and card print portraits of the celebrated American Indians he met in his travels all over North America. Views within Minnesota include members and structures related to the Episcopal mission as well as Dakota Indians at Morton and Birch Coulee (both part of the Lower Sioux Indian Community) and Ojibwe on the White Earth Reservation. The images that document the Episcopal ministry at these locations include church programs intended for education and vocational training.[3]

Whipple's collection is complemented by the roughly three hundred images in the Sibley House Historic Site collection that was developed by a Minnesota chapter of the Daughters of the American Revolution. They acquired the Whipple objects now held by the Minnesota Historical Society, including photographic views and identified portraits of American Indians from the midwestern and western United States. Minnesota views include the Lower Sioux Indian Community, Leech Lake Indian Reservation in Minnesota, and photographs associated with Bishop Whipple.

Whipple and his wives (he was widowed and remarried) and colleagues collected a series of portraits of celebrated American Indian individuals made primarily by photographer F. A. Rinehart, including people belonging to Dakota/Lakota, Assiniboine, Apache, Salish, Kiowa, Omaha, Cheyenne, and other tribes across North America. This tribally diverse collection of images speaks to the absence of gashkibidaaganag as a key regalia component among these primarily non–Great Lakes portraits. Another group of images was more personal and made by local Minnesota photographers. These include a number of images of American Indian members of the Episcopal mission congregations. In all the images where people wear street dress, they wear no beadwork of any kind. A few photographs do include a portrait of beadwork artist and bag maker Sophia Smith at White Earth and several images of Dakota and Ojibwe lace makers. For more on Whipple's collection of gashkibidaaganag, see page 200.

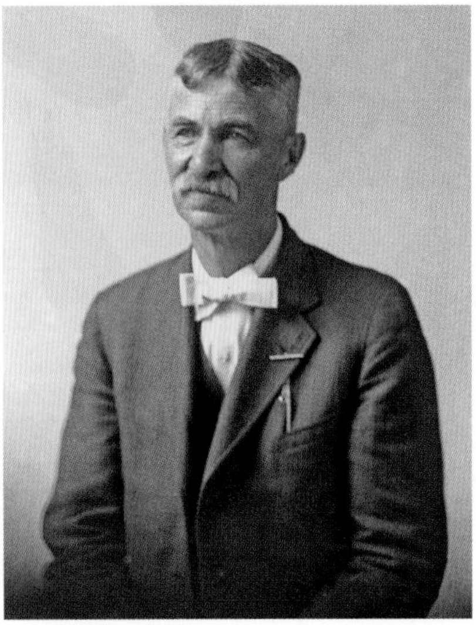

4.03 *(above)* Robert G. Beaulieu, c. 1910. *MNHS E97.1B p17*

4.04 *(right)* Moccasin game, White Earth Reservation, 1920. *MNHS E97.38 r4*

Robert G. Beaulieu

Of particular importance is the collection of images made by a photographer of Ojibwe ancestry, Robert G. Beaulieu (Figure 4.03; 1858–1935). His large Ojibwe-French family was influential on the White Earth Reservation, and sixteen of his 115 related images include gashkibidaaganag. While the majority of the images bear witness to the colonization efforts of religious organizations and the US government's assimilationist policies upon the Ojibwe at White Earth from the 1870s to the 1930s, his image of men playing the moccasin game features a player wearing a magnificent gashkibidaagan over western clothing (Figure 4.04).[4]

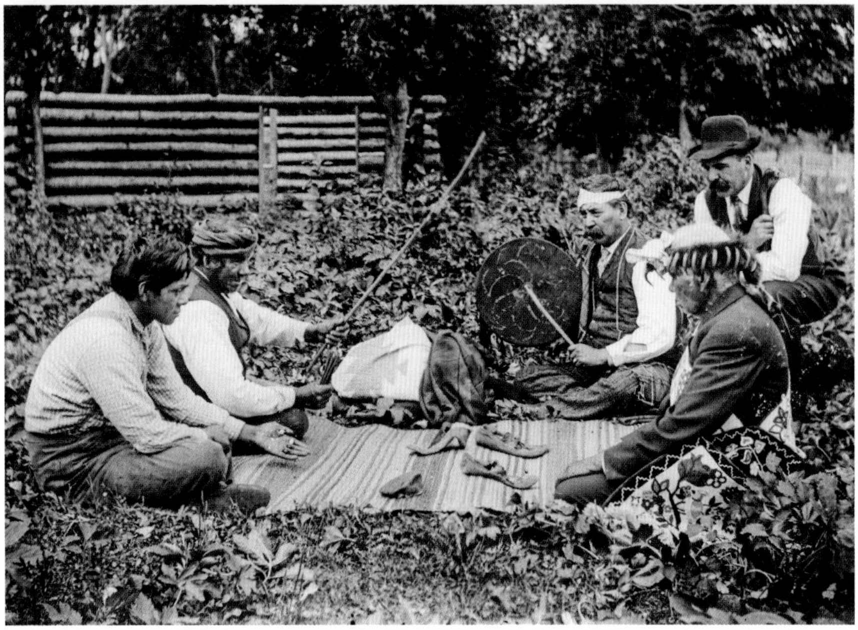

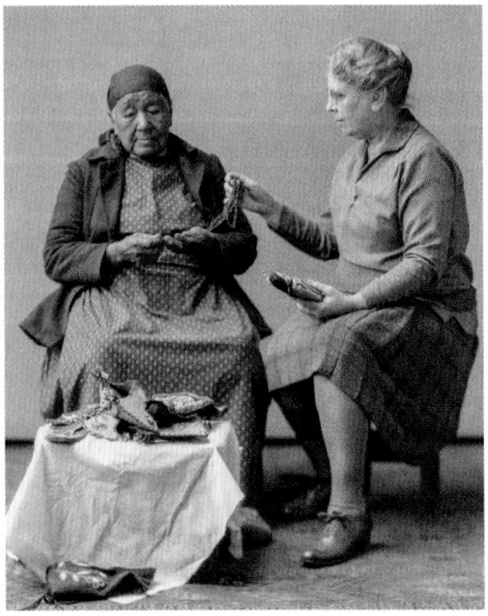

4.05 Susan Windgrow (Makawastewin), a Dakota woman from the Prairie Island Community, with Frances Densmore, c. 1830. *MNHS E91.1M r9*

Frances Densmore

Nearly two hundred images related to American Indians were collected or produced by ethnographer and musicologist Frances Densmore (Figure 4.05; 1857–1967). A native of Red Wing, Minnesota, she began working with American Indians in Minnesota and other tribal nations across the United States in the 1890s. Densmore's collection of family and professional photos includes views taken by her and by others, documenting Indians in Minnesota and elsewhere to illustrate her US Bureau of Ethnography publications on Ojibwe music, plants, and customs. She recorded individuals, clothing, housing, wild ricing, maple sugaring, canoe building, and various Indian crafts, including basketry, beadwork, and moccasin making. Her annotations on specific photographs are of particular interest. The manuscript holdings at the Minnesota Historical Society contain many images Densmore submitted for publication and some that were not selected. Her documented interviews with Native informants and the resulting publications are an invaluable resource on the Ojibwe and Dakota of Minnesota and their beadwork.

Densmore's photograph of the women's dance at the White Earth annual celebration (Figure 4.06) provides important, useful data about gashkibidaaganag. Her written historical observations about the exchange of gashkibidaaganag and other regalia pieces at such dances not only support other published records, but they also demonstrate Densmore's personal interests and perspective. A note in her handwriting on the back of this image says: "Picture taken at Fourteenth of June White Earth a 'Woman's Dance' in which Articles received as gifts are carried—these gifts—accompanying invitation to dance—a few yards of calico was a common gift, and a woman has it on her shoulder. Probably taken in 1907." The calico recipient is in the immediate foreground. Notice the man at the center wearing two gashkibidaaganag.

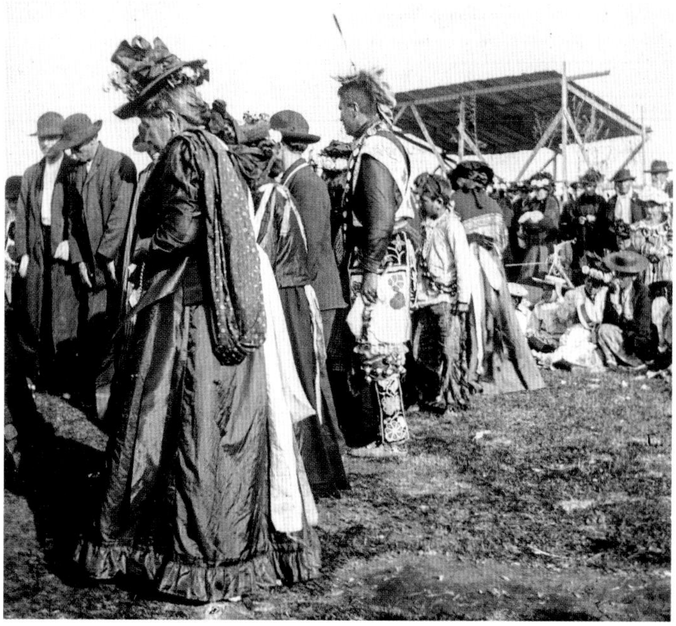

4.06 The women's dance at White Earth, c. 1907. *MNHS E97.37 r5*

Monroe P. Killy

Monroe P. Killy (Figure 4.07; 1910–2010) was a collector and documenter of American Indian material culture and lifeways in the Minnesota region. Holdings at the Minnesota Historical Society include more than seven hundred photographs, slides, and films documenting Indians in Minnesota between 1930 and the 1970s, primarily Ojibwe at Nett Lake, Mille Lacs, Grand Portage, Leech Lake, and Itasca State Park. The images document individuals, clothing, housing, wild ricing, maple sugaring, canoe building, and various Indian crafts, including basketry, beadwork, and moccasin making. For more on Monroe Killy, see page 116.

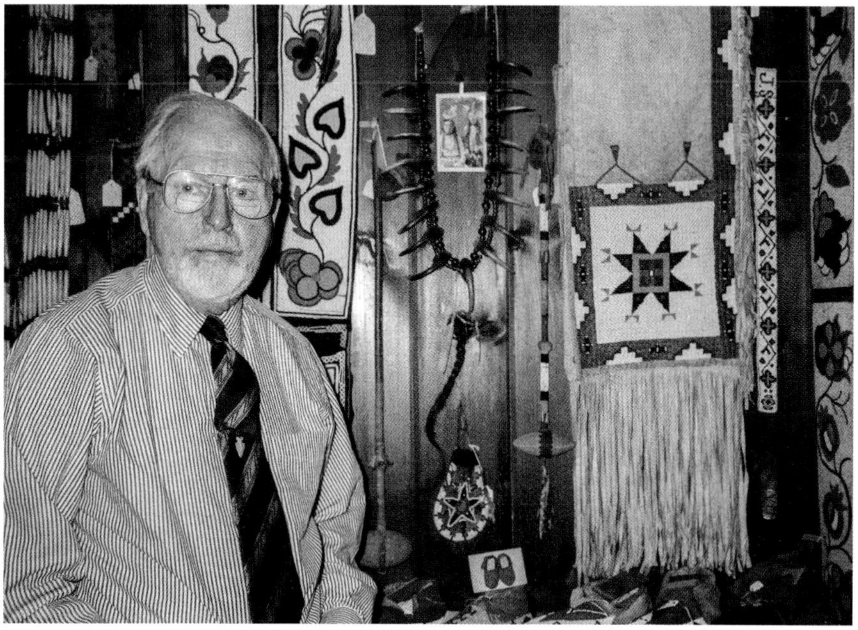

4.07 Monroe Killy, c. 1990. *Author's collection*

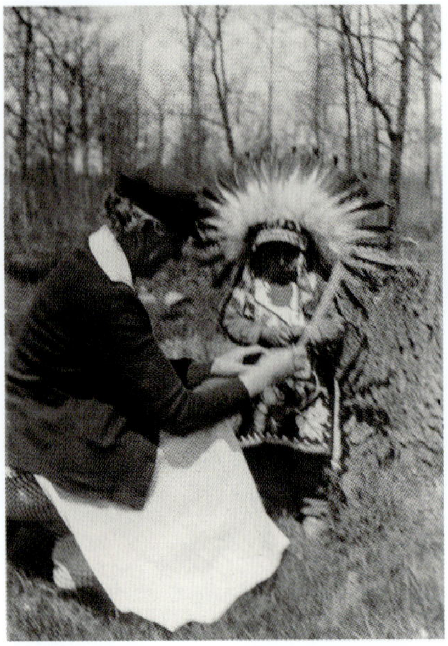

4.08 *(above)* Jeannette Ayer sets up a photo shoot with band member Frankie Hanks in 1937. Ayer uses dance aprons and beaded belts to represent a diminutive gashkibidaagan on Frankie. *MNHS E97.1H r2*

4.09 *(right)* The resulting postcard produced for sale at Mille Lacs Indian Trading Post. *MNHS E97.1H r3*

Harry and Jeanette Ayer collections

Harry (1878–1966) and Jeannette (1883–1966) Ayer of the Mille Lacs Indian Museum and Trading Post both created and accumulated several hundred visual documents of "traditional" Ojibwe lifeways and the interaction of cultures in the entrepreneurial tourism setting of the Mille Lacs Indian Museum and Trading Post. Harry was a professional photographer and botanist. The Ayers, who were at Mille Lacs between 1914 and 1959, made and sold several photographic postcards as souvenirs at the store (Figures 4.08 and 4.09). Their photographs, made from the 1920s to the 1960s, include views of the Mille Lacs Indian Museum and Trading Post as well as individuals, clothing, housing, wild ricing, maple sugaring, canoe building, wigwam construction, moccasin games and dance programs for tourists, and various Indian crafts, including basketry, beadwork, and moccasin making, serving as a rich resource of east-central Minnesota Ojibwe material culture. For more on the Ayers, see pages 146 and 155.

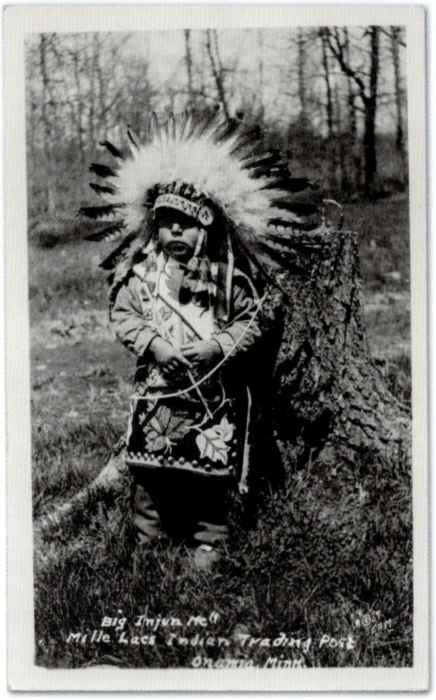

Nineteenth-century Minnesota photographers

Also of particular value are the 150 or so rather well-documented images made by nineteenth-century Minnesota photographers Joel E. Whitney, Charles A. Zimmerman, Benjamin Franklin Upton, James Martin, Harry E. Hoard and Charles A. Tenney, Frank Jay Haynes, and Truman W. Ingersoll. These men created photographs and recorded events that survive as the primary early images of Minnesota's first people and the objects they prized most.[5]

In the last half of the nineteenth century, photographers created many studio portraits of Indians produced as the pocket-sized cartes de visite that were popularly sold and collected. Many studio portraits show Indian subjects wrapped in blankets, perhaps reflecting the subject's preference—or the photographer's. By the late 1850s, "blanket Indian" was used as shorthand for those who maintained tribal custom and costume. These images fed the interests of collectors who had read newspaper stories about the subjects' roles as political or military leaders.

In addition, these photographers made a smaller but significant group of studio portraits that documented the apparel of the indigenous people of the region and particularly those who returned to the St. Paul and Fort Snelling area after the establishment of reservations. While some of the pieces of clothing or accessories can be found in more than one image, suggesting that they were studio props used by the photographers, the images document the items available at the time.

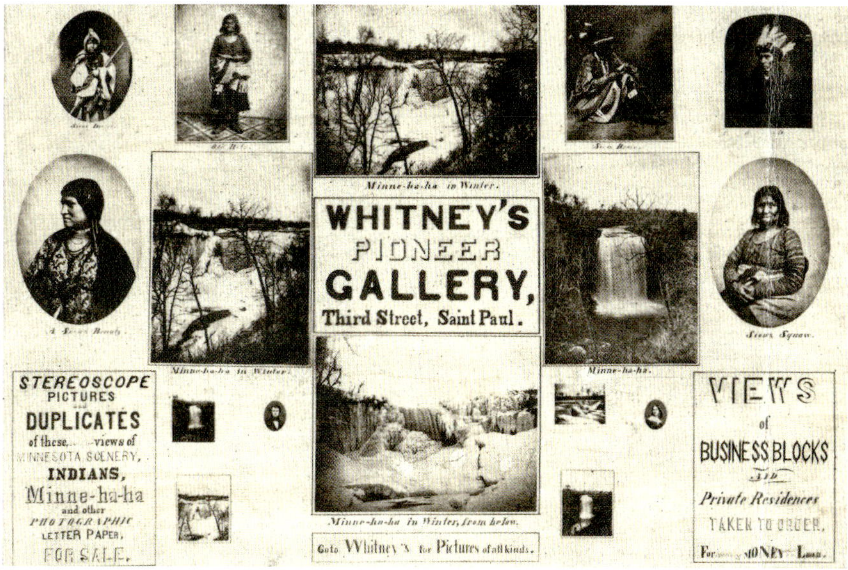

4.10 Advertisement for Whitney's Gallery, 1867. *MNHS N2.6 r6*

An 1867 advertisement of image types offered by Whitney's Gallery (Figure 4.10) shows that early established firms of this type produced fine photographs as well as "stereoscopic pictures and duplicates of these views of Minnesota scenery, Indians, Minne-ha-ha and other."

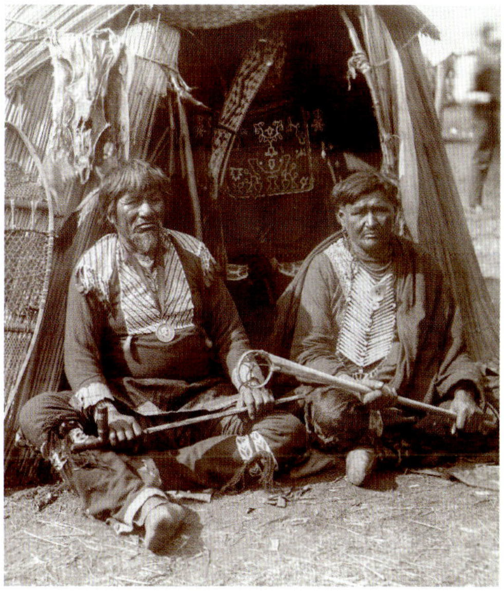

4.11 *(left)* Black Hawk and Green Cloud, 1897. *MNHS E98 p2*

A pair of images shows the value of a collection with depth, which can make it possible to identify individuals and objects in one image using the data provided in others. Truman Ingersoll created several images, perhaps on the same day, including Black Hawk, Green Cloud, and a third man. In Figure 4.11, Black Hawk and Green Cloud sit in a wigwam doorway, while the third man stands in the shadows, wearing a distinctive gashkibidaagan and a spot-stitched dance apron. In Figure 4.12, the two men are seated at front left, wearing nearly the same clothing, while the third man is now standing behind the drum but without the bag; Black Hawk and Green Cloud are not identified in this image. Sometimes they are misidentified culturally in other images, but they are both Ho-Chunk men, and it is likely that the other individuals and the three visible bags seen here are Ho-Chunk as well.

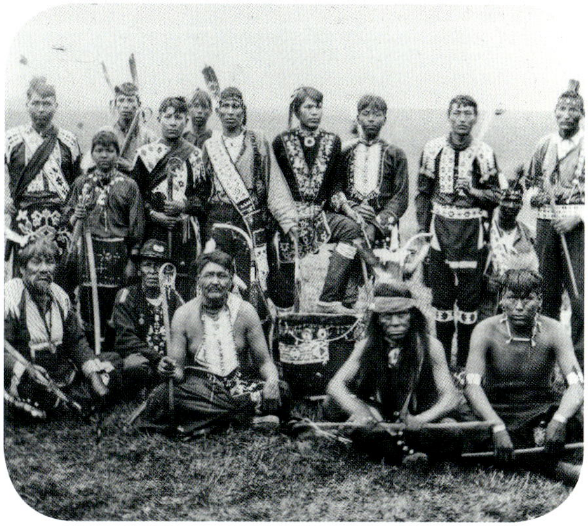

4.12 *(below)* Group of Ojibwe men, circa 1900. *MNHS E91.1 r54*

Other photographic resources

The collection groups at the Minnesota Historical Society that document American Indians in Minnesota are still being augmented and developed to provide the greatest possible depth of resources for future users. Other Minnesota Historical Society collections of use include the work of Frank Jay Haynes (1853–1921; active 1860s–1920), Ole Flaten (1854–1933; active 1870s–1920s), and Carl Gustaf Linde (1882–?; active 1910s–1920s).

In addition to reviewing the valuable resources at the Minnesota Historical Society, I have examined historical photograph collections at other museums and historical organizations over the last thirty years to learn about tribal preferences for the popular use of these bags. Significant collections, many now online, clearly illustrate wardrobe preferences by those being photographed in a variety of settings, including studio portraits, treaty signings, staged images, informal or nonpolitical activities (dances, powwows), recorded events, and snapshots.[6]

The study of these photographs supports my premise that gashkibidaaganag from the late nineteenth through the mid-twentieth centuries were worn predominantly by Woodland Indians of the Great Lakes region. The bags appear with greatest consistency among the Ojibwe in multiple settings. Of other regional groups, Potawatomi, Menominee, Ho-Chunk, and Meskwaki people occasionally wore gashkibidaaganag.

Because of their value and beauty, gashkibidaaganag and particularly Ojibwe gashkibidaaganag can be found all over the world. Although they were traded west for ponies, in the bulk of extant imagery, they rarely appear as the regular "traditional" or typical preferred garb for other indigenous communities. The number of individuals wearing the bags (as in Figure 4.13) and the quantity of images documenting this activity suggests that, for the Ojibwe of Minnesota, the bags were a marker of indigeneity, a representation of culture, and that they were more than just a bag, serving rather as vibrant, wearable shorthand for who they were and are: Ojibwe-anishinaabeg.

4.13 Leech Lake Band members at Walker, Minnesota, c. 1920. While it lacks fine detail, this image clearly conveys the predominance of gashkibidaaganag in the regalia of these men. It is one of my favorite gashkibidaagan records. *MNHS E97.37 p80;* *see also page ii*

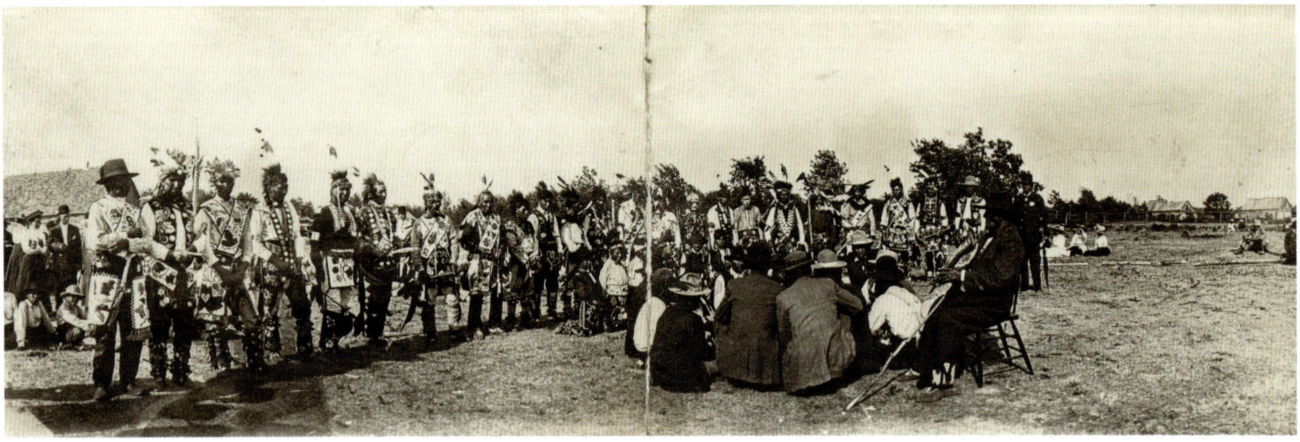

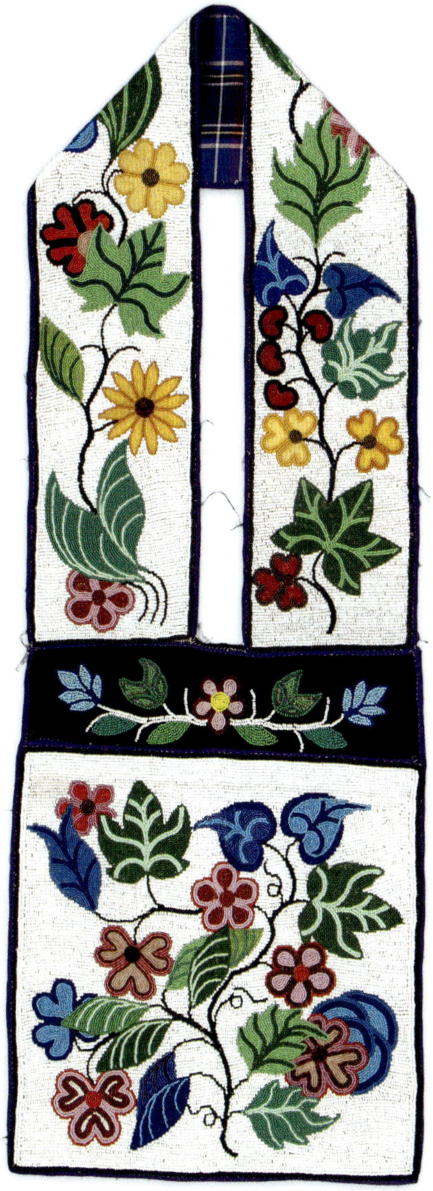

Chapter 5

Handicraft and Commerce

American Indian products and design were popularized during the first quarter of the twentieth century as the Arts and Crafts movement celebrated the craft traditions of American Indians, particularly those from the Southwest. Countless photographs of Victorian interiors record pastiches and cozy corners embellished with all forms of ephemeral and exotic goods, including embroideries, photographs, Persian textiles, paisley shawls, crazy quilt throws, Navajo rugs, and Indian "curiosities."

American Indian crafts were recognized as relevant to several early twentieth-century interior design trends for their handmade quality and their uniqueness. A 1901 article in the *Minneapolis Journal*, urging readers to buy local, argues that Indian products rival Oriental products in design and quality: "There is evidence on every hand of an increasing demand for the art products of North American Indians. . . . Americans are awakening to the fact that while they have been sending merchants to scour the Orient for things quaint and curious with which to adorn their dwellings a rich treasure was lying neglected at their doors."[1]

The typical eclectic Victorian room setting in Figure 5.01 is probably this woman's bedroom or sitting room, where she displays her collection of American Indian objects among period bric-a-brac. The back wall holds a spot-stitch appliqué gashkibidaagan and three loom-woven panels that have not been made into bags. The latter, sometimes referred to as stained glass or window illumination panels, were made in many sizes, but rarely on the scale of a gashkibidaagan, and they were often hung in windows.

The exchange of beaded goods took place within Ojibwe families and communities as well as with tourists, Twin Cities consumers, art collectors, ethnographers, the owners of curio stores and trading posts, and even people learning the newly popular craft of beadwork. While bandolier

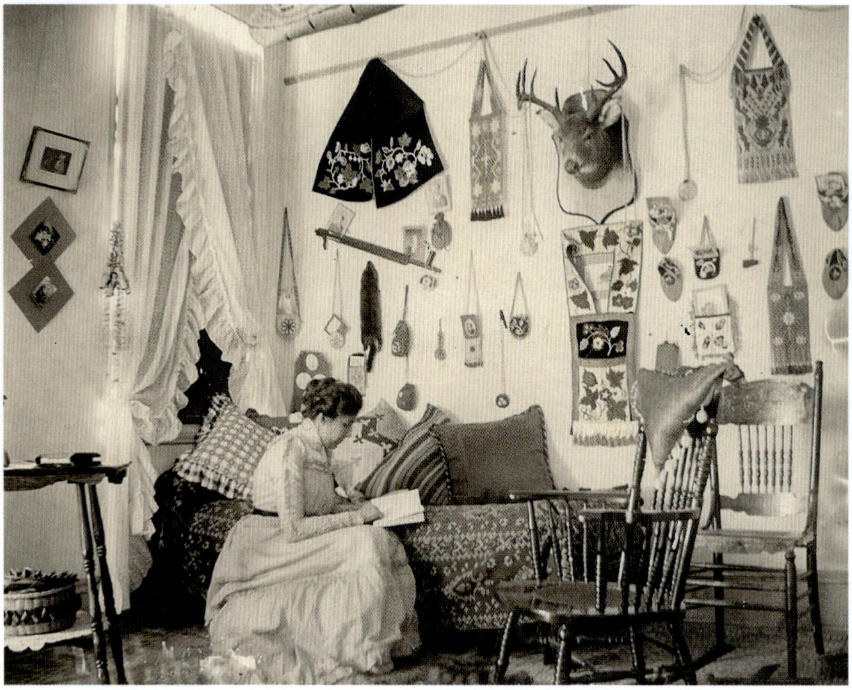

5.01 Room interior, 1885, White Earth Reservation. *BCHS 14.11.36*

bags seemed to remain in a separate category, many items of Indian material culture were commodified: small beaded bags, moccasins, belts, and birchbark canoes. The *Bemidji Pioneer* described a 1908 window display at Crane & Gould, a local merchant: "Their windows are filled with Indian pictures and pillows, and Indian and Mexican handicraft of everything under 'the sun' in that line. The goods are exceptionally well selected and are the best that money can buy. As a striking effect to the whole display is a life-size form of an Indian clad in beadwork and Indian stuff. The window is trimmed with festooning and has a back ground of latticed woodwork. The whole display is of exceptional merit."[2]

People bought the bead artwork of Ojibwe women because they liked it, because they could afford it, because they wanted to support the beadworkers, because it would help them remember a trip taken to northern Minnesota, and probably for other reasons. Some craft objects, lacking functional purposes, may have been less marketable, but sales did provide needed income and an apparent but perhaps unanticipated incentive to preserve traditional crafts.

Yet Minnesotans in the late nineteenth and early twentieth centuries held conflicting views regarding the value, quality, and market appeal of Ojibwe and other American Indian beadwork. Some paternalistic voices, including those of educators, missionaries, and Indian agents, openly argued that other methods of earned income must be found for Indian women because their beadwork was of poor quality and without a commercial market. Naysayers were patronizing and influential. In an article published in 1898 in the *New York Times,* Sybil Carter, who had established lacemaking schools for American Indians in Minnesota and around the country, noted that lacemaking was growing among Ojibwe women at Leech Lake. She asserted that lacemaking would provide steady employment, whereas no market existed for the beadwork the Ojibwe women made.[3]

In 1952 Karen Daniels Petersen (1910–2007), a staff member at the Science Museum of Minnesota who wrote books on subjects related to the Plains and Ojibwe Indians, started the Episcopal Church Indian Crafts Program, which was intended to help Ojibwe people in northern Minnesota become self-supporting. The written correspondence between

Petersen and band members gives a rich picture of the challenges the Indians faced, from seasonal availability of natural materials, to preferences for brain-tanned hides over commercial, to pressing family issues, as well as the frustration of not having funds to buy supplies before being paid for the finished items. Petersen's records give clues about the craft workers' incomes: Beaded coin purses made by Mrs. Alice Lokken sold for $5.00 in Redby, but she sold them to Petersen for $4.00. Mrs. J. L. Thompson charged $1.50 for beaded chains for belts. Mrs. Ed J. Fairbanks of Bena sold Petersen earrings and bracelets at $0.75.[4]

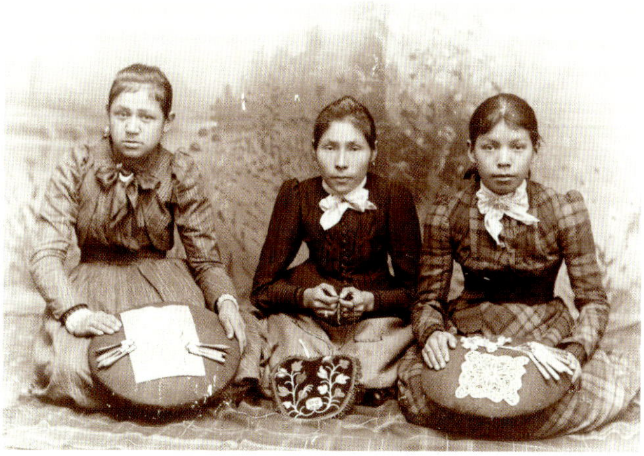

5.02 Young women with lace and beadwork, c. 1900. *MNHS Collection III.40.100*

Photographers documented the progress of the lacemaking classes in northwestern Minnesota. In Figure 5.02, young women pose at White Earth with pillow lace in process and a beaded purse or bag form of the type made regularly for sale to collectors and tourists. The inclusion of the beadwork suggests that even after the introduction of lacemaking, beadwork continued to represent cultural significance for the Ojibwe and their customers.

Some Minnesotans, including F. T. Gustavson, Harry and Jeannette Ayer, Neva L. Munson Williams, and certain missionaries of the Episcopal Church, worked diligently to promote the traditional arts of the Ojibwe. In 1936, when Neva Williams was young, her family, the Weltys, moved to Vineland Resort on Mille Lacs Lake. Her father eventually found a spot on Wigwam Bay that had enough land, was close to a good fishing ground, and had good access to the recently built US Highway 169. They ran the Wigwam Inn Resort from 1938 until about 1952. Neva remembers that in the 1930s, "Almost every resort had small items for sale. Mostly birch bark work, some beadwork." Neva was involved in a number of mid-twentieth-century efforts to support Minnesota Indian artisans in making and selling their work. She had multiple goals: to provide funding to individuals in Minnesota's reservation communities, to ensure the creation of authentic Indian-made objects in an era when copies of Indian crafts were being mass-produced overseas and sold across North America as Indian made, and to find creative venues for the sale of or access to authentic products.[5]

For the most part, Indian artists and craftspeople were not paid much for their work, even when it was being promoted by sympathetic concerns. At the Mille Lacs Museum and Trading Post, order books and store inventories show the prices the Ayers paid to Ojibwe craft vendors during the 1940s and 1950s. A strength of the trading post's stock was the products made from birch bark and basswood. In 1940 the Ayers paid $0.25 each for basswood dolls (150 single units purchased). In 1947–50 they purchased birdhouses in two sizes: small at $1.25, and large at $1.85 (38 single units purchased). For makaks (birchbark containers), they paid $0.40 and $0.50 during this period (125 single units purchased), but the containers most likely did not have beaded decorations like one elaborate beaded example that survives. Mille Lacs craft workers also sold beaded napkin rings; the ones recorded in the Ayers' books were purchased for just $0.10 each. And band members who made the popular birchbark teapots received only $0.20 for each teapot. The trading post records do not include the prices the Ayers received from the items they sold.[6]

Some gashkibidaaganag sold for up to forty or fifty dollars at the turn of the twentieth century. But a 1916 advertisement demonstrates the fickle nature of the market: a merchant offered his gashkibidaagan stock at five dollars each, possibly closing out the business.[7]

Fine Ojibwe beadwork was recognized in awards offered in competitions, including those at reservation fairs or expositions as well as at many county fairs. At the Second Annual Red Lake Indian Fair in 1914, the *Bemidji Pioneer* noted, "Indians only can compete for prizes or premiums.... Exhibits included agricultural, domestic, school booth, Indian beadwork, etc."[8]

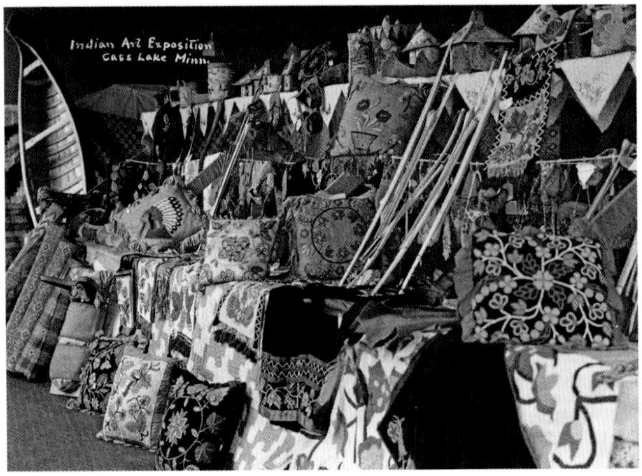

5.03 Cass Lake Indian Art Exposition, c. 1914–20. *MNHS E97.29 p3*

At least four gashkibidaaganag, as well as several beaded pillow tops, are visible in Figure 5.03, a Leech Lake Reservation image of the Cass Lake Indian Art Exposition, dating between 1914 and 1920. Displays at the Minnesota State Fair by Mahnomen County in 1917 and by the Minnesota Archaeological Society in 1939 also included gashkibidaaganag.[9]

Curio shops, newspaper advertisements, and occasional articles confirm that Indian beadwork surfaced in varied roles in Minnesota's economy during the late nineteenth and early twentieth century. A photograph of M. A. Smith's Curio Store in Duluth (Figure 5.04) shows all manner of American Indian–made souvenirs crowding the shop. Above the cash register, the owners prominently positioned the most significant pieces in the inventory, two gashkibidaaganag: one in the loom-woven style and a second embellished with beads in the spot-stitch appliqué style.[10]

In the Cass Lake area, local merchants and government traders Louisa J. Lynch and Robert P. Fairbanks placed at least thirty-four advertisements in the *Tomahawk* in 1903 and 1904 alone, claiming "Indian beads silk and fancy work a specialty" and "Indian fancy work a specialty." The quantity and the size of their advertisements suggest a significant and persistent market for Ojibwe beadwork in the Cass Lake area, countering the assertions of the lacemaking organizer Sybil Carter.[11]

American Indian crafts often attracted well-meaning but patronizing supporters. An article in the *Minneapolis Journal* on April 3, 1903, noted that a Mrs. Vrooman, who was "a generous patron of native handicrafts and has given much time, thought and money to the encouragement of fine handwork of all kinds," would sponsor a display of fine beadwork from Red Lake and White Earth Reservations at Vrooman's Little Shop in Minneapolis: "It is her desire to assist in establishing the Indian beadwork and other industries native to the tribes upon a permanent and paying basis." She also advertised free beadwork lessons for children on Saturday mornings.[12]

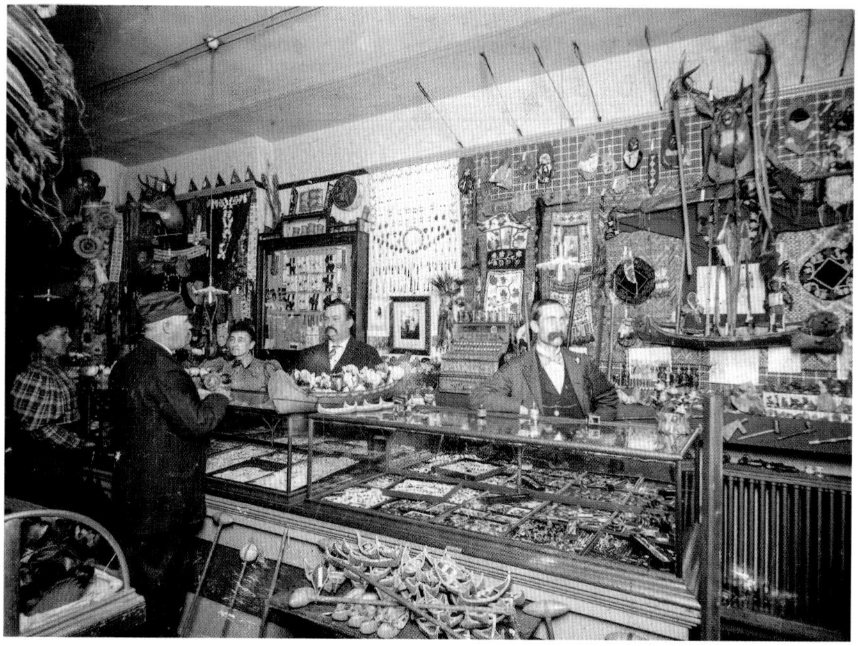

5.04 M. A. Smith's Curio Store at 410 West Superior Street in Duluth, 1896, from a city booster booklet published by a Duluth newspaper. *KAMLASC S2386b48*

In the era just before US Highway 169 opened in Minnesota, a 1929 travel guide was promoting tourism. Called *The Minnesota Book: Land of Pleasure, Land of Treasure*, this guidebook proclaimed that the major use of the state's ten thousand lakes was for fishing and hunting, along with full-service resorts with beaches, dancing, and amenities appealing to families with children. Clearly, investments had already been made in recreational opportunities in the Mille Lacs and Cass Lake areas. The construction of Highway 169, beginning in 1931, improved transportation to these areas, following an established development pattern.

Many of the resorts invented names by playing off elements of the Ojibwe and Dakota languages. A few of these resort monikers included Wabi-kon (Cass Lake), Wah-We-Yes-Cumig Resort (Waubun), I-O-Wana Beach (Bena), Aun-Way-Be-Win (Ogema), and Ojibway (Cass Lake), but few incorporated indigenous material culture in the décor or made any other reference to the cultures that inspired their names.

A handful of resort areas in Minnesota did provide Native guides. Mahnomen County, Ogema in Becker County, Bemidji in Beltrami County, and Crane Lake in St. Louis County were among the few that elaborated on the role of American Indians in the history of their areas. The Ayers' trading post at Mille Lacs was one of a minority of resort-area businesses that promoted access to local American Indians and their crafts and relics.[13]

In the 1930s and 1940s, the Mille Lacs Indian Museum and Trading Post promoted itself as one of the leading tourist attractions in the state (see also page 155). It was a "two and a half hours' scenic drive from Minneapolis on Highway 169," as noted in the trading post's ad in the *Mille Lacs Lake Travel Guide* (Figure 5.05). The ad promoted the trading post's handmade American Indian items from far and wide, plus its local Ojibwe products: "The finest of Indian Bead-workers, they produce neck chains, girdles [belts], moccasins, wrist bands, fobs, purses, gauntlets, etc." No mention is made of more significant pieces such as the many gashkibidaaganag displayed on the trading post's walls (Figure 5.06).

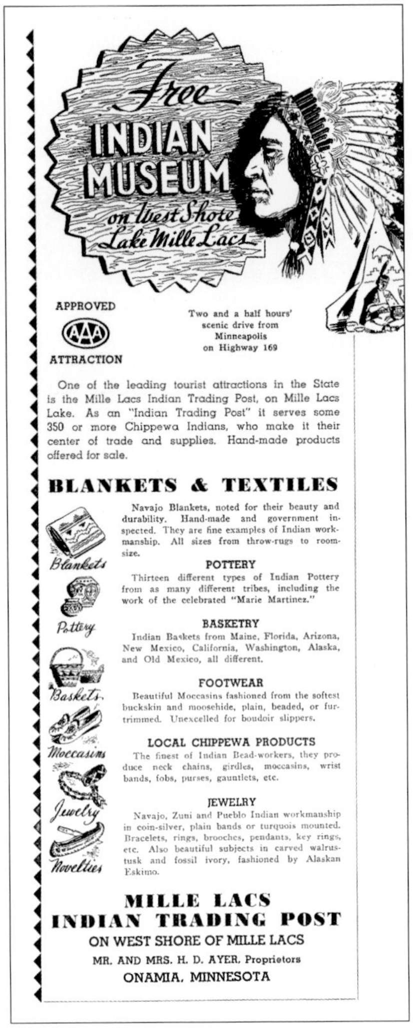

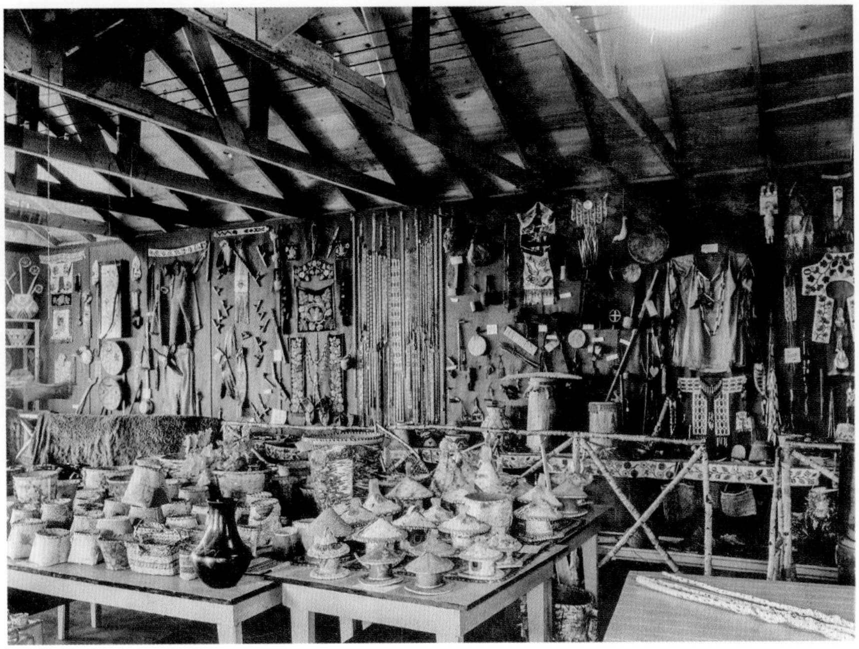

5.05 *(above)* Advertisement. *Mille Lacs Lake Travel Guide, 1942, page 57*

5.06 *(above right)* Interior of Mille Lacs Indian Trading Post, 1935. *MNHS MM6.7M r62*

The Ayer's advertisement was paired with a typically racially charged promotional commentary on the people of the Mille Lacs area: "The 300 or so Chippewa who make this region their home are one of its chief attractions. During the summer it is still possible to see [women] bent over charcoal fires and small Indian children playing with primitive toys fashioned out of willow thongs. Each September, before the wild rice harvest begins, these Indians stage their ceremonial 'rice dance' at which visitors are always welcome."[14]

All or parts of easily ten spot-stitch appliqué gashkibidaaganag are visible in Figure 5.07, taken at the 1910 Annual White Earth Reservation Celebration. In anticipation of the 1922 annual celebration the *Minneapolis Morning Tribune* opined: "Storekeepers on the reservation report that for several months past they have been unable to buy beaded moccasins or bags. During the fall and winter months—when cash is scarce—the Indians freely part with these treasures. As the annual festival approaches, every bit of handmade finery is saved to be worn when the great day rolls around. The stock of Indian beadwork is low and no merchant sees a chance of replenishing his supply until after the big powwow is over."[15]

Grand Portage gashkibidaagan maker Ellen Olson responded eloquently to the newspaper's blithe mention of beadworkers "freely" selling their "treasures" as she reflected on her early years as a bead artist: "Women became important because their beadwork had monetary value and they often became the moneymakers. The old ways were disappearing and that left men on the reservation fewer sources of income. Women could sell [beadwork like] moccasins in the lumber camps or trade them for food when money was in short supply and there were no stores nearby."[16]

These observations offer a sampling of the diverse views on the value of American Indian beadwork in Minnesota from the late nineteenth

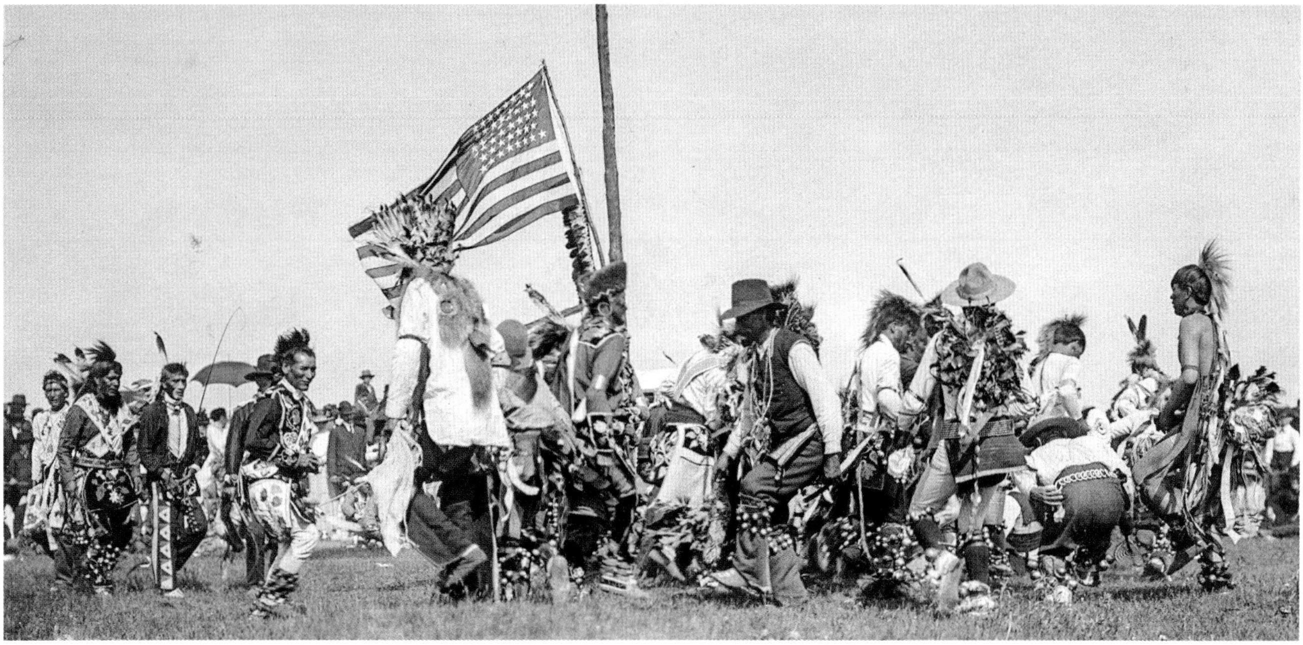

5.07 Annual White Earth Reservation Celebration, 1910. *MNHS Collection I.364.17*

century well into the mid-twentieth century. For the most part, they illustrate the varied perspectives of non-Indians regarding the availability, value, and appeal of traditional and tourist market crafts made by the Ojibwe of Minnesota. At the same time, the examples discussed here reveal the complex but significant cultural roles occupied by the Ojibwe bead artists of Minnesota. The pervasive presence of small, affordable examples of Ojibwe beadwork familiarized tourists and more serious collectors with their artistry. Those purchases led, no doubt, to client demand, encouraging the bead artists to create more elaborate products, like the gashkibidaagan, with potentially greater aesthetic appeal and market value. Given the transaction value and cultural prominence of the gashkibidaagan, it became the supreme symbol of a bead artist's skill. Whatever the scale of the product, beadwork and its availability positioned Ojibwe women to provide economic stability and objects of status for their families and communities well into the twentieth century.

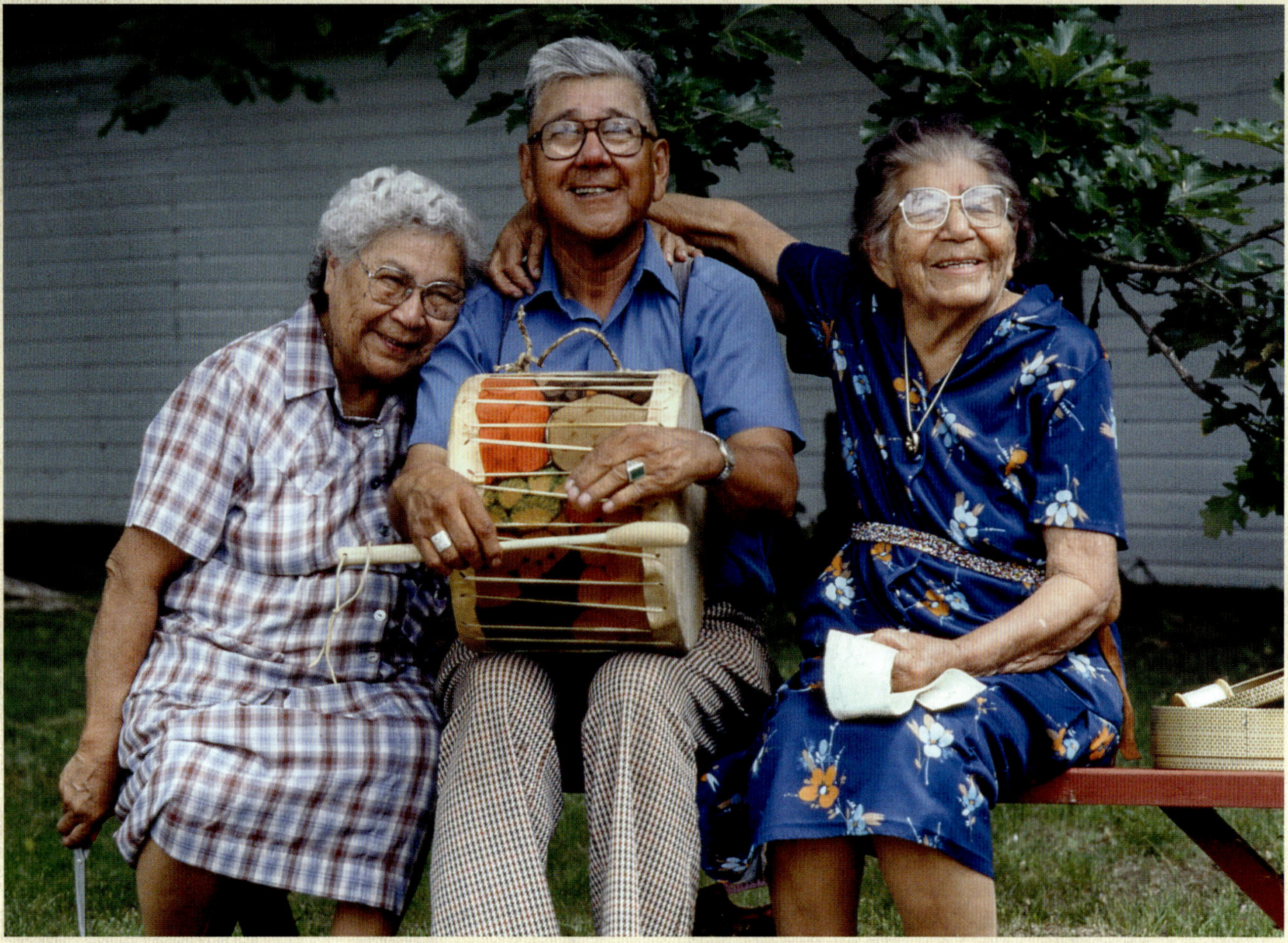

Beadworkers Batiste Sam and Maude Kegg pause to relax with Fred Benjamin at Mille Lacs, c. 1994. *MNHS Mille Lacs Exhibit Materials*

Part 2

Reservation Stories

In the 1860s, at about the same time that Ojibwe people had begun to make gashkibidaaganag, the state and federal governments were pushing Minnesota's Ojibwe and Dakota people to cede their land and move to reservations. During this difficult time, many people left their homes to move onto the traditional lands of other Ojibwe tribal bands. Reservations became home to bands that had not previously shared territory. And they also became places where bead artists could learn from each other, as well as be exposed to influences from missionaries and others eager to teach them Euro-American culture. While the work of bead artists associated with particular reservations has survived in greater quantities than on others, it is clear that Ojibwe people throughout the state made and in some ways solidified their cultural identities by wearing gashkibidaaganag during this challenging period. Through the twentieth century and into the twenty-first, the continuation of this tradition has brought honor and beauty to family life and cultural events and provided an artistic outlet for creative bead artistry.

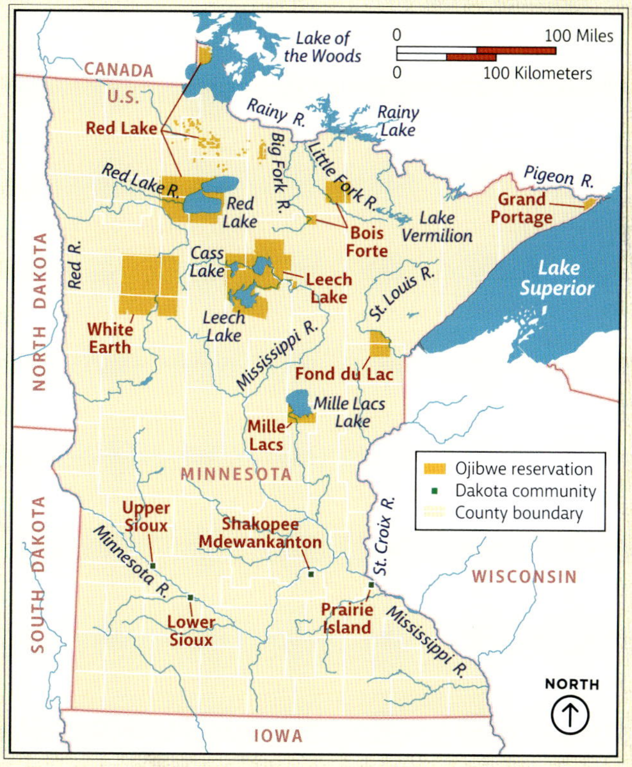

Ojibwe reservations in Minnesota *Map by Matt Kania, Map Hero, Inc.*

Each chapter in the second part of this book tells stories of gashkibidaaganag associated with one of Minnesota's seven reservations. Some reservations provide more bag examples than do others; the productivity of bead artists may be a significant factor, but it is also clear that the preferences of non-Indian collectors and ethnologists have created many of the records. Assigning these stories to specific reservations can be challenging as well. Motifs on other beaded objects with known provenance—belts, dance aprons, leggings, and yokes—can sometimes support some reservation attributions. But the most obvious evidence is missing: most bandolier bags come to us without dates, without clear association to specific reservations, and without their makers' names. White collectors either did not understand or did not care about specific band associations. This is especially true for the beadworking traditions of Leech Lake, Red Lake, and White Earth, which many whites referred to as "the Cass Lake area." The stories tied to these reservations often overlap.

In this section of the book, I present the evidence that I have been able to find, making my best judgment on which stories are most closely associated with which reservations. Because the written records on gashkibidaaganag in large collections have mostly been kept by non-Indians, a great number of these stories reflect Western ways of knowing. Many of the records contain inaccurate information, misspellings, and misattributions, which complicate efforts to identify named individual Ojibwe. While I am grateful to bead artists and others who have taught me so much, I am also aware of how much I *don't* know. For instance, because of the deep genealogical knowledge that is alive on Minnesota's reservations, other band members will no doubt recognize relatives and connections that remain invisible to me.

The words of the beadworkers themselves, though, bring readers closer to the tradition and its experience. Before you read these reservation stories, I invite you to listen to Bois Forte poet Linda LeGarde Grover, who shows beadworking through a child's eyes on a hot summer day. She makes it easy to see the loving relationships and cultural identities that are stitched into gashkibidaaganag.

Mary Remembering, on a July Afternoon

Linda LeGarde Grover

An afternoon like this reminds me of my grandma,
way back when she taught us how to bead
one summer. On a day like today, warm,
Summers, she wore a gray cotton house dress
washed so soft it fluttered light as silk
when she walked. On a day like today, warm
she stretched carpet thread on a wooden loom,
forgetting about dishes, laundry, ironing,
chores that could wait that afternoon
as flowers grew and bloomed beneath her hands.
Large knuckles she had, and knobby fingers
that lifted beads carefully from a jar lid
with her needle counting
two blue two red eight white two white four green
Four white two green two blue six white two blue.
A steamy afternoon it was; we sat
at her table, Grandma flanked and squeezed
by me and Cynthia getting closer and closer,
yet she never said to move, or make more room,
only that the warm air from our open mouths
as we breathed and watched limbered her fingers,
and the waxed threads, felt good.
One day she gave us little wooden looms
she'd made, and our own needles, fast and silvery
to try out beading, and we felt honored
to do what Grandma did; honored
we watched, and then we did what Grandma did.
Threaded our looms
picked up beads with our needles
pressed up and wove
into no pattern at all, just beads,
but you know? She praised us,
praised us anyway, said that looks good.
It's been eighty years since I saw my Grandma
but I remember when we learned to bead,
that summer just before my father died,
and mother in her sadness never thrived
again, but passed nights drinking, days asleep
til the Indian agent noticed and sent me
to boarding school, where I was to forget
what Grandma taught me, and learn other ways.
But I never forgot how we learned to bead
and when we brought our bracelets into town,
a long, hot walk with Grandma to the store.
We sold our "just beads" bracelets for five cents,
And Grandma got four bits apiece for hers.
She said, you girls keep your money, as
she bought blue yarn, white sugar, brown flannel
and three red suckers for the long walk home,
along with endless days, I would have thought,
of Mother, singing as she sewed and cooked
of Father, cutting wood and hauling scrap
and Grandma, flanked and squeezed by two small girls
who watched her work. I never did forget
that summer when she taught us how to bead,
and held it in my heart those lonely days
at school. Marching to class, learning English,
scrubbing the floors, I held it in my heart,
that summer when she taught us how to bead,
her strong brown hands, that soft gray dress, the steam
from summer heat, and concentrating mouths
limbering her fingers and the threads,
that summer Grandma taught us how to bead.

Chapter 6

Bois Forte

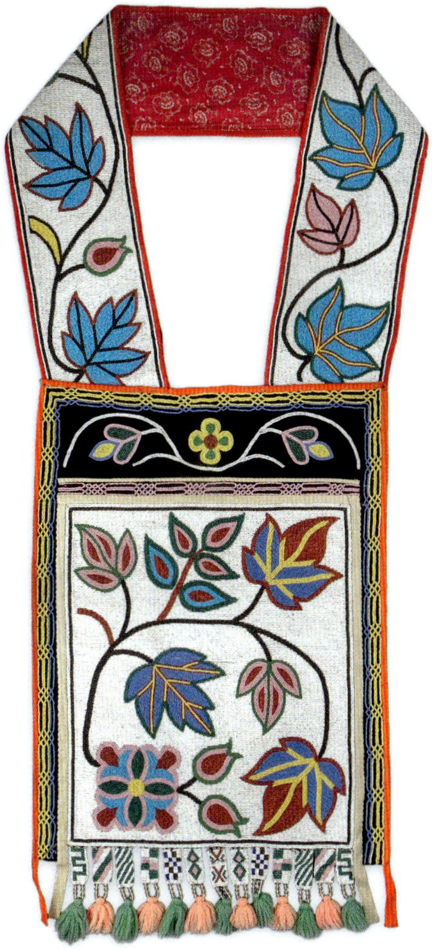

The Bois Forte Band of Chippewa is made up of three Ojibwe groups that were living in the area when French and British people arrived: the Zagwaandagaawininiwag, or People of the Strong Woods; the Lake Vermilion Band of Lake Superior Chippewa; and the southern half of the Little Forks Band of Rainy River Saulteaux. The Bois Forte Reservation, established in 1866, lies in St. Louis, Koochiching, and Itasca Counties. Named for the thick forests that used to cover the region—*bois forte* is French for "strong wood"—it is composed of three sectors. Today, most band members live at Nett Lake, which is reported to be the largest producer of wild rice in the United States. The Vermilion sector, on Lake Vermilion near the city of Tower, is home to the band's Fortune Bay Casino and the Bois Forte Heritage Center. The Deer Creek sector is administered as a natural resource reserve.[1]

Many of the bags associated with Bois Forte are unusually large compared to the majority of gashkibidaaganag made between 1850 and 1940. The two gashkibidaaganag associated with the Bois Forte Reservation, Figures 6.01 and 6.02, were acquired by Albert Reagan and sold to the Canadian Museum of Civilization (now the Canadian Museum of History) in 1912. The bags were loaned to the Bois Forte Heritage Center when it opened in 2001, but they have since been returned to Canada.[2]

Bois Forte is a relatively isolated place. Few photographers appear to have visited it—and even fewer documented the early beadwork of the Bois Forte Reservation communities in the last half of the nineteenth century. Figure 6.03, an image taken by anthropologist William Jones, shows Chief Debwawendunk, or Moses Day, with his wife Sahkahmequaybeake at Nett Lake. He wears two gashkibidaaganag and displays a third. The bags each appear to have full-width pockets and some sort of decorated space above the pocket opening. While the bag's visible loom-woven motifs do not match those on the loom-woven bag in Figure 6.02, they all appear to be of the same large scale. The visible zigzag strap motifs and exploding X themes on Debwawendunk's pocket panels are similar in scale to the bags in Figures 6.01 and 6.02.[3]

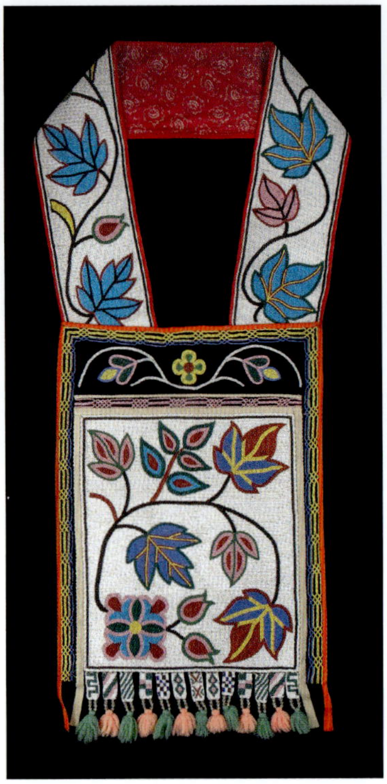

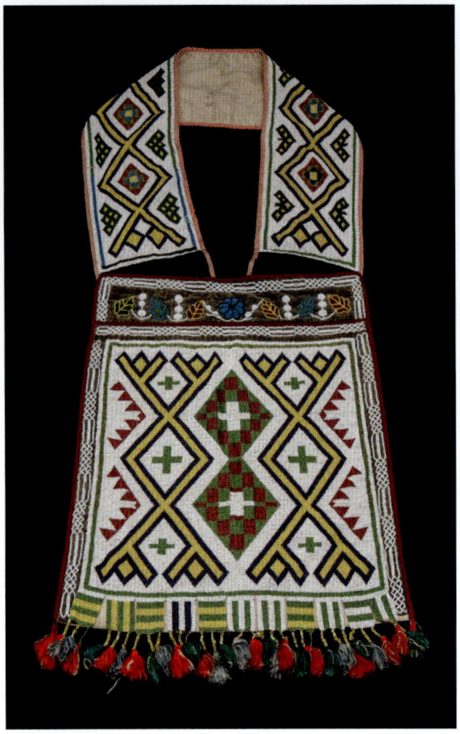

6.01 *(right)* Spot-stitched bag, Bois Forte Reservation, before 1912. *CMH III-G-53*

6.02 *(far right)* Loom-woven bag, Bois Forte Reservation, before 1912. *CMH III-G-54*

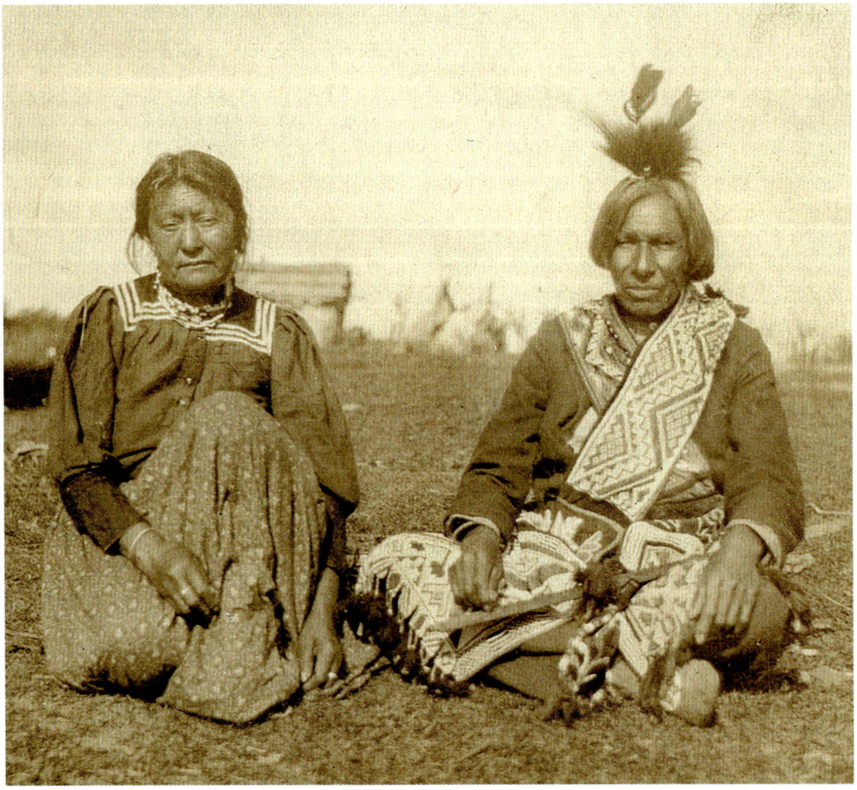

6.03 Debwawendunk (Moses Day) with his wife, Sahkahmequaybeake, at Nett Lake, c. 1904. *Photo by William Jones, American Philosophical Society 3645*

Francis Henry Pequette, missionary

Some of the best Bois Forte gashkibidaaganag are found in photographs made of a missionary who served on the reservation. Francis "Frank" Henry Pequette (Ped-way-way-geshig), possibly a member of the L'Anse Band of Ojibwe, was born in 1856 in Zeba, Michigan. He became a Methodist missionary and served in the Northern Minnesota Conference from about 1899 until his death in 1937. In 1907 the mission where he served as deacon was relocated from Wakemup Bay to Nett Lake on the Bois Forte Reservation. Pequette's wife Georgina and his niece, Bessie Lightfoot, accompanied him in his work. His preaching circuit ranged from Vineland to Nett Lake.[4]

Photographs show Pequette wearing both ecclesiastical garb and Euro-American street wear—and gashkibidaaganag. These images, held in a number of repositories, document his ongoing interaction with Minnesota's non-Indian communities as well as the members of the nations and missions he served. Because he was fluent in both Ojibwe and English, he served in various regional capacities beyond his role as a missionary. A newspaper account notes that in about 1910, a contest was held to name a new tuberculosis sanatorium near Fond du Lac. Pequette won the contest by submitting the name *Nopeming*, which means "out in the woods" in Ojibwe. He made two trips to Washington, DC: in 1907 he served as Chief Moses Day's interpreter, and in 1913 he was a member of a delegation from Fond du Lac Reservation.[5]

Pequette was well connected in northern Minnesota, and he likely spent much time traveling among his many mission locations. He assisted British ethnographer Beatrice Blackwood during her collecting visits to Minnesota in 1925 and 1939. Images of Pequette and several Ojibwe stories he recounted are found in the Blackwood collections held by the Pitt Rivers Museum in Oxford, England.

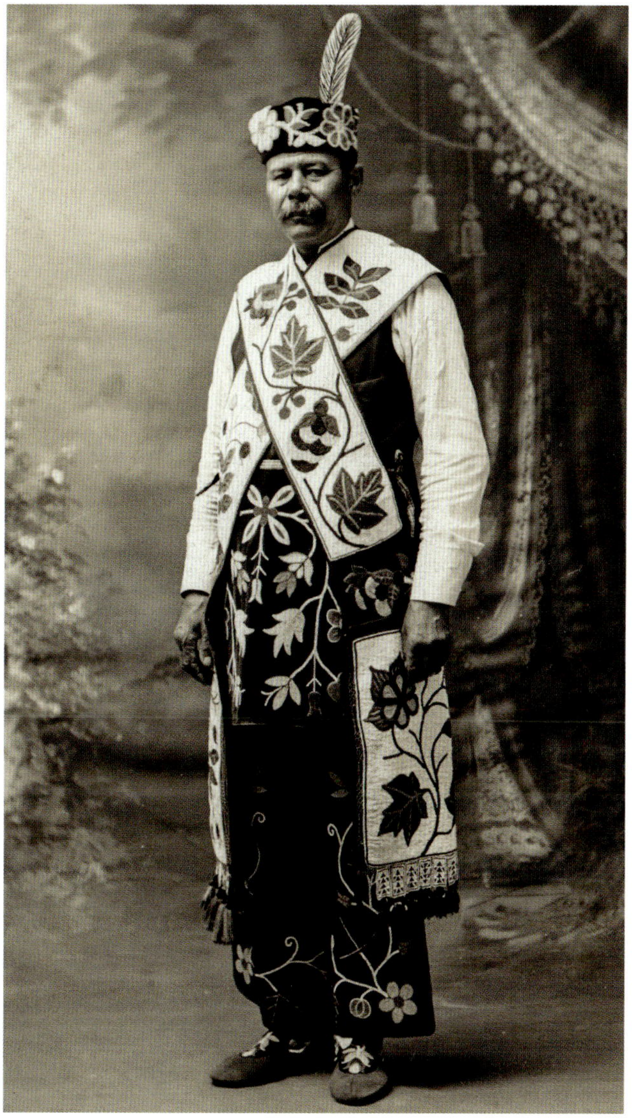

6.04 Reverend Frank Pequette in Indian clothing, c. 1909–12. *MNHS E97.1P r5*

Pequette had also worked with musicologist Stella Stocker in 1916, and her albums include images of him wearing gashkibidaaganag. In Figure 6.04, Pequette wears two oversized spot-stitched bags with attached loom-woven tab and tassel fringe. The composition of the bags indicates that the pocket openings were the full width of the pocket, but their large size also suggests that they may simply have been panel bags with no functioning pocket. The floral motifs are not entirely

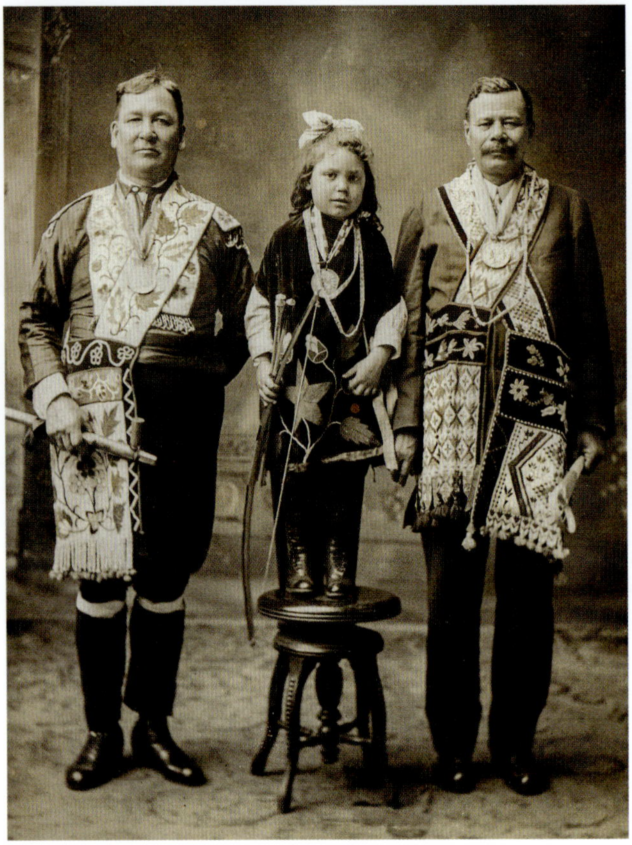

6.05 Reverend Frank Pequette (*right*) with Reverend Duane Porter and his daughter, c. 1910. *MNHS E97.1P r9*

dissimilar to those used by other Minnesota Ojibwe women, and even though the bags are greatly oversized, the motifs still seem to flow, reflecting the freedom of design seen in most spot-stitch appliqué bags made by Minnesota Ojibwe bead artists.[6]

In Figure 6.05, Pequette wears two loom-woven bags. The one on his left hip is more typical of documented Minnesota forms, with the exploding X pocket panel, full-width pocket opening, and integrated loom-woven tab fringe finished in wool yarn tassels. The one on his right hip features the smaller-scale repetitive motif more common among Great Lakes nations outside of Minnesota. Reverend Duane Frank Porter, an Ojibwe man and Methodist missionary whose family had lived in what became Pine County, wears one spot-stitch appliqué bag and a spot-stitched yoke underneath.[7]

Who made the visually striking and massive bags shown in these historical images? Pequette's wife was variously registered as born in Michigan or Canada; listed as Mrs. F. H. Pequette, Georgina, Georgiana, Georgenia, Georgianna, Ishquaahchebequoquay, or Ishquashehebequoquay; and recorded as a full-blood member of the L'Anse Band of the Mackinac Agency in Michigan. Georgina may very well have been the creator of all the bags Frank is shown wearing, and particularly the spot-stitch appliqué ones. Her mother, Nancy Bedell, was born in Michigan in about 1830 and was also recorded as a member of the L'Anse Band in the Mackinac Agency. It is also possible that Nancy was a bead artist who taught her daughter to bead or may even have worked on bags with her daughter while living with the Pequettes in Minnesota.[8]

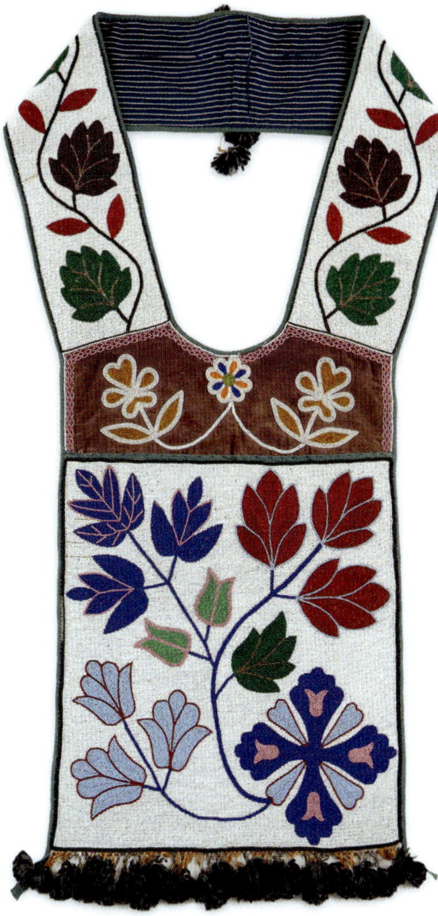

Chapter 7

Fond du Lac

Ojibwe people have long lived in the area that is now Duluth, Minnesota, and Superior, Wisconsin. An ancient portage crossed Minnesota Point at about the place where the ship canal now flows under Duluth's Lift Bridge. The name now used for the Fond du Lac Reservation—Nagaajiwanaang, or Where the Flow of the River Stops—referred to the slowing of the St. Louis River below the rapids. In 1679, Daniel Greysolon, Sieur du Lhut, arrived at the westernmost point of Lake Superior, which he called the *fond du lac*, or "bottom of the lake." He met with Ojibwe and Dakota people, attempting to establish a peace that would further French fur-trading interests. In the years that followed, Ojibwe families from several small bands traded with French, British, and American fur companies until 1854, when, under pressure from Euro-Americans, the Fond du Lac Reservation was established in Carlton and St. Louis Counties. About four hundred Ojibwe living in the area moved up the St. Louis River to a location that became the reservation for the Fond du Lac Band of Lake Superior Chippewa. The three reservation districts include the tribal headquarters in Cloquet as well as Brookston and Sawyer.[1]

Today the Fond du Lac Band of Lake Superior Chippewa has established both the Fond du Lac Tribal and Community College and the Fond du Lac Reservation Cultural Center and Museum in Cloquet. The bag in Figure 7.01 is on display at the cultural center, and those in Figures 7.02, 7.03, and 7.04 can be found at the Min No Aya Win Human Services Center nearby. All four bags are of the type seen more frequently on the eastern side of the state and often north of Duluth. What distinguishes them as typically from Fond du Lac includes a group of characteristics: all have a scooped edge between the straps above the pocket, are larger than average, have a symmetrical design above the pocket opening, and appear to have full-width pocket openings. In addition, all four of the bags have a darker color palette than is generally seen in bags from White Earth and other northwestern Minnesota reservations. Three of the bags are spot-stitch appliqué, and the bag in Figure 7.03 is decorated with loom-woven panels and spot-stitch appliqué above the faux pocket opening. The words "Paul Piska Basswood Lake" are beaded in the area above the pocket panel in Figure 7.04. Basswood is a border lake now located in the Superior National Forest near Fall Lake, Minnesota, crossing into Canada. Generations of Piska family members have lived in the Thunder Bay area, associated with the Thunder Bay Reserve.

Fond du Lac Band member Mary LaFave, born in 1909, fondly remembered her childhood and the warm feelings that rituals, beadwork, and other cultural traditions brought her as a young girl:

> I remember a lot of happiness and a lot of rituals. In one, we went into a wigwam. There was nothing going on in there, but boy you should see the pretty things they had up. Nice blankets and nice beadwork they had up in there around the inside of the wigwam. I don't know if they done this

7.01 *(below)* Spot-stitch appliqué bag, Fond du Lac Reservation, twentieth century. *FDLCCM*

7.02 *(below right)* Spot-stitch appliqué bag, Fond du Lac Reservation, twentieth century. Excluding the color palette, this bag more closely resembles examples from the Cass Lake area in northwestern Minnesota. *MNAWHSC*

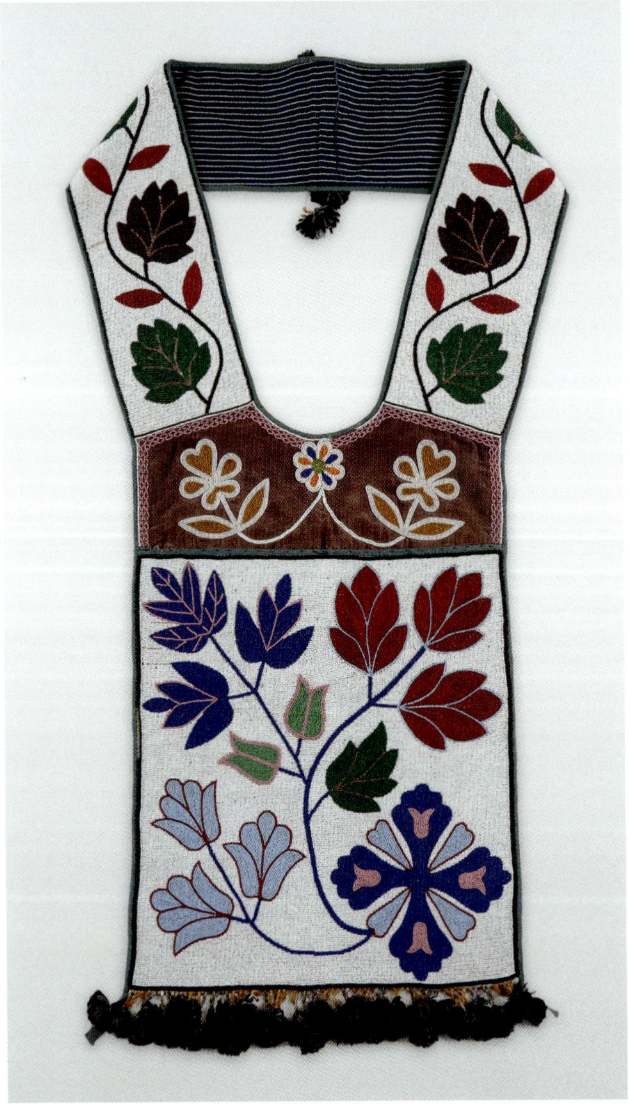

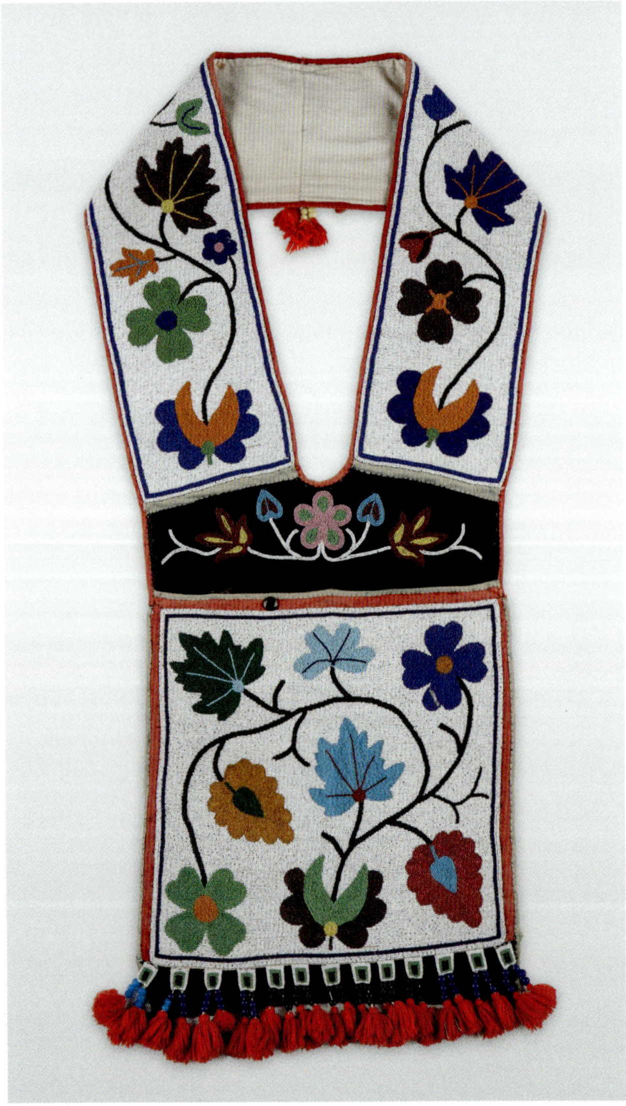

for people to see, but I sure thought it was pretty. They had deerskins that were tanned. They had some kind of baskets where they used to keep their tobacco. There was great big beadwork that they put over their shoulders.[2]

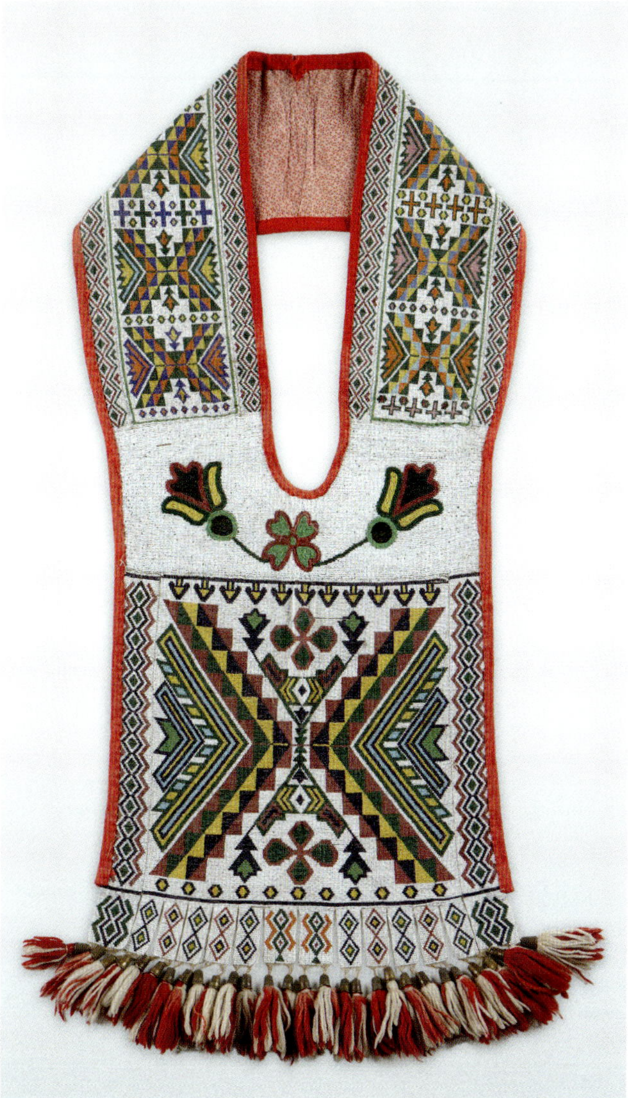

7.03 Bag decorated with loom-woven panels and spot-stitch appliqué above the faux pocket opening, Fond du Lac Reservation. The printed cotton backing has a floral sprig design and a red with pink palette popular in the 1870s and 1880s, but the size of the bag and the motif repetition suggest a twentieth-century creation. *MNAWHSC*

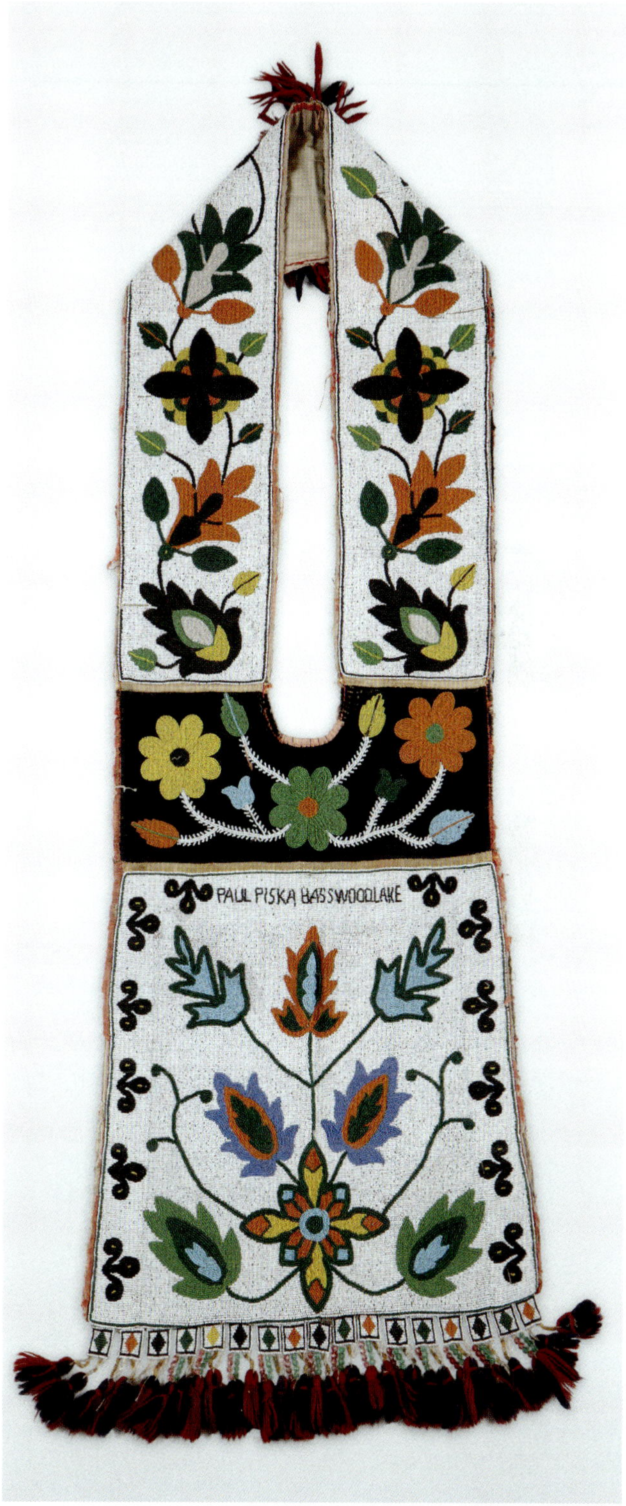

7.04 Bag associated with Paul Piska of Thunder Bay, Canada, twentieth century. It also has a false or faux pocket opening mimicking a full-width opening. *MNAWHSC*

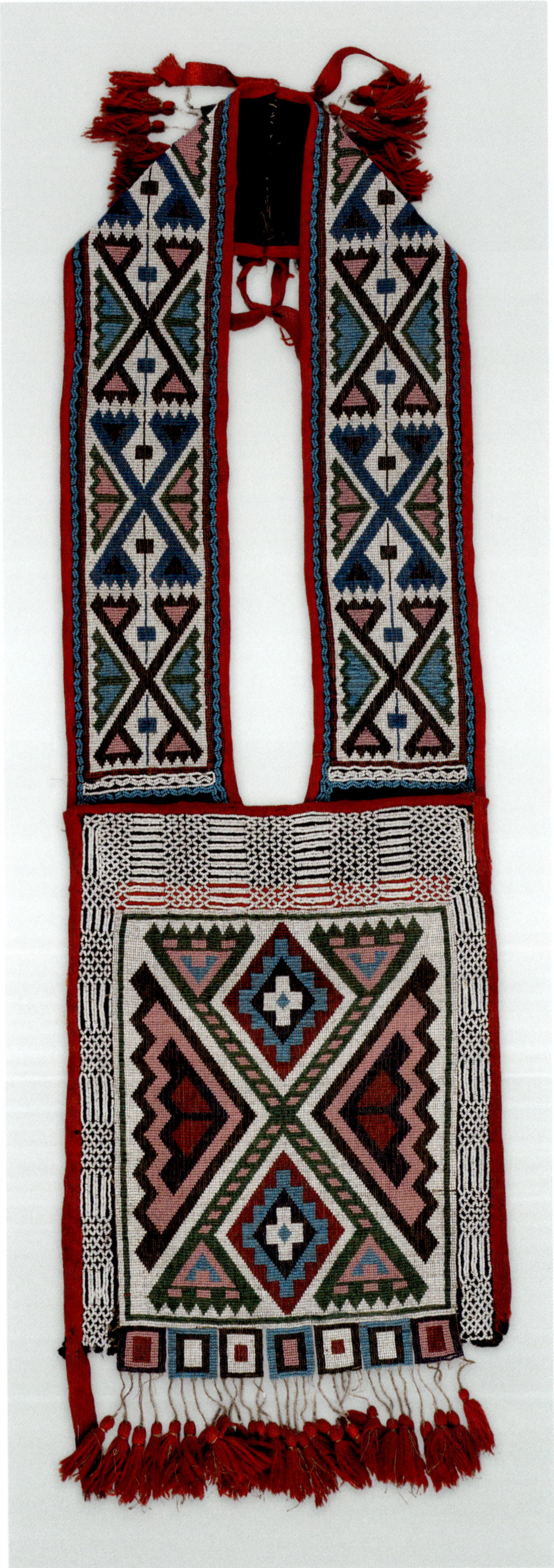

Frank C. Berry, collector

Frank C. Berry (1859–1914), a white collector of gashkibidaaganag, lived for many years in Duluth, about forty miles from the Fond du Lac Reservation. For twelve years he worked as a "commercial traveler"—a traveling salesman—for the Wright-Clarkson Mercantile Company, a role in which he was well regarded and successful. His territory included Douglas, Todd, Wadena, Hubbard, Cass, Beltrami, Itasca, Aitkin, and Crow Wing Counties in northern Minnesota—an area that also contained the Bois Forte, Leech Lake, Red Lake, and Mille Lacs Reservations. In addition, White Earth and Fond du Lac Reservations were also easily accessible from Berry's regular route and from his home county of St. Louis. It's reasonable to think that he had contact with merchants serving these reservation communities and with the Ojibwe themselves. In May 1910, Berry was promoted and his work was then based in the central office in Duluth. His collecting activities probably predated his promotion. Shortly before his death in 1914, Berry moved to Mississippi for health reasons.[3]

While it is impossible to know their exact reservation sources, eight gashkibidaaganag collected by Frank C. Berry provide a sampling of several styles of loom-woven and spot-stitched bags made in northern Minnesota before 1910. The three bags with loom-woven beadwork in Figures 7.05, 7.06, and 7.07 are all from a later phase of loomed bags, probably 1880s to early 1890s. Their larger bag size and larger motifs, as well as their floral motifs, speak to the stylistic shifts in later loom-woven bags. Each bag treats the area above the pocket differently, but all three still incorporate characteristics more common among earlier bags, such as integrated woven tab fringe and the exploding X as the primary motif on the pocket panel. The bags in Figures 7.05 and 7.06 retain the otter-track pattern as the primary edging; each has straps covered with loom-woven strips and additional fringe at the center, where the strips meet; their color palettes are common in

7.05 Loom-woven bag, Frank Berry collection, before 1910. *MNHS 6333.6.E; see also Figure 3.12*

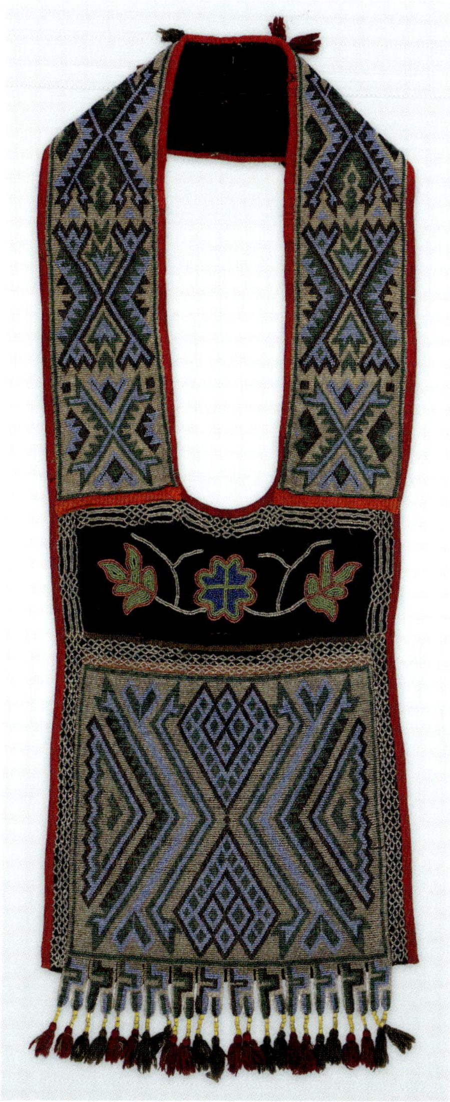

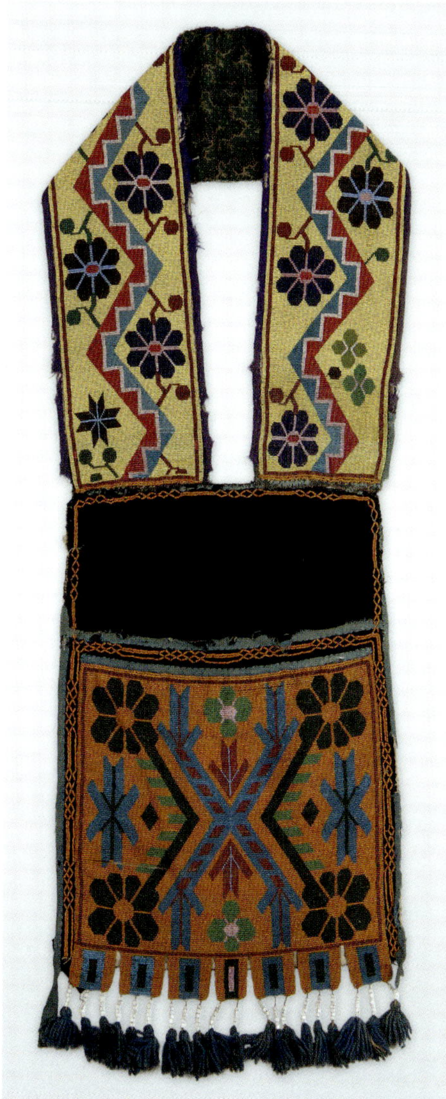

7.06 *(far left)* Loom-woven bag, Frank Berry collection, before 1910. *MNHS 6333.6.G; see also Figure 3.26*

7.07 *(left)* Loom-woven bag, Frank Berry collection, before 1910. *MNHS 6333.6.F; see also Figure 3.42*

Minnesota loom-woven bags. The bead background of the bag pocket panel in Figure 7.07 is created in "greasy yellow," a color that was less common and is thus favored by collectors.

The spot-stitch appliqué styles shown in Figures 7.08–11 existed simultaneously. Figures 7.08, 7.09, and 7.10 show the range of bag styles in the late nineteenth to early twentieth centuries. All three incorporate a common looped-thread fringe strung with bugle beads and wool tassels. Figures 7.09 and 7.10 include the larger-scale border motifs that were replacing the smaller otter-track line designs common in earlier bags, while Figure 7.08 combines a single line of otter-track beadwork with a larger zigzag variation. Figure 7.11 is typical of a later phase, seen well into the 1940s, when the pockets began to disappear, until eventually the pocket panel and the area above the pocket opening were merged to become a single beaded panel. This bag continues to incorporate a full-width pocket opening and it retains the earlier style of loomed tab fringe, but visually the pocket represents a continuous beaded panel from the fringe to the strap.[4]

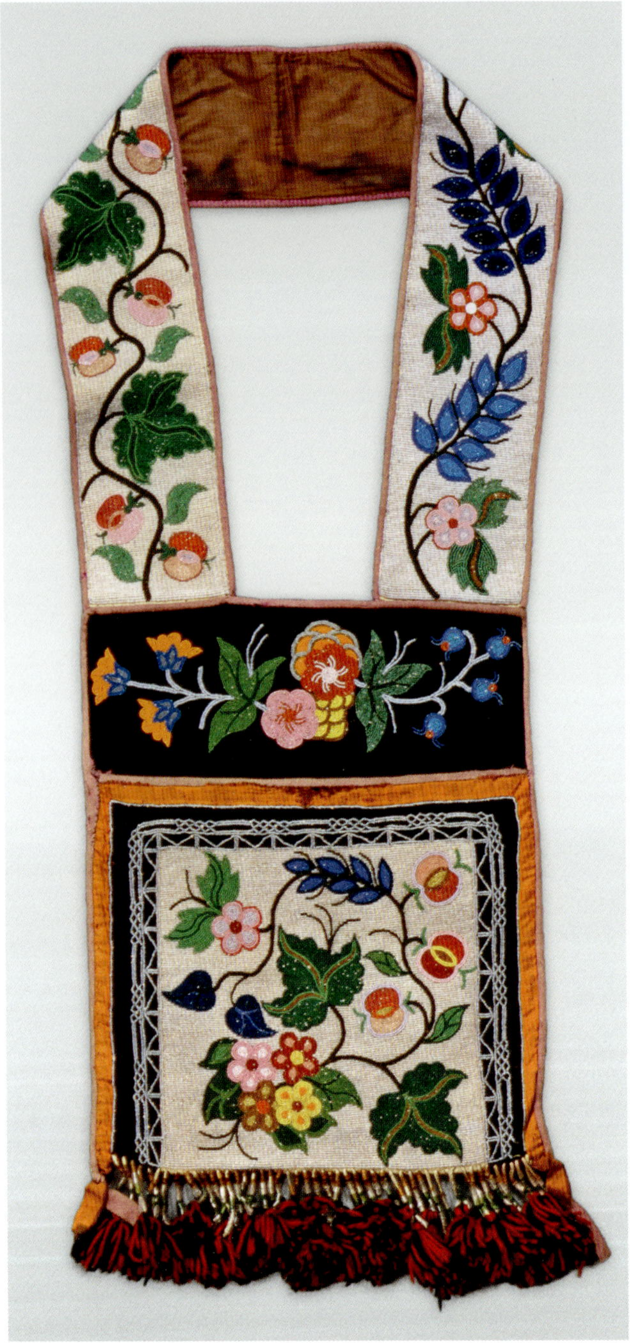

7.08 Spot-stitch appliqué bag, Frank Berry collection, before 1910. *MNHS 6333.6.D*

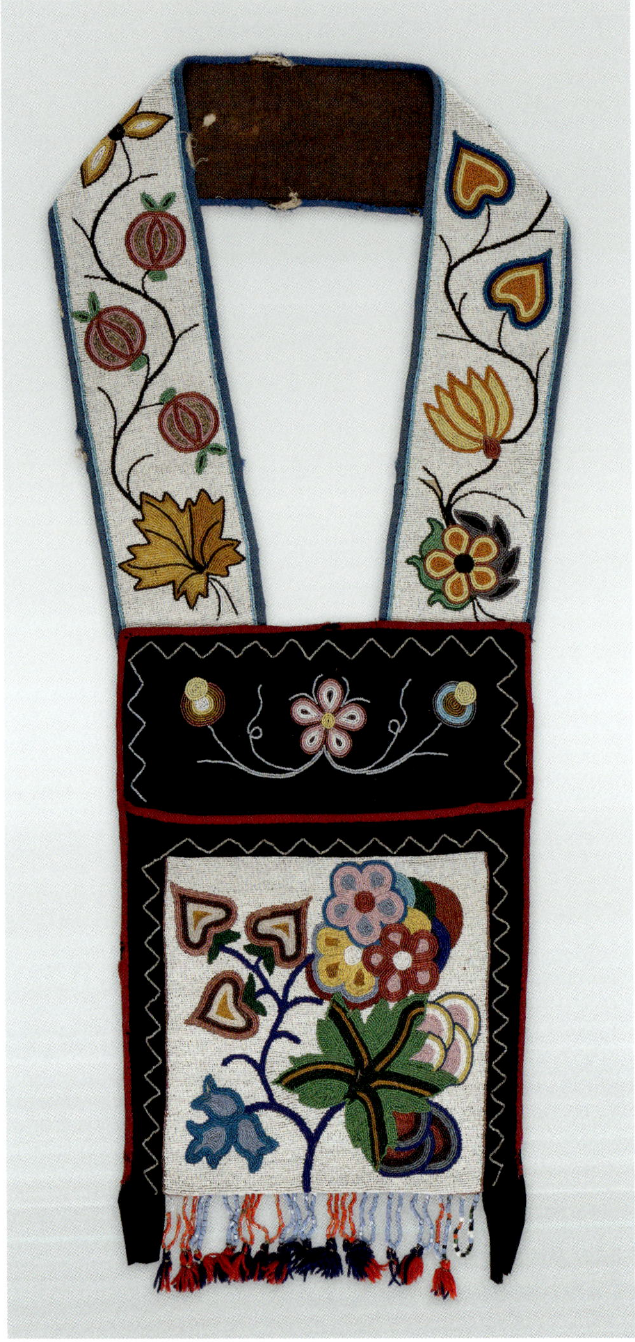

7.09 Spot-stitch appliqué bag, Frank Berry collection, before 1910. *MNHS 6333.6.H; see also Figures 3.14, 3.61, 3.67*

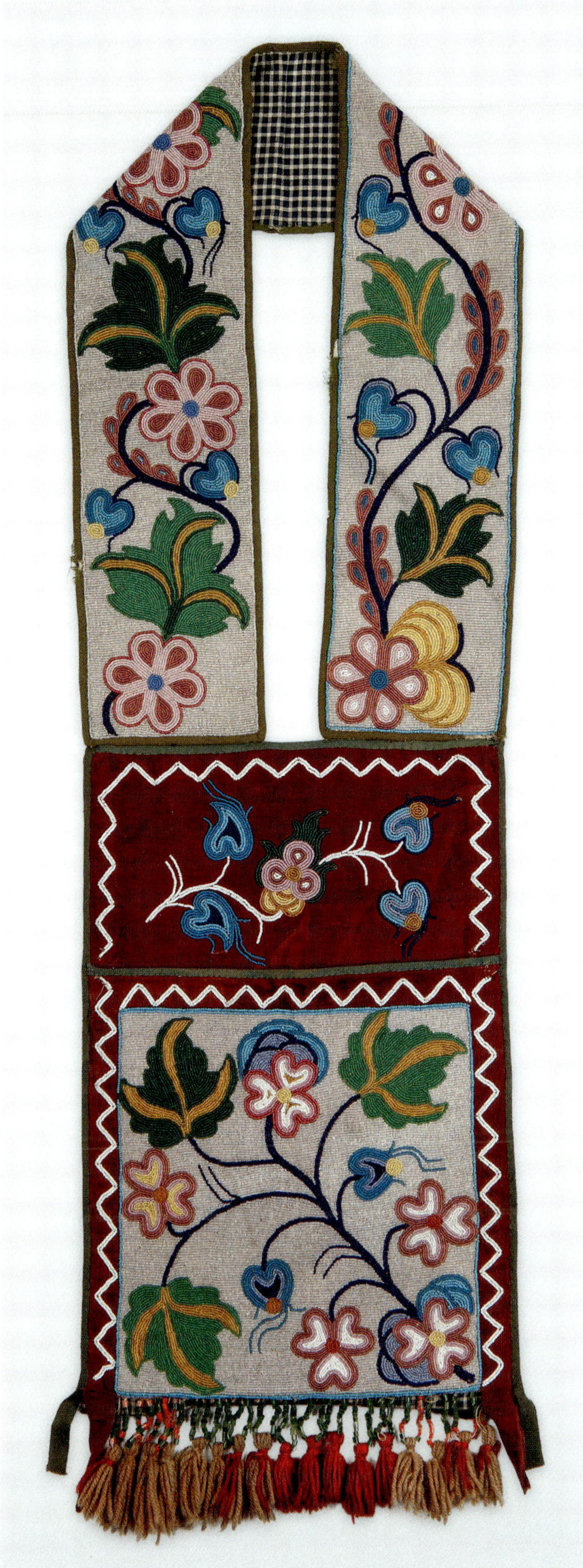

7.10 Spot-stitch appliqué bag, Frank Berry collection, before 1910. *MNHS 6333.6.A; see also Figure 3.48*

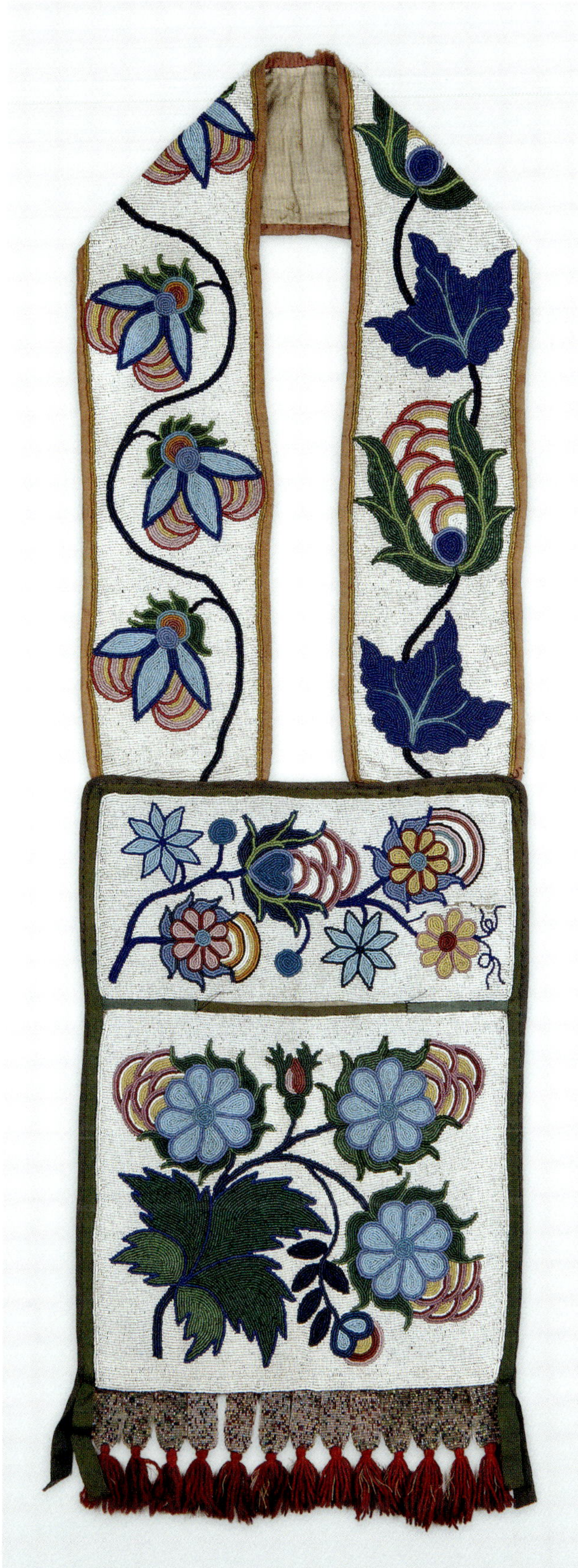

7.11 Spot-stitch appliqué bag, Frank Berry collection, before 1910. *MNHS 6333.6.C*

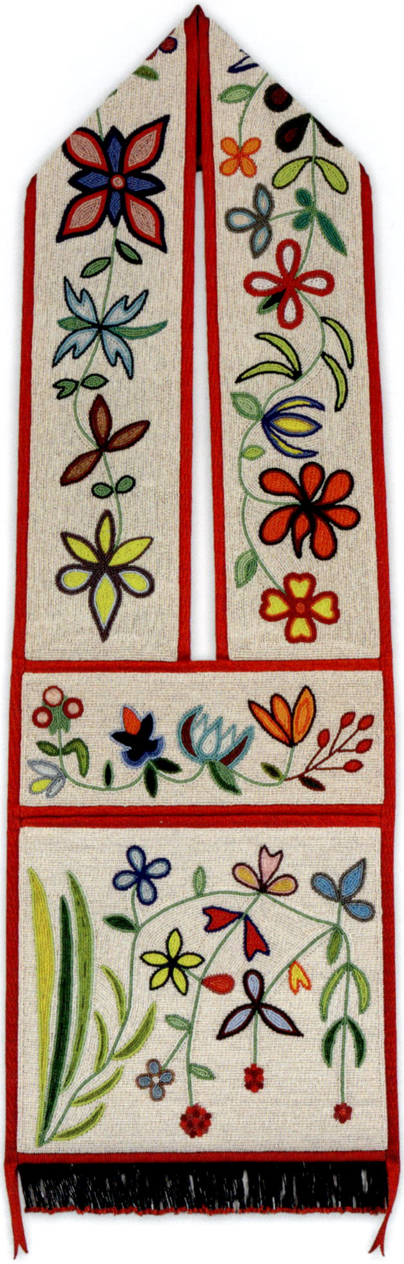

Chapter 8

Grand Portage

The Ojibwe community at Grand Portage (Gichi-onigamiing) has a long and culturally rich history. Grand Portage takes its name from the nine-mile track bypassing the waterfalls and rapids of the lower Pigeon River as it drops down to Lake Superior. At the western end of the portage are the waterways that carried traders into the heart of the continent—and furs back out. By the 1740s this strategic location had made Grand Portage the major fur trading depot on Lake Superior, and the Grand Portage Ojibwe interacted with fur traders; with the many Ojibwe communities to the north, in what would become Canada; and with the Assiniboine, the Cree, and other tribes. American influence began in earnest after the War of 1812, and the Treaty of 1854 established the Grand Portage Reservation. Today, the Grand Portage Band continues its interaction with many cultures through historical demonstrations at the National Park Service's Grand Portage National Monument.[1]

Surviving gashkibidaaganag associated with this community are rare, as are historical photographs of them. The majority of existing bags fall into two groups. The first group of bags was created in the 1930s to 1940s as part of a large New Deal art project for the Works Progress Administration (WPA); the second group spans bag makers from three generations of one Grand Portage family.

Some of the Grand Portage beadwork made for the WPA project is held in the Tweed Museum in Duluth. Other examples in the collections of the National Park Service at the Grand Portage National Monument Heritage Center include two gashkibidaaganag, one of them shown in Figure 8.01. Band member Joe Hunter wears this bag in Figures 8.02 and 8.03. Joe's wife, Nancy Hunter, wears another bag in Figure 8.02 that is also seen in several other images from 1939 and 1940. The pocket portions of two of the three bags visible in Figures 8.02 and 8.03 provide evidence of a frequent preference in Grand Portage gashkibidaagan construction: they have a curved cutout at the top edge of the area above the pocket panel. The majority of documented Minnesota Ojibwe bags from reservation communities other than Fond du Lac have a straight edge in this location.[2]

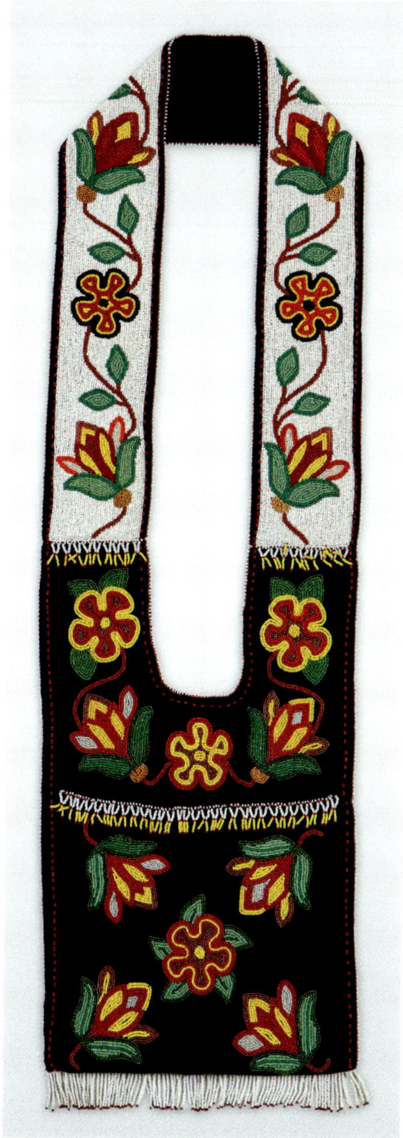

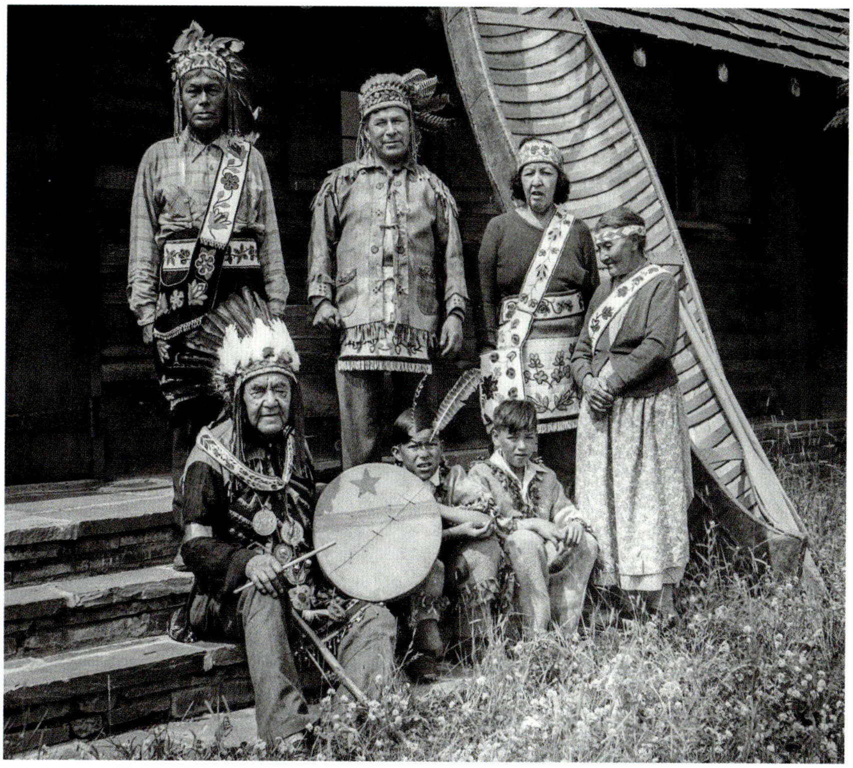

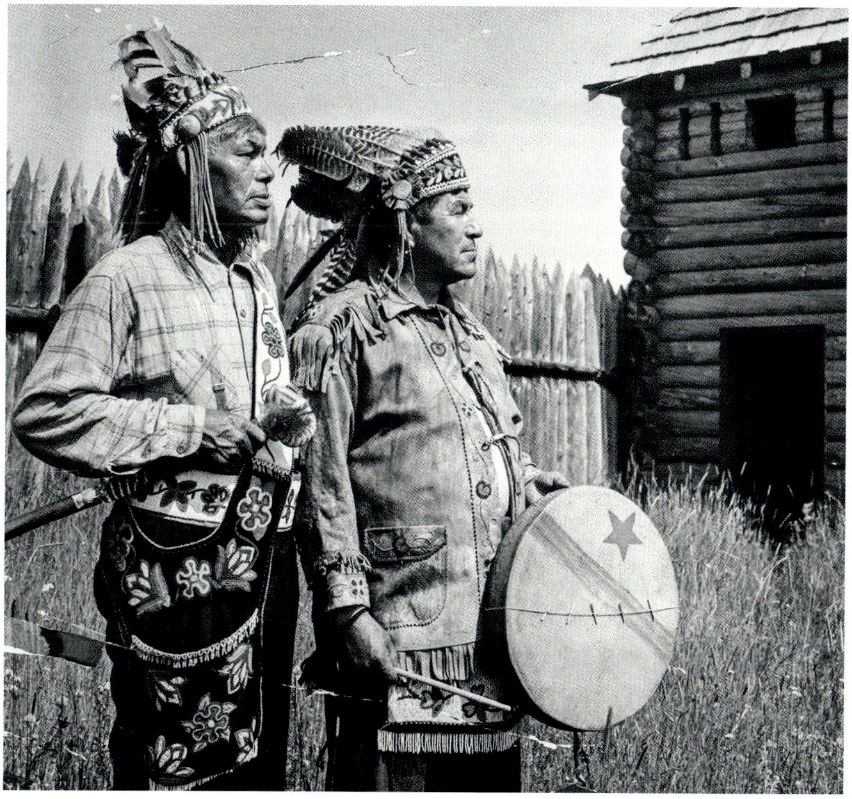

8.01 *(above)* Spot-stitch appliqué bag made as part of a Works Progress Administration program, Grand Portage National Monument, c. 1930s–1940s. *GPNM 1252*

8.02 *(above left)* Grand Portage, 1945. *Back row*: Joe Hunter, Alec Bushman, Nancy Hunter. *Front row*: Chief Nahbugdway (Mike Flatte), Francis Hunter, Tony LeSage, and Nancy LaPlante. *MNHS E97.1F p10*

8.03 *(left)* Joe Hunter and Alec Bushman wearing Grand Portage beadwork, 1945. *MNHS E97.1 p53*

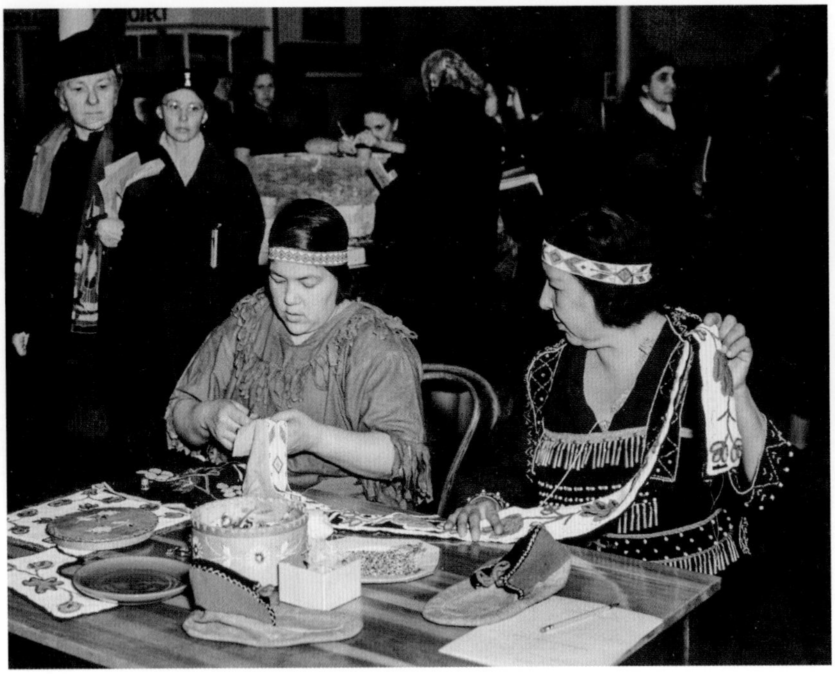

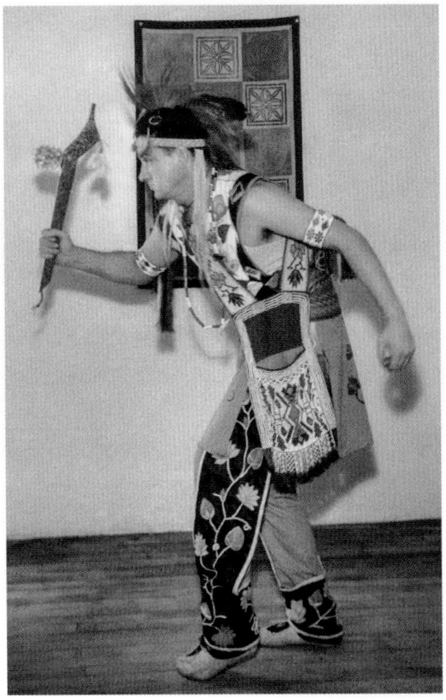

8.04 *(above)* Christina LeSage and Nancy Hunter, 1939. *MNHS E445.6 r14*

8.05 *(above right)* Striking a pose, probably at the photographer's direction, to show a gashkibidaagan, Grand Portage, c. 1938. *MNHS E97.22 r2*

In Figure 8.04, two Grand Portage women—Christina LeSage and Nancy Hunter—assemble the bag worn in Figure 8.02 by Nancy Hunter. They were participating in a 1939 Duluth beadwork demonstration as part of an "American Hands in Action" WPA event.[3]

The WPA project at Grand Portage also produced the beadwork shown in Figure 8.05. The man wears a spot-stitch appliqué bib collar and a loom-woven gashkibidaagan. The current whereabouts of these two items is unknown.[4]

A second group of Grand Portage bags were made by three artists who represent three generations of a family—the only three-generation group of gashkibidaagan makers I have been able to document. These beadworkers are Mary Posey (Sangwaywaince or Sangwekwe, possibly a diminutive form of her Ojibwe name; 1880–1964), Ellen Bushman Olson, and Marcie McIntire. According to Ellen Olson, Mrs. Posey made all the beadwork worn by her husband, Alec Posey, including his beaded yoke. She also made gashkibidaaganag and other dance regalia for other members of the Grand Portage Reservation community, including all of Alex LeSage's beaded regalia.[5]

Ellen said that Alec Posey sometimes carried tobacco and long pipes in his bandolier bag, shown in Figure 8.06. Like the bags in Figures 8.02 and 8.03, Alec Posey's bag has a curved cutout at the top edge of the area above the pocket panel. Both the pocket and the strap incorporate loom-woven geometric motifs, and the area above the pocket and at the bottom ends of the strap feature spot-stitched floral motifs. The fringe consists of short loom-woven tabs, each with a glass bead strung onto warps twisted to form a single strand that terminates in a tassel made from red and white flat ribbons. Tassels are also repeated at the center top of the strap.

The bag appears in several photographs in the 1930s, worn by Alec and by other members of the Grand Portage community, which suggests that Mary may have made it in the 1920s. Studies of those historical images also suggest that the current pristine ribbon fringe is a later replacement or addition. It's easy to imagine that it must have been a difficult decision for the Poseys to sell this family heirloom to collector Monroe Killy in 1937.[6]

The Poseys became Ellen Bushman's foster parents when she was young (Figure 8.07). Now Ellen Bushman Olson, she has been a beadworker for much of her life. Ellen's daughter Marcie McIntire represents a contemporary perspective on Ojibwe beadwork and the creation of a gashkibidaagan. Their stories are told below, pages 118 and 122.

A historical photo shows two bags from the same era as Mary Posey's work. At a 1924 Grand Portage celebration on July 4, two members of the LeGarde family each wear a distinctive gashkibidaagan (Figure 8.08). On the left, Frank LeGarde's bag is constructed with a barely visible curved cutout above the pocket panel, while his son Paul wears a bag with a straight edge above the pocket. Both bags are decorated with loom-woven beadwork and are also embellished above the pocket opening with spot-stitch appliqué.[7]

Another Grand Portage bag includes elements similar to LeGarde's and Posey's. In 1914 collector Albert Green Heath acquired a bag (Figure 8.09) from the Grand Portage Reservation that features a cutout at the top edge

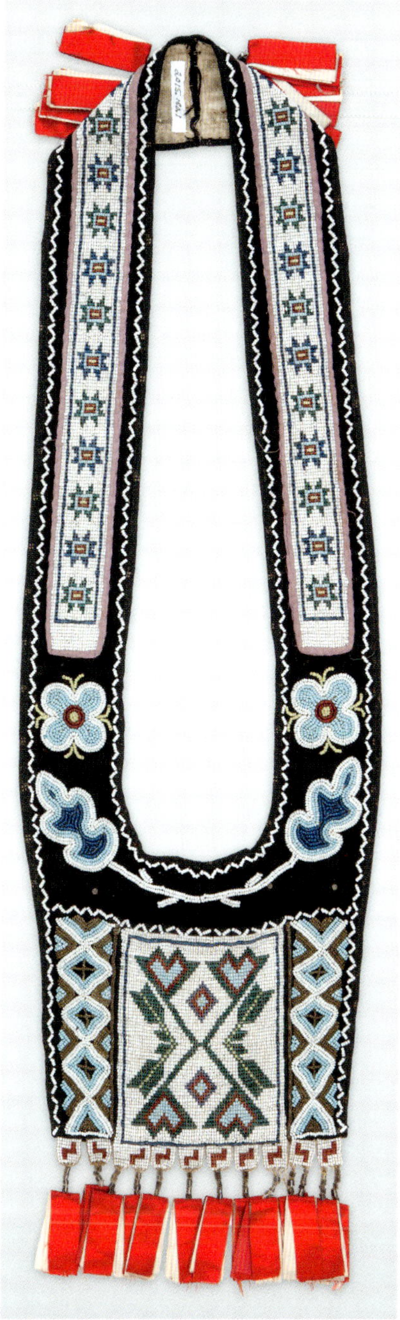

8.06 *(above)* Gashkibidaagan Mary Posey made for her husband, Alec, c. 1920s. *MNHS 2015.180.1*

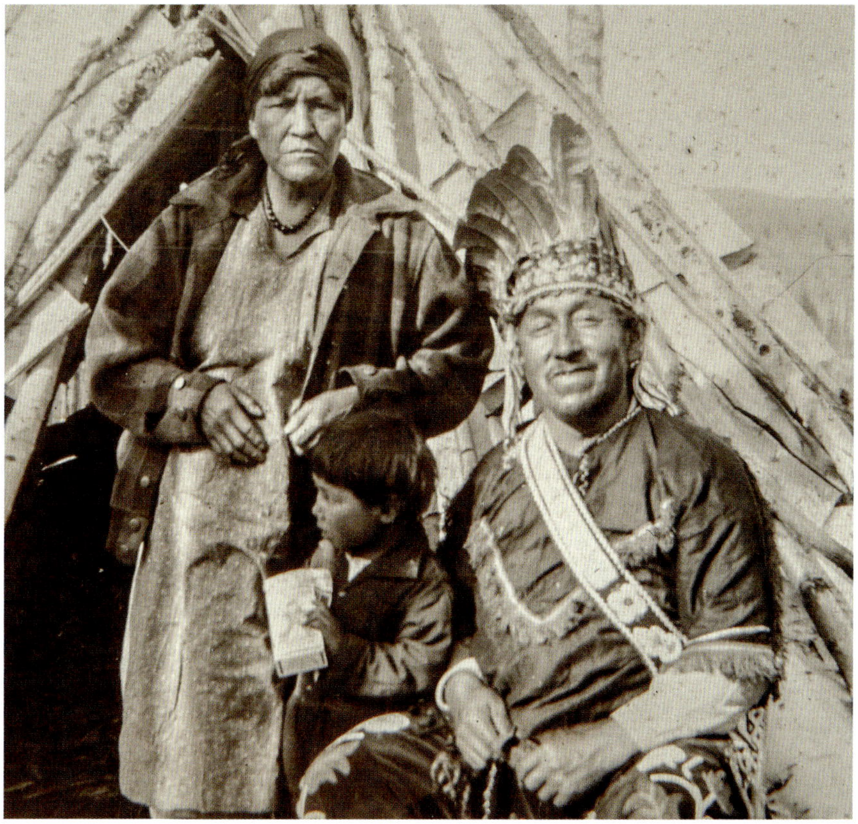

8.07 *(left)* Mary and Alec Posey with their foster daughter Ellen, Grand Portage, 1930. Alec wears Mary Posey's bag. *Courtesy Ellen Olson*

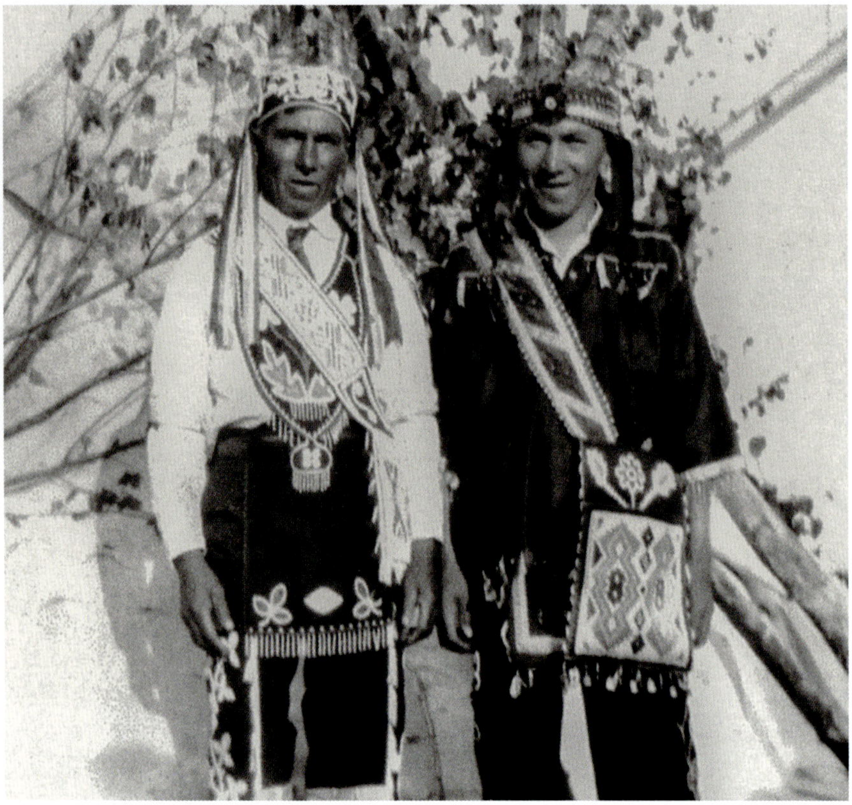

8.08 Frank and Paul LeGarde, Grand Portage, 1924. *CCHS M868.21*

of the pocket and distinctive bright green-and-white contrasting motifs. The fringe, very similar in style to that on the bag made by Mary Posey, consists of short loom-woven tabs, with warps twisted to form three strands that terminate in a red bead and with tassels made from red and white flat ribbons. Ribbon tassels are also found at the center top of the strap.

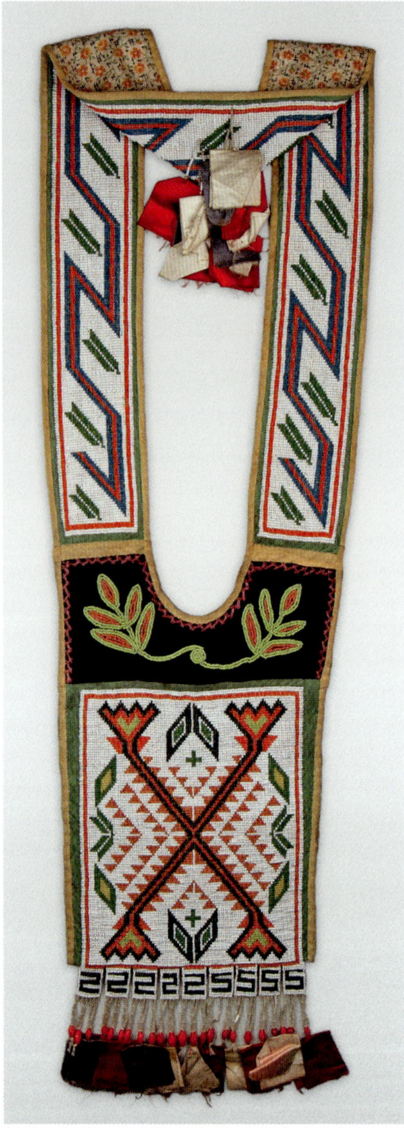

8.09 Loom-woven bag, Grand Portage, collected in 1914. *LMA 31161*

Monroe Killy, collector

In the 1930s, photographer Monroe Killy (1910–2010) began to record American Indian culture in Minnesota. He worked at his father's camera store in Minneapolis when he was a young adult. He visited Minnesota Ojibwe reservations annually with his father, who went north to hunt and fish, often with Ojibwe guides. As a hunter and also a photographer, Monroe developed relationships with many members of the reservation communities, including Nett Lake, Mille Lacs, Grand Portage, and Leech Lake. His photo documentation of indigenous Minnesotans is a rich resource used worldwide by American Indians, scholars, and the general public.

The Minnesota Historical Society holds more than five hundred Killy images taken between 1926 and 1974 documenting Indian life in Minnesota and North Dakota.

Like Frances Densmore, Killy soon extended his photographic efforts and began collecting material culture objects of American Indians (Figure 8.10). He made two complete collections in his lifetime. In the early 1970s, feeling threatened by the American Indian Movement's activity in Minneapolis, he sold the first, and then began collecting again; he sold the second collection to William and Barbara Schoenwetter of Wayzata a few years before his death in 2010.[8]

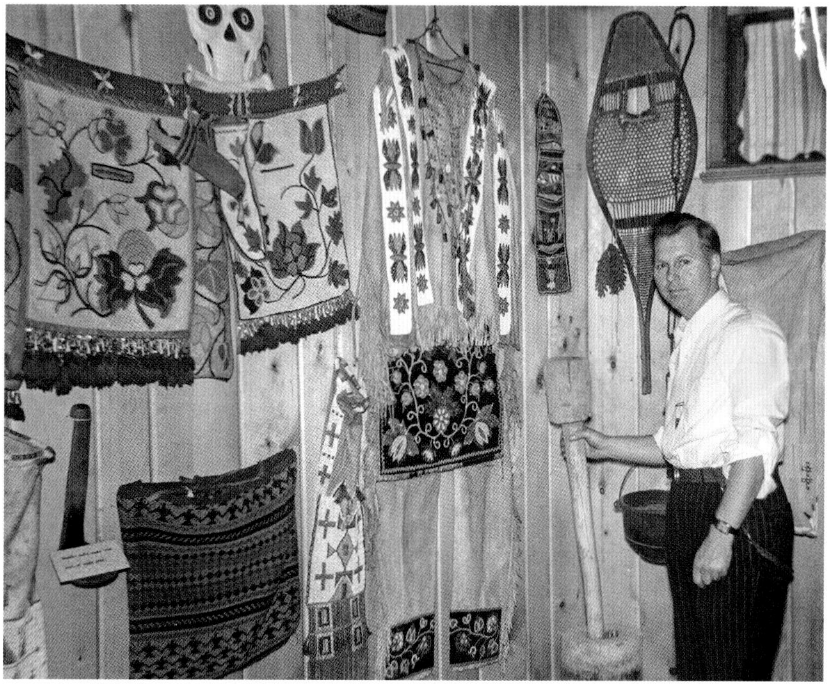

8.10 Monroe Killy with a view of his collection, displayed in his Minneapolis basement, no date. *Author photo*

As his collection grew, and whenever possible, Killy tried to document each transaction by photographing the objects with their makers or users. The most historically significant gashkibidaagan he collected is the rare example from Grand Portage, the bag created by Mary Posey (Figures 8.11 and 8.06). The Schoenwetters donated it to the Minnesota Historical Society in 2015.[9]

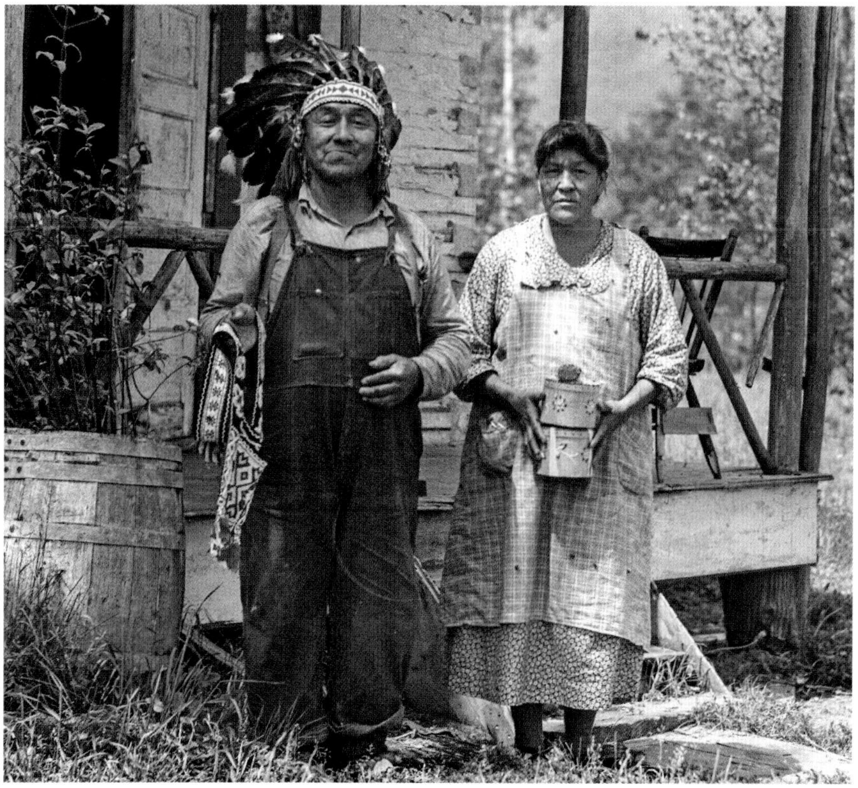

8.11 Alec and Mary Posey in front of their home at Grand Portage, 1937. Alec holds a small gashkibidaagan made by Mary, and she holds two of her quill-worked birchbark boxes. *Photo by Monroe Killy, MNHS E97.1P p15*

Ellen Bushman Olson, bead artist

Ellen Bushman Olson (Figures 8.12 and 8.14) is a bead artist, an elder, and an enrolled member of the Grand Portage Band of Lake Superior Chippewa. As Mary Posey's foster daughter and Marcie McIntire's mother, she represents the middle of three generations of Grand Portage women who have made gashkibidaaganag. A knowledgeable woman with a generous spirit, she agreed to share information in hopes that the words and images of this book would help "the people who make bandolier bags come to life."

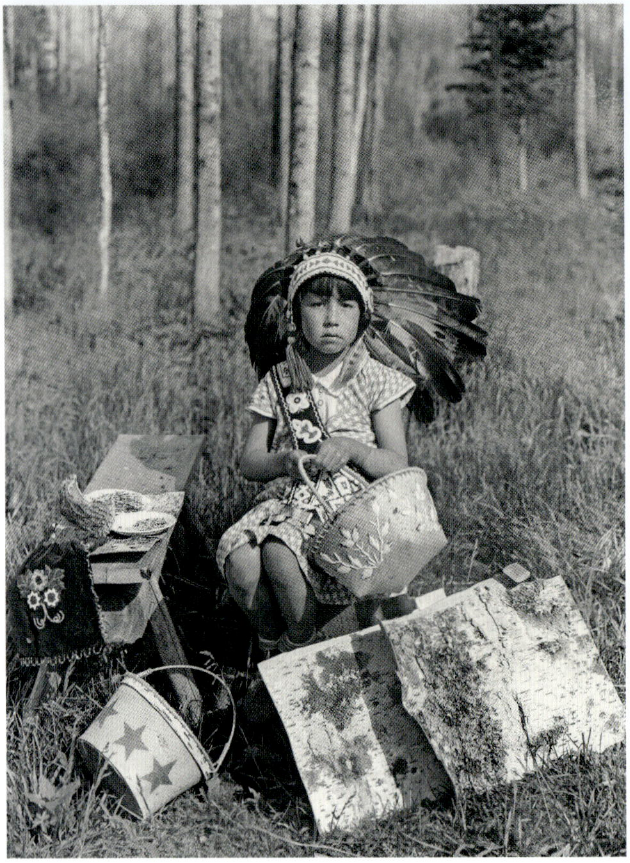

8.12 Ellen Bushman in 1936, surrounded by birchbark and beaded objects. Visible on her right shoulder is the strap of the gashkibidaagan made by her foster mother, Mary Posey. *MNHS E97.1P p1*

Ellen was born in 1929 to Sophie LeSage Crawford and Peter Bushman. Her biological father, Menaheegonce, was from Canada, and her mother's family came from the Maple Hill area of Minnesota, just north of Grand Marais, and from Garden River, Ontario, east of Sault Ste. Marie. She was raised by Alec and Mary Posey, her foster parents. Mary Posey didn't work outside the home. She walked Ellen to school, and Alec picked Ellen up after school daily.[10]

The fur trade was long gone when Ellen was a child, but Grand Portage continued to be a meeting place for Ojibwe people. Families from Nett Lake visited; others came by boat from Canada to pick berries and also walked over the border from the nearby Canadian reserves. Ojibwe regularly came from Canada to play lacrosse (for the men) and stickball (for women), and sometimes they would stay for nearly a month. Others came to Grand Portage to collect their treaty payments and to get farm equipment and animals from government representatives. Early on, some Grand Portage members also lived in Inger, Minnesota, and at Leech Lake. Ellen observed that intermarriage likely led to a loss of material culture specific to the Grand Portage area.

Interactions with people who came from other places provided opportunities for trade. Grand Portage members traded berries for wild rice, as there wasn't much ricing nearby. At busy tourist stands on the northern and southern edges of the reservation, Grand Portage women sold their crafts, including birchbark and beadwork items, as well as soda and candy (Figure 8.13).

Mary Posey's mother, Mrs. Spruce, taught Mary to bead, and Ellen learned beadwork and other skills by watching Mary and three aunties: Eva LeSage, Cecelia LeSage Hendrickson, and Christina LeSage. During the Great Depression, when Ellen was about ten years old, Mary gave her some used twill weave red wool, green bias tape, colorful ribbon, and glass beads. Ellen took these materials and made them into a belt for Alec, who wore it often and bragged that his little girl made it for him.

"From the time I was a child it was my ambition to do beadwork," said Ellen. "I was especially interested in someday making bandolier bags and full regalia." She also knew that it could take years to make one of these bags.

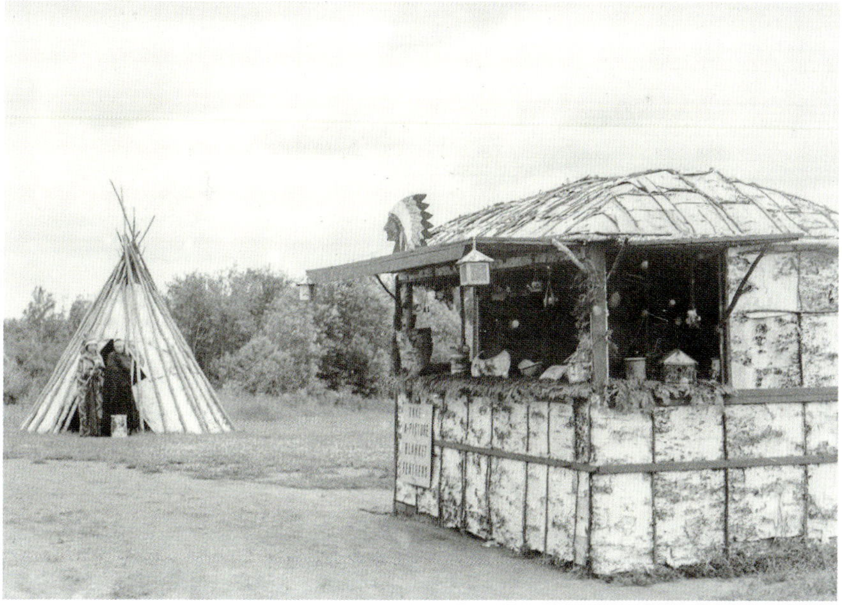

8.13 Souvenir stand at Mineral Center, on the northern edge of the Grand Portage Reservation, c. 1940. *MNHS HF4.9 r49*

In the late 1920s, echoing the pattern of the fur trade, a man came from Montreal annually to sell beads, ribbon, and cloth at Grand Portage. Ellen recalled that beads cost about fifteen cents a tube during the Depression. By 1935 the trading post on nearby Susie Island, run by Effie Falconer McClean, always had beads for sale, and the beadworkers at Grand Portage bought from her.[11]

Ellen remembers that during the Depression, the Ojibwe found resourceful ways to make many kinds of bags out of "nothing." They used nettle fibers, they unraveled blankets, and they recycled lots of other materials. New cloth and ribbons were scarce. If one of the women had a stash of fabric and beads, she shared it with others. Bags and other fabric-based items were made with flour sacks and old blankets. To decorate her beaded cloth items, Mary Posey used cotton thread and, when she could get it, grosgrain ribbon from France. During this tough economic time, "Women became important because their beadwork had monetary value," Ellen noted, "and they often became the moneymakers. The old ways were disappearing, and that left men on the reservation fewer sources of income."

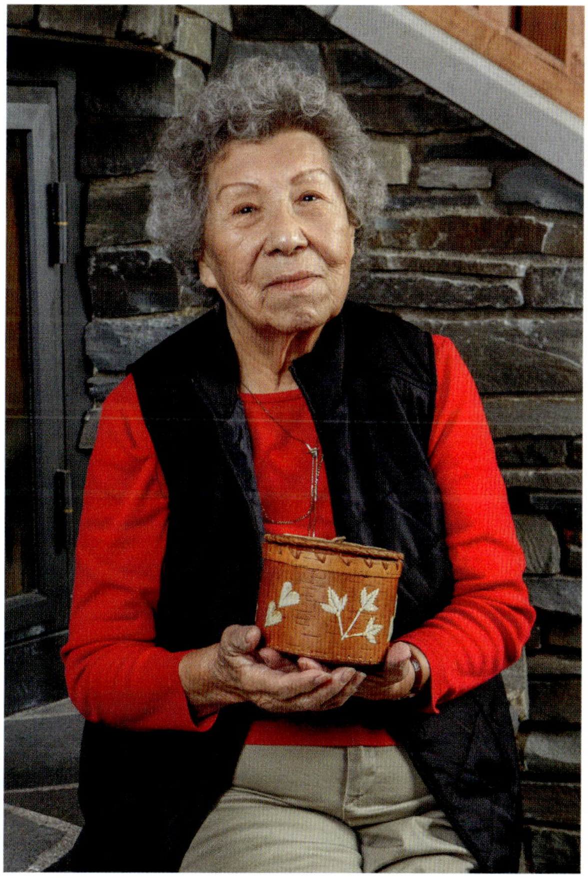

8.14 Ellen Olson at the Grand Portage Heritage Center, 2016. *Photo by James Castle*

The WPA employment program at Grand Portage, overseen by the Minnesota Historical Society, ran from approximately 1937 to 1939. While many Grand Portage men were occupied building the log school up the hill, the program for women focused on demonstrating craft activities to tourists. There were no formal teachers, and the WPA workers were band members living around Grand Portage. All the WPA craft activity took place inside the area that is now the Grand Portage National Monument. Three women would demonstrate at a time in the Crawford Cabin, and tourists came and went while the women worked. The women made quilled baskets, plain baskets,

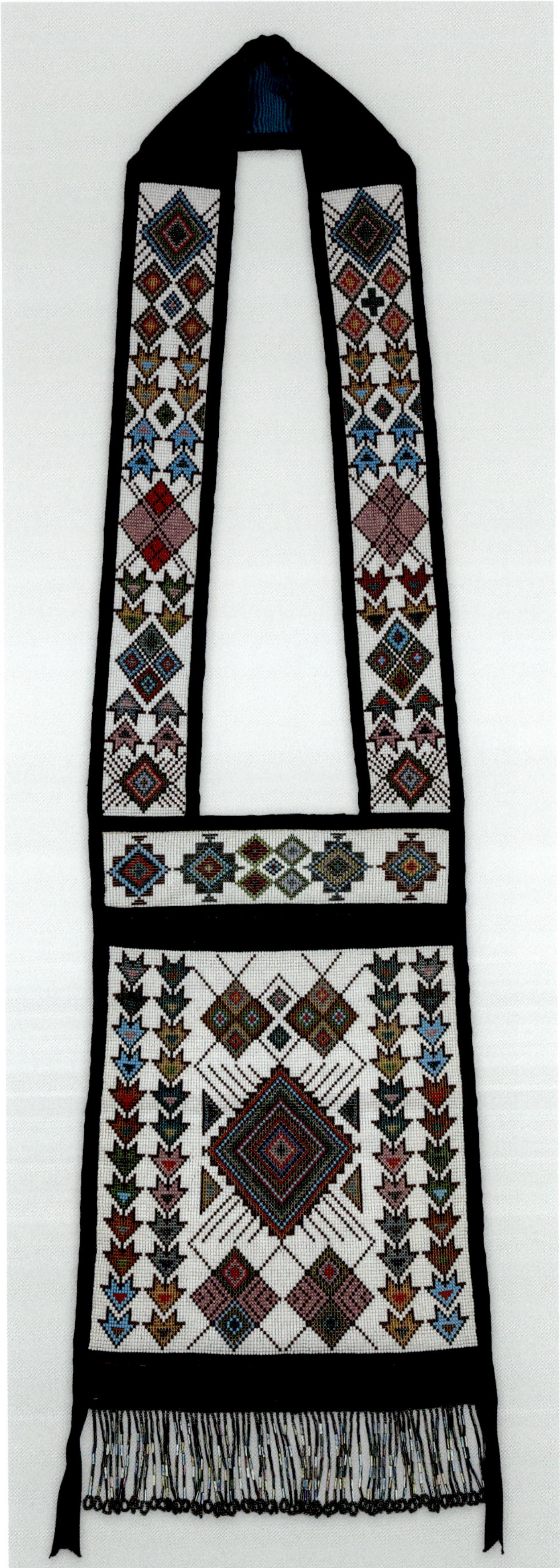

leather clothing, and gashkibidaaganag. Ellen believes the quilled and beaded pieces were made by Nancy LaPlante, Ida Frost, and Ellen's aunt Christina LeSage. The two gashkibidaaganag made during that period that are in the collections of Grand Portage National Monument (see Figure 8.01) are among the objects rotated in the exhibits at the monument's Heritage Center.

The Grand Portage bags that Ellen recalls were mostly decorated with loom-woven panels that were mounted on black velvet, and the fringe was generally made of tabs, not tassels. "Bandolier bags weren't made as often or as frequently as other kinds of bags," she notes. "They were just made for special occasions and were mainly decorative." She remembers that the Midewiwin practitioners at Grand Portage did not wear gashkibidaaganag, and she also recalls specific bags people owned. Mrs. LeSage had what Ellen called a small "lady's size" bag. Chief Mike Flatte had one gashkibidaagan. When asked if more than one member of the Grand Portage community might use the same bag, Ellen replied that people would borrow beadwork for pictures and special ceremonies. Many gashkibidaaganag didn't remain in the community for too long, as they were presented as special gifts, mostly to government officials.

When her daughters were young, Ellen did little beadwork, mostly focusing on small loom-woven projects. When she returned to Grand Portage in 1970, after living in Minneapolis, she made belts, moccasins (both the old-fashioned pointed ones and the "lazy lady" kind—in the gathered round-toe construction style), and medallions that could be worn as necklaces. Ellen thinks she has made eight gashkibidaaganag, including one now at the National Museum of the American Indian. While she has sold most of her larger projects, she still owns the last bag she made. She has decorated her bags with both loom-woven panels and spot-stitch appliqué.[12]

Ellen sketches her own patterns or motifs, getting ideas by observing natural forms. "I try to employ old geometrics without copying and I often make a bead

8.15 Ellen Olson's most recent, loom-woven bandolier bag, 2016. *Photo by James Castle*

tab fringe. I call this bag design 'butterfly' [shown in Figure 8.15] because the beads are iridescent and my background color is chalk white beads. My most recent one, this is a woman's bag because it is smaller than the size I would make for a man's bag."

Ellen draws her design in color and clips the paper to a string with clothespins in the room where she is working, using it as a reference as she weaves beads. She makes her own simple looms from scrap lumber, built to the size of the work she intends to create. "I prefer loom work because it's the oldest kind, the most outstanding," said Ellen. Her mother made cedar mats with the same kinds of designs and same colors and that inspired Ellen's loom beadwork designs.

Ellen uses nylon thread "for longevity and strength." In their early work Ellen and Marcie used button-and-carpet thread for the warp and cotton thread for the weft. Now they both use Nymo, a nylon monofilament thread that became available about 1971. Ellen has used both black and white thread. Her beadwork has won awards at several art fairs, and in 1992 the Plains Art Museum in Fargo, North Dakota, commissioned a colorful spot-stitch appliqué bag (Figure 8.16).

Ellen offered some additional thoughts on beadworking in 2012.

> After visiting museums and looking at collections, I believe indigenous bead artists should keep to our own traditions, incorporating old designs and materials, like velvet. I knew how precious bandolier bags were to my people, and I wanted to make some of my own. Much of my beadwork was made for shows, competitions, and collections. I was one of the few doing old-style bandolier bags, clothing, and moccasins. It was and still is difficult to get some supplies like good tanned leather. I create this beadwork for all my female relatives, the ones who came before me, and to be a "beadwork lady." And I'm still doing it today. I'm especially pleased that my daughters do beadwork and that they each have a wonderful eye for color and design.[13]

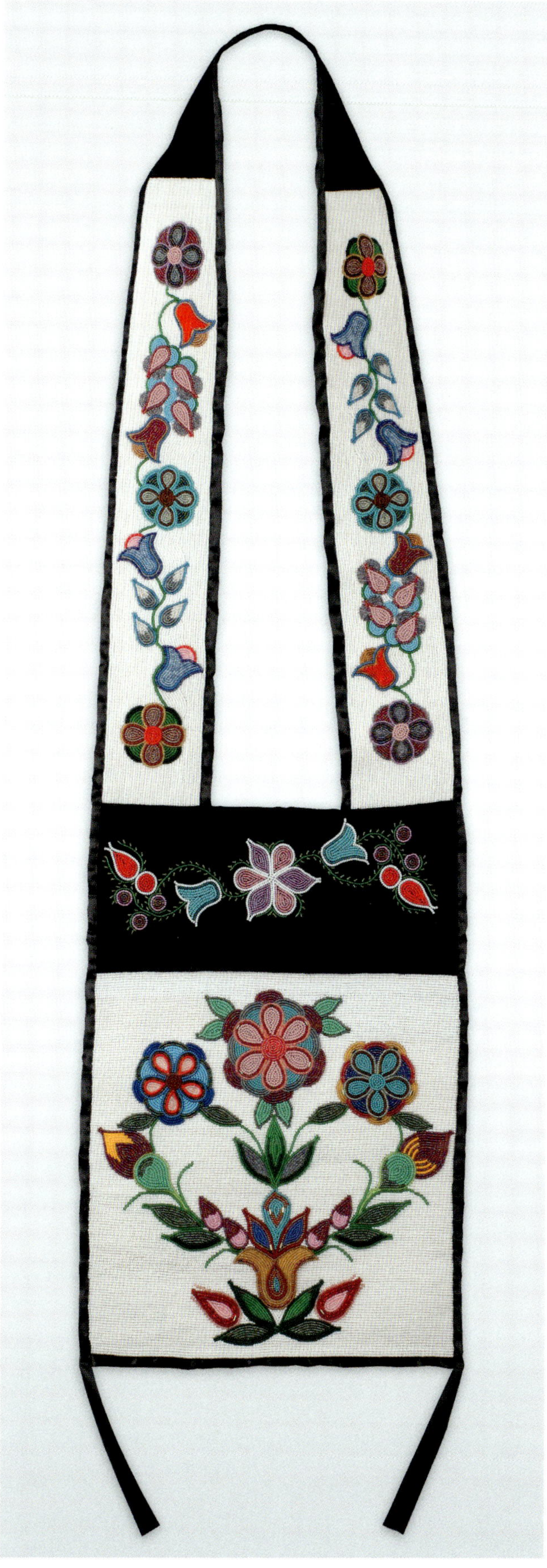

8.16 Ellen Olson's spot-stitched bag.
PAM 1992.002.001

Marcie McIntire, bead artist

Marcie McIntire (Figure 8.17) is a third-generation gashkibidaagan maker from Grand Portage who works nearly full time as a bead artist. She runs the Ningii-Ozhitoomin Ojibwe Art Gallery in Grand Portage close to the powwow grounds, where much of what she makes is for sale. Marcie has made four gashkibidaaganag, one of which was purchased by the Grand Portage Band and is displayed in a conference room at the Reservation Tribal Council offices. In 2009 she was the featured artist at the holiday bazaar held by the Mitchell Museum of the American Indian in Evanston, Illinois. She also teaches beadwork and other crafts at the North House Folk School in Grand Marais.[14]

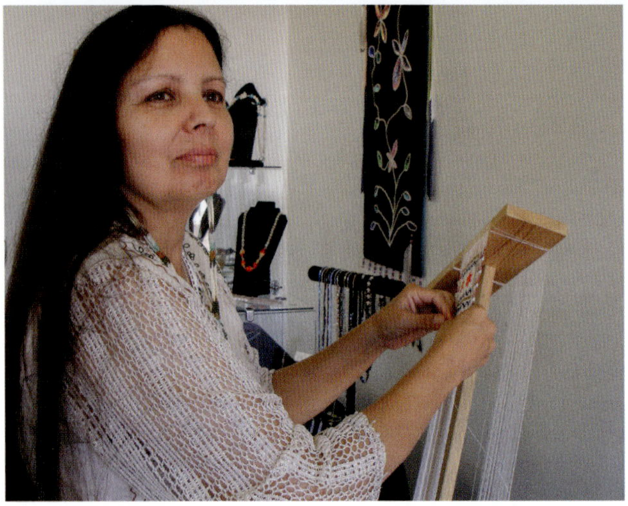

8.17 Marcie McIntire, 2009. *Photo by Cheryl Walsh Bellville*

The chance to meet and work with Marcie and her mother Ellen Olson over so many years represents a particularly rewarding aspect of contemporary curatorial research and collecting. It is all too rare for a curator of historical objects to actually meet active artisans, visit them in their home or studio environments, and document their work, in addition to the standard curatorial role of acquiring examples for an institutional collection.

Marcie designed her own degree program at Antioch University, and she wrote a major paper that incorporates Grand Portage Ojibwe perspectives from tribal and family oral histories, as well as her experiences learning to bead from relatives, in a discussion of the form. Marcie is one of the few bag makers I have interviewed who actually had the opportunity to reflect on the origin of the bags, why she creates them, and what this kind of personal expression means to her as an Ojibwe woman. The text that follows is an excerpt; Figures 8.18, 8.19, and 8.20 show her gashkibidaaganag.[15]

In my experience I have observed that any object created with beads seems, invariably, to produce a certain excitement in the viewer. I have seen this reaction in adults and especially in children. Those observations have led me to believe beadwork can be appreciated even without an understanding of its place in the context of history.[16]

The Anishinaabe excelled in weaving, beadwork, and birchbark arts. Certainly the foliate patterns are a well-known Anishinaabe design style, often accompanied by the ancient line designs in beadwork borders along the edges of the magnificent bandolier bags.

Ethnographer Carrie Lyford observed that the older floral designs were characterized by their delicacy. The newer designs became larger and bolder. Lyford indicated the change in design may have had to do with the changing art objects among the Anishinaabe in the nineteenth century such as the introduction of the large bandolier bags.[17]

Discussing the beadwork designs as being original but having been influenced or derived from European culture is an analysis solely within the realm of European viewpoints and language. The function of art in Native society has been denied. Instead it was assumed that, "taking their inspiration from floral patterns on the white man's cloth, Indian women improvised their own designs." Such viewpoints fulfill the early ethnologists' view that any acculturation is synonymous with a "tragic loss of valuable ethnological material." As historian Carolyn Gilman wrote, "It never occurred to Frances Densmore and others that Chippewa culture might be resilient enough to assimilate portions of white culture, and yet retain its unique identity."[18]

As a beadwork artist, I learned through association with other artists that my use of floral designs was traditional, albeit fairly recent. It never dawned on me that my designs could be associated with the colonizers. The older designs were the geometric ones, like the kind I used in loom work. Nevertheless, the geometric designs were also based on foliate forms.

Whether Anishinaabe beadworkers were using geometric or floral designs, they were depicting the flora in the world around them. Grand Portage member Duane Goodwin noted, "In my beadwork, you've noticed, there's a lot of floral design. That comes from having a special caring feeling for flowers, natural essence in nature."[19]

The assumption that designs are derived from another source besides the culture or individual who produced the art seems rather comical in relation to my own experience with beadwork. At the beginning of my beadwork career, John Bushman, a Grand Portage elder, told me, "You have to use your own designs. When you are just learning, you can use other people's designs. But later on, you'll have to use your own designs."[20] Thus I learned there was individual creativity in Anishinaabe art. I always did my own designing. It was also apparent that one needed special permission or direction to use other people's designs, like dream designs, for example.

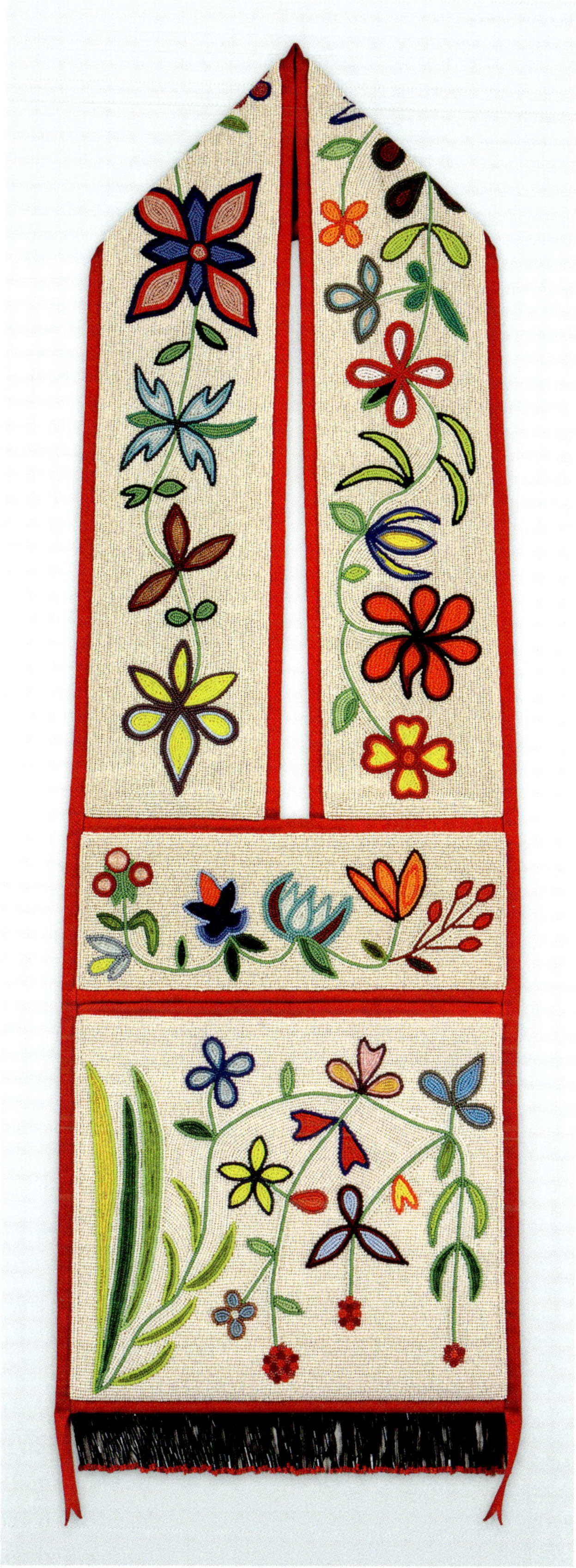

8.18 A spot-stitched bag by Marcie McIntire with full-width open front pocket, Grand Portage, 1989. *Photo by James Castle*

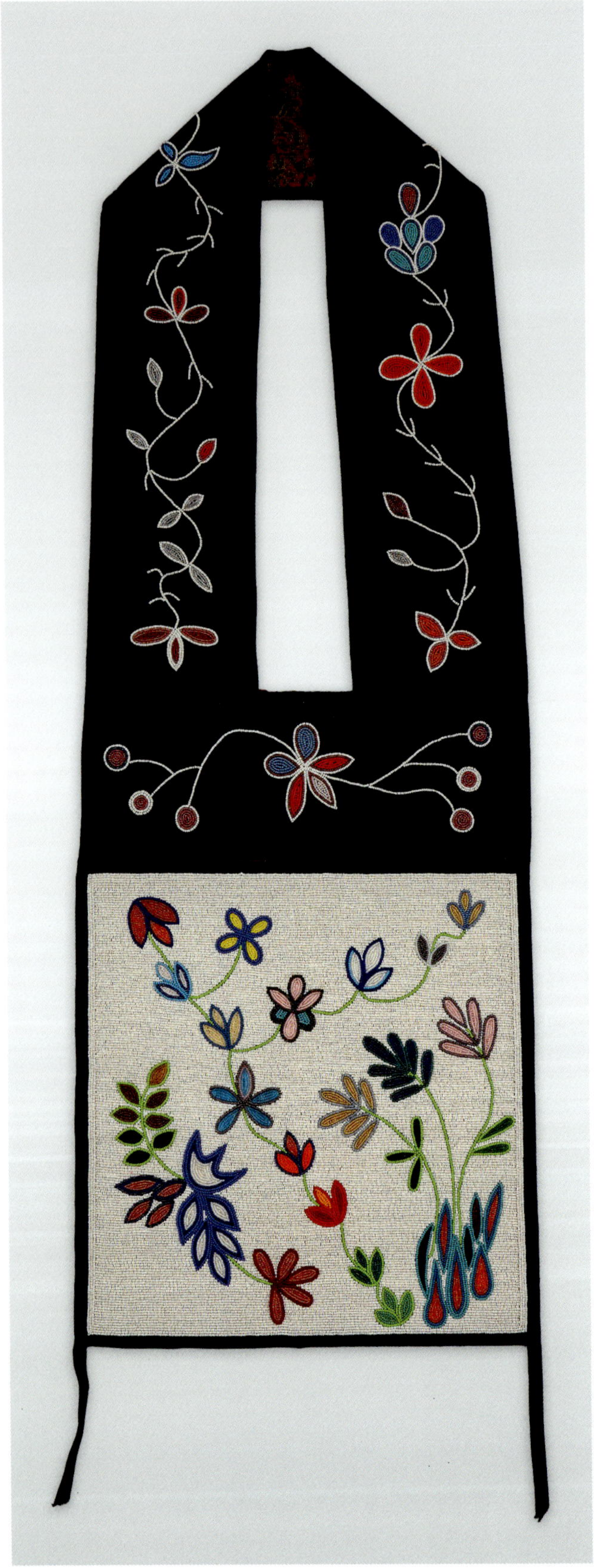

8.19 A spot-stitched bag by Marcie McIntire with full-width open front pocket, strap spot stitched on black velveteen, Grand Portage, 1993. *Photo by James Castle*

The bead embroidery technique has been variously referred to in the literature as appliqué, applied design, couching, spot stitching, and overlay. Although bead embroidery has predominantly been used for floral design, geometric designs have been used, especially in contemporary times. Further, the so-called geometric line designs were used exclusively for the bead embroidery technique of border design. "The simple border patterns," notes Lyford, "are of ancient origin and were popular in all the old Algonquin quillwork."[21] The border designs were used along the edges of artwork, mainly on clothing. They were also used to decorate the borders of bandolier bags once they became popular.

The use of color in beadwork has been addressed most frequently by contemporary commentators. One distinctive aspect is the large assortment of colors used in a single work. I know I have tried to use as many different shades of colors as possible in my own work. Regarding my own work, the harvest of colors I use is directly related to the variety of beads available from the Czech Republic. Subtleness in color is an aspect characterizing my own work.

I made my first piece of beadwork, a bracelet, under watchful eyes. As a child and a young adult, I concentrated on making my work as bright and brilliant as possible. But I think I added a subdued effect with the shading, using two different hues of one shade. Even though the colors are brilliant, they are subdued in a certain way. The fact that the color combinations are not garish is an apt description of my own work. I consciously seek the subdued effect when I am choosing colors for a particular work. My use of color involves the selection of the very brilliant colors. I combine colors. It was an aspect of beadwork that I learned from my mother, Ellen Bushman Olson. She said bright colors, like red, yellow, and blue, were the Indian colors. I had to learn how to use color to make it look bright, as Indian people used a lot of bright colors. The literature indicates an interest in the color of the background in comparison to that of the design components. Such a separation never occurred in my mind. When I choose colors, the color of the background is part of the combination. The background color must have a pleasing effect along with the rest of the colors comprising the combination. When I am choosing colors for a particular work, I will lay the beads out to decide. Placing the beads side by side in the arrangement in which they will be beaded is a way to determine how they will appear on the finished piece. I outline my floral patterns, as described in ethnographic literature. So [as I plan a piece] I line the beads up in the same order as the outlining and filling in of the flower parts. Then I can decide on replacements if I have chosen a noxious color combination.

Although I have my own beadwork style and do a certain amount of experimentation, I have been told my work is too traditional. This means that my vests, belts, bags, and dance outfit accessories are not objects that can be hung on the wall of an office or den. They are utilitarian objects that could only be sold if they were framed. I admit I have been quite conservative by staying within the confines of the Anishinaabe culture. Using my own designs, I have always said they are *Anishinaabe* designs. I create my own designs within a specific cultural context. I think my work reflects unique aspects of craftsmanship. I come from a tradition in which my grandmother's grandmother did beadwork.

While studying at Antioch University, I realized that the beadwork tradition originates in antiquity. It has a forerunner in the porcupine quillwork techniques and designs. I believe [the writings of Andrew Hunter] Whiteford and others have shown that ancient techniques and designs have persisted to contemporary times. I did not realize I was practicing an art with ancient antecedents. I had thought I was practicing an art which developed after Venetian beads arrived on this continent. I assumed my art was less than two hundred years old as deduced from knowledge of my family tradition. Now I realize it has an ancient cultural basis within my family and my community.

I feel I have been lucky to come from a family of beadworkers, in which the women and probably some of the men did beadwork all the way back to the early nineteenth century. Some Anishinaabe people do not have a beadwork tradition in their family and they learn it as adults. I think that is worthy too.

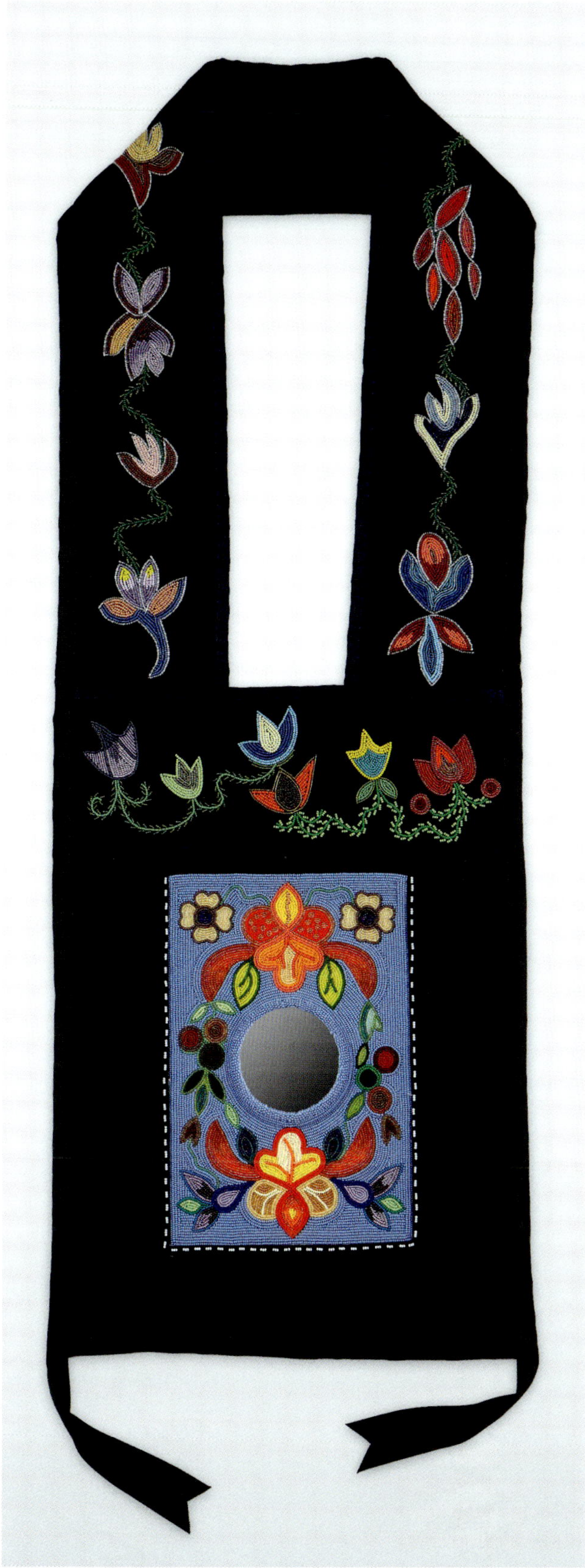

8.20 A spot-stitched bag by Marcie McIntire with a circular mirror at center of pocket panel and full-width open front pocket, Grand Portage, 2014. *Photo by James Castle*

I think the tradition of having beadwork in my family and community makes my work unique. I have always made things by hand and I have always been around people, male and female, who make things. I think one learns techniques, methods, and craftsmanship by example. Beadwork involves the fine motor skills connected with handcraft. I learned beadwork by watching. But part of that learning experience involved all forms of handcraft I have had the opportunity to observe.

Beadwork is an art which has proven to be a satisfying and fulfilling experience for me. I receive a great deal of pride and enjoyment from my work. Beadwork is an aspect of my life which makes me extremely happy. Happiness contributes to an individual's sense of self-esteem and feeling of self-worth. Self-esteem is especially important for a woman living in a predominantly patriarchal society. I believe the art of beadwork has given me permission to function as an autonomous individual. My art has given me the freedom to feel integrated and whole. When I am doing beadwork I feel like I have been freed from the dehumanizing effects of sexism and racism, creating a much more satisfying life. The happiness derived from creating art provides meaning for life. For me, it is the ultimate reality, providing the greatest sense of peacefulness an individual can experience.

Chapter 9

Leech Lake

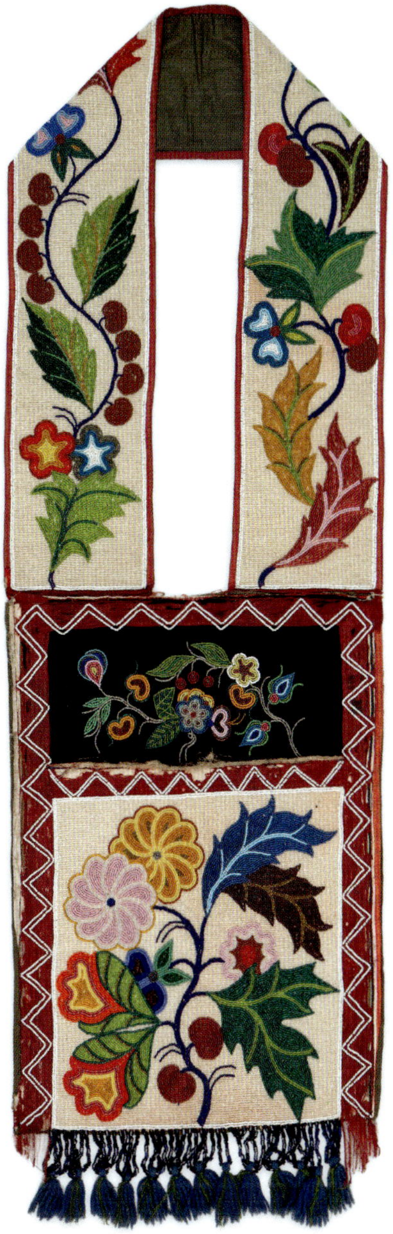

Ojibwe people had moved into northwestern and north-central Minnesota by the late 1700s and lived throughout the area, with the Pillager Band, a group especially known for its military power, in the vanguard. But in 1855, when the US government forced the sale of their lands, the Pillagers, along with people from the Lake Superior and Mississippi Bands, were concentrated on three smaller reservations in this area. In 1934 these three reservations were combined to make up the Leech Lake Reservation—Gaa-zagaskwaajimekaag, in Ojibwemowin—that now encompasses portions of Beltrami, Cass, Hubbard, and Itasca Counties.

The area is immensely beautiful. Three of Minnesota's largest lakes lie within the reservation's boundaries: Leech Lake (third largest), Lake Winnibigoshish (fourth largest), and Cass Lake (eighth largest). In the late 1890s, after the Dawes Act forced band members to accept eighty-acre plots, the bulk of the reservation was slated to be sold, and timber companies were the likely buyers. In 1902, responding to the lobbying of early conservationists, the US Congress created the Minnesota Forest Reserve, made up mostly of former reservation lands. The forest reserve, enlarged and renamed the Chippewa National Forest in 1928, now takes up 85 percent of the reservation; band members own just 5 percent of the land.[1]

The lakes and forest played a significant role in attracting tourists to the region. Local businesses in the off-reservation town of Cass Lake did their part, promoting the area for fishing, swimming, boating and canoeing, hiking, golf, touring, and "restful living." The lake itself—originally known as Ga-misquawakokag, or Red Cedar Lake—was renamed in 1820 for Michigan territorial governor Lewis Cass. That renaming may have been the subject of the centennial celebration depicted in Figure 9.01, which is captioned with customary racist language. One of the women in this image wears two and perhaps three spot-stitch appliqué bags, two

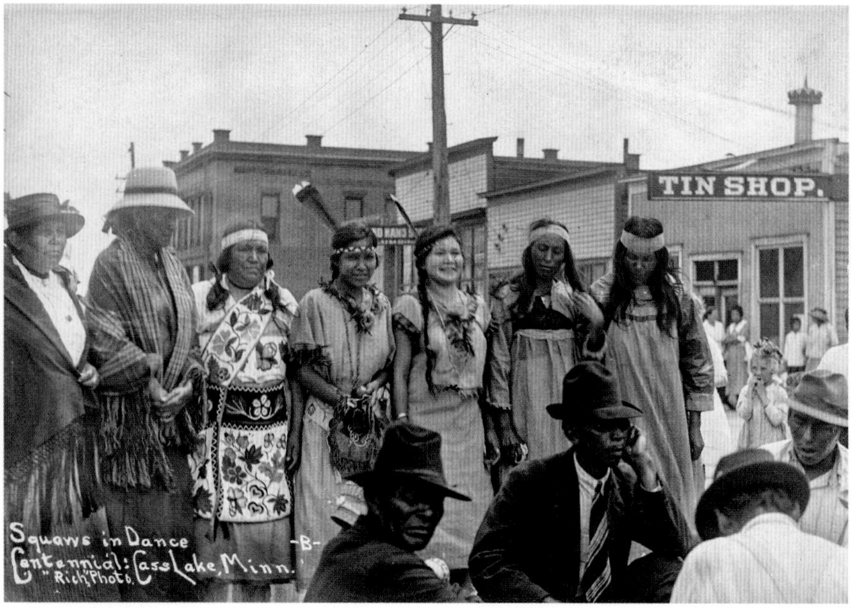

9.01 Cass Lake centennial celebration, c. 1925. *Photo by Arthur Richardson. MNHS MC3.9 CL9 r9*

with full-width pocket openings visible.[2]

Leech Lake was also the site of one of the last military engagements between US armed forces and indigenous nations in the United States. At the center of the conflict was Bagone-giizhig (Bug-O-Nay-Ge-Shig, or Hole-in-the-Day). In Figure 9.02, taken in 1897, he stands at far left wearing a spot-stitch appliqué bag with a possible slit pocket opening. The pocket portion of the bag has an oversize zigzag border of ribbon appliqué. The man next to him also wears a spot-stitch appliqué bag with a wide pocket border.[3]

In September 1898, Bagone-giizhig was protesting timber fraud when authorities arrested him and another man as witnesses to a bootlegging case. Not wanting to be taken to Duluth, they escaped with others to Sugar Point. The Indian agent requested military assistance, and in the ensuing battle, on October 5, six white soldiers were killed.

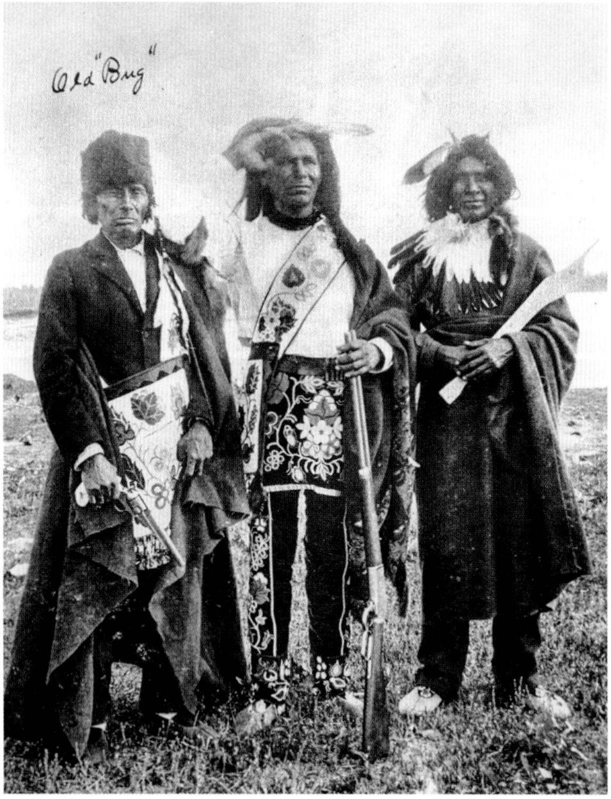

9.02 Bagone-giizhig *(left)* with two Pillager men on Bear Island, Leech Lake, 1897. *MNHS E97.1B p8*

In Figure 9.03, Major Elias D. Libbey, National Guard commandant of the Minnesota batteries during the battle at Leech Lake, poses in 1898 with several Ojibwe people and other National Guard members. Libbey wears a Minnesota spot-stitch appliqué gashkibidaagan of the form most common at the turn of the twentieth century; no information is available on how he came to wear the bag. Either because there is something in the pocket or because of the weight of the beads, the bag's pocket sags open, displaying the plaid fabric of the inner pocket. And as often happens in posed images, the bag is worn in apron manner to best display the full complement of the bag components and the artistry of the maker, who may be one of the women facing the camera.[4]

US commissioner of Indian affairs William A. Jones traveled to Leech Lake in October 1898 to meet with band leaders and investigate the battle. Jones is second from right in Figure 9.04, a photo of the council; a man seated at the table, left of center, is wearing two spot-stitch appliqué bags, and it appears that the man seated two back from him may also be wearing one, as a portion of a shoulder strap is visible.

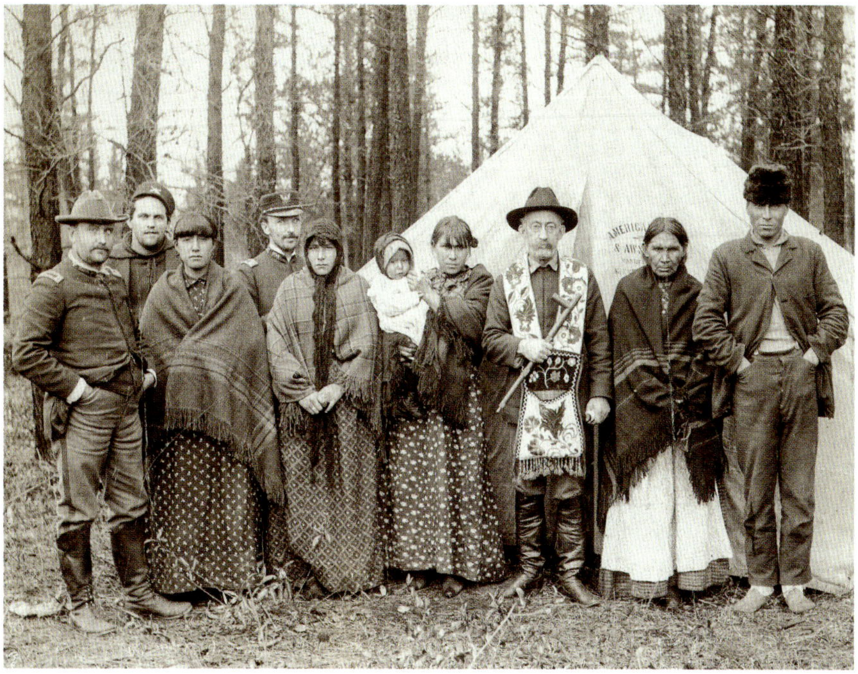

9.03 Ojibwe people at Leech Lake pose with Major Elias D. Libbey, who wears a gashkibidaagan, 1898. *MNHS E97.1 r111*

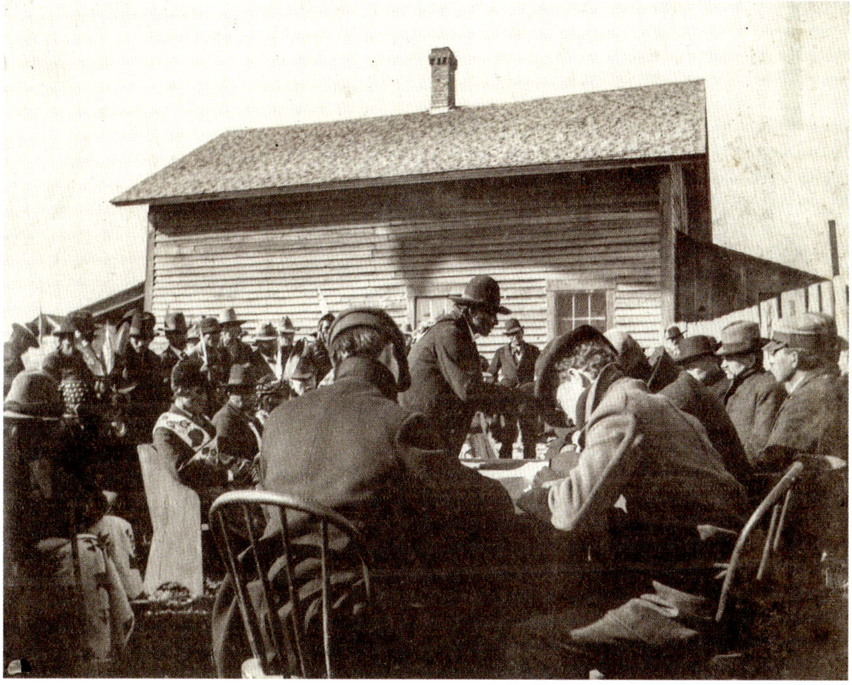

9.04 Council at Leech Lake, 1898. *WHS 29227*

The Leech Lake, Red Lake, and White Earth Reservations make up the area of heaviest gashkibidaagan production in Minnesota, and this large northwestern region saw much tourist activity. Well into the twentieth century, "Cass Lake" served as the moniker for a regional recreation area that encompassed the Leech Lake, Red Lake, and White Earth Reservation destinations as well as many other lakes and numerous camping, fishing, hunting, and beach resorts in northwestern Minnesota. The events documented in photographs frequently took place in towns such as Walker or Cass Lake, all in easy travel distance from Leech Lake, Red Lake, and White Earth Reservations. Ojibwe families often came from all three reservations to participate in events and celebrations, which means that images of gashkibidaaganag are often associated with a lake or a city rather than attributed to a reservation. Still, enough photos were taken and preserved that individual examples can be dated and connected to each of these reservations.

The reservations located the farthest north include some bandolier bags that deviate from the most common Minnesota Ojibwe spot-stitch appliqué forms. A few examples are evident in Figures 9.05, 9.06, and

9.07. These three bags are all part of an anonymous donation built as a collection in the Cass Lake region, without specific documentation or attribution. They all use bolder hues than is typical in other areas of the state; some shared motifs; bead-strung, single-thread fringe; red wool tape binding; and the later styles for spot-stitch appliqué pockets (either a faux opening or no pocket reference). The designs on both pocket panels and straps, with an emphasis on bilateral symmetry and a formality of motif placement, are more static and less animated than many floral bags from other regions within Minnesota. All this suggests they were made by a woman or group of women with similar inspirations or training.

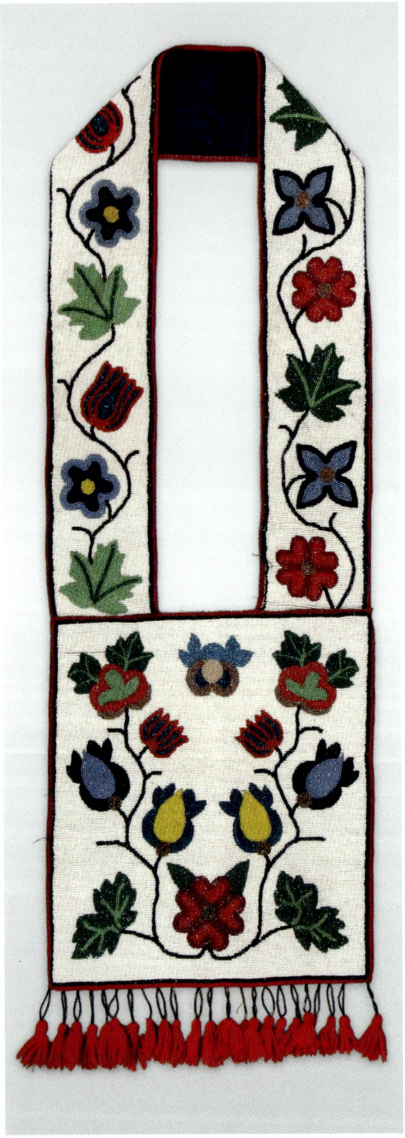

9.05 Gashkibidaagan, possibly from Leech Lake, first half of twentieth century. *MNHS 2011.208.146*

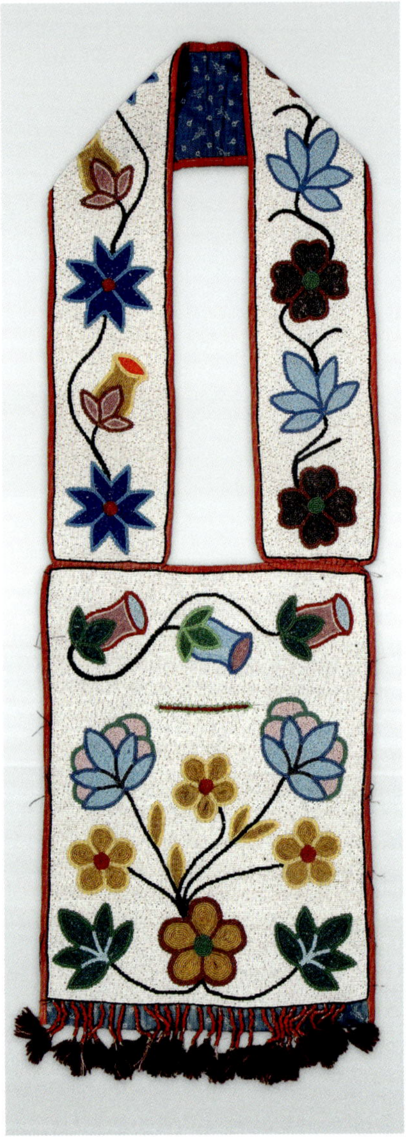

9.06 Gashkibidaagan, possibly from Leech Lake, c. 1890–1915. *MNHS 2011.208.149*

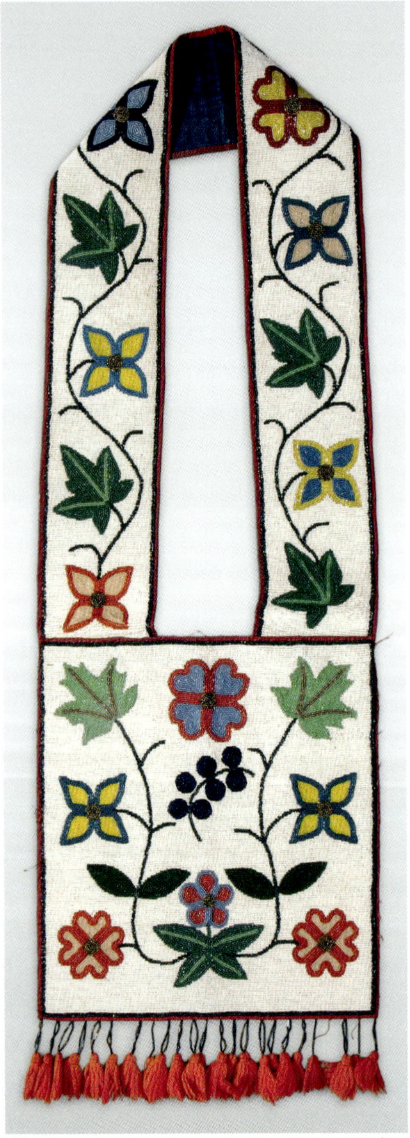

9.07 Gashkibidaagan, possibly from Leech Lake, first half of twentieth century. *MNHS 2011.208.150*

In contrast, the bags in Figures 9.08, 9.09, and 9.10, with Cass Lake or general Leech Lake provenance, represent the most common animated design approach seen in spot-stitch appliqué bags among Minnesota Ojibwe. They also are all embellished with many of the motifs seen on a great number of bags associated with White Earth and the Cass Lake region. The bag in Figure 9.08 was described by its collectors, Paul and Nellie Hankins, as a "medicine bag," acquired at Cass Lake about 1916. Generally, gashkibidaaganag were worn on various special occasions. While this spot-stitch appliqué bag may have been owned and worn by a medicine man, the motifs it incorporates on the pocket (large leaf, love apple, and cloud or pinecone) are not associated with formal Midewiwin practices, according to some of the beadworkers I interviewed. The strap also incorporates heart-petaled flowers and ivy-like leaves. Figure 9.09 includes several popular motifs, including the folded leaf, pear, strawberry, arrowhead leaf, gear flower, heart-petaled flower, and an unusual green layered podlike motif at lower right that attempts a three-dimensional representation. The two separate straps that tie together allowed the bag to be stored flat. Figure 9.10 incorporates heart-petaled flower, pinecone, oak leaf, pointed petal flower, and inverted coneflower motifs. All three bags have the full-width pocket opening.[5]

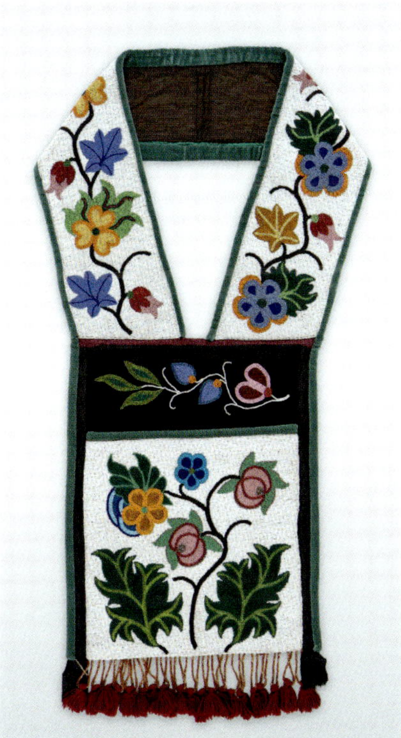

9.08 *(below left)* Gashkibidaagan acquired at Cass Lake, on Leech Lake Reservation, by Paul and Nellie Hankins in 1916. *MNHS 1981.119.1*

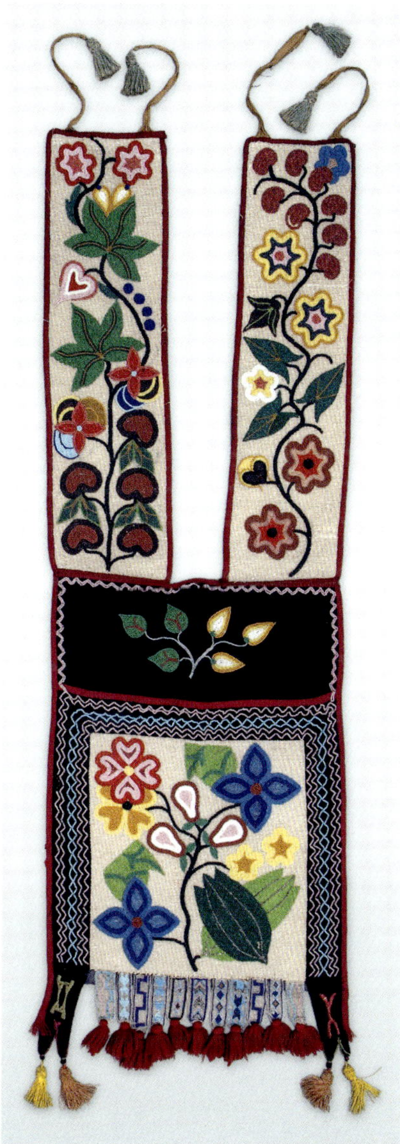

9.09 *(below center)* Gashkibidaagan, possibly from Leech Lake, probably c. 1900. *MNHS 2011.208.145; see also Figure 2.08*

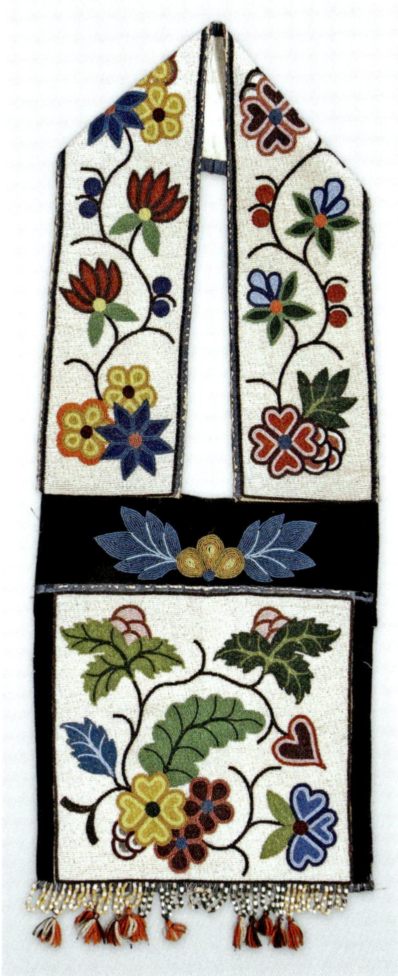

9.10 *(below)* Gashkibidaagan, possibly from Leech Lake, probably c. 1900. *MNHS 2011.208.147*

In the late 1890s, photographer De Lancy W. Gill, who worked for the Bureau of American Ethnology in Washington, DC, took portraits of some visiting Leech Lake Band members. In Figure 9.11, Wabununi (White Feather), seated far left, wears a bag with a strap decorated in spot-stitch appliqué on a dark cloth background. While bag makers of modern times often use the dark background for effect, this was not common at that time. Gay-she-gwanay-aush, seated far right, wears the same spot-stitch appliqué bag and beaded strap in both this photo and Figure 9.12.[6]

Bags and images of bags with a dark ground on the strap are rare; there are just two in the Minnesota Historical Society's holdings, one collected by Eva Mudge, shown in Figure 9.13. This bag has some similarities to the one worn in Figure 9.14 by the Ojibwe leader Midriff, or Diaphragm, in Washington, DC, in 1899, which has a ribbon-work appliqué border visible on the area above the pocket opening. These two bags, as well as the one worn by Wabununi in Figure 9.11, appear to have functioning pockets, full-width pocket openings, and pocket panels with white beaded background.[7]

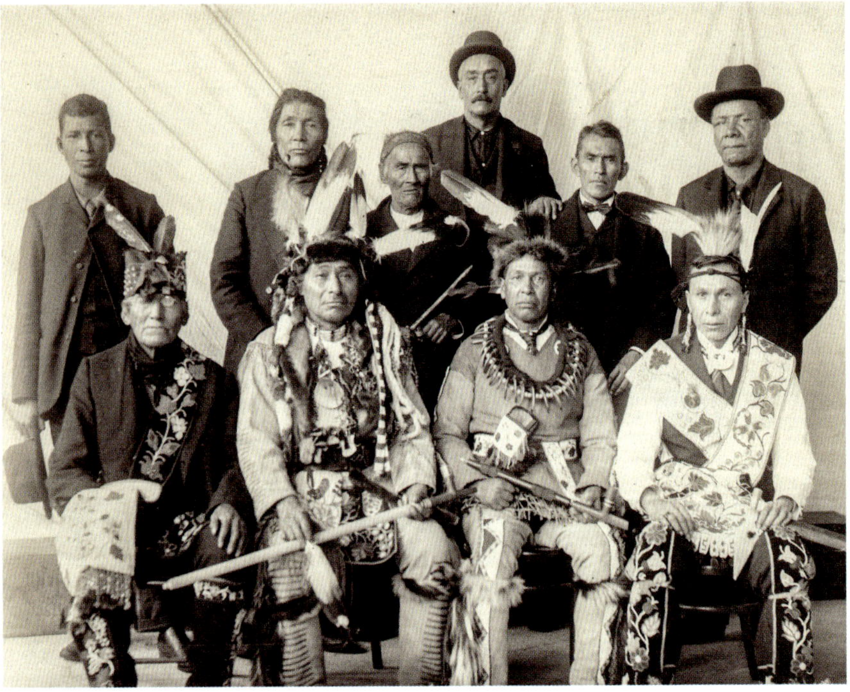

9.11 *(below)* Leech Lake delegation to Washington, DC, February 1899. *MNHS E97.51 p9*

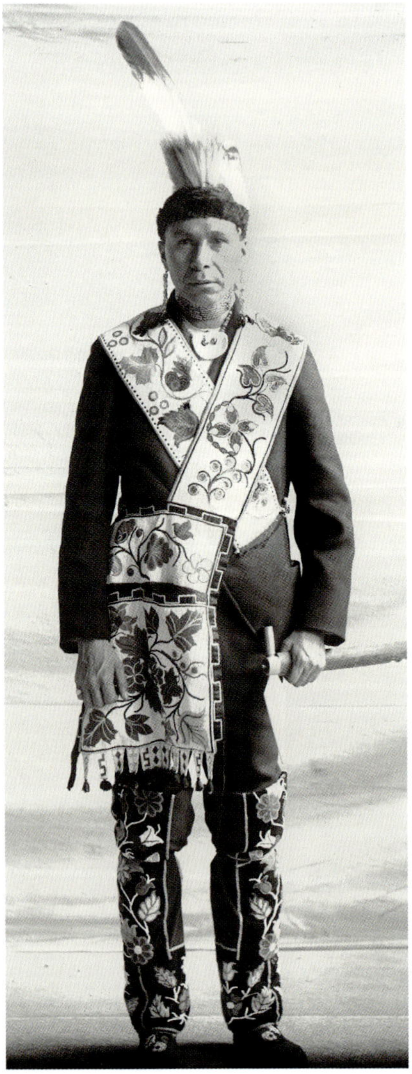

9.12 *(below right)* Gay-she-gwanay-aush, 1899. *NAA-SI BAE GN 00509B 06140000*

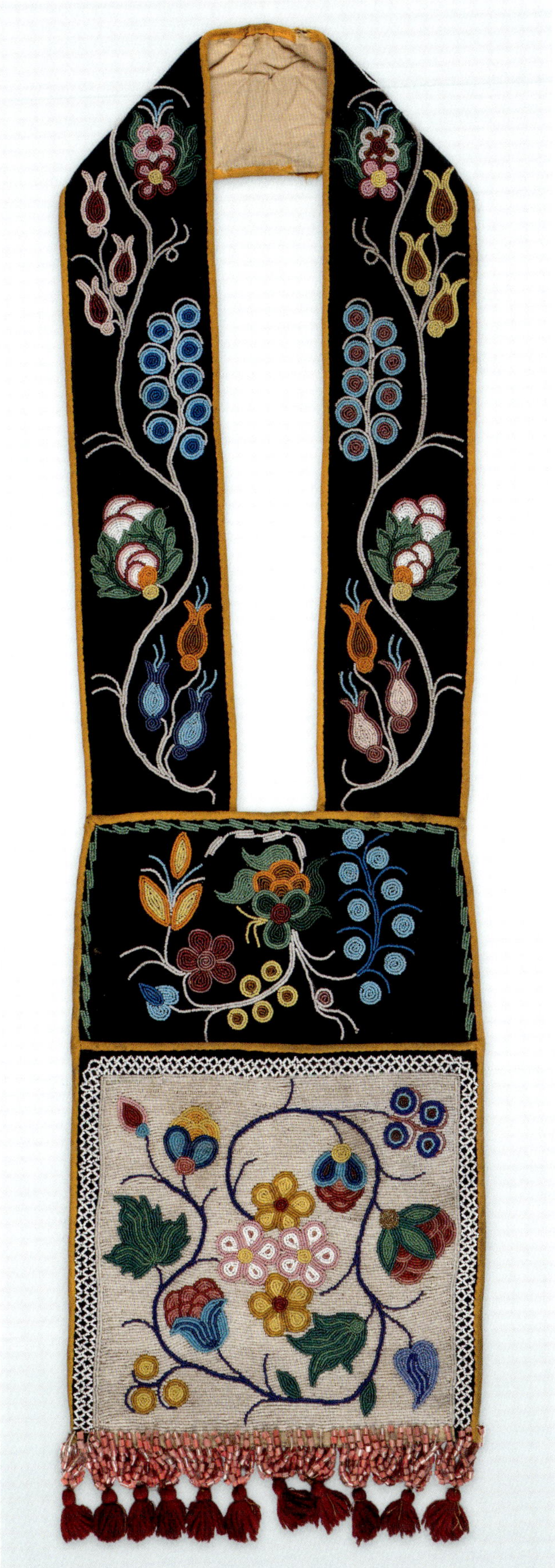

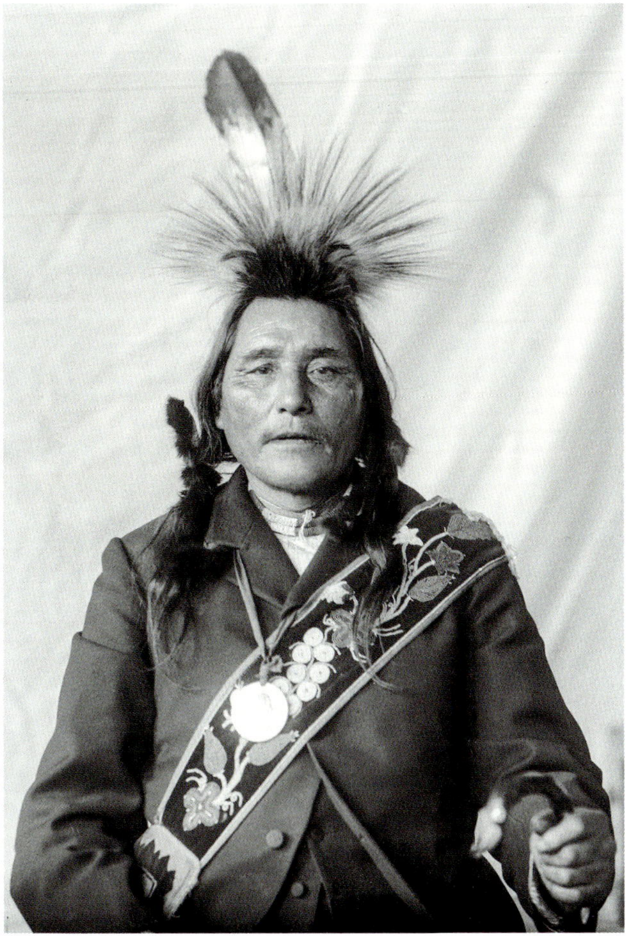

9.13 *(left)* Gashkibidaagan, possibly from Leech Lake, 1880s, collected by Eva Mudge. *MNHS 9666.8; see also Figure 3.47*

9.14 *(above)* Midriff, 1899. *NAA-SI BAE GN 00585A 06152800*

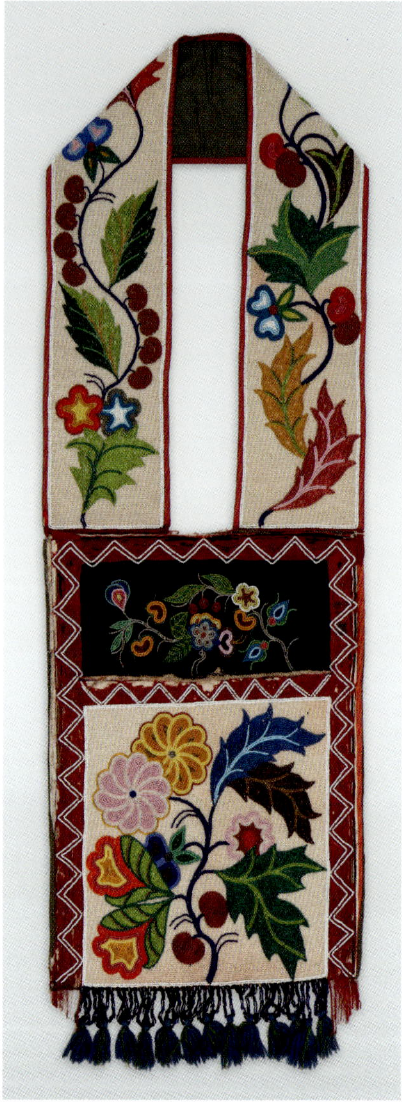

While building roads in the Cass Lake region with the Minneapolis contracting firm of Barnard Curtis in about 1920, Neal Gednay Barnard and his wife, Marguerite, acquired several pieces of dance regalia, including a gashkibidaagan (Figure 9.15) associated with Kay-zhe-baush-kung (Otto Bismark, c. 1874–1937) at Onigum on Leech Lake. Kay-zhe-baush-kung was a Leech Lake allottee who lived at Whipholt, about ten miles east of Walker. His wife, Ozowe-ge-shigoke (Mary), likely made all his beaded garments, including the gashkibidaagan. This bag incorporates many common elements on bags from this area made between 1890 and 1920, including the contrasting color for a pocket frame, the oversized edging motif (here a zigzag), and the folded leaf motif seen in the panel above the pocket opening. Other popular Minnesota Ojibwe motifs used on the bag include the arrowhead leaf on the strap, cherry/berry forms, heart flower, rosebuds, and the common vine and tendril structural elements that link the other motifs together into a cohesive design.[8]

A pair of images by Minneapolis photographer A. F. Raymond captures two gashkibidaagan roles within Ojibwe culture. He documented men wearing gashkibidaaganag at a politically motivated event in 1913 (Figure 9.16), the signing of a controversial declaration of allegiance to the United States. And in about 1923 Raymond recorded a Leech Lake family proudly posing outside their dwelling of reeds, elm, and birch bark (Figure 9.17). The father wears two lively spot-stitch appliqué bags. Both of his bags have full-width pocket openings and zigzag, white-bead border treatments. Perhaps the woman sitting off to the left, barely visible in this image, is his wife and the bags' maker.[9]

9.15 *(above)* Bag used by Kay-zhe-baush-kung, Leech Lake Reservation, before 1920. *MNHS 1984.156.3*

9.16 *(right)* Leech Lake signing of declaration of allegiance, 1913. *Photo by A. F. Raymond, MNHS E97.5 r2*

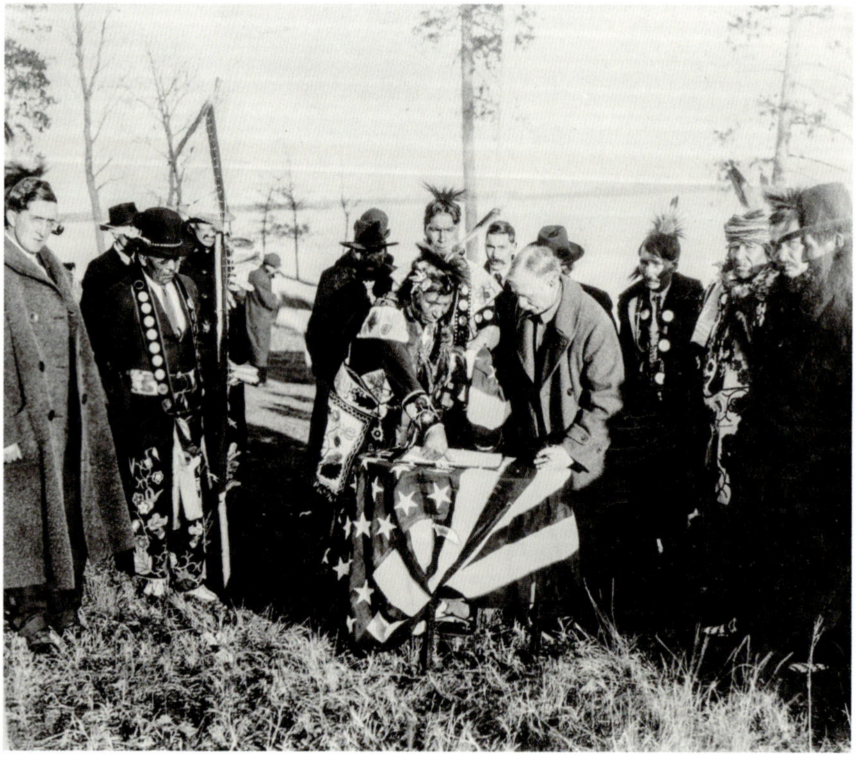

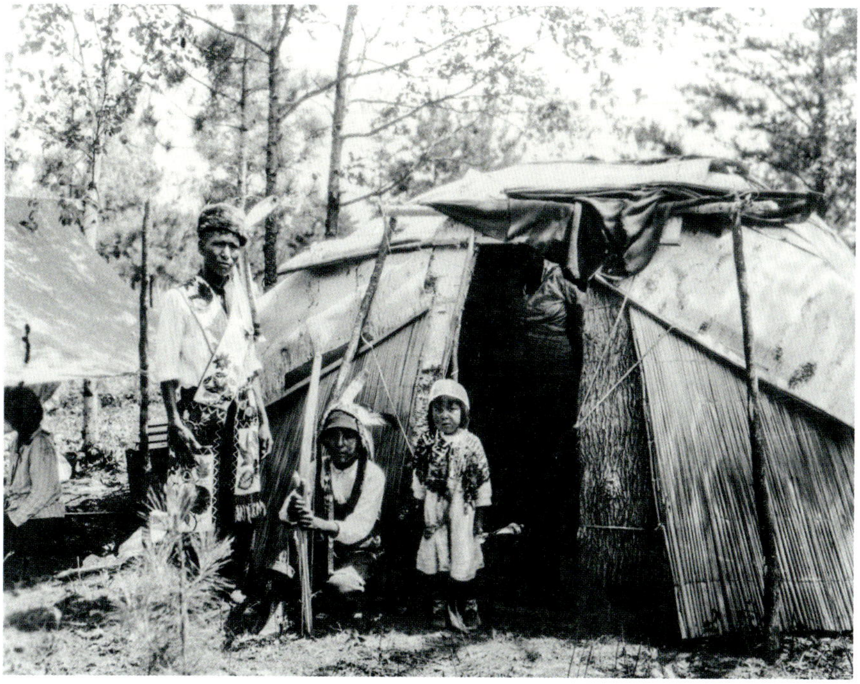

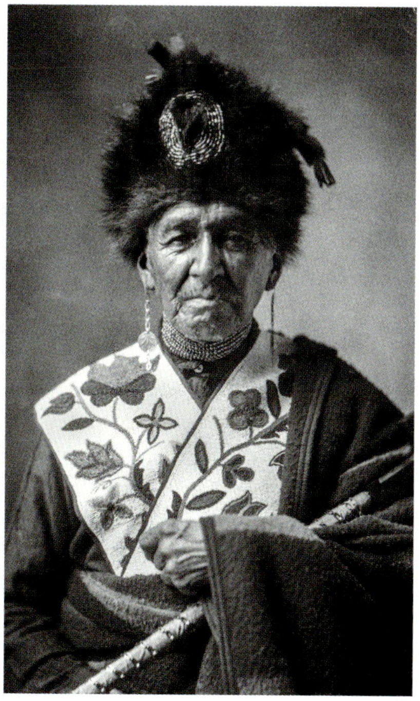

Another kind of image, a portrait, shows a bag worn by Chief Jim Greenhill of the Leech Lake Reservation, a man who was also frequently photographed. In Figure 9.18, taken about 1940, he wears two gashkibidaaganag with unusually wide straps. The pockets are hidden under the blanket, but the motifs on the straps were commonly seen in Minnesota Ojibwe beadwork.

9.17 *(above left)* Leech Lake family, c. 1923. *Photo by A. F. Raymond, MNHS E97.31 r94*

9.18 *(above)* Chief Jim Greenhill, c. 1940. *MNHS E97.1G r13*

Large-scale motifs

Gashkibidaaganag from the Leech Lake, White Earth, and broader Cass Lake areas often feature a single enlarged motif as the primary pocket element (Figure 9.19). Many historical photographs show bags featuring one large, serrated leaf (possibly representing those of the wild grape, maple tree, thimbleberry, or others). Several additional examples can be found in museums, but they have no association data. The other favored primary pocket motif, a tulip or waterlily, also appears on bags from the Cass Lake area (Figures 9.20 and 9.21).[10]

Another clue to this bag design appears in a historical photo (Figure 9.22). Many of the area's resorts had American Indian–related names, but their resort building exteriors and interior decor was inspired more by the rustic log cabin look or Arts and Crafts–style furnishings than by the regional history, material culture, and crafts of the indigenous people. An exception was the Glyken Hotel, a floating lodge off of Cass Lake's Star Island, an especially popular area for church camps and private cabins dating to the 1910s. In about 1930, the Glyken featured a gashkibidaagan with a large tulip or waterlily pocket motif suspended in the center of its dining area.[11]

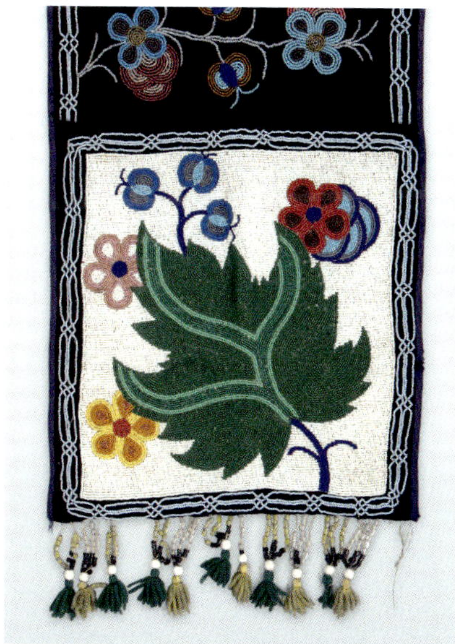

9.19 Bag with large leaf motif, c. 1900. Collected in Cass Lake area by Alfred H. Peterson. *MNHS 2011.208.152*

9.20 *(right)* Bag with single flower on pocket, probably late nineteenth or early twentieth century. *MNHS 2006.168.2; see also Figure 3.51*

9.21 *(far right)* Gashkibidaagan, early twentieth century; beads and cloth, 107.95 × 31.12 cm; gift of Marjorie Marie Underwood. *MIA 91.67*

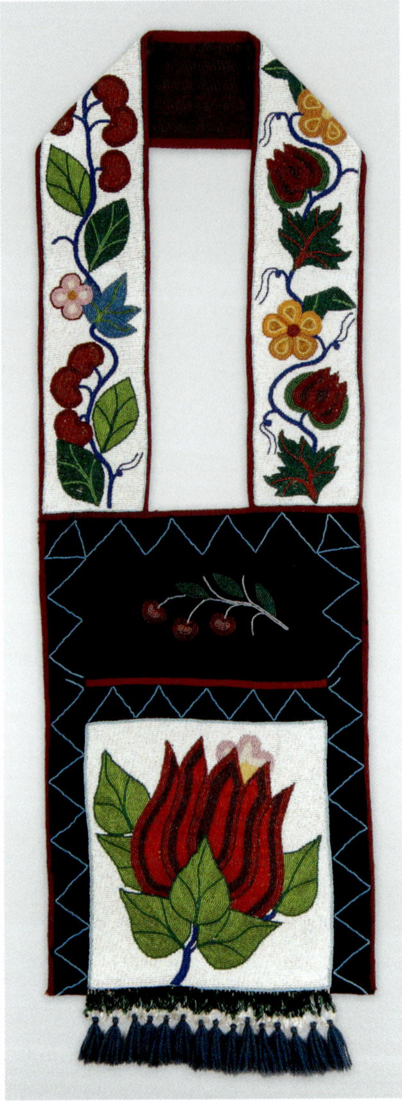

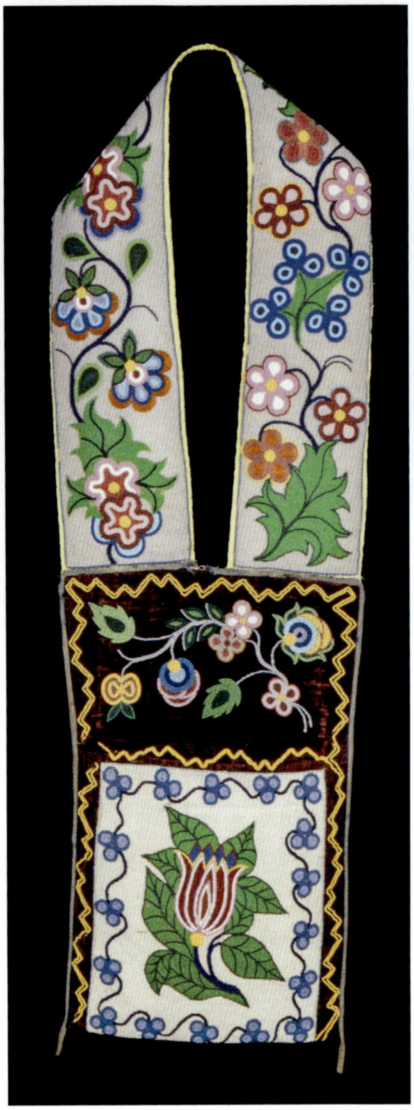

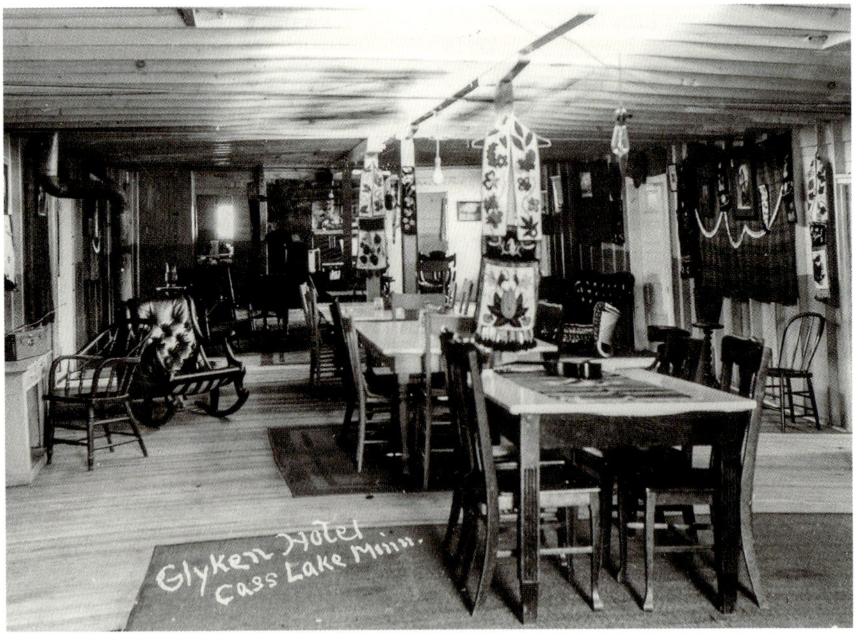

9.22 Glyken Hotel interior, Cass Lake, c. 1930. At least three spot-stitch appliqué bags are partially visible, including one with a single motif on the pocket *(center)*. *MNHS HF5.4 r91*

Jack Negonegwonabe King and Metigogwon King

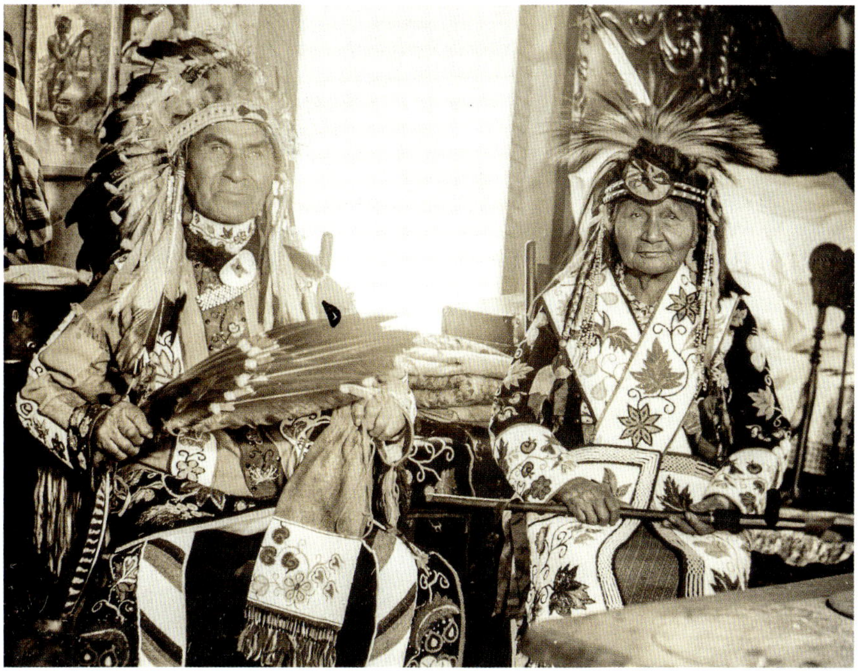

9.23 *(left)* Negonegwonabe King and Metigogwon King, Leech Lake Reservation, 1931. *MNHS Neg 35496*

9.24 *(below)* Negonegwonabe King and Metigogwon King, Leech Lake Reservation, 1931. *MNHS Neg 35497*

Adorned from head to toe for collector Monroe Killy's camera, the Kings, Pillager Band Ojibwe living at Onigum on Leech Lake, sat for a portrait in January 1931 (Figures 9.23 and 9.24). Metigogwon wears two gashkibidaaganag, an elaborately beaded blouse, a headdress, and moccasins. Her husband, Jack Negonegwonabe, wears a dance apron, leggings, a headdress, and moccasins; he holds a feather fan and a tobacco bag. Over his leggings Mr. King also wears dance drops, beaded strips that hang from the belt to the shin, which are evidence of the ongoing exchanges between the Dakota and the Ojibwe at occasions such as the Annual White Earth Celebration and Pow Wow.

These photographs record both the quality of Mrs. King's work and her productivity. Metigogwon told Killy that she made beadwork for herself and her husband only. The gashkibidaagan on her right hip in Figure 9.24 gives a view of a faux or small slit opening on the front of her panel style spot-stitch appliqué bag. The bag on her left hip probably has the same pocket style, given the other similarities in the edging stitches, finished size, and motifs. Other examples of her beadwork are visible in the interior background, as well. Killy purchased several objects from the Kings, but their location today is unknown, as his collection was sold off in 1978.[12]

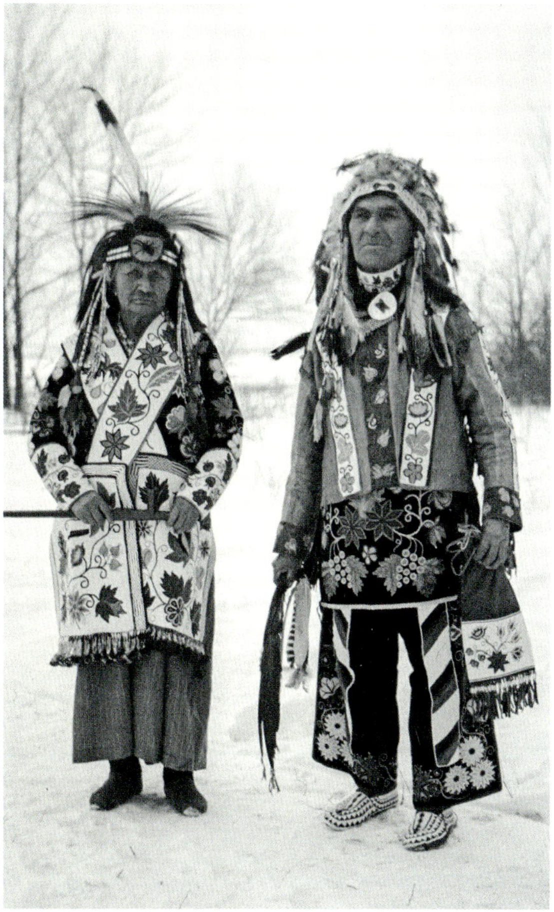

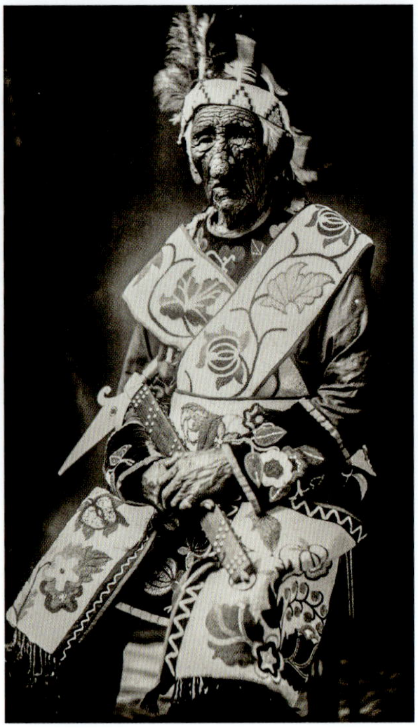

9.25 John Smith, c. 1912. *MNHS E97.1K r71*

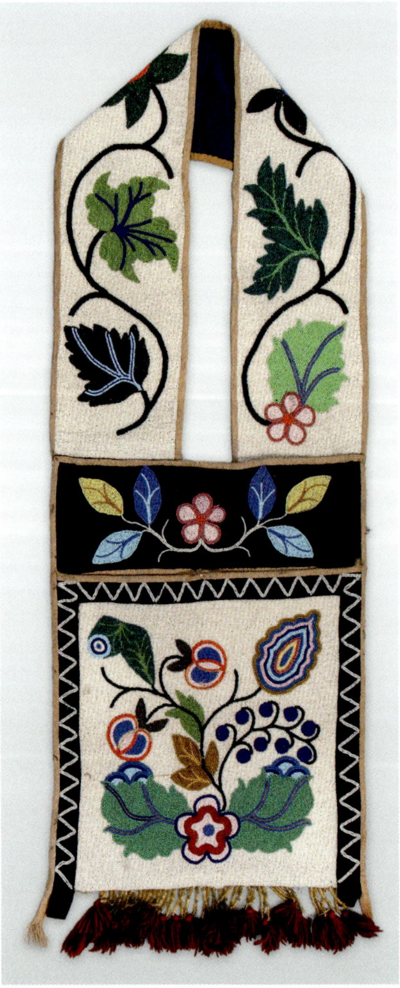

Chief John Smith

Ka-be-nah-gwey-wence (Kah-be-na-gwi-wens, Dah-be-hah-que-wince), or Chief John Smith, from Leech Lake was known as the man who lived in three centuries. Wearing regalia as well as non-Native dress, he posed for countless postcards, including a story series with his family. After his death in 1922, reportedly at the age of 137, his adopted son Tom and other individuals continued to pose for images wearing some of this beadwork.[13]

Two items shown in Figure 9.25, the bag on Smith's left knee and his shirt, which he wore for many pictures, were both in the collection of Alfred H. "Gafe" Peterson of Walker, Minnesota, and eventually came to the Minnesota Historical Society in an anonymous gift. The bag itself is shown in Figure 9.26. The strap detail in Figure 9.27 depicts a different bag with a folded leaf motif, tipped with a target-like element—and the same target element, with another folded leaf, is also visible on the pocket of the bag strap shown in Figure 9.26, suggesting that they are made by the same bag maker. From various dated images of Smith, we can deduce that the bag probably was produced between 1900 and 1912.[14]

John Smith's bag and shirt and sixteen other gashkibidaaganag from Peterson's collection feature many Ojibwe motifs common across Minnesota, but some of the motifs may relate particularly to women with ancestral ties to the northwestern part of Minnesota. Women in the Cass Lake area perhaps shared some motif and color preferences with the Métis and Ojibwe bead artists in the nearby communities of Pembina and Turtle Mountain, North Dakota.

Several of the pieces in Peterson's collection have motifs rendered in blue, red, and white bands of color (Figure 9.28); neither the motifs nor the colors are usually found in beadwork from other Minnesota Ojibwe reservations. Before the Métis women in this region began working with glass beads, they frequently rendered their quillwork in a palette of blue, red, and white (Figure 9.29). The roundels, medallions, or target motifs created with rings or bands of contrasting colors (color layering) that are found in the beadwork of this area were popular in regional quillwork. Medallion motifs are also common among the Turtle Mountain Band of Chippewa in North Dakota, which is primarily made up of descendants of the Pembina Band. The use of different colors of bead rings inside a single motif such as the leaf on the bag in Figure 9.26; the use of blue, red, and white color combinations; and the target-like motif all show how beadworkers continued to use old methods, techniques, and motifs but render them in newly available materials.[15]

9.26 John Smith's bag, gifted anonymously to the Minnesota Historical Society, c. 1900–1912. Note the blue target element at the tip of the folded leaf. *MNHS 2011.208.153*

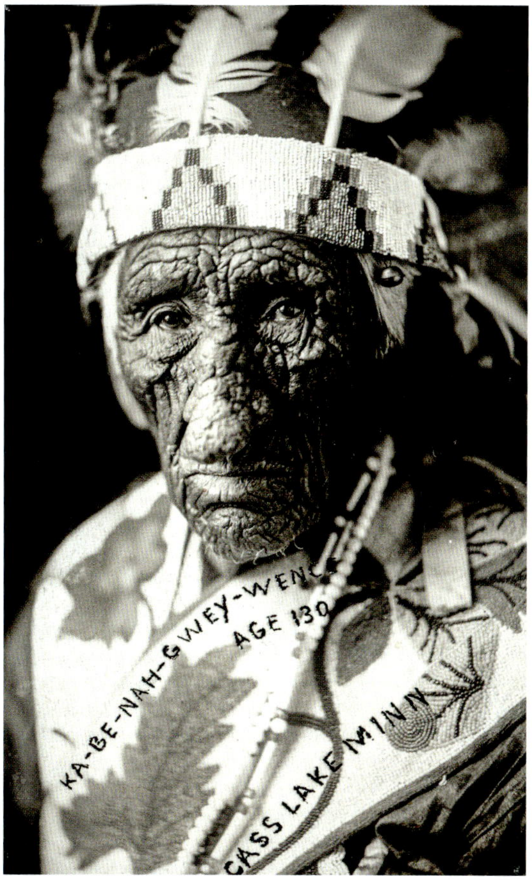

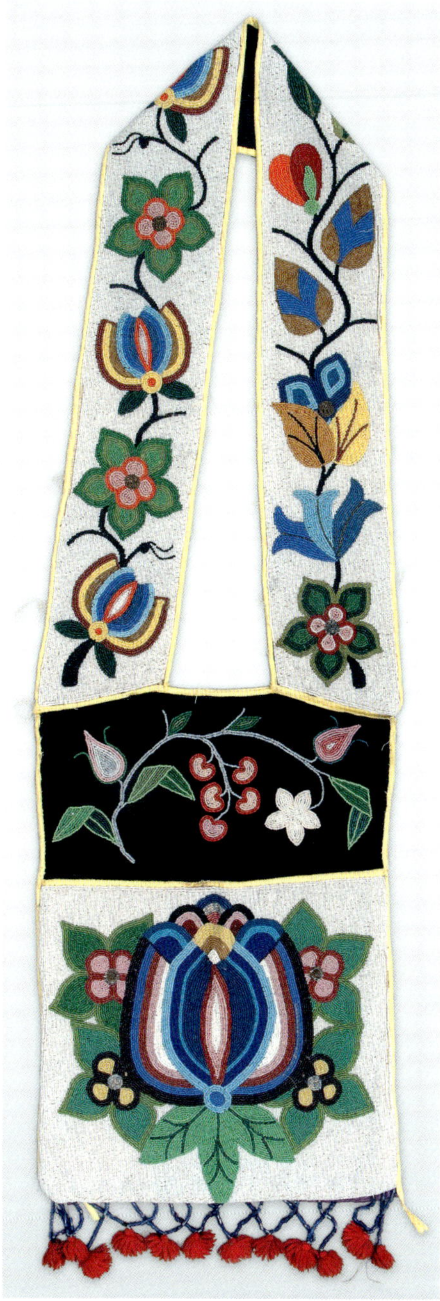

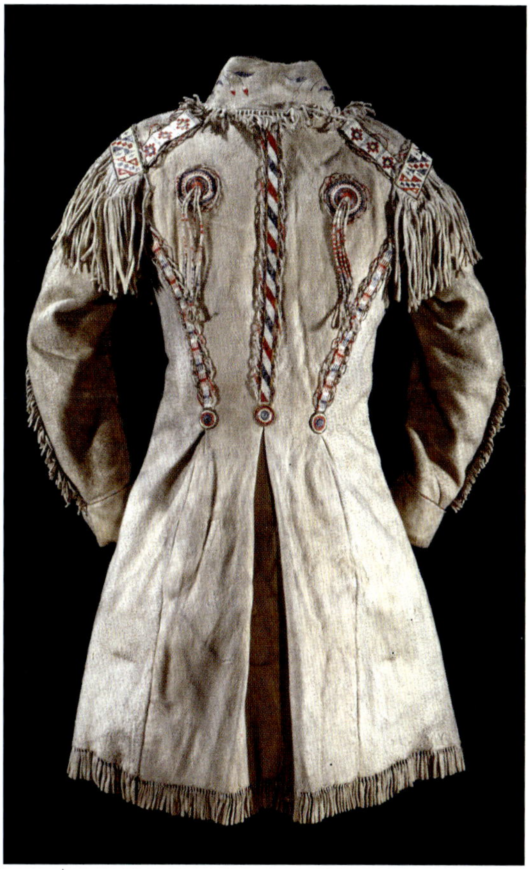

9.27 *(above left)* John Smith, c. 1912. Note the target element on folded leaf under "MINN," lower right. *MNHS E97.1K r72*

9.28 *(above)* Bag from Cass Lake, likely in use after 1890 and before 1920, with a large motif rendered in the blue, red, and white color palette found in Métis communities. The bead artist also used a folded leaf motif. *MNHS 2011.208.160; see also Figure 3.57*

9.29 *(left)* Leather frock coat with blue, red, and white quillwork, mid-nineteenth century. The coat was probably made by a Métis artist, and Alexander Ramsey, the Minnesota territorial governor, may have brought it back from one of the treaty signings he attended in 1851. Ramsey's granddaughters later donated the coat to the Minnesota Historical Society. *MNHS 8303.2*

Melvin Losh, bead artist

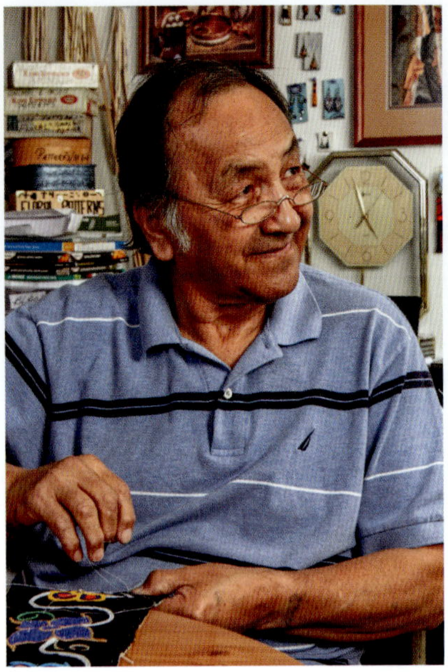

9.30 Bead artist Mel Losh, 2016. The stack of boxes over Mel's right shoulder holds his meticulously organized bead and quill patterns. *Photo by James Castle*

Melvin W. (Mel) "Bear" Losh (Figure 9.30) is a renowned quill and bead artist. He was born in 1946 in Cass Lake, Minnesota, one of Charles and Irene Johnson Losh's eight children. Both of his parents were from the Leech Lake Reservation and were members of the Minnesota Chippewa Tribe. Charles was born at Bena and was known for the birchbark baskets he made. Irene was from the Onigum–Squaw Point area and was regarded as a talented beadworker who also made braided rugs. Melvin, an enrolled member of the Leech Lake Band of Ojibwe, has lived in Bena, Chicago, and Duluth. He worked for the Leech Lake Band for thirty-seven years, first as an accountant in the financial aid office and then as the financial aid director for Leech Lake College.

A great many female Ojibwe beadworkers influenced Mel's work. When he was in high school, he took a loom-work class from Josephine (Josie) Ryan at the Bena Town Hall. Josie was skilled in many mediums, making beadwork, baskets, moccasins, and more, and she got him interested in the craft. She later became a marketing agent for many Ojibwe artisans, buying their work and selling it to businesses and to some collectors. Mel would never copy her beadwork because it was unique, but, he says, "Josie and my mother Irene taught me the actual beading techniques that I use."

He recalls that the most respected beadworkers in the areas around Leech Lake, Bena, and Cass Lake when he was learning to bead were his mother, Irene; Josie Ryan; his aunts Hattie (Losh) Hillstrom, Susan (Losh) Harstad, and Ida (Losh) Donnell (his father's three sisters enrolled in the Leech Lake Band); Clarice Richardson (at Ryan's Village near Bena); Esther Wakonabo (at Inger); and Paula White. Good beadworkers were also active at Cross Lake, Squaw Point, and Onigum. Josie introduced Mel to Mamie Humphrey, a Leech Laker living at Bena, who was a great beadworker on velvet. She made belts, bags, moccasins, and even jingle dresses of black velvet.

Irene Losh made vests, belts, beaded bags, moccasins, and side strips (dance drops), and she took orders for powwow clothing. Irene also learned from other Onigum beadworkers, whose names Mel didn't know. She started actively beading again after her children grew up. When time allowed, his mother and aunts enjoyed making velvet beaded bags, medallions, and moccasins, working on their craft both indoors and outdoors. Most of them also made braided rugs, which was a year-round activity.

Mel is very specific about the methods, materials, and techniques he uses when he beads. His mother left him all her floral patterns, some of which were given to her by another beadworker, Kate Sherman from Lake Winnibigoshish. Irene cut them out of thick paperboard from tea or potato chip boxes; then she traced them onto the cloth with flour paste, or with white pen or pencil on muslin. Mel uses her patterns in both his quill- and beadwork: "I need a pattern for everything I design," he notes.

Mel was once an active powwow dancer, and he started making his own beaded clothing in 1960 (Figure 9.31). After he retired from working for the band, he became restless, so he began doing quill- and beadwork full time. Beadwork has become a major source of income for him. His intention is to create pieces of art, not bags to be worn. When beading, he says, "I completely lose track of time, I think most of the time I am like I am in a trance. When I do bead- and quillwork, it is like an addiction for me, and a challenge."

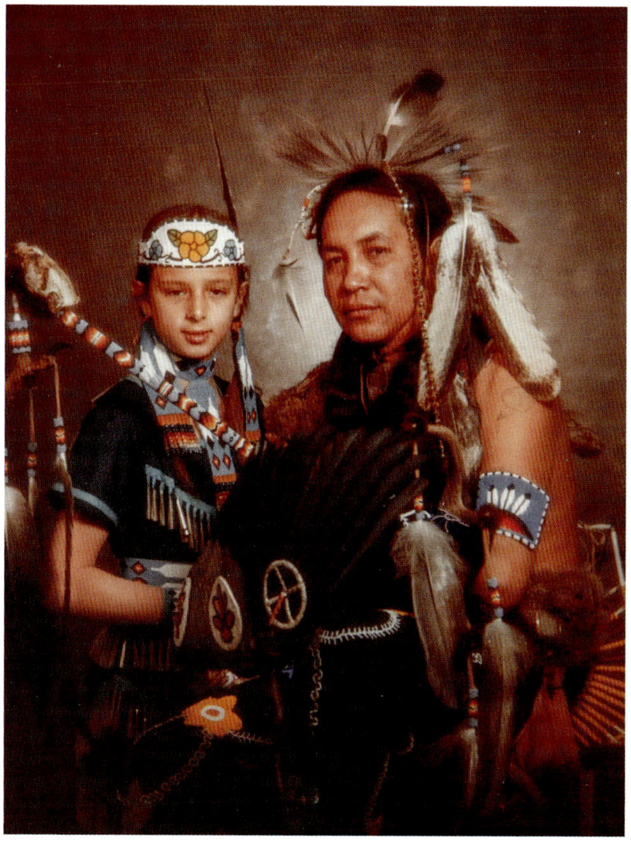

9.31 *(above)* Mel, wearing his dance regalia, posed in the early 1960s with his niece, Laura Losh (now Stangel), who was the first Miss Leech Lake. All the beadwork Laura wore was made by Mel; Mel's mother Irene Losh made her jingle dress. *Photo courtesy Mel Losh*

Mel beads the two straps, the pocket, and the section above the pocket on the gashkibidaaganag he makes. His patterns are always floral. The Ojibwe women who influenced him took their patterns from what they saw in the woods, as well as from what their ancestors handed down to them. But he notes that some other women simply did freehand drawing as they were laying out a design for a gashkibidaagan or other beaded item. The first bags he made have pockets, but the more recent ones don't and are backed with various materials such as felt, wool, or bark cloth (Figure 9.32).

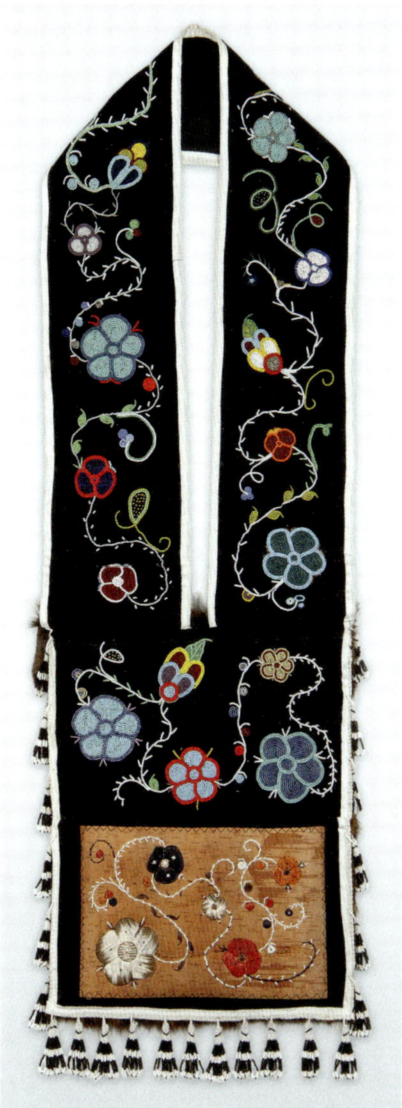

9.32 *(left)* Mel made this bag between 1980 and 1986. Acquired from him for the Minnesota Historical Society's collections, this bag is unusual in that the pocket panel is actually quillwork on birch bark, and the back side of the bag is lined with animal fur. *MNHS 1988.340.1*

Mel buys his beads from many places, including Morrells in Bemidji, Beadin' Path of Fargo, Superior Beads in Duluth, and the Chewe Gift Shop in Cass Lake. Representatives of Hibbing's Blackhawks gift store used to travel to powwows by bus to sell their wares, and Mel bought a lot of beads from them because they had bead types no one else carried. He hasn't seen them lately when he's scouting powwow stands for beads. Mel uses all sizes of beads: 10s, 11s, 13s, and sometimes 15s or 16s if he has a small enough needle. He sews with lots of needles and always uses size D Nymo thread. Because he uses left-over beads from each project, Mel hasn't yet made one gashkibidaagan with all new beads, so he's never counted the number of beads used in one of his bags.

Mel's preferred fabric base for beadwork is cotton velvet (Figures 9.33 and 9.34). He used to go to a variety of stores trying to find cotton velvet because the silk or rayon velvet is too slippery—the beads slip, or the beadwork "crumbles" (doesn't lie flat). His mother had warned him about this, too. Now, he looks for cotton velvet or velveteen at rummage sales, at Goodwill, and at big fabric stores, or friends find it and give it to him.

9.33 *(right)* Mel beading a strap on cotton velvet, 2016. *Photo by James Castle*

9.34 *(below right)* Mel beading, 2016. *Photo by James Castle*

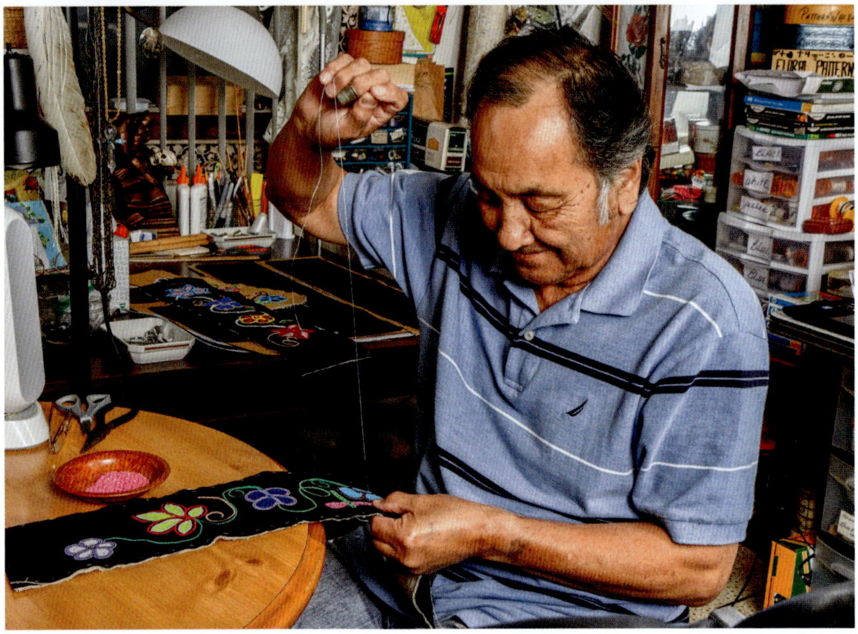

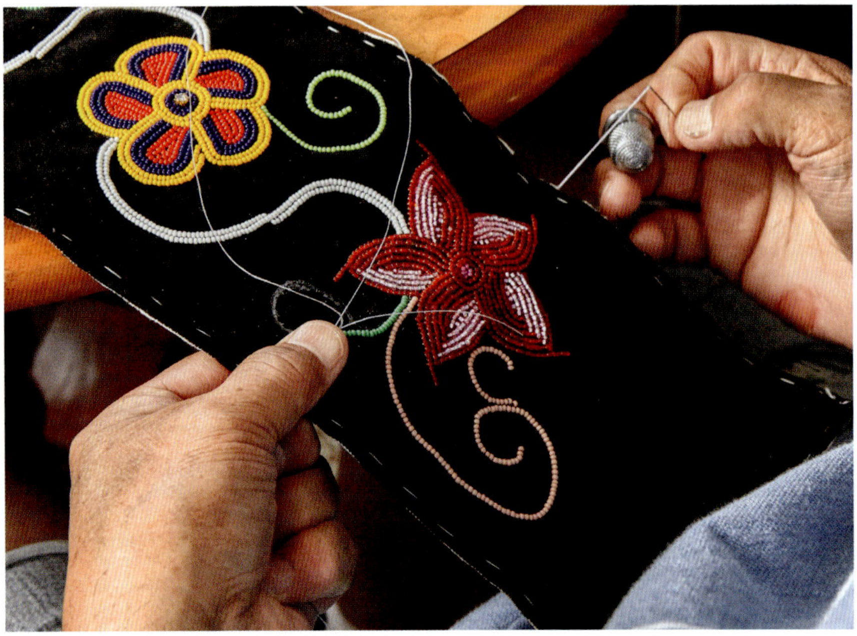

Mel's interfacing material usually consists of paper sack pieces layered between the velvet and the muslin. When paper sacks weren't available he used four layers of newspaper (his mother had suggested that). His lining or backing cloth is unbleached muslin. When he plans to bead the entire surface, with no fabric showing, he also uses unbleached muslin, instead of velveteen, for the ground.

Mel binds his bag edges with cotton bias tape purchased at fabric stores. He always uses white. People tell him he should use dark colors, as the old bags do, but he likes how the white binding "makes the colors pop." For Mel, the biggest challenge of making bandolier bags is piecing the bag together so that it fits well and sewing on the bias tape binding smoothly and evenly. His bags don't have the typical wool yarn tassel fringe or woven tabs. Instead he makes individual bead tassels that each take two to four hours to create, and he usually attaches them to the sides and bottom of the pocket portion of the bag.

Mel's first interest in gashkibidaaganag came when he saw a picture of an Indian woman holding a fully beaded bag in the late 1960s. It was the most beautiful piece of beadwork he had ever seen. He told his parents he was interested in making one. They encouraged and challenged him to do so. Mel had only read about gashkibidaaganag and had only seen them in historical photos and in museums; he can't recall seeing anyone wear or dance them back in the days when he was dancing. He notes that the various Ojibwe forms he is aware of are floral beadwork with both background and patterns fully beaded (spot-stitch appliqué), geometric loom-woven designs, and spot-stitched beadwork on wool or velvet.

In late 2016 Mel had completed his twenty-ninth bag (Figure 9.35) and was working on his thirtieth bag. These days, Mel's bags are almost always sold before he finishes them. Somehow he also has time to make quilled birchbark boxes, embellished with the same colorful flowers he is known for—and often, somewhere on the object, his signature: a ladybug.[16]

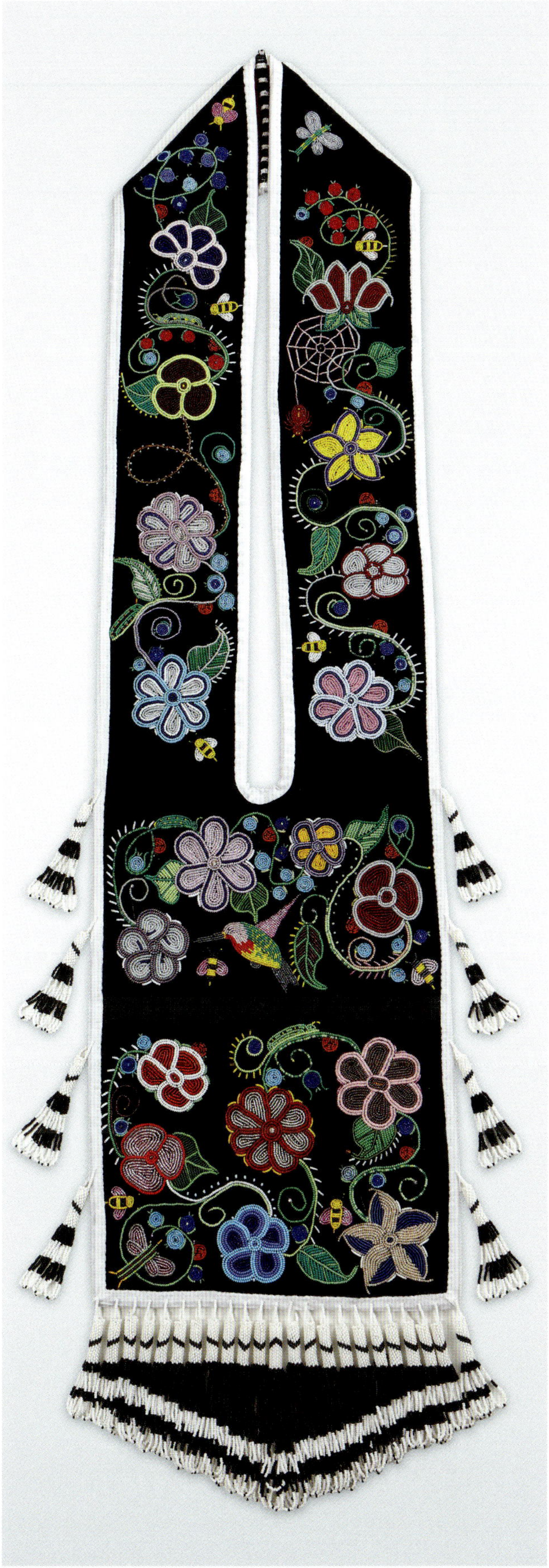

9.35 Melvin Losh's twenty-ninth gashkibidaagan, 2016. *Photo by James Castle*

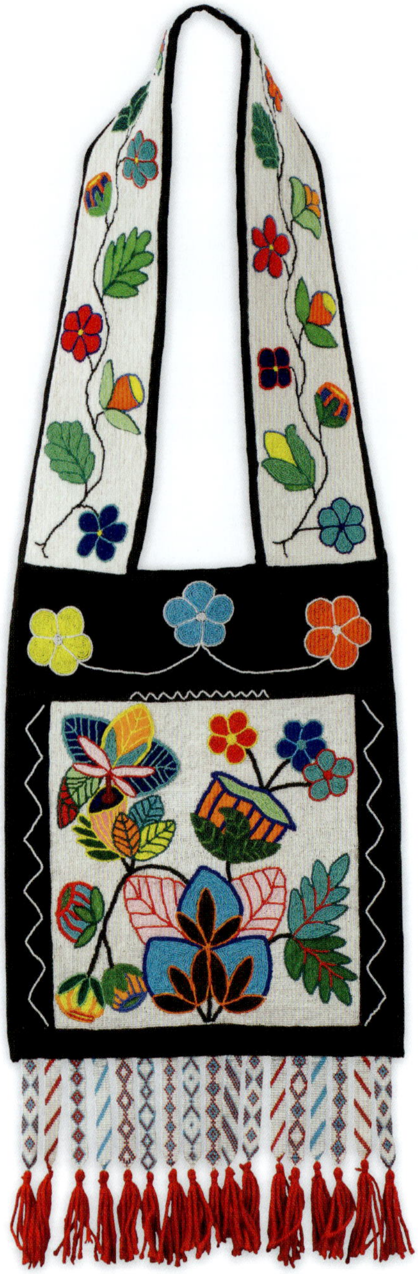

Chapter 10

Mille Lacs

People have been living on the shores of Mille Lacs Lake for thousands of years. It is a beautiful place, rich in fish, wild rice, and other game. When the first Europeans visited the lake, Dakota people lived there, but by the mid-1700s, the Ojibwe had taken over the area. The most intensive occupation of the Mille Lacs area appears to coincide with the beginning of the use of wild rice in the Woodland Period from about 2,150 to 350 years ago. The area on the far eastern edge of the reservation, near the Wisconsin border, has long been regarded as an important crossing for animals and travelers.[1]

The Mille Lacs Reservation, established in 1855, is called Misi-zaaga'ig-aniing in Ojibwemowin, meaning Great Lake. The Mille Lacs, Sandy Lake, and Rice Lake Bands of Mississippi Chippewa, and the Snake and Kettle River Bands of St. Croix Chippewa, were subsumed into the current Mille Lacs Reservation. While the band has property in seven Minnesota counties, Mille Lacs and Pine Counties contain the primary population centers: Vineland, Onamia, Garrison, Isle, Wigwam Bay, Wahkon, Bay Lake, and Milaca.

In 1889 Congress passed the Nelson Act, which forced the allotment of Minnesota's Ojibwe reservations (except Red Lake). The Office of Indian Affairs created the US Chippewa Commission, charged to persuade Ojibwe people throughout Minnesota to take their allotments at White Earth, so that the state's Indian population could be concentrated in one area. Many band members refused removal, and some of the families who did remove later returned to Mille Lacs to be on their land and close to friends and family. Those who stayed became known as the Non-removable Mille Lacs Band.

The beadwork traditions of the Mille Lacs Band are deep rooted and well documented. Jacob Brower, a land surveyor and historian who published a monograph on Mille Lacs in 1900, included a photo of Mille Lacs headmen Na-gwa-ne-be and Aish-pun (Figure 10.01). The man on the left wears a beaded yoke and belt underneath a spot-stitch appliqué bag with a full-width pocket opening, a wide zigzag border treatment, and fringe terminating in wool yarn tassels. The man on the right wears a gashkibidaagan with loom-woven panels on the pocket and strap, a spot-stitch appliqué strip embellishing the top edge of the full-width pocket opening, and related spot-stitch embroidery on the area above the opening. The repetitive motifs on the loom-woven pocket panel and the roundels embroidered above the full-width pocket opening, however, suggest it may have been made by a Wisconsin Ojibwe or other Great Lakes bead artist.[2]

In August 1902, Major James McLaughlin of the US Indian Department visited the Mille Lacs Band, hoping to persuade members to relocate to White Earth. In Figure 10.02, he is the third standing man from the left, holding the rifle he used to kill the steer that those present will soon feast on. The Ojibwe man standing at center left is wearing a spot-stitch appliqué bag with a colored bead background on both the strap and pocket panel. The bag also incorporates a full-width pocket opening and long loom-woven tab fringe terminating in wool yarn tassels. The man to his left wears a brightly patterned bandana over his spot-stitch appliqué beaded bib collar.

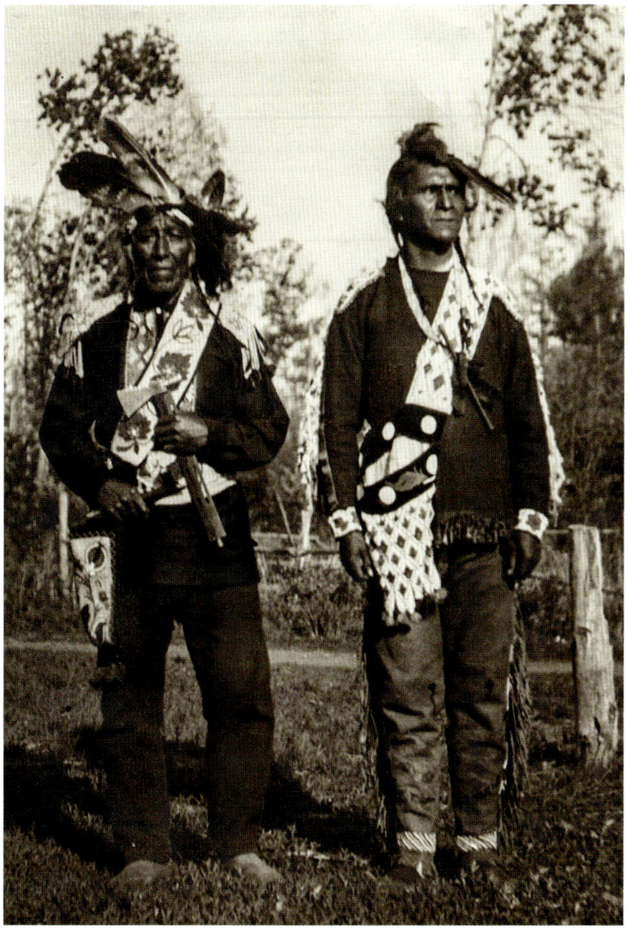

10.01 Mille Lacs leaders Na-gwa-ne-be and Aish-pun, 1901. *MNHS E97.1N m3*

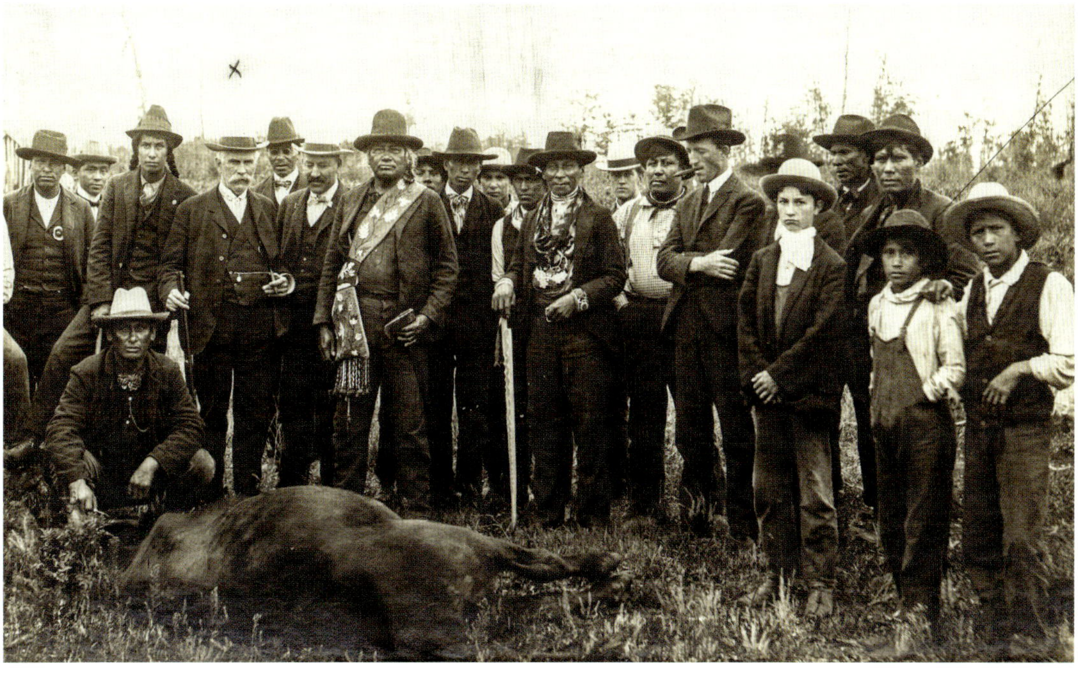

10.02 James McLaughlin of the US Indian Department and Mille Lacs Band members, 1902. *MNHS E97.5 p5*

A fairly late addition to this story of people and the land is the Mille Lacs Indian Museum and Trading Post on Highway 169 in Onamia. The trading post building was operated by Harry and Jeanette Ayer, who developed close personal and working relationships with many band members. Between 1918 and 1959 their roles as employers, friends, vendors of locally made goods, merchants, adoptive parents, and legal guardians earned them a measure of community status and respect rarely attained by non-Indians; the Ayers have also come to be seen as paternalistic and opportunistic by some in later generations. In 1959 they donated their impressive collections of Ojibwe artifacts and the post itself to the Minnesota Historical Society, where researchers can use them to learn about the history of the Mille Lacs Indian community, the craft products of North American Indian artisans, tourism in the area, and the entrepreneurial personalities of the Ayers. For more on the Ayers, see page 155.

Many scholars who published reference works on the culture and traditions of American Indians in the twentieth century contacted the Mille Lacs Indian Trading Post to locate informants and examples of material culture. Anthropologist Albert Ernest Jenks, a professor at the University of Minnesota, did work at Mille Lacs. Frances Densmore, Sister Bernard Coleman, and Beatrice Blackwood of the Pitt Rivers Museum in Oxford, England, to name a few, all worked with the Ayers and Mille Lacs Band members to observe and record stories, cultural traditions, and methods. These researchers also documented the work of Mille Lacs Indian artisans through the purchase and study of objects they created. Sometimes the researchers were directly introduced to individuals who created products at their request. At other times the objects were made available from the trading post's existing inventory. The generosity of knowledgeable band members in providing accurate cultural information, backed by the collections available through the post, gave the Mille Lacs Indian Trading Post and its products a reputation for legitimacy that stands to this day.

Between the 1940s and the 1960s, ten or fifteen band families established roadside stands along Highway 169 to sell to tourists (Figure 10.03). Families sat on quilts or under temporary bark shelters making crafts that were usually suspended from lashed wood structures at the road's edge.[3]

The owner of another enterprise on the west side of Mille Lacs Lake also worked closely with members of the Mille Lacs Band. Sherman Holbert operated Fort Mille Lacs a few miles south of the Ayer facility. The success of the Ayers' enterprise, Holbert's attractions, and the family stands was due to a precipitous convergence of critical elements. American Indians were making their history, region, and lifeways accessible through entrepreneurial invention while interacting with two successful commercial tourism businesses and a Euro-American public. For more on Holbert, see page 163.

Mille Lacs beadworkers used motifs representing primarily two different styles. One is typical of the floral motifs, folded leaf, and arrangements commonly found in bags also associated with the White Earth, Red Lake, and Leech Lake Reservations. The second group is similarly arranged and connected with vinelike elements but incorporates motifs and juxtapositions that are rarely found elsewhere: cornucopias, columns, floral forms with three lobes or petals (possibly representing trilliums), trumpet-shaped flowers, pod forms, layering of unrelated motifs, and unusual sprays or clusters of noncompatible motifs bursting forth from another single motif. Examples of the former can be seen in a number of images that capture gashkibidaaganag in a variety of Mille Lacs settings. In Figure 10.04, the woman standing in the back row wears a full spot-stitch appliqué panel bag with a typical arrangement of leaves and flowers attached to meandering vines as well as a narrow slit or faux opening on the pocket panel. The pocket appears to be outlined with what resembles a hexagonal dot motif that is more common on older loom-woven bags from the 1860s to the 1880s.

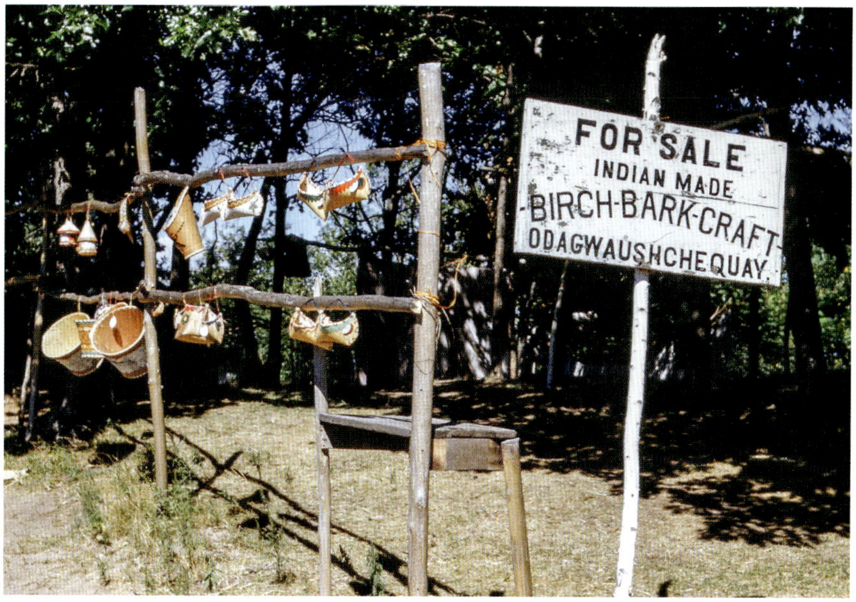

10.03 *(above)* A Mille Lacs family's roadside stand alongside Highway 169, September 1946. *MNHS I.69.165*

10.04 *(below)* People posed in front of Einen's store in Onamia, c. 1909–12. *MNHS E97.1 r17*

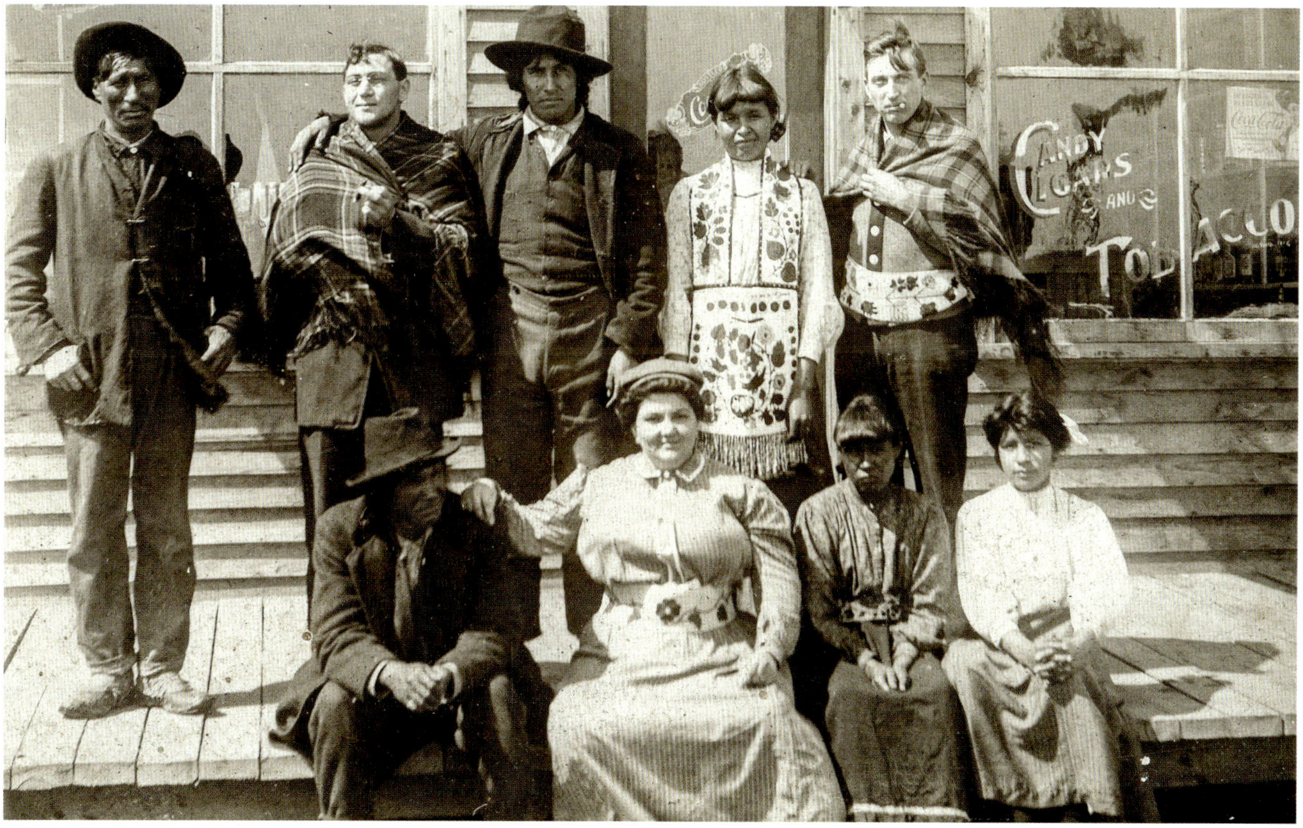

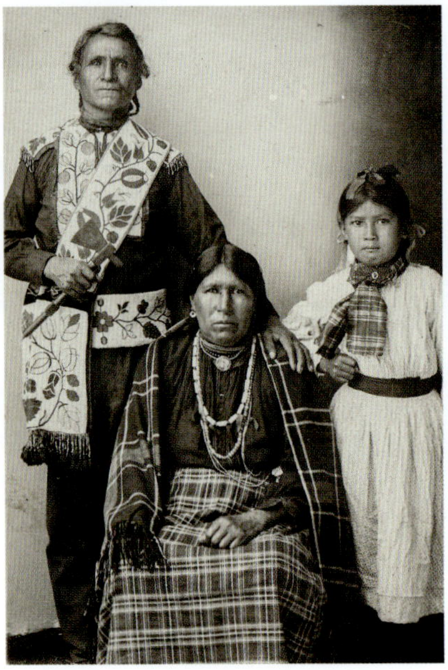

10.05 *(above)* Shingobe family, Mille Lacs, c. 1909–12. The girl is identified as Susan Sam Razor. *MNHS E97.1S r11*

10.06 *(right)* Mille Lacs postcard, c. 1927. *Pat Albers Collection GL05A*

10.07 *(below)* Tom Shingobe, 1967. *MNHS Collection I.69.51*

In Figure 10.05, a typical studio portrait family grouping, Mrs. Shingobe wears fabrics and blankets, often woven in plaid patterns and rendered in a drab palette, that are so common among the Ojibwe women of Minnesota in the twentieth century. Beaded necklaces, simple earrings, and perhaps a cameo brooch provide her ornamentation. Mr. Shingobe wears a yoke, a belt, and a spot-stitch appliqué gashkibidaagan with a full-width pocket opening and long strung-bead fringe finished with wool yarn tassels.

A rare historical image (Figure 10.06) features three women dancing six gashkibidaaganag. A man on the far left wears one bag. Fully visible bags are all spot-stitch appliqué with full-width pocket openings, and at least four have the wide zigzag border treatments popular in the early decades of the twentieth century.[4]

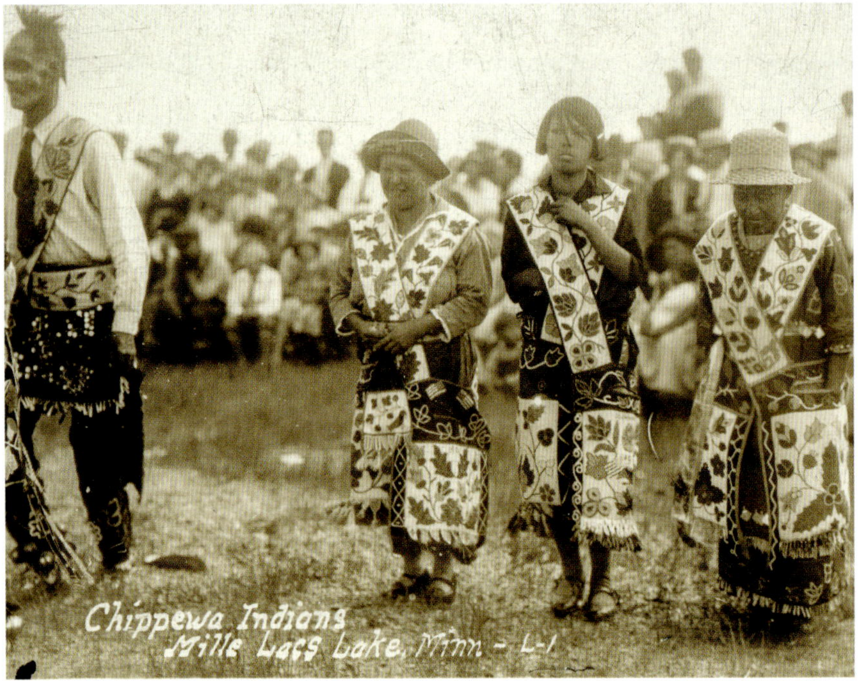

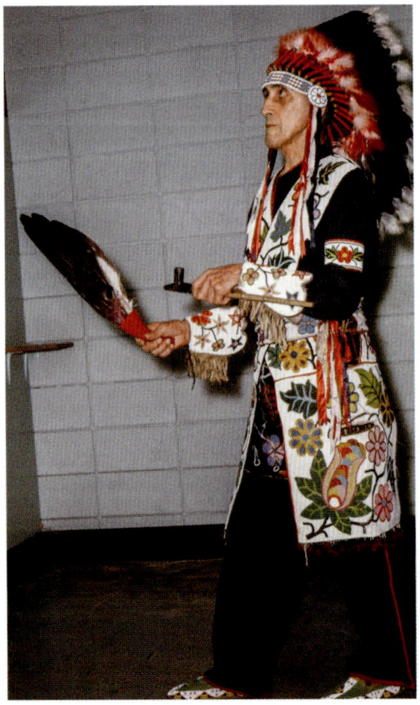

Two slides taken by collector Monroe Killy in 1967 record Mille Lacs Band member Tom Shingobe wearing two elaborate spot-stitch appliqué panel bags with narrow slit pocket openings and fringe with glass beads and yarn tassels. The lower left corner of the fully visible bag in Figure 10.07 incorporates one of the distinctive tulip or lilylike motifs seen in other Minnesota Ojibwe bags.[5]

Images taken outside of Minnesota occasionally show individuals wearing gashkibidaaganag that feature the unusual cornucopia-like motif; when the origin of a bag bearing this motif can be traced to a specific place, that origin has thus far always been Mille Lacs. It is not surprising that influences would be shared between the Ojibwe of eastern Minnesota and western Wisconsin. Members of the St. Croix Band were split by the state boundary; trade, visits, and marriages can certainly explain the potential migration of motifs.

Wawweyaycumig and Nawajibigokwe

Chief Wawweyaycumig (Round Earth), born about 1853, and his wife, Nawajibigokwe (Central Rock Woman), were both highly regarded for their traditional knowledge. They gave Frances Densmore information that she used in *Chippewa Customs*, and Nawajibigokwe also helped Densmore with *Uses of Plants by the Chippewa Indians*. They appear together in many photographs.[6]

Until 1903 Chief Wawweyaycumig and Nawajibigokwe lived at Mille Lacs. For many years, Wawweyaycumig had protested the removal of his family and others from Mille Lacs to White Earth. Darwin Hall, chairman of the US Chippewa Commission (see page 197), spent many years working to persuade Wawweyaycumig and other Mille Lacs Band members to move. In the late 1890s, Wawweyaycumig became more convinced that he had no other option, and he helped encourage many other band members to move as well. He and his family (Figure 10.08) moved in 1903.[7]

Wawweyaycumig wore a total of six different gashkibidaaganag, always two at a time, when he was photographed on three different occasions. The bags likely were made by Nawajibigokwe. In Figure 10.09, taken at Elbow Lake on the White Earth Reservation, Nawajibigokwe holds a small beaded bag. As in other images, she wears several loom-woven bead chains, suggesting she is a prolific bead artist and perhaps indicating her pride in her work and her status in her community. Her beadwork is rooted in the stylistic qualities of Mille Lacs, but after the family moved to White Earth in 1903, collectors would probably assume it was of White Earth stylistic origins. Wawweyaycumig wears two bags. The ones worn by the man at the other end of the back row are more difficult to assess, but the one worn by the young boy in the first row appears to be a full panel spot-stitch appliqué bag, possibly having no functional pocket.

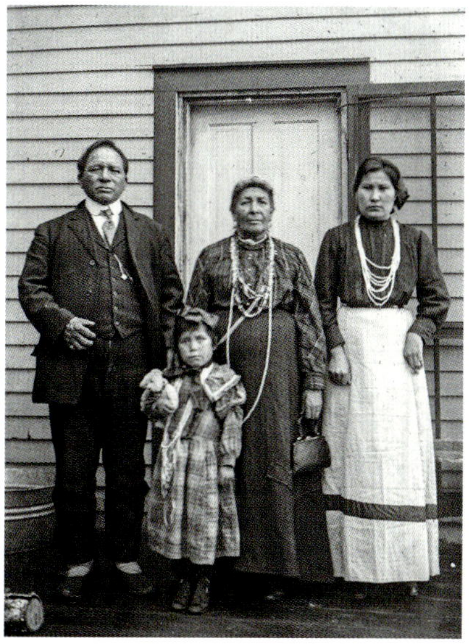

10.08 Wawweyaycumig family photograph showing three generations, White Earth Reservation, c. 1905. *Photo by Robert G. Beaulieu, MNHS E97.1W r5*

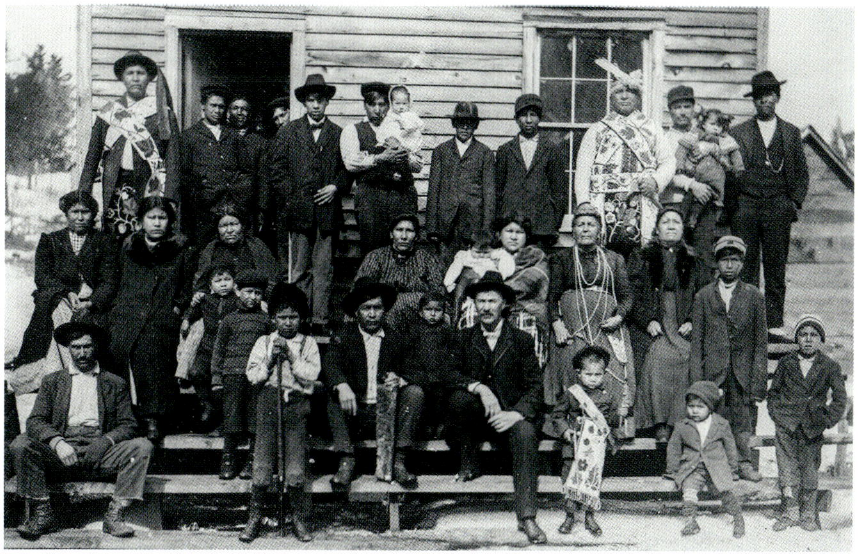

10.09 Wawweyaycumig *(back row, third from right)*, his wife *(second row, third from right)*, and other Mille Lacs removals to White Earth, Elbow Lake, c. 1905. *Photo by Robert G. Beaulieu, MNHS E97.5 r4*

Wawweyaycumig wears the same bag on his left hip in both Figures 10.09 and 10.10. Figures 10.10, 10.11, and 10.12 were all taken by De Lancy Gill in Washington, DC, in February 1908. After one photo, the two bags were switched and the beaded waist belt was dropped slightly, revealing more bag details. Unlike the bags in Figure 10.09, these are full panel bags either with no pocket or with a narrow, likely nonfunctional pocket opening, with multiple rows of otter-track edging on both bags, and with loom-woven tab fringe. Figure 10.12 reveals a linear border on the bag strap, one or two beads in width, created to mimic the old-style strap construction in which two separate strips met at center top.[8]

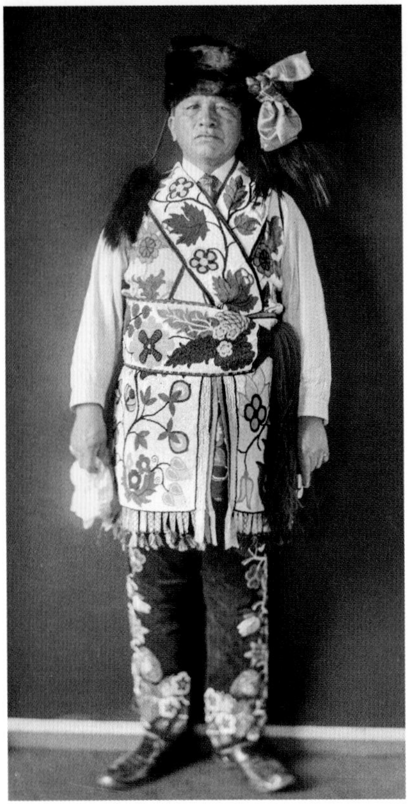

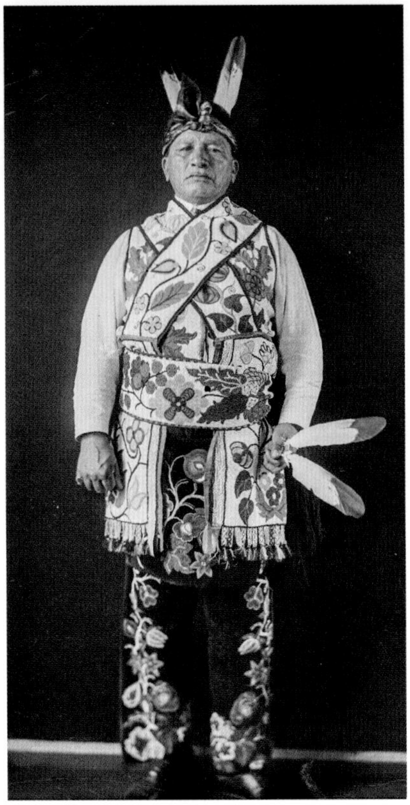

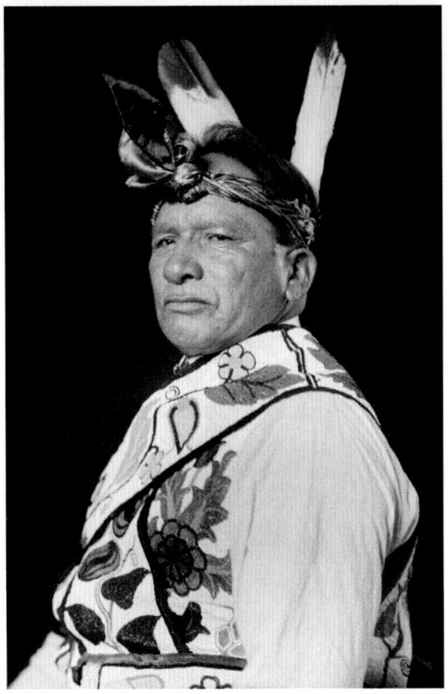

10.10 *(above)* Wawweyaycumig, 1908. *Photo by De Lancy Gill, NAA-SI BAE GN 00532C 06143900*

10.11 *(above center)* Wawweyaycumig, 1908. *Photo by De Lancy Gill, NAA-SI BAE GN 00533B 06144100*

10.12 *(above right)* Wawweyaycumig, with shoulder strap details, 1908. *Photo by De Lancy Gill, NAA-SI BAE GN 00533A 06144000*

White Earth superintendent John R. Howard collected materials from many White Earth artisans in the first quarter of the twentieth century, and in about 1963 his family donated to the Mille Lacs Indian Museum thirty objects that were then cataloged as part of the Ayer collection. One of the items was labeled "Belt. Chippewa Chief's from White Earth Reservation" (Figure 10.13). It is, in fact, the same belt worn by Wawweyaycumig in most of these photos. None of his bags have been located, but this sash provides a fine example of his beadwork regalia and its maker's artistry.[9]

This collection of photos, together with others taken by Stella Stocker, is particularly useful because it includes so many remarkable bag images and good documentation to allow us to make suggestions about the bead artist herself. Since Wawweyaycumig and Nawajibigokwe are from longtime Mille Lacs families removed to White Earth, these photos also

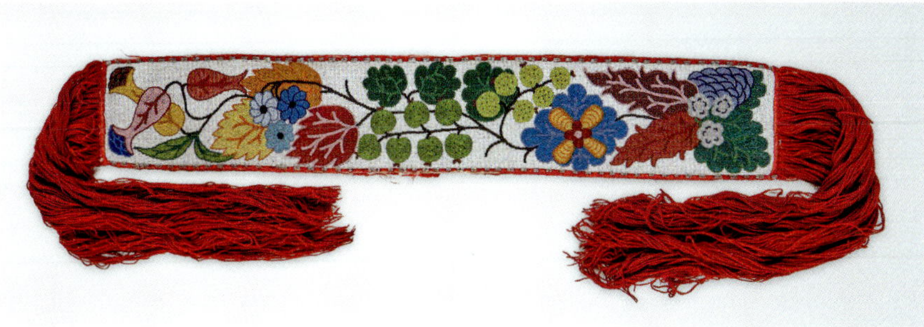

10.13 Wawweyaycumig's beaded belt, c. 1900, no later than 1908. *MNHS 10000.716*

contribute to an understanding and documentation of Minnesota Ojibwe beadwork from different bands blending together as reservations were established.[10]

Lake Lena

Not much is known about the small group of twentieth-century gashkibidaaganag associated with the Ojibwe community of Lake Lena, on the St. Croix River about twenty-two miles east of Hinckley, Minnesota. Today that location serves as the administrative center for the Mille Lacs Reservation's District Three. These bags share design characteristics, the beaded words "Lake Lena, Minn.," and a date. Beaded representations of words and numbers, like images of animals and people, are not frequently seen on Minnesota Ojibwe bags. Some of the Lake Lena bags also feature the outline floral decoration above the pocket opening that was more typically seen in Ho-Chunk, Menominee, Potawatomi, or Meskwaki beadwork. A local theory suggests that the Lake Lena bags may have been made specifically for presentation to Ojibwe men returning from military service, or in recognition of their military service.

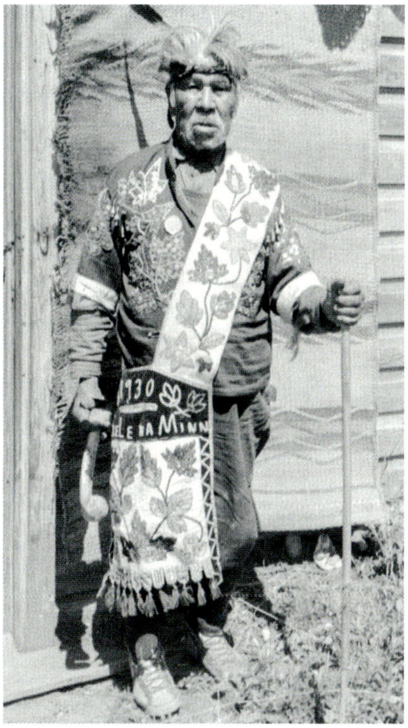

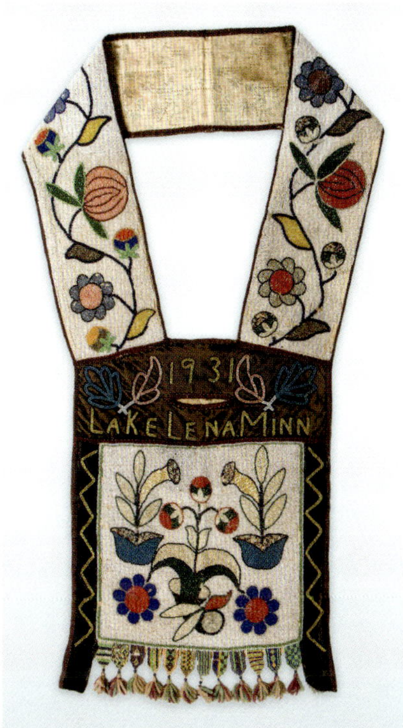

10.14 *(above left)* Zhonii'a Giishig, 1941. *MPM 5747*

10.15 *(above)* Lake Lena bag, 1931. *MNHS 2005.193.1*

In Figure 10.14, Zhonii'a Giishig (Sky Money), or John Mink, wears a 1930 Lake Lena bag. Mink lived from 1850 to 1943, was described as a Midewiwin priest and drum religion leader, and resided on the Lac Courte Oreilles Reservation, about seventy-five miles east of the Lake Lena community, in Wisconsin. The Minnesota Historical Society acquired another Lake Lena bag, shown in Figure 10.15 and dated 1931, from the Sherman

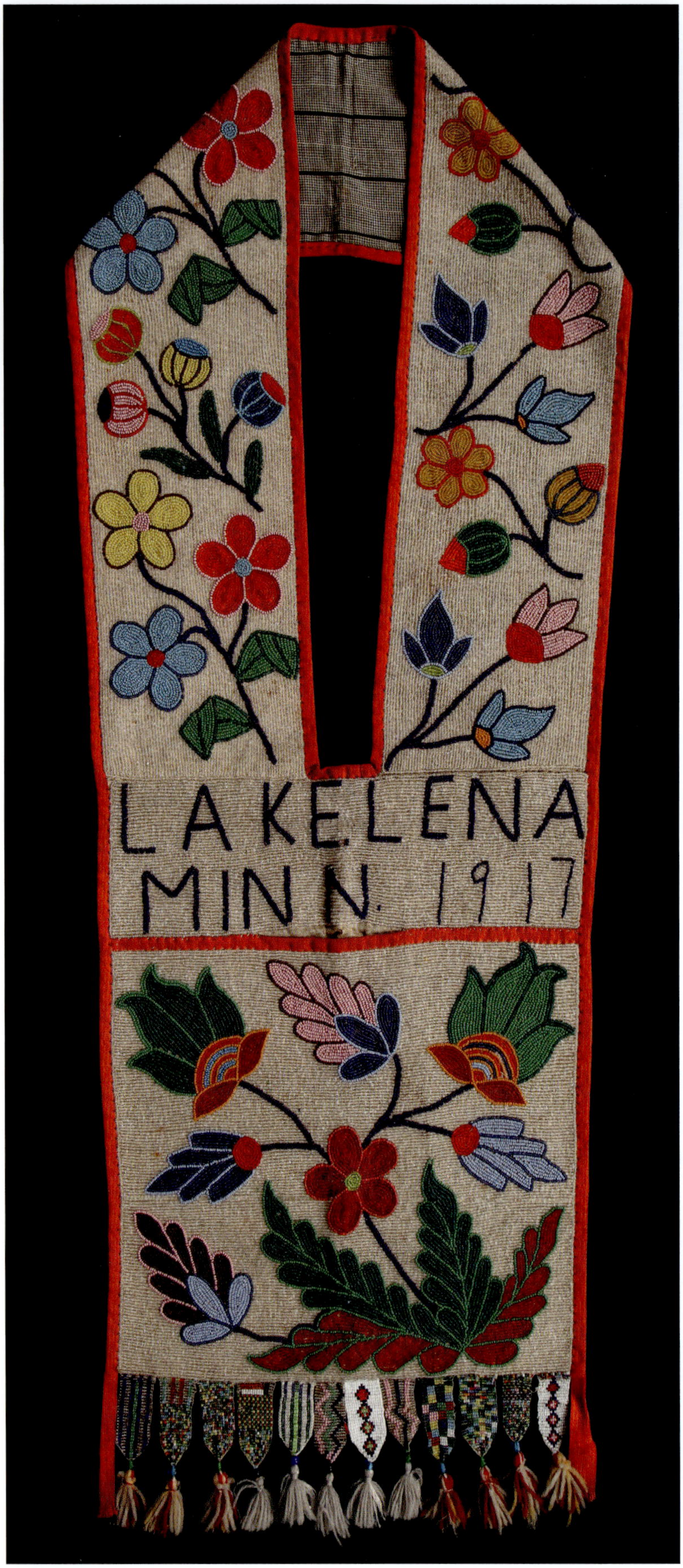

Holbert collection. At the time he acquired it, Holbert was told it had been designed by Mille Lacs Band member Jim Clark and made by women in his family. The two bags are very similar, having the same zigzag border treatment, narrow slit pocket opening, and beaded outline floral motifs above the pocket panel. The 1931 pocket panel is also decorated with three images representing creative interpretations of the tree-of-life motif used by cultures around the globe.[11]

Another narrow slit pocket opening (4.25 inches) is found on the Lake Lena bag in Figure 10.16, dated 1917. Unlike the other two bags, however, this one also includes the folded leaf motif on one side of the strap. Formerly displayed in the Mille Lacs Indian Baptist Mission, the bag is now in the collections of Bethel University's History Center in St. Paul. Yet another 1917 bag (Figure 10.17) was owned by Monroe Killy, then purchased by William and Barbara Schoenwetter, who donated it to the Minnesota Historical Society in 2016. It includes a cornucopia motif, a folded leaf, and several other heavily layered motifs on the strap, as well as the place name. The artist represented a pocket opening using red binding fabric; she has filled the space above the bag pocket with an elegant symmetrical motif incorporating leaves, birds, and a central flower. All four Lake Lena bags also have loom-woven tab fringe, with nonrepeating motifs, which is rarely found on spot-stitch appliqué bags.

The similarities in these bags—their shared unique motifs and similar arrangement of elements—suggest that the bags were made by women from one family or a community of women in the Lake Lena, Minnesota, area.[12]

10.16 Lake Lena bag, 1917. *HCABU 0001*

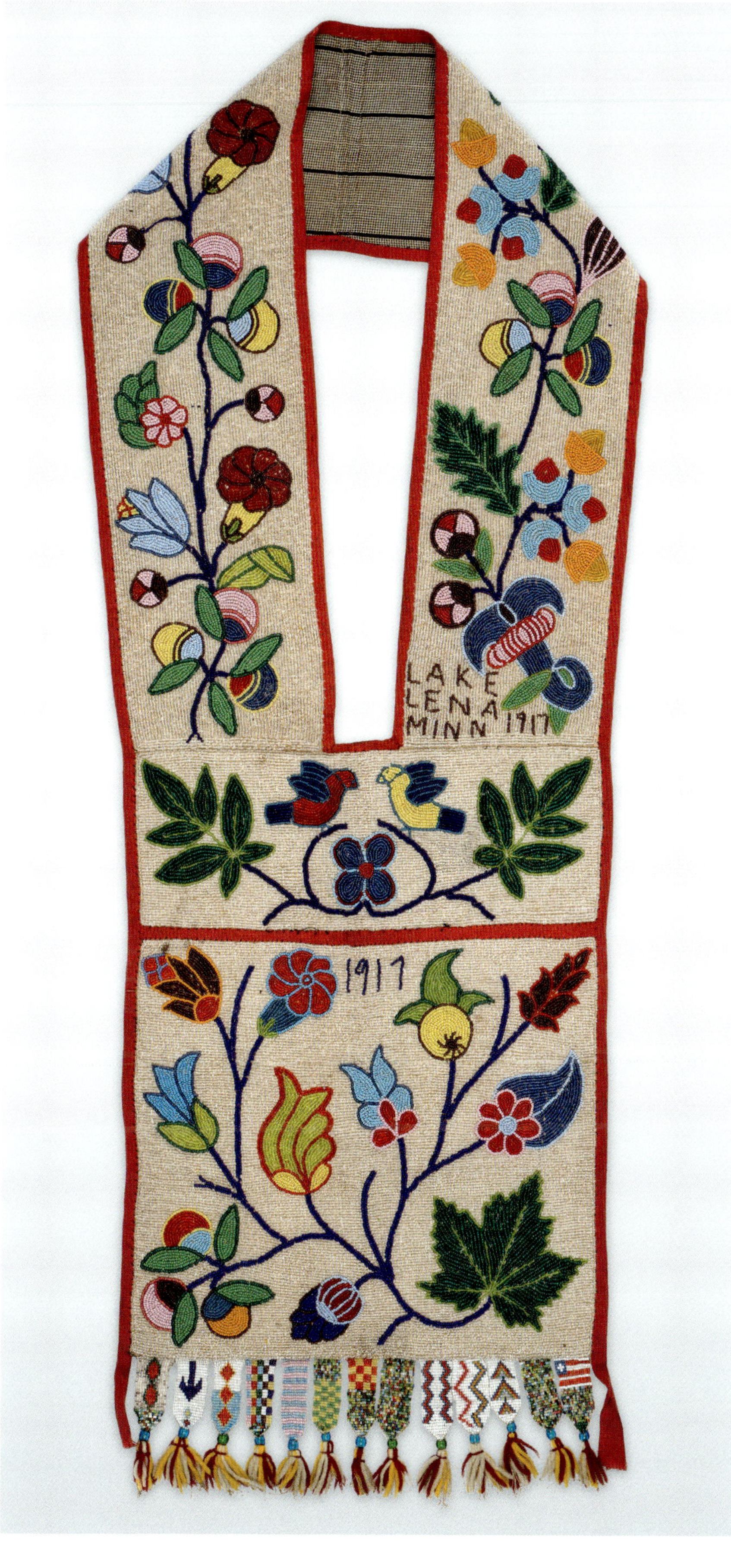

10.17 Lake Lena bag, 1917.
MNHS 2016.160.1

Pete Moos

In the 1910s, photographer Ross A. Daniels operated his business in Sandstone (ten miles north of Hinckley) and then in Pine City (fourteen miles south of Hinckley). Among his customers were Pete Moos (Moose) and other members of the Mille Lacs Band in Pine County. Three of his portraits record gashkibidaaganag for which we have no other records.[13]

The beadwork in the two gashkibidaaganag worn by Pete Moos in Figures 10.18 and 10.19 is remarkable, and the size of the bags and their motifs suggest they were made in the early twentieth century, at about the time the portraits were made. Despite the different dates provided by catalogers, these studio images were clearly taken the same day in the same setting, and they capture two spot-stitch appliqué bags featuring complex layered and assembled motifs that are associated with the Mille Lacs Band, like leaf-wrapped cornucopias, trumpet- or horn-shaped flowers, and three-lobed or -petaled flowers (possibly representing trillium). The more common Minnesota motifs include the folded leaf, vines decorated with numerous motifs, and a realistic rosebud. Both bags have attached loom-woven tab fringe and full-width pocket openings. Moos also wears an elaborate spot-stitch appliqué fringed yoke, a belt, and moccasin cuffs.

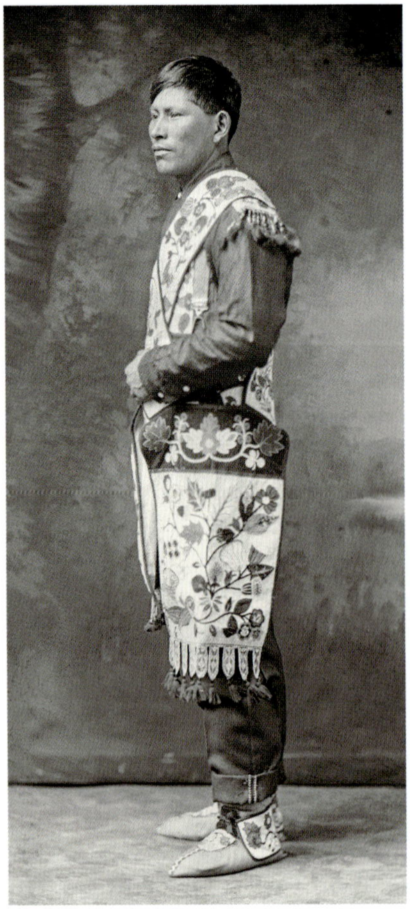

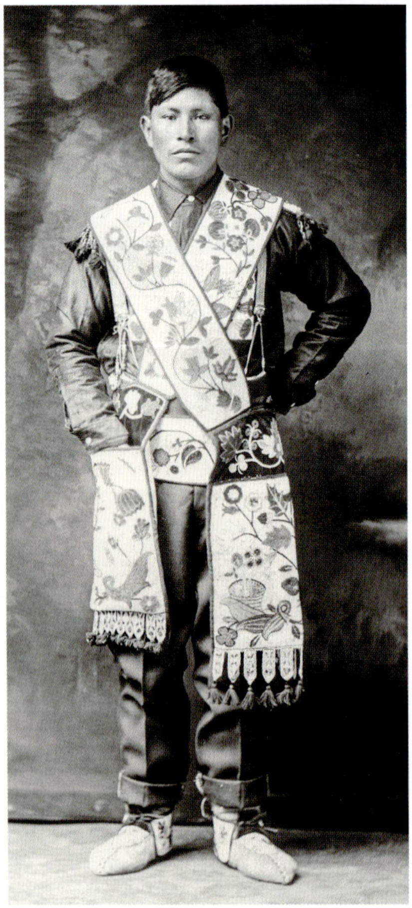

10.18 *(right)* Pete Moos, c. 1912.
MNHS E97.1 p60

10.19 *(far right)* Pete Moos, c. 1913.
MNHS E97.1 r170

The Ayers, owners of the Mille Lacs Trading Post

Harry and Jeanette Ayer began regular visits to the Mille Lacs Reservation area in 1914, but they didn't become full-time residents until 1918, when they took over the H. D. Robbins Trading Post on the western shore of Mille Lacs Lake. The Ayers were never official Indian agents, but they were licensed to trade with the Ojibwe. The husband and wife both eventually learned the Ojibwe language and developed close personal and working relationships with many band members. As early as the 1920s, the Ayers encouraged band members to make crafts for sale, opening a new sales room to attract tourists in 1926 (Figures 10.20 and 10.21). The lovely shores of the lake were within easy driving distance for residents of the Twin Cities of Minneapolis and St. Paul who had begun buying cars, and the entrepreneurial Ayers saw opportunities for members of the Non-removable Mille Lacs Band. The trading post became an important and regular destination for weekend travelers heading "up to the lake," along scenic Highway 169.[14]

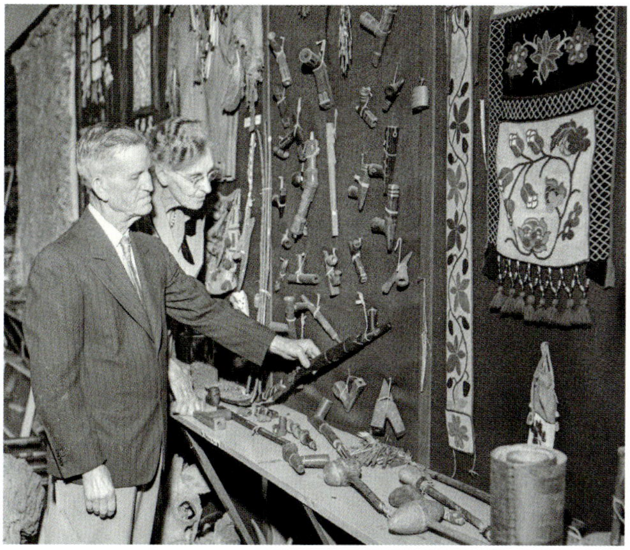

10.20 *(above)* Harry and Jeanette Ayer in their trading post, 1959. *MNHS por 72 p4*

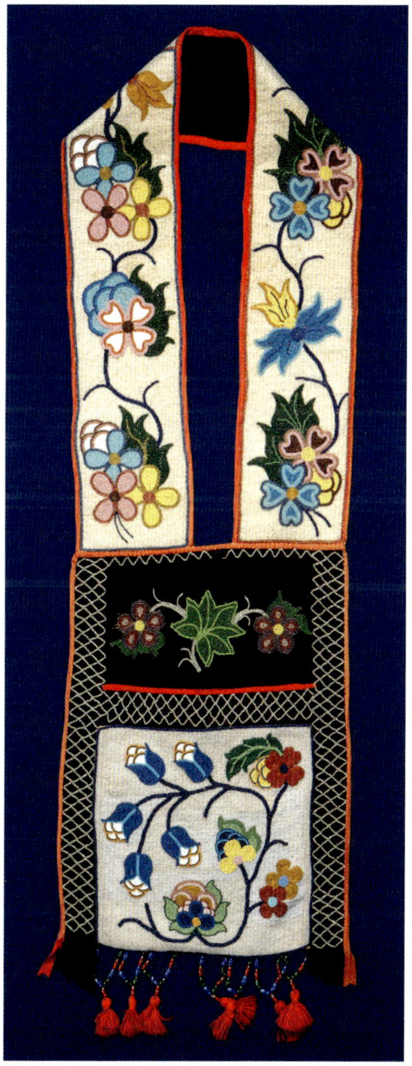

10.21 *(left)* The gashkibidaagan visible in Figure 10.20, c. 1875–1925. *MNHS 10000.610; see also Figures 2.09 and 3.17*

The Ayers' collection of about fourteen hundred items—woven yarn bags, birchbark containers, dolls, smoking equipment, beaded garments, textiles, and games—is supplemented with extensive photographs, trading post and store records, and correspondence. This combined body of materials provides a rare perspective on twentieth-century reservation life and commerce. The trading post and museum at Mille Lacs, now a Minnesota Historical Society historic site, enables the society and descendants of Mille Lacs artisans to maintain the ongoing relationships and to continue documenting

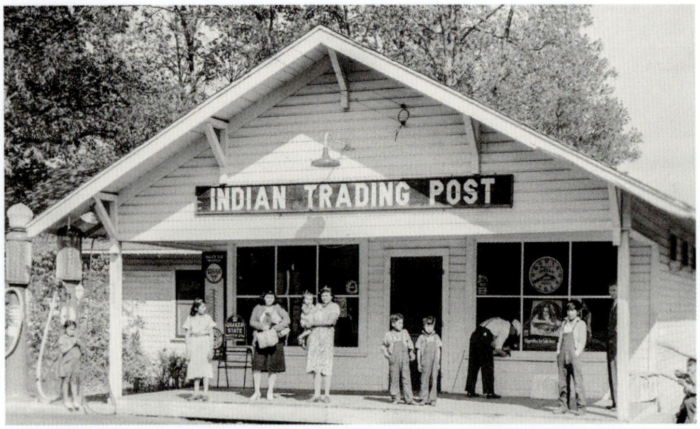

10.22 The Ayers' trading post, c. 1929. *MNHS MM6.7M r81*

the crafts, tourist trade, culture, customs, and practices of this Ojibwe community.[15]

The Ayers purchased contemporary American Indian crafts to sell in their trading post (Figure 10.22) directly from craftspeople as well as from their representatives. According to interviews with band members, the Ayers received their first objects as gifts at dances held by Indian people at Mille Lacs. They asked people to make specific items for their collection and also purchased and took artifacts in exchange for groceries and other goods. They were interested not only in the work of local Ojibwe but also in the work of Native artisans from the Southwest, from the greater Upper Midwest, and from Alaska. They also carried stock that was appropriate for bead artists' needs, including printed cottons, oilcloth, bead needles, needle threaders, beads, and assorted ribbons. The Ayers encouraged submissions of craftwork that would appeal to seasonal tourists as well as serious collectors, leading to innovative as well as "traditional" forms.[16]

Many of the pieces in this large collection were displayed at the trading post as part of the Ayers' marketing strategy to build their reputation as a quality resource for the purchase of authentic American Indian material culture. The Ayers sometimes acquired more costly objects that they used for display and demonstration, never intending to offer them for sale (Figure 10.23). These beautiful items were artfully arranged on the walls inside the trading post or secured in glass cases. Images of the trading post taken in 1935 (see Figure 5.06) and in 1948 (Figure 10.24) reveal that many of the same objects remained on long-term display. As many as fourteen gashkibidaaganag were on display at one time. Some of those same bags, however, are worn by band members in photographs taken of performances for tourists, which demonstrates a partnership between the Ayers and Mille Lacs tribal members. In the 1920s and 1930s, the Minnesota

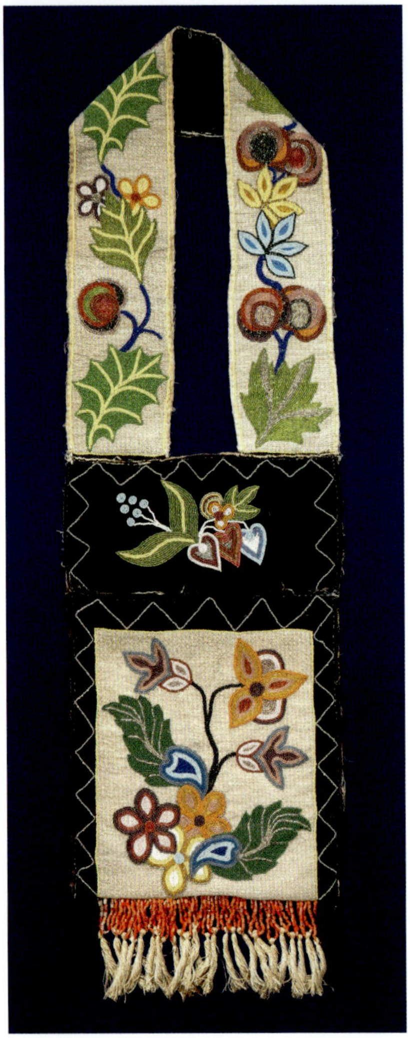

10.23 *(above)* A spot-stitched bag collected by the Ayers, c. 1875–1925. *MNHS 10000.154*

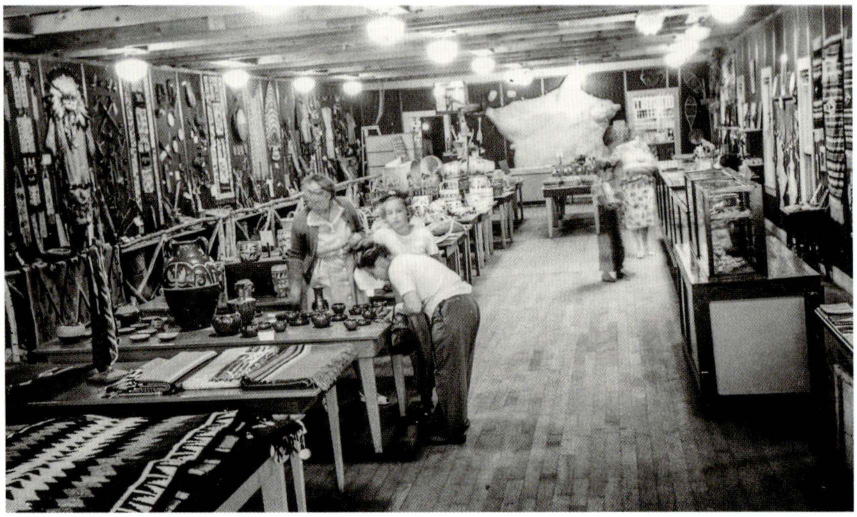

10.24 *(right)* Mille Lacs Indian Trading Post, 1948. Bandolier bags hang on the walls. *MNHS MM6.7M r139*

Historical Society regularly offered member trips from St. Paul to the trading post for these cultural demonstrations and activities.

We know the names of some of the women who made gashkibidaaganag and sold them to the Ayers, but in most cases we don't know which of the surviving bags were made by whom. Twenty-four beaded objects, including gashkibidaaganag, in the Ayer collection cover a range of beadworking styles used over several decades, with the majority likely made after 1900. Some bags are associated with specific Mille Lacs families, including the Skinaways (see page 160) and the Boyds, meaning these bags were either used by or made for members of these families. The beautifully designed and executed bag in Figure 10.25 is associated with Charlie Gahbow of the Mille Lacs Band. It's possible that his wife, at his side in Figure 10.26, made the bag that became part of the Ayer collection.[17]

The three bags in Figures 10.27, 10.28, and 10.29 were collected at White Earth in the early 1900s by Agent John R. Howard and then given to the Ayers by Howard's children. They have obvious shared motifs and assembly elements, suggesting a single maker or perhaps a family group; their dates suggest they were made at Mille Lacs and taken to White Earth during the removal of 1889. The motif arrangements are somewhat unusual, with fewer and larger motifs and more open space between them than typical, but the overall presentation remains fluid. What appears to be a prairie coneflower motif sits at the base of the strap

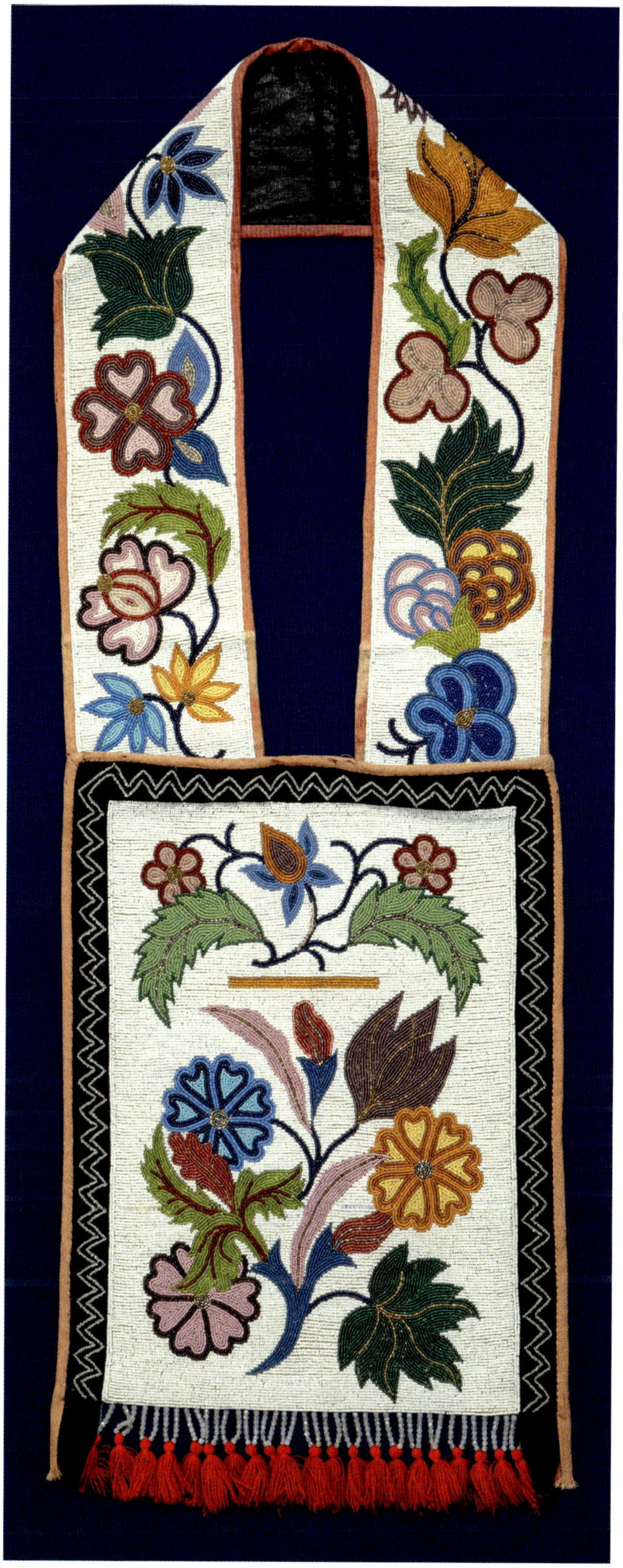

10.25 *(above)* Bag that the Ayers associated with Charlie Gahbow, c. 1875–1925. *MNHS 10000.625*

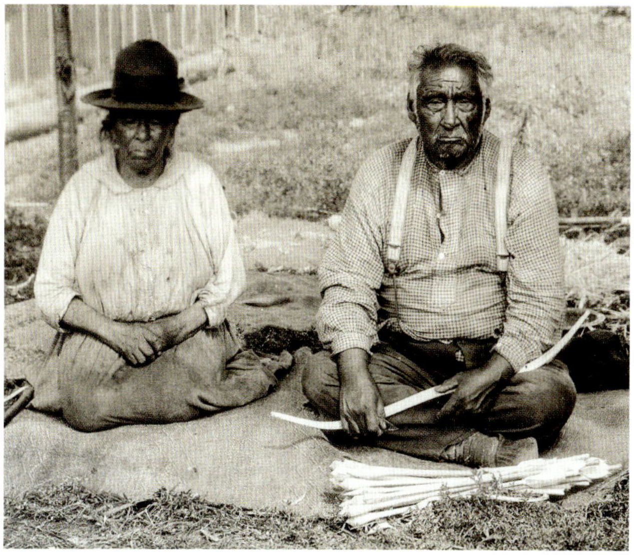

10.26 *(left)* Mr. and Mrs. Charlie Gahbow making a bow and arrows, c. 1925. *MNHS E97.34 r13*

on the left of all three bags. The bags in Figures 10.27 and 10.28 also have what may have been intended to represent a trillium on the strap and an oak leaf on the pocket. The motifs are boldly articulated, and no doubt these bags would each have helped their wearer make a striking impression while circling with the other dancers on the powwow grounds.

In 1921 Charley Boyd, his wife Quaykosh, and their young son Raining posed beside Mille Lacs Lake (Figure 10.30). Raining's cradleboard is wrapped with beaded cloth bands, probably made by Quaykosh or her female relatives. These beadworkers may have been makers of an unusual gashkibidaagan in the Ayer collection (Figure 10.31) associated with Charley. The fall color palette and the flowers with circular petals are not common among bags known to be made by Minnesota Ojibwe artists, but the variations on the coneflower motif are typical of the unusual imagery seen often in bags attributed to Mille Lacs.[18]

The Ayers took care to keep a representative sampling of the types of souvenirs sold at their trading post, and as a result, a broad range of Indian crafts made for sale from the 1890s to the 1950s eventually came into the Minnesota Historical Society's collections in 1959. Much of this same material was then incorporated into exhibits at the new Mille Lacs Indian Museum that opened in 1960. In 1995 a newer museum facility

10.27 *(below left)* Bag collected at White Earth by Agent John R. Howard, early 1900s. *MNHS 10000.149; see also Figure 3.97*

10.28 *(below center)* Bag collected at White Earth by Agent John R. Howard, early 1900s. *MNHS 10000.150*

10.29 *(below right)* Bag collected at White Earth by Agent John R. Howard, early 1900s. *MNHS 10000.153; see also Figure 3.63*

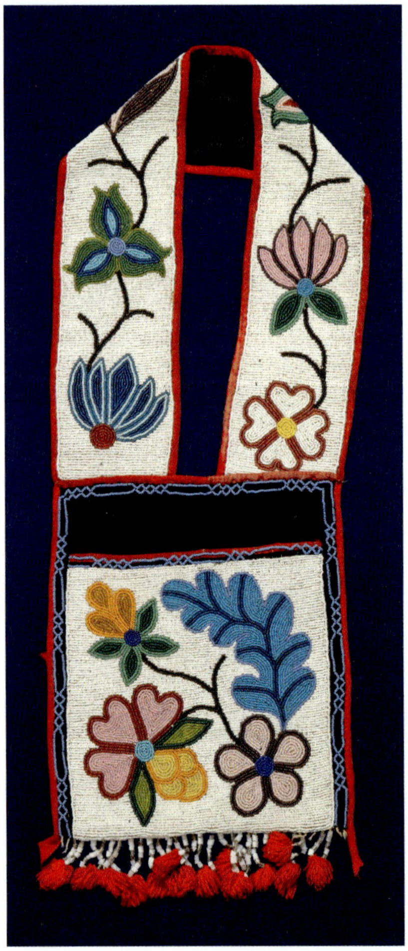

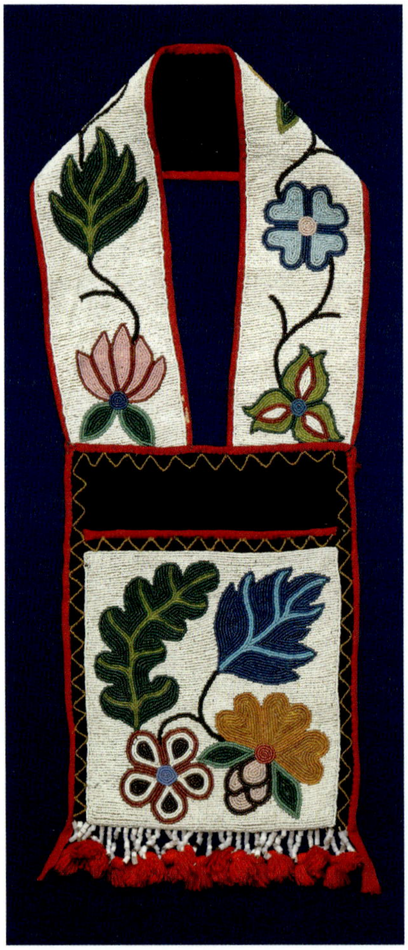

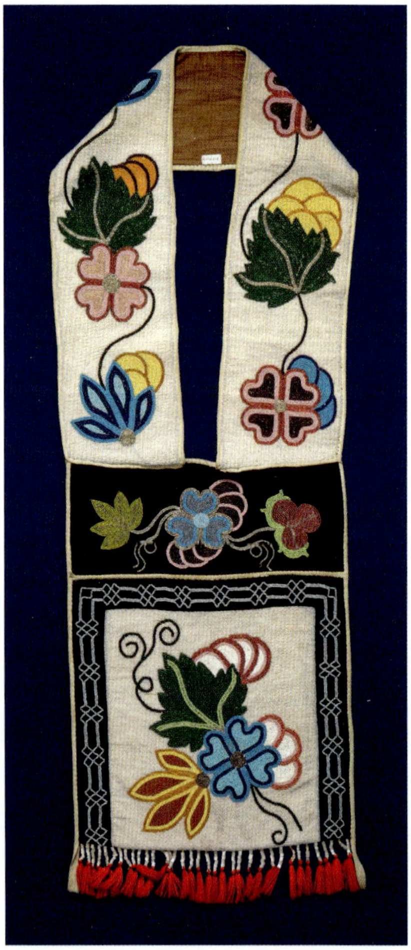

and a restored and interpreted trading post were completed in collaboration with members of the Mille Lacs Band.

The Ayers' personal relationships with so many band members as vendors, interpreters, and employees no doubt made it possible for them to build such an extensive collection. Stock at the post today still includes work by Mille Lacs Band artisans, as well as by other Ojibwe in Canada and Minnesota, and pottery by Dakota artisans.

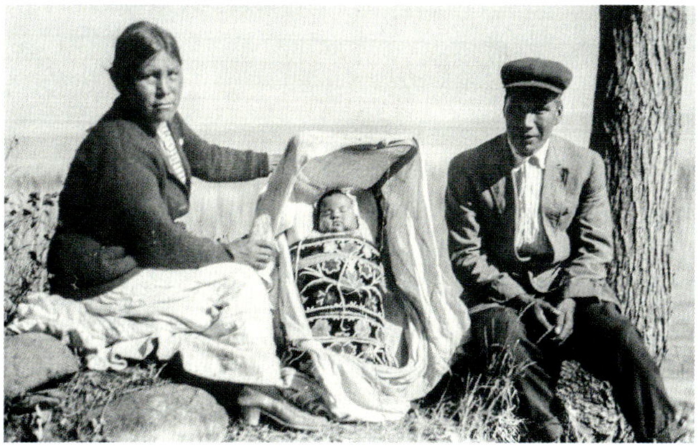

10.30 *(above)* Charley Boyd, his wife Quaykosh, and their son Raining at Mille Lacs Lake, 1921. *MNHS E97.33p35*

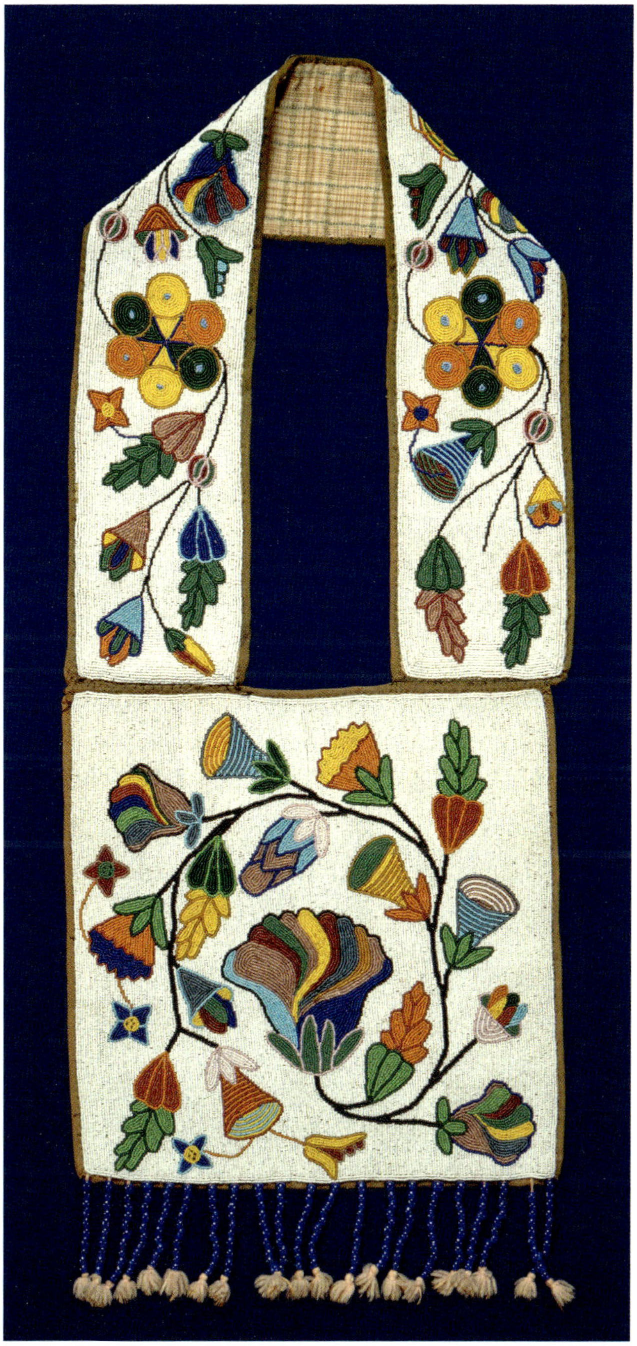

10.31 *(left)* Spot-stitch appliqué bag, c. 1875–1925. A small, yellowed, paper tag marked "Charlie Boyd" was pinned to the bag. *MNHS 10000.620*

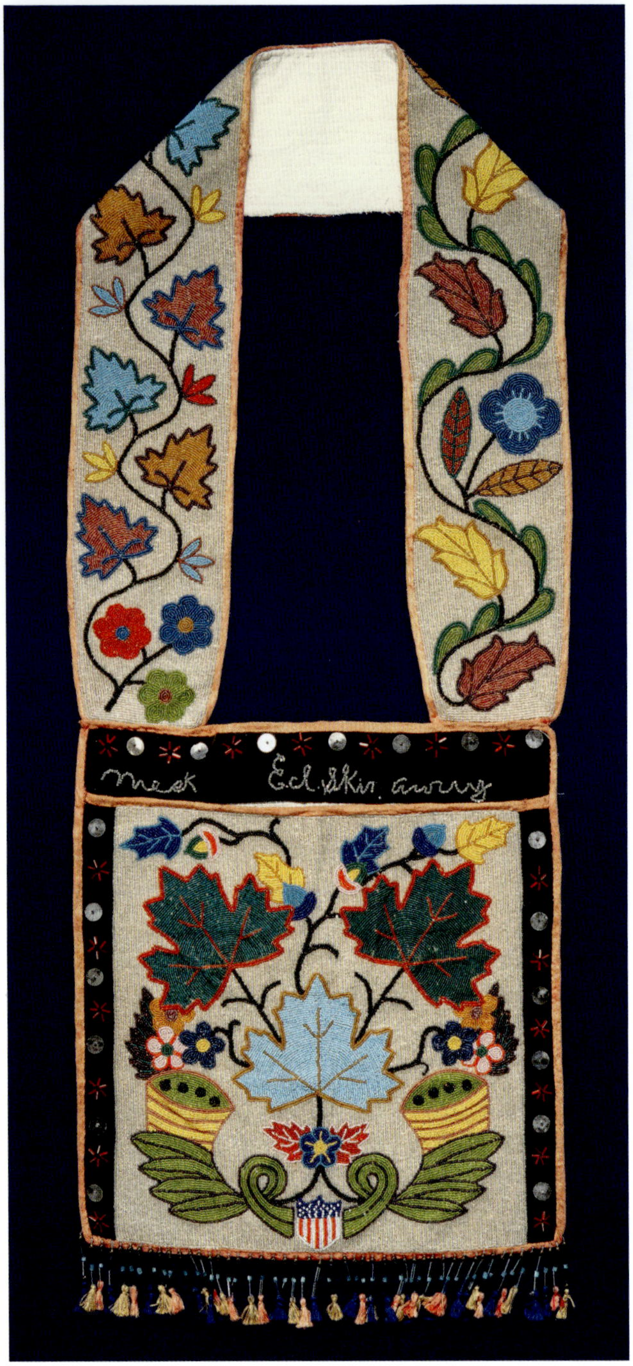

10.32 *(above)* Spot-stitch appliqué bag, with Ed Skinaway's name beaded on the bag. *MNHS 10000.615; see also Figure 3.87*

10.33 *(right)* Ed Skinaway and Mary Wind, Mille Lacs, c. 1930. *MNHS E97.15 r17*

The Skinaways, transmitters of Mille Lacs lifeways

A number of members of the Skinaway family worked for the Ayers, demonstrating the Ojibwe maple sugar harvest, performing for tourists at the trading post, working in the Ayers' boat-building business, and posing in front of their family residence. In fact, during the Great Depression, the Frank Skinaway family provided all of the demonstrations for tourists.

Four bags in the Ayer collection have Skinaway connections. A namesake bag (Figure 10.32), with "mesk Ed Skinaway" beaded above the pocket opening, may refer to Miskoogwaniash, or Ed Skinaway (Figure 10.33), who was born in 1900 and is listed in the 1937 Indian Census rolls as Maiscogwanayaush. The bag may have been made for his use or to commemorate him. The bead motifs include maple leaves, acorns, cornucopias, a US shield, and a star. This bead artist worked outside the norm, employing large sequins to border the pocket rather than a more traditional fine-line running bead stitch.[19]

Chief Tom Skinaway (Manido'bijiki, or Spirit Buffalo) was a frequent participant in the cultural demonstrations at the Ayers' trading post. He and his wife, Mary (O-gah-bay-bah-kah-co-nah-o-quay), also worked with Frances Densmore. Their daughter, Jennie Mitchell, was remembered into the 1980s as a good beadworker. In Figure 10.34, Tom Skinaway wears the bandolier bag shown in Figure 10.35, which is part of the Ayer collection. This gashkibidaagan is a classic example of distinctive Mille Lacs beadwork, featuring some of the unusual motifs associated with this community: The cornucopia with an architectural column layered across the base of the horn and the stacked

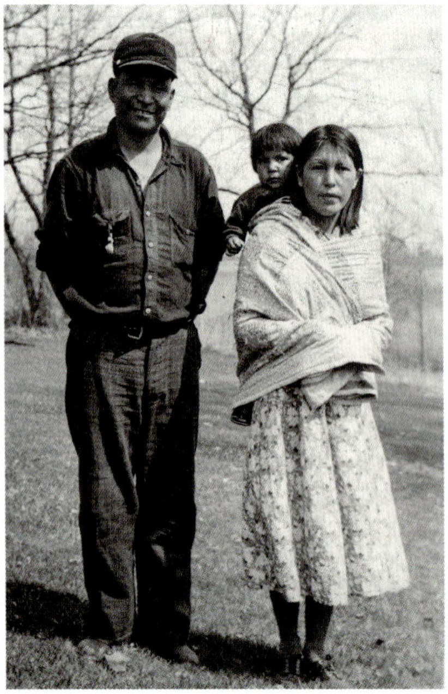

compositions of trumpet forms and flowers are among the unique Mille Lacs motifs less closely associated with natural forms. The arrowhead leaf motif featured on this bag pocket and strap represents a plant that still grows in marshy areas and on the edges of lakes over much of Minnesota, including Mille Lacs Lake. Like Ed Skinaway's bag in Figure 10.32, the bag in Figure 10.35 uses sequins on the decorated panel above the pocket opening.[20]

In Figure 10.36, Tom Skinaway wears a different, particularly large Ayer bag; Figure 10.37 shows this bag in detail. The repetitive use of a primary leaf motif, its bilateral symmetry and stilted leaf positioning, and the scooped area above the pocket are less common not just in Mille Lacs but also in Minnesota Ojibwe beadwork in general. In Figure 10.38, Skinaway wears yet another bag, which has not been located. Because Tom Skinaway was photographed wearing each of these three bags at Mille Lacs in the 1920s and early 1930s, all three of them may have been made by women in the Skinaway family.[21]

10.34 *(below left)* Tom Skinaway, c. 1925. *MNHS E97.1S r5*

10.35 *(below)* Gashkibidaagan worn in Figure 10.34, made in the 1920s. *MNHS 10000.609; see also Figure 3.86*

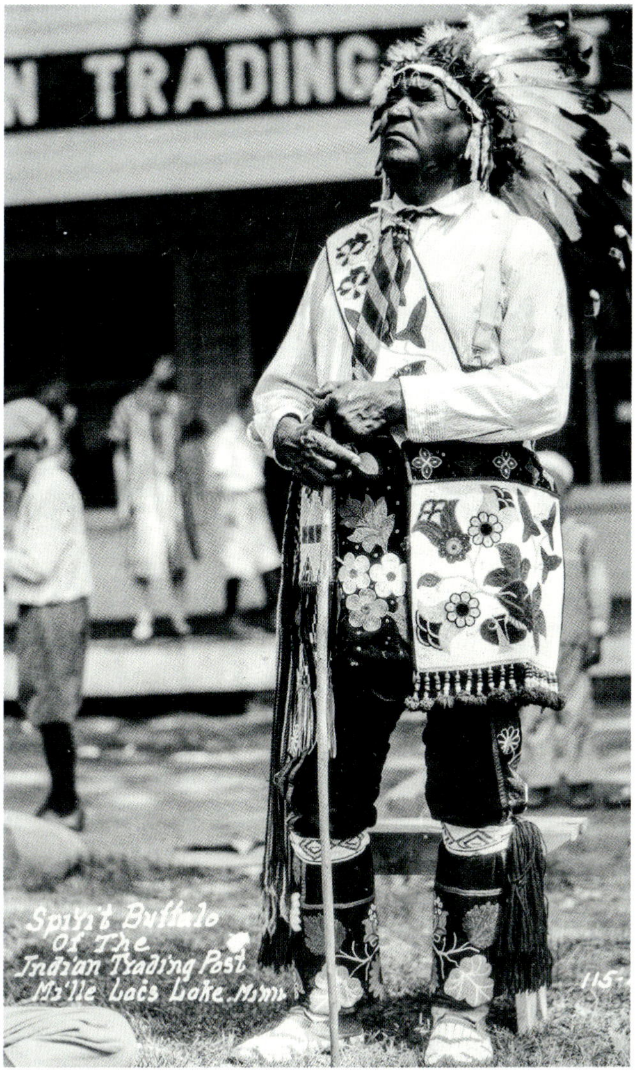

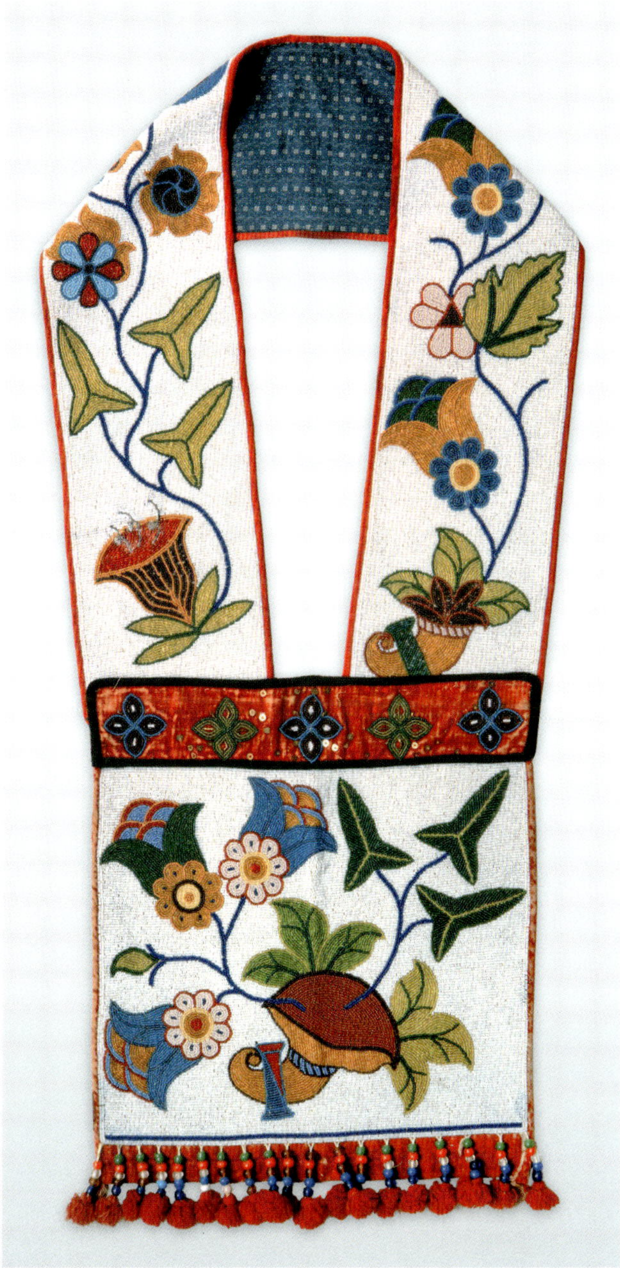

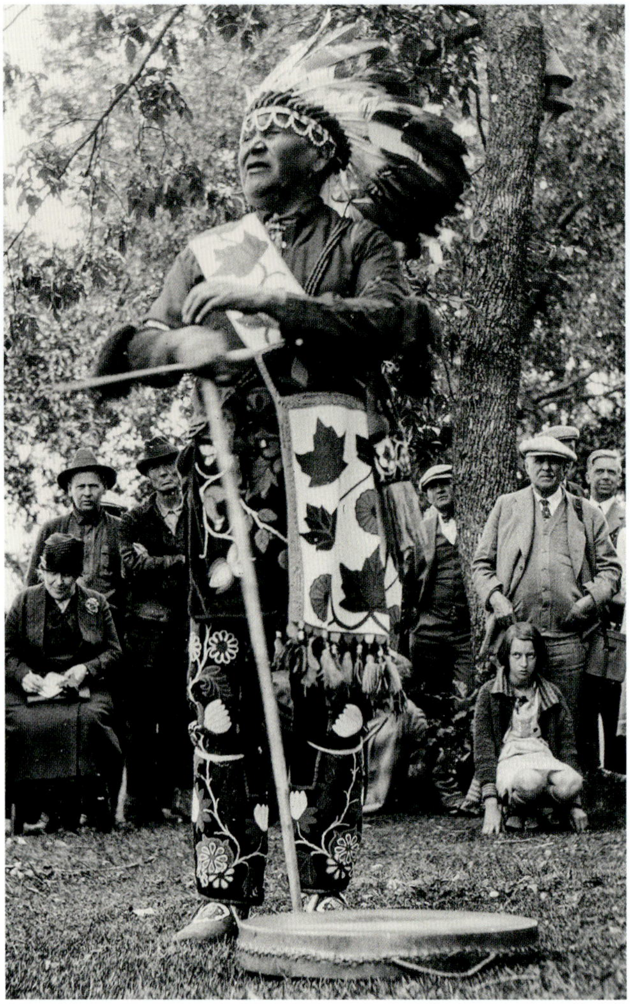

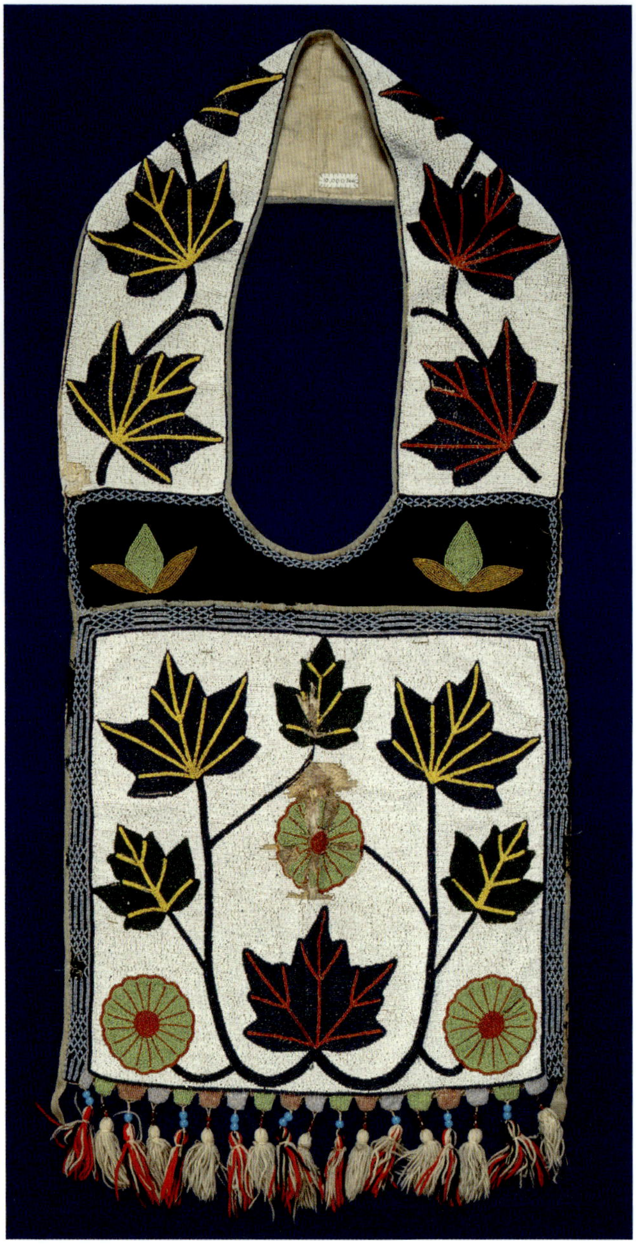

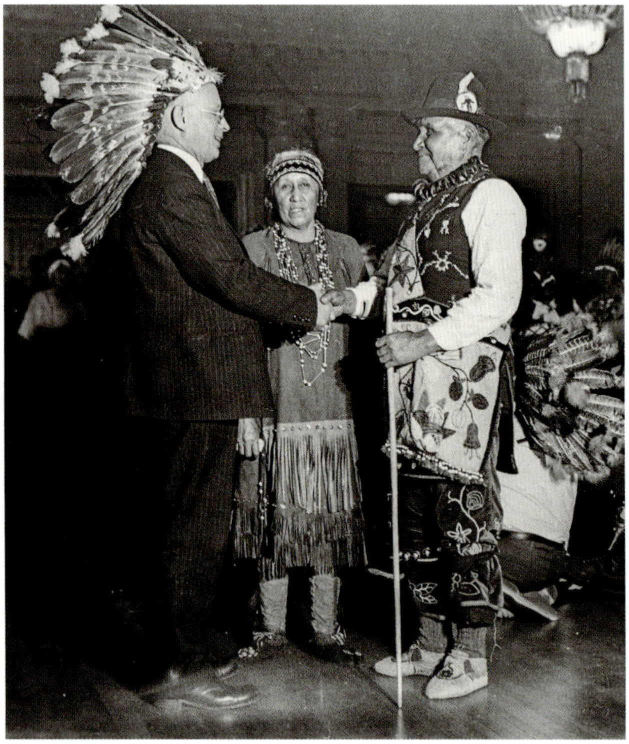

10.36 *(above left)* Tom Skinaway addresses a tour of Minnesota Historical Society members at Mille Lacs, 1928. *MNHS E97.15 r4*

10.37 *(above)* Bag worn by Skinaway in Figure 10.36. *MNHS 10000.366*

10.38 *(left)* Minneapolis mayor William A. Anderson and Tom Skinaway, 1930s. *MNHS Reserve Album 243, page 132*

Sherman A. Holbert, entrepreneur and collector

Sherman Holbert (1916–2013) owned and operated Fort Mille Lacs, a tourist center just south of the Mille Lacs Indian Museum and Trading Post. In interviews and in an article in the *Mille Lacs Messenger* in 1999, Holbert shared some of the history of his family's time in the Mille Lacs Lake area and his objectives for his tourist center at Fort Mille Lacs.[22]

Holbert was raised partially by his grandparents, who lived on Wigwam Point (also known as Sherman Point and Shabashkung Point). His grandfather C. A. Sherman was the publisher of the *Mille Lacs Messenger* until his death in the 1930s. Holbert played with many Mille Lacs Band members when he was young, and he learned to speak Ojibwemowin. He left Mille Lacs as a teenager, began work as a salesman, served in the Army Air Corps during World War II, married, and returned to Mille Lacs in 1946. He and his wife, Maxine, started a maple sugar–processing operation, which he sold in 1952; he then began a business marketing wild rice across the country, ran local sawmills, and traded in artifacts related to American Indians.

In 1952 Sherman and Maxine opened the Fort Mille Lacs gift shop. His new great passion became developing the gift shop into a tourist destination, complete with a restaurant, an animal park, a miniature golf course, and a motel. Holbert persuaded the Churchill family from Lake Lena to perform weekend powwows, which continued for nearly two decades. This soon led to the re-creation during the 1950s and 1960s of an early nineteenth-century Ojibwe village, in which Mille Lacs Band members demonstrated various aspects of their culture. Holbert turned to Mille Lacs tribal member John Clark (Beginning Day, or Niigaanigiizhig) to set this up. At first Clark was assisted by his wife, Lucy (Omadwe), who was born a Kegg (Figure 10.39). By the late 1950s, the Clarks' three adult children had all moved to the fort and become full-time employees; this included Dorothy (later, Dorothy Sam), Norman, and Zhaawan (Millie Benjamin). Holbert also recruited Jim Hanks (Naawakwegiizhig) to build canoes. The multigenerational staffing by band members provided a more realistic family setting and merged the knowledge of elders with the energy and strength of the younger

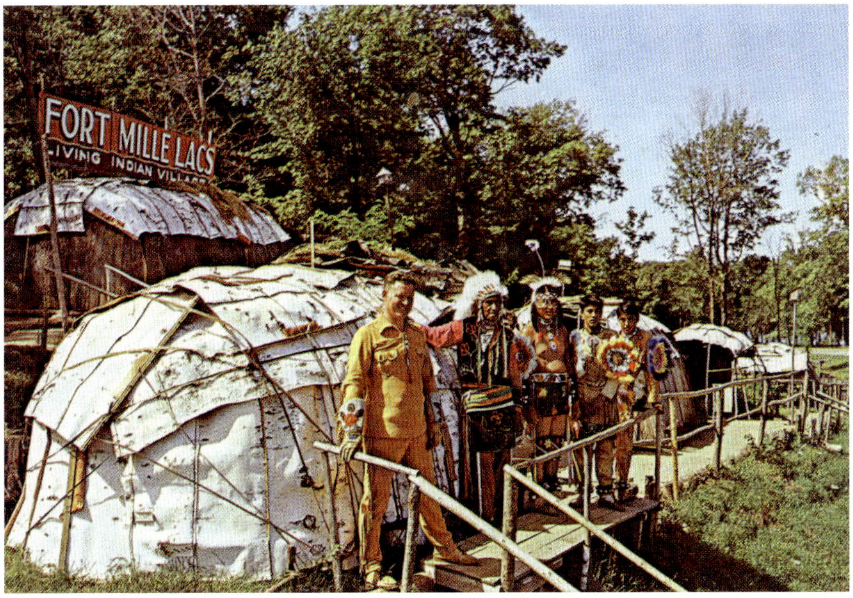

10.39 Postcard of the Indian village at Fort Mille Lacs, c. 1950. *MNHS Holbert Papers*

members. Created to bring in tourists and to improve the sale of Indian crafts, this village became a big part of Fort Mille Lacs' attraction.[23]

Each summer, the Indian village housed four families—the Clarks, the Benjamins, the Pendegayoshes, and the Nayquonabes. Mrs. Bearheart, a Ho-Chunk woman from Wisconsin, was also an occasional participant. On the weekends, the staff expanded to include the Churchill, Gahbow (Garbow), and Skinaway families.

When interviewed for a 1999 newspaper article, Millie Benjamin noted that she believed the Mille Lacs Band, as a whole, benefited from the Fort Mille Lacs village activities: "People worked hard to remember things they had learned. That helped them bring back things that might have been lost," she said. "I think it helped preserve the culture."[24]

The business was controversial, though, and as tourist interest dwindled, Indian activists protested against Fort Mille Lacs, drawing attention to how much money Holbert had made from the work of Ojibwe people over the years. Eventually, all that remained was the gift shop and museum, where Holbert sold and displayed arts and crafts made by members of the Mille Lacs Band. In the 1990s Holbert developed catalogs of his holdings and began selling off his collection. He sold the property to the Mille Lacs Band, and in 1999 his facility was closed. Between 2002 and 2005 the Minnesota Historical Society purchased a number of his holdings to acquire examples of products made by band members who were identified by name. Included in this acquisition were two of at least fifteen gashkibidaaganag he had owned.[25]

At some point earlier in his collecting, when trading with a collector in Chicago, Holbert found a beaded object of particular interest—a bag that had been disassembled and remade into a dance apron, with the addition of a red wool backcloth (Figure 10.40). It had the name John Shewap beaded into it, which Holbert recognized as the name of a Mille Lacs Band member, so he bought the item. Later, in his own materials, he found a photograph of "Shawap" (also possibly Shawab) wearing the bag as it was

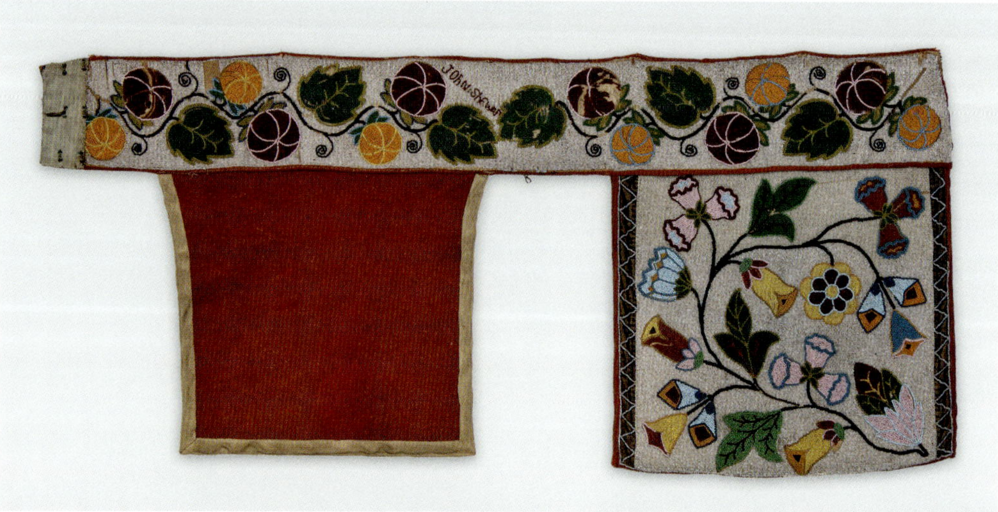

10.40 Gashkibidaagan converted to a dance apron, collected by Sherman Holbert, mid-twentieth century or earlier. *MNHS 2002.259.4*

originally made, and for many years he displayed the dance apron and the photo together; another photograph may depict the bag's maker (Figure 10.41). When Holbert began selling off the collections and dismantling the exhibits and buildings, his photograph was lost. Luckily, a duplicate image survives of the bag being worn in its original condition (Figure 10.42).[26]

Potential relatives of John Shewap (Shewab), the Shewaabs, appear in Figure 10.43; the Mille Lacs Band has property in Kanabec County, where the photo was taken. This young man and woman wear or hold a roach headdress and nine beaded items, exceptional pieces of Mille Lacs beadwork. All but the loom-woven pipe bag were made using the spot-stitch appliqué technique. Distinctive Mille Lacs motifs on the yoke (Figure 10.44) include the cornucopia, the trumpet flower, the seed pod, and the layering of unrelated motifs.[27]

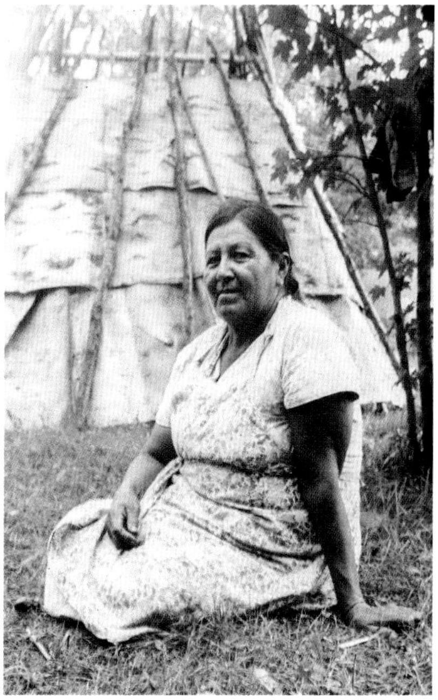

10.41 *(above)* Mrs. John Shawab of Mille Lacs, possibly the maker of the bag worn in Figure 10.42, c. 1940. *MNHS E97.1S r18*

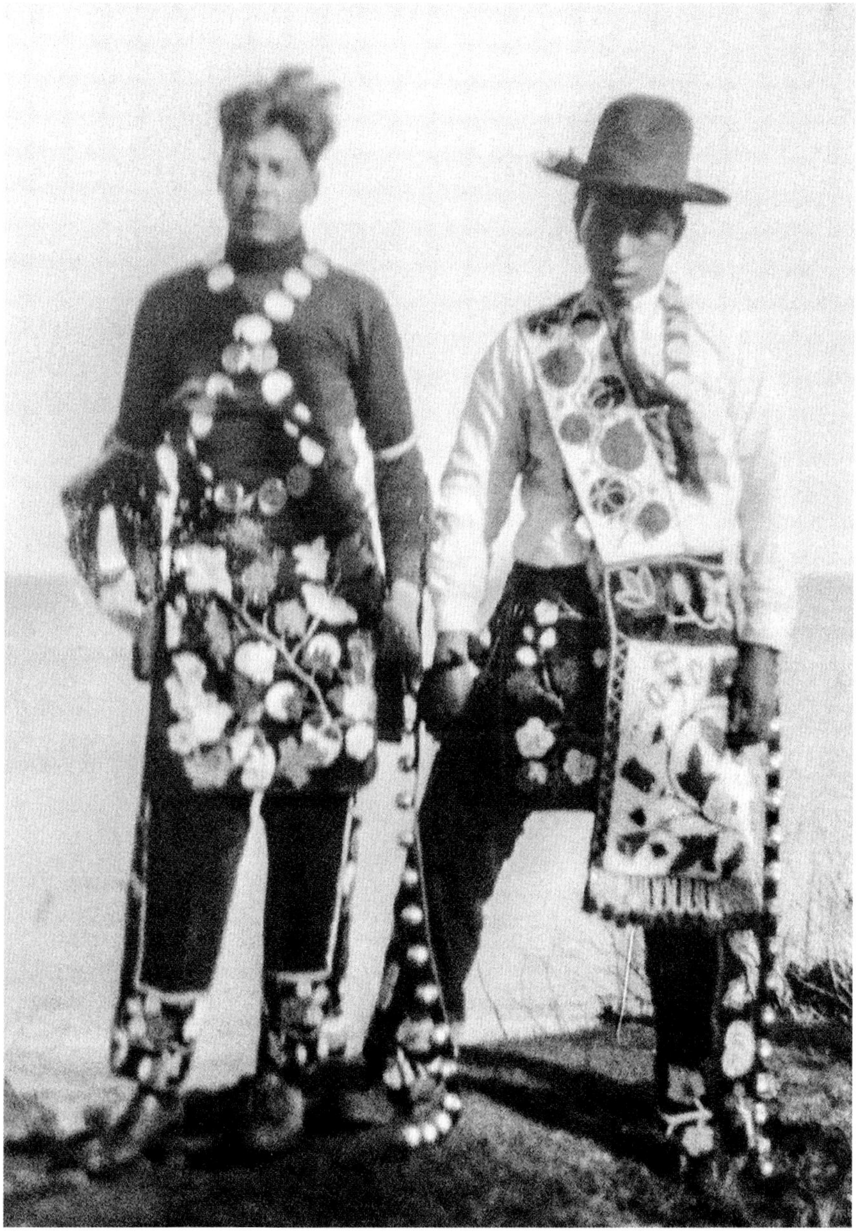

10.42 *(left)* John Shewap *(right)*, wearing the bag before its conversion to a dance apron (Figure 10.40), and a man identified as Otto Kegg. *Author copy of Holbert's original photo*

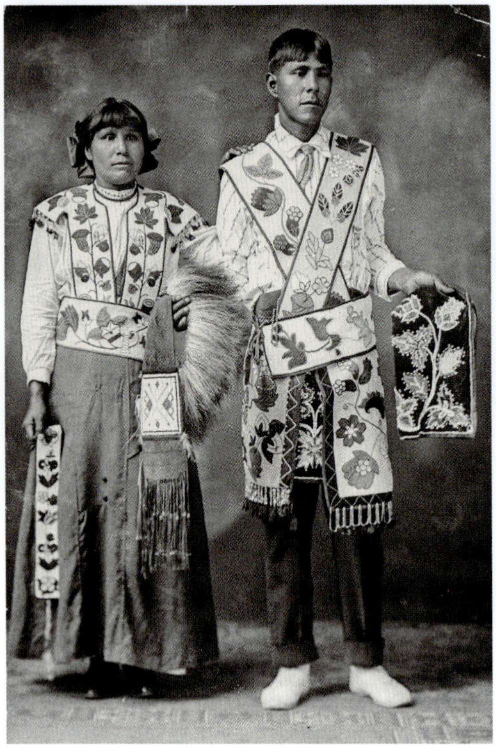

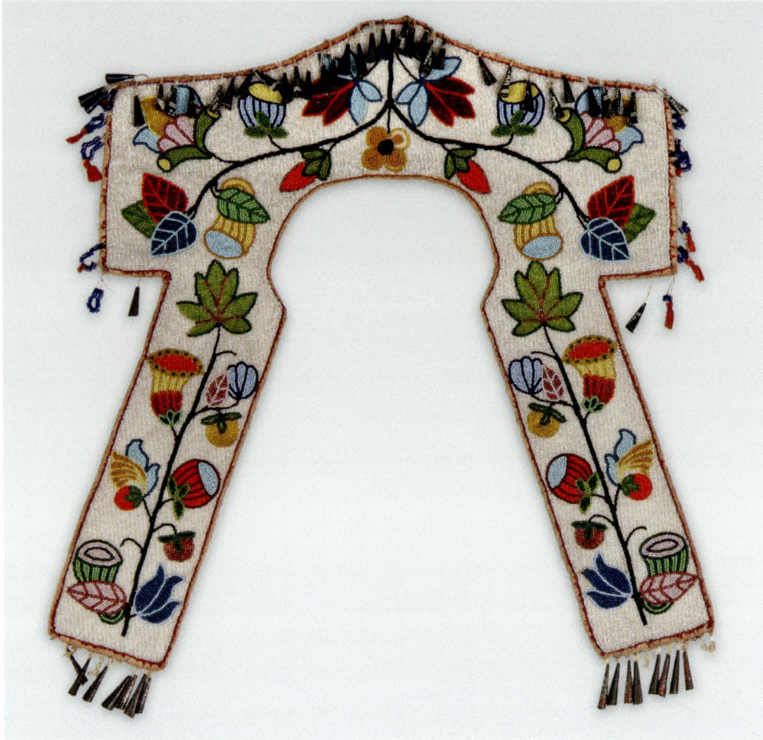

10.43 *(above)* Naabaw *(right)* and Ma'iingan (Wolf) Shewaab in dancing costume, Kanabec County. *MNHS E97.37 r20*

10.44 *(above right)* Yoke with Mille Lacs motifs worn by Ma'iingan in Figure 10.43, c. 1890–1915. *MNHS 2007.47.1.A*

Maude Kegg and Batiste Sam, bead artists

In 1982 my colleague Kathy Hussey-Arntson and I went to the Mille Lacs Indian Museum and Trading Post to interview Maude Kegg and Batiste Sam (Figure 10.45) about beadwork. We knew very little about bandolier bags, but we knew it was important to interview these two women who together embodied an enormous wealth of experience and knowledge about Ojibwe culture. They had also served as guides at the museum and for decades had given interpreted tours of its Four Seasons Room, an exhibition hall where a life-sized diorama depicting traditional Ojibwe life and activities interprets the cycles of the seasons.

Maude Ellen Mitchell Kegg (Nah-wah-cumig-goo-quay, Naawakamigookwe, Middle of the Earth Woman) was born August 26, 1902, and died January 6, 1996. Her parents were Charles and Nancy (Pine) Mitchell, and she was raised by her maternal grandmother Margaret Pine near Portage Lake, north of Mille Lacs Lake. In 1990 Maude Kegg was granted one of thirteen National Heritage Fellowships awarded by the National Endowment for the Arts in recognition of her status as a Native American storyteller, craftswoman, and tradition bearer.[28]

Batiste (Batise, Bapise) Gahbow Sam (Quay-zaince) was born October 3, 1914, and died January 25, 1998. In 1996 the National Congress of American Indians named her Tribal Elder of the Year, recognizing her contributions to Ojibwe art, culture, and language.[29]

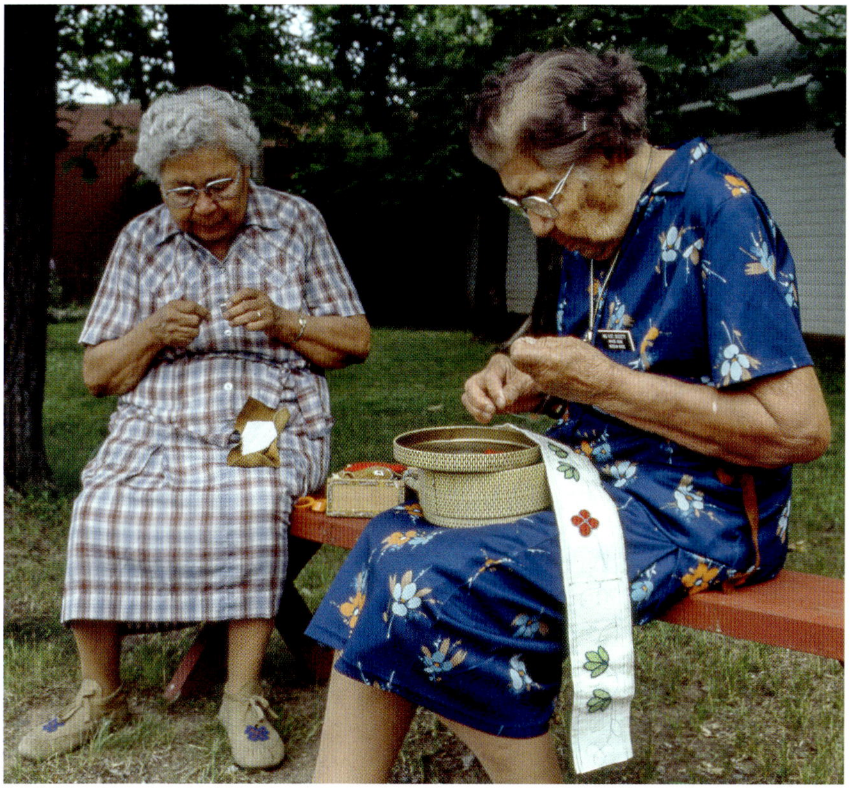

10.45 Maude Kegg *(left)* and Batiste Sam beading outside the Mille Lacs Indian Museum and Trading Post, with their bead and pattern boxes at the ready, c. 1994. *MNHS Mille Lacs Exhibit Materials*

Maude and Batiste answered our questions and discussed with each other how they learned to bead, what the mechanics of beadwork were for them, and what they knew about bandolier bags. Because they were such close friends, and we interviewed them together, they delivered their stories as a duet.

Maude learned to do beadwork from her grandmother on Bay Lake, northwest of Mille Lacs Lake. When she was very small, there was a gathering near her home for a Midewiwin ceremony. She was watching women do beadwork during a break, and when she asked them for beads, her grandmother taught her how to ask for them in a traditional way. Maude went from one wigwam to the next, saying, "I'm poor, I'm poor in beads." And at one doorway after another, a woman came out laughing and gave her beads, and she got what she wanted. When she was a young girl, Maude recalled that her grandmother and her aunt did lots of beadwork, especially purses. "They'd show me [how to bead], but I didn't care. She kept tearing out my work, and I just got tired, and quit."

The women did not know beadworkers from other reservations, although they had seen the work of Josie Ryan from Leech Lake; Josie was the daughter of Cecelia Rock, who lived at Mille Lacs and worked for the Ayers in the trading post store. When Kathy and I asked if some or most of the Ojibwe women Maude and Batiste knew as young women were good beadworkers, we didn't get a definitive answer from either of them. But Maude did observe that most women of their generation could still make birchbark baskets.

By the early 1980s, they said, young Ojibwe women were educated, worked in offices, and didn't want to learn to make bags. Not even many old people were still making bags. "When we were younger," they said, "more people were making bandolier bags. Beads were cheaper—a dime to twenty-five cents a hank. Now they are more expensive." They also noted that by the early 1980s women were making birchbark items and other things to sell that could be made more quickly than bandolier bags. "Nobody makes bandolier bags, that's why we don't see them in powwow regalia," said Batiste.

Most of the bead artists I've met keep their patterns, tools, and some beads in a container—usually some found item, rarely bought in a store. Batiste noted, "Mr. Ayer kept rocks in the old cigar boxes, when they were emptied [I] took two." That's where she kept her beads and patterns, some cut out of candy and gum wrappers. Maude sometimes kept her patterns in a cigar box, too. Maude also noted that her aunt used to trace flowers and make paper patterns.

In beadworking, Maude said, one needs to plan the design first, then decide what to use, but she liked opaque white seed beads for a background color. She didn't use the clear ones, since they would get dirty more easily. Batiste agreed and commented that she would use leftover beads or buy new ones, but she always needed lots of white beads. When Batiste was making smaller items such as eyeglass cases, she used different background colors. Neither woman beaded at night. Maude commented that it was hard to see colors at night. Batiste's grandmother told her and others not to do beadwork at night because it was not good for their eyes.

Maude thought that, perhaps due to so much intermarriage among clans and tribes in her lifetime, Ojibwe and Dakota beadworkers learned from and inspired each other's designs. Neither Maude nor Batiste had any recollection of Ojibwe making loom-woven bags during their lifetime. When asked if some motifs or designs had special meaning, Batiste observed while looking at some floral beadwork, "these flower designs, they don't mean anything." Maude noted that one couldn't use four leaves in a bandolier bag pocket design, since that represented Midewiwin imagery, so a bead artist would either need to add a fifth leaf or use fewer leaves.[30]

Both women agreed that Ojibwe bead artists work from the front side of an object and draw their pattern there. And both used the two-by-two appliqué technique (couching beads down every two beads) to keep the beadwork surface flat and smooth. Maude used the two-needle technique, and Batiste used a single needle, but both started with their glass seed beads strung on nylon thread. Batiste recalled that when they were younger, they used cotton thread size 40 for beadwork on cloth, size 60 for loom work.

They both always bought their seed beads from the Ayers at the trading post; neither remembered where she got her larger beads. The trading post had lots of bead colors at twenty-five cents for a big hank, so they didn't have to order special colors. Maude commented that she tried using some of the cut-steel beads, but they cut the threads and the beads fell off.

Maude said it was important to make sure the beads were not too crowded or forced. If they were, then you wouldn't end up with a smooth surface. Batiste preferred to bead on cotton velvet, also known as velveteen, because it is thicker and easier to sew on. The silk velvet fabric gets out of shape when it is used for a beading surface. Maude used printed cotton or other available cloth for backing or lining material, while Batiste preferred a white backing of muslin.

Bags were used by both men and women, but "especially the chief, always the chief," who used them to carry tobacco, especially at ceremonial dances. Maude said the chief's wife, an *ogichidaakwe* (ceremonial headwoman or wife of a ceremonial headman), could wear one. A woman could also make a bag for herself. Both women said a woman would make a bandolier bag for her husband. Batiste noted that some bandolier bags were given away, and if a family wanted to have a horse, a bag could be used to buy it. "Nothing else was traded for a horse," she said.

If you needed to ask someone to make a bandolier bag for you, even if it was a relative, you would have to furnish the beads and materials and also pay them. Maude and Batiste weren't sure how often this might have happened since you couldn't be sure someone else would finish a big project like a gashkibidaagan. Batiste remembered watching her aunt, Quaykosh, make bandolier bags for someone who had hired her.

Maude's grandmother and aunt made many bandolier bags and brought them to the trading post to sell. While her family no longer owned any bandolier bags, and they had no early photos of bandolier bags made by family members, Maude recognized some bags in the Ayer collection as ones that her family made. When asked how so many bags ended up in the hands of collectors, museums, and individuals, Batiste replied, "Want some money, so sell them."

We asked the beadworkers what they were particular about when they made their bags. Maude said that she used whatever she had on hand to make the bag thicker, in order to provide support to hold the weight of the beads and make the bag hang properly. When Kathy and I noted that some of the bags in the Minnesota Historical Society's collections incorporated layers of paper or newsprint, she said she never used paper and wished she could still get more old oilcloth.[31]

Maude's bag (Figure 10.46) was commissioned by the Plains Art Museum, and she took about three years to make it, from 1979 to 1982. When we asked Maude about the inspiration for her bag, she replied, "I just copied a bag at the trading post" (Figure 10.47)—but, as usual, while the bead artist was inspired by another bag, she introduced her own changes. Maude was pretty true in her use of the motifs and layout of the pocket panel, where she rendered her version of the unusual Mille Lacs composite motifs in vivid colors, but she introduced a different woven tab fringe,

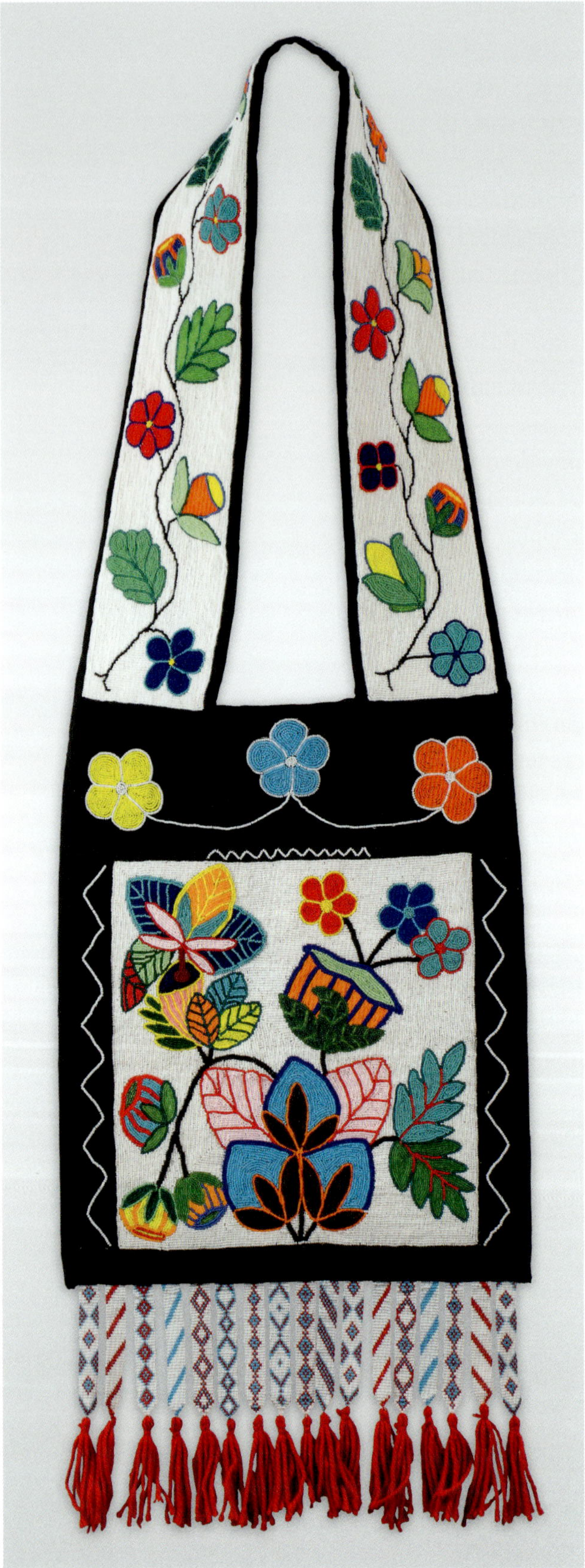

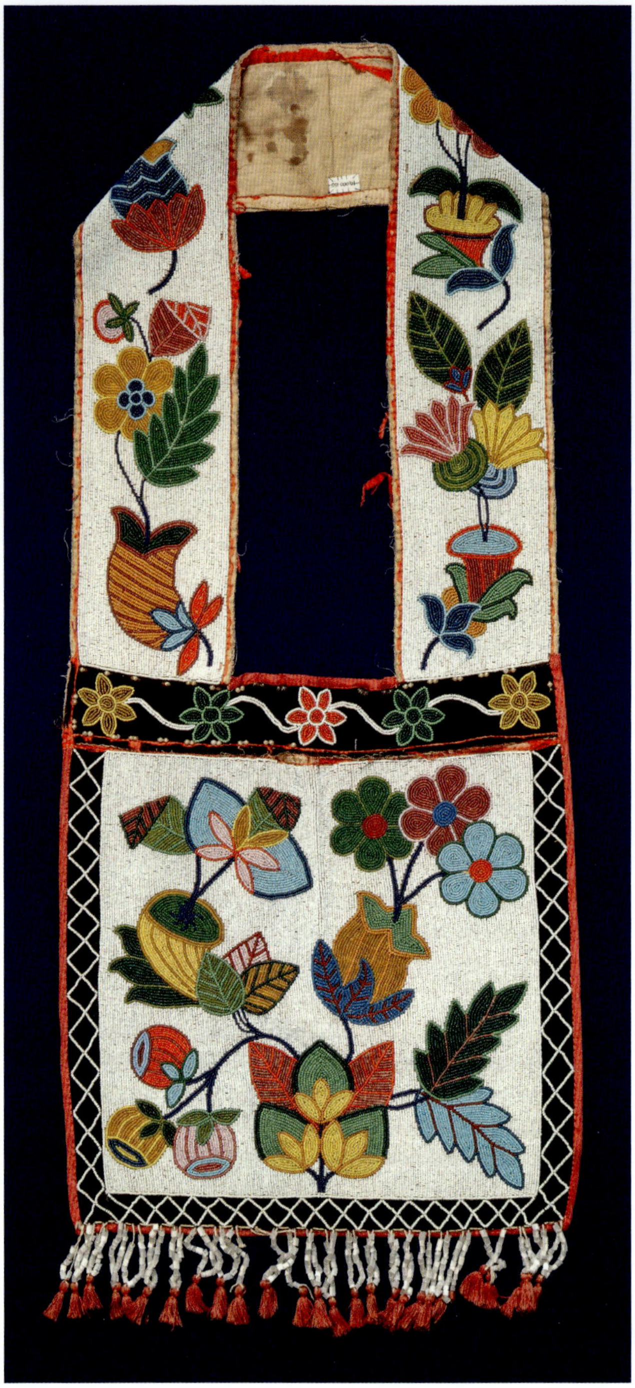

10.46 *(left)* Gashkibidaagan made by Maude Kegg, 1982. *PAM 1991.019.0001*

10.47 *(above)* Spot-stitch appliqué bag, Mille Lacs area, c. 1875–1925. Maude modeled her bag on this one. *MNHS 10000.155*

a large zigzag border, a much simplified flower chain above the pocket panel, and less complex motifs to decorate the strap. Maude's bag was, like most Ojibwe gashkibidaaganag, filled with the fluidity, enthusiasm, and unique signature of the individual bead artist.

Batiste's bag was about as big as she was (Figure 10.48). After looking at bandolier bags at the Mille Lacs Museum, she decided that she wanted to finish such a project. Mille Lacs Band member and friend Jessie Clark assisted her in drawing motifs onto a black cotton velour foundation fabric, and Batiste spot-stitch appliquéd glass seed beads in a bilaterally symmetrical floral design. In her usual meticulous fashion, Batiste made the size and spacing of her floral motifs complement the scale of the bag, a testament to her design sense. Batiste was pleased that when she completed her bag in 1995, the Minnesota Historical Society purchased it.

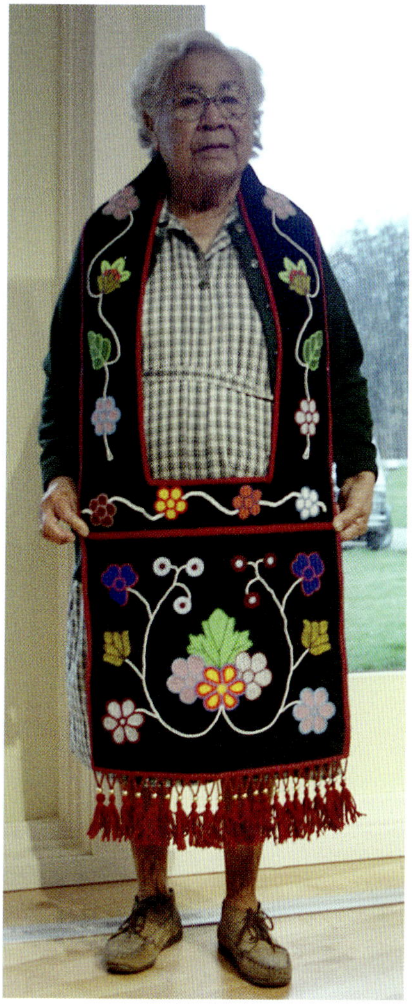

10.48 Batiste Sam with her gashkibidaagan, 1995. *MNHS Mille Lacs Exhibit Materials; bag is MNHS 1996.201.1*

We lost both of these talented and generous women, cultural treasures, in the 1990s. I was blessed to have had the time I did with them, and I still miss them both.

Cheryl Benjamin Minnema, bead artist

When she was a little girl learning to bead, Cheryl Benjamin Minnema (Figure 10.49) made dance regalia for her Barbie doll. One of six children, Cheryl was born in Minneapolis in 1973. Her family moved to Harding, Minnesota, when she was three, then to Onamia Junction, and then to the Mille Lacs Reservation. She attended school in Onamia through the sixth grade, then transferred to Nay Ah Shing School on the reservation, where she attended high school—except for her eighth grade year at Flandreau Indian School, a boarding school in South Dakota. She has an associate of arts degree from Central Lakes College in Brainerd and a bachelor of arts in elective studies from St. Cloud State. She was married in 1999 and has two sons, Sean and Ethan.

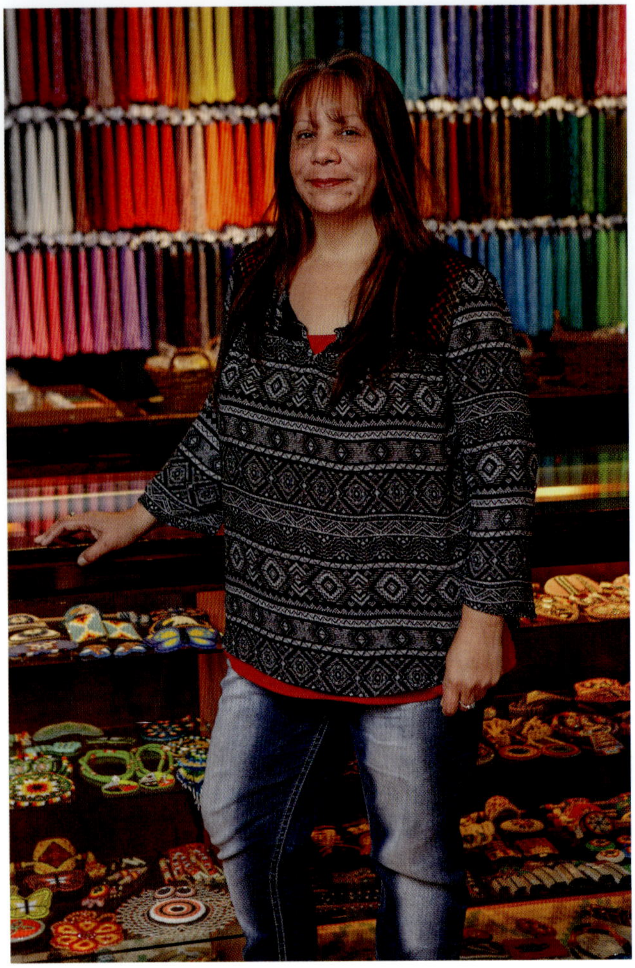

10.49 Cheryl Minnema in front of the bead sales display at the Mille Lacs Trading Post, 2016. *Photo by James Castle*

Cheryl's exposure to beadwork began early. She learned from well-known and respected female elders at Mille Lacs, including her great-grandmother Ke-che-quay-zaince, her grandmother Omadwe (Lucy Kegg Clark), Batiste Sam, Margaret Hill, Maude Kegg, and Jesse Clark. Cheryl notes specifically that when she was a child, she and others learned from older women by watching them, not through formal instruction.

Due to her aging eyesight and hands, Omadwe didn't do much beading during Cheryl's early beading years. But Cheryl recalls that Omadwe was always busy making birchbark baskets, teapots, birdhouses, and canoes; quilts for ceremonial dances that occurred in the fall and spring; basswood dolls; and purses. Although Omadwe did little beading, Cheryl remembers seeing her beads threaded up and wound around some cloth within her sewing box.

Cheryl's greatest influence was her mother Zhaawan (Millie Benjamin). Zhaawan taught Ojibwe culture at the Nay Ah Shing School, and Cheryl felt she was lucky to have her mother as an influence both at home and at school. In both places, Cheryl learned how to make Ojibwe crafts, how to harvest wild rice and maple syrup, and how to speak Ojibwe. She had fun learning new phrases in school and then rushing home to repeat them to Grandma, who knew very little English.

Cheryl learned how to bead on a loom, making simple floral and symmetrical designs copied out of a beading book. First projects included dance outfit pieces such as belts, armbands, headbands, and barrettes. After learning how to bead with appliqué stitches from Zhaawan, Cheryl made beaded leggings, moccasins, capes, and the Barbie doll regalia.

Beadwork was always present within Cheryl's family. A faded snapshot of her great-grandfather Young Kegg (Figure 10.50) is a testament to the family's beading tradition. Young wears and holds two large spot-stitch appliqué bags with

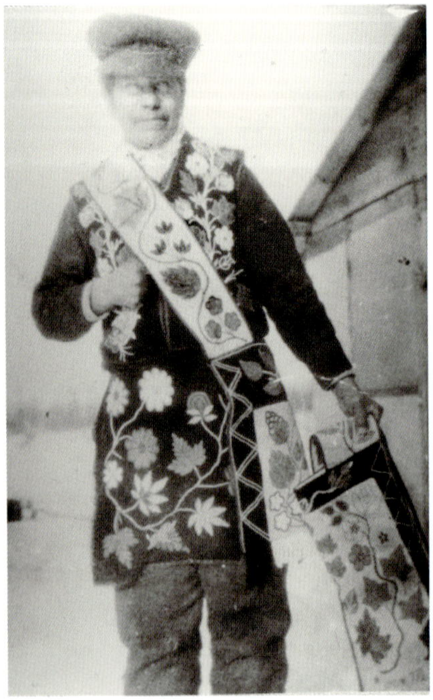

10.50 Young Kegg, Cheryl's great-grandfather, c. 1910s. *Courtesy Cheryl Minnema*

oversized zigzag borders; the one he wears appears to have a pocket, while the one in his left hand seems not to have one. He also wears a beaded vest and dance apron.

Many people hired Cheryl's mother or her sisters to make belts, leggings, vests, and hair ties. Zhaawan made Cheryl's high school graduation outfit, which included a beaded velvet cape, a buckskin dress, and beaded moccasins. Earlier, Omadwe had made a pair of beaded moccasins for Cheryl's dance outfit. As an adult, Cheryl is often asked to make beaded moccasins for dancers or leather moccasins for funerals.

As is true for so many Ojibwe bead artists today, Cheryl doesn't remember her mother or grandmother mentioning bandolier bags or gashkibidaaganag when she was growing up. As did other bead artists, she saw bags at the Mille Lacs Trading Post and in books by Frances Densmore and other ethnographers. It wasn't until Cheryl began making her first bag that she became aware of gashkibidaaganag in unpublished historical photographs. When Cheryl finished her bag in 2007 (Figure 10.51), the first person her mother wanted to show it to was Margaret Hill. Margaret had made a gashkibidaagan many years earlier and had recalled how much work it was. Margaret also had recalled seeing gashkibidaaganag at the ceremonial dances when she was young, in the 1930s or 1940s.

The Mille Lacs Band purchased Cheryl's bag, and its pocket motif also served as inspiration for the Minnesota Historical Society's Shoulder Bag Kit, produced for use with elementary schoolchildren. Available in classroom sets and as a retail product, the kits offer children a chance to learn about bandolier bags, motifs, and Ojibwe culture—and to decorate their own fabric bags, printed with Cheryl's design.[32]

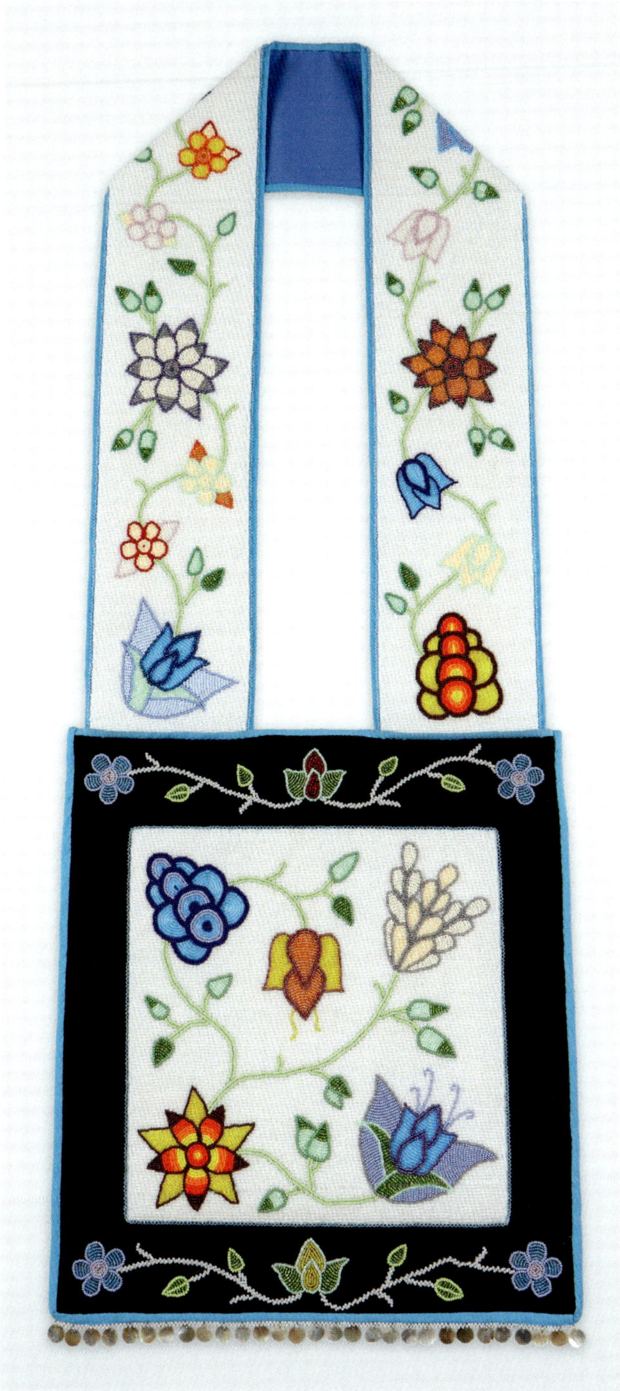

10.51 Cheryl's first gashkibidaagan, completed in 2007. *Photo by James Castle*

Cheryl uses mostly size 11 beads, which she buys at the Mille Lacs Indian Museum and Trading Post because it's readily accessible. Zhaawan once told her how to assess the quality of the beads before purchasing them. "If you hold up the hank of beads and it hangs and looks smooth, the beads are good," she said. "If they appear lumpy and uneven, they are bad beads and won't yield the smooth surface a good beadworker seeks."

Foundation materials for Cheryl's bags include black cotton velveteen (she doesn't use silk velvet because it is too deep; the beads sink and the fabric is hard to cut), nonwoven interfacing, cotton bias tape (Cheryl

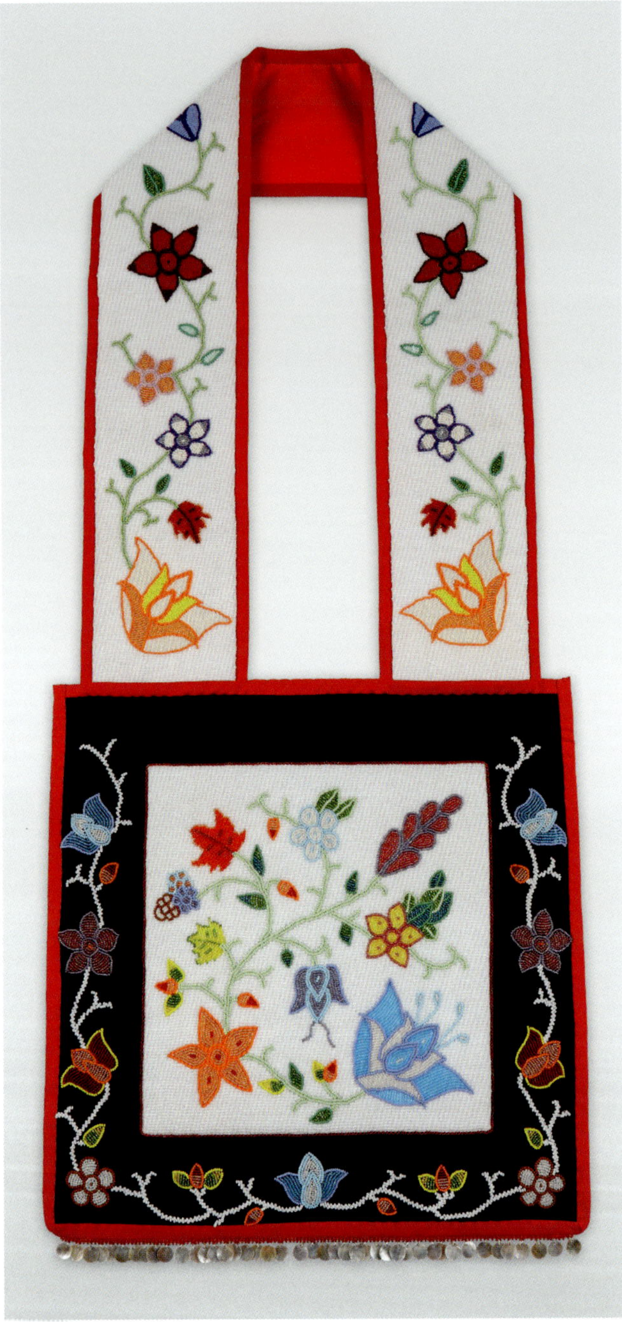

10.52 Cheryl's second gashkibidaagan, completed in 2008, is owned by the Mille Lacs Band and displayed at the Government Center. *Photo by James Castle*

prefers red, because she likes a colorful edging), plain or printed cotton lining (she uses fabric she has on hand, only buying new cotton prints if nothing she has matches). Her second bag (Figure 10.52) shows these elements. She sews her bags with Nymo thread and prefers size B; she uses size D for sewing leather.

Cheryl says the quantity of beads is crucial for her gashkibidaaganag. She has had the trading post order beads for her, when necessary, to get adequate quantities (usually the white background color). If the trading post doesn't have enough hanks of a bead color she needs, she may drive to Duluth or the Twin Cities to find them. Because the difference in bead dye lots can be discernible, beadworkers must sometimes purchase a large number of beads from the same lot at one source.

Omadwe used the double-needle appliqué technique, but Cheryl uses the single-needle technique as she works (Figures 10.53 and 10.54). Zhaawan admired the two-needle technique but she used the single-needle technique most of the time as well. Good spot-stitch appliqué beadwork on a textile surface should "roll easily." If it is stiff, the bead artist has pulled the thread too tight.

Cheryl does most of her beading in an office at home, but she also enjoys beading outside when it's warm and there's not too much wind. She remembers how her grandmother, Omadwe, often scolded the women within their family: "'*Gego* [Don't],' she would say, while we were hunched over by a little lamp in the dark, still trying to sew. She would tell us not to sew after dark; it was bad for your eyes." Omadwe sewed during the day, taking advantage of the natural light.

Cheryl is a tireless bead artist, always interested in tackling the next Ojibwe regalia piece for a new challenge. She has a full life as a working mother, author, student, and self-described "bead woman." Though sewing is an element of everyday life for her, she didn't think of herself as a bead artist until someone called her one. She sees the work she does as originally part of Ojibwe women's everyday lives, but now it is mostly for other uses, such as making miniatures for sale to tourist markets.

> I try to use floral beadwork because that is what we [Ojibwe] are known for. I do have more contemporary ideas that I would like to try, adding more imagery. I like to look at pictures of real flowers and also create my

own flowers by adding to those existing flowers. One of my mother's greatest talents was drawing; I loved to watch her draw many different kinds of flowers, leaves and vines. When I am designing a piece of work, it has to flow. I learned what materials to use in doing my beadwork by watching what my mother bought for her sewing.[33]

Cheryl's third gashkibidaagan, created in 2010, commemorates her mother in the year of her death. The bag, which incorporates Zhaawan's favorite colors and love of sunflowers, has been purchased by the school district in Elk River, Minnesota. Cheryl's fourth bag (Figure 10.55) was purchased for resale by the Mille Lacs Band in 2016.

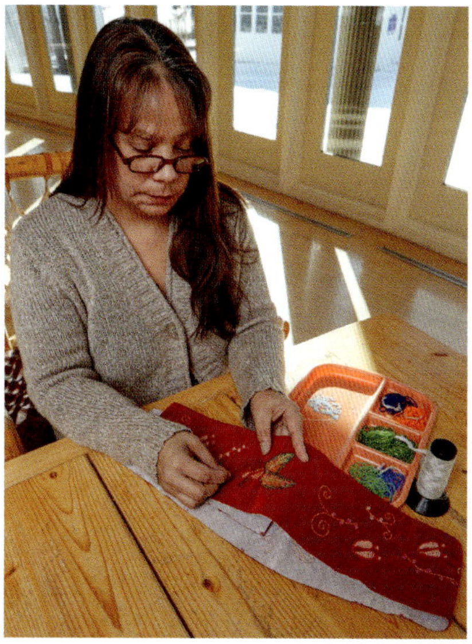

10.53 *(right)* Cheryl demonstrates beading at the Mille Lacs Indian Museum, 2016. *Photo by James Castle*

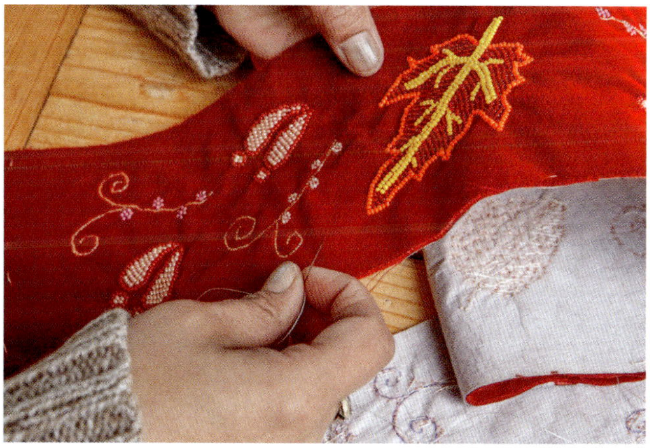

10.54 *(below)* Cheryl beading a floral pattern on the strap of her "fall" bag, part of a four seasons project underway in 2016. *Photo by James Castle*

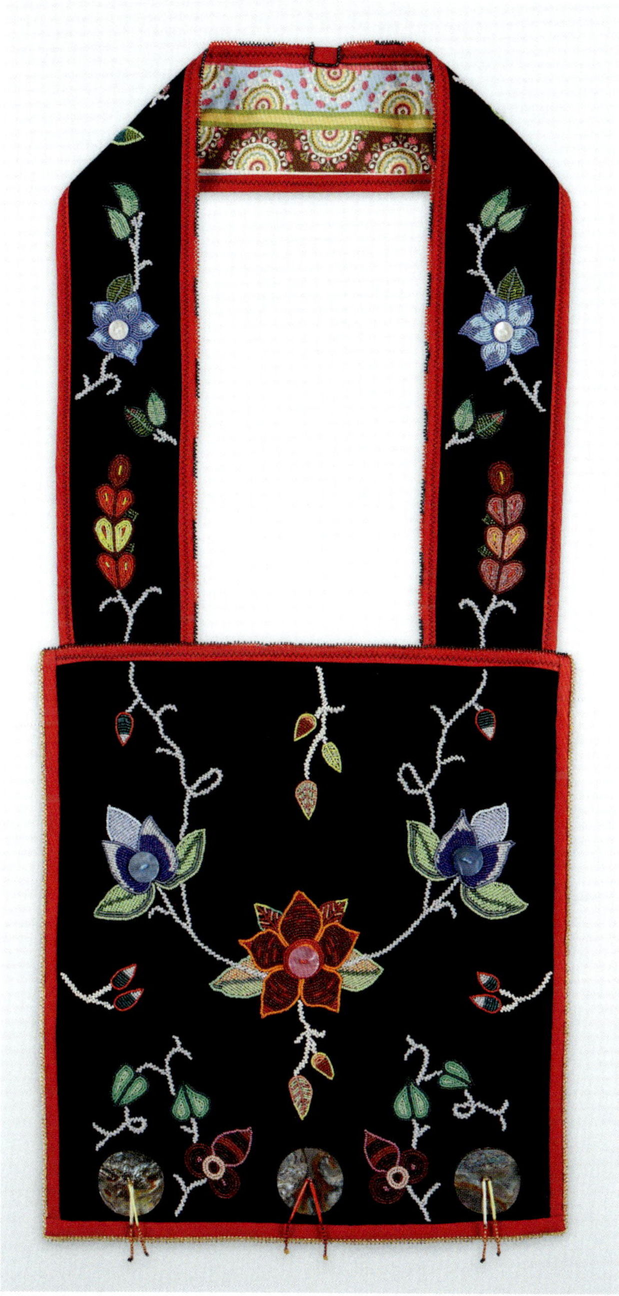

10.55 Cheryl's fourth gashkibidaagan, completed in 2012. *Photo by James Castle*

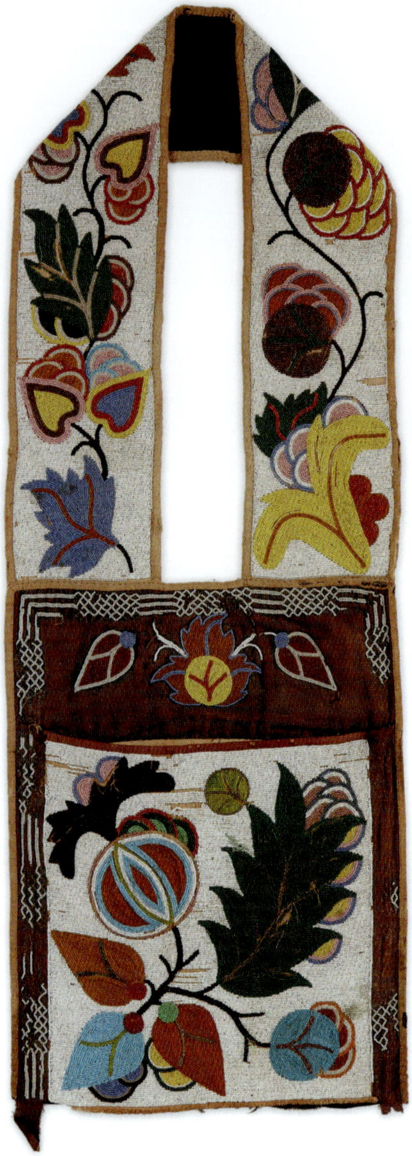

Chapter 11

Red Lake

The Red Lake Reservation is one of only two reservations in the United States that has not been divided by allotment: the people of the Red Lake Nation hold the land in common. Red Lake's leaders and people also were adamant and unusually successful in resisting the US government's other pressures to change. The tribe never surrendered jurisdiction over crimes committed on the reservation, and Red Lake has the greatest number of Ojibwe speakers of any reservation in the state. The people of Red Lake developed the first modern indigenous democratic governance system in the United States, decades before any other tribe, but they also maintained their system of hereditary chiefs.[1]

The Ojibwe name for the Red Lake Nation is Miskwaagamiiwi-zaaga'igan—People of Red Lake. The reservation was established in 1863 and 1864, primarily in Beltrami and Clearwater Counties of northwestern Minnesota; its four main communities are Little Rock, Ponemah, Redby, and Red Lake. Nearby metropolitan areas include Bemidji and Thief River Falls, where the Red Lake Band manages its Seven Clans Casino. Red Lake is the largest freshwater lake in the country wholly contained within one state.

The products of Red Lake's creative beadworkers are visible in many photographs and collections. The folded leaf motif may have originated at Red Lake with the bead artist associated with Giwita-bines (see page 78). The first Episcopal bishop of Minnesota, Bishop Henry Whipple, collected an extraordinary bag (Figure 11.01), which may be from Red Lake or another nearby reservation, that features folded leaves on the pocket panel. The border framing the pocket is an oversize looped embroidery stitch similar to examples seen in other gashkibidaaganag from northwestern Minnesota Ojibwe reservations.

In Figure 11.02, Qui-wi-zhen-shish (Bad Boy), a well-respected member

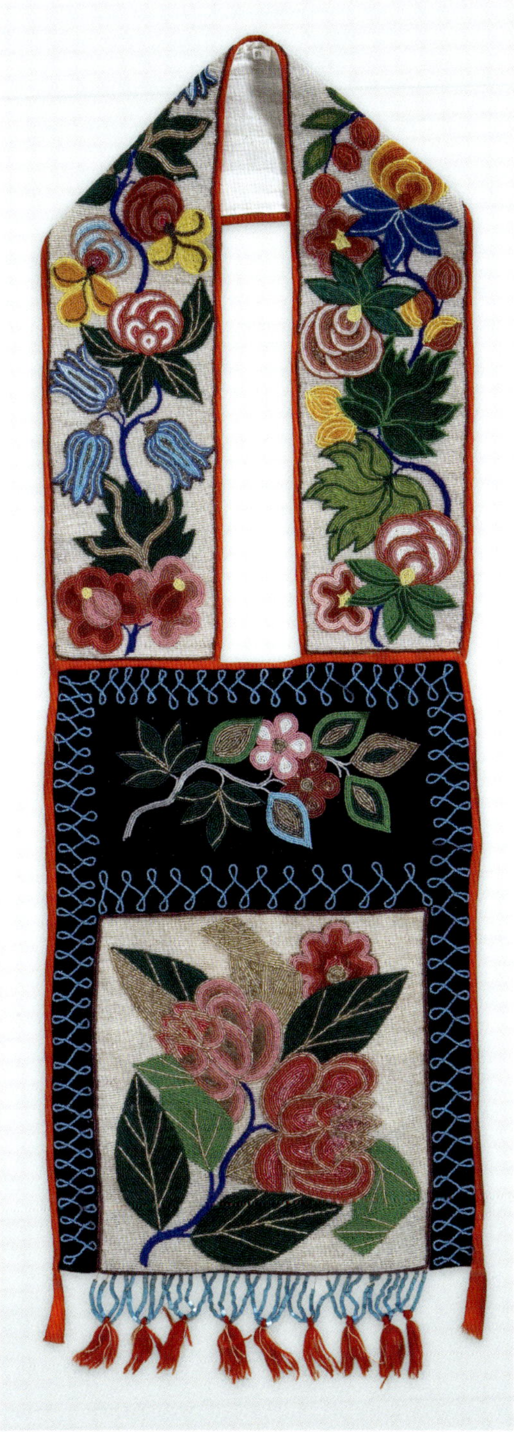

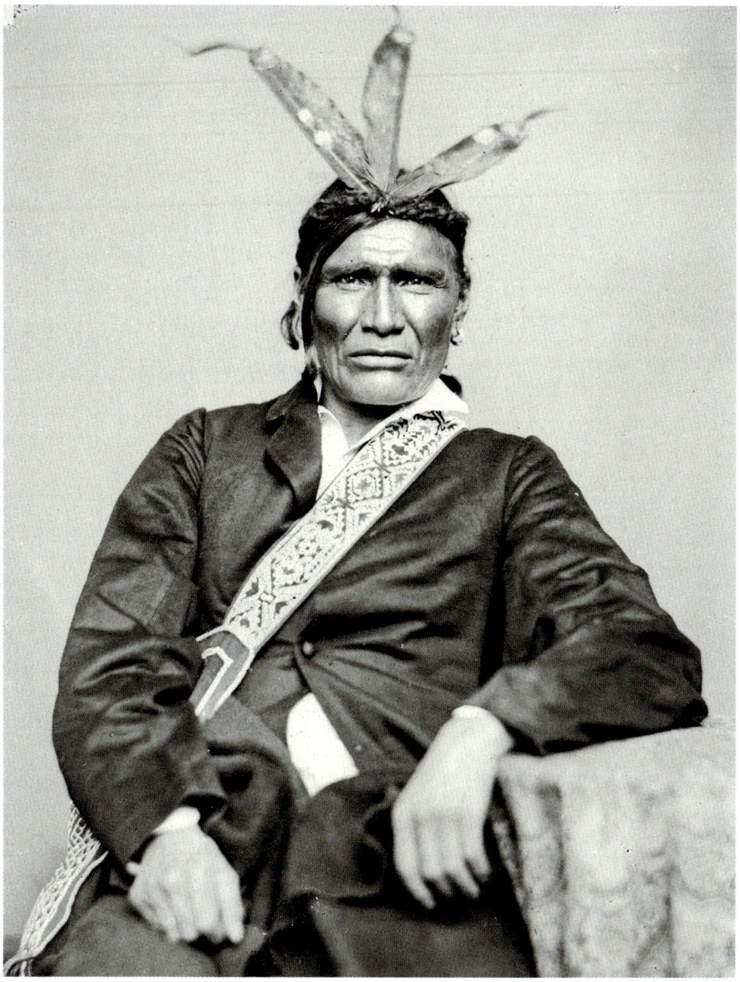

11.01 *(left)* Gashkibidaagan collected by Bishop Henry Whipple before 1901. *MNHS 1828*

11.02 *(above)* Qui-wi-zhen-shish (Bad Boy), an influential Red Lake leader and a successful warrior, hunter, and farmer, photographed before 1872. *NAA-SI BAE GN 00572A 06150600*

11.03 *(right)* Loom-woven strap similar to that worn in Figure 11.02. *MNHS 6020.8; see also Figure 2.31*

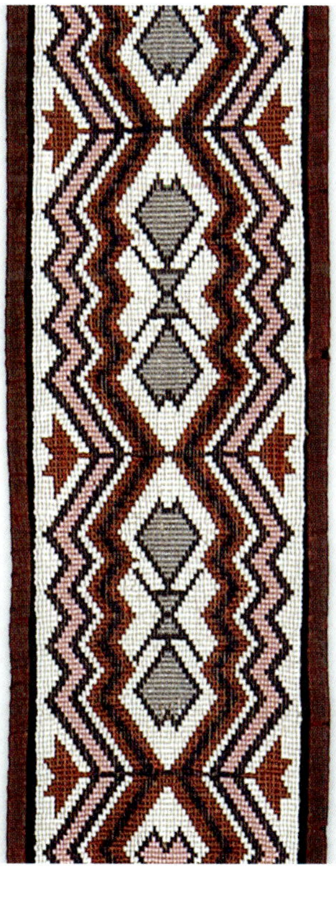

of the Red Lake Band, is wearing an early gashkibidaagan featuring a full-width pocket opening, a loom-woven pocket panel with tab fringe, and a loom-woven panel strap including lozenge-shaped hexagons and thunderbirds; there is probably no spot stitching above the pocket opening. The pocket panel is a loom-woven interpretation of the zigzag designs beaded into the finger-woven sashes of the 1830s to the 1850s, and the strap design is very similar to the elongated octagons on the strap of the bag in Figure 11.03.[2]

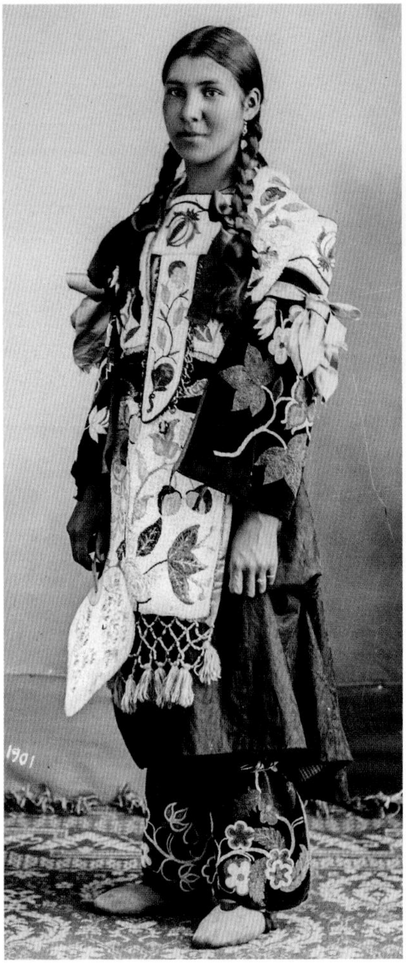

Figure 11.04, a 1901 studio portrait of an unidentified Indian woman, was made by Niels Larson Hakkerup of Bemidji. She is enveloped in spot-stitch appliqué beadwork, including moccasins, leggings, a gashkibidaagan worn apron style, a dance apron on each arm, and a belt around her shoulders with a dance drop or false knife sheath suspended from it. The netted fringe on her bag is not particularly common, but other examples exist in the Whipple collection at the Minnesota Historical Society (see page 200). This type of fringe was popular on early twentieth-century embroidered shawls and other examples of eighteenth- and nineteenth-century decorative furnishing textiles. Figure 11.05, a photo taken at the White Earth Benedictine boarding school in 1895, shows girls making crazy quilt tops and doing embroidery; the table at center is draped with a textile also embellished with a similar netted fringe (which is also similar to fringes found on Chinese embroidered shawls).[3]

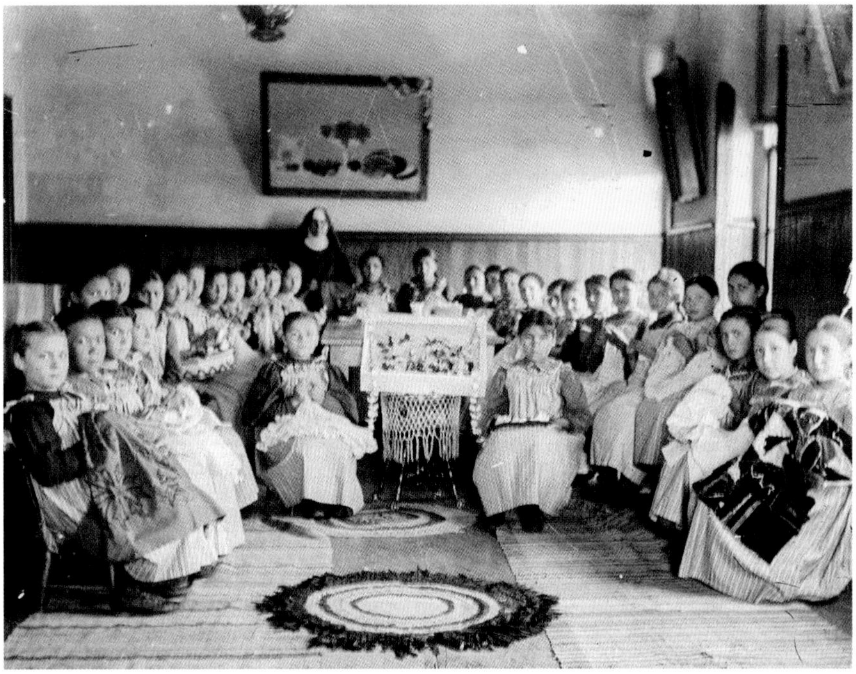

11.04 *(above)* Indian woman, 1901. *Photo by Niels Larson Hakkerup, MNHS E97.1 r14*

11.05 *(right)* Lace makers, White Earth, 1895. *St. Benedict's Monastery Archives*

In Figure 11.06, six Red Lake women and six children pose on the front steps of St. Mary's Catholic Church at Red Lake with Father Thomas Borgerding, a Benedictine missionary, in about 1910. The young boy in the front row wears a spot-stitch appliqué gashkibidaagan, dance apron, and leggings, all scaled down to child size to fit him properly. The bag has a full-width pocket opening, large-scale zigzag border, gear flower and love apple motifs, and fringe of bugle beads strung in loops and finished with wool yarn tassels. Perhaps it is his mother and bead artist who sits to his left.[4]

In the early 1900s, William R. Spears's store at Red Lake (Figure 11.07) displayed a variety of regular merchandise as well as at least three spot-stitch appliqué gashkibidaaganag, a beaded pillow, moccasins, model canoes, many loom-woven bead chains on the counter, and an extraordinary

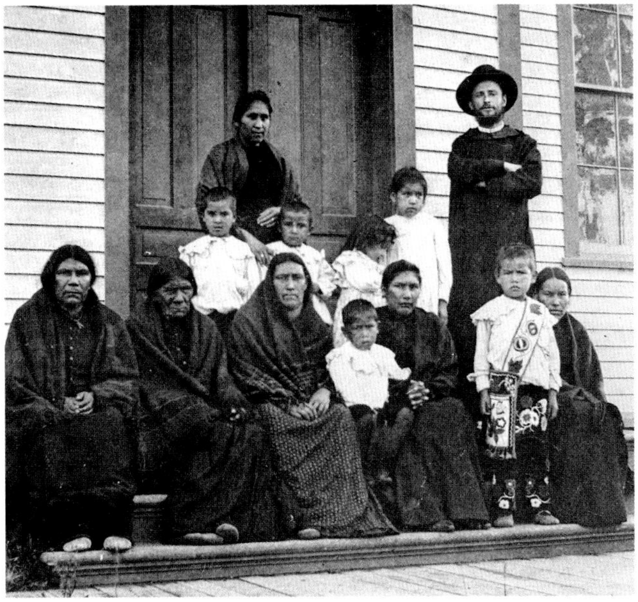

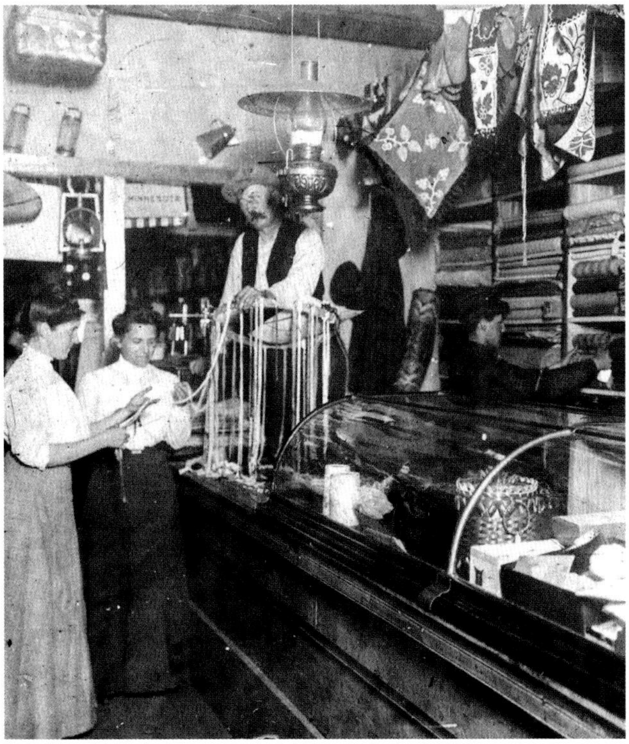

11.06 *(above)* Father Thomas Borgerding with Red Lake women and children, c. 1910. *MNHS E97.7R p15*

11.07 *(above right)* William R. Spears's store, Red Lake. *St. John's Abbey Archives*

11.08 *(right)* Red Lake powwow, 1933. *Photo by Monroe Killy, MNHS E97.37 p70*

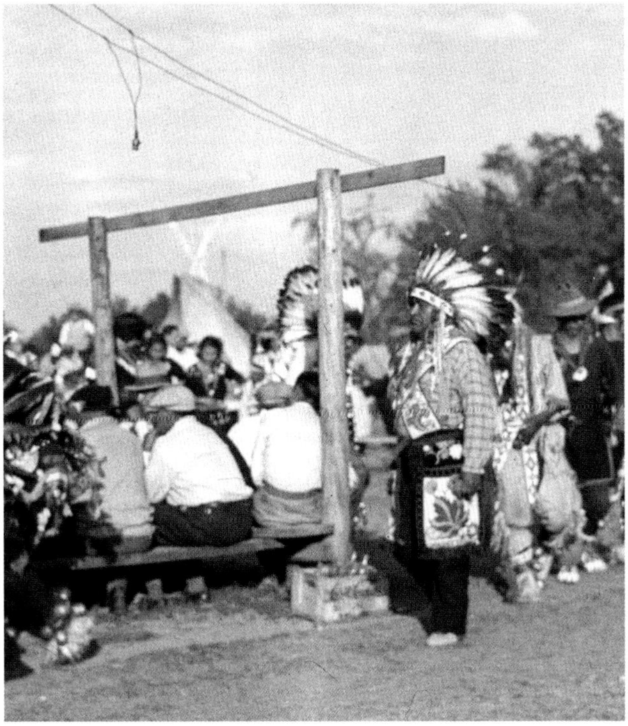

amount of cloth yardage. Spears was a longtime trader, and he advertised regularly in the *Red Lake News*, especially between 1915 and 1920.[5]

Figure 11.08, a Red Lake scene taken on June 4, 1933, by Monroe Killy, beautifully isolates a single participant, dancing his bag on the powwow grounds. A spot-stitch appliqué bag with full-width pocket, it features a single oversized motif on the pocket panel, a leaf. This bag style is often seen in historical images related to the Ojibwe reservations in the northwestern part of Minnesota, but the surviving bags are more likely to feature more complex arrangements of multiple floral motifs on the pocket panel.[6]

John English

John English, who was enrolled at Red Lake, was married to Mary Warren English of White Earth. He stands at the right in Figure 11.09, a photo taken of the last official Red Lake delegation to Washington, DC, in 1909. The bag that English displays features a common gashkibidaagan motif in the upper left corner of the bag's pocket panel. The motif may be a large seedpod, a rosehip, a gooseberry, the cross section of an apple, or the popular love apple.[7]

In 2008 a Mille Lacs Band employee brought the gashkibidaagan shown in Figure 11.10 to the Minnesota History Center for a condition assessment. In 2015 I discovered it was the same bag worn by English in Figure 11.09.

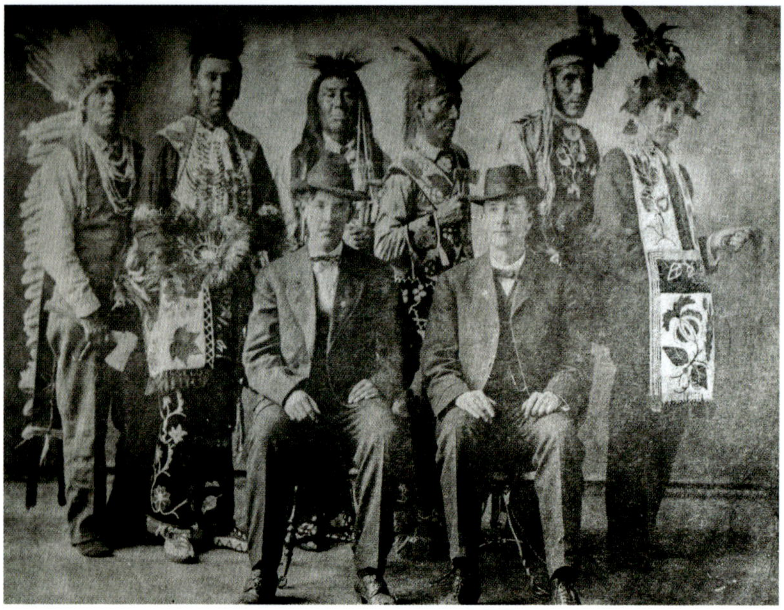

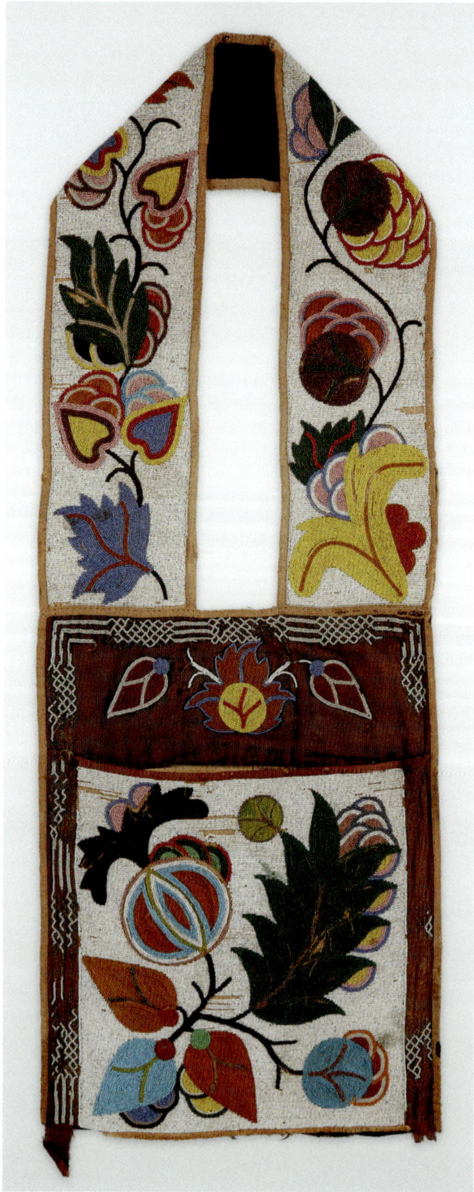

11.09 *(above)* Red Lake treaty delegation in Washington, DC, 1909. Standing, from left: Peter Everwind, Joe Mason, George Highlanding, Ane we gwan abe, Nodin, and John English. Seated: Paul H. Beaulieu and Judge Gibbons. *MNHS E97.51 p4*

11.10 *(right)* The gashkibidaagan associated with John English, created before 1909, is now owned by the Mille Lacs Band of Ojibwe. *Photo by James Castle*

The love apple motif can be found in many sizes on other bags and in other photographs relating to Red Lake. Figure 11.11, a portrait of Red Lake tribal member Ni-Be-Da-Ah-Nah-Gwod (George Burnette), made in Washington, DC, in 1907, shows a similar interpretation of this motif on his gashkibidaagan strap. The bag in Figure 11.12 (as well as 2.02, 3.90, and 9.19, for example) illustrates the love apple's versatility in the hands of Ojibwe bead artists.[8]

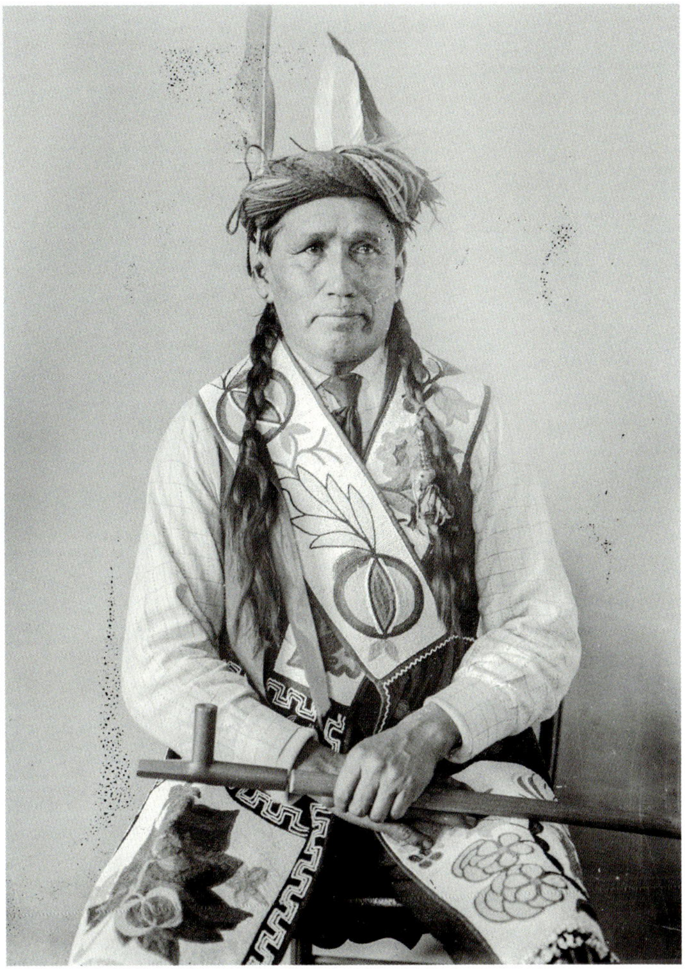

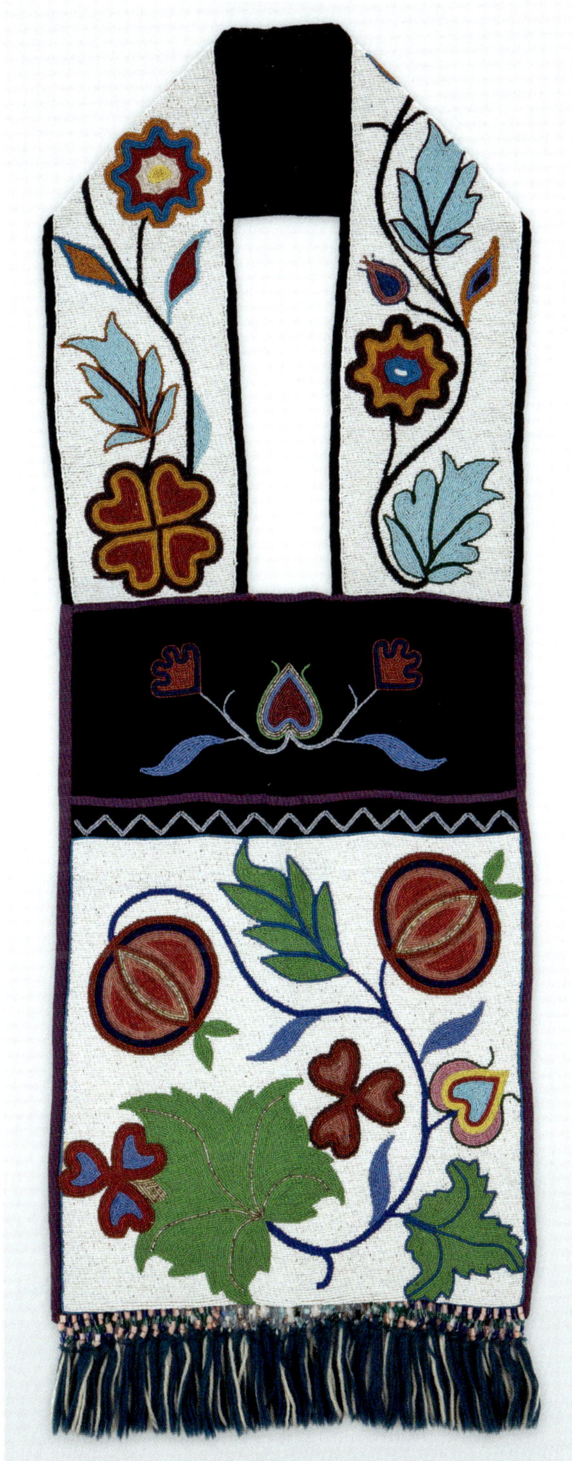

11.11 *(above)* George Burnette, 1907. *Photo by De Lancy Gill, NAA-SI BAE GN 00512A 06140400*

11.12 *(right)* Spot-stitch appliqué bag, before 1911. *MNHS 1982.67.9*

Photographers in the Red Lake area

Some of the finest images of nineteenth-century Minnesota Ojibwe wearing gashkibidaaganag were taken by photographer Jacob Borry. Borry's Photograph Gallery, located on Main Street in Thief River Falls, Minnesota, operated from 1912 to 1920, but he began taking photos in the late 1890s. Because Thief River Falls is one of the larger towns near the Red Lake Reservation, Borry's Indian customers were probably Red Lake Ojibwe.

Borry's images all appear to be studio shots ranging from formal to casual. His subjects are usually serious, dressed in visually rich, beaded regalia, and they face the camera with authority. John Strong (Red Feather, Kiviniguanjasj, and John Strong son of Red Robe) was a grandson of Moose Dung (Mons-o-mo or Mons-o-moh), a powerful leader of the mid-nineteenth century at Red Lake. Strong is pictured alone and in group photographs, including one (Figure 11.13) where he appears to be shown with his family. It's quite possible the unidentified woman seated on the floor is the bead artist of the regalia worn in this image.[9]

Borry's undated image of Chief Poh-ah-be-one and Ponyhoof (Figure 11.14) provides no further clues to the individuals depicted. The central pocket motif on the boy's bag is similar to the motifs on the bags worn by

11.13 *(below)* John Strong *(right rear)*, probably with his family. *Photo by John Borry, PCHS 1999–007–011*

11.14 *(below right)* Chief Poh-ah-be-one and Ponyhoof. *Photo by John Borry, PCHS 0000–000–020*

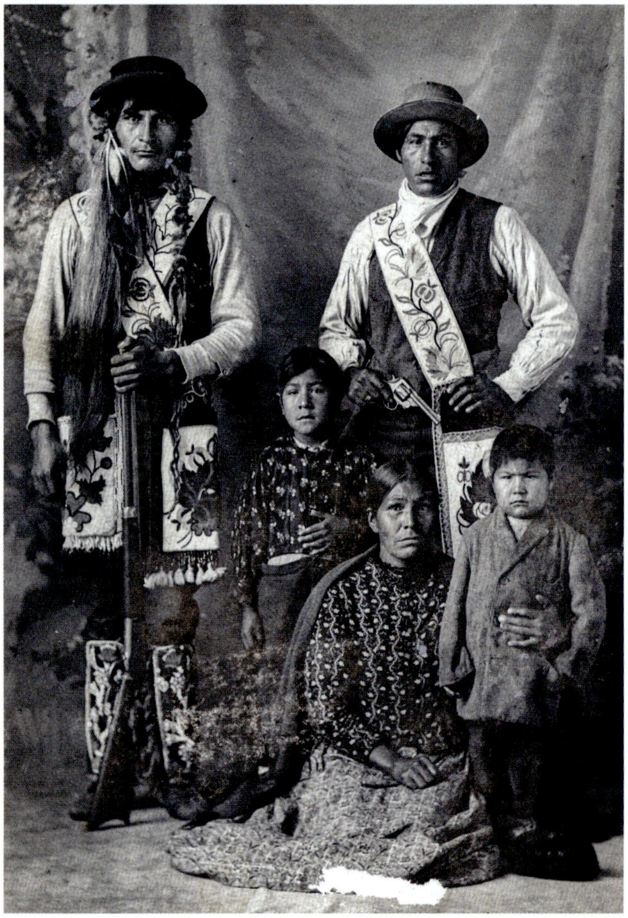

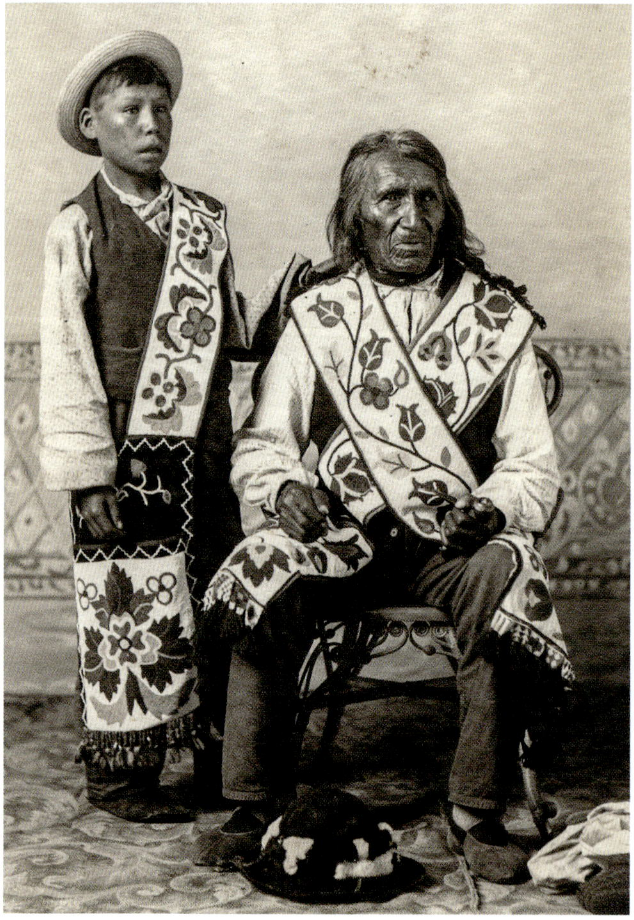

both women in Figure 11.15, taken at the White Earth Reservation Mission School run by St. Benedict's Monastery.[10]

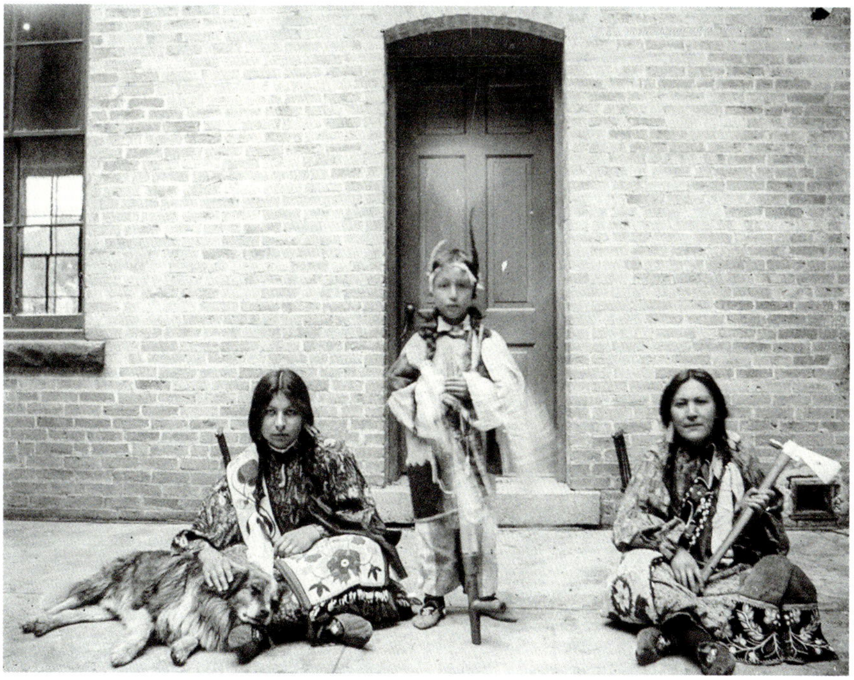

11.15 White Earth Reservation Mission School, 1883. *St. Benedict's Monastery Archives SBM.06f*

Other photography studios in the area contributed records of gashkibidaaganag. A photographer named Smith in Thief River Falls took a picture of the Red Lake leader Red Robe with Albert Stately (Figure 11.16). In Figure 11.17, four men wear eight loom-woven gashkibidaaganag. The pocket panels on the six most visible bags all incorporate some variation of the exploding X motif, and all but two clearly have full-width pocket openings. Five of the six visible bags have no embellishment in the area above the pocket opening. Two of the men also wear fully developed floral spot-stitch appliqué leggings, two wear dance aprons, and one wears a vest.[11]

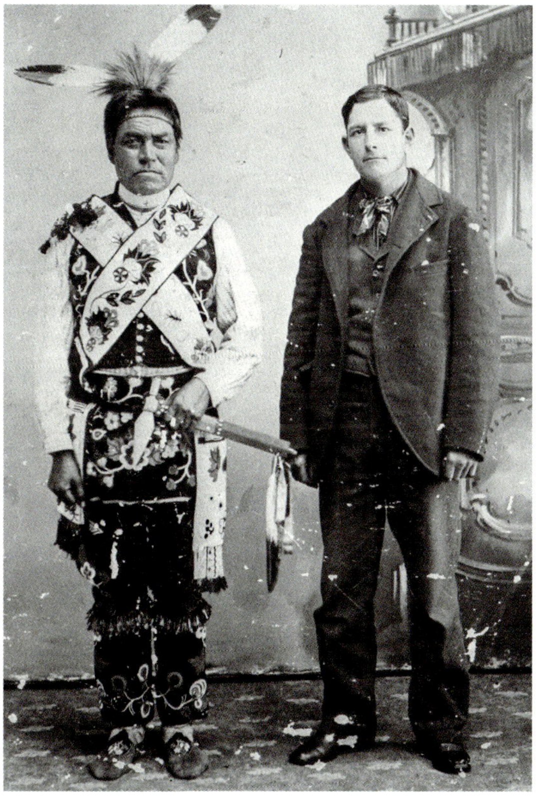

11.16 Red Robe and Albert Stately, c. 1885. *Photo by Smith photography, MNHS E97.1R r4*

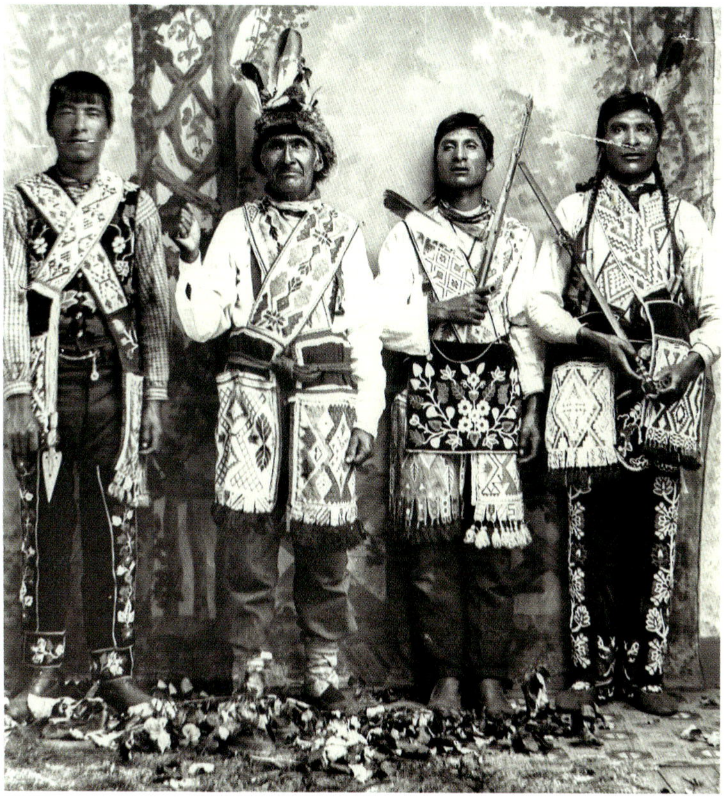

11.17 Ojibwe band members Jim Cobenas, Tigoble of Red Lake, and Joe and Charles Cobenas *(holding ceremonial pipes)*, Jadis Township, Roseau County, 1890. *Photo by Ole Alex Holm, Roseau County HS 4276*

Roland Reed, photographer

Roland W. Reed (1864–1934) created images of North American Indians in the pictorialist style of Edward Curtis, memorializing what he perceived as America's vanishing race. Reed opened a studio in Ortonville, a town in west-central Minnesota, in 1899 and began a full-fledged photography career. Over the next few years, he made occasional visits to reservation communities in Minnesota, and in 1907 and 1908 he embarked on an extended visit to the Ojibwe of Cass Lake, Leech Lake, Red Lake, and Rainy Lake.[12]

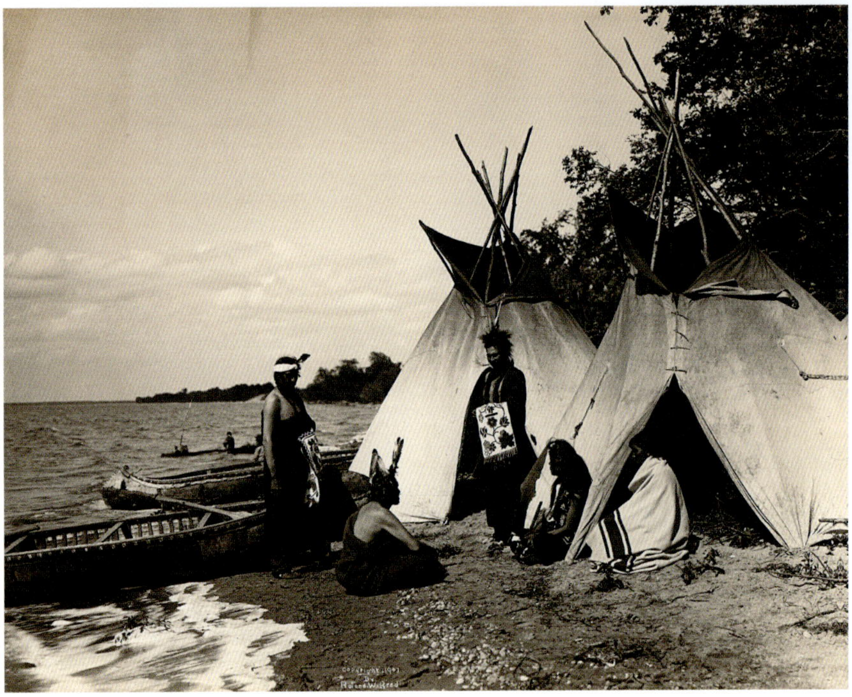

11.18 *Confusion*, by Roland W. Reed, 1907. *Courtesy Kramer Gallery, St. Paul*

Like Curtis, Reed had an inventory of props that he used in his photographs. Red Lake area trader John G. Morrison served as Reed's material culture specialist and recommended the sort of clothing and accessories he should acquire and use for particular subjects. A series of photographs rich in material culture objects with beached canoes on a lakeshore were likely all shot in the same location on the Red Lake Reservation. Gashkibidaaganag were among the accessories Reed used to represent the Ojibwe of Minnesota in three of these images from 1907. One bag is visible in *The First Sail*; two are visible in *Friend or Foe* and in *Confusion* (Figure 11.18). The bags are draped over a man or a woman's arm, with the strap hanging down in back, rather than being worn. Both bags are of the spot-stitched style, one having the single pocket panel form with a faux or narrow slit pocket opening. The other bag appears to be of an earlier form, with a cloth panel above the pocket opening as well as the oversize zigzag or feather stitch border so often seen on the Ojibwe gashkibidaaganag of northwestern Minnesota. The motifs and components are also quite typical of Minnesota Ojibwe work, and considering Morrison's contacts, the bags may very well have been made by a Red Lake bead artist.[13]

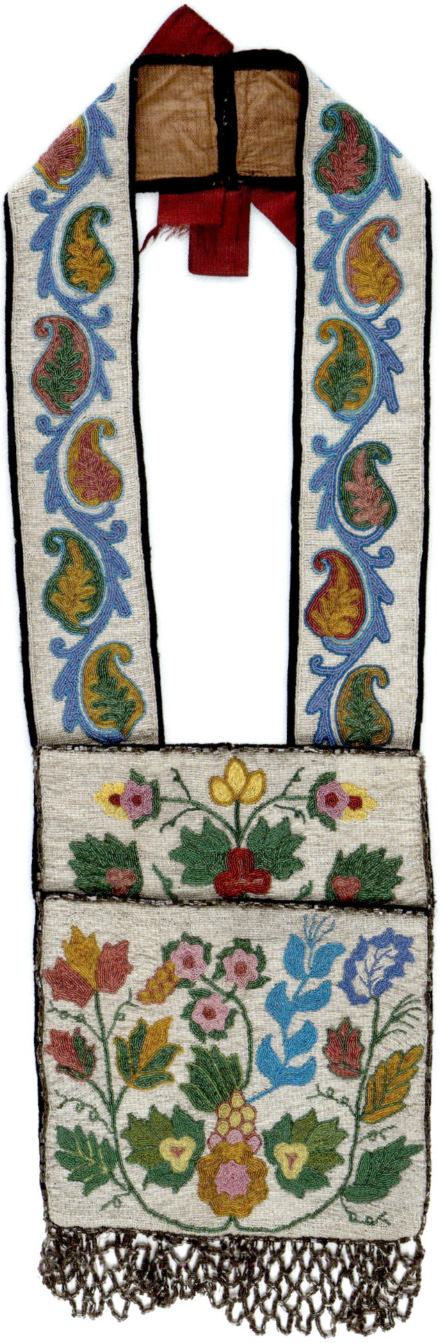

Chapter 12

White Earth

White Earth Reservation (Gaa-waabaabiganikaag) was created in 1867 as a result of a treaty between the US government and the Mississippi Band of Chippewa Indians. The government initially planned to persuade or force all the Ojibwe and Dakota people of the region to move to either White Earth or Red Lake, thus opening their former reservations to non-Indian farmers and lumbermen. Some people from Ojibwe communities across Minnesota relocated to White Earth, the largest numbers being from the Gull Lake Mississippi Band, the Mille Lacs Band, and the Pillager Band. By 1920, however, broad populations had relocated to White Earth for a number of reasons. The reservation populates and impacts the communities of Becker, Clearwater, and Mahnomen Counties and includes the communities of Bagley, Callaway, Clearwater, Detroit Lakes, Elbow Lake, Mahnomen, Naytahwaush, Ogema, Pine Point, Ponsford, Rice Lake, Waubun, and White Earth.[1]

White Earth is part of what was loosely referred to, well into the mid-twentieth century, as the Cass Lake area (see page 99). Many gashkibidaaganag may be identified as "Cass Lake," but this term must be considered carefully because it can relate to Ojibwe from different reservation communities. Gashkibidaaganag associated with the White Earth area are perhaps the most elaborate and distinctive of all Ojibwe bandolier bags. They demonstrate the considerable skills and talents of their makers.

For the most part, Minnesota Ojibwe people conformed outwardly to the roles established within the cultural and political limits assigned to reservation life at the turn of the nineteenth century. While Ojibwe men and women were prevented from engaging in many of their religious and economic practices, they found ways to push at the constraints, resisting where they could, seeking out opportunities to demonstrate elements of traditional culture and retain mastery over their own lives.

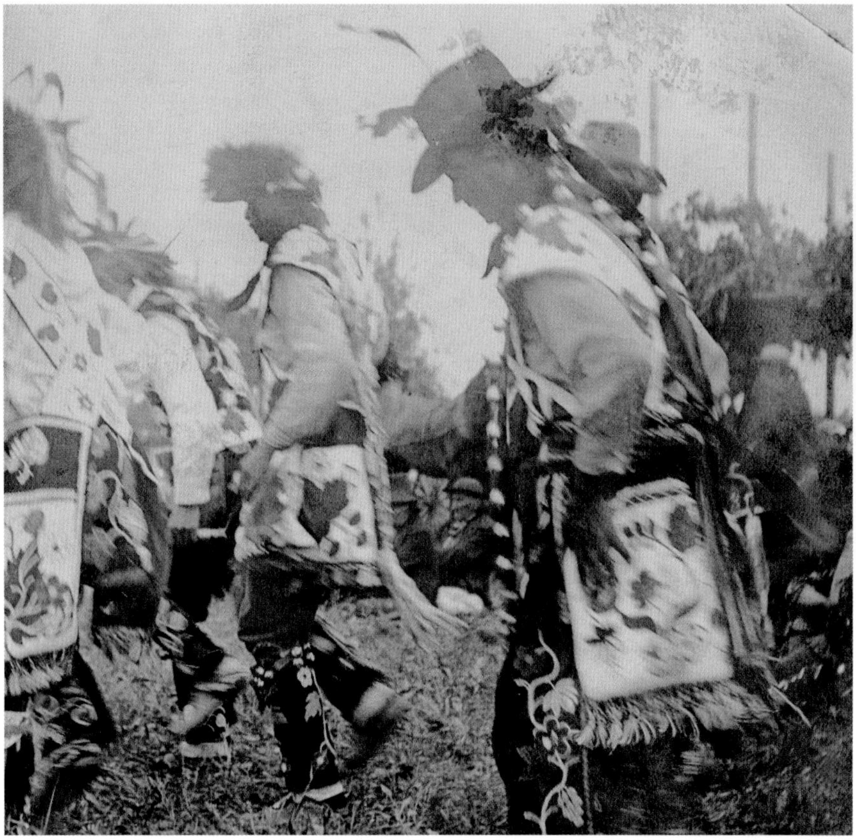

12.01 Dancers at Annual White Earth Reservation Celebration, c. 1900. The photographer (possibly Edward A. Bromley) captured the fluid motion of the bags and their fringe as the men move in concert around the dance circle. Note the enlarged leaf motifs on two of the three visible pockets. *MNHS E97.37 r7*

The Annual White Earth Reservation Celebration (Figure 12.01) became the community's most significant opportunity to publicly celebrate elements of the traditional life members were otherwise forbidden or discouraged from practicing openly. As Frances Densmore noted, "The Indian agents usually discourage the dances but the Ojibwa at White Earth, Minn., are allowed to hold an Annual Council Fire and Dance to celebrate their removal from Gull Lake to their present location." The making and wearing of gashkibidaaganag and other regalia was an important part of the event and of Ojibwe identity.[2]

The first celebration was a small affair held June 14, 1873, at the Episcopal church, organized by Clement H. Beaulieu and Enmegahbowh (Reverend John Johnson). It was advertised as a picnic, with speeches (by notable chiefs and prominent men of the reservation) and charades by Kish-Kun-Ah-Kud, the sexton of the church. Considering his long career with the church and accomplishments on so many levels, it is not surprising that Enmegahbowh succeeded in convincing the White Earth Reservation community that there was reason to celebrate their initial removal to the reservation in June 1868. The celebration has been held on an almost uninterrupted annual basis ever since, counting its start with the 1868 move, rather than with the year it first took place.[3]

At first, the White Earth annual celebration was managed by the Episcopal Church. For tourists, the celebration served as a summer road trip to see colorful historical performances and unusual dances and to learn about another culture. But for members of the Ojibwe and Dakota communities who attended and participated in the programs, the experience incorporated evolving and complex roles packed with mixed messages and experiences: building relationships between the two tribes, historical and contemporary performances, opportunities to represent themselves politically, a way to transmit cultural knowledge, as well as visits and competitions with friends and families from near and far. This reservation community accommodated two to three thousand visitors in a weekend. Political speeches made by officials from the Indian agency and from Minnesota's government were essential program components, and officials from the US Bureau of Indian Affairs spoke regularly alongside important Ojibwe chiefs and leaders. Reservation bands played church social music and music for bowery dances, in which those who wanted to dance paid a nickel and then chose a dance partner. Reservation police—not local non-Indian authorities—handled security. This all took place simultaneously with "sham battles," scalp dances, tableaus of historical and contemporary Indian life, footraces, canoe races, sharing of gifts and food, the communal gathering of friends and family, the sharing of songs, stories, and dances—and, of course, the wearing of elaborate regalia.[4]

The act of wearing gashkibidaaganag played a key role in transforming a Eurocentric-inspired "celebration" into an opportunity for members of the White Earth Band and their indigenous visitors to express cultural pride in a setting where participants and attendees brought their own various and mixed agendas. Over the course of several decades, the pervasive and highly visible gashkibidaaganag became a vehicle for Indians to present their historical, real, and imagined roles as they interacted with Indian agents, US government officials, tourists, other tribes, and representatives of the Episcopal and Catholic mission churches (Figure 12.02).

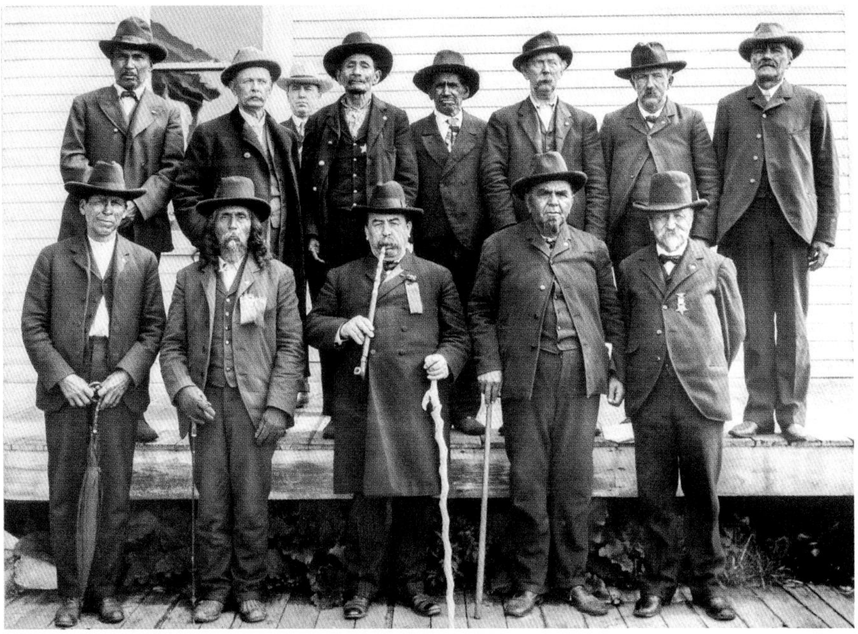

12.02 Minnesota governor Samuel Van Sant *(front row center)* posed proudly in 1903 with fellow soldiers present at the anniversary of the occupation of White Earth Reservation. *MNHS E97.5 h1*

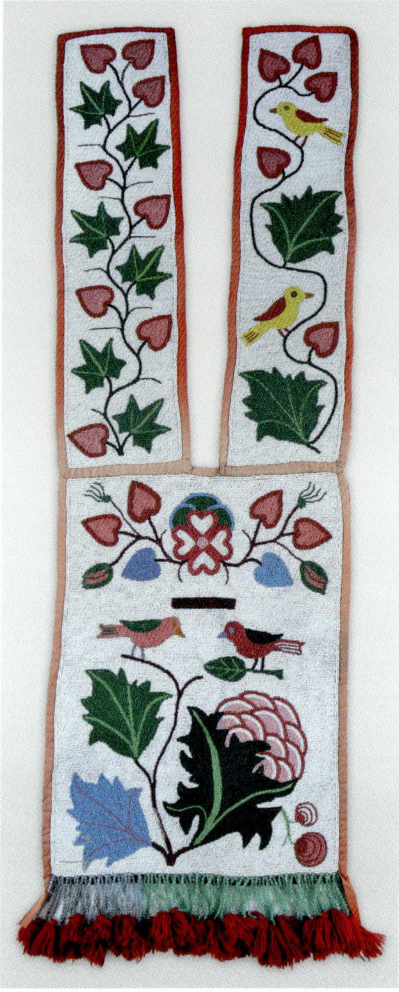

12.03 Spot-stitch appliqué bag from White Earth Reservation, c. 1890s. *Maryhill Museum of Art 1981.4.6*

In the early twentieth century, the descriptive title and the reservation community's "ownership" gradually shifted. By the 1920s, the Annual White Earth Reservation Celebration managed by the Episcopal church had evolved into a greater presentation of personal and community Ojibwe cultural identity, eventually identified as the Annual White Earth Reservation Celebration and Pow Wow, as it is today. Articles published through these years do not explicitly address the shift, but the change may have had as much to do with the way the event was viewed by outsiders as with changes in the eyes of White Earth Ojibwe themselves.[5]

The White Earth powwow is one of the best documented of the regional public dances among the Ojibwe in Minnesota. Community observers, attendees, participants, and ethnographers have left detailed information about the programs, particularly in the pages of the *Tomahawk*, the *Chippeway Herald,* and the *Progress* newspapers. Additional accounts come from celebrated guests, participants, and members of other tribes in the form of invitations, personal journals, ethnographic records, and photographs.[6]

In the first quarter of the twentieth century, white Americans were taking note of things "Indian," as the influences of the Arts and Crafts movement brought an upsurge in their popularity. As people in other states and countries became aware of bandolier bags, these objects of great beauty told the compelling story of human beings immersed in the creation of cultural identity. Ojibwe artists used their extraordinary artistic and beadworking talents to take advantage of this evolving popular culture movement, and for this reason we find bandolier bags in private and public collections around the world.

The purchasers of the bandolier bag in Figure 12.03 may have been among those collectors. Mr. and Mrs. George Ochsner lived in Idaho, and they acquired this bag and other objects from the White Earth Reservation at the turn of the twentieth century or earlier, perhaps during visits

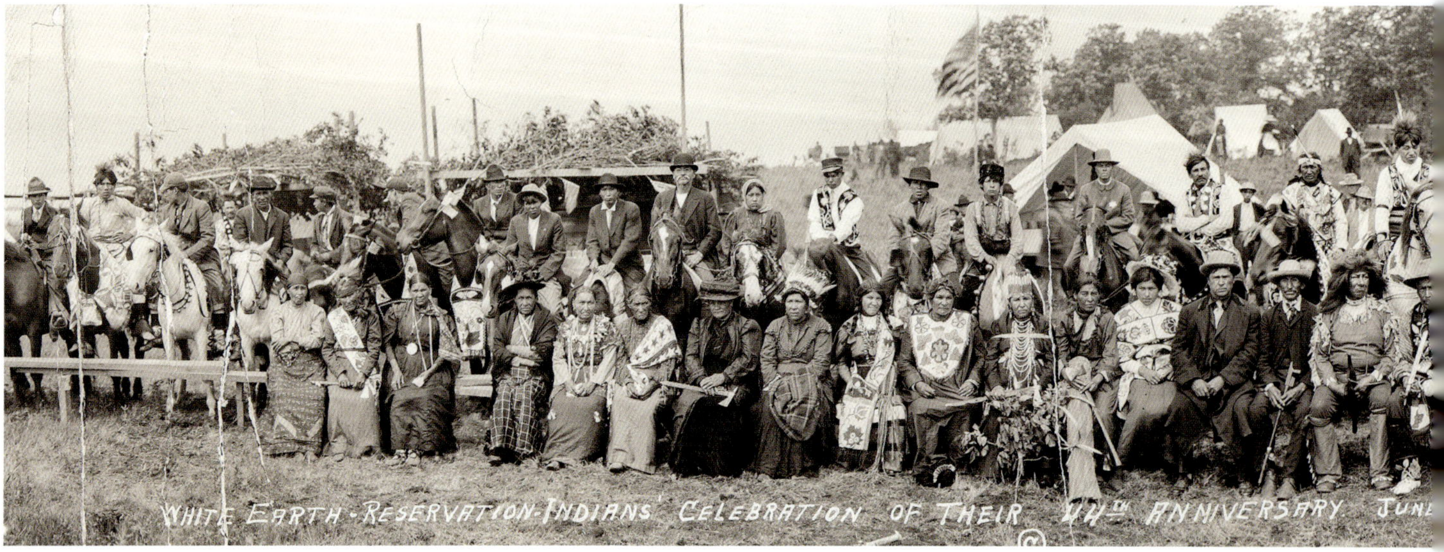

to the annual celebration. The bag represents the later spot-stitched full-panel style with a beaded faux slit pocket opening, two styles of heart flowers, ivy leaves, oversized leaves, a pinecone, and four birds in profile. As is typical of the full panel bags, the decorative border around the pocket is no longer present. The Ochsners donated the bag to the Maryhill Museum of Art in Washington State.[7]

Most remarkably, gashkibidaaganag of extraordinary quality and in great quantity worn at this annual celebration are well recorded photographically, particularly in 1900, 1910, 1912, and 1916. Photographs from the annual celebration, as well as many other images, record the abundance of these bags and the strong cultural identity they conveyed. The images document the distinctive bag types and beadwork motifs between 1890 and 1930 from the area often loosely termed as the Cass Lake resort region.

In a 1912 panorama of the forty-fourth annual celebration (Figure 12.04), twenty-four floral spot-stitch appliqué gashkibidaaganag can be clearly identified. This staged setting positioned just outside the dance ground stands is particularly rich in communicating the complex relationships at work at the time. Men and women are seated and on horseback, in a mix of natural and "studio" bodily attitude. Reservation police, lay ministers, dancers, chiefs, and others all came together for this portrait. People wear many forms of dress, but the twenty-four bags have the place of honor on the outermost surface and are worn in traditional style across the chest, like aprons, piled on in layers for effect. Even the fifth and sixth horses from the left wear them, martingale style: over the horse's head, with the bag pocket facing forward. The people's facial expressions are serious, somber, and dignified. One woman in the front row (above the "A" of "Anniversary") wears a fashionable skirt and blouse with a stylish large store-bought "peach basket" hat and three bandolier bags. The subjects wear a host of elaborate beaded accessories, but the bags are all clearly displayed as showpieces and worn with great pride.

12.04 White Earth Reservation Celebration, 1912, collected and donated by Frances Densmore. *Photo by Randolph R. Johnston, MNHS E97.37 pan 1*

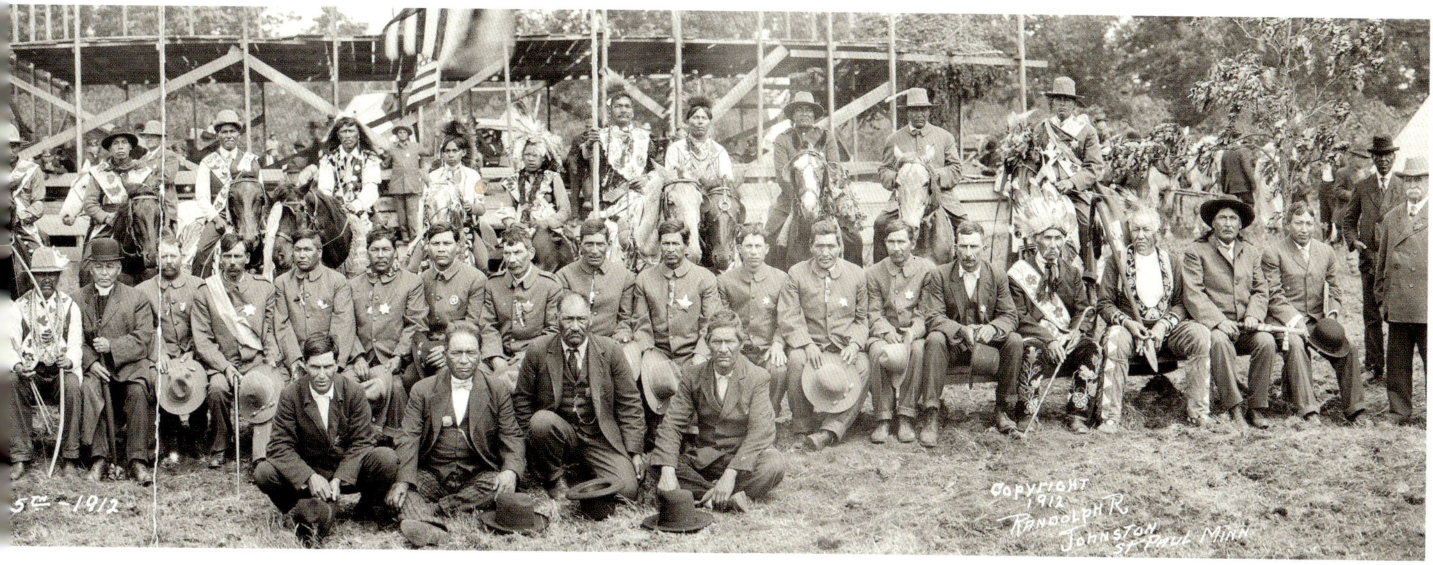

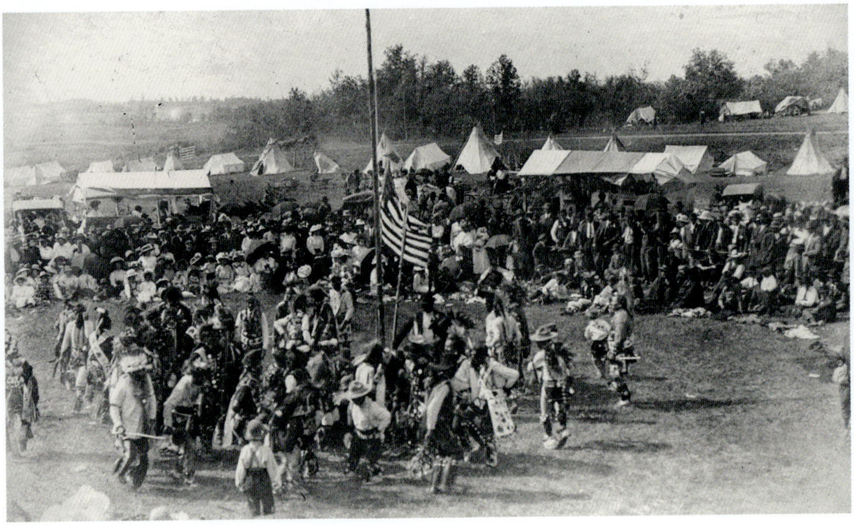

12.05 Annual White Earth Reservation Celebration, no date. *Photo by Rich, MNHS E97.37 p5*

Photographer Arthur A. Richardson had a studio in Bemidji in the 1910s and 1920s as well as a traveling outfit called the Rich Photo Craft Car. In one of Richardson's photos (Figure 12.05) he captured an example of the re-enacted war, sham battle, and scalp dances performed for visitors at the Annual White Earth Reservation Celebration. Gashkibidaaganag worn and danced by participants outshone both the striped awnings of the food wagons and the fashionable apparel of the non-Indian females in attendance.[8]

Once gashkibidaaganag left the hands of the bead artist and her community, where they represented recognition and honor, the role and meaning of the bags morphed. Gashkibidaaganag provided economic purchase power with the Dakota, and in many cases were created and sold to non-Indians simply to provide a family with needed cash. Bags associated with White Earth are particularly representative of the multitude of ways the surviving bags left the ownership of bead artists and tribal leaders and were preserved by collectors or museums. Stories shared in this chapter include bags that were purchased for display at the 1893 World's Columbian Exposition, that were presented to a non-Indian by band members, that were collected by an Indian agent and commissioner, that were purchased by or given to Minnesota's longtime Episcopal bishop Henry Whipple, that were associated with an Ojibwe leader, and that were commissioned by a missionary.[9]

Gashkibidaaganag are no longer as prevalent as they once were, but today the Annual White Earth Reservation Celebration and Pow Wow continues to be held on the weekend closest to June 14. Family and friends come to visit or camp out for the week, so they can participate in the annual craft show and sale, buy their commemorative band T-shirts, and attend the powwow. The bags are rarely seen or danced with any regularity, but contemporary bead artists like Ivy Ailport have kept the gashkibidaagan tradition alive at White Earth, and more Ojibwe bead artists are now creating these treasures to be danced at powwows.

1893 World's Columbian Exposition

In 1893 Minnesota, like thirty-five other states, erected a building at the World's Columbian Exposition in Chicago to showcase the state's attractions and accomplishments. Visitors entered through a square portico, where they came upon a statue of Henry Wadsworth Longfellow's fictional Ojibwe character Hiawatha carrying the figure of Minnehaha. The exhibits displayed on the main floor included mounted caribou, moose, deer, bear, and gamebirds, as well as photographs of fishing resorts; sheaves of wheat, timothy, and other grasses provided decoration. Sharing space on that same floor were Ojibwe and Dakota cultural objects, described by one non-Indian observer, clearly a person of his time, as "Indian curios, some of them reviving memories of the massacres of early days."[10]

The Minnesota Board of World's Fair Managers had considered assembling a Minnesota Indian village, which did not materialize, and the Indian curio display was put together rather hurriedly in the early months of 1893. The display was successful primarily due to the efforts of Mrs. Nancy Judson and the Women's Auxiliary Board. The exhibit included a personal collection of American Indian objects on loan from Stephen Jewett, a collector in Faribault, Minnesota, and a remarkable assemblage of Ojibwe beaded pieces purchased for the World's Fair. The purchased objects were probably made by or acquired from White Earth Band members, mostly women, through an agency identified as the Becker County Indian Industries. Some of the objects from the installation that are now in the Minnesota Historical Society collections were apparently acquired from the private collection of Jessie Campbell West, including the bag on the right in Figure 12.06. Given the tight timeline, the Columbian Exposition committee probably selected bags from those already in existence on the White Earth Reservation.[11]

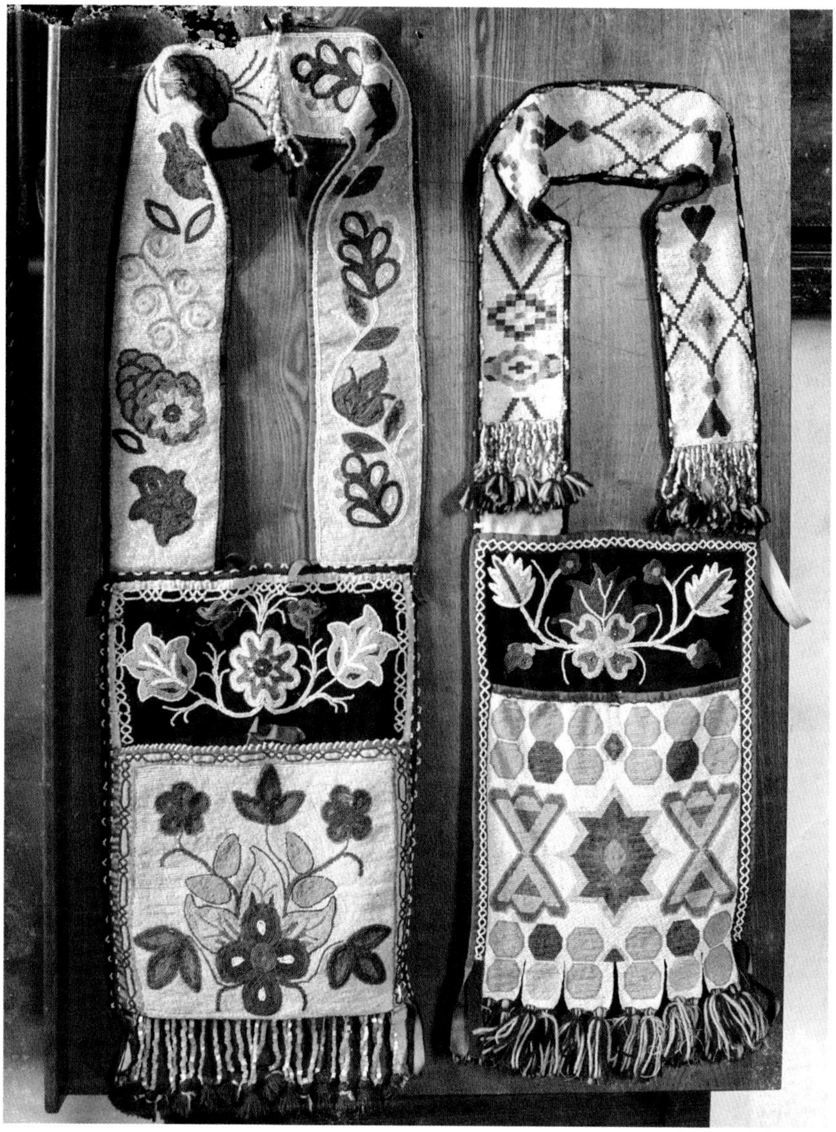

12.06 Columbian Exposition Indian curio exhibit case, 1893. *MNHS E97.22 p3; see also Figures 1.05 and 12.08*

At the close of the exposition, Stephen Jewett's personal collection was returned to him, and the nonperishable exhibits—furniture, fixtures, and the like—were distributed among the sponsoring organizations and other state-affiliated agencies. The Minnesota Historical Society received a large group of objects, including twenty-two beaded objects from the Indian exhibit. Because of their remarkable condition, the certainty that they were

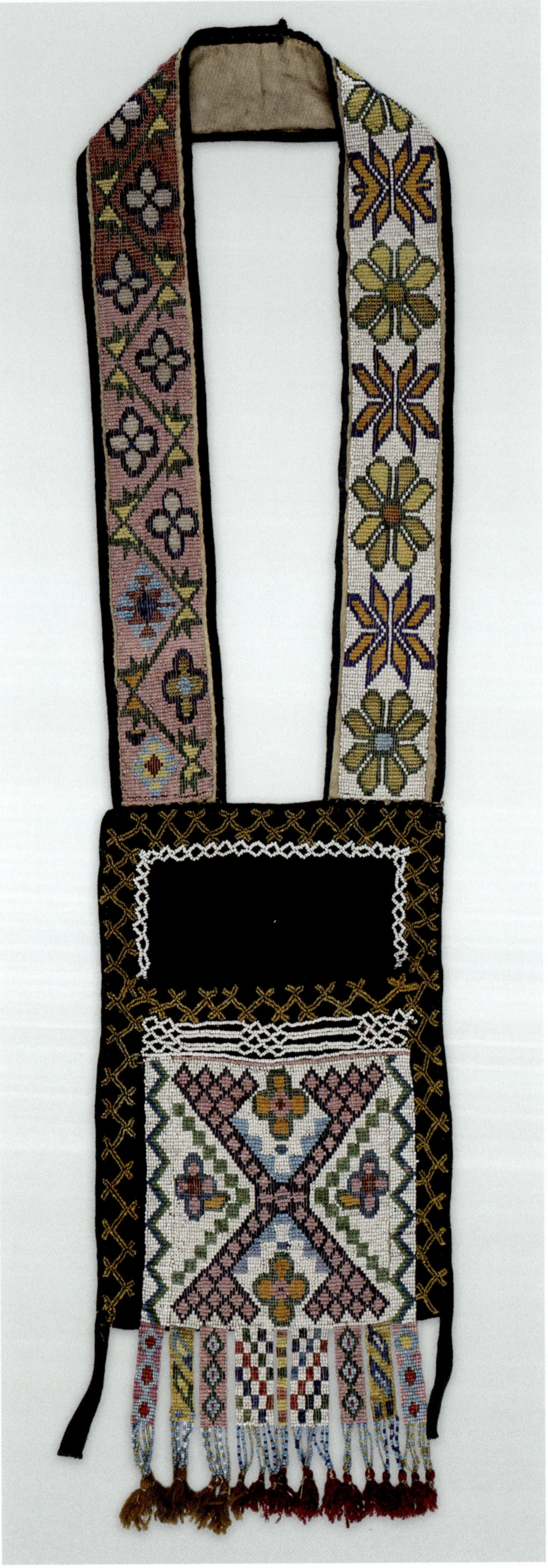

made before 1893, and their provenance, these twenty-two items represent important historical resources for the study of material culture techniques, design elements, materials use, and evolving regional traditions. They also show the diversity of design themes incorporated by Ojibwe women of Minnesota and particularly those of the White Earth Reservation. The beaded pieces, including five gashkibidaaganag, have been researched and published extensively by scholars, collectors, and other researchers.[12]

Two of the bags are fine examples of the variations found in loom-woven bags. The bag in Figure 12.07 is much smaller in overall scale than average, but the strap length is comparable to that of larger bags. The pocket is overflowing with simple shapes and line stitches, including zigzag, otter track, and feather stitches, as well as triangles, rectangles, and diamonds. Other components include the integrated loom-woven tab fringe, the empty space above the pocket, the exploding X, and the halfway break in design on the strap that references or mimics the earlier two-piece straps.[13]

The loom-woven bag in Figure 12.08 is one of the finest designed bags of its type in the Minnesota Historical Society's collections. The arrangement, the balance, the use of a challenging color palette consistently and creatively in all three different bag elements, the quality of the embroidery work above the pocket opening, and the overall fine workmanship attest to the skills of this bead artist. She uses an unusual and very early motif, the circle or dot (hexagon), while at the same time fully embracing the growing shift to larger-scale motifs on the pocket panel. The bag, as a painter's canvas, is united by the artistic and balanced appliquéd motif above the pocket opening.

Three spot-stitch appliqué bags all have some typical motifs, but each also has atypical elements; without the clear White Earth provenance for Columbian Exposition objects, it would be difficult to assume they were necessarily of Minnesota Ojibwe manufacture. The bag in Figure 12.09 employs many common motifs, including rosebuds, berries, gear flowers,

12.07 Loom-woven bag from Columbian Exposition display, 1893 or earlier. *MNHS 512.E137*

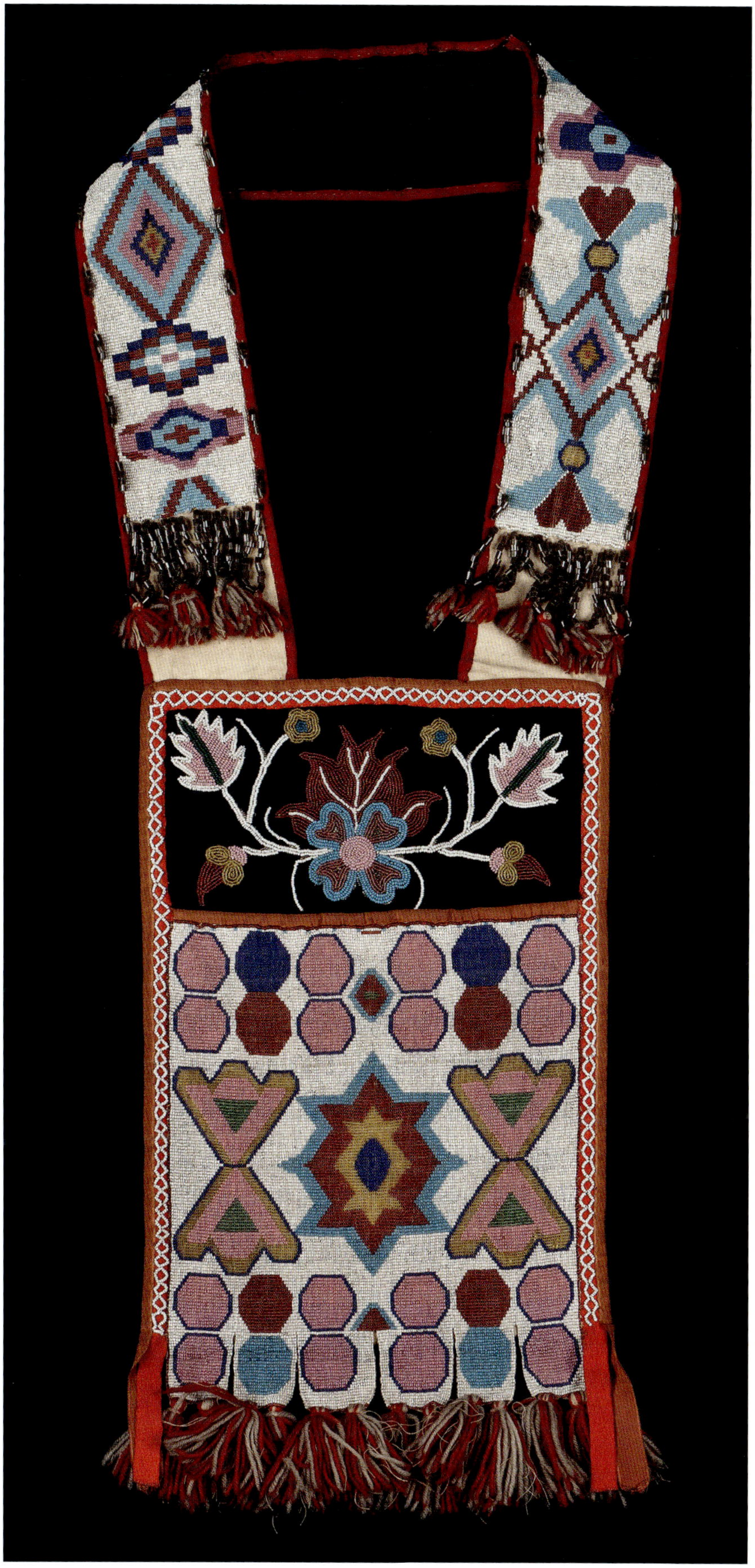

12.08 Spot-stitch appliqué bag from Columbian Exposition display, 1893 or earlier. *MNHS 532.E157; see also Figure 2.18*

pinecones, vines, and tendrils. The ribbon appliqué pocket border, however, is out of scale with, and distracts from, the delicate presentation of the floral motifs, an unusual shortcoming for Ojibwe beadwork. In Figure 12.10, the pocket panel and area above the pocket opening are smaller than usual and densely filled with floral motifs, while the strap uses the meandering vine format with a much more generous spacing approach. The pocket panel is bordered with otter track and anchors its design with the leaf-and-flower cluster motif so common among Minnesota Ojibwe bags.

The most mysterious example of this collection is in Figure 12.11. The pocket portion is typical of Minnesota bags with its layered motifs, leaves, vines, and tendrils, but the strap incorporates an atypical motif: the ancient teardrop shape known as a cone, buta, pine, or paisley. Popular in the nineteenth century, the buta appeared in wool and silk shawls that

12.09 *(below left)* Spot-stitched appliqué bag from Columbian Exposition display, 1893 or earlier. *MNHS 514.E139*

12.10 *(below center)* Spot-stitch appliqué bag from Columbian Exposition display, 1893 or earlier. *MNHS 521.E146.2; see also Figure 3.71*

12.11 *(below right)* Spot-stitch appliqué bag from Columbian Exposition display, 1893 or earlier. *MNHS 525.E150*

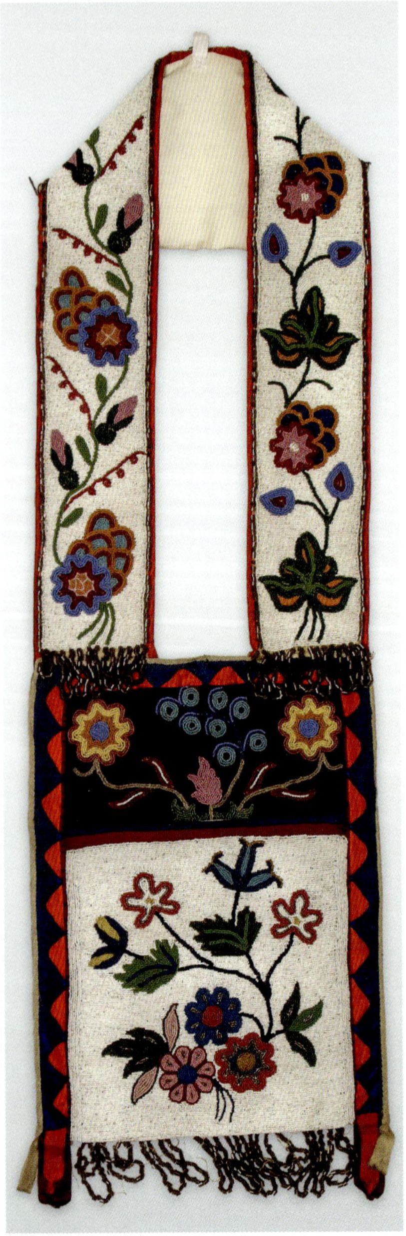

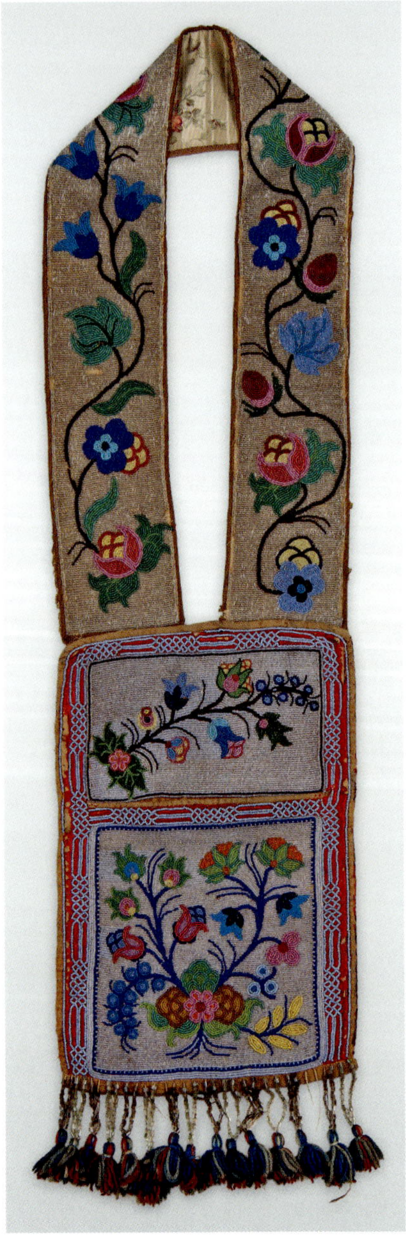

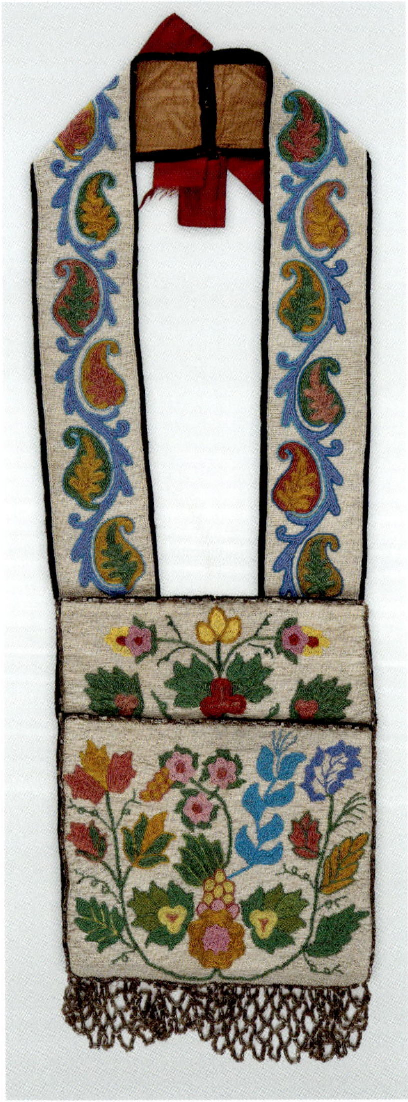

were fashionable accessories for European and American women from about the 1830s through the 1880s. By the 1870s and 1880s, everyday cotton-printed fabrics incorporated both the motif and a popular color palette of rusts, reds, oranges, browns, blacks, tans, beiges, and whites. This remarkable gashkibidaagan accurately captures the buta decorative motif, but its creator coordinates it effectively with the pocket below, using the color palette and placement preference of this specific bag form. While the netted bugle-bead fringe is not seen frequently, it is found on a few other bags in the Minnesota Historical Society's collection.

Why did this artist select paisleys to decorate her bag and to illustrate her skills? Did she create the bag for her own pleasure—to take a chance, show off her particular talents, make a statement? Did she have an apron or pieced quilt at home that incorporated paisley fabric? Did she copy the variations of this motif present in her everyday life, where artists often go for their inspiration? Did she intend to give or sell it to someone? We'll likely never know. But this bag will always be special and always arouse the curiosity and interest of those who are exposed to its charms and vibrancy.[14]

More than 120 years after the 1893 World's Columbian Exhibition, its Indian exhibit objects can still be found in the Minnesota Historical Society's collections and we continually learn from them. These five bags make up an amazing collection of documented material. The provenance it brings weaves together with the society's other documented collections to create an important resource for the study of beadwork and gashkibidaaganag in Minnesota.

Stafford King, politician

Stafford King (1893–1970) served as Minnesota state auditor from 1931 to 1969, prepared a map of Minnesota showing the state parks in 1930, and was inducted into the White Earth Band in the 1920s. During that ceremony, King received a gashkibidaagan, a magnificent beaded velvet smoking jacket, and smaller pieces of beadwork as well (Figures 12.12 and 12.13). The bead artists were not identified, but it is unlikely that King would have been given anything *not* made by members of the White Earth Band.[15]

King's bag is beaded in spot-stitch appliqué and incorporates several Minnesota Ojibwe motifs: folded leaf, oak leaf, large contrast-veined leaf, heart-shaped flower and flower petals, pointed-petal flower, pinecone, and love apple. The single panel pocket is transitional in form, with a narrow slit opening and a design treatment above the slit that mimics the separate cloth band formerly seen on the area above the pocket opening. The white beaded background is spot stitched in the typical horizontal rows. The fringe is composed of bugle beads threaded in single loops, each finished with a yarn tassel. I believe that the motif of the waterlily and lily pad with folded lanceolate leaf on the strap is a representation of the same image on the bandana cloth backing found on the Red Lake bag in chapter 3 (see Figures 3.82, 3.83, and 3.84).

12.12 Gashkibidaagan presented to Stafford King in the 1920s. *MNHS 1990.502.5; see also Figure 3.85*

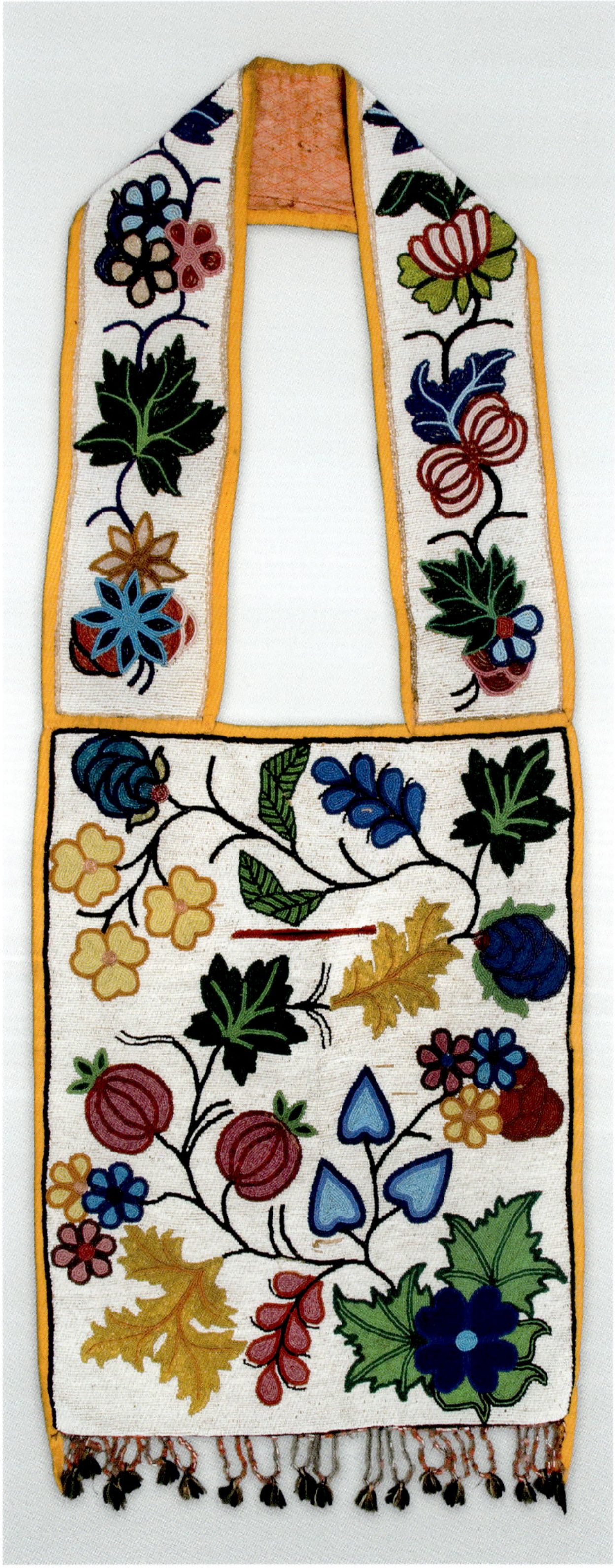

The collar of King's velvet smoking jacket (Figure 12.14) incorporates a flower or flower cluster motif superimposed on a leaf cluster background. Likewise, the pocket motif arrangement on King's bag begins with a similar, though less complex, cluster motif with a flower superimposed on leaves in the lower right corner. This motif arrangement is similar to others frequently found on gashkibidaaganag in White Earth images attributed to the last quarter of the nineteenth century and on twentieth-century bags.[16]

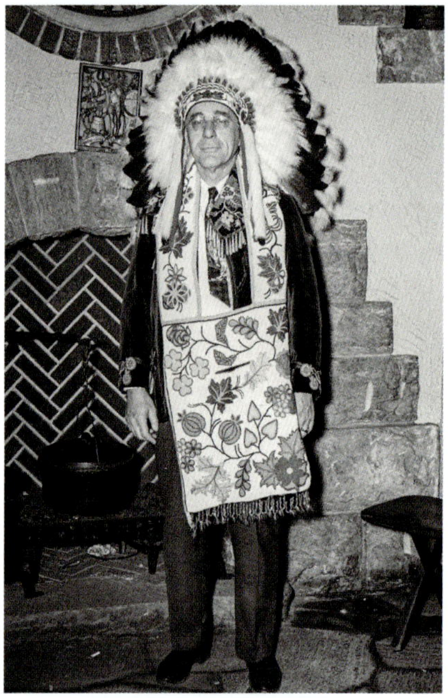

12.13 King wearing both the bag and the smoking jacket, 1949. *MNHS por 6151 p8*

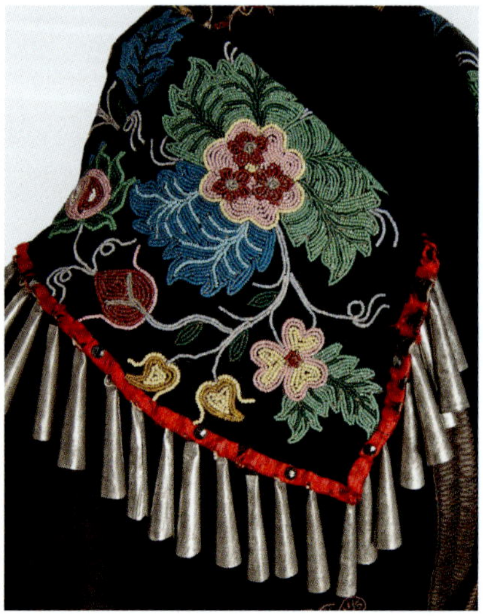

12.14 Collar detail on King's smoking jacket. *MNHS 1990.502.1*

Darwin Scott Hall, collector

The Honorable Darwin "Dar" Scott Hall (1844–1919) had a long and productive career of service to the state, to the federal government, and to the communities in which he lived: Birch Cooley, Hebron, Preston Lake, Benson, Minneapolis, and Olivia. In 1891 President William Henry Harrison appointed Hall to serve as the chairman of the US Chippewa Commission. His main duties in this difficult assignment were to convince Mille Lacs Band members to relocate and take allotments on the newly established White Earth Reservation. While his complete dates of service are unclear, he served as chairman of the commission in 1891 and in 1897. Hall built relationships with Ojibwe individuals, and several times over the course of his chairmanship he met with and traveled to White Earth with Mille Lacs members in an effort to convince them to make the move. In 1899 he accompanied representatives of White Earth, Red Lake, and Leech Lake to Washington, DC. Considering the diverse roles he held in his interactions with the Ojibwe of Minnesota, newspaper accounts during Hall's various campaigns for government positions and political office not surprisingly presented a mixed view of his personal qualities and experience.[17]

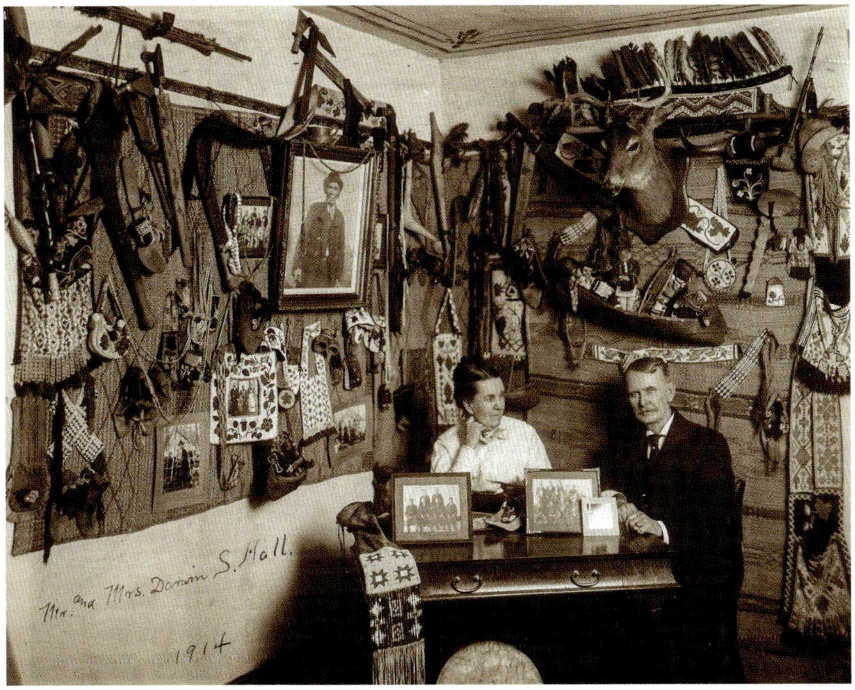

12.15 Darwin and Mary Hall in their "Indian Room," 1914. *MNHS Por 3172 p2*

In 1918 Hall donated about 130 items, including objects and photographs, to the Minnesota Historical Society. He identified the majority of his objects as being from White Earth, but some pieces likely were made by Mille Lacs Band members—both those who stayed at Mille Lacs and those who removed to White Earth. For instance, his collection included the photo, Figure 10.09, of Chief Wawweyaycumig, his wife, and other removals from Mille Lacs.

While some of the material culture objects that came to the Minnesota Historical Society from Hall's collections may have been given to him by White Earth Ojibwe visiting him in 1918 to 1919, his last years, a photograph taken in 1914 (Figure 12.15) suggests he had long before that acquired a large and diverse collection representing many aspects of Ojibwe life. Hall's donation included four bags, three of which are shown in Figure 12.15. He and his wife, Mary, are surrounded by American Indian material culture objects and photographs in what was typically called their "Indian

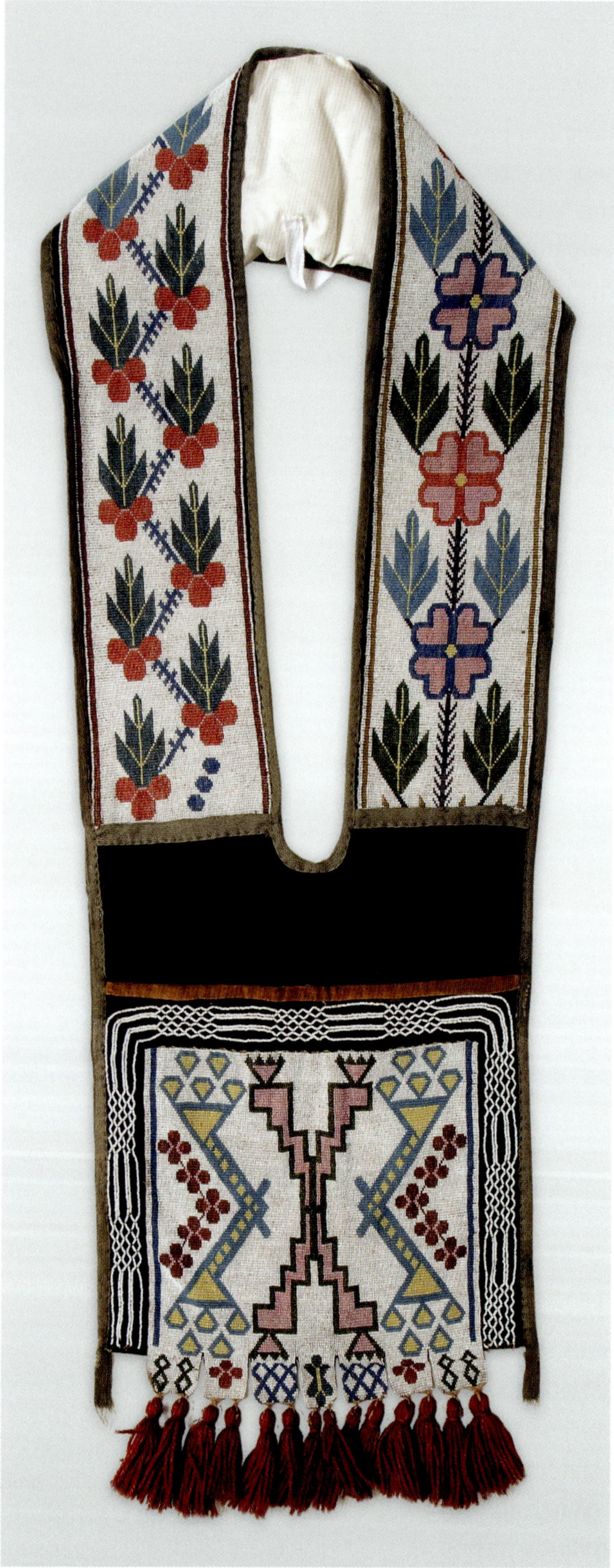

12.16 Loom-woven bag, exploding X motif, collected by Darwin Hall c. 1891–1914. *MNHS 285.E81; see also Figures 3.39 and 3.45*

Room." Hall noted at the time of his gift that the bags are from White Earth Reservation, which suggests that the objects date to the 1890s or earlier, because that was when Hall was actively engaged with the White Earth community.[18]

Fortunately, the four bags Hall gave the Minnesota Historical Society illustrate the evolving styles of Ojibwe gashkibidaaganag in Minnesota, as well as the varied nineteenth-century forms commonly seen in Minnesota Ojibwe loom-woven panel bags.

Two of the bags feature loom-woven panels whose bead artists were beginning to represent floral motifs rendered in a boxy appearance, due to the grid restrictions of the loom-weaving process. Many Ojibwe loom-woven bags featured a large centered X motif on the pocket, and the bag in Figure 12.16 illustrates the evolution of that common motif into what I refer to as the exploding X. This bag's maker left the area above the pocket opening undecorated, which was more common in the very earliest bandolier bags. The bag also features the curved cutout in the panel above the pocket, which is less common in Minnesota bags, found primarily in some Fond du Lac and Grand Portage bags. Later, in bags made toward the end of the nineteenth century, bead artists also began to spot stitch an asymmetrical floral motif in the area above the pocket opening, demonstrated in the Hall bag in Figure 12.17. This bag's acquisitions record listed a name, O-Meoh-Yah-Wub-e-tung, in parentheses, suggesting that the bag was owned by or otherwise connected to this person.

The bag in Figure 12.18 incorporates some of what are probably the earliest design motifs of the four bags. Vertical stripes of simple geometric motifs adorn the pocket, with the floral interpretation motifs beginning to emerge on the loomed strap panel; the motifs on the integrated loom-woven fringe tabs are repeated, rather than varied. The bag includes a balanced and near symmetrical spot-stitch appliqué design above the pocket opening, plus a floating spot-stitched strip attached to the top edge of the pocket panel. The latter is most often seen on early Ojibwe gashkibidaaganag (1850s to 1870s); in this case, the spot-stitched strip is beaded in a nontypical Ojibwe style that is seemingly more reminiscent of the Iowa, Mesqwaki, Menominee, or Ho-Chunk of the Great Lakes region.

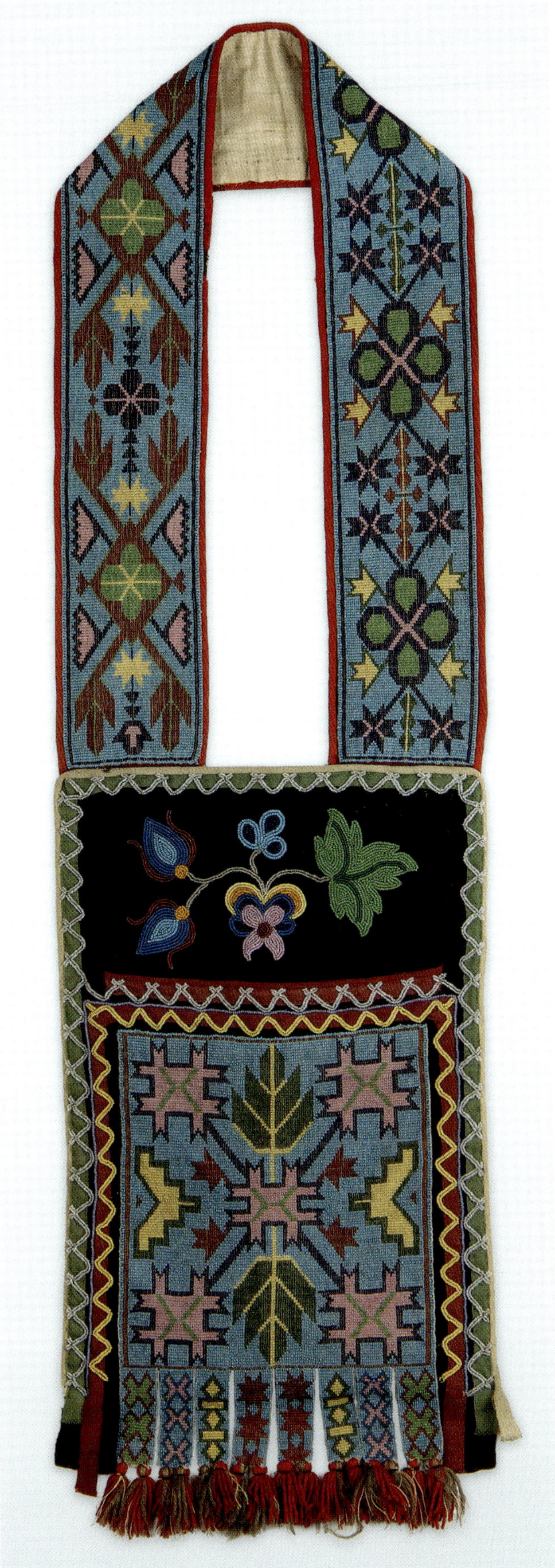

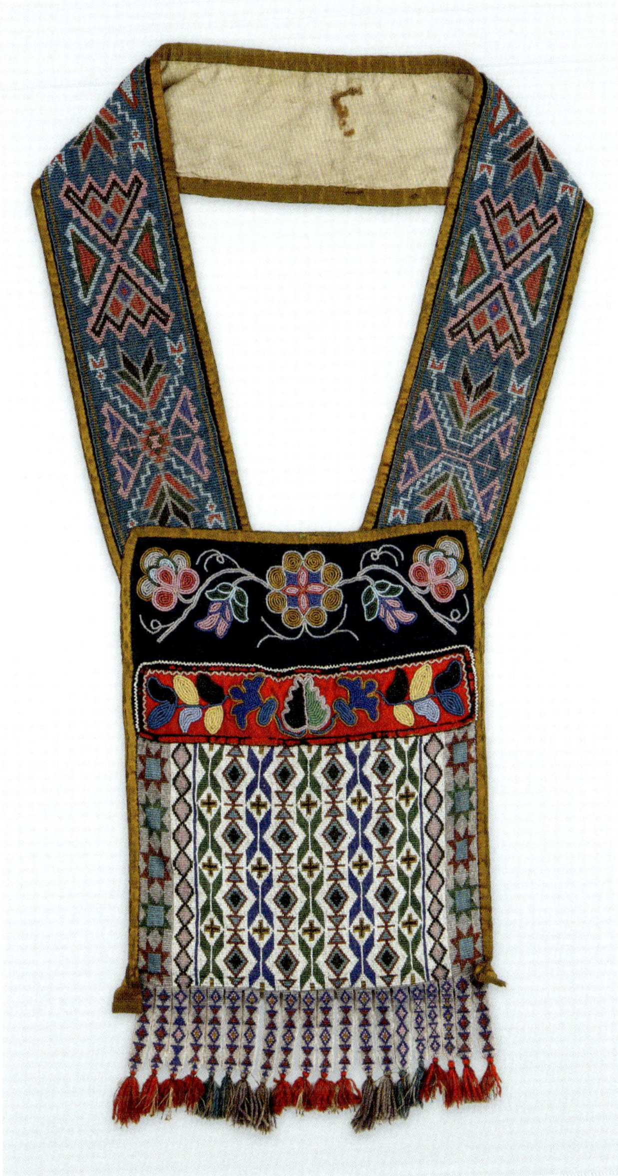

12.17 *(left)* Loom-woven bag with spot stitching above the pocket, collected by Darwin Hall c. 1891–1914. *MNHS 272.E68; see also Figure 2.10*

12.18 *(above)* Loom-woven bag with floating spot-stitched strip, collected by Darwin Hall c. 1891–1914. *MNHS 268.E64; see also Figure 2.07*

12.19 Loom-woven bag with X and floral motifs, collected by Darwin Hall c. 1891–1914. *MNHS 262.E58.2*

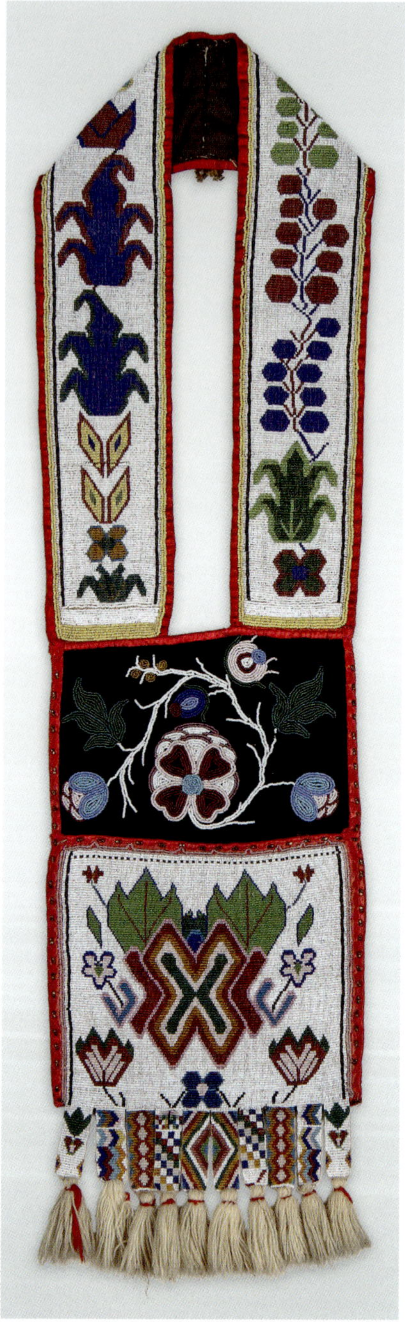

The fourth bag (Figure 12.19) is not visible in the 1914 photo. With the exception of its integrated woven tab fringe, the bag's parts are almost entirely filled with floral motifs. The artist's last paean to earlier loom-woven bags is her central X, a shrunken and manipulated version that perhaps represents a flower surrounded by leaves and other blossoms. The panel above the pocket features a larger central motif surrounded by an encircling vine carrying other floral motifs. Because this circular arrangement of motifs requires so much space to render, it is most frequently seen on the square panels made for dance aprons.

Henry Benjamin Whipple, Episcopal bishop and collector

Bishop Henry Benjamin Whipple (1822–1901) arrived in Minnesota in 1859, a year after it became a state and at a time when many European settlers were moving to the area. This influx of immigrants represented a true disaster for the region's indigenous people, who were forced to give up their homelands through treaties and who endured unrelenting attempts to extinguish their cultural and religious practices. Whipple dedicated his life to defending Indians in Minnesota, within the church, and on the national stage. But like most reformers of his time, he believed—mistakenly—that Indians had to abandon their traditional ways and adopt European customs in order to survive. Although he had genuine respect for Indians and their culture, he was nonetheless committed to converting them to his own Christian faith.

Whipple accumulated photographs and the material culture of the North American indigenous people that he met on his many travels and during his missionary work in Minnesota. Those travels included regular visits to the Episcopal mission to the Ojibwe, based on the White Earth Reservation and staffed by Joseph A. Gilfillan and Enmegahbowh. Unfortunately for us, Whipple did not leave systematic documentation of his collection. The great variety in his collection is probably evidence of many factors, including his diverse interests; his interactions with both Ojibwe and Dakota people in Minnesota and with other indigenous nations farther afield; as well as the numbers, variety, and quality of gifts given to a widely traveled man of his status. In his memoir, *Lights and Shadows of a Long Episcopate*, Whipple gives an account of the Episcopal lacemaking project (see page 75) and describes the gift of a beaded stole from Ne-gon-e-bin-ais (Flatmouth the Younger), but beyond this he did not record elements of his collection.[19]

Such exclusions suggest Whipple did not view himself as a collector, but rather considered the objects as gifts, much like a key to the city or a bouquet of flowers given a visiting dignitary. Other objects, like the lace samples in the Whipple collection, may have been retained as a document of special Episcopal mission projects. Usually, such items are saved but rarely recorded or managed as a collection. Also, many of the attributed Whipple pieces were gifts to his wives, presented to or made for them. Other examples in the collection still retain their original price tag, which suggests they were purchased.

Fortunately, Whipple had enough regard for his collection to keep it together and often displayed it in the private office at his residence, later transferring much of it to St. Mary's Hall (now Shattuck–St. Mary's School) for the education of girls. While his collection documents indigenous cultures from the far corners of North America, the majority of the objects are from Minnesota and the Great Lakes area, with specific emphasis on the Dakota and Ojibwe of the region.

After the death of Whipple's second wife, Evangeline, in 1930, the American Indian collection was broken up. The Sibley House Association of the Minnesota Society of the Daughters of the American Revolution purchased 309 Whipple objects through an antiques dealer, and these were eventually transferred to the Minnesota Historical Society. The other 191 Whipple objects were held in the historical collections at the Shattuck–St. Mary's School in Faribault, Minnesota, before being acquired by the Science Museum of Minnesota. Together, the two museums hold twenty-one gashkibidaaganag: the Minnesota Historical Society holds one primarily loom-woven and eleven spot-stitched bags; the Science Museum of Minnesota holds one spot-stitched and eight primarily loom-woven bags. A smaller collection of Whipple objects is also held at the Rice County Historical Society in Faribault.[20]

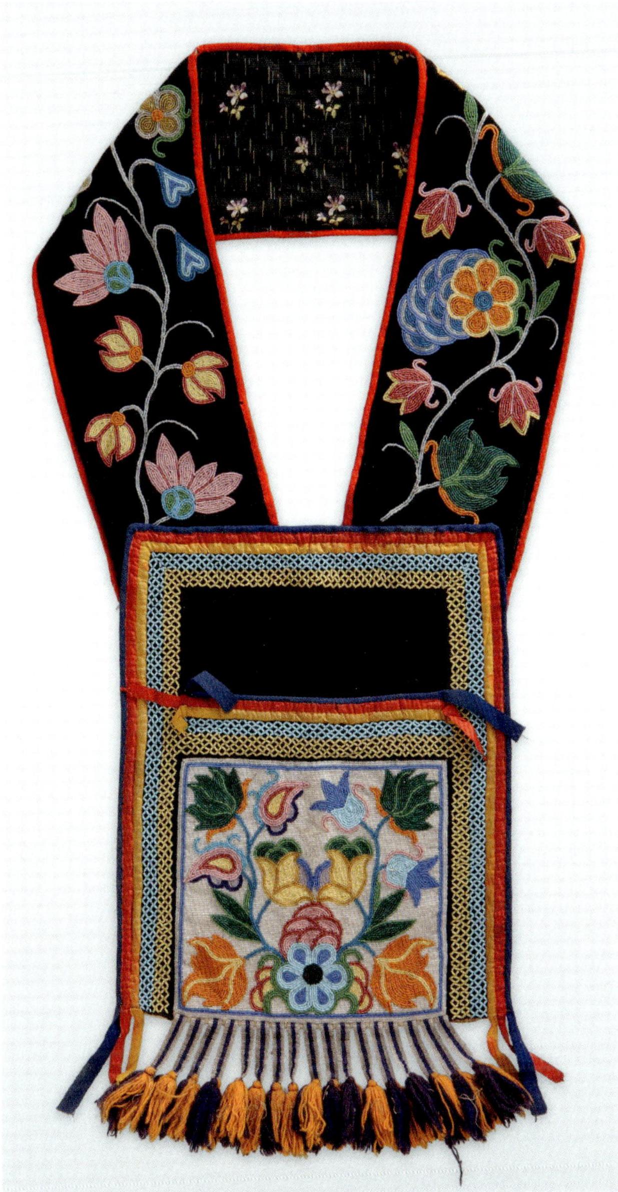

12.20 Spot-stitch appliqué bag, Bishop Whipple Collection, c. 1860–1901. *MNHS 1825*

The Whipple collection of gashkibidaaganag represents a wide range in both era and form. Two of his gashkibidaaganag are among the finest bag examples in the Minnesota Historical Society's holdings (Figures 12.20 and 11.01), representing the best of Ojibwe spot-stitch appliqué bead art. Dating to the last quarter of the nineteenth century, both bags are in remarkable condition and both excel in successful spatial use while integrating a multitude of elegantly rendered motifs of different sizes.

Two loom-woven bags from the Science Museum of Minnesota's holdings (Figures 12.21 and 12.22) feature variations on the exploding X motif, integrated woven tabs, and the smaller overall dimensions of earlier gashkibidaaganag. Outline-filled spot-stitch appliqué decorates the area above the pocket in Figure 12.21; the cross motif is incorporated in the area both above and below the pocket opening. The cross motif appears infrequently

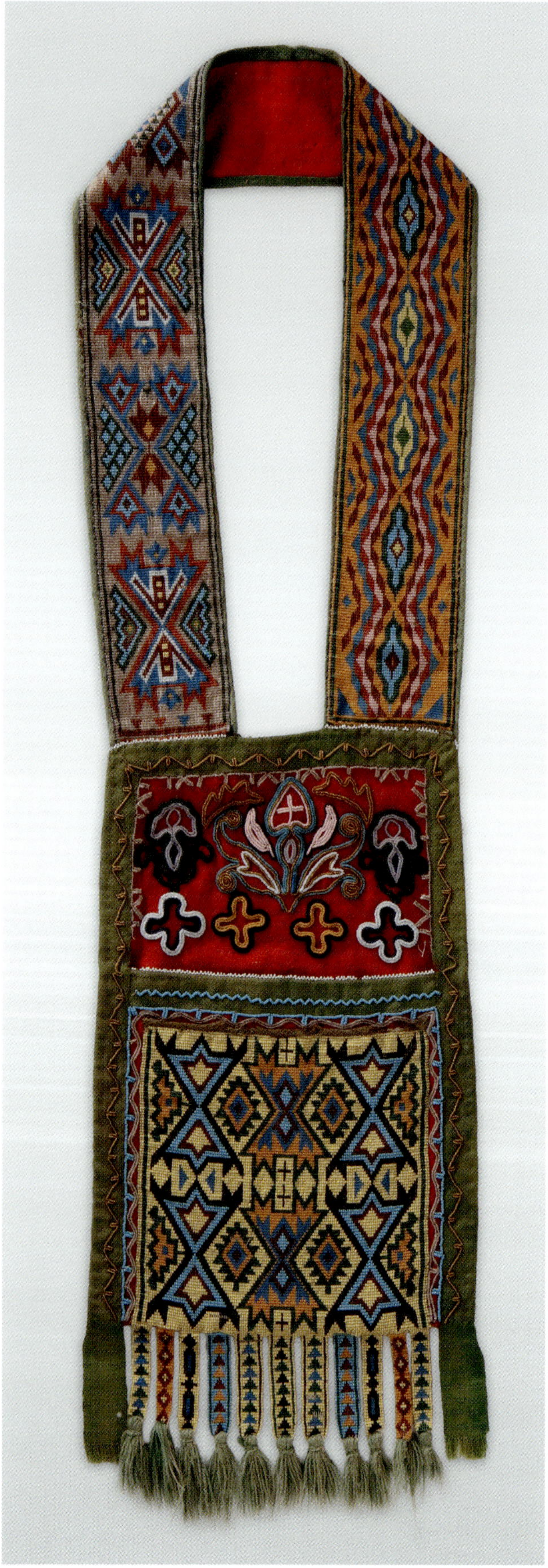

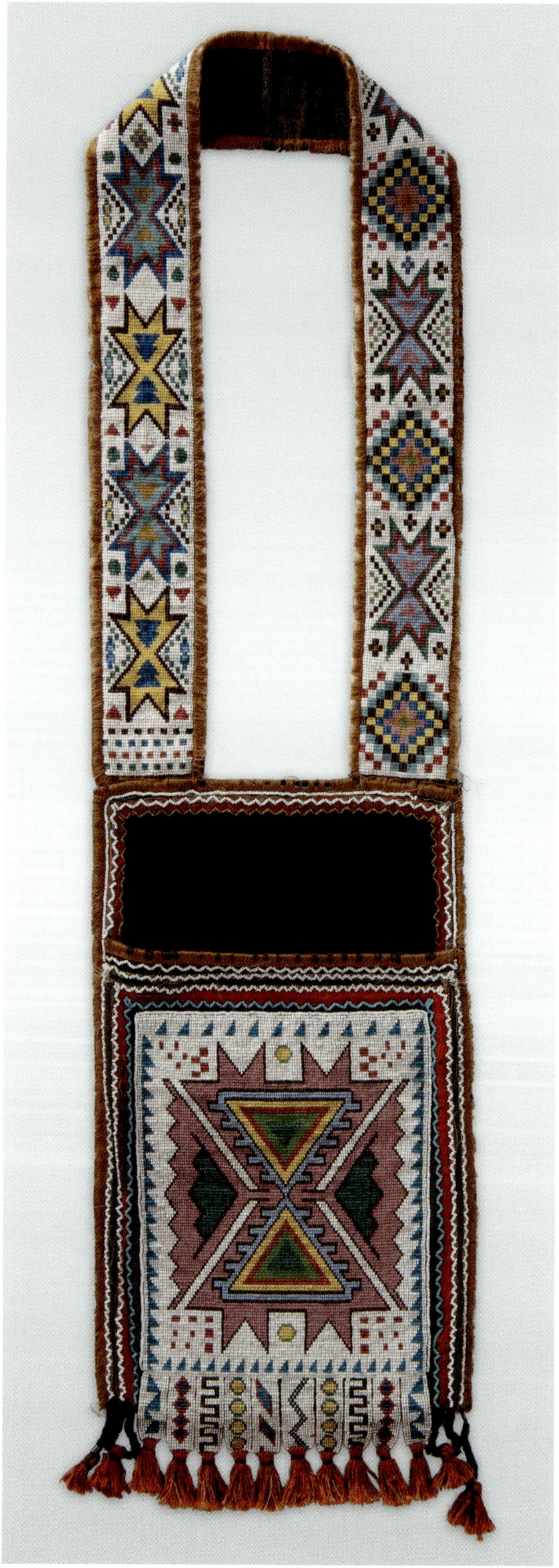

in Ojibwe gashkibidaaganag, and its presence on this bag may indicate that it was made specifically for a Christian, perhaps for Whipple.

Whipple's collection also includes the exquisite work of bead artist Sophia Smith (see below).

The diversity of Whipple's collection helps document the vast changes experienced by American Indians in Minnesota in the nineteenth century as they lost their land, were removed to reservations, and then were missionized, robbed of their culture in government schools, and alienated from their friends and families. As all this was taking place, Indian people continued to derive inspiration from their environment, learn from their elders, and adopt selected aspects of white culture—along with the beads, sequins, yarn, ribbons, thread, and other supplies that changed how they embellished everything from moccasins to dance aprons to gashkibidaaganag.

12.21 *(facing page left)* Loom-woven bag from Whipple's collection, c. 1860–1901. *SMM A79:4:65*

12.22 *(facing page right)* Loom-woven bag from Whipple's collection, c. 1860–1901. *SMM A79:4:67*

Sophia Smith, bead artist

Born sometime in the mid-nineteenth century, Sophia Smith was described as the finest mat and beadworker at White Earth. In a large oval card print (Figure 12.23), she holds a gashkibidaagan she made; this is one of only a handful of images documenting a specific bag and its identified maker. Information on the reverse side of the print records that the bag she holds was the last "fire bag" (one of many names for a bandolier bag) made for Bishop Whipple, who died in 1901. Sophia wears fashionable clothing from about 1902 to 1904, which suggests that the bag was completed after Whipple's death.[21]

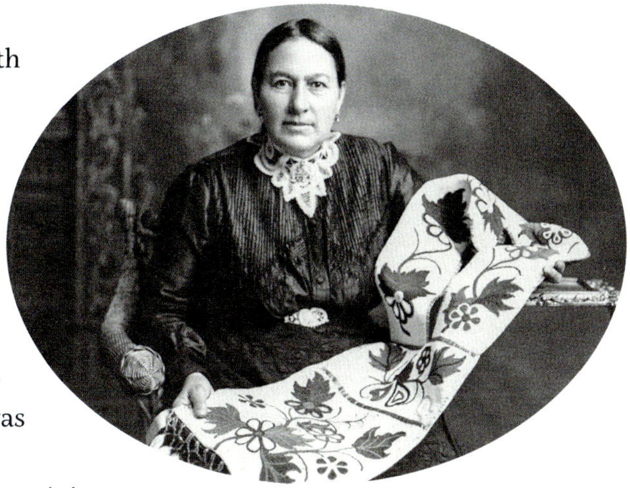

12.23 Sophia Smith, perhaps 1902–04. *MNHS Collection III.40.74*

Bead artist Sophia Smith and her husband, Episcopal lay minister Frederick "Fred" W. Smith, spent most of their married years on the White Earth and Red Lake Reservations. Fred studied for the Episcopal ministry for three years at White Earth and was ordained by Bishop Whipple in July 1876. On January 1, 1877, Reverend Joseph A. Gilfillan led the families of Reverend Samuel Madison and the Smiths to Red Lake to establish an Episcopal mission. Gilfillan usually sought out married men with two or three children for his lay ministers, no doubt counting on their wives' supporting roles in their husband's missionary work. Fred and Sophia initially lived and served their converts in a log cabin; they continued their service in the Red Lake communities until 1888, when Fred's illness compelled them to end his work there. Both of Fred's brothers were also serving as ministers in parts of the Red Lake Reservation, and Sophia and her sisters-in-law likely formed a strong bond. In spite of Fred and Sophia's obligations at White Earth, life at Red Lake must have been dear to them, because they were still there in 1910.[22]

12.24 *(below)* Spot-stitch appliqué bag made by Sophia Smith, Bishop Whipple Collection, c. 1901. *MNHS 1520*

12.25 *(below right)* Spot-stitch appliqué bag associated with Sophia Smith, Bishop Whipple Collection. *MNHS 1498*

Sophia's work is included in the Bishop Whipple Collection at the Minnesota Historical Society. The gashkibidaagan she holds in her portrait is shown in Figure 12.24. Two other bags in the collection, shown in Figure 12.25 and Figure 1.02, also exhibit characteristics of her work, or perhaps of a family or community of beadworkers she may have participated in. Commonalities among these three bags include the half-flower motif, large leaf motifs, heart motifs, and pinecone or cloud motifs. Other beaded

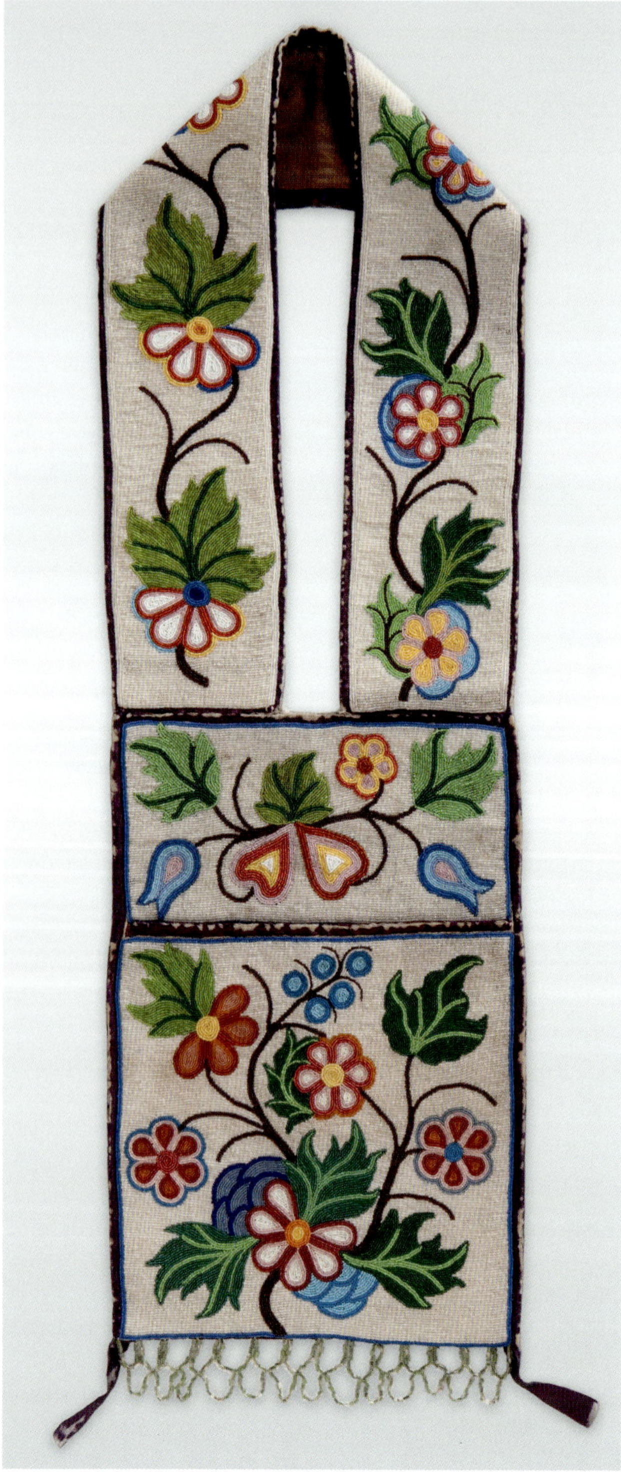

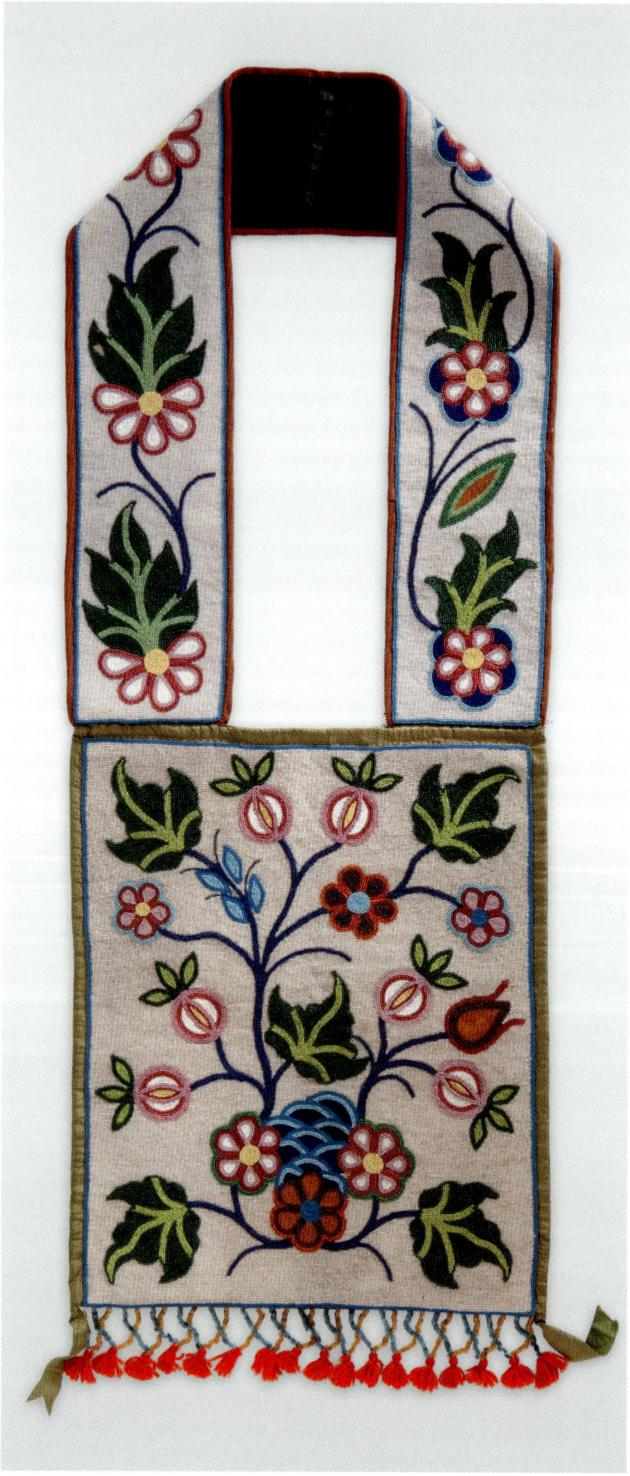

items in the Whipple collection also suggest Sophia may have been either the bead artist or involved in some aspects of their production. Through her missionary work with Fred, Sophia probably interacted with women at the Ojibwe communities on the White Earth Reservation and at Red Lake, Redby, and Ponemah on the Red Lake Reservation, and she may have done beadwork with them as a traditional social activity.

But most likely, the commonalities among the three bags suggest one maker. The half-flower motif on all three bag straps is unique among Minnesota Ojibwe beadwork pieces. Other shared motifs on the three bags include a nearly identical large leaf, heart forms, the pinecone, and vine and tendril combinations—all commonly seen on other bags of the northwestern region of Minnesota. Other similarities include netlike fringe made with bugle beads, bag component dimensions, and bead color palettes. The beadwork on each of the three bags clearly represents the work of a highly skilled maker with technical and artistic maturity.[23]

Joseph Charette, White Earth leader

Joseph Charette, or Critt (Iahbaykewenzie Wenjemahdub, or Where He Moves from Sitting), was born in 1836 at Whitefish Lake, Minnesota, and died in 1921 at Pine Point in Becker County, Minnesota. During the Civil War he served in the Ninth Minnesota Infantry, Company G, from August 1862 to August 1865. Charette was a White Earth leader well known by missionary Joseph Gilfillan and US Chippewa commissioner Darwin Hall. Recognized and respected by Ojibwe and non-Indians alike, he regularly interacted with members of his community as well as whites who represented state offices and federal agencies. Gilfillan celebrated his oratory skills:

> While many are admirable speakers, there is only one who is a genius, a truly remarkably eloquent man. He is the Chief Wendji-madub (Where he moves from sitting), or, as his French name is, Joseph Charette. . . . I consider him perhaps the best speaker, the greatest orator, I have ever met. Although without education—he does not know a letter—his powers are remarkable. He has all the vehemence, the fire, the energy, command of language, range of thought, of the true orator. As another said, "Every word comes like an electric spark from his heart." I think he would be considered a wonderful speaker in any nation.[24]

Musicologist Stella Stocker met with Charette at Fond du Lac in 1916 and recorded in her notes that his father was French. No doubt her meeting with him, as with other Ojibwe elder informants, influenced the song lyrics she developed for her musical pageant entitled *Sieur du Lhut*.[25]

Charette's frequent interaction with individuals from all walks of life suggested his role as a spokesman and identified him as a likely wearer of gashkibidaaganag. As a result of his many contacts across cultures, historical images of him survive in several public repositories. Fourteen images of Charette taken between 1896 and 1916 are found in the collections of the Smithsonian Institution and the Minnesota Historical Society, and in six of them he is shown wearing a variety of gashkibidaaganag over his frequent "uniform" of dark shirt, suit coat, and pants.[26]

In Figure 12.26, Charette wears either a gashkibidaagan with a loom-woven strap or a single loom-woven sash. Like the strap on a bag collected by Darwin Hall (see Figure 12.18), Charette's strap features a vivid interpretation of the X motif, with partial star points (or claws) at the end of zigzag arms, a theme often seen in Minnesota Ojibwe loom-woven bags.

In February 1899 De Lancy Gill recorded Charette's participation as a member of the White Earth delegation to Washington, DC (Figure 12.27). Charette wore a spot-stitch appliqué bag with four folded leaf motifs visible on the strap.[27]

12.26 *(below)* Joseph Charette, 1896, at the Bureau of American Anthropology. *Photo by William Dinwiddie, NAA-SI BAE GN 00438A 06132100*

12.27 *(below right)* Joseph Charette, 1899. *Photo by De Lancy Gill, NAA-SI BAE GN 00586 06153000*

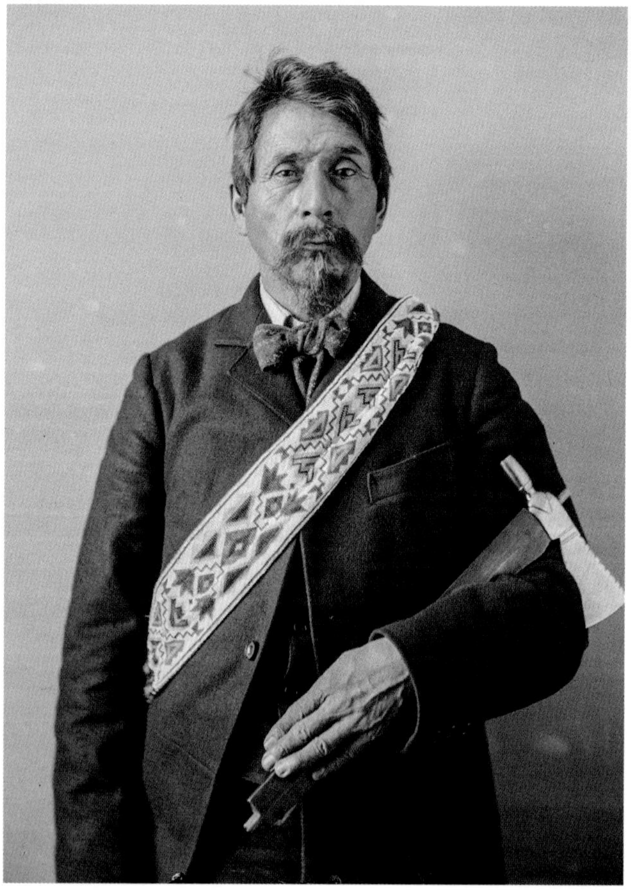

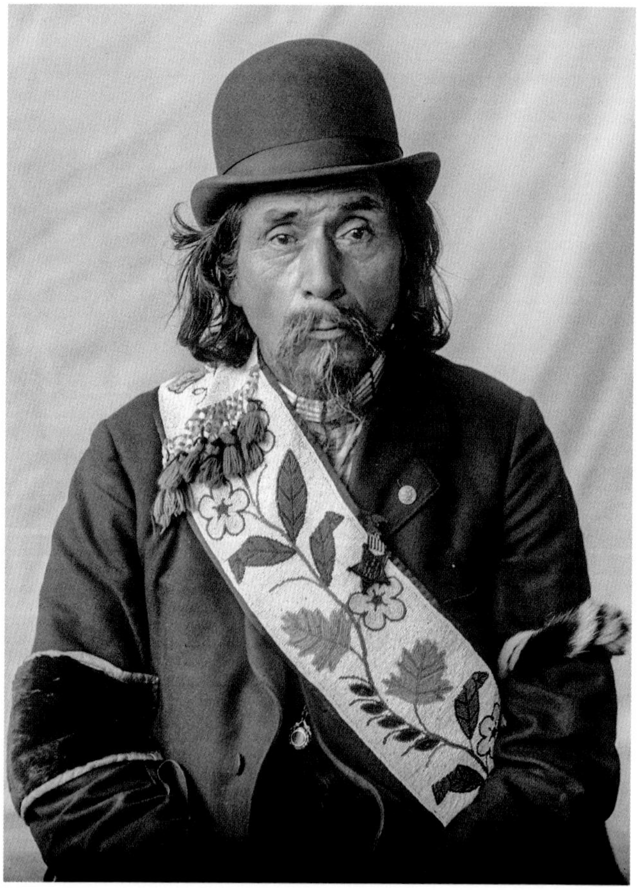

Joseph A. Gilfillan, missionary

Reverend Joseph Alexander Gilfillan (1838–1913) served as an Episcopal missionary to the Ojibwe of northern Minnesota for twenty-five years assigned to St. Columba Episcopal Church at White Earth. His papers are filled with colorful accounts of life among the Ojibwe, travels between missions, the successes and failures of missionary work, and newspaper and Episcopal newsletter clippings on many topics. He learned Ojibwemowin, and he made a special study of Ojibwe place names.[28]

A lengthy article titled "Agricultural Fair at White Earth," probably written by Gilfillan, includes perhaps the earliest references to the economic role of the gashkibidaagan. Published in 1879 in the *Minnesota Missionary,* the article notes, "Their ponies they got last summer, or the summer before, from the Sioux, who seem to have an inexhaustible supply of them. One otter skin and one beaded tobacco-pouch, made by a Chippewa woman, is the price they paid for each pony on the Missouri River or at Devil's Lake."[29]

In "The Ojibways in Minnesota," a paper Gilfillan published in 1901, he again addressed the value of the gashkibidaagan: "One of the bead-work pouches is the great ornament of an Ojibway, and any person wearing it is considered to be in full dress; it is worth a pony among the Sioux. Thus the stock of horses is every summer replenished."[30]

In 1893 Gilfillan donated a pair of dolls to the Minnesota Historical Society (Figures 12.28 and 12.29). They were made for him, at his direction, to replicate "traditional Ojibwe apparel" as accurately as possible. The male doll is shown wearing two gashkibidaaganag in the transitional style of the late nineteenth century. The beadwork on these diminutive bags is loom woven, but the pocket panel motifs reflect the transition away from earlier geometric motifs as beadworkers attempted to render more naturalistic flora (such as the leaf or tree motif on the bag on the right) but were still challenged in their efforts by the boxy quality resulting from the use of the loom-woven technique. The bag on the left is a good representation of the patchwork-quilt "flower basket" pattern.

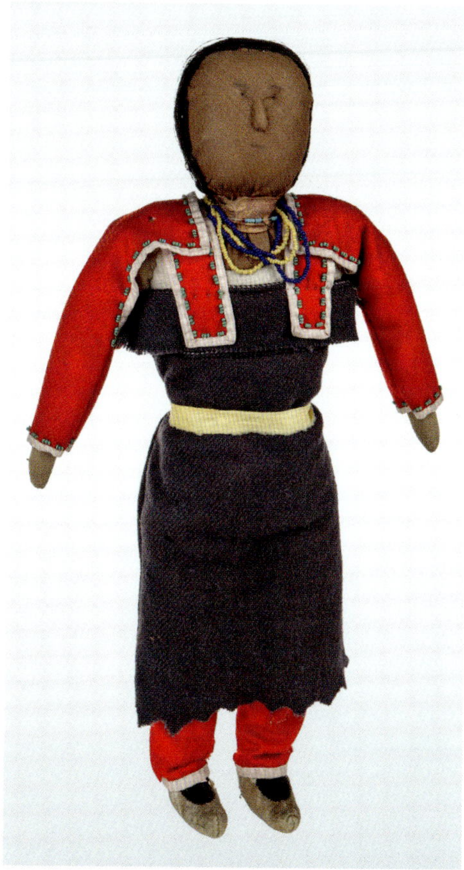

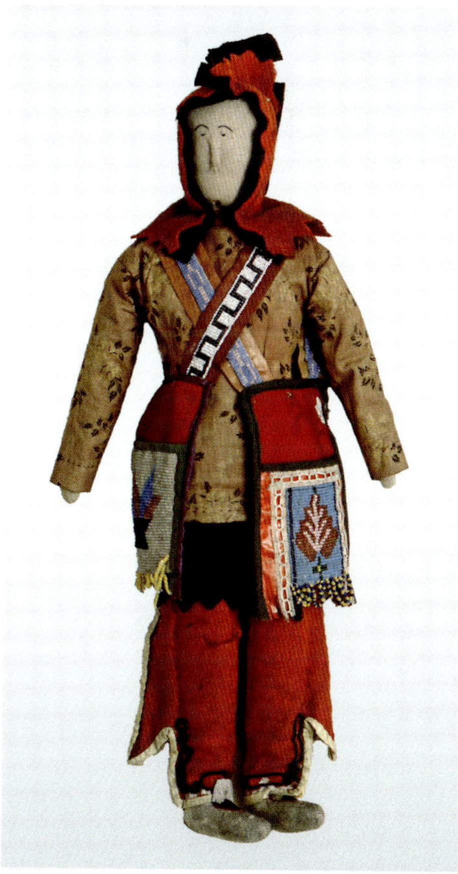

12.28 *(above right)* Female Ojibwe doll donated by Joseph Gilfillan, 1893. *MNHS 163.E32.A*

12.29 *(right)* Male Ojibwe doll donated by Joseph Gilfillan, 1893. *MNHS 163.E32.B*

Ivy Ailport, bead artist

Ivy Jean Norcross Ailport (Figure 12.30) was born at White Earth, Minnesota, in 1938 and raised at Ponsford and Pine Point, where she attended school. She grew up with eight siblings and several foster siblings in a log house with her parents, Josephine and George Norcross. Her grandparents George and Katherine Lightning lived nearby, and the two families shared many things, including a love of gardening and bead artistry. Ivy died at Ogema, Minnesota, on July 9, 2012.

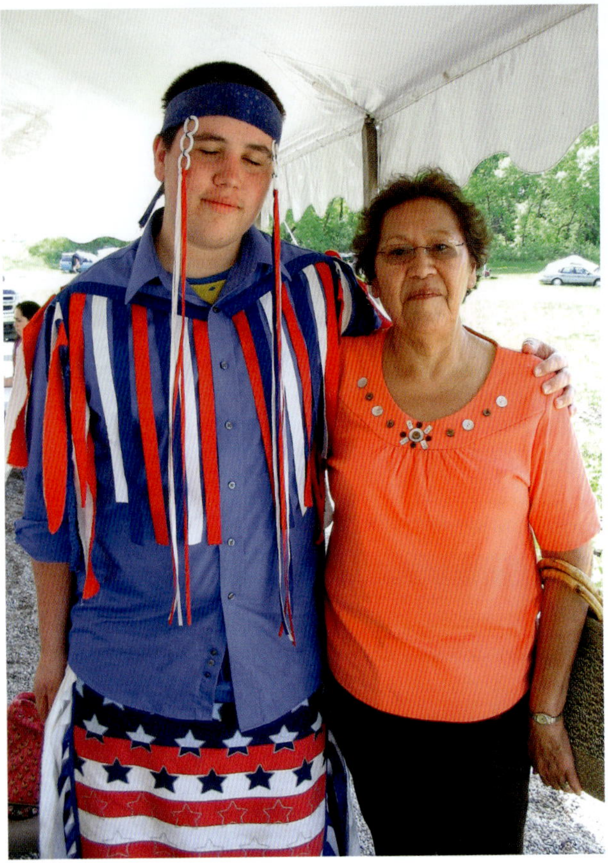

12.30 Ivy Ailport and her grandson, 2009. *Author photo*

The Depression era had little perceived impact on Ivy's family. They were already poor but never went hungry and rarely got sick. The children were raised on the foods of seasonal Ojibwe life in Minnesota: fish, deer meat, maple sugar, wild berries, and wild rice. Her mother baked bread daily, canned food year round, and also raised flowers in her garden, sharing them with the community at wakes and on other occasions.

Ivy was raised as a Catholic, but her grandmother Katherine was a respected member of the Midewiwin, a traditional healer, and a midwife. Ivy was fascinated with the padlocked log outbuilding where Katherine kept her medicines—herbs and plants in trunks, hanging on the walls, or stored in jars.

Ivy had early and typical exposure to Ojibwe beadwork. She remembered her grandmother Katherine was always sitting and beading moccasins. She often saw her mother Josephine beading as well. As is often the case for adults, Ivy regretted she did not spend more time learning from her mother and grandmother, but she was busy with her own small children and couldn't find the time to ask them about beading. Still, both women educated and inspired Ivy in her pursuit of bead artistry.

Josephine did both loom and spot-stitch appliqué beadwork and made belts and headbands for Ivy's children for powwow dancing. Ivy recalls that her mother kept her patterns "in a big old can." At one point, Josephine decided she wanted to make a black beaded vest for Ivy. She showed Ivy the patterns in the can, traced copies for Ivy, and told her they were original Ojibwe flower and leaf designs. One is the typical five-petaled flower with rounded petal edges; this is what Ivy used on her bag many years later. Josephine said she wanted Ivy to use them in her beadwork.

At some point, many years ago, Ivy and her husband, Harry, wanted some beaded clothing for powwows. They couldn't find anyone to do beadwork for hire, so they taught themselves. They began with belts and made some moccasins. Like her mother, Ivy made beadwork for her grandkids, and she held onto the beadwork she made for them when they outgrew it, taking care of it until they were old enough to value and assume responsibility for it. The only piece of her mother's work that Ivy still had in her possession was a long, beaded pipe bag.

Harry wanted a special piece for himself, a bandolier bag. Ivy had no memory of seeing these bags when she was younger, but she had seen many in photographs. She believed they must have been tied to rank or prestige, and she noted that many men wore two. Ivy said during her lifetime there really wasn't much in the way of powwows until the 1970s, when dancing became more popular again and there were more occasions to dance. Many people who did dance at White Earth in the 1970s had only minimal dance regalia or beadwork.

Ivy talked with her mother about how to make a gashkibidaagan and was told that a traditional pocket panel should always have four leaves on it. According to Josephine: "In Ojibwa beadwork, motifs either need to touch each other or be joined by lifelines [the traditional vine element]. The four leaves on the pocket panel point in the four directions. In the past, bags could also be made for Midewiwin, and they were required to have four leaves [or four motifs] in the design."

Ivy's typical process began with a week of planning the bag and each of the bag's designs and components. She had to think about it and visualize it first, often using big sheets of white paper to sketch her ideas. Then she cut out the patterns. Ivy also did much of the beadwork and assembled the finished bag. While she sometimes allowed Harry to help with the actual beading, she made a point of telling me that she selected the motifs and did all the design work. They both had insomnia and would occasionally get up in the night and sit and bead. All her bags were made using the spot-stitch appliqué process, with some loom work employed for the tab fringe. Ivy was very proud of her gashkibidaaganag. She admitted that when she started out she didn't think she would actually be able to make one.

In Figure 12.31, taken early in 2002, Harry wore Ivy's first bag along with the other pieces of his dance regalia that she had made. Harry pointed out that if not enough space was left between the strap ends when they were attached to the pocket section, the bag would buckle when worn. Ivy used her mother Josephine's pointed-petal flower and oak leaf designs on this bag, but added some new motifs of her own. It took at least three months to make, even with Harry's help beading late at night. In 2002 Ivy worked on her second bag (Figure 12.32), designed to memorialize the lives lost in the attacks of September 11, 2001. Harry wore the finished bag to powwows and to a special veterans' event in Detroit Lakes, Minnesota.

Ivy made her third bag (Figure 12.33) between September 2002 and July 2003. Wanting to do something different for this bag, she gathered fall leaves from a maple tree in her yard and carefully pressed them in a book for later inspiration. She found bead colors to interpret the broad range of hues in the turning leaves. Ojibwe bead artists nearly always mixed leaves, flowers, berries, and scale of the motifs on their bags, and, in that spirit, Ivy incorporated acorns with the maple leaves. The white beaded border pattern of diamonds was intended to function like a picture frame. The bag was constructed using size 11 glass seed beads from Czechoslovakia, purchased from Elliott Green, New York. Ivy's materials included black cotton velvet, cotton cloth binding, cotton print lining, and polyester tassels. According to her, in the old days, the pocket opening on the gashkibidaaganag would sag, so Ivy liked to bead a faux opening on the front and add a zippered opening on the back side. The loomed fringe tabs incorporate a bear paw motif in honor of Ivy's membership in the bear clan.[31]

Harry died in 2008. It was hard for Ivy to tackle any large bead projects after Harry's death. But she continued doing quillwork and other projects and described herself as always busy, always thinking of something to do and make. Ivy was a gracious woman who loved life and her family. Her death in 2012 was a great loss.

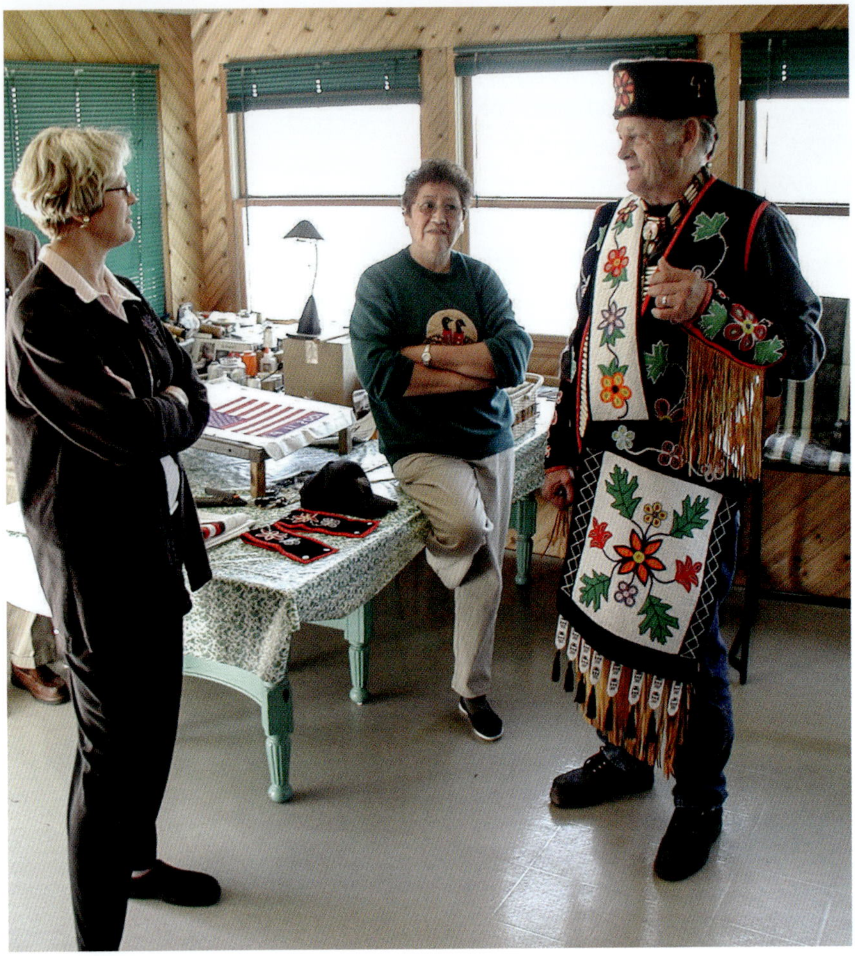

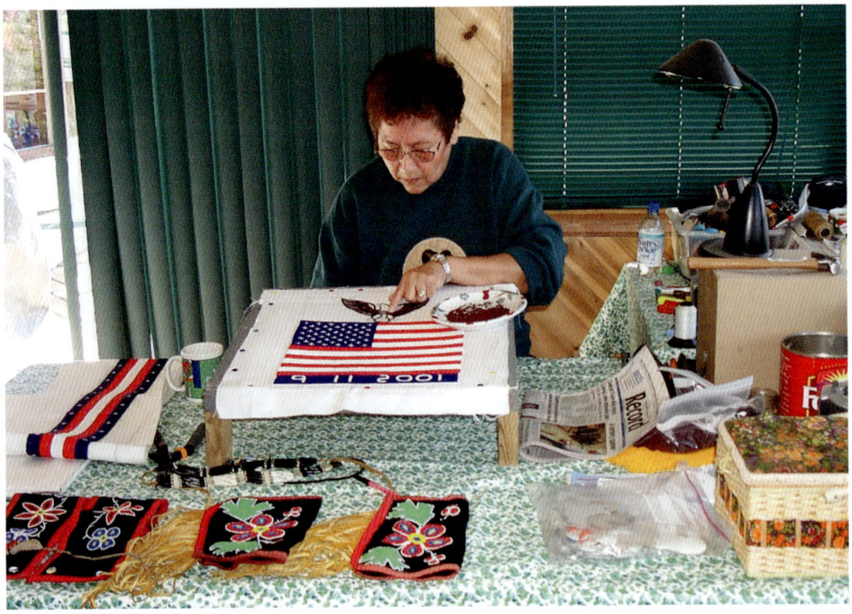

12.31 *(above left)* Marcia Anderson, Ivy Ailport, and Harry Ailport in Ivy's studio, 2002. Harry is wearing Ivy's first bag. *Author photo*

12.32 *(left)* Ivy beading on her second bag, which memorializes the victims of September 11, 2001. *Author photo*

12.33 *(facing page)* Ivy Ailport's third gashkibidaagan, "Fall Leaves." The pocket panel flower with the pointed petals is one of Ivy's mother's original beadwork motifs. *MNHS 2003.159.1*

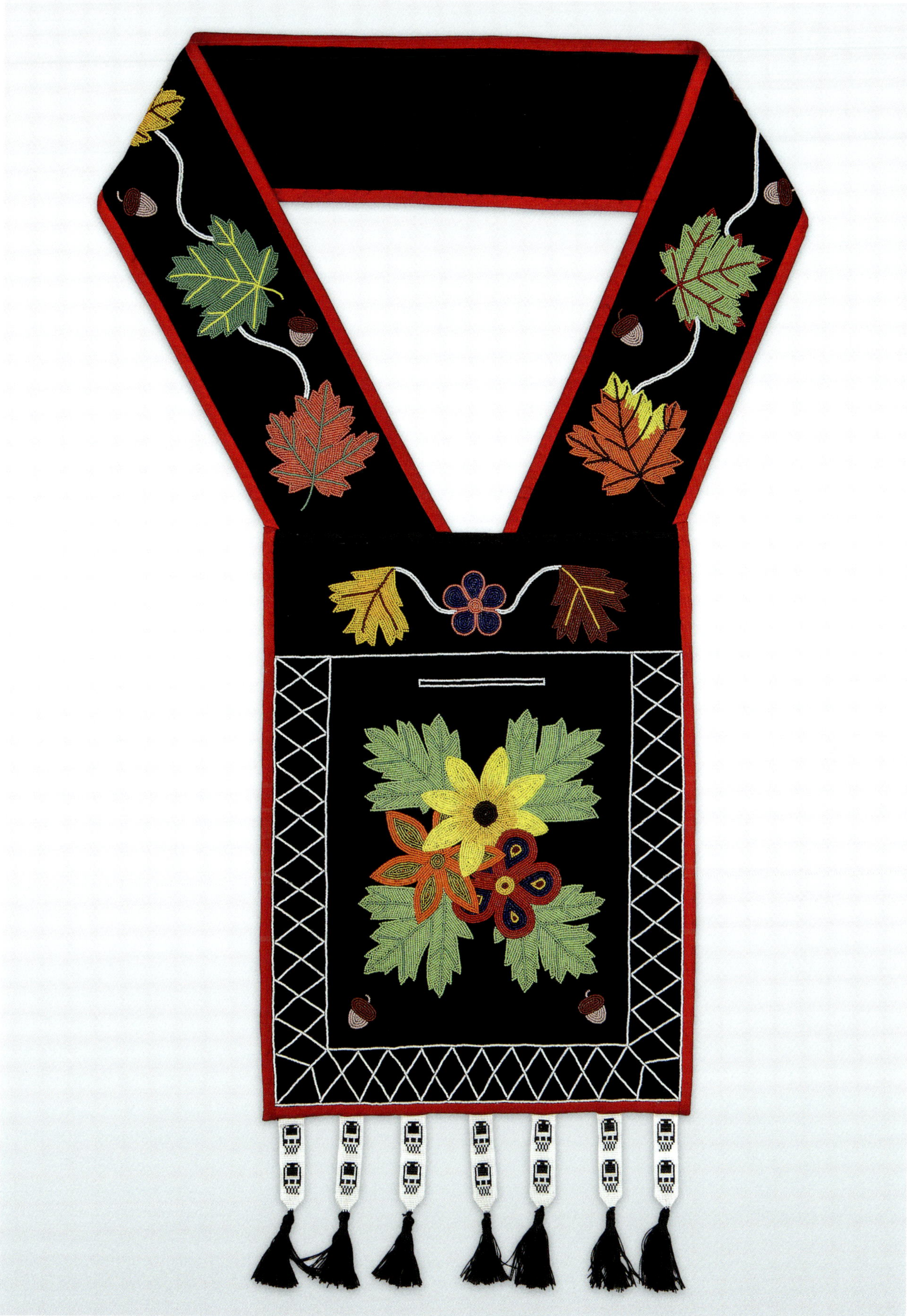

Conclusion

When I picked up that first gashkibidaagan in 1981, I knew almost nothing about it. I see that bag very differently now. I can speculate about when and where it was made, how the bead artist used the forms and structures that were common at that time, and what is perhaps out of the ordinary about the bag.

In this book, I have offered a bit of the history and cultural significance of the bags; a rough chronology of their forms; a glimpse into the bead artists' creativity (especially in making such remarkable objects from not much); an overview of motifs and designs; and stories about a few specific bags and bead artists on Minnesota's reservations. I've included, too, photographs that show the dignity and pride of gashkibidaaganag wearers in the past and more recent wearers carrying on a living tradition.

I hope you consider this book as a welcome into the larger story of Ojibwe gashkibidaaganag and into the even larger story of North American bandolier bags. Now that you have read this book, I encourage you to page back through it, or to look at gashkibidaaganag images online, and to see what you can guess about a bag's structure, age, and likely cultural affiliation—and then, of course, to check your work.

Even after thirty years of studying these bags, I remain fascinated by the stories they tell, and I know that there are other stories out there yet to be told. I hope that other researchers will document more bead artists and will further explore connections and influences, as well as the meanings of these amazing pieces of art and culture.

I especially look forward to the work of others who explore the design exchanges and interactions between Ojibwe bead artists on Canadian reserves and the Ojibwe in northern Minnesota and Wisconsin, indeed the whole Great Lakes region. How did this interaction affect design preferences, perhaps distinguishing Ojibwe reserves, reservations, and individual artists from each other?

More interviews and more research in reminiscences, manuscript collections, newspapers, and other records might yield more specifics about the instructions, publications, and images employed at government and church boarding schools to train and thereby influence Ojibwe bead artists.

Additionally, might a broader look at documented collections of other accessories—including yokes, belts or sashes, dance aprons, leggings, and vests—provide more specifics on reservations or regional motifs or traits?

It is clear, though, that evidence in museums and archives can take us only so far. Historical records are often incomplete, inaccurate, or missing altogether, and this makes it difficult to accurately identify the makers of the bags, the wearers of the bags, and the role of the bags within their community. The rest of this story is, quite rightfully, in private homes—in family photos, in family stories, and in beadwork held by families as heirlooms. I applaud the families that have kept these treasures safe, and I hope this work supports their continued safekeeping.

Grand Portage elder and bead artist Ellen Olson, a knowledgeable woman with a generous spirit, agreed to share information for this book in hopes that its words and images would help "the people who make bandolier bags come to life." She also explained, "I create this beadwork for all of my female relatives, the ones who came before me, and to be a beadwork lady." The Ojibwe beadwork ladies and men who follow her can perhaps find inspiration in the work of their relatives shown in these pages.

Acknowledgments

There are so many to thank for their encouragement, guidance, and assistance over the course of this decades-long project. I hope I haven't forgotten any of you who have helped to make this book possible.

First, I must thank all the bead artists, through all the years, whose gashkibidaaganag have enriched so many lives. It is my hope that this book will help to bring more of these wonderful bags, and the stories of their makers, to light.

The contemporary bag makers I interviewed gave generously of themselves and shared their passion for beadwork and their culture with me—Maude Kegg, Batiste Sam, Ellen Olson, Ivy Ailport, Melvin Losh, Marcie McIntire, and Cheryl Minnema.

Others from originating communities who provided cultural support, information, direction, and inspiration include Elisse Aune, Kathryn "Jody" Beaulieu, Brenda Boyd, Andy and Mary Favorite, Linda LeGarde Grover, Betty Kegg, Ron Libertus, Nokomis Paiz, Victoria Raske, Joycelyn Shingobe, Sara Spears, Ruth Waukazo, Karissa White Isaacs, Travis Zimmerman and the Mille Lacs Indian Museum and Trading Post staff, Jeff Savage and Jarvis Paro of Fond du Lac Reservation and Tribal Museum, Sonya Skogland and Willie Reponen of Min No Aya Win Human Services Center, David Niib Aubid, and members of the Minnesota Historical Society's Indian Advisory Committee.

My advisors Kate Duncan, Brenda Child, and Annette Atkins kept my nose to the grindstone and helped me to focus the work. My writing groups and others provided support, technological direction, critiques, and gracious editorial commentary: Marx Swanholm, Annette Atkins, Debbie Miller, Carol Ryan, Jeff Kolnick, Jane Carroll, Michael Lansing, Shannon Smith, and Rosa Corral.

So many colleagues shared resources and provided access to collections, the benefits of their knowledge, and the necessary ongoing encouragement. Thanks to Tilly Laskey, independent curator and my partner in so many discoveries; Kathy Hussey-Arntson, scholar and former MNHS colleague; Barbara Hail, curator emerita of the Haffenreffer Museum of anthropology at Brown University, Providence, RI, and her staff; Diana Pardue, curator of collections at the Heard Museum, Phoenix, AZ; Nancy Blomberg, chief curator and curator of native arts at the Denver Art Museum; Laura Peers, director of the Pitt Rivers Museum in Oxford, England; Nicolette Meister, curator of collections at the Logan Museum of Anthropology, Beloit College, Beloit, WI; Marsha Rooney, curator of history at the Northwest Museum of Art and Culture, Spokane, WA; Patricia Maus, program director at the University of Minnesota Duluth Kathryn A. Martin Library Archives and Special Collections; Sister Moira Wild, Sister Mariterese Woida, and the late Sister Ruth Nierengarten at the Haehn Museum and the archives at St. Benedict's Monastery, St. Joseph, MN; Brother David Klingeman, archivist at St. John's Abbey Archives, Collegeville, MN; Steve Cotherman and Sheree Peterson of Madeline Island Museum, La Pointe, WI; Mary Warner and Ann Marie Johnson of Morrison County Historical Society; Tim Cochrane and Bill Clayton of Grand Portage Monument Heritage Center; Diane Magnuson, director of archives at The History Center, Archives of Bethel University and Converge Worldwide—BGC. Additional thanks to Tom Shaw, Bruce White, Cory Wilmott, Alice Scherer, Carol James, Cindy Hall-Duran, Earl Gutnik, and John Pearson.

Thanks also to Rachel Harvieux and Wisconsin Historical Society staff; Dawn Scher Thomae and Milwaukee Public Museum collections staff; collections staff at the Smithsonian Institution's National Museum of the American Indian and National Museum of Natural History; Native American Art Studies Association colleagues; and the many staff members at Minnesota's county and local historical societies who responded to surveys sent between 1985 and 2001.

Collectors of photographs, objects, and information shared much: Monroe Killy, Dick Nelson, Neva Williams, Alan Woolworth, Pat Albers, Tom Amble, David DeTar Newbert, Mike Johnson, and William and Barbara Schoenwetter.

Staff members in the MNHS's collections and reference areas have been both generous and enthusiastic: head of collections Brian Szott; photographers Eric Mortenson and Peter Latner, videographers Matt Anderson and Lori Williamson, image data managers Jean Moberg and Janet Christensen, CMS/EMU specialist Karen Lovaas, registrar Nicole Delfino, head curator Adam Scher, associate curator Linda McShannock, associate curator Sondra Reierson, and NAGPRA coordinator and heritage collections consultant Leah Bowe. My editor at the MNHS Press, Ann Regan, has been a patient, empathetic professional who shares my passion for the telling of women's stories.

Volunteers Kathy Johnson and Meghan Berry Evans worked tirelessly for years to assist me in research—comparing historic photos to surviving bags, mailing inquiries to museums and collectors, and filing the findings—and then in recataloging each of the bags. Bill Jolitz, Chris Evans, and James Castle lovingly made beautiful new images to record these bags. And textile conservation lab volunteers created storage mounts designed by conservator Ann Frisina to rehouse and preserve the bags.

Special thanks to Barbara O'Sullivan, Ann Meline, Margaret Solberg, Kelly Marshall, and my book club friends who never let me quit when the going got tough.

I am grateful for the financial and institutional support provided through a 2002 Minnesota Humanities Center Works in Progress Grant, which allowed me to spend a month researching bandolier bags and related archival holdings at the Smithsonian's National Museum of the American Indian and National Museum of Natural History. In 2002 the Ken and Nina Rothchild Fund for Business History and Women's History at the MNHS helped to fund my travel to the Museum of Civilization in Hull, Ontario, to research Minnesota and relevant Canadian bandolier bag object, archival, and photographic collections. Further study was supported by the Charles Eugene Flandrau Fund of the MNHS, 2009–10.

And to all the individuals over the years who treasured these bags and donated them to the Minnesota Historical Society and other collections, my sincerest gratitude!

Appendix 1

Bandolier Bags at the Minnesota Historical Society

This list includes bandolier bags and bag fragments held in the collections of the Minnesota Historical Society in 2017. Interested parties may search bags by their catalog numbers, typed in quotation marks, at http://search.mnhs.org/. Figure numbers are provided for images of gashkibidaaganag that appear in this book.

"Acquisition date" means the date a bag was physically received by MNHS; the formal date of accessioning may be later. Information that is not available is indicated by "N/A." "Date attributed by source" is usually the date provided by the donor, but when no such date is available, it is an approximate date provided by collections staff, either at the time of the donation or later; it is sometimes contradicted by the evidence or by the bag itself. If the author has an informed estimate, it is provided as the "Date attributed by MGA"; sometimes this informed estimate confirms the source's attribution. If the author has no further information, the author's attribution line is not included. A source listed as anonymous prefers to remain unnamed.

The strap width is measured at the widest point. (Because many of the strap ends are hidden beneath backing cloth, it is generally not possible to measure their lengths accurately or completely; a few measurements are provided in this listing.) In pocket panel dimensions, height precedes width. The measurement for "area above pocket panel" provides the height of that space. Fringe measurement reflects the average fringe length. If no measurement is given, the bag does not include that feature. For instance, no dimensions are given for the area above the pocket panel for a full panel bag.

64.155.29 Loom-woven panel bandolier bag. *See p. 11 and Figs. 1.14, 3.10*
Acquisition date: 9/16/1964
Date attributed by source: c. 1880–87
Date attributed by MGA: c. 1880s
Maker/Culture/Location: Probably Ojibwe; Mille Lacs Reservation
Source: Drucilla Paist McGill
Provenance: Presented to Minnesota governor Lucius Frederick Hubbard (1882–87) by five Ojibwe chiefs from the Mille Lacs Band of Ojibwe
Overall length: $38\frac{1}{4}$"; strap width: 5"; pocket panel: 10" × $10\frac{1}{2}$"; area above pocket panel: $5\frac{3}{4}$"; applied decorated band: $2\frac{3}{8}$" × $10\frac{3}{4}$"; pocket opening: $9\frac{7}{8}$"; fringe: $3\frac{1}{2}$"

69.41.5 Miniature loom-woven panel bandolier bag
Acquisition date: 3/18/1969
Date attributed by source: c. 1880
Maker/Culture/Location: Possibly Ojibwe, possibly Red Lake Reservation
Source: Donald C. Heath
Provenance: From collection made by the donor's father, Willard B. Heath, who taught at Red Lake Reservation, 1881–84
Overall length: $15\frac{1}{2}$"; strap width: N/A; pocket panel: $3\frac{3}{4}$" × $3\frac{1}{8}$"; area above pocket panel: $1\frac{1}{2}$"; pocket opening: 3"; integrated fringe: $2\frac{1}{2}$"

69.138.5 Spot-stitch appliqué bandolier bag, peacock motif. *See Fig. 3.95*
Acquisition date: 9/26/1969
Date attributed by source: c. 1900
Maker/Culture/Location: Probably Ojibwe; acquired at Akeley, Hubbard County, MN

Source: Theodore S. Walker and Kenneth R. Walker
Provenance: Originally collected by Eveline Van Winkle Sammis and Fletcher Loren Walker
Overall length: 44″; strap length: 46″; strap width: $6\frac{1}{8}$″; pocket panel: $14\frac{1}{2}$″ × $13\frac{1}{8}$″; area above pocket panel: 6″; pocket opening: $11\frac{3}{4}$″; fringe: 3″

70.90 Spot-stitch appliqué bandolier bag. *See p. vi and Fig. 2.49*
Acquisition date: 9/3/1970
Date attributed by source: 1880; not later than 1888
Maker/Culture/Location: Ojibwe; Cass Lake, MN
Source: Mrs. Helen D. Barnes and Do Denley
Provenance: Presented to Rev. William Denley by an Ojibwe chief of Cass Lake, MN
Overall length: 41″; strap width: 5″; pocket panel: $18\frac{3}{8}$″ × 13″; pocket opening: $4\frac{1}{8}$″; fringe: $3\frac{1}{2}$″

74.32.5 Spot-stitch appliqué bandolier bag. *See p. 55 and Fig. 3.16*
Acquisition date: 6/12/1974
Date attributed by source: c. 1880–90
Date attributed by MGA: c. 1880–1890s
Maker/Culture/Location: Probably Ojibwe; MN
Source: Monroe family
Provenance: Printed cotton pocket lining c. 1880s–1890s
Overall length: 45″; strap length: $46\frac{3}{4}$″; strap width: 5″; pocket panel: 13″ × $12\frac{1}{2}$″; area above pocket panel: $7\frac{3}{8}$″; pocket opening: $11\frac{7}{8}$″; fringe: $2\frac{3}{4}$″

163.E32.B: Male Ojibwe doll wearing two loom-woven panel bandolier bags. *See Fig. 12.29*
Acquisition date: 9/2/1898
Date attributed by source: Before 1898
Maker/Culture/Location: Ojibwe; White Earth Indian Reservation
Source: Rev. Joseph A. Gilfillan
Provenance: Creation requested by Gilfillan
Overall length: N/A; *Bag 1:* strap: $10\frac{1}{2}$″ × 1″; pocket panel: 5″ × $3\frac{1}{2}$″; area above pocket panel: $1\frac{1}{2}$″. *Bag 2:* strap: $11\frac{1}{4}$″ × $1\frac{1}{16}$″; pocket panel: $5\frac{1}{2}$″ × $3\frac{3}{4}$″; area above pocket panel: $1\frac{7}{8}$″

262.E58.2 Loom-woven panel bandolier bag. *See Fig. 12.19*
Acquisition date: 8/13/1918
Date attributed by source: c. 1891–99
Date attributed by MGA: Possibly 1891 or earlier, but not later than 1919
Maker/Culture/Location: Probably Ojibwe; White Earth Reservation
Source: Darwin S. Hall
Provenance: N/A
Overall length: 37″; strap width: $4\frac{1}{4}$″; pocket panel: $9\frac{5}{8}$″ × $7\frac{3}{4}$″; area above pocket panel: $6\frac{1}{4}$″; integrated fringe: $4\frac{3}{4}$″; bead loops at center seam of strap: 1″

268.E64 Loom-woven panel bandolier bag. *See p. 3 and Figs. 2.07, 12.18*
Acquisition date: 8/13/1918
Date attributed by source: 1910
Date attributed by MGA: Possibly 1891 or earlier, but not later than 1914
Maker/Culture/Location: Probably Ojibwe; White Earth Reservation
Source: Darwin S. Hall
Provenance: See bag in 1914 MNHS por 3172 p2 (*Fig. 12.15*)
Overall length: 38″; strap width: $4\frac{3}{4}$″; pocket panel: $14\frac{3}{8}$″ × 12″; area above pocket panel: $3\frac{3}{4}$″; integrated fringe: $4\frac{3}{8}$″

272.E68 Loom-woven panel bandolier bag. *See Figs. 2.10, 12.17*
Acquisition date: 8/13/1918
Date attributed by source: 1900
Date attributed by MGA: Possibly 1891 or earlier, but not later than 1914
Maker/Culture/Location: Probably Ojibwe; White Earth Reservation
Source: Darwin S. Hall
Provenance: See bag in 1914 MNHS por 3172 p2 (*Fig. 12.15*). Sacking cloth backing stamped "M. W. JENSEN & CO/McINTOSH, MINN."
Overall length: 41″; strap width: $4\frac{3}{8}$″; pocket panel: $16\frac{1}{8}$″ × $11\frac{5}{8}$″; area above pocket panel: 5″; integrated fringe: $4\frac{1}{2}$″

285.E81 Loom-woven panel bandolier bag. *See Figs. 3.39, 3.45, 12.16*
Acquisition date: 8/13/1918
Date attributed by source: c. 1900
Date attributed by MGA: Possibly 1891 or earlier, but not later than 1914
Maker/Culture/Location: Probably Ojibwe; White Earth Reservation
Source: Darwin S. Hall
Provenance: See bag in 1914 MNHS por 3172 p2 (*Fig. 12.15*)
Overall length: $39\frac{1}{2}$″; strap width: $5\frac{1}{2}$″; pocket panel: $14\frac{1}{4}$″ × $12\frac{1}{4}$″; area above pocket panel: 4″; integrated fringe: 4″

512.E137 Loom-woven panel bandolier bag. *See Fig. 12.07*
Acquisition date: 12/1/1893
Date attributed by source: Not later than 1893
Date attributed by MGA: Not later than 1893
Maker/Culture/Location: Probably Ojibwe-made at White Earth Reservation; acquired in Becker County, MN
Source: Minnesota World's Fair Commission
Provenance: Exhibited at the 1893 Columbian Exposition, Chicago. Attributed to Becker County Indian Industries; some objects that are part of this accession are documented as created by American Indian students who attended an industrial or boarding school located in Becker County, MN.
Overall length: 32″; strap width: $2\frac{1}{2}$″; pocket panel: $7\frac{1}{4}$″ × $7\frac{5}{8}$″; area above pocket panel: $3\frac{5}{8}$″; pocket opening: $5\frac{3}{4}$″; integrated fringe: $4\frac{1}{4}$″

514.E139 Spot-stitch appliqué bandolier bag. *See Fig. 12.09*
Acquisition date: 12/1/1893
Date attributed by source: Not later than 1893

Date attributed by MGA: Not later than 1893
Maker/Culture/Location: Probably Ojibwe-made at White Earth Reservation; acquired in Becker County, MN
Source: Minnesota World's Fair Commission
Provenance: Exhibited at the 1893 Columbian Exposition, Chicago. Attributed to Becker County Indian Industries; some objects that are part of this accession are documented as created by American Indian students who attended an industrial or boarding school located in Becker County, MN.
Overall length: 40"; strap width: 4¼"; pocket panel: 16¼" × 12½"; area above pocket panel 4½"; fringe: 2⅜"

521.E146.2 Spot-stitch appliqué bandolier bag. *See Figs. 3.71, 12.10*
Acquisition date: 12/1/1893
Date attributed by source: Not later than 1893
Date attributed by MGA: Not later than 1893
Maker/Culture/Location: Probably Ojibwe-made at White Earth Reservation; acquired in Becker County, MN
Source: Minnesota World's Fair Commission
Provenance: Exhibited at the 1893 Columbian Exposition, Chicago. Attributed to Becker County Indian Industries; some objects that are part of this accession are documented as created by American Indian students who attended an industrial or boarding school located in Becker County, MN.
Overall length: 41½"; strap width: 4⅝"; pocket panel: 9⅝" × 11"; area above pocket panel: 6⅛"; pocket opening: 8⅝"; attached fringe: 4"

525.E150 Spot-stitch appliqué bandolier bag, paisley motif on strap. *See p. 185 and Fig. 12.11*
Acquisition date: 12/1/1893
Date attributed by source: Not later than 1893

Date attributed by MGA: Not later than 1893
Maker/Culture/Location: Probably Ojibwe-made at White Earth Reservation; acquired in Becker County, MN
Source: Minnesota World's Fair Commission
Provenance: Exhibited at the 1893 Columbian Exposition, Chicago. Attributed to Becker County Indian Industries; some objects that are part of this accession are documented as created by American Indian students who attended an industrial or boarding school located in Becker County, MN.
Overall length: 42½"; strap width: 4½"; pocket panel: 10¾" × 13¼"; area above pocket panel: 5"; netted fringe: 3"

532.E157 Loom-woven panel bandolier bag. *See Figs. 2.18, 12.08*
Acquisition date: 12/1/1893
Date attributed by source: Not later than 1893
Date attributed by MGA: Before 1893
Maker/Culture/Location: Probably Ojibwe-made at White Earth Reservation; acquired in Becker County, MN, from the collection of Mrs. Jessie Campbell West
Source: Minnesota World's Fair Commission
Provenance: Exhibited at the 1893 Columbian Exposition, Chicago. Some objects that are part of this larger accession are documented as part of the personal collection of Mrs. Jessie Campbell West. See photograph of her collection at BCHS, #4969 (*Fig. 1.05*).
Overall length: 36¾"; strap length: 41½"; strap width: 3¾"; pocket panel: 15¼" × 11"; area above pocket panel: 4¾"; pocket opening: 11"; integrated fringe: 4"

---

753 Loom-woven bandolier bag
Acquisition date: Unknown
Date attributed by source: c. 1875–1925
Maker/Culture/Location: Possibly Ojibwe
Source: Unknown
Provenance: N/A

Overall length: 33¾"; strap width: 2⅛"; pocket panel: 7½" × 6¼"; area above pocket panel: 3"; pocket opening: 7½"; integrated fringe at top shoulder strap: 5¼"; integrated fringe at bottom: 6"

1139 Loom-woven panel bandolier bag
Acquisition date: 1996; originally acquired by Sibley House Association, 1937
Date attributed by source: 1900 or earlier
Maker/Culture/Location: Mrs. Friday; probably Ojibwe; probably made at Lac Courte Oreilles Reservation, WI
Source: Transfer from Sibley House Association; originally donated by Mrs. Luella Weymouth
Provenance: Acquired by donor's husband about 1900; made by Mrs. Friday, Lac Courte Oreilles Band of Lake Superior Chippewa Indians of Wisconsin
Overall length: 39"; strap width: 4⅝"; pocket panel: 14⅜" × 12½"; area above pocket panel: 3⅛"; pocket opening: 14⅜"; integrated fringe: 4"

1496 Spot-stitch appliqué bandolier bag. *See Figs. 2.15, 3.65*
Acquisition date: 1996; originally purchased by the Sibley House Association, 1939
Date attributed by source: c. 1860–1901
Date attributed by MGA: Probably before 1910
Maker/Culture/Location: Possibly Ojibwe
Source: Transfer from the Sibley House Association
Provenance: Bishop Henry Benjamin Whipple collection
Overall length: 38½"; strap width: 4⅝"; pocket panel: 11⅜" × 11¾"; area above pocket panel: 5⅝"; pocket opening: 9¾"; fringe: 4"

1498 Spot-stitch appliqué bandolier bag, pocket on reverse. *See Fig. 12.25*
Acquisition date: 1996; originally purchased by the Sibley House Association, 1939

Date attributed by source: c. 1860–1901
Date attributed by MGA: Before 1910
Maker/Culture/Location: MGA attributes to Sophia Smith and/or associated group; Ojibwe; possibly White Earth Reservation or Red Lake Reservation
Source: Transfer from the Sibley House Association
Provenance: Bishop Henry Benjamin Whipple collection; tag attached, "$40.00."
Overall length: 45¼″; strap width: 5⅝″; pocket panel: 18¾″ × 15¾″; pocket opening on reverse: 6½″; fringe: 2¾″

1520 Spot-stitch appliqué bandolier bag. *See Fig. 12.24*
Acquisition date: 1996; originally purchased by the Sibley House Association, 1939
Date attributed by source: c. 1895–1901
Date attributed by MGA: Probably no later than 1902–04
Maker/Culture/Location: Sophia Smith; Ojibwe; possibly White Earth Reservation or Red Lake Reservation
Source: Transfer from the Sibley House Association
Provenance: Bishop Henry Benjamin Whipple collection; see photograph of Sophia Smith holding bag (MNHS Collection III.40.74, *Fig. 12.23*), identifying her as maker and noting bag as made specifically for Bishop Whipple
Overall length: 45″; strap width: 5¾″; strap length: 45½″; pocket panel: 13½″ × 13⅛″; area above pocket panel: 6¾″; fringe: 2¼″

1825 Spot-stitch appliqué bandolier bag. *See Fig. 12.20*
Acquisition date: 1996; originally purchased by the Sibley House Association, 1939
Date attributed by source: c. 1860–1901
Date attributed by MGA: Before 1910; floral backing print cotton c. 1890s
Maker/Culture/Location: Probably Ojibwe
Source: Transfer from the Sibley House Association
Provenance: Bishop Henry Benjamin Whipple collection
Overall length: 39¾″; strap width: 6¾″; pocket panel: 13¾″ × 11⅛″; area above pocket panel: 5¾″; pocket opening: 8¾″; fringe: 4½″

1826 Spot-stitch appliqué bandolier bag, pocket on reverse. *See Figs. 3.55, 3.98*
Acquisition date: 1996; originally purchased by the Sibley House Association, 1939
Date attributed by source: c. 1860–1901
Date attributed by MGA: Before 1910
Maker/Culture/Location: Probably Ojibwe
Source: Transfer from the Sibley House Association
Provenance: Bishop Henry Benjamin Whipple collection
Overall length: 34¾″; strap width: 6⅛″; pocket panel: 17½″ × 14½″; pocket opening: 5″; fringe: 3½″

1827 Spot-stitch appliqué bandolier bag, beaded overall with bugle beads
Acquisition date: 1996; originally purchased by the Sibley House Association, 1939
Date attributed by source: Before 1939
Date attributed by MGA: Before 1910
Maker/Culture/Location: Probably Ojibwe
Source: Transfer from the Sibley House Association
Provenance: Bishop Henry Benjamin Whipple collection
Overall length: 45¼″; strap width: 6⅜″; pocket panel: 20″ × 16″; pocket opening: 15″; fringe: 3½″

1828 Spot-stitch appliqué bandolier bag, folded leaf motif. *See Fig. 11.01*
Acquisition date: 1996; originally purchased by the Sibley House Association, 1939
Date attributed by source: c. 1860–1901
Date attributed by MGA: Before 1910. Printed cotton pocket lining c. 1890s–1915
Maker/Culture/Location: Probably Ojibwe
Source: Transfer from the Sibley House Association
Provenance: Bishop Henry Benjamin Whipple collection
Overall length: 46″; strap width: 6¼″; pocket panel: 15⅛″ × 14⅛″; area above pocket panel: 7″; fringe: 3½″

1829 Spot-stitch appliqué bandolier bag with loom-woven strap. *See Fig. 3.46*
Acquisition date: 1996; originally purchased by the Sibley House Association, 1939
Date attributed by source: c. 1860–1901
Date attributed by MGA: Before 1910
Maker/Culture/Location: Possibly Ojibwe; probably Great Lakes
Source: Transfer from the Sibley House Association
Provenance: Bishop Henry Benjamin Whipple collection
Overall length: 39⅛″; strap width: 3⅞″; pocket panel: 11¾″ × 11″; area above pocket panel: 4″; pocket opening: 10″; fringe: 4½″

1830 Spot-stitch appliqué bandolier bag
Acquisition date: 1996; originally purchased by the Sibley House Association, 1939
Date attributed by source: c. 1860–1929
Date attributed by MGA: Before 1910; printed cotton backing is mid-1890s
Maker/Culture/Location: Probably Ojibwe
Source: Transfer from the Sibley House Association
Provenance: Bishop Henry Benjamin Whipple collection
Overall length: 48⅛″; strap width: 5½″; pocket panel: 13¾″ × 14½″; area above pocket panel: 5¼″; pocket opening: 11¾″; fringe: 3″

1831 Spot-stitch appliqué bandolier bag, pocket on back. *See Fig. 1.02*
Acquisition date: 1996; originally purchased by the Sibley House Association, 1939

Date attributed by source: c. 1860–1901
Date attributed by MGA: Before 1910
Maker/Culture/Location: MGA attributes to Sophia Smith and/or associated group; Ojibwe; probably White Earth Reservation or Red Lake Reservation
Source: Transfer from the Sibley House Association
Provenance: Bishop Henry Benjamin Whipple collection; tag attached, "$40.00."
Overall length: 45¾"; strap width: 6⅜"; pocket panel: 20" × 16½"; pocket opening: 7¾"; fringe: 3"

1844 Miniature spot-stitch appliqué bandolier bag
Acquisition date: 1996; originally purchased by the Sibley House Association, 1939
Date attributed by source: c. 1860–1901
Date attributed by MGA: Before 1910
Maker/Culture/Location: Possibly Car-ka-be-she-gue; probably Ojibwe; probably MN
Source: Transfer from the Sibley House Association
Provenance: Bishop Henry Benjamin Whipple collection; note in bag: "From Car-ka-be-she-gue two bags for Mrs. Whipple."
Overall length: 18¾"; strap width: 2⅛"; pocket panel: 6¾" × 6⅞"; area above pocket panel: 3"; pocket opening: 5½"; fringe: 1¾"

1976.37.5 Spot-stitch appliqué beaded panel, likely a bandolier bag pocket fragment
Acquisition date: 4/14/1976
Date attributed by source: c. 1932
Maker/Culture/Location: Ojibwe; made in Ponsford, Becker County, White Earth Reservation
Source: Mrs. Isabelle Robideau Long
Provenance: Obtained at White Earth Reservation
Pocket panel: 21¾" × 16⅛"; pocket opening (on back of panel): 5⅜"

1978 Spot-stitch appliqué bandolier bag. *See p. 2 and Fig. 2.16*
Acquisition date: 1996; originally purchased by the Sibley House Association, 1939
Date attributed by source: c. 1860–1901
Date attributed by MGA: No later than 1901
Maker/Culture/Location: Probably Ojibwe; probably White Earth Reservation
Source: Transfer from the Sibley House Association
Provenance: Bishop Henry Benjamin Whipple collection; note found in bag: "To our Bishop Rt. Rev. Henry Benjamin Whipple, Faribault, Minn. Christmas present from Mr. Wm. Wilkins Davis Smith and Mrs. Emily Smith. White Earth, Becker Co. Minn."
Overall length: 37½"; strap width: 5¼"; pocket panel: 11½" × 13½"; area above pocket panel: 5⅞"; pocket opening: 12"; fringe: 4½"

1978.23.3 Spot-stitch appliqué bandolier bag
Acquisition date: 1/1/1978
Date attributed by source: Created before 1973
Maker/Culture/Location: N/A
Source: Northern Pacific Railroad collection
Provenance: N/A
Overall length: 44½"; strap width: 6"; pocket panel: 14" × 12½"; area above pocket panel: 6⅛"; pocket opening: 10¾"; fringe: 3¾"

1978.23.4 Loom-woven panel bandolier bag, red wool foundation cloth, no backing
Acquisition date: 1/1/1978
Date attributed by source: Created c. 1880
Date attributed by MGA: Last third of 19th century; printed cotton pocket lining c. 1870s–1880s
Maker/Culture/Location: Probably Ojibwe
Source: Northern Pacific Railroad collection
Provenance: N/A
Overall length: 42½"; strap width: 4⅝"; pocket panel: 10¾" × 11½"; area above pocket panel: 6⅝"; pocket opening: 9⅞"; fringe: 6½"

1981.4.71 Spot-stitch appliqué bandolier bag
Acquisition date: 1/1/1981
Date attributed by source: Probably early 20th century
Date attributed by MGA: Probably no later than 1959
Maker/Culture/Location: Documented during inventory at the Mille Lacs Indian Museum and Trading Post, 1981
Source: Harry Darius Ayer and Jeannette Ora Foster Ayer
Provenance: The Mille Lacs Indian Museum and Trading Post on Highway 169 in Onamia, MN, was operated by Harry and Jeanette Ayer. They developed working relationships with many Mille Lacs Band members between 1918 and 1959.
Overall length: 44½"; strap width: 5⅞"; pocket panel: 14½" × 13¼"; area above pocket panel: 4¼"; pocket opening: 11¾"; fringe: 5½"

1981.119.1 Spot-stitch appliqué bandolier bag. *See p. 8 and Fig. 9.08*
Acquisition date: 11/1/1981
Date attributed by source: 1916
Maker/Culture/Location: Ojibwe; Cass Lake, MN
Source: Lawrence D. Hankins
Provenance: Original collectors Paul and Nellie Hankins described this as a "medicine bag" made by the Ojibwe of Cass Lake, MN.
Overall length: 48"; strap width: 7½"; pocket panel: 16⅝" × 14¾"; area above pocket panel: 6"; pocket opening 14"; fringe: 4"

1982.11.28 Miniature loom-woven panel bandolier bag
Acquisition date: 1982
Date attributed by source: Before 1899
Maker/Culture/Location: Possibly Ojibwe
Source: N/A
Provenance: N/A
Overall length: 11½″; strap width: 1″; pocket panel: 3¼″ × 3¾″; area above pocket panel: 3¼″; pocket opening: 2¼″; fringe: 2¼″

1982.67.1 Loom-woven panel bandolier bag. *See Fig. 3.02*
Acquisition date: 9/28/1982
Date attributed by source: c. 1877–86
Date attributed by MGA: Probably after 1877, not later than 1886
Maker/Culture/Location: Possibly Ojibwe or Dakota
Source: Donald M. Stewart
Provenance: Bag was probably collected by Oscar E. Garrison (1825–86) of Crow Wing County, MN; purchased by Donald M. Stewart from Mr. Gerald L. Garrison.
Overall length: 39½″; strap width: 3¾″; pocket panel: 8½″ × 8⅞″; area above pocket panel: 4″; pocket opening: 8″; integrated tassel and fringe at top shoulder: 5″; integrated tassel and fringe at bottom: 3¼″

1982.67.6 Pocket panel for loom-woven bandolier bag; bag fragment with buildings, smoke, tree, and possible thunderbird motifs. *See Fig. 3.37*
Acquisition date: 9/28/1982
Date attributed by source: c. 1900 (Sorenson)
Date attributed by MGA: Last third of 19th century
Maker/Culture/Location: Probably Ojibwe; probably MN
Source: Purchased in 1967 from Mrs. Florence Sorenson by Donald M. Stewart
Provenance: Panel was purchased from the granddaughter of the collectors, who owned a hotel in Detroit Lakes, MN.
Overall length: 10 7/16″; strap width: N/A; pocket panel: 8⅛″ × 8⅛″; integrated fringe: 2¼″

1982.67.9 Spot-stitch appliqué bandolier bag. *See Fig. 11.12*
Acquisition date: 9/28/1982
Date attributed by source: Possibly 1911 or earlier
Maker/Culture/Location: Probably Ojibwe; probably White Earth Reservation
Source: Donald M. Stewart obtained bag from Ms. Lucylle Warren Zastrow, originally from White Earth Reservation.
Provenance: Letter found in pocket, from "Rose" to Mrs. George Huefner, Huron, SD, Aug. 9, 1911
Overall length: 45¾″; strap width: 6½″; pocket panel: 15⅞″ × 15⅝″; area above pocket panel: 6½″; pocket opening: 14⅜″; fringe: 4″

1983.4.10 Male doll wearing two miniature loom-woven panel bandolier bags
Acquisition date: Unknown
Date attributed by source: N/A
Maker/Culture/Location: Probably Ojibwe
Source: N/A
Provenance: N/A
Bag 1: overall length: 7″; strap width: ½″; pocket panel: 2⅜″ × 2⅛″; area above pocket panel: ¾″; pocket opening: 1⅞″; fringe: 1¼″. *Bag 2:* Overall length: 7¼″; strap width: ½″; pocket panel: 2¼″ × 2½″; area above pocket panel: ⅞″; pocket opening: 1¾″; fringe: 1¼″

1983.81.1 Spot-stitch appliqué bandolier bag, no pocket
Acquisition date: 3/15/1983
Date attributed by source: About 1915
Maker/Culture/Location: Probably Ojibwe
Source: Theordore L. Losby; bag was purchased by her parents, Mr. and Mrs. Fred W. Bagley, at Mille Lacs Lake, MN
Provenance: Beaded name "MARY PiKe" on bag may refer to Mary Riegert Pike, born May 1900.
Overall length: 45″; strap width: 5⅝″; pocket panel: 18⅜″ × 14⅞″; area above pocket panel: 4″; fringe: 1½″

1984.6.1 Spot-stitch appliqué bandolier bag. *See Fig. 2.45*
Acquisition date: 1/1/1980
Date attributed by source: Probably early 20th century
Date attributed by MGA: Probably early 20th century
Maker/Culture/Location: Probably Ojibwe; MN
Source: Charles A. Lindbergh, Sr.
Provenance: Gift to Charles A. Lindbergh, Sr.
Overall length: 41½″; strap width: 6″; pocket panel: 14⅜″ × 12⅝″; area above pocket panel: 4⅛″; pocket opening: 13¾″; fringe: 2¾″

1984.156.3 Spot-stitch appliqué bandolier bag, folded leaf motif. *See cover, p. 127, and Fig. 9.15*
Acquisition date: 11/1/1984
Date attributed by source: Not later than 1920
Maker/Culture/Location: Associated with Kay-zhe-baush-kung (Otto Bismark); Ojibwe; Leech Lake Reservation
Source: Marguerite P. Barnard
Provenance: Purchased c. 1920 by Marguerite Barnard and her husband Neal as one component of an Ojibwe dance outfit associated with Kay-zhe-baush-kung (Otto Bismark)
Overall length: 48½″; strap width: 6″; pocket panel: 15¼″ × 14¼″; area above pocket panel: 6¾″; pocket opening: 11⅞″; attached fringe: 3¾″

1986.203.1 Spot-stitch appliqué bandolier bag
Acquisition date: 9/1/1986
Date attributed by source: First quarter 20th century
Date attributed by MGA: First quarter 20th century

Maker/Culture/Location: Ojibwe; Ogema, Becker County, MN
Source: Merrill Mettler
Provenance: Printed inner fabric visible at the top of the bag, on the back, appears to be from the early 20th century, possibly 1900–1910.
Overall length: 39½"; strap width: 5½"; pocket panel: 12" × 13¾"; area above pocket panel: 5⅞"; pocket opening (sewn shut): 11¾"; fringe: 1½"

1987.48.2 Loom-woven panel bandolier bag, strap atypically attached
Acquisition date: 2/19/1987
Date attributed by source: Second half 19th century
Maker/Culture/Location: Possibly Ojibwe
Source: Purchase at Sotheby's
Provenance: N/A
Overall length: 31½"; strap width: 3 1/16"; pocket panel: 11" × 7¼"; area above pocket panel: 6½"; pocket opening: 10⅛"; fringe: 3¾"

1988.340.1 Spot-stitch appliqué and quill-worked bandolier bag, pocket on reverse. *See Fig. 9.32*
Acquisition date: 1/1/1988
Date attributed by source: Made between 1980 and 1986
Maker/Culture/Location: Mel Losh; Ojibwe; Leech Lake Reservation
Source: Purchased from Mel Losh, Leech Lake Band of Ojibwe
Provenance: Maker, Mel Losh
Overall length: 46"; strap width: 6½"; pocket panel: 13⅜" × 16½"; birchbark panel: 10⅞" × 7⅛"; area above birchbark panel: 8½"; attached fringe: 2½"

1990.502.5 Spot-stitch appliqué bandolier bag, slit pocket. *See Figs. 3.85, 12.12*
Acquisition date: 9/14/1990
Date attributed by source: 1920
Maker/Culture/Location: Likely Ojibwe; White Earth Reservation
Source: Ms. Louise E. King (daughter-in-law of Stafford King)
Provenance: White Earth Nation induction gift to Stafford King, c. 1920
Overall length: 45¾"; strap width: 5¾"; pocket panel: 17½" × 21⅞"; pocket opening: 4½"; fringe: 2¾"

1990.506.5A and **1990.506.5B** Spot-stitch appliqué bandolier bag, faux pocket; strap detached from bag. *See Figs. 1.15, 2.12*
Acquisition date: Probably 6/8/1989
Date attributed by source: Not later than 1920
Maker/Culture/Location: Ojibwe; White Earth Reservation
Source: Herbert S. McDuffee, Jr., Marilyn Vincent, and Kathryn Breuer
Provenance: Presented to Herbert S. McDuffee by the Ojibwe of the White Earth Nation in recognition of his military service
Overall length: 43½"; overall strap length: 46½"; strap width: 6"; pocket panel: 15⅝" × 18½"; faux pocket opening: 4⅜"; fringe: 2½"

1993.260.10 Spot-stitch appliqué bandolier bag. *See Figs. 2.04, 2.05, 2.06*
Acquisition date: 5/6/1993
Date attributed by source: 1900–1950
Maker/Culture/Location: Probably Ojibwe; White Earth Reservation
Source: Mrs. Marcella J. Wage
Provenance: Owned by source's husband, Paul Wage of the White Earth Nation
Overall length: 47½"; strap width: 6½"; pocket panel: 15¾" × 14¾"; area above pocket panel: 7⅜"; pocket opening: 14⅝"; fringe: 3"

1994.19.4 Spot-stitch appliqué bandolier bag strap fragment
Acquisition date: 3/3/1993
Date attributed by source: c. 1905
Maker/Culture/Location: Probably Ojibwe
Source: Thomas T. Hale
Provenance: Purchased by Clara Ames (Mrs. J. T.) Hale of Duluth and St. Paul, MN
Overall length: 26 to 26½"; width: 6⅞"

1994.19.7 Spot-stitch appliqué bandolier bag slit pocket; ear of corn and bird motifs. *See Fig. 2.14*
Acquisition date: 3/13/1993
Date attributed by source: c. 1905
Maker/Culture/Location: Ojibwe; MN
Source: Thomas T. Hale
Provenance: Purchased at the Hage Store in Deerwood, MN
Overall length: 43½"; strap width: 5¼"; pocket panel: 14⅛" × 18¼"; pocket opening: 5⅛"; fringe: 4"

1995.46.11 Spot-stitch appliqué bandolier bag, faux pocket
Acquisition date: 9/7/1993
Date attributed by source: c. 1900
Maker/Culture/Location: Probably Ojibwe; White Earth Reservation
Source: L. Wynn Carr
Provenance: Acquired by Byron Carr, government cruiser on White Earth Reservation, c. 1900
Overall length: 45¼"; strap width: 6⅞" to 7¼"; pocket panel: 18" × 19½"; faux pocket opening: 3¾"; fringe: 3½"

1995.46.16 Spot-stitch appliqué bandolier bag, slit pocket. *See Fig. 3.94*
Acquisition date: 9/7/1993
Date attributed by source: c. 1900
Maker/Culture/Location: Likely Ojibwe; White Earth Reservation
Source: L. Wynn Carr
Provenance: Acquired by Byron Carr, government cruiser on White Earth Reservation, c. 1900
Overall length: 34¾"; strap width: 6¼"; pocket panel: 15¼" × 17"; pocket opening: 5⅜"; fringe: 4¼"

1995.95.2 Spot-stitch appliqué bandolier bag, faux pocket. *See Fig. 2.50*
Acquisition date: 6/1/1976
Date attributed by source: Possibly 1890–1930
Maker/Culture/Location: Probably Ojibwe; MN
Source: Emily Peake

Provenance: Possible association with White Earth Reservation or Red Lake Reservation; bag was a gift given to donor's grandmother Elizabeth Peake (Gitchi-wab-ogema-equay, Big White Boss Woman)
Overall length: 42¼″; strap width: 6⅝″ to 7″; pocket panel: 15⅝″ to 16¼″ × 16⅝″; faux pocket opening: 4⅛″; no fringe

---

1995.95.3 Spot-stitch appliqué bandolier bag, faux pocket
Acquisition date: 6/1/1976
Date attributed by source: Possibly 1890–1930
Maker/Culture/Location: Probably Ojibwe; MN
Source: Emily Peake
Provenance: Possible association with White Earth Reservation or Red Lake Reservation; bag was a gift given to donor's grandmother Elizabeth Peake (Gitchi-wab-ogema-equay, Big White Boss Woman)
Overall length: 43″; strap width: 6″; pocket panel: 15⅞″ × 18¾″; faux pocket opening: 5¼″

1996.201.1 Spot-stitch appliqué bandolier bag. *See Fig. 10.48*
Date attributed by source: Completed by maker 1995
Maker/Culture/Location: Made by Batiste Sam with assistance from Jessie Clark; Ojibwe; Mille Lacs Reservation
Source: Purchased from Batiste Sam, Mille Lacs Band of Ojibwe
Provenance: Maker, Batiste Sam
Overall length: 47¾″; strap width: 5⅞″; pocket panel: 18½″ × 15⅜″; area above pocket panel: 3″; pocket opening: 17⅞″; fringe: 4½″

2002.259.4 Dance apron reassembled from spot-stitch appliqué bandolier bag. *See Fig. 10.40*
Acquisition date: 2002
Date attributed by source: c. 1940–2002
Date attributed by MGA: Mid-20th century or earlier
Maker/Culture/Location: Probably Ojibwe; Mille Lacs Reservation
Source: Purchased from Sherman Andrews Holbert
Provenance: Original bandolier bag strap is signed "JOhN ShEWap"; undated photograph of John Shewap and Otto Kegg shows Shewap wearing the original bandolier bag
Overall strap length/waist band: 44¾″; strap width: 5¾″; visible portion of pocket panel: 16¾″ × 14¼″

2003.159.1 Spot-stitch appliqué bandolier bag, faux pocket; pocket on reverse. *See Fig. 12.33*
Acquisition date: 7/29/2003
Date attributed by source: 2003
Maker/Culture/Location: Ivy Ailport; Ojibwe; White Earth Reservation, Ogema, MN
Source: Purchased from Ivy Ailport, White Earth Nation
Provenance: Maker, Ivy Ailport
Overall length: 52″; strap width: 6¼″; pocket panel: 15¾″ × 16¾″; area above pocket panel: 4⅝″; faux pocket opening: $4\frac{11}{16}$″; fringe: 6¼″

2005.193.1 Spot-stitch appliqué bandolier bag, slit pocket. *See Fig. 10.15*
Acquisition date: 6/22/2005
Date attributed by source: No later than 1931
Date attributed by MGA: No later than 1931
Maker/Culture/Location: Ojibwe; associated with Lake Lena, Mille Lacs Reservation
Source: Purchased from Sherman Andrews Holbert
Provenance: Beaded above pocket: 1931/ LAKE LENA, MINN
Overall length: 45″; strap width: 6¼″; pocket panel: 16″ × 12⅝″; area above pocket panel: 4½ to 6⅛″; pocket opening: 3⅞″; fringe: 3¼″

2006.168.2 Spot-stitch appliqué bandolier bag, large single motif on pocket. *See Figs. 3.51, 9.20*
Acquisition date: 10/26/2006
Date attributed by source: c. 1890–1920
Date attributed by MGA: Probably late 19th or early 20th century
Maker/Culture/Location: Probably Ojibwe; possibly from Cass Lake area, MN
Source: Purchased at Cowan's Auctions, Inc.
Provenance: N/A
Overall length: 47¼″; strap width: 5¼″; pocket panel: 14¾″ × 13½″; area above pocket panel: 7½″; pocket opening: 10⅞″; fringe: 3¾″

2008.9.1 Bandolier bag with loom-woven panel pocket and spot-stitch appliqué straps. *See Figs. 2.13, 2.42, 3.53*
Acquisition date: 2/16/2007
Date attributed by source: c. 1880–1925
Date attributed by MGA: Probably last third of 19th century
Maker/Culture/Location: Probably Ojibwe; MN
Source: Robert G. and Beth S. Huntley
Provenance: N/A
Overall length: 40¼″; strap length: 24½″; strap width: 5¼″; pocket panel: 11½″ × 9⅛″; area above pocket panel: 3¾″; pocket opening: 8″; fringe: 3⅞″

2009.25.1 Spot-stitch appliqué bandolier bag
Acquisition date: 7/9/2007
Date attributed by source: c. 1910
Date attributed by MGA: Probably late 19th to early 20th century
Maker/Culture/Location: Possibly Ojibwe; MN
Source: JoAnn Bakken
Provenance: N/A
Overall length: 44¼″; strap width: 5¼″; pocket panel: 10¾″ × 16″; area above pocket panel: 6″; pocket opening: 7″; fringe: 3⅝″

2011.208.144 Spot-stitch appliqué bag, slit pocket
Acquisition date: 5/19/2008
Date attributed by source: c. 1900–1950

Date attributed by MGA: Probably 1890s–1920s
Maker/Culture/Location: Probably Ojibwe; MN
Source: Anonymous
Provenance: Part of the collection made by Alfred H. Peterson in Cass Lake, MN; collector was active 1920–74.
Overall length: 41¼"; strap width: 6¼"; pocket panel: 15½" × 16½"; pocket opening: 4"; fringe: 6¼"

2011.208.145 Spot-stitch appliqué bandolier bag. *See p. 31 and Figs. 2.08, 9.09*
Acquisition date: 5/19/2008
Date attributed by source: c. 1900–1950
Date attributed by MGA: Probably c. 1890–1900
Maker/Culture/Location: Probably Ojibwe; MN
Source: Anonymous
Provenance: Part of the collection made by Alfred H. Peterson in Cass Lake, MN; collector was active 1920–74.
Overall length: 51"; strap width: 6½"; pocket panel: 16" × 14½"; area above pocket panel: 6⅝"; pocket opening: 14"; fringe: 4 to 5¼"

2011.208.146 Spot-stitch appliqué bandolier bag, pocket on reverse. *See Fig. 9.05*
Acquisition date: 5/19/2008
Date attributed by source: c. 1900–1950
Date attributed by MGA: Possibly first half of 20th century
Maker/Culture/Location: Possibly Ojibwe; MN
Source: Anonymous
Provenance: Part of the collection made by Alfred H. Peterson in Cass Lake, MN; collector was active 1920–74.
Overall length: 45"; strap width: 5⅛"; pocket panel: 16" × 14⅝"; pocket opening on reverse: 4½"; fringe: 3"

2011.208.147 Spot-stitch appliqué bandolier bag. *See Fig. 9.10*
Acquisition date: 5/19/2008
Date attributed by source: c. 1900–1950
Date attributed by MGA: Probably c. 1900; pocket is backed with a navy and white cotton print c. 1895–1915
Maker/Culture/Location: Possibly Ojibwe; MN
Source: Anonymous
Provenance: Part of the collection made by Alfred H. Peterson in Cass Lake, MN; collector was active 1920–74.
Overall length: 41½"; strap width: 6¾"; pocket panel: 13⅜" × 16"; area above pocket panel: 4"; pocket opening (sewn shut): 16"; fringe: 3"

2011.208.148 Spot-stitch appliqué bandolier bag. *See Figs. 2.02, 3.95*
Acquisition date: 5/19/2008
Date attributed by source: c. 1900–1925
Date attributed by MGA: Probably 1890s–1920s; printed cotton backings and pocket lining may date c. 1895–1915
Maker/Culture/Location: Possibly Ojibwe; MN
Source: Anonymous
Provenance: Part of the collection made by Alfred H. Peterson in Cass Lake, MN; collector was active 1920–74.
Overall length: 45"; strap width: 6"; pocket panel: 14¼" × 15"; area above pocket panel: 6"; pocket opening: 11¾"; attached fringe: 3"

2011.208.149 Spot-stitch appliqué bandolier bag, faux pocket. *See Fig. 9.06*
Acquisition date: 5/19/2008
Date attributed by source: c. 1890–1915
Date attributed by MGA: c. 1890–1915; bag is backed with a blue and white cotton print featuring a leaf and floral sprig, c. 1895–1915
Maker/Culture/Location: Possibly Ojibwe; MN
Source: Anonymous
Provenance: Part of the collection made by Alfred H. Peterson in Cass Lake, MN; collector was active 1920–74.
Overall length: 43½"; strap width: 5⅜"; pocket panel: 18" × 14¼"; faux pocket opening: $4\frac{3}{16}$"; attached fringe: 3"

2011.208.150 Spot-stitch appliqué bandolier bag, pocket on reverse. *See Fig. 9.07*
Acquisition date: 5/19/2008
Date attributed by source: c. 1900–1950
Date attributed by MGA: First half of 20th century
Maker/Culture/Location: Possibly Ojibwe; MN
Source: Anonymous
Provenance: Part of the collection made by Alfred H. Peterson in Cass Lake, MN; collector was active 1920–74.
Overall length: 44"; strap width: 5⅛"; pocket panel: 15⅝" × 14⅜"; pocket opening on reverse: 4½"; integrated fringe: 3¼"

2011.208.151 Spot-stitch appliqué full panel bag, slit pocket
Acquisition date: 5/19/2008
Date attributed by source: c. 1900–1950
Date attributed by MGA: Possibly first third of 20th century
Maker/Culture/Location: Possibly Ojibwe; MN
Source: Anonymous
Provenance: Part of the collection made by Alfred H. Peterson in Cass Lake, MN; collector was active 1920–74.
Overall length: 45"; strap width: 5⅞"; pocket panel: 19⅜" × 15"; pocket opening: 3¾"; fringe: 2¾"

2011.208.152 Spot-stitch appliqué bandolier bag, single large central pocket motif. *See Fig. 9.19*
Acquisition date: 5/19/2008
Date attributed by source: c. 1900–1950
Date attributed by MGA: c. 1900
Maker/Culture/Location: Possibly Ojibwe; MN
Source: Anonymous
Provenance: Part of the collection made by Alfred H. Peterson in Cass Lake, MN; collector was active 1920–74.
Overall length: 43¾"; strap width: 5"; pocket panel: 13" × 12⅞"; area above pocket panel: 6⅝"; pocket opening: 10¾"; integrated fringe: 3"

2011.208.153 Spot-stitch appliqué bandolier bag, folded leaf motif. *See p. 83 and Fig. 9.26*
Acquisition date: 5/19/2008
Date attributed by source: c. 1900–1912
Date attributed by MGA: c. 1900–1912
Maker/Culture/Location: Possibly Ojibwe; MN
Source: Anonymous
Provenance: Part of the collection made by Alfred H. Peterson in Cass Lake, MN; collector was active 1920–74. Documented in photographs as worn by Chief John Smith (MNHS E97.1K r71, *Fig. 9.25*).
Overall length: 45½″; strap width: 6¾″; pocket panel: 15⅜″ × 15¾″; area above pocket panel: 5⅜″; pocket opening: 15⅛″; attached fringe: 3″ to 3½″

2011.208.154 Spot-stitch appliqué bandolier bag
Acquisition date: 5/19/2008
Date attributed by source: c. 1900–1950
Maker/Culture/Location: Possibly Ojibwe; MN
Source: Anonymous
Provenance: Part of the collection made by Alfred H. Peterson in Cass Lake, MN; collector was active 1920–74.
Overall length: 47″; strap width: 5¾″; pocket panel: 13¾″ × 14⅝″; area above pocket panel: 7⅜″; pocket opening: 11⅜″; attached fringe: 3½″

2011.208.155 Loom-woven panel bandolier bag
Acquisition date: 5/19/2008
Date attributed by source: c. 1880
Date attributed by MGA: Last third of 19th century
Maker/Culture/Location: Possibly Ojibwe; MN
Source: Anonymous
Provenance: Part of the collection made by Alfred H. Peterson in Cass Lake, MN; collector was active 1920–74.
Overall length: 43¼″; strap width: 5⅛″; pocket panel: 11½″ × 13″; area above pocket panel: 4″; pocket opening: 12″; integrated fringe: 5¾″

2011.208.156 Spot-stitch appliqué bandolier bag. *See Fig. 3.69*
Acquisition date: 5/19/2008
Date attributed by source: c. 1900–1950
Date attributed by MGA: Probably 1890s to 1920s
Maker/Culture/Location: Possibly Ojibwe; MN
Source: Anonymous
Provenance: Part of the collection made by Alfred H. Peterson in Cass Lake, MN; collector was active 1920–74.
Overall length: 41¾″; strap width: 5½″; pocket panel: 13½″ × 12¾″; area above pocket panel: 5¾″; pocket opening: 10⅞″; attached fringe: 2¼″

2011.208.157 Spot-stitch appliqué full panel bag, slit pocket
Acquisition date: 5/19/2008
Date attributed by source: c. 1900–1950
Date attributed by MGA: Probably first third of 20th century
Maker/Culture/Location: Possibly Ojibwe; MN
Source: Anonymous
Provenance: Part of the collection made by Alfred H. Peterson in Cass Lake, MN; collector was active 1920–74.
Overall length: 42″; strap width: 6⅞″; pocket panel: 18⅛″ × 17⅝″; pocket opening: 4¾″; attached fringe: 2½″ to 3½″

2011.208.158 Spot-stitch appliqué bandolier bag. *See p. 91 and Figs. 3.52, 3.73*
Acquisition date: 5/19/2008
Date attributed by source: c. 1900–1950
Date attributed by MGA: First half of 20th century
Maker/Culture/Location: Possibly Ojibwe; MN
Source: Anonymous
Provenance: Part of the collection made by Alfred H. Peterson in Cass Lake, MN; collector was active 1920–74.
Overall length: 41¾″; strap width: 6⅜″; pocket panel: 16¼″ × 15¼″; area above pocket panel: 3¾″; pocket opening: 14½″; no fringe

2011.208.159 Spot-stitch appliqué bandolier bag. *See Fig. 3.49*
Acquisition date: 5/19/2008
Date attributed by source: c. 1900–1950
Date attributed by MGA: First half of 20th century
Maker/Culture/Location: Possibly Ojibwe; MN
Source: Anonymous
Provenance: Part of the collection made by Alfred H. Peterson in Cass Lake, MN; collector was active 1920–74.
Overall length: 47½″; strap width: 6¼″; pocket panel: 17″ × 14⅞″; area above pocket panel: 7⅜″; pocket opening: 14⅞″; attached fringe: 3½″

2011.208.160 Spot-stitch appliqué bandolier bag, large single floral motif. *See Figs. 3.57, 9.28*
Acquisition date: 5/19/2008
Date attributed by source: c. 1900–1950
Date attributed by MGA: After 1890 and before 1920
Maker/Culture/Location: Possibly Ojibwe; MN
Source: Anonymous
Provenance: Part of the collection made by Alfred H. Peterson in Cass Lake, MN; collector was active 1920–74.
Overall length: 48″; strap width: 5¼″; pocket panel: 14″ to 14½″ × 12½″; area above pocket panel: 6½″ to 7½″; pocket opening: 13⅝″; attached fringe: 3″

2015.180.1 Loom-woven panel bandolier bag. *See Fig. 8.06*
Acquisition date: N/A
Date attributed by source: c. 1920s
Date attributed by MGA: Made before 1930
Maker/Culture/Location: Mary Posey; Ojibwe; Grand Portage Reservation
Source: William and Barbara Schoenwetter
Provenance: Documented in numerous dated photographs of Posey family members and in interviews with Mary Posey's foster daughter, Ellen Olson

Overall length: 35″; strap width: 9¼″; pocket panel: 5¾″ × 4¾″; area above pocket panel: 2″; pocket opening: 4¼″; attached fringe: 4″

2016.160.1 Spot-stitch appliqué full panel bandolier bag, no pocket; folded leaf, birds, and cornucopia motifs. *See Fig. 10.17*
Acquisition date: 12/16/2016
Date attributed by source: 1917
Maker/Culture/Location: Ojibwe; Lake Lena, Mille Lacs Reservation
Source: William and Barbara Schoenwetter
Provenance: Beaded "LAKE LENA MINN 1917" on strap, "1917" on pocket
Overall length: 40½″; strap width: 6½″; pocket panel: 12¼″ × 14″; area above pocket panel: 5″; fringe: 4″

6020.8 Loom-woven panel bandolier bag, thunderbird motifs. *See Figs. 2.31, 11.03*
Acquisition date: 4/15/1920
Date attributed by source: c. 1870–90
Date attributed by MGA: Probably 1870–1890s
Maker/Culture/Location: Possibly Ojibwe
Source: James C. Ferguson
Provenance: Printed cotton strap backing of stripes in bright blue, bright turquoise, and bright gold is typical of 1873 prints in sample books at the American Textile History Museum.
Overall length: 39½″; strap width: 3⅞″; pocket panel: 10⅞″ × 9¼″; area above pocket panel: 6⅝″; pocket opening: 8⅝″; integrated fringe on shoulder strap: 4½″; integrated fringe at bottom: 5½″

6020.9 Spot-stitch appliqué bandolier bag, ribbon appliqué. *See p. 1 and Figs. 2.17, 3.03, 3.21*
Acquisition date: 4/15/1920
Date attributed by source: c. 1880
Date attributed by MGA: c. 1860s–1880s
Maker/Culture/Location: Possibly Ojibwe
Source: James C. Ferguson
Provenance: N/A
Overall length: 41″; strap width: 4¾″; pocket panel: 9⅞″ × 10½″; area above pocket panel: 6¾″; pocket opening: 8⅜″; integrated fringe on shoulder strap: 3¾″; integrated fringe at bottom: 5½″

6020.10 Loom-woven panel bandolier bag. *See p. 10 and Fig. 3.40*
Acquisition date: 4/15/1920
Date attributed by source: Before 1920
Date attributed by MGA: c. 1870s–1920
Maker/Culture/Location: Possibly Ojibwe
Source: James C. Ferguson
Provenance: N/A
Overall length: 37″; strap width: 4⅜″; pocket panel: 8¼″ × 8½″; area above pocket panel: 5 5/16″; pocket opening: 7¾″; attached fringe at shoulder strap: 2″; integrated fringe at bottom: 4″

6037.4 Miniature loom-woven panel bandolier bag. *See Fig. 3.19*
Acquisition date: 6/19/1920
Date attributed by source: c. 1880
Date attributed by MGA: 1920 or earlier
Maker/Culture/Location: Probably Ojibwe
Source: Margaret C. Spencer
Provenance: N/A
Overall length: 33″; strap width: 4½″; pocket panel: 6½″ × 8½″; area above pocket panel: 4⅛″; pocket opening: 4⅞″; tab extensions (no fringe): 4″

6288.1 Spot-stitch appliqué bandolier bag, bird motifs. *See Fig. 3.50*
Acquisition date: 5/3/1923
Date attributed by source: Before 1923
Maker/Culture/Location: Probably Ojibwe; MN
Source: Clara Hill Lindley (daughter of James J. and Mary Hill of St. Paul)
Provenance: Beaded at top center of strap: "M.F."
Overall length: 48″; strap width: 5¾″; pocket panel: 14¾″ × 17″; area above pocket panel: 4¾″; pocket opening: 16″; attached fringe: 3⅝″

6333.6.A Spot-stitch appliqué bandolier bag. *See Figs. 3.48, 7.10*
Acquisition date: 10/4/1923
Date attributed by source: c. 1890
Maker/Culture/Location: Probably Ojibwe; MN
Source: Harriet M. Berry, wife of the collector Frank C. Berry (1859–1914)
Provenance: Berry made his collection while working as a traveling salesman for a mercantile company in northern Minnesota counties; the bags were probably collected before he was promoted to offices in Duluth in 1910.
Overall length: 44⅛″; strap width: 5⅝″; pocket panel: 12⅞″ × 12¼″; area above pocket panel: 6½″; pocket opening: 12⅛″; fringe: 3¼″ to 4¼″

6333.6.C Spot-stitch appliqué bandolier bag, no pocket. *See Fig. 7.11*
Acquisition date: 10/4/1923
Date attributed by source: c. 1880
Maker/Culture/Location: Probably Ojibwe; MN
Source: Harriet M. Berry, wife of the collector Frank C. Berry (1859–1914)
Provenance: Berry made his collection while working as a traveling salesman for a mercantile company in northern Minnesota counties; the bags were probably collected before he was promoted to offices in Duluth in 1910.
Overall length: 41″; strap width: 5½″; pocket panel: 17″ × 13″; area above pocket panel: 5¾″; fringe: 3½″

6333.6.D Spot-stitch appliqué bandolier bag. *See Fig. 7.08*
Acquisition date: 10/4/1923
Date attributed by source: c. 1880
Maker/Culture/Location: Probably Ojibwe; MN
Source: Harriet M. Berry, wife of the collector Frank C. Berry (1859–1914)
Provenance: Berry made his collection while working as a traveling salesman for a mercantile company in northern Minnesota counties; the bags were probably collected before he was promoted to offices in Duluth in 1910.

Overall length: $38\frac{1}{2}$"; strap width: $4\frac{3}{4}$"; pocket panel: $14\frac{1}{2}$" × 12"; area above pocket panel: $5\frac{3}{16}$"; pocket opening: $13\frac{3}{8}$"; fringe: $3\frac{1}{2}$"

6333.6.E Loom-woven panel bandolier bag, no pocket. *See Figs. 3.12, 7.05*
Acquisition date: 10/4/1923
Date attributed by source: c. 1880
Maker/Culture/Location: Probably Ojibwe; MN
Source: Harriet M. Berry, wife of the collector Frank C. Berry (1859–1914)
Provenance: Berry made his collection while working as a traveling salesman for a mercantile company in northern Minnesota counties; the bags were probably collected before he was promoted to offices in Duluth in 1910.
Overall length: $37\frac{3}{4}$"; strap width: $4\frac{1}{2}$"; pocket panel: $13\frac{3}{4}$" × 12"; fringe: $4\frac{3}{4}$"

6333.6.F Loom-woven panel bandolier bag. *See Figs. 3.42, 7.07*
Acquisition date: 10/4/1923
Date attributed by source: c. 1880
Maker/Culture/Location: Probably Ojibwe; MN
Source: Harriet M. Berry, wife of the collector Frank C. Berry (1859–1914)
Provenance: Berry made his collection while working as a traveling salesman for a mercantile company in northern Minnesota counties; the bags were probably collected before he was promoted to offices in Duluth in 1910.
Overall length: 43"; pocket panel: $14\frac{1}{2}$" × $12\frac{3}{4}$"; area above pocket panel: $5\frac{5}{8}$" to $6\frac{1}{4}$"; pocket opening: $12\frac{1}{2}$"

6333.6.G Loom-woven panel bandolier bag. *See Figs. 3.26, 7.06*
Acquisition date: 10/4/1923
Date attributed by source: c. 1880
Maker/Culture/Location: Probably Ojibwe; MN
Source: Harriet M. Berry, wife of the collector Frank C. Berry (1859–1914)
Provenance: Berry made his collection while working as a traveling salesman for a mercantile company in northern Minnesota counties; the bags were probably collected before he was promoted to offices in Duluth in 1910.
Overall length: $37\frac{1}{2}$"; pocket panel: $13\frac{1}{2}$" × $11\frac{1}{4}$"; area above pocket panel: $4\frac{5}{8}$" to $5\frac{1}{8}$"; pocket opening: 10"; fringe: $4\frac{1}{8}$"

6333.6.H Spot-stitch appliqué bandolier bag. *See p. iv (left) and Figs. 3.14, 3.61, 3.67, 7.09*
Acquisition date: 10/4/1923
Date attributed by source: c. 1880
Maker/Culture/Location: Probably Ojibwe; MN
Source: Harriet M. Berry, wife of the collector Frank C. Berry (1859–1914)
Provenance: Berry made his collection while working as a traveling salesman for a mercantile company in northern Minnesota counties; the bags were probably collected before he was promoted to offices in Duluth in 1910.
Overall length: $42\frac{3}{8}$"; strap width: $5\frac{1}{2}$"; pocket panel: $14\frac{1}{2}$" × $13\frac{1}{4}$"; area above pocket panel: $6\frac{1}{4}$"; pocket opening: $14\frac{1}{4}$"; fringe: $3\frac{3}{8}$"

6447 Miniature spot-stitch appliqué bandolier bag pocket without strap
Acquisition date: 2/19/1925
Date attributed by source: c. 1900
Maker/Culture/Location: Possibly Ojibwe
Source: Mrs. Frank C. Berry
Provenance: Unknown
Overall length: 11"; pocket panel: $6\frac{1}{2}$" × 6"; area above pocket panel: $1\frac{5}{8}$"; pocket opening: $5\frac{1}{4}$"; fringe: $2\frac{1}{2}$"

6507.12 Loom-woven panel bandolier bag. *See Figs. 2.01, 3.28*
Acquisition date: 11/21/1925
Date attributed by source: Before 1925
Date attributed by MGA: Mid to late 19th century
Maker/Culture/Location: Probably Ojibwe; MN
Source: National Society of Daughters of Founders and Patriots of America, Minnesota Chapter
Provenance: N/A
Overall length: $37\frac{1}{4}$"; strap width: $4\frac{3}{4}$"; pocket panel: 8" × $12\frac{1}{8}$"; area above pocket panel: $3\frac{3}{8}$"; pocket opening: $9\frac{7}{8}$"; floating panel: $2\frac{1}{8}$" × $10\frac{3}{8}$"; fringe: $5\frac{3}{8}$"

6585.3 Bandolier bag with loom-woven panels on black velvet
Acquisition date: 10/16/1926
Date attributed by source: c. 1890
Maker/Culture/Location: Possibly Ojibwe or Meskwaki (Sac and Fox)
Source: Ursula Stewart Wheaton
Provenance: N/A
Overall length: $35\frac{1}{4}$"; strap width: 2"; loomed top panel: $6\frac{3}{4}$" × $12\frac{1}{8}$"; spot-stitched bottom panel: $6\frac{1}{8}$" × $12\frac{7}{8}$"; pocket opening: $12\frac{1}{8}$"; fringe: $1\frac{1}{2}$"

7373.1 Loom-woven panel, bandolier bag pocket fragment. *See Fig. 2.30*
Acquisition date: 3/22/1935
Date attributed by source: c. 1890
Date attributed by MGA: Last half of 19th century
Maker/Culture/Location: Probably Ojibwe; MN
Source: Miss Ellen Wheelock
Provenance: Loom-woven bag panel imitating the bead pattern of a finger-woven sash
Overall length: $11\frac{1}{8}$"; pocket panel: $7\frac{1}{2}$" × 8"; fringe: $3\frac{3}{4}$"

7373.2.1,2 Loom-woven straps, bandolier bag fragments
Acquisition date: 3/22/1935
Date attributed by source: c. 1890
Date attributed by MGA: Last half of 19th century
Maker/Culture/Location: Probably Ojibwe; MN
Source: Miss Ellen Wheelock
Provenance: May be mates to 7373.1 as parts of a disassembled bandolier bag
Strap 1 (gold beads): strap length: $24\frac{1}{2}$"; strap width: $2\frac{1}{4}$" to $2\frac{5}{16}$"; integrated fringe: $6\frac{1}{4}$" to $6\frac{3}{8}$". *Strap 2 (pink beads):* strap length: $24\frac{7}{8}$"; strap width: $2\frac{5}{16}$" to $2\frac{3}{8}$"; integrated fringe: $6\frac{3}{8}$"

7418.7 Loom-woven panel bandolier bag. *See Fig. 3.41*
Acquisition date: 10/4/1935
Date attributed by source: c. 1880
Date attributed by MGA: Not earlier than 1860 and not later than 1910
Maker/Culture/Location: Probably Ojibwe; MN
Source: Mr. and Mrs. George Chase Christian
Provenance: Purchased by donors at the estate sale held on 6/5/1933 at Bishop Whipple's Faribault, MN, residence
Overall length: 38½″; strap width: 4⅞″; pocket panel: 12″ × 13¼″; area above pocket panel: 4¾″; pocket opening: 10½″; fringe: 3″

8014.1 Male Ojibwe doll wearing two spot-stitch appliqué bandolier bags
Acquisition date: 8/21/1940
Date attributed by source: Before 1940
Date attributed by MGA: Possibly 1900–1940
Maker/Culture/Location: Ojibwe; White Earth Reservation
Source: Miss Irene Hudson
Provenance: Acquired by donor at the White Earth Reservation
Overall length of doll: 13⅛″; *Bag 1, berry cluster motif:* strap width: $1\frac{1}{16}$″; pocket panel: 3½″ × 2¼″; pocket slit: ⅞″; fringe: ¾″. *Bag 2, yellow flower motif:* strap width: 1⅛″; pocket panel: 3¼″ × 2⅜″; pocket slit: ⅞″; fringe: ⅞″

8033.1 Loom-woven panel bandolier bag. *See Fig. 3.29*
Acquisition date: 10/12/1940
Date attributed by source: c. 1880
Date attributed by MGA: c. 1880
Maker/Culture/Location: Probably Ojibwe
Source: Margaret Wharton Fitzgerald Willis
Provenance: Includes cross motifs
Overall length: 38½″; strap length: 45″; strap width: 4⅜″; pocket panel: $10\frac{1}{16}$″ × 9⅛″; area above pocket panel: $4\frac{9}{16}$″; pocket opening: 8⅜″; fringe: 4″

8034.14 Spot-stitch appliqué bandolier bag. *See Fig. 3.91*
Acquisition date: 10/24/1940
Date attributed by source: c. 1900
Date attributed by MGA: Probably made between 1900–1940
Maker/Culture/Location: Probably Ojibwe
Source: Charles B. Lyon and C. P. Lyens
Provenance: N/A
Overall length: 44¼″; strap length: 41½″; strap width: 5⅝″; pocket panel: 15⅞″ × 18½″; area above pocket panel: 6⅝″; pocket opening: 15⅝″; fringe: 3¼″

8616.15 Loom-woven panel bandolier bag. *See Fig. 3.20*
Acquisition date: 11/25/1946
Date attributed by source: 1880–89
Maker/Culture/Location: Probably Ojibwe
Source: Eugene C. Alder
Provenance: Collected at Pine Ridge Reservation, SD
Overall length: 41″; strap length: 44″; strap width: 4″; pocket panel: 11″ × 10″; area above pocket panel: 6⅝″; pocket opening: 9¾″; fringe: 5″ (integrated fringe at bottom of bag), 3¾″ (integrated fringe at top of bag on shoulder strap)

8662.1 Miniature loom-woven panel bandolier bag. *See Fig. 3.32*
Acquisition date: 6/18/1947
Date attributed by source: Before 1947
Date attributed by MGA: Made before 1947
Maker/Culture/Location: Probably Ojibwe
Source: Mrs. H. C. Lawton
Provenance: N/A
Overall length: 19″; strap width: 1⅝″; pocket panel: 4⅛″ × 4″; area above pocket panel: 2″; pocket opening: 3¾″; integrated fringe: 2″

8701.1 Spot-stitch appliqué bandolier bag. *See p. vi and Fig. 3.05*
Acquisition date: 1/16/1948
Date attributed by source: c. 1890
Date attributed by MGA: c. 1890
Makcr/Culturc/Location: Probably Ojibwe
Source: Mrs. Carl W. Jones
Provenance: Reportedly collected through William F. "Buffalo Bill" Cody
Overall length: 44″; strap width: 6″; pocket panel: 13″ × 13″; area above pocket panel: 5½″; pocket opening: 11¼″; attached fringe: 4″

8723.6 Spot-stitch appliqué bandolier bag, no pocket. *See Fig. 3.92*
Acquisition date: 7/7/1948
Date attributed by source: c. 1885
Date attributed by MGA: Possibly 1890–1905
Maker/Culture/Location: Probably Ojibwe
Source: F. H. Holmes
Provenance: Associated with Warroad, Roseau County, MN
Overall length: 49″; strap width: 8″; pocket panel: 17⅛″ × 16¼″; area above pocket panel: 2¾″; fringe: 4″

9023.2 Miniature loom-woven panel bandolier bag. *See Fig. 3.35*
Acquisition date: 10/14/1953
Date attributed by source: c. 1925
Maker/Culture/Location: Probably Ojibwe
Source: Mrs. Beatrice Berthold and Gladys A. Fellows
Provenance: Donors attributed to Cass Lake region, MN, 1925
Overall length: 26½″; strap width: 2½″; pocket panel: 8½″ × 6¾″; area above pocket panel: 3⅝″; pocket opening: 6″; integrated fringe: 3½″

9120.2 Loom-woven panel bandolier bag. *See p. v and Fig. 1.01*
Acquisition date: 2/23/1954
Date attributed by source: c. 1890
Date attributed by MGA: Probably last third of 19th century
Maker/Culture/Location: Probably Ojibwe
Source: Mrs. Muriel S. Dean

Provenance: N/A
Overall length: 39 3/8"; strap width: 4 3/8"; pocket panel: 11 1/2" × 10 1/2"; area above pocket panel: 5 1/8"; pocket opening: N/A; integrated fringe on strap: 4 1/2"; integrated fringe at bottom: 4 1/2"

9606 Spot-stitch appliqué bandolier bag, slit pocket
Acquisition date: 3/13/1959
Date attributed by source: c. 1880
Maker/Culture/Location: N/A
Source: Mr. Cecil Yapp
Provenance: Bag was a gift to Mr. Yapp from Abby Day Starkey of NY. Abby's father was an Episcopalian minister; her parents were missionaries to Dakota Territory.
Overall length: 41 7/8"; strap width: 5 1/6"; pocket panel: 16 1/4" × 13 3/8"; pocket opening: 3 1/2"; no fringe

---

9666.7 Loom-woven panel bandolier bag. *See Figs. 3.30, 3.79*
Acquisition date: 7/8/1959
Date attributed by source: c. 1880
Date attributed by MGA: Probably 1880 or earlier
Maker/Culture/Location: Probably Ojibwe
Source: Dudley Hersey Mudge and Grace Warner Mudge
Provenance: Originally in the collection of Eva A. Mudge
Overall length: 42 1/4"; strap width: 3 1/2"; pocket panel: 9 3/8" × 10 3/16"; area above pocket panel: 8 1/2"; pocket opening: 9"; integrated fringe: 4 1/2"

9666.8 Spot-stitch appliqué bandolier bag. *See Figs. 3.47, 9.13*
Acquisition date: 7/8/1959
Date attributed by source: c. 1890
Date attributed by MGA: Probably 1890–1920s
Maker/Culture/Location: Probably Ojibwe
Source: Dudley Hersey Mudge and Grace Warner Mudge
Provenance: Originally in the collection of Eva A. Mudge
Overall length: 42"; strap width: 4 3/8"; pocket panel: 11 3/8" × 10 5/16"; area above pocket panel: 6 1/4"; pocket opening: 10 7/8"; attached fringe: 3"

9859.19 Spot-stitch appliqué bandolier bag
Acquisition date: 8/16/1960
Date attributed by source: c. 1900
Date attributed by MGA: Probably 1900–1930s
Maker/Culture/Location: Probably Ojibwe; possibly Teton Dakota
Source: Mrs. W. C. Bryant
Provenance: Center of strap beaded "Eathons," possible misspelling of Canadian department store Eaton's; acquired at Cheyenne River Reservation, SD
Overall length: 42 1/4"; strap width: 5 3/8"; pocket panel: 14 1/2" × 15 1/8"; pocket opening (at top edge): 14 1/2"; fringe: 4"

9907 Spot-stitch appliqué full panel bandolier bag, slit pocket
Acquisition date: 1960
Date attributed by source: Not later than 1900
Date attributed by MGA: Probably first third of 20th century
Maker/Culture/Location: Possibly Ojibwe
Source: Mrs. Grace Stillwell Boswell
Provenance: Collected by Eugene J. Stillwell
Overall length: 41 1/2"; strap width: 5 5/8"; pocket panel: 15 5/8" × 12 7/8"; pocket opening: 4 3/8"; integrated fringe: 3"

10000.128 Possible bandolier bag strap, fragment
Acquisition date: 1959
Date attributed by source: c. 1875–1925
Date attributed by MGA: Possibly earlier than 1918 but no later than 1959
Maker/Culture/Location: Probably Ojibwe; probably Mille Lacs Reservation
Source: Harry Darius Ayer and Jeannette Ora Foster Ayer
Provenance: The Mille Lacs Indian Museum and Trading Post on Highway 169 in Onamia, MN, was operated by Harry and Jeanette Ayer. They developed working relationships with many Mille Lacs Band members between 1918 and 1959.
Strap: 40" × 6 1/4"

10000.148 Small loom-woven panel bandolier bag. *See Fig. 3.38*
Acquisition date: 1959
Date attributed by source: Before 1959
Date attributed by MGA: Possibly earlier than 1918 but no later than 1959
Maker/Culture/Location: Probably Ojibwe; probably Mille Lacs Reservation
Source: Harry Darius Ayer and Jeannette Ora Foster Ayer
Provenance: The Mille Lacs Indian Museum and Trading Post on Highway 169 in Onamia, MN, was operated by Harry and Jeanette Ayer. They developed working relationships with many Mille Lacs Band members between 1918 and 1959.
Overall length: 28 1/2"; strap width: 1 1/4"; pocket panel: 8 1/4" × 6 1/2"; area above pocket panel: 3 3/4"; pocket opening: 7"; fringe: 2 3/4"

10000.149 Small spot-stitch appliqué bandolier bag. *See Figs. 3.97, 10.27*
Acquisition date: 1959
Date attributed by source: c. 1875–1925
Date attributed by MGA: Possibly earlier than 1918 but no later than 1959
Maker/Culture/Location: Probably Ojibwe; probably Mille Lacs Reservation
Source: Harry Darius Ayer and Jeannette Ora Foster Ayer
Provenance: The Mille Lacs Indian Museum and Trading Post on Highway 169 in Onamia, MN, was operated by Harry and Jeanette Ayer. They developed working relationships with many Mille Lacs Band members between 1918 and 1959.
Overall length: 27 3/4"; strap width: 4 1/8"; pocket panel: 9 7/8" × 9 1/8"; area above pocket panel: 2 1/2"; pocket opening: 8 1/4"; fringe: 2 3/8"

10000.150 Small spot-stitch appliqué bandolier bag. *See Fig. 10.28*
Acquisition date: 1959
Date attributed by source: c. 1875–1925
Date attributed by MGA: Possibly earlier than 1918 but no later than 1959
Maker/Culture/Location: Probably Ojibwe; probably Mille Lacs Reservation
Source: Harry Darius Ayer and Jeannette Ora Foster Ayer
Provenance: The Mille Lacs Indian Museum and Trading Post on Highway 169 in Onamia, MN, was operated by Harry and Jeanette Ayer. They developed working relationships with many Mille Lacs Band members between 1918 and 1959.
Overall length: 28⅜″; strap width: 4½″; pocket panel: 9¾″ × 9⅝″; area above pocket panel: 2¾″; pocket opening: 8¼″; fringe: 2¼″

10000.151 Loom-woven panel bandolier bag. *See Fig. 3.04*
Acquisition date: 1959
Date attributed by source: c. 1850–1900
Date attributed by MGA: Late 19th century
Maker/Culture/Location: Probably Ojibwe; probably Mille Lacs Reservation
Source: Harry Darius Ayer and Jeannette Ora Foster Ayer
Provenance: The Mille Lacs Indian Museum and Trading Post on Highway 169 in Onamia, MN, was operated by Harry and Jeanette Ayer. They developed working relationships with many Mille Lacs Band members between 1918 and 1959.
Overall length: 38″ (with extensions); strap width: 5¼″; pocket panel: 11½″ × 12″; area above pocket panel: 2¼″; pocket opening: 5½″; fringe: 2¾″

10000.152 Loom-woven panel bandolier bag, thunderbird motifs. *See Figs. 2.32, 3.25*
Acquisition date: 1959
Date attributed by source: c. 1850–1900
Date attributed by MGA: Possibly mid to late 19th century
Maker/Culture/Location: Probably Ojibwe; probably Mille Lacs Reservation
Source: Harry Darius Ayer and Jeannette Ora Foster Ayer
Provenance: The Mille Lacs Indian Museum and Trading Post on Highway 169 in Onamia, MN, was operated by Harry and Jeanette Ayer. They developed working relationships with many Mille Lacs Band members between 1918 and 1959.
Overall length: 36″; strap width: 4″; pocket panel: 10½″ × 9½″; area above pocket panel: 6⅝″; pocket opening: 8⅜″

10000.153 Spot-stitch appliqué bandolier bag. *See p. iv (right) and Figs. 3.63, 10.29*
Acquisition date: 1959
Date attributed by source: c. 1875–1925
Date attributed by MGA: Possibly earlier than 1918 but no later than 1959
Maker/Culture/Location: Probably Ojibwe; probably Mille Lacs Reservation
Source: Harry Darius Ayer and Jeannette Ora Foster Ayer
Provenance: The Mille Lacs Indian Museum and Trading Post on Highway 169 in Onamia, MN, was operated by Harry and Jeanette Ayer. They developed working relationships with many Mille Lacs Band members between 1918 and 1959.
Overall length: 44″; strap width: 6½″; pocket panel: 14⅝″ × 13½″ to 14″; area above pocket panel: 5⅞″; pocket opening: 5″; fringe: 3″

10000.154 Spot-stitch appliqué bandolier bag. *See Fig. 10.23*
Acquisition date: 1959
Date attributed by source: c. 1875–1925
Date attributed by MGA: Possibly earlier than 1918 but no later than 1959
Maker/Culture/Location: Probably Ojibwe; probably Mille Lacs Reservation
Source: Harry Darius Ayer and Jeannette Ora Foster Ayer
Provenance: The Mille Lacs Indian Museum and Trading Post on Highway 169 in Onamia, MN, was operated by Harry and Jeanette Ayer. They developed working relationships with many Mille Lacs Band members between 1918 and 1959.
Overall length: 44½″; strap width: 5″; pocket panel: 12¾ to 13″ × 14″; area above pocket panel: 6″ to 6⅜″; pocket opening: 12¼″; fringe: 5″

10000.155 Spot-stitch appliqué bandolier bag, no pocket; folded leaf, cornucopia, and pod motifs. *See Fig. 10.47*
Acquisition date: 1959
Date attributed by source: c. 1875–1925
Date attributed by MGA: Possibly earlier than 1918 but no later than 1959
Maker/Culture/Location: Probably Ojibwe; probably Mille Lacs Reservation
Source: Harry Darius Ayer and Jeannette Ora Foster Ayer
Provenance: The Mille Lacs Indian Museum and Trading Post on Highway 169 in Onamia, MN, was operated by Harry and Jeanette Ayer. They developed working relationships with many Mille Lacs Band members between 1918 and 1959. This bag was the inspiration for the bag made by Maude Kegg, Ojibwe bead artist of Mille Lacs Reservation (PAM 1991.019.0001)
Overall length: 42″; strap width: 5⅜″; pocket panel: 16½ to 17″ × 15½″; area above pocket panel: 2¼″; fringe: 3¼″

10000.156 Spot-stitch appliqué bandolier bag, oak leaf motif. *See Fig. 3.54*
Acquisition date: 1959
Date attributed by source: c. 1875–1925
Date attributed by MGA: Possibly earlier than 1918 but no later than 1959
Maker/Culture/Location: Probably Ojibwe; probably Mille Lacs Reservation
Source: Harry Darius Ayer and Jeannette Ora Foster Ayer
Provenance: The Mille Lacs Indian Museum and Trading Post on Highway

169 in Onamia, MN, was operated by Harry and Jeanette Ayer. They developed working relationships with many Mille Lacs Band members between 1918 and 1959.
Overall length: 38″; strap width: 5⅞″; pocket panel: 14″ × 12″; area above pocket panel: 4⅝″; pocket opening: 13¾″; fringe: 3″

10000.157 Spot-stitch appliqué full panel bandolier bag, no pocket. *See Fig. 2.52*
Acquisition date: 1959
Date attributed by source: Before 1925
Date attributed by MGA: Possibly earlier than 1918 but no later than 1925
Maker/Culture/Location: Probably Ojibwe, probably Mille Lacs Reservation
Source: Harry Darius Ayer and Jeannette Ora Foster Ayer
Provenance: The Mille Lacs Indian Museum and Trading Post on Highway 169 in Onamia, MN, was operated by Harry and Jeanette Ayer. They developed working relationships with many Mille Lacs Band members between 1918 and 1959. Bag worn by Ojibwe dancer at Mille Lacs Reservation before 1925 (MNHS E97.37 p37).
Overall length: 40″; strap width: 7⅝″; pocket panel: 16⅜″ × 16¼ to 17″; fringe: 3½″

10000.158 Spot-stitch appliqué full panel bandolier bag, faux pocket. *See Fig. 3.06*
Acquisition date: 1959
Date attributed by source: c. 1875–1925
Date attributed by MGA: Possibly earlier than 1918 but no later than 1959
Maker/Culture/Location: Probably Ojibwe; probably Mille Lacs Reservation
Source: Harry Darius Ayer and Jeannette Ora Foster Ayer
Provenance: The Mille Lacs Indian Museum and Trading Post on Highway 169 in Onamia, MN, was operated by Harry and Jeanette Ayer. They developed working relationships with many Mille Lacs Band members between 1918 and 1959.
Overall length: 40½″; strap width: 5½″ to 5¾″; pocket panel: 15¼″ × 17⅝″; faux pocket opening: 5⅜″; fringe: 2¾″

10000.159 Spot-stitch appliqué full panel bandolier bag, no pocket. *See Fig. 2.51*
Acquisition date: 1959
Date attributed by source: c. 1875–1925
Date attributed by MGA: Possibly earlier than 1918 but no later than 1959
Maker/Culture/Location: Probably Ojibwe; probably Mille Lacs Reservation
Source: Harry Darius Ayer and Jeannette Ora Foster Ayer
Provenance: The Mille Lacs Indian Museum and Trading Post on Highway 169 in Onamia, MN, was operated by Harry and Jeanette Ayer. They developed working relationships with many Mille Lacs Band members between 1918 and 1959.
Overall length: 44½″; strap width: 6½″; pocket panel: 14⅞″ × 17½″; fringe: 3¾″

10000.245 Possible loom-woven bandolier bag pocket, fragment. *See Fig. 3.31*
Acquisition date: 1959
Date attributed by source: c. 1875–1900
Date attributed by MGA: Probably between 1875 and 1900
Maker/Culture/Location: Probably Ojibwe; probably Mille Lacs Reservation
Source: Harry Darius Ayer and Jeannette Ora Foster Ayer
Provenance: The Mille Lacs Indian Museum and Trading Post on Highway 169 in Onamia, MN, was operated by Harry and Jeanette Ayer. They developed working relationships with many Mille Lacs Band members between 1918 and 1959.
Pocket panel: 10¼″ × 9¾″; fringe: 5⅜″

10000.366 Spot-stitch appliqué bandolier bag. *See Fig. 10.37*
Acquisition date: 1959
Date attributed by source: Before 1929
Date attributed by MGA: Possibly earlier than 1918 but no later than 1928
Maker/Culture/Location: Probably Ojibwe; probably Mille Lacs Reservation
Source: Harry Darius Ayer and Jeannette Ora Foster Ayer
Provenance: The Mille Lacs Indian Museum and Trading Post on Highway 169 in Onamia, MN, was operated by Harry and Jeanette Ayer. They developed working relationships with many Mille Lacs Band members between 1918 and 1959. This bag worn by Tom Skinaway at Mille Lacs Indian Trading Post, 1928 (MNHS E97.1S r4).
Overall length: 44½″; strap width: 6¾″; pocket panel: 19⅝″ × 18½″; area above pocket panel: 4½″; pocket opening: 17¾″; fringe: 5″

10000.609 Spot-stitch appliqué bandolier bag, no pocket; arrowhead, cornucopia, and "Greek" column motifs. *See Figs. 3.86, 10.35*
Acquisition date: 1959
Date attributed by source: c. 1920–29
Date attributed by MGA: Possibly earlier than 1918 but no later than 1925
Maker/Culture/Location: Probably Ojibwe; probably Mille Lacs Reservation
Source: Harry Darius Ayer and Jeannette Ora Foster Ayer
Provenance: The Mille Lacs Indian Museum and Trading Post on Highway 169 in Onamia, MN, was operated by Harry and Jeanette Ayer. They developed working relationships with many Mille Lacs Band members between 1918 and 1959. This bag is worn in two photographs of Tom Skinaway at Mille Lacs Indian Trading Post about 1925 (MNHS E97.1S r5 [*Fig. 10.34*] and E97.38 r8).
Overall length: 39″; strap width: 6½″; pocket panel: 14½″ × 14⅞″ (includes floating panel); floating panel: 2⅞″; fringe: 2½″

10000.610 Spot-stitch appliqué bandolier bag. *See Figs. 2.09, 3.17, 10.21*
Acquisition date: 1959

Date attributed by source: c. 1875–1925
Date attributed by MGA: Possibly earlier than 1918 but no later than 1959
Maker/Culture/Location: Probably Ojibwe; probably Mille Lacs Reservation
Source: Harry Darius Ayer and Jeannette Ora Foster Ayer
Provenance: The Mille Lacs Indian Museum and Trading Post on Highway 169 in Onamia, MN, was operated by Harry and Jeanette Ayer. They developed working relationships with many Mille Lacs Band members between 1918 and 1959.
Overall length: 49½"; strap width: 5¾"; pocket panel: 13½ to 14⅜" × 12⅞"; area above pocket panel: 6¾"; pocket opening: 10½"; fringe: 4½"

10000.615 Spot-stitch appliqué bandolier bag. *See Figs. 3.87, 10.32*
Acquisition date: 1959
Date attributed by source: c. 1875–1925
Date attributed by MGA: Possibly earlier than 1918 but no later than 1959
Maker/Culture/Location: Probably Ojibwe; probably Mille Lacs Reservation
Source: Harry Darius Ayer and Jeannette Ora Foster Ayer
Provenance: The Mille Lacs Indian Museum and Trading Post on Highway 169 in Onamia, MN, was operated by Harry and Jeanette Ayer. They developed working relationships with many Mille Lacs Band members between 1918 and 1959. A namesake bag with "mesk Ed Skinaway" beaded above the pocket opening may refer to Ojibwe Miskoogwaniash, or Ed Skinaway of the Mille Lacs Reservation.
Overall length: N/A; strap length: 23⅝"; strap width: 5⅛"; pocket panel: 17⅛" × 16 17/32"; pocket opening: N/A; no fringe

---

10000.616 Spot-stitch appliqué full panel bandolier bag, slit pocket
Acquisition date: 1959
Date attributed by source: c. 1875–1925
Date attributed by MGA: Possibly earlier than 1918 but no later than 1959
Maker/Culture/Location: Probably Ojibwe; probably Mille Lacs Reservation
Source: Harry Darius Ayer and Jeannette Ora Foster Ayer
Provenance: The Mille Lacs Indian Museum and Trading Post on Highway 169 in Onamia, MN, was operated by Harry and Jeanette Ayer. They developed working relationships with many Mille Lacs Band members between 1918 and 1959.
Overall length: 42½"; strap width: 6½"; pocket panel: 17⅝" × 21"; pocket opening: 4"; fringe: 3⅜"

10000.620 Spot-stitch appliqué full panel bandolier bag, no pocket. *See Fig. 10.31*
Acquisition date: 1959
Date attributed by source: c. 1900–1925
Date attributed by MGA: Possibly earlier than 1918 but no later than 1959
Maker/Culture/Location: Probably Ojibwe; probably Mille Lacs Reservation
Source: Harry Darius Ayer and Jeannette Ora Foster Ayer
Provenance: The Mille Lacs Indian Museum and Trading Post on Highway 169 in Onamia, MN, was operated by Harry and Jeanette Ayer. They developed working relationships with many Mille Lacs Band members between 1918 and 1959. Ayers associated this bag with Ojibwe "Charlie Boyd," Mille Lacs Reservation.
Overall length: 36½"; strap width: 5½"; pocket panel: 14⅝" × 14⅜"; fringe: 3¾"

10000.625 Spot-stitch appliqué full panel bandolier bag, faux pocket. *See Fig. 10.25*
Acquisition date: 1959
Date attributed by source: c. 1875–1925
Date attributed by MGA: Possibly earlier than 1918 but no later than 1959
Maker/Culture/Location: Probably Ojibwe, probably Mille Lacs Reservation
Source: Harry Darius Ayer and Jeannette Ora Foster Ayer
Provenance: The Mille Lacs Indian Museum and Trading Post on Highway 169 in Onamia, MN, was operated by Harry and Jeanette Ayer. They developed working relationships with many Mille Lacs Band members between 1918 and 1959. The Ayers associated this bag with Mille Lacs area Ojibwe Charles Gahbow (son of John Gahbow).
Overall length: 41½"; strap width: 5½"; pocket panel: 14¾" × 18⅜"; faux pocket opening: 4⅜"; fringe: 2¾"

10000.647 Miniature leather-backed loom-woven panel bag
Acquisition date: 1959
Date attributed by source: c. 1925–59
Date attributed by MGA: Possibly earlier than 1918 but no later than 1959
Maker/Culture/Location: Probably Ojibwe; probably Mille Lacs Reservation
Source: Harry Darius Ayer and Jeannette Ora Foster Ayer
Provenance: The Mille Lacs Indian Museum and Trading Post on Highway 169 in Onamia, MN, was operated by Harry and Jeanette Ayer. They developed working relationships with many Mille Lacs Band members between 1918 and 1959.
Overall length: 11½"; strap width: 1½"; pocket panel: 4¼" × 3½"; pocket opening: 1⅜"; fringe: 3"

10000.714 Spot-stitch appliqué full panel bandolier bag, slit pocket. *See Figs. 2.11, 3.80, 3.96*
Acquisition date: 1959
Date attributed by source: c. 1875–1925
Date attributed by MGA: Possibly earlier than 1916
Maker/Culture/Location: Probably Ojibwe; possibly Mille Lacs Reservation or White Earth Reservation
Source: Harry Darius Ayer and Jeannette Ora Foster Ayer
Provenance: The Mille Lacs Indian Museum and Trading Post on Highway

169 in Onamia, MN, was operated by Harry and Jeanette Ayer. They developed working relationships with many Mille Lacs Band members between 1918 and 1959. This bag probably collected by John Howard Reed, superintendent at the White Earth Reservation 1910–16, and donated to the Ayers in 1963 by Reed's daughters, Mrs. Watson and Mrs. Fierke.

Overall length: 42½″; strap width: 5⅜″; pocket panel: 13⅝ to 14½″ × 18″; pocket opening: 4½″; fringe: 4″

10000.715 Loom-woven panel bandolier bag. *See Fig. 3.88*

Acquisition date: 1959

Date attributed by source: c. 1875–1925

Date attributed by MGA: Possibly mid to late 19th century

Maker/Culture/Location: Probably Ojibwe; probably Mille Lacs Reservation

Source: Harry Darius Ayer and Jeannette Ora Foster Ayer

Provenance: The Mille Lacs Indian Museum and Trading Post on Highway 169 in Onamia, MN, was operated by Harry and Jeanette Ayer. They developed working relationships with many Mille Lacs Band members between 1918 and 1959.

Overall length: 43½″; strap width: 6⅜″; pocket panel: 13⅝ to 15⅝″ × 13″; area above pocket panel: 8″; pocket opening: 14⅝″; fringe: 4¾″

10000.1248 Leather male doll wearing two miniature loom-woven panel bandolier bags

Acquisition date: 1959

Date attributed by source: Before 1959

Date attributed by MGA: Possibly earlier than 1918 but no later than 1959

Maker/Culture/Location: Probably Ojibwe; probably Mille Lacs Reservation

Source: Harry Darius Ayer and Jeannette Ora Foster Ayer

Provenance: The Mille Lacs Indian Museum and Trading Post on Highway 169 in Onamia, MN, was operated by Harry and Jeanette Ayer. They developed working relationships with many Mille Lacs Band members between 1918 and 1959.

Both bags: Overall length: 11″; strap width: 1⅛″; pocket panel: 3″ × 2¼″; area above pocket panel: 1⅝″; pocket opening: 2½″; fringe: 1½″

110IN.21 Miniature spot-stitch appliqué bandolier bag

Acquisition date: Unknown

Date attributed by source: c. 1890

Maker/Culture/Location: Possibly Ojibwe

Source: Unknown

Provenance: N/A

Overall length: 10½″; strap width: ½″; pocket panel: 3¹¹⁄₁₆″ × 3½″; area above pocket panel: ⅝″; pocket opening: 3″; fringe: 2¼″

130IN.4 Miniature spot-stitch appliqué bandolier bag

Acquisition date: Unknown

Date attributed by source: c. 1900

Maker/Culture/Location: Possibly Ojibwe

Source: Unknown

Provenance: N/A

Overall length: 9½″; strap width: ⁵⁄₁₆″; pocket panel: 2⅛″ × 3″; area above pocket panel: 2¼″; pocket opening: 2⁹⁄₁₆″; fringe: 1″

505IN.1 Spot-stitch appliqué bandolier bag in three pieces

Acquisition date: Unknown

Date attributed by source: N/A

Maker/Culture/Location: Possibly Ojibwe

Source: Unknown

Provenance: N/A

Overall length: 42″; strap length: 23⅝″ to 24″; strap width: 7⅝″; pocket panel: 18″ × 16¾″; fringe: 3⅜″

X.1.506 Loom-woven pocket panel

Acquisition date: 1996 (transfer of ownership to MNHS)

Date attributed by source: c. 1880–1950

Date attributed by MGA: Probably last half of 19th century

Maker/Culture/Location: Possibly Ojibwe

Source: Sibley House Association

Provenance: N/A

Overall length: 12½″ × 12⅝″; fringe tabs: 5″ including warp extensions

Appendix 2

Bandolier Bag Care, Handling, Storage, and Cleaning

Ann Frisinia, Minnesota Historical Society Textile Conservator

Basic care

Bandolier bags are fragile composite objects that may be fabricated with many combinations of layers of silk, cotton, and wool textiles, newspaper, oilcloth, linen and cotton threading material, glass beads, sequins, faceted metal beads, wool yarn, and metal tinkler cones. Each of these materials ages in specific ways at differing rates. It is very important to support a bag while handling it, in order to prevent undue flexing and folding. Excessive manipulation of a bag could result in tearing friable fabrics, especially when they are applied in layers; breaking fragile cotton thread; loosening glass beads, sequins, tinkler cone or tassel fringe; and other damage. Take care not to wear jewelry that can catch and tear loose embellishments or fringe. For more detailed information, see *Caring for American Indian Objects: A Practical and Cultural Guide,*" edited by Sherelyn Ogden (St. Paul: MNHS Press, 2004).

Basic storage

Store bags flat with a small supportive pillow or scrunched-up piece of acid-free tissue along the folds of the shoulder band. A shallow acid-free box lined with unbuffered acid-free tissue is ideal, but a pillow case or a muslin case supported on a flat board will work as well. Enclosed storage also prevents the loss of beads. Dust and general atmospheric pollutants will eventually result in damaging the fibers and discoloring the bag. Finally, high humidity or rapid temperature fluctuations are to be avoided, as they stress all materials as well as promote glass disease and the rusting of metal faceted beads and tinkler cones.

Detailed instructions for bandolier storage mounts can be found on the MNHS website at http://www.mnhs.org/preserve/conservation/reports/bandolier_storage.pdf. Depending on your skill level, it should take approximately four hours to complete a storage mount.

Glass bead issues and disease

Glass disease affects certain glass beads due to a problem in their manufacturing. Signs of glass disease include sweaty, sticky surface, crusty deposits, crizzling, or a white haze. Finally, beads with glass disease will bleach the fabric at points of direct contact. The only way to prevent glass disease is to keep the beads dry and cool. It is also important to note that some bugle beads have layers of colored film inside them. These layers of colored film can delaminate and flake off with abrasive handling or threading material. Take care when you see bugle beads to check for this issue and handle accordingly.

Basic display

Bandolier bags are not self-supporting and will flop and flex if not properly displayed. A flat or slanted padded board will support most bags well enough. Avoid vertical hanging, as the bag may not be strong enough to support itself, especially if there is heavy beading. Keep all fragile textiles out of direct sunlight to prevent fading and weakening of fibers. Cover bandolier bags with a plexi-box or shadow box to prevent dust and dirt from building up on the surface.

Basic cleaning

Surface cleaning can be successful, if done with care. Before surface cleaning, be sure to examine the textile thoroughly for loose beads, sequins, or fringes; open seams; or splits or areas of loss within the fabric. Bag loose pieces and document their location. You can clean the surface with a low-suction vacuum cleaner fitted with a micro suction attachment (available at fabric stores). Place the soft brush of the nozzle on the textile in a systematic row-by-row manner. By methodically cleaning the textile, you can be assured of equal cleaning throughout.

If the beads are dirty after surface cleaning, and the threading material is strong and stable, you may use a swab dampened slightly with isopropyl (rubbing) alcohol or your own saliva for a more thorough method of surface cleaning. Be sure to choose a rubbing alcohol that does not contain glycerin, as this will leave behind a sticky water-attractive surface. Conservators within the museum community use saliva instead of rubbing alcohol to clean beads because of its mild enzymatic cleaning action. When swabbing, take care not to wet the threading material, as this could result in mechanical damage or promote mold colonies to establish within the beads. Gently roll the swab across the surface and immediately discard it when it becomes dirty. Do not rub back and forth, as this will drive dirt deep into the crevices.

Appendix 3

Bags in Other Collections

These repositories hold one or more bandolier bags that are either identified as Minnesota Ojibwe gashkibidaaganag or are likely examples.

American Museum of Natural History, Washington, DC
Canadian Museum of History, Gatineau, Quebec
Denver Art Museum
Ely-Winton Historical Society, Ely, MN
Field Museum of Natural History, Chicago, IL
Grand Portage National Monument, Grand Portage, MN
Grand Rapids Public Museum, Grand Rapids, MI
Grant County Historical Society, Elbow Lake, MN
Haffenreffer Museum of Anthropology, Providence, RI
Heard Museum, Phoenix, AZ
Lake of the Woods Museum, Kenora, Ontario
Logan Museum of Anthropology, Beloit College, Beloit, WI
Madeline Island Museum, La Pointe, WI
Maryhill Museum of Art, Goldendale, WA
McCord Museum, Montreal, Quebec
Milwaukee Public Museum
Minneapolis Institute of Arts
Missouri Historical Society, St. Louis, MO
Montana Historical Society, Helena, MT
Morrison County Historical Society, Little Falls, MN
Mower County Historical Society, Austin, MN
National Cowboy and Western Heritage Museum, Oklahoma City, OK
National Museum of the American Indian, Smithsonian Institution, Washington, DC
National Museum of Natural History, Smithsonian Institution, Washington, DC
Nebraska Historical Society, Lincoln, NE
Northwest Museum of Arts and Culture, Spokane, WA
Peabody Essex Museum, Salem, MA
Peabody Museum of Archaeology and Ethnology, Harvard University, Cambridge, MA
Science Museum of Minnesota, St. Paul, MN
Tweed Museum of Art, University of Minnesota Duluth
Wisconsin State Historical Society, Madison, WI

Notes

Abbreviations Used in Notes and Captions

BAE	Bureau of American Ethnology, Smithsonian Institution, Washington, DC
BCHS	Becker County Historical Society, Detroit Lakes, MN
CCHS	Cook County Historical Society, Grand Marais, MN
CMH	Canadian Museum of History, Gatineau, Quebec
CVM	Chippewa Valley Museum, Eau Claire, WI
DIA	Detroit Institute of Arts
FDLCCM	Fond du Lac Cultural Center and Museum, Fond du Lac Reservation, MN
GPNM	Grand Portage National Monument, Grand Portage, MN
HCABU	History Center, Archives of Bethel University and Converge Worldwide—BGC, St. Paul, MN
KAMLASC	Kathryn A. Martin Library Archives and Special Collections, University of Minnesota Duluth
LMA	Logan Museum of Anthropology, Beloit College, Beloit, WI
MIA	Minneapolis Institute of Art
MNAWHSC	Min No Aya Win Human Services Center, Fond du Lac Reservation, MN
MNHS	Minnesota Historical Society, St. Paul, MN
MPM	Milwaukee Public Museum
NAA-SI	National Anthropological Archives–Smithsonian Institution, Washington, DC
NMAI	National Museum of the American Indian, Smithsonian Institution, Washington, DC
NMNH	National Museum of Natural History, Smithsonian Institution, Washington, DC
PAM	Plains Art Museum, Fargo, ND
PCHS	Pennington County Historical Society, Thief River Falls, MN
SMM	Science Museum of Minnesota, St. Paul, MN
WHS	Wisconsin Historical Society, Madison, WI

Location Details for Uncaptioned Gashkibidaaganag

page iii	Figure 1.13
page iv	Figures 7.09, 8.15, 10.29
page v	Figure 1.01
page vi	Figures 3.05, 2.49
page 1	Figure 3.03
page 2	MNHS 1978
page 3	Figure 12.18
page 8	Figure 9.08
page 10	Figure 3.40
page 11	Figure 1.14
page 31	Figure 9.09
page 55	MNHS 74.32.5
page 83	Figure 9.26
page 91	MNHS 2011.208.158
page 101	Figure 6.01
page 105	Figure 7.01
page 112	Figure 8.18
page 127	Figure 9.15
page 144	Figure 10.46
page 176	Figure 11.10
page 185	Figure 12.11

Notes to Preface

1. A pronunciation is available at the Ojibwe People's Dictionary, http://ojibwe.lib.umn.edu/main-entry/gashkibidaagan-na; for a discussion of the word itself, see Chapter 1. Minnesota Historical Society (hereafter, MNHS) collections staff weighed a sample of twelve items, August 2016. Ten gashkibidaaganag, including early small loom-woven examples and oversize mid-twentieth-century spot-stitched ones, weighed between 1 and 3.65 pounds. A beaded red wool precursor bag weighed 5 ounces and a late nineteenth/early twentieth "stained glass panel" or beaded wall hanging weighed 7 ounces. By catalog numbers, all MNHS: 69.138.5 = 2.5 pounds, 74.32.5 = 2.1 pounds, 532.E157 = 1.6 pounds, 19892.67.1 = 1.1 pounds, 1990.4502.5 = 3.25 pounds,

1993.260.10 = 3.2 pounds, 1995.46.11 = 3.7 pounds, 8033.1 = 1.5 pounds, 8034.14 = 3 pounds, 8616.15 = 1.4 pounds.

2. People of this group use both *Ojibwe* and *Anishinaabe* to refer to themselves. *Ojibwe* (and *Chippewa,* a misspelling of the same name) have been used throughout the last two centuries to refer to the people. Anishinaabe, which means *original man,* carries the larger meaning of an indigenous person, as distinct from a non-indigenous person. In this book, which introduces many other terms and quotes from many historical sources, I have chosen to use the more familiar *Ojibwe.*

Notes to Chapter 1

Epigraph: Gilfillan, "Ojibways in Minnesota," 101–2. The earliest known version of this comment is in Gilfillan's Scrapbook 1872–98, p. 42–45; it is clipped from the *Minnesota Missionary* (Faribault, MN) 3.1 (October 1879): 2, in Gilfillan papers, MNHS.

1. Ojibwe People's Dictionary; Picken, *Fashion Dictionary,* 14; Nichols and Nyholm, *Concise Dictionary,* 26, 49.

2. Important Minnesota and other regional gashkibidaaganag are found worldwide. See, for example, two bags described in Feest and Kasprzycki, *Peoples of the Twilight,* 266, 280: a bag with finger-woven pocket and loom-woven strap collected 1855–62 by Hermann Domeier at Chengwatana (Pine City), Minnesota, and held at the Sammlung des Instituits für Ethnologie, Universität Göttingen, Germany (Am 3138); and a bag with loom-woven beadwork collected 1861–76 in Minnesota or Wisconsin by Ivan Čebul and held at the Slovenski Etnografski Muzej, Ljubljana, Slovenia (E2877). A finger-woven bag attributed by Frederick Baraga to southwestern Chippewa and collected 1835–36 at La Pointe, Wisconsin, is also held at the Slovenski Etnografski Muzej (E2868); see Feest, "Native American Collection I of Friderik Baraga," 305. A finger-woven pocket panel mounted on a cloth foundation is the only surviving portion of another early bag collected at LaPointe in 1854; it was acquired by H. C. Gilbert and is held by the Indian Dormitory Museum on Mackinac Island: Feest and Kasprzycki, *Peoples of the Twilight,* 292.

3. Figure 1.06 is printed in Mittelholtz and Graves, *Historical Review of the Red Lake Indian Reservation,* following p. 48. No original negatives or prints have been located for the images in this publication. The O. W. Thum Co. of Grand Rapids, Michigan, was founded c. 1884–85 and soon became known worldwide for its Tanglefoot flypaper, patented in 1887; see Bauer, "125-year-old Tanglefoot Company."

4. On Rolette, see White, "The Power of Whiteness," 180–97. Rolette's wife, Angelique Jerome, was a Métis woman and may have made the bag he is wearing. Schoolcraft describes items 3, 10, 11, 12, and 13 in Figure 1.11 as a rush mat, bark baskets filled with maple sugar called *moke-ocks,* quilled moccasins, and shot pouches, items of the type brought in by the tribes for sale at Michilimackinac Island. He notes that they are regarded as fancy goods of Indian fabrication, generally in demand as articles of curiosity. In a later entry, Schoolcraft describes the use of naturally dyed porcupine quills for decoration in the preferred colors of red, blue, black, green, and yellow. Schoolcraft, *Narrative Journal,* 122, 127. A Dakota slit pouch or bag with similar dimensions and white bead edging, also incorporating metal cone fringe and a quillwork panel, was collected in Minnesota in 1856; it was acquired by Vojta Náprstek and is held by the Náprstek Museum in Prague, Czech Republic: Feest and Kasprzycki, *Peoples of the Twilight,* 222–23. An ear pouch sample at the MNHS includes wool, buckskin, a bird skin, glass seed beads, dyed quills, tinkler cones made of scrap metal, and calico cotton. (Because the bag was collected during the tumultuous US–Dakota War of 1862 and may have been taken as a trophy of war, it is designated as a Culturally Sensitive Object and restricted from further study.)

5. Some examples of early/precursor bag types can be found in the collections of the Wisconsin Historical Society, Florida State Museum, Neville Public Museum, Detroit Institute of Arts, Field Museum of Natural History, Mackinac Island Historical Museum of History, Historic Fort Wayne, and the Nelson-Atkins Museum of Art.

6. Peterson and Brown, eds., *The New Peoples.* The historical homeland of the Métis is generally defined as all of Manitoba, Saskatchewan, and Alberta, and parts of Ontario, British Columbia, the Northwest Territories, North Dakota, Montana, and Minnesota.

7. Hilger notes, "Tribal custom did not require more than one attire for each person.... No storage space was needed for clothing for one costume was worn on all occasions, it being replaced only when worn-out. Several pairs of moccasins, however, were always on hand, and so were tanned skins. These and any personal belongings, such as bows and arrows, sewing material, etc., were stored in rolls of birch bark or in woven bags of cedar bark, and were placed along the walls of the wigwam." *Chippewa Families,* 115–17.

8. Lyford, *Ojibwa Crafts,* 128–29.

9. Coleman, *Decorative Designs,* 35.

10. See MNHS 8707.4.2 (a military sash from the 1860s) and MNHS Collection I.379.178 (an officer of the First Minnesota Infantry Regiment wearing a sash at his waist). The British Museum holds a watercolor by John White in the 1580s, after a lost drawing by Jacques Le Moyne in the 1560s, showing the wife of a Timucuan chief of Florida with a garment draped over her right shoulder and worn like a sash (1906,0509.1.23).

11. As quoted in White, *We Are at Home,* 44. Jones, *History of the Ojebway,* distinguishes between medicine bags and "pouches" several times. "Their pouches, containing their pipes and tobacco, are fastened to their belts" (p. 76). At religious feasts, "The guests bring with them their pouches, pipes, and calumet.... He then places his medicine-bag, pouch and images, by his side" (p. 95).

12. "Minnesota Chief Sees Roosevelt," *Minneapolis Tribune,* February 16, 1908, p. 15. On May Zhuck-ke-ge-shig, see Winchell, *Aborigines of Minnesota,* 717.

13. Gilfillan, "Ojibways in Minnesota," written in 1897, describes tobacco pouches as kashkibitagunug. Gilfillan spoke Ojibwemowin, and his usage is likely tied to the White Earth area, where he spent most of his time; he also worked with

members of the Mille Lacs and Gull Lake communities. Andy Favorite and Ivy Ailport, members of the White Earth community, also provided the term gashkibidaagan when I asked what word represented bandolier bag in Ojibwemowin. Favorite and Ailport interviews, both 2010.

14. Ojibwe People's Dictionary. Niingaabii'anook (Gerri Howard) of the Cha-cha-bah-ning community of the Leech Lake Reservation, is an Ojibwe language teacher at the Niigaane Immersion School at Bena. She was recorded for the Ojibwe People's Dictionary and verified the use of this term in June 2011, stating that it should be written as aazhoningwii'igan.

15. Nichols and Nyholm, *Concise Dictionary*, 20, 23, 49, 78, 84, 142, 246.

16. Gilfillan, "Agricultural Fair at White Earth."

17. Hoffman, "Menomini Indians," 269.

18. Gilfillan, "Ojibways in Minnesota," 101–2. For a portrait of Chief Joseph wearing a bag, see MNHS E99.1 r53.

19. Burleson, "White Earth," 107. A newspaper article about the collection of White Earth Indian agent Simon Michelet (Micholet) makes a similar observation on the White Earth celebration: "During the proceedings, the medicine bags are traded for ponies, and other things, one pony bringing two medicine bags": *Minneapolis Morning Tribune*, May 6, 1910, p. 4.

20. Lyford, *Ojibwa Crafts*, 129.

21. Hilger, *Chippewa Child Life*, 113. Until the mid-twentieth century, whites referred to the women's dance as the "squaw dance." The term is now considered derogatory and is no longer used. Lurie, *Wisconsin Indians*, 62, provides a definition of powwow: "Powwow, an eastern Algonkian word for religious leaders and the rituals they performed, was adopted into English by whites in the eighteenth century to describe a noisy, usually political, gathering. By the end of the nineteenth century it gained currency among whites to describe hired performances of Indian dancing and singing before paying audiences." Treuer brings the explanation of the powwow into contemporary times: "Many tribes in the Great Lakes and Plains have ancient warrior societies and ceremonies that gave birth to the powwow. In the 1970s, powwow customs evolved further to include traditional community powwows and contest powwows, where dancers compete against one another in numerous styles of dance": *Warrior Nation*, 338–39.

22. Gilfillan, "Agricultural Fair at White Earth."

23. Densmore, *Chippewa Customs*, 37.

24. Coleman, *Decorative Designs*, 58.

25. Hoffman, "Mide'wiwin," 299. Portions of loom-woven and spot-stitch appliqué bags can be seen in photographs taken in Midewiwin lodges in Keshena, Wisconsin, in 1891 (MNHS E96 p2, E96 p3, and E96 p4) and at Elbow Lake on the White Earth Reservation in 1909 (NAA INV 9259600).

26. Reagan, "Bois Fort Chippewa," 122.

27. Warner, *Big Hearted Paleface Man*, 101–8.

28. McDuffee, "Reminiscences."

29. Coleman, *Decorative Designs*, 35; Reagan, "Bois Fort Chippewa," 122.

30. Blessing, "Contemporary Costuming," 7.

31. The Limon bags may be found by searching "Bandolier Bag Project" at http://fineartamerica.com.

Notes to Chapter 2

1. "Samples of Indian Art," *Minneapolis Journal*, April 2, 1903, p. 6.

2. Lyford, *Ojibwa Crafts*, 128–30.

3. See MNHS 8616.15, 74.32.5 (Figure 3.16), 2005.193.1 (Figure 10.15), and 1990.502.5 (Figures 3.85 and 12.12).

4. MNHS also holds several beaded belts or bands decorated in the same fashion, using two vines of motifs going in opposing directions and meeting at the center of the belt. See 10000.717, 267.E63, 10000.125.

5. Mitchell interview, 1991, p. 4, 5, 26–27. Sally notes that the medicine lodge at Mille Lacs was "constructed of poles and beautiful quilts. They called them blankets, but we would call them quilts because they were of pieced material." This suggests the many blankets presented at dances may have been something other than what many have long believed them to be. Ulrich, *Age of Homespun*, discusses the Algonkian use of blankets in the same manner as the furs they replaced. Her observation substantiates the habit of cultures to use newly available materials to create replacements for those no longer preferred or as easy to obtain (e.g., beads to replace quillwork).

6. In the nineteenth century, this wool tape was available from milliners, dressmakers, dry goods stores, and even itinerant peddlers. It was used on military uniforms and it served as hem-saver tape on women's dresses that were to be worn on the street (visiting or day dresses, not dinner dresses or ball gowns). The tape was meant to protect the hem edge and was replaced when it showed wear. A functional material of this type would eventually become obsolete stock when fashions and hem lengths changed; it could then be repurposed and sold to traders very cheaply. So it was no doubt readily available to Indian women from several sources. See http://www.wmboothdraper.com/, "Tape and lace" tab.

7. An example of beadwork instruction is *Indian Bead Craft*, published by the Walco Bead Company in 1935. Ojibwe bead artists had access to the same instruction books available to non-Indians. Popular how-to books were no doubt available to anyone ordering beads, and one such publication was found in the reference library at St. Benedict's Monastery. It teaches loom work techniques and gives instructions for products including beaded belts, watch fobs, wrist straps, sautoir neck chains, hat bands, and girdles or belts. It includes a cross-stitch-like interpretation of a naturalistic rose (see p. 5 and 6); a similar pattern is seen today in loom work from Mille Lacs.

8. The Ayer collection from the Mille Lacs Indian Trading Post includes twenty-three bead sample cards from New York firms Walco Bead Co., American Bead Company, Inc., Walter A. Yokel, Inc., S. A. Frost's Son, Theo L. Stern & Co., and A. L. Hettrich Co. of San Francisco. The Albert G. Heath collection at the Logan Museum contains twenty-five bead sample cards from the same era, with four from Walco Bead Co.

9. The faceted metal beads marked on the Ayer sample cards were identified by various names, including cut colored metal beads, natural cut steel—not colored, torse colored metal beads, and aluminum unies.

10. Moss and Scherer, *New Beadwork*, 105; Ewers, "Three Ornaments."

11. Barbeau, "Assomption Sash." See additional related headgear images in MNHS collections: E97.1W r21, E97.31 p6, 6784, E97.1M r38, E97.1Pr26, E97.1Sr21, Reserve album 255 no 45.

12. The images in Figures 2.25–27, along with MNHS E97.1 h1 no29 and E97.1A r16, were all distributed by three early St. Paul photographers. Ke-bay-nah-kay and Ah-ah-shaw-we-ke-shick are both posed standing against an anonymous background. Aw-ke-wen-zee and Aw-Monse are both shown seated, on the same carpet in Martin's Art Gallery. All of these photographers functioned independently but also had some business arrangement with one of the others, and all were active in St. Paul during the 1860s, while one was also active in the 1850s and two were also active in the 1870s.

13. While there are other portraits that include small bags of this type, this one has provenance as to date, culture, and location. Brookes was hired by the Wisconsin Historical Society to paint Souligny and the portrait of another Native leader that became part of the collections before Brookes's death in 1867. Wisconsin Historical Society, "Shu'nuni'u (Souligny)."

14. For examples of additional bags related to this early form, see SMM A79.4.73, NMNH E357768–0, NMAI 230126.000, NMAI 012601.000, NMNH E357768, NMNH ET01764, NMAI 180729.000, NMAI 17/9691, NMAI 247026.000, NMAI 180729.000, Nebraska HS 7621–4, DIA 1988.28, MPM (LCO bag) 2289300864655; Penney, *Art of the American Indian Frontier*. An example at the Peabody Museum of Archaeology and Ethnology at Harvard University (PMH 27–17–10/98248) combines a finger-woven sash bag with a loomed bead strap, suggesting one possible evolution to the fully loom-beaded gashkibidaagan form; it may also simply represent a contemporary replacement of a worn strap with an available newer and sturdier one.

15. Orchard, *Beads and Beadwork*, 89–90. To confirm the possible use of this technique in the region over time, I studied the method employed for early documented sashes and garters in MNHS collections. I also looked at examples with Minnesota attribution in the collections at the Logan Museum of Anthropology at Beloit College in Wisconsin. The majority of the bags and other loomed pieces whose manufacture provided access to selvages and had Ojibwe attribution used the same square stitch method, even examples dating to the mid-nineteenth century.

The biggest challenge in studying loom-woven panel bags is finding bags and historic images with good documentation. My goal in this study has been to find as many examples of these bags and related images as possible to serve as a point of departure for much-needed further research. I have compiled the data related to the MNHS collection of bags providing most often a window of dates and possible reservation association. The dated images are inclusive of the broader region, including Ojibwe and other Great Lakes people living in Minnesota and Wisconsin in the nineteenth and twentieth centuries.

16. Jackson, *Descriptive Catalog*, 71. While it is not so identified, it is possible that this paperboard-mounted composite image (MNHS E97.1 h1) was displayed in the window of Whitney's Gallery to advertise American Indian portraits for sale; it helpfully provides an order number on each carte de visite. Noon Day was also photographed in 1863 at Whitney's Gallery (MNHS E97.1N r18). Plenty Hail is included on the composite in images 27 and 67.

17. Berg, "Agents of Cultural Change," 165. An image (MNHS E97.7W r27) taken in the exact same location dated 1881 includes two identifiable clergy. None of the men pictured wear bags, but Abbot Edelbrock, who laid the cornerstone for the new church in 1881 (completion in 1882), traveled between White Earth, Red Lake, and Collegeville, Minnesota, until his death in 1908. The other Benedictine is Hermanutz, who was at Red Lake from 1883 to 1888 (intermittent) and White Earth from 1878 to 1929. So it is likely that the images are from the 1880s, and perhaps even the dates listed (Wilmott, personal communication, 2015; Leah Bowe graciously provided some of this information). An illustration in Lindblad, *Full of Fair Hope*, 21, shows Reverend Ignatius Tomazin, diocesan priest and pastor at White Earth 1870–78, with two seated men, each wearing a loom-woven panel decorated bag. A third bag is lying on the ground between them.

18. For other images of Chief White Cloud, see MNHS E97.1W r18 (he wears a spot-stitch appliqué bag), E97.1W p9, E97.1W r20, E97.1W p11, E97.1W r30, E97.1W r17, E97.1W r33.

19. Orchard, *Beads and Beadwork*, 115 (plate 127).

20. Ojibwe People's Dictionary.

21. For other bags like that in Figure 2.50, see also MIA 74.63.6, and possibly MNHS 2011.208.151. All three bags appear to be by the same maker(s).

Notes to Chapter 3

1. Ulrich, *Age of Homespun*, 55–56, writing about seventeenth-century relations between the Algonkians and settlers in Virginia and New England, argues that some twentieth-century scholars are wrong to say that because "Indians had no woven cloth before the arrival of European traders and settlers, it took time for their women to learn sewing skills. Others assume that Indians were attracted to woven fabrics because they were lighter and more colorful than animal skins and nearly as warm, as though the replacement of one form of clothing for another were a simple matter of consumer choice. Indians didn't adopt English blankets because they were superior to their traditional clothing but because furs and hides purchased new products like iron pots, knives, and guns [and beads]. It is hardly surprising that the wearers chose to use their new clothing very much as they had the old. Nor did Indian women have any reason to take up English textile tasks when they were so fully occupied with their own. A trucking-cloth blanket might replace a mantle of skins, but it could not roof or furnish a wigwam.

Trade with Europeans had a profound impact on male hunting and on the trading and manufacture of wampum, which became a kind of currency in the fur trade, but it had little effect on women's other textile work. A hundred years after contact, Algonkian women were still weaving mats for wigwams and baskets to store and carry food."

2. Densmore, *Chippewa Customs,* 183.

3. Densmore, *Chippewa Customs,* 184.

4. Densmore, *Chippewa Customs,* 63, 83; Orlofsky and Orlofsky, *Quilts in America,* 61–62, 312.

5. On birchbark biting, see Densmore, *Chippewa Customs,* 184–85; Kohl, *Kitchi-Gami,* 413–14.

6. See Milwaukee Public Museum collections online for bag #14601 acquired from Radin about 1908–13 while he was associated with the Bureau of American Ethnology, Washington, DC: https://www.mpm.edu/research-collections/anthropology/online-collections-research/bandolier-bag-collection/collection (p. 4).

7. Hoffman, "Menomini Indians," 269. Hoffman references garter and other beadwork patterns and states that "Many if not all of these designs used in beadworking have been introduced among the Menomini by intercourse with the Ojibwa, with whom they have been friendly neighbors from the earliest historic times. This is shown not only by the identical patterns existing among both tribes, but it is evident also from the frequent intertribal traffic, existing even at this day."

8. Densmore, *Chippewa Customs,* 173.

9. Densmore, *Chippewa Customs,* plate 84.

10. For discussions of these designs, see Pomedi, *Living with Animals*; http://www.thecanadianencyclopedia.ca/en/article/aboriginal-art-in-canada. For a wampum belt, probably Haudenosaunee (Iroquois), see Peabody Essex Museum E39.383: pictured in Grimes, et al., *Uncommon Legacies,* 103.

11. Densmore, *Chippewa Customs,* 186 (plate 80), 193 (figure 27); Lyford, *Ojibwa Crafts,* 142 (plate 86). While I believe the common wild rose, with its heart-shaped petals, could easily have inspired the motifs discussed above, there is another potential source of influence in silver trade goods. Silver brooches were produced in quantity in the eighteenth and nineteenth centuries for the fur trade, both in a popular circular form and in single and double heart shapes. The circular forms are well documented as worn by the Ho-Chunk of this region; the heart-shaped ones appear less commonly. The Grand Portage National Monument's Heritage Center's collections include a heart-shaped silver brooch found on the monument site. Frederickson, *Covenant Chain,* 21; Densmore, *Chippewa Customs,* 138–42.

12. Coleman, *Decorative Designs,* 93–96. *Peterson's Magazine* and *Godey's Lady's Book* were both fashion and pattern books available across North America and throughout Minnesota.

13. Densmore notes, "Every woman who did beadwork had patterns cut from stiff birch bark which she laid on the material to be decorated. Mrs. English said that she remembered when patterns were pricked with a stiff fishbone around the outline and then cut with scissors. In this way the pattern was evident to the eye before the cutting was begun. With very few exceptions the cut patterns collected by the writer show no trace of a marking implement, the appearance being that the patterns are cut without tracing": "Uses of Plants," 390. For examples of patterns collected by Densmore, see MNHS 6935.32.1.1-.42.

14. Popular quilt patterns in the 1920s–30s were called love apple, pomegranate, or pineapple; see Hall and Kretsinger, *Romance of the Patchwork Quilt,* 106–7, 108–9, 110–11.

15. *Chippeway Herald,* November 1908 ("Miss Sybil Carter" obituary), and January 1906 ("Lace-Work Among the Indians Begun at White Earth"). More instructors arrived in October 1890, in August 1891, and on March 1, 1892. Lace makers also went to teach the Dakota at Birch Cooley, Red Lake, and Leech Lake Ojibwe reservations. A discussion of the teaching of lacemaking is in the reminiscences of Pauline Colby, an Episcopal missionary and teacher at White Earth and Red Lake (1892–1932), at MNHS.

16. Forbes, "Lace Making," 613–16; Sybil Carter Indian Mission, Annual Report 1908, p. 7. Schools at White Earth and Red Lake were closed at the time of this report. *Lace Made by North American Indians,* published in 1904 and probably written by Mrs. W. Bayard Cutting, the organization's president, lists Lower Sioux as "Birch Coulee."

17. Several other examples can be found at the Cooper Hewitt, Smithsonian Design Museum.

18. Gittinger, *Master Dyers to the World,* 175–91 (images p. 178, 179, 182).

19. Picken, *Fashion Dictionary,* 13, 193, includes definitions for bandanna and kerchief. For other historical images at MNHS featuring bandanas, see E97.1B r13 (John Belogin and Pudigan, approx 1870), E97.1M r43 (Maw-je-ke-jik, c. 1863), E99.1 r29 (War Eagle, c. 1880), PCHS 2000–073–007 (Native American Brave—Kiviniguanjasj, n.d.), and Collection I.364.13 (a handsome bandana example tied to Charette's accessories blows in the breeze). For other examples of portraits of men wearing printed bandanas, see MNHS E97.1 r154 and E91.1M p2. For ex amples of bandanas themselves, see MNHS 7330.1, 67.230.163, 1983.90.1039, 1988.264.1, 7829.32B.

20. Heath (1888–1953) traveled extensively throughout North America, buying, trading, and selling Native American objects. His collection, which includes fourteen gashkibidaaganag (seven from White Earth, Red Lake, Leech Lake, and Grand Portage), was donated to the Logan Museum of Anthropology in 1955; information on Heath and images of his collection may be found at the museum's website. Densmore recorded eighteen songs with Gi'wita'bines (Spotted Bird), who was about fifty years old, was fluent in English, and sent his children to the government schools. He "took special pride in his singing, which he said was in the 'regular old Indian way'": Densmore, *Chippewa Music,* 173.

21. Of the bags at MNHS, two with folded leaf motifs, 1990.502.5 and 1995.46.16, have specific attribution to White Earth. The majority of the other bags with folded leaf motifs have only general association with the broader White Earth,

Cass Lake, and Leech Lake region: 2011.208.153, 2011.208.160, 2011.208.145, and 1984.156.3 (which appears on this book's cover).

Notes to Chapter 4

1. For discussions of issues in American Indian photography, see Hoelscher, *Picturing Indians*; Sandweiss, *Print the Legend*; Johnson, ed., *Spirit Capture*; White, *We Are at Home*.

2. Petrulis, *Metropolitan Postcard Club*. A second postcard (MNHS E97.31 r120), made from another image taken the same day of Migizi and Janie Mitchell, Mildred Mitchell, and Mrs. John Mitchell, is dated c. 1920. That postcard's back imprint dates from 1926–1940s.

3. Whipple's life and work are discussed on page 200.

4. White, *We Are at Home*, 89–94.

5. The MNHS acquired many of these images in 1927, with the purchase of the E. A. Bromley collection. Bromley was active in Minneapolis from the 1890s to the 1920s. His collection included thousands of negatives made by early Minnesota photographers, including Benjamin F. Upton, William Henry Illingworth, Joel Emmons Whitney, and others.

6. Video interviews with Ivy Ailport, Batiste Sam, and Ron Libertus; taped interviews with Maude Kegg and Batiste Sam. Collections reviewed in person and online in addition to those discussed here include images from the Smithsonian, National Museum of the American Indian, Minnesota Historical Society (and C. N. Christiansen, Frank Jay Haynes), Science Museum of Minnesota, Milwaukee Public Museum, American Philosophical Society, Minnesota Reflections, photograph archives of the Mille Lacs and Red Lake Bands, Wisconsin State Historical Society, Wisconsin History, Charles Van Schaick of Black River Falls, WI, F. A. Rinehart Trans Mississippi & International Exposition 1898 images at the Omaha Public Library, Canadian Museum of Civilization, Heard Museum, Nebraska Historical Society, Peabody Museum of Archaeology and Ethnology at Harvard University, McCord Museum, St. John Abbey Archives, St. Benedict's Monastery Archives, postcard collections of Pat Albers and Tom Amble, World Wide Web and Facebook photograph collections, and many more. Different collections provide varying documentation and must be thoroughly assessed to determine their possible value.

Notes to Chapter 5

1. "Indian Handicrafts," *Minneapolis Journal*, November 15, 1901, p. 11.

2. "Bemidji Window Display," *Bemidji Daily Pioneer*, December 22, 1908. American Indian–made goods of all sizes and prices could be found statewide, at varied locations, sometimes out of town at the highway's edge. For examples, some documented by MNHS photographs, see Fort Mille Lacs Indian Village; Buckskin Trading Post and Wikiup Indian Craft & Souvenirs (Walker area, 1950s); Wigwam Inn Resort; Nick's Indian Gift Shop (north of Onamia, 1956, MM6.3 r33); Mille Lacs Curio Shop (c. 1940, MM6.3 r34); Nisswa Indian Trading Mart (c. 1947, HF4.9 r54); Johnson's Trading Post (Orr, c. 1952, MS2.9 OR r6); Roe's Trading Post (Pipestone, approximately 1935, HF4.9 r58). In the far northwest corner of the state at Lake Bronson, Frank Palmer worked out of a storefront with a painted sign proclaiming "Indian Trader" and dated 1877 (photo c. 1900, MK6.9 LBr2). An 1898 Leech Lake photograph shows an unidentified man posing in front of the store of the Wright Brothers, who sold "Indian Curios" (E97.4 r22). The Ayers also regularly carried a large stock of pottery, silver and turquoise jewelry, and textiles from the Southwestern tribes in support of the early twentieth-century interior design trend. At Vineland Resort, individual Mille Lacs Band families sold from roadside stands; Sherman Holbert personal interviews, 2002 and 2005.

3. "Indians as Lace Makers," *New York Times*, October 23, 1898.

4. See correspondence with Lokken, May 1954, and Thompson, March 3, 1954, in Correspondence, 1956–62, Indian Crafts of the Episcopal Church in Minnesota Organization Records, MNHS.

5. Williams interview. See also *Minnesota CEP [Concentrated Employment Program] Newsletter* 2.4 (n.d.).

6. Inventories of the Indian Room and the Souvenir Room are in vols. 102–4, Harry D. Ayer and family papers, 1787–1982, MNHS.

7. "Abercrombie's Closing Out Sale," *Bemidji Daily Pioneer*, March 7, 1916. MNHS bags 1498 and 1831, probably no later than 1901, retain their original paper price tags, each marked $40.

8. "Second Annual Red Lake Indian Fair," *Bemidji Daily Pioneer*, September 1, 1914.

9. Some of the objects that can be identified in Figure 5.03 include approximately eight heavily beaded pillows (some in European embroidered style, others decorated in Ojibwe dance apron style); two quilts (one log cabin pieced and one tulip appliqué pattern); six spot-stitch appliqué gashkibidaaganag (four fringed with strung bead loops and yarn tassels, while two have woven tabs); a beaded dress; birchbark birdhouses; embroidered doily linens; moccasins; other beadwork; small bags; bows with stunning arrows; four woven mats; miniature canoes; a full-size canoe; and a cradleboard complete with doll. For images of the state fair displays, see MNHS FM6.55S p46 and FM6.55X p14.

10. The photo in Figure 5.04 appears in "Illustrated Duluth 1896," a pamphlet at KAMLASC.

11. Advertisements for Louisa J. Lynch and Robert P. Fairbanks appear in the *Tomahawk*, August 2, 1903. Louisa J. Lynch's advertisement closed with "Indian beads Silk and Fancy Needle work, a specialty." Robert P. Fairbanks had been active in the area as a licensed government trader since the 1860s; his ad included the statement "Indian fancy beadwork a specialty."

12. "Samples of Indian Art," *Minneapolis Journal*, April 2, 1903, p. 6.

13. Ten Thousand Lakes Greater Minnesota Association, *The Minnesota Book*.

14. *Mille Lacs Lake Travel Guide*, 1942.

15. "Sioux and Chippewas Hit Trail for White Earth," *Minneapolis Morning Tribune,* June 11, 1922, p. D11.

16. Olson interviews.

Notes to Chapter 6

1. For Bois Forte Reservation history, see http://www.boisforte.com/history.htm and http://mn.gov/indianaffairs/tribes_boisforte.html.

2. Reagan, "Chief Moses Day," "Bois Fort Chippewa," and "Plants Used by the Bois Fort Chippewa"; Latady personal communication.

3. White, *We Are at Home,* 219. In Figure 6.03, as in images by De Lancy Gill (Washington, DC, 1901, BAE GN 00569A 06150100, NAA-SI), and by musicologist Stella Stocker (1916–17, KAMLASC, 2882-9 S3089 B1Vol1), Debwawendunk is pictured holding or wearing beadwork. Because the images by Jones and Stocker were both made at Nett Lake, it is probable that the beadwork is from there, and likely was made by his wife, Sahkahmequaybeake.

4. The United Methodists had established short-lived missions on the Mississippi and in central Minnesota from the 1830s to the 1850s. In 1888 they returned to the area and established a mission among the Ojibwe in the Tower area south of Lake Vermilion. Purdham, *Fragile Starts,* 1–12; Hingley, "Visit to the Pagan Indians," 12–13; Methodist Episcopal Church, Northern Minnesota Conference, *Official Journal of the . . . Session,* 1938:379; and Methodist Church, Northern Minnesota Conference, *Official Journal of the . . . Session* 1943:622; *Duluth Herald,* November 27, 1937 (obituary); Pequette death certificate 1937-MN-014624. His obituary indicates Pequette married in 1879. US Indian Census Rolls 1885–1940 indicate the couple had no children who survived to maturity. In the 1900 US Census for Baraga County, Michigan, L'Anse township, Pequette and his wife are listed without other family members and were possibly recorded with other residents of the L'Anse Ojibwe Reservation. He is variously listed in government records and newspapers as living at Nett Lake, Sawyer, Fond du Lac, and Virginia, Minnesota.

5. Christine Carlson, "A Disease," *Nahgahchiwanong Dibahjimowinnan,* December 8, 2009, p. 8–9; Reagan, "Chief Moses Day," 519–22; Christine Carlson, "Joseph Northrup Family," *Nahgahchiwanong Dibahjimowinnan,* February 2012, p. 6.

6. For other Stocker images, see KAMLASC 2846-9 S3089 B1Vol1 (available at MDL umn241475) and MNHS E97.1P p9. Original images are in photo album, 1916, in Stocker papers, KAMLASC.

7. Duane Frank Porter (1850–1944) was the son of Duane Porter and Mary Mun-nee LaPrairie Porter. He became active in the Methodist Church in 1891, was ordained a deacon in 1899, and was a minister by 1906. He served the White Earth community at Pine Bend from 1899 until his death in 1944. His niece, Susie Porter Bunker, remembered there was a large group of Indian women at the Pine Bend Indian Mission who spoke no English and formed a Ladies Aid sewing club: "They made such lovely quilts, aprons, knitted mittens and socks, moccasins, beaded chains and many other things. The club made a lot of money at their sales." Porter himself noted that during the annual summer Methodist Camp Meeting in 1908 or 1909, "The Ladies Aid Society of the church handled the refreshments and made enough money from the sale of goods during the meeting to pay all the expenses of the camp meetings. . . . Bead work and souvenirs were sold to help the cause." Porter, "From the Reverend Duane F. Porter's Notebook," 11, 19; Bunker's 1962 reminiscences of Porter are typed at the end of this transcript. See also the *Christian Advocate* 85 (September 8, 1910): 20.

8. Pequette is listed in the 1910 census as clergyman for the Methodist Episcopal Church, and he served as census enumerator for the Bois Forte Reservation. He listed himself as half Chippewa and half German, while his wife and seventy-five-year-old mother-in-law, Nancy Bedell, are listed as "full-blood Chippewa." US Indian Census Rolls for the Pequettes show them living at Nett Lake or Bois Forte nearly every year from 1913 to 1937. Nancy Bedell died March 19, 1928, at L'Anse, Baraga, Michigan; see Michigan, Deaths and Burials Index, 1867–1995. Bags of a similar scale to Pequette's in the MNHS collections include 1827, 8723.6, 69.138.5, 2003.159.1, 10000.157.

Notes to Chapter 7

1. For Fond du Lac history, see http://www.fdlrez.com; Peacock, *A Forever Story*; http://mn.gov/indianaffairs/tribes_fonddulac.html; White, et al., "Ethnographic Study of Duluth," 21.

2. As quoted in Peacock, *A Forever Story,* 241–42. Mary LaFave was born February 3, 1909, and died on November 1, 1985.

3. "Frank C. Berry Dead," *Bemidji Daily Pioneer,* February 7, 1914; *Stillwater Gazette,* August 15, 1906 (on his territory); *Bemidji Daily Pioneer,* May 20, 1910 (on promotion).

4. The bags were donated to the MNHS in 1923 by Berry's widow.

Notes to Chapter 8

1. For Grand Portage history, see http://www.grandportage.com/heritage.php; http://mn.gov/indianaffairs/tribes_grandportage.html. Olson interviews provided information on beadworking at Grand Portage; see also Plains Art Museum, *Aazhoniingwa'igan: Ojibwe Bandolier Bag,* a 1992 video recording that features the work of Ellen Olson and Maude Kegg, with additional interviews by Jessie Ehlert, Renee Senogles, and Marcie McIntire.

2. Two other Grand Portage men wear gashkibidaaganag in a photo taken at the 1942 dedication of the monument. See CCHS, PHB350.

3. Raske interviews. The spellings *LeSage* and *LaSage* are used almost interchangeably. Most census documents record the name as *LeSage,* which is used here for consistency.

4. The bag and collar are also visible in MNHS E97.22 r5.

5. Olson interviews. Two other MNHS images, both dated August 22, 1931, show Alec Posey wearing the bag: E97.1 r123 and E97.37 r114.

6. See also MNHS E97.34 p1 (c. 1940), E97.37 m2 (1934), E97.37 r108 (1934). While Posey's first name is spelled differently in many documents (Alex, Alexis, and Maymashawash), the family refers to him as Alec. He died on January 23, 1951, and Mary Posey was born July 15, 1880, and died July 16, 1964; see Minnesota death certificates.

7. Raske interviews.

8. Killy interview, 1987, by Bonnie Wilson; interviews and personal communications with the author, 2008 and 2009. Interviews with Monroe were held over several years at his home in Minneapolis. He noted that he began by collecting lithics, and that most of the American Indian material culture collectors in Minnesota were members of the Minnesota Archaeological Society. He attended powwows at Red Lake, Nett Lake, Grand Portage, Mille Lacs, and Hayward, WI. MNHS's Monroe Killy collection (1910–2010) includes family photos as well. Over five hundred of his images related to the Ojibwe of Minnesota can be seen at mnhs.org.

9. See also MNHS E97.1 r125.

10. Much of the information in this section is from my interviews with Ellen Olson, 2009–14.

11. McClean, a schoolteacher and a historian at Grand Portage from the 1920s to the late 1930s, was born on Susie Island and bought the post after the death of its founder, Pete Gagnon, "for a few hundred dollars and an old car," said Dewey Albinson: Gilman, *Grand Portage*, 125.

12. Ellen's bags are in the collections of the Smithsonian, Washington, DC, and the Plains Art Museum, Fargo.

13. Olson interview.

14. A brief overview of her career is in *Trib Local Evanston* (Illinois), November 19, 2009.

15. Marcie's fourth bag, finished in July 1989 and acquired by the Grand Portage Band, is on display in the Tribal Council Government Office. The bag's pocket panel is spot stitched with a pearl-white beaded background; it has a full-width open front pocket and red binding. There are spot-stitched floral motifs on the black velveteen strap and the area above the pocket opening. McIntire interviews; see also http://www.crossingbordersstudiotour.com. The paper excerpted below is titled "Anishinabe Beadwork."

16. Abrams and Ackerman, *Theories of Criticism*, 38.

17. Lyford, *Ojibwa Crafts*, 145.

18. Grand Rapids Public Museum, *Beads*, 13; Hail and Duncan, *Out of the North*, 153; Gilman, "Collection with a Mission," 6.

19. As quoted in Garte, *Circle of Life*, 12.

20. Joseph Bushman, Grand Portage Anishinaabe, conversation, December 1971.

21. Lyford, *Ojibwa Crafts*, 127.

Notes to Chapter 9

1. For Leech Lake Reservation history, see http://www.llojibwe.com and http://mn.gov/indianaffairs/tribes_leechlake.html. See also Cass Lake Commercial Club, "Cass Lake"; Tim Brady, "Real Story of the Chippewa National Forest"; Treuer, *Ojibwe in Minnesota*, 35.

2. An article in the *Tomahawk*, August 3, 1922, is titled, "Indian Treaty Fete in 1926 Proposed." In the first part of the twentieth century, entrepreneurs sometimes gathered popular images from events like a centennial celebration and sold them in souvenir packets. One such packet of twelve images of the Cass Lake celebration taken by Arthur Allen Richardson (known as "Rich") is in the archives at St. John's Abbey, Collegeville, MN. These and other photographs of this particular event, variously dated between 1920 and c. 1930, seem to have also been sold individually. Twenty-three images on the mnhs.org website (thirteen by Rich) are related to the centennial. In various images, women wear one or two spot-stitch appliqué gashkibidaaganag, and in the street dancer images five or more spot-stitch appliqué bags are visible.

3. Matsen, "Battle of Sugar Point," 269–75. This Bagone-giishig should not be confused with the men of the same name, elder and younger, who were of the Mississippi Band. The Leech Lake Bagone-giizhig had been arrested in the spring of 1898 and taken to Duluth, where not enough evidence existed to convict him on trivial or trumped up bootlegging charges. He was released and had to walk over 130 miles home. Commissioner Jones noted this in his report, which criticized local officials; Bagone-giizhig was not captured at that time.

4. On Libbey, see 1901 *Legislative Manual of the State of Minnesota*, 648.

5. Eight bags and two bag straps at MNHS are specifically associated with Leech Lake, Cass Lake or Walker, Minnesota: 70.90, 9023.2, 9023.3, 9023.5, 9023.6, 1981.119.1, 1984.156.3, 2011.208.145, 2011.208.147, and 2011.208.160.

6. See also INV 06140000 and INV 06139900, both at NAA-SI. Rebecca Kugel identifies the man seated on the far right as Gay-she-gwanay-aush. The gashkibidaagan he wears is also worn by an Otoe man named George Arkektah in another NAA image (INV 10014000) that was made in December 1898. I believe the bag worn by the two men was made by a Minnesota Ojibwe woman and was not an NAA studio prop. Kugel, *To Be the Main Leaders*, 102–3.

7. See also MNHS bags 1988.340.1, 2003.159.1, and 2008.9.1.

8. The 1920 US Census records Otto Bismark as born in 1861, fifty-nine years of age, and living in Clearwater County on the Red Lake Reservation. In 2009 I interviewed Ron Libertus, an emeritus professor of American Indian Studies at the University of Minnesota who was born at Onigum, Minnesota, and is enrolled at White Earth, about MNHS bandolier bags 1984.156.3, 6020.8, 532.E157, 272.E68, and a bag he brought in, which had been owned by his family.

9. A. F. Raymond's studio was the Minneapolis Standard Photo Company, and he was in business from the 1900s to the 1940s. For more on the controversial declaration of allegiance, see Barsh, "An American Heart of Darkness," 91–115.

10. For another example of a bag featuring a large leaf

without association data, see Pomona College Museum of Art Collection Online, P1609. A bag nearly identical to Figure 9.21 at the Peabody Museum of Archaeology and Ethnology at Harvard University appears to be by the same unidentified bead artist; see catalog number 995-29-10/73425.

11. Ryan, *Star Island,* 4–5.

12. Killy interview.

13. Smith and Smith, *Being the Life History.*

14. For Smith's shirt, see MNHS 2011.20.8.40 and E97.1K p27. The beaded cuffs, bib front collar, and yoke appear to have been removed from a previous shirt and reattached to a lightweight cotton shirt.

15. See dance aprons employing the same blue, red, and white color palette in MNHS 2011.208.137 and 2011.208.141.

16. Losh interviews; Lundquist, "Melvin Losh." Mel was among three Minnesota Native artists interviewed in the Plains Art Museum's film *On the Border: Native American Weaving Traditions of the Great Lakes and Prairie,* which documents the continuity of traditional American Indian arts, as well as the artists' innovations.

Notes to Chapter 10

1. For Mille Lacs Reservation history, see http://millelacsband.com and http://www.indianaffairs.state.mn.us/tribes_millelacs.html. For place name, see http://www.ojibwe.org/home/about_anish_glossary.html.

2. Brower, *Mille Lac.* An Ojibwe man in two different photographs, c. 1920s (likely taken the same day), wears a bag that employs roundel motifs above the pocket opening that are similar to those in Figure 10.01. The location given for MNHS E97.1 r28 is "on reservation near Hayward, Wisconsin"; the location for MNHS E97.31 r138 is Reserve, Wisconsin. But the bag pocket and belt he wears in both photographs are also similar to gashkibidaagan 10000.148 in the Ayer collection, MNHS.

3. Blessing, "Contemporary Costuming," discusses the economic situations of the Ojibwe families selling at roadside stands.

4. Other images in the MNHS collections that document dances and powwows at Mille Lacs include E97.37 r53, E97.37 r54, E97.37 r55 (all from a 1920 Mille Lacs powwow, including one gashkibidaagan and other beadwork); E97.37 r19 (dancers at Wahkon, Minnesota, c. 1909–12, including one gashkibidaagan and other beadwork).

5. For another photo of Shingobe taken by Killy in 1969, see MNHS Collection I.69.52.

6. Winchell, *Aborigines of Minnesota,* 729; Densmore, *Chippewa Customs,* 2; Densmore, "Uses of Plants," 282; Densmore, "State History Convention speech." Wawweyaycumig's Ojibwemowin name appears with many phoenetic versions.

7. "Red Man Must Go: Mille Lacs Indians will be Removed to White Earth," *Minneapolis Tribune,* February 27, 1898, A5; White, *We Are at Home,* 54–57.

8. De Lancy Gill made two to three thousand portraits of American Indians for the Smithsonian's Bureau of American Ethnology (BAE) between 1889 and 1932. *Report of S. P. Langley,* 43.

9. A letter from Howard's daughter, Ruth Howard Fierke, to Harry Ayer, July 22, 1963, offers to donate Howard's collection to Ayer and includes information on the belt. The letter is in the MNHS collection file; items in the Howard donation are cataloged as 10000.700–10000.730.

10. See snapshots taken by Stella Stocker at the White Earth Celebration in 1916 (KAMLASC umn241590 and umn241592) that show Wawweyaycumig with family members and bags. Both bags in umn241590 apparently have full-width pocket openings on the front, a separately spot-stitched unbalanced motif on the dark panel above the pocket, and oversized beaded zigzag pocket border edging. The arrowhead leaf motif can be seen on the pocket of the bag on his left hip, and the folded leaf motif is visible on the strap of the bag resting on his right hip. In another Stella Stocker snapshot (KAMLASC umn241593), Round Earth holds his grandchild wearing yet another gashkibidaagan.

11. On Mink, see Facts on File, Encyclopedia of Native American Religions. MNHS holds eight photographs that are related to a Mr. and Mrs. John Mink of Mille Lacs; only E97.32M r23 shows John Mink, and he does not resemble the John Mink of Lac Courte Oreilles in Figure 10.14.

12. Yet another Lake Lena bag, dated 1917 and similar in design and motifs, has been in the private collection of Mike Johnson, Walsall, West Midlands, England.

13. White, *We Are at Home,* 185–87. The MNHS's online collection includes sixty-four images made by Daniels, including turn-of-the-century interiors of his Pine City studio, self-portraits, numerous formal portraits, and various photographs of people and landscapes.

14. Superintendent John H. Hinton to Harry Ayer, November 20, 1918. Hinton approved the departure of H. D. Robbins, filed the proper papers, recommended the Ayers receive trader's license, and gave them free occupancy of the Robbins house and permission to use the front room as a store. All this was compensation for the Ayers' service as custodians of the grounds and other buildings. Members of the Non-removable Band lived in nearby communities, including Onamia, Isle, Garrison, East Lake, Pine City, Hinckley, Lake Lena, Minnewawa, Sandy Lake, Aitkin, Wahkon, Malmo, and McGregor, which greatly benefited the Ayers.

15. For a discussion of the museum's development as an MNHS site, see Lonetree, *DeColonizing Museums,* 29–72. In his 1979 consultant report for an NEH self-study of the Mille Lacs Indian Museum and Trading Post, Thomas Vennum, Jr., described the Ayer collection as "one of the richest tribal treasures in the country": "Minnesota Historical Society Self-Study Report, December 31, 1979," p. 548, copy in MNHS Reference Library.

16. Ayer Trading Post Volumes, Day Books, Volume 87, Ayer and family papers; MNHS Museum Collections accession file

for Ayer collection, 10000.1959; Hussey-Arntson, "Report on Ayer Collections." Other interior images of the Trading Post at MNHS include MM6.7M r1, MM6.7M r2, MM6.7M r19, MM6.7M r20, MM6.7M r22, MM6.7M r23, MM6.7M r29, MM6.7M r55, MM6.7M r56, MM6.7M r58 and MM6.7M r59 (c. 1935), MM6.7M r61, MM6.7 r143, MM6.7 r142, MM6.7 r144 (1940–45).

17. The bag is also worn by Migizi in MNHS E97.1M r29. Other bags from the Ayer collection are captured in historical photographs, including bags 10000.157 and 10000.159 worn in a posed shot by Cecilia Rock, an employee at the Ayers' store (MNHS E97.1R r2).

18. Raining died in 2009, and his obituary states that his parents were Charley and Quaykosh Boyd. The MNHS photo documentation mistakenly identifies Charley as Quaykosh and his wife as Poeschewzigan. The 1930 US Census lists Charley, born about 1893 in Minnesota, as residing at Kathio, Mille Lacs, Minnesota. His spouse is listed as Duaykosh Boyd. Mrs. Boyd is also listed as Quay Kosh Boyd, born about 1890 in Minnesota and living at Kathio, Mille Lacs, Minnesota. Their two children are listed as Raney, nine, and Suesness, five.

19. Hussey-Arntson, "Report on Ayer Collections." The US Indian Census of 1937 lists Ed Skinaway as widowed and living at White Earth; he was born in 1900 to Tom and Lucy Skinaway.

20. Densmore, *Chippewa Customs,* 4; Sam interview. Batiste Sam thought Jenny Mitchell was a good beadworker. Other household members listed in the 1930 US Indian Census as living with Mary (O-gah-bay-bah-kah-Co-nah-o-quay, age sixty, full blood), at Kathio, Mille Lacs, included her daughter Jennie Mitchell (thirty-one). There are two Tom Skinaways of Ojibwe background in Minnesota during this period. In 1923 Tom (Mun-e-do-be-zhe-kee, born about 1868), married to Mary (born about 1870) and father of Jennie Mitchell (born about 1899), was listed in the US Indian Census as a member of the Removable Mille Lac Mississippi Chippewa living at Cass Lake. The other Tom Skinaway (O-shing-aun-ah-quod, born about 1873) was married to Lucy (Naynahcowege Shigoquay, born about 1874); their son Edward was born in 1900. Lucy and Tom Skinaway were listed as Removable Mille Lac Mississippi Chippewa at White Earth on the US Indian Census, June 30, 1929.

21. Additional historic images of Tom Skinaway, husband of Mary, include Reserve Album 243, p. 119 (1926), E97.1S r5 (c. 1925, wearing 10000.609), E97.38 r8 (c. 1925, wearing 10000.609), E97.1S r4 (1928, wearing 10000.366), E97.37 r4 (1928). In E97.37 r62 (c. 1925), Tom wears an unidentified bag and stands with Harry Ayer. Several other images show partial views of him wearing a gashkibidaagan.

22. *Mille Lacs Messenger,* July 9, 2013 (obituary).

23. "End of an Era," *Mille Lacs Messenger,* November 3, 1999.

24. "Fort Mille Lacs Indian Village," *Mille Lacs Messenger,* November 10, 1999.

25. Holbert interviews; Holbert papers; *Mille Lacs Messenger,* November 10, 1999. The Sherman Holbert collection of over two hundred photographic images was made primarily by him and his associates. It also includes examples made by his grandmother Sherman, a professional photographer, in the late nineteenth and early twentieth centuries. The images document Holbert's early maple syrup, wild rice, and commercial tourist businesses and more fully his Fort Mille Lacs Indian Village on the shore of Mille Lacs Lake. The collection includes individuals/portraits, clothing, housing, wild ricing, maple sugaring, canoe building, wigwam construction, dance programs for tourists, and various Indian crafts. Of the bags in his sales brochures, eleven were spot-stitch appliqué (one with the folded leaf motif), one had a loom-woven strap and spot-stitch appliqué pocket, and one was entirely decorated with loom-woven panels.

26. Lyford, *Ojibwa Crafts,* plate 144, shows a motif very similar to fruit motifs in the strap element of 2002.259.4. What seems to be a cropped version of the image of Shewap is shown in *Mille Lacs Messenger,* November 10, 1999, p. 24. The 1880 US Census lists a John Shawab at Princeton, Minnesota, born about 1870 to Benjamin and Helen Shawab of Princeton, Mille Lacs, Minnesota. A Mrs. John Shawab of Mille Lacs, c. 1940, appears in MNHS E97.1S r18.

27. An 1892 photograph (HE2.3 r62) made by Darwin Hall is labeled, "On the road from Mille Lacs Lake to Mora. Captain C. H. Beaulieu, Mr. Potts, the driver, Shawab, an Indian."

28. In the 1910 US Indian Census, Maude was six years old and living with Margaret, who was seventy-four, born about 1846, at Crow Wing County, Bay Lake Township, Minnesota. In the 1920 US Census, Maude is listed as married to Martin Kegg, Bay Lake.

29. US Indian Census, 1928, lists Batiste's father, Me-zhe-show-e-ge-shig (Dick Gahbow), born about 1879, and her mother, Pe-dway-way-quay or Bedwagquey, as born about 1882.

30. Plains Art Museum, *Aazhoniingwa'igan.* In this video, which features Maude and Ellen Olson, the Ojibwe word Maude used for bandolier bag sounded like gashkibidaagan.

31. Sam oral history interview (Anderson, 1997).

32. More than two hundred schools and districts are using the Ojibwe Shoulder Bag Kit in the classroom, and over seven thousand students decorate their own bags each year. Many of the schools are in Minnesota, but some are as far away as Alaska, Washington, DC, Alabama, and Canada. Matt Horstman, personal communication.

33. Regan, "Cheryl Minnema Beads Her Way"; Minnema interviews; CherylMinnema.com.

Notes to Chapter 11

1. For Red Lake history, see http://www.redlakenation.org; http://mn.gov/indianaffairs/tribes_redlake.html; Treuer, *Warrior Nation,* 341–43.

2. On Bad Boy, see Jackson, *Descriptive Catalog,* 10.

3. Other MNHS bags with netted fringe include 1520, 1826, and 1978.

4. Reverend Father Thomas Borgerding was the pastor at St. Mary's from 1888 to 1923, so the image must date from no earlier than October 1888; see "Red Lake and White Earth Mission list," St. John's Abbey Archives.

5. For an example of Spears's advertisements, see *Red Lake News,* February 15, 1915.

6. The ongoing conflict regarding "dances," both among the clergy and between them and the Ojibwe, must have been more complex than can now be guessed. The annual celebration at White Earth was over a decade old, and there were dances at Red Lake, Mille Lacs, and throughout the general Cass Lake area. Yet Gilfillan's remarks in 1886 indicate a distaste for the practice and a complete lack of understanding of the cultural role of this activity: "There is something about dancing, that as the Indian clergymen say, takes the moral fibre out of the Indian's heart and demoralize[s] him utterly. The dance is the devil's very instrument to destroy in them what God has been building up. . . . The Cass Lake Indian settlement where Rev. John Coleman is, has also suffered from the scourge of dancing the past winter." Gilfillan, "Indian Notes," 2.

7. Wilcox and West, *A Pioneer History of Becker County,* 253. John English was a policeman at Red Lake and was part of the 1909 delegation to Washington, DC, on treaty grievances and claims against the government. Mary Warren English, one of three sisters of the Ojibwe historian William Whipple Warren, was an important source for Frances Densmore's ethnographic work at White Earth; Brenda Child, "Introduction," in Densmore, "Uses of Plants," reprinted as *Strength of the Earth,* viii.

8. On the love apple, see Hall and Kretsinger, *Romance of the Patchwork Quilt,* 106–7. For other love apple motifs, see MNHS 1498, 1826, 1983.81.1, 1990.502.5, 2005.193.1, 2011.208.148, 2011.208.151, 2011.208.153, 2011.208.154, 2011.208.159, 10000.158, 10000.159. A George Brunette, born in Minnesota in 1868 and probably the same as George Burnette, is listed as a "half breed" on National Archives, RG 75, Entry 364, "Treaty of April 12, 1864, Red Lake and Pembina Half-Breeds," Scrip Stubs, available at http://www.maquah.net/Historical/Scrip/list.html.

9. On John Strong's family, see David Thorstad, "Sad Legacy of Moose Dung."

10. Berg, "Agents of Cultural Change," 167. Berg's article includes a second image (MNHS N5.9 r14) that shows the same girls and gashkibidaaganag that are in Figure 11.15. That image, provided by the Archives of St. John's Abbey, is dated 1910 and is identified as the Children's Band, Drexel Indian School, White Earth; there is no clear way to reconcile the disparity in the dates. The school was opened in 1878 and closed in 1945.

11. Photographer Ole Alex Holm of Holm Studio identified Figure 11.17 as being taken of local band members in Jadis Township. Holm moved his business back and forth between Roseau and Jadis between 1894 and 1915.

12. Lawrence, *Alone with the Past,* 32, 35–45, 156, 221.

13. Reed's display in the Indian Arts Building at the Panama-California Exposition in San Diego, 1915–16, focused on American Indians of the southwest, but it included a spot-stitch appliqué bag (see Beltrami County Historical Society BCHS-1309; published in Lawrence, *Alone with the Past,* 156). His photos were used in Halesia Foster's booklet *Mille Lacs: Where Nature Reigns,* which provided highly romanticized comments on Ojibwe people while justifying the taking of their land. The booklet is undated, but it features Reed's "The Moose Call" (1908) and "The Pathfinders" (originally titled "The Pass Finders," 1912).

Notes to Chapter 12

1. For White Earth history, see http://whiteearth.com/history.html and http://mn.gov/indianaffairs/tribes_whiteearth.html. White Earth, never the historical homeland of any Ojibwe group, was established to become the home of all of the Ojibwe and Dakota in the state. Not all bands, however, wanted to give up their own reservation and move onto a single new reservation. Mississippi Band members from Gull Lake were the first group to move to White Earth Village in 1868. The 1920 census reflected those who had moved to White Earth: 4,856 were from the Mississippi Band including 1,308 from Mille Lacs, the Pillager Bands had 1,218, Pembina Band 472, and 113 had come from Fond du Lac of the Superior Band. Towns associated with the reservation include Callaway, Ogema, Mahnomen, White Earth, Naytahwaush, Beaulieu, Ponsford, Waubun, and Elbow Lake.

2. Densmore, "An Ojibwa Council Fire." Figure 12.01 was acquired by the MNHS with the E. A. Bromley collection.

3. On the founding of the celebration, see "June 14, 1915: Senator Clapp will be present: A Big Time Expected," *The Tomahawk,* June 3, 1915, p. 1; "Forty-Eight Years Ago Yesterday: Chippewas Settled Upon This Reservation: Event Now Being Celebrated as Usual," *The Tomahawk,* June 15, 1916, p. 1. In the latter article, a portrait of Clement Beaulieu carries a caption saying, "Clement H. Beaulieu, who aided Rev. Johnson Enmegahbowh to organize the first 14th of June Celebration in June 1873." Enmegahbowh was credited with inaugurating the Fourteenth of June celebration as early as 1903, and for decades following, whenever a large history of the celebration was part of the annual newspaper coverage. No doubt a portion of the extraordinary popularity of this June celebration in an isolated location in western Minnesota was due to the same appeal of Indians performing in their "natural environment," as promoted by the Wild West shows popular at this time. However, the White Earth celebration was started for different reasons, was very well attended but was only occasionally economically successful, and existed primarily as a participatory and commemorative event, with limited staged "performances." In about 1920, it appears that the phrase "and Pow Wow" was added to its name.

4. "Red Men Celebrating," *Minneapolis Tribune,* June 15, 1900, p. 3; "White Earth Indian Celebration Is Like a Picture of Prehistoric Days," *Minneapolis Morning Tribune,* July 1, 1917, p. 12. On the Bowery dance, see http://www.encyclopediadubuque.org. Bowery dances are often listed in programs for the Annual Celebrations or mentioned in reviews published shortly after the events. See, for example, "The Celebration," *The Tomahawk,* June 20, 1918, p. 8.

5. See, for example, "21st Anniversary Celebration," *The Progress,* June 8, 1889, [p. 4]; "Annual Celebration," *St. Paul*

Globe, June 16, 1896, p. 5; "Indian pow wow," *Winona Republican Herald,* June 20, 1904, p. 2; "White Earth Reds Hold Grand Pow Wow," *St. Paul Globe,* June 21, 1903, p. 28; "Thirty-Eighth Anniversary Celebration," *Little Falls Herald,* June 8, 1906, p. 3. An article in the *Minneapolis Sunday Tribune,* June 21, 1914, p. 15, uses "pow wow" in the headline and content of the article, also mentioning celebration or annual powwow descriptors later in the text.

6. "Indians on White Earth and Red Lake Reservations," *Minneapolis Tribune,* August 26, 1900, p. B2; "May-Zhuck-Ke-Ge-Shig—Lowering Day," *The Chippeway Herald,* April 1904; "White Earth Indian Reservation," *The Chippeway Herald,* May-June 1909; "Indians' Pow-Wow Brings Hundreds to White Earth," *Minneapolis Journal,* June 15, 1914; "The Celebration," *The Tomahawk,* June 20, 1918, p. 8. The same "White Earth History" was repeated annually in the newspaper coverage, and some photographs were re-used, but there was also original reporting of speeches by politicians, chiefs, and guests, descriptions of events, and general commentary before and after the event.

7. Maryhill Museum of Art accession files for 1981.4.6 includes correspondence with donors and descendents.

8. For an image of his traveling photo car at the Annual White Earth Celebration, c. 1910, see MNHS E97.37 r107.

9. These bags in MNHS collections all have some sort of association with White Earth: 163.E32.B, 258.E54, 262.E58.2, 268.E64, 272.E68, 285.E81, 8014.1, 10000.714, 1976.37.5, 1982.67.9, 1990.502.5, 1990.506.5.A,B, 1993.260.10, 1995.95.2, 1995.95.3, 2003.159.1, 2011.208.145, 2011.208.160.

10. Bancroft, *Book of the Fair,* 812–13.

11. Women's Auxiliary Board correspondence and reports, 1892–93, in Minnesota, Board of World's Fair Managers, World's Columbian Exposition Records. In acquiring the Indian objects from Becker County Industries, the auxiliary sought assistance from US Indian agent Charles A. Ruffee and Captain Charles Beaulieu. Theodore H. Beauliou (Beaulieu), a White Earth community member, participated in the process to develop the exhibits. The exposition representative who negotiated the exhibit was George N. Lamphere. Nothing further was learned about the Becker County Indian Industries.

12. Minnesota Board of World's Fair Managers, *Final Report,* 28, 77, 137, 140. The Woman's Auxiliary Board submitted a list of articles purchased with state funds that included "2 silk portiers, Indian school work" and "22 articles Indian exhibit" for a total of $274. See also Jewett to D. A. Monfort, April 10 and April 21, 1893, in Women's Auxiliary Board correspondence, World's Columbian Exposition Records.

13. Some of the bead artists I interviewed suggested that this may have been intended to be a "woman's bag."

14. Anderson, "Treasures for the Millennium," 455–57.

15. Stafford King papers; Stafford King photograph collection. The photo collection includes snapshots of King at his induction at White Earth or a later event. Twenty-one images document King and others wearing beadwork (see I.287.81-.94 and .96-.102).

16. Figure 11.15 shows Ojibwe women wearing gashkibidaaganag with pocket motifs similar to the one seen on the collar of the velvet smoking jacket. For other bags with pockets employing motifs perhaps inspired by this early example, see MNHS bags 10000.156, 10000.159, 1995.46.16, 1978.23.3, 526.E151, 521.E146.2; NMAI 2/7346.

17. On Hall, see *Olivia Times,* February 27, 1919 (obituary); data provided by Hall attached to the 1916 portrait of him by Lee Studios, MNHS por 3172 Lee 1; White, *We Are at Home,* 54–55, 59. An obituary of Hall's wife, Mary, noted that "Mr. Hall is very well known here, and is very popular among the members of this reservation, and many of them will no doubt feel that his sorrow is also theirs": *The Tomahawk,* October 26, 1916. On the move to White Earth, see also Doerfler, *Those Who Belong.* For a photograph of Hall in Washington with the delegation, see MNHS E97.51 p8.

18. *Olivia Times,* February 27, 1919.

19. Whipple, *Lights and Shadows,* 48, 173–74.

20. On Whipple, see Casagrande and Ringheim, *Straight Tongue*; Anderson and Laskey, "American Indian Art in the Whipple Collections." MNHS and SMM hold about five hundred Whipple objects; twenty-one of them are gashkibidaaganag. See MNHS bags 1496, 1498, 1520, 1825, 1826, 1827, 1829, 1830, 1831, 1844, 1978, 7418.7; SMM bags A79:4:65, A79:4:66, A79:4:67, A79:4:68, A79:4:69, A79:4:70, A79:4:71, A79:4:72, A79:4:73, A79:4:74. In 2011 Tilly Laskey and I created a website that pulls together the two institutional collections; see http://www.inhonorofthepeople.org.

21. Sophia Smith, Sophia Larush (La Roche) Smith, a member of the Minnesota Chippewa Tribe, White Earth allotment, was born 1853 or 1863 and was married sometime prior to 1873. The 1910 US Census lists her as forty-seven years old and living in Red Lake. See also http://www.inhonorofthepeople.org/people/sophia-smith-sophia-larush-smith-laroche.

The MNHS holds nine copies of the portrait shown in Figure 12.23 (DAR 1451C, Collection III.40.74 Copy 1–Copy 9). The reverse side of each of the ten includes a white sticker with catalog information and a description printed in ink, all in the same hand, that reads "Mrs. Fred Smith (and) Bishop Whipple's Last Fire Bag." The handwriting on the sticker labels and in the description on each card back appears to be the same. In addition, on the front of print III.40.74, Copy 5, written in script in pen and ink, is "Last Fire Bag made for Bishop Whipple, by Sophia, full blood Chippewa, wife of Rev. Fred Smith, finest mat and beadworker at White Earth." This appears to be the original inscription and is the source of the historical data found on the back of each of the copies. The front of the card stock is imprinted with "N. E. Grantham, Detroit City, MINN." Grantham, listed with the alternate name of "Mrs. N. B. Grantham" in the Directory of Minnesota Photographers (http://www.mnhs.org/people/photographers/), operated in the 1890s and 1900s. Her studio took other significant images now in the Whipple collection, including those of Fred Smith, Enmegahbowh (John Johnson), and Buskisigan. Another Grantham image (MNHS

Collection III.40.75) pictures Sophia holding the gashkibidaagan and wearing a white dressing sacque or combing jacket over the clothes she wears in the other image. The photo was probably taken just before or shortly after Whipple's death in 1901. The taking of the portrait and the number of surviving prints suggest that Sophia and her work were highly regarded. What use Whipple or others may have intended for the images remains a mystery. Why various keepers of these photographs over the last century retained multiple copies is also curious. Whatever the original intention, the image remains one of the most significant and extraordinary documents known of these material culture objects.

Sophia's tape lace collar may have been made at one of the Episcopal mission Indian lace schools first established in Minnesota in 1893; it is not very high. The bodice sleeves, in a style dating to the early 1900s and known as a "bishop sleeve," are fairly loose and fitted at the arms, but with fullness at the wrist. Her cinched waist is at the natural waistline, not the high waist seen about 1907–09. The belt buckle style also suggests the earlier date: McShannock and Morehouse personal communications.

22. US Department of the Interior, "'Open House' Red Lake Reservation"; Gilfillan, *Domestic Missions,* 1–4, 547–56; Gilfillan, "The Spirit of Missions," 2. Frederick Willis Smith appears on US Census, 1910, microfilm roll T624_690, p. 11A.

Rarely do we get the name of a historic bag maker, and even less often may we get a glimpse of her personal life. In 1880 Bishop Whipple remarked that on a visit to Red Lake, "A hearty welcome greeted us, and all fatigues are soon forgotten at the Christian home of Rev. Fred Smith, whose wife is a model Indian housewife. Every nook and corner of the house is neat—the floors are white, the beds clean—food, however plain, well cooked—and such berries!"; see Whipple, "The Indian Country," 4.

In 1886 Reverend Gilfillan recorded sad news on another visit to Red Lake that "Rev. Fred Smith has sustained a grief in losing two of his children this past winter; one a lovely daughter, a young woman who had been at school in Philadelphia, and one an infant. Grace sustains him and his wife under these trials": Gilfillan, "Indian Notes."

23. A fourth bag, held in a private collection, may be by the same hands.

24. Gilfillan. "Ojibways in Minnesota," 74. Various documents on Charette are available by searching his name at maquah.net. Charette's name is spelled in numerous ways in printed and photographic records, including Wainchemadub, Wenje-madub, Wenji-mada, Wenpinadub, "Moves from where he sits," Chief Joseph Charette, Joseph Charrette, Joe Charette, Joe Critt, Joseph Sharette, Jr., Crett, and Krett. He is buried in St. Columba's Cemetery at White Earth.

25. Diary, 1916, p. 1, Stocker papers.

26. For examples at MNHS, see E97.1W r34 (ca. 1897), E97.51 p8 (1899), E97.51 m1, E97.51 m2, E97.5 h1 (1903), E97.1m p11 (ca. 1905), E97.1W r23 (1907), E97.1W p2 (1910), MN2.7F/r170 (1914). For examples at the Smithsonian, see NAA INV 06132100, NAA INV 06132200 (1896), NAA INV 06154700, NAA INV 06154800 (1899), NMAI N27539 (1906). A photo of Charette taken at White Earth between 1906 and 1912 (MNHS Collection I.364.13) shows Charette wearing an extraordinary beaded collar and a floral spot-stitched gashkibidaagan.

27. In 1908 De Lancy Gill also made a portrait of Joe Broad (Gah-Gos-Sha-De-Bay), another White Earth Band member wearing a spot-stitch appliqué bag with a full-width pocket opening (BAE GN 00539A1 06145600). Broad wears the same bag in MNHS E97.1G p3, a photo taken by Robert G. Beaulieu in 1915.

28. [Gilfillan], "Archdeacon Gilfillan."

29. Scrapbook, 1872–98, p. 42–45, Gilfillan papers.

30. Gilfillan, "Ojibways in Minnesota," 101–2.

31. Ailport interviews; Ailport video oral history, 2010.

Bibliography

Interviews and personal communications

Ailport, Ivy. Interview by Marcia G. Anderson, 2010.

Bowe, Leah. Personal communications, 2013–16.

Favorite, Andrew. Interview by Marcia G. Anderson, 2010.

Holbert, Sherman. Interviews by Marcia G. Anderson, 1995–2002.

Kegg, Maude. Interview (with Batiste Sam) by Marcia G. Anderson and Kathy Hussey-Arntson, Onamia, MN, 1982.

Killy, Monroe. Interview by Bonnie Wilson, Minneapolis, January 15, 1987. Transcript in Minnesota Photographers Oral History Project. Minnesota Historical Society.

———. Personal communications and interviews by Marcia G. Anderson, Minneapolis, September 3, 2008, and October 9, 2009.

Libertus, Ron. Interview by Marcia G. Anderson, St. Paul, MN, July 13, 2009.

Losh, Melvin. Interviews by Marcia G. Anderson at Bena, Leech Lake, and Ponemah, MN, Summer 2009, February 25, 2010, March 26, 2010, April 26, 2010, Summers 2012 and 2014.

McIntire, Marcie. Interviews by Marcia G. Anderson, Grand Portage and St. Paul, MN, multiple interviews since the late 1980s, Summer 2009, Summer 2013.

McShannock, Linda. Personnal communication, December 15, 2006.

Minnema, Cheryl Benjamin. Interview by Marcia G. Anderson, Milaca, MN, 2007, Summer 2009, June and September 2014.

Mitchell, Sally. Interview by Anthony Godfrey, Vineland, MN, November 8, 1991. Mille Lacs Indian Trading Post Oral History Project. Minnesota Historical Society.

Morehouse, James. Personal communication, December 22, 2006.

Niingaabii'anook (Gerri Howard). Interview by Marcia G. Anderson, 2011.

Olson, Ellen. Interviews by Marcia G. Anderson, Grand Portage, MN, 2009–14.

Raske, Vicky L. Interviews by Marcia G. Anderson, Grand Portage, MN, 2000–2015.

Sam, Batiste. Interview (with Maude Kegg) by Marcia G. Anderson and Kathy Hussey-Arntson, Onamia, MN, 1982.

———. Oral history, Onamia, MN, 1997. Marcia G. Anderson, interviewer. Videotape. Minnesota Historical Society.

Shingobe, Julie. Interview by Anthony Godfrey, August 5, 1992. Oral History Interviews of the Mille Lacs Ojibwe Social History Project. Minnesota Historical Society.

Wedll, Don. Personal communications, St. Paul and Garrison, MN, 2008, 2015.

Williams, Neva Munson. Interview by Marcia G. Anderson, Deerwood, MN, October 3, 2009.

Wilmott, Cory. Personal communication, 2015.

Manuscript collections

Ayer, Harry Darius. Harry D. Ayer and family papers, 1787–1982. Minnesota Historical Society.

Bardon, John A. John A. Bardon papers, 1845–80, 1935. Minnesota Historical Society.

Cass Lake Centennial Souvenir Photograph Packet. St. John's Abbey Archives, Collegeville, MN.

Colby, Pauline. Reminscences and related materials, 1931?, 1937, 1944. Minnesota Historical Society.

Durfee, W. R. Ledger sheet, Superior, WI, August 16, 1869. John A. Bardon papers, Minnesota Historical Society.

Gilfillan, Joseph A. Joseph A. Gilfillan and family papers, 1872–1940. Minnesota Historical Society.

Heath, Albert Green. Albert Green Heath Collection. Logan Museum of Anthropology, Beloit College, Beloit, WI.

Holbert, Sherman. Sherman Holbert and family papers, 1888–2005. Minnesota Historical Society.

Indian Crafts of the Episcopal Church in Minnesota. Organizational Records, 1952–77. Minnesota Historical Society.

King, Stafford. Papers, 1898–1969. Minnesota Historical Society.

Minnesota. Board of World's Fair Managers. World's Columbian Exposition Records, 1884–85, 1891–94. Minnesota Historical Society.

———. *Final Report of the Minnesota Board of World's Fair*

Managers. [St. Paul?: The Board, 1894].
Stocker, Stella Prince. Papers. Kathryn A. Martin Library Archives and Special Collections, University of Minnesota Duluth.
Whipple, Henry Benjamin. Henry B. Whipple papers, 1833–1934. Minnesota Historical Society.

Newspapers

Bemidji Pioneer
Chippeway Herald (White Earth, MN)
Duluth Herald
Mille Lacs Messenger
Minneapolis Journal
Minneapolis Morning Tribune
Nahgahchiwanong Dibahjimowinnan (Cloquet, MN)
Olivia Times
St. Paul Globe
The Tomahawk (White Earth, Becker County, MN)
Winona Daily Republican

Books, articles, exhibits, pamphlets

Abrams, M. H., and James Ackerman. *Theories of Criticism: Essays in Literature and Art.* Occasional papers of the Council of Scholars. Washington, DC: Library of Congress, 1984.
Albinson, Elmer. Grand Portage motion picture footage, c. 1940–49. Minnesota Historical Society.
———. *My Chippewa Home Revisited: National Monument Site, Grand Portage, Minnesota.* Motion picture featuring Ellen Bushman [Olson] and her daughter Shelly, 1982[?]. Copy at Minnesota Historical Society.
Anderson, Marcia G. "Selections from the Bishop Whipple Collection of American Indian Art." Exhibition. Minnesota Historical Society, 2008.
———. "Treasures for the Millennium." *Minnesota History* 56 (Winter 1999–2000): 452–58.
Anderson, Marcia G., and Kathy L. Hussey-Arntson. "Ojibwe Bandolier Bags in the Collections of the Minnesota Historical Society." *American Indian Art Magazine* 11 (1986): 46–57.
———. "Ojibway Beadwork Traditions in the Ayer Collections." *Minnesota History* 48 (Winter 1982): 153–57.
Anderson, Marcia G., and Tilly Laskey. "American Indian Art in the Bishop Henry Benjamin Whipple Collections." Paper presented at Native American Art Studies Association Conference. Oklahoma City, OK, 2009.
———. "In Honor of the People." Website created 2011. http://www.inhonorofthepeople.org/ (accessed 2016).
Bancroft, Hubert Howe. *The Book of the Fair.* Chicago, San Francisco: Bancroft Company, 1893.
Barbeau, Marius. *Assomption Sash.* Department of Mines and Resources, National Museum of Canada. Bulletin 93, Anthropologoical Series No. 24, 1972.
Barsh, Russell Lawrence. "An American Heart of Darkness: The 1913 Expedition for American Indian Citizenship." *Great Plains Quarterly* 13 (Spring 1993): 91–115.
Bauer, Julia. "125-year-old Tanglefoot Company of Grand Rapids sold to Contech Enterprises of Canada." *Mlive.com.* October 28, 2009. http://www.mlive.com/business/west-michigan/index.ssf/2009/10/125-year-old_tanglefoot_compan.html (accessed March 5, 2014).
Berg, Carol J. "Agents of Cultural Change: The Benedictines at White Earth." *Minnesota History* 48 (1982): 158–70.
Blessing, Fred K. "Contemporary Costuming of Minnesota Chippewa Indians." *Minnesota Archaeologist* 20 (October 1956): 1–8.
Brady, Tim. "The Real Story of the Chippewa National Forest." *Minnesota Conservation Volunteer* (November–December 2004): 22–30.
Brower, Jacob V. *Mille Lac.* St. Paul: [H. L. Collins Company,] 1900.
Burleson, H. E. "White Earth." *The Young Christian Soldier* (1902): 107.
Casagrande, Louis B., and Melissa M. Ringheim. *Straight Tongue: Minnesota Indian Art from the Bishop Whipple Collections.* St. Paul: Science Museum of Minnesota, 1980.
Cass Lake Commercial Club. "Cass Lake 'The Permanent Home of the Pine': An Eye-full of Cass Lake." [Cass Lake, MN]: The Club, [c. 1920].
Coleman, Sister Bernard M. *Decorative Designs of the Ojibwa of Northern Minnesota.* Catholic University of America Anthropological Series No. 12. Washington, DC: Catholic University of America Press, 1947.
———. *Where the Water Stops: Fond du Lac Reservation.* Duluth, MN: College of St. Scholastica, 1967.
Corbiere, Alan. "Anishinaabe Headgear: Symbolic, Linguistic and Cultural Meanings." *American Indian Art Magazine* 37 (2012): 38–47.
"Crazy Patchwork: All the New Fancy Stitches Illustrated and Plain Instructions for Making the Patchwork." *PieceWork Magazine* (March/April 1998): 98.
Culkin, William E. "Tribal Dance of the Ojibway Indians." *Minnesota History Bulletin* 1.3 (August 1915): 83–93.
Danziger, Edmund J., Jr. "They Would Not Be Moved: The Chippewa Treaty of 1854." *Minnesota History* 43 (1973): 175–85.
Densmore, Frances. *Chippewa Customs.* Smithsonian Institution Bureau of American Ethnology Bulletin 86. Washington, DC: Government Printing Office, 1929. Reprint: St. Paul: Minnesota Historical Society Press, 1979.
———. *Chippewa Music.* Smithsonian Institution Bureau of American Ethnology Bulletin 46. Washington, DC: Smithsonian Institution, 1910.
———. "An Ojibwa Council Fire." *The Indian School Journal* (December 1906): 21.
———. "State History Convention Speech." *Minnesota History* 21 (September 1940): 284–93.
———. "Uses of Plants by the Chippewa Indians." In *Forty-Fourth Annual Report of the Bureau of American Ethnology.* Washington, DC: Government Printing Office, 1928. Reprint: *The Strength of the Earth: The Classic Guide to Ojibwe Uses of*

Native Plants. St. Paul: Minnesota Historical Society Press, 2006.

Doerfler, Jill. *Those Who Belong: Identity, Family, Blood, and Citizenship among the White Earth Anishinaabeg.* East Lansing: Michigan State University Press, 2015.

Dubin, Lois Sherr. *North American Indian Jewelry and Adornment: From Prehistory to the Present.* New York: Harry N. Abrams, Inc., 1999.

Emery, Irene. *The Primary Structures of Fabrics: An Illustrated Classification.* Washington, DC: The Textile Museum, 1980.

Ewers, John C. "Three Ornaments Worn by Upper Missouri Dandies in the 1830s." In J. C. Ewers, *Indian Life on the Upper Missouri.* Norman: University of Oklahoma Press, 1968.

Feest, Christian. "The Native American Collection I of Friderik Baraga: Comparative and Contextual Aspects." Available at Researchgate.net; republished from *Etnolog* (Ljubljana) 8.59 (1998): 285–311.

Feest, Christian F., and Sylvia S. Kasprycki. *Peoples of the Twilight: European Views of Native Minnesota, 1823 to 1862.* Afton, MN: Afton Historical Society Press, 1999.

Forbes, Mrs. A. S. C. "Lace Making by Indian Women." *Out West: A Magazine of the Old Pacific and the New* 16 (June 1902): 613–16.

Foster, Halesia Sperry. *Mille Lacs: Where Nature Reigns.* Minneapolis: Foster & Williams, n. d.

Frederickson, N. Jaye. *The Covenant Chain: Indian Ceremonial and Trade Silver.* Ottawa: National Museums of Canada, 1980.

Garte, Edna. "Circle of Life: Cultural Continuity in Ojibwe Crafts." Exhibition at the Depot St. Louis County Heritage and Arts Center, Duluth, MN, 1984.

Gilfillan, Joseph A. "Agricultural Fair at White Earth." *Minnesota Missionary* 3.1 (October 1879).

———. *Domestic Missions: The Indian Deacons at White Earth.* [N.p., 1880?]

———. "from The Spirit of Missions." [Typescript, 1874.] Joseph Alexander Gilfillan Papers. Minnesota Historical Society.

———. "History of the Indian Missions in Minnesota." *Church Review* (October 1885): 547–56.

———. "Indian Notes." *Minnesota Missionary* (May 1886): 2.

———. "The Ojibways in Minnesota." *Collections of the Minnesota Historical Society* 9 (1901): 55–128.

[Gilfillan, S. C.] "Archdeacon Gilfillan; His Life and Work." *The Red Man* (December 1913): 158–60.

Gilman, Carolyn. "Collection with a Mission: Frances Densmore's Chippewa Artifacts." In Joan Jensen and Michelle Wick Patterson, eds., *Travels with Frances Densmore: Her Life, Work, and Legacy in Native American Studies.* Lincoln: University of Nebraska Press, 2015.

———. *The Grand Portage Story.* St. Paul: Minnesota Historical Society Press, 1992.

Gittinger, Mattiebelle. *Master Dyers to the World: Technique and Trade in Early Indian Dyed Cotton Textiles.* Washington, DC: The Textile Museum, 1982.

Grand Rapids Public Museum. *Beads: Their Use by Upper Great Lakes Indians.* Grand Rapids, MI: The Museum, 1977.

Grimes, John R., Christian F. Feest, and Mary Lou Curran. *Uncommon Legacies: Native American Art from the Peabody Essex Museum.* New York/Seattle: American Federation of Arts/University of Washington Press, 2002.

Hail, Barbara A., and Kate C. Duncan. "Out of the North: The Subarctic Collection of the Haffenreffer Museum of Anthropology." *American Anthropologist* 93 (June 1991): 528–29.

Hall, Cary A., and Rose G. Kretsinger. *The Romance of the Patchwork Quilt in America.* Caldwell, ID: Caxton Printers, 1935.

Hilger, M. Inez. *Chippewa Child Life and Its Cultural Background.* Smithsonian Institution Bureau of American Ethnology Bulletin 146. Washington, DC: Government Printing Office, 1951.

———. *Chippewa Families: A Social Study of White Earth Reservation.* St. Paul: Minnesota Historical Society Press, 1998. First published as *A Social Study of One Hundred Fifty Chippewa Indian Families of the White Earth Reservation of Minnesota.* Washington: Catholic University of America, 1939.

Hingley, Rev. Joseph B. "The Visit to the Pagan Indians." *Northwestern Christian Advocate* 55 (September 4, 1907): 12–13.

Hoelscher, Steven D. *Picturing Indians: Photographic Encounters and Tourist Fantasies in H. H. Bennett's Wisconsin Dells.* Madison: University of Wisconsin Press, 2008.

Hoffman, Walter James. "The Menomini Indians." In *Fourteenth Annual Report of the U.S. Bureau of Ethnology.* Washington DC: Government Printing Office, 1896.

———. "The Mide'wiwin or 'Grand Medicine Society' of the Ojibwa." *Seventh Annual Report of the US Bureau of Ethnology.* Washington, DC: Government Printing Office, 1891.

Hussey-Arntson, Kathy. "Report on the Jeannette and Harry Ayer Collections." Minnesota Historical Society, Museum Collections, 1982.

Jackson, William Henry. *Descriptive Catalogue of the Photographs of the United States Geological Survey of the Territories, for the Years 1869 to 1873, Inclusive.* Washington, DC: Government Printing Office, 1874. Reprint: Emereo Publishing, 2012.

James, Carol. *Sprang Unsprung: An Illustrated Guide to Interlinking, Interfacing and Intertwining.* N.p.: Carol James Sashweaver, 2011.

Jensen, Joan, and Michelle Wick Patterson, eds. *Travels with Frances Densmore: Her Life, Work, and Legacy in Native American Studies.* Lincoln: University of Nebraska Press, 2015.

Johnson, Tim, ed. *Spirit Capture: Photographs from the National Museum of the American Indian.* Washington, DC: Smithsonian Institution Press, 1998.

Jones, Rev. Peter (Kahkewaquonaby). *History of the Ojebway Indians; with Especial Reference to their Conversion to Christianity.* London: A. W. Bennett, 1861.

Jones, Tom, et al. *People of the Big Voice: Photographs of Ho-Chunk Families by Charles Van Schaick, 1879–1942.* Madison: Wisconsin Historical Society Press, 2011.

Jorgensen, Ruth J. *The Story of Herb Nyquist: White Man Indian.* N.p.: 1976.

Kohl, Johann Georg. *Kitchi-Gami: Life Among the Lake Superior Ojibway.* London: Chapman and Hall, 1860. Reprint: St. Paul: Minnesota Historical Society Press, 1985.

Kugel, Rebecca. *To Be the Main Leaders of Our People: A History of Minnesota Ojibwe Politics, 1825–1898.* East Lansing: Michigan State University Press, 1998.

Lace Made by North American Indians. Pamphlet, June 1904. Copy in the collections of the Cooper Hewitt, Smithsonian Design Museum, New York.

Langley, S. P. *Report of S. P. Langley, Secretary of the Smithsonian Institution, for the Year Ending June 30, 1903.* Washington, DC: Government Printing Office, 1903.

Lawrence, Ernest R. *Alone with the Past: The Life and Photographic Art of Roland W. Reed.* Afton, MN: Afton Press, 2012.

Lonetree, Amy. *DeColonizing Museums: Representing Native America in National and Tribal Museums.* Chapel Hill: University of North Carolina Press, 2012.

Lindblad, Owen, OSB. *Full of Fair Hope: A History of St. Mary's Mission, Red Lake, Minnesota.* St. Joseph, MN: Park Press Quality Printing, 1997.

Lundquist, Monica. "Melvin Losh: Reviving a Tradition." *PieceWork Magazine* (November/December 1994): 74–81.

Lurie, Nancy Oestreich. *Wisconsin Indians: Revised and Expanded Edition.* Madison: Wisconsin Historical Society Press, 2002.

Lyford, Carrie A. *Ojibwa Crafts.* Washington, DC: US Department of the Interior, 1943. Reprint: Stevens Point, WI: Richard C. Schneider, Publishers, 1982.

Markusen, Ann, and Marcie Rendon. *Native Artists: Livelihoods, Resources, Space, Gifts.* Minneapolis: Humphrey Institute of Public Affairs, University of Minnesota, 2009.

Matsen, William E. "The Battle of Sugar Point: A Re-Examination." *Minnesota History* 50 (Fall 1987): 269–75.

McDuffee, Herbert. "Reminiscences." July 1920. Typescript. Minnesota Historical Society.

McIntire, Marcie. "Anishinabe Beadwork." Student paper. Antioch University, Yellow Springs, OH, March 2000.

Methodist Church. Northern Minnesota Conference. *Official journal of the . . . Session.* Brainerd, MN: Edited and published by the Secretary, [1939?–1947?].

Methodist Episcopal Church. Northern Minnesota Annual Conference. Session. *Official journal of the . . . Session.* Duluth: Thwing-Stewart Co., 1907–[1938?].

Meyer, Diana Lambdin. "Little Spirits on a Thread: Ojibwa Bead-Embroidered Bandolier Bags." *PieceWork Magazine* (March/April 2005): 31.

Mille Lacs Lake Travel Guide. 1942. Copy in Minnesota Historical Society Pamphlet Collection.

Minnesota Historical Society. Directory of Minnesota Photographers. http://www.mnhs.org/people/photographers/ (accessed January 2, 2017).

———. Records Center. Exhibits Department. Mille Lacs Indian Museum Files, 1990–95.

Minnesota Quilt Project. *Minnesota Quilts: Creating Connections with Our Past.* Stillwater, MN: Voyageur Press, Inc., 2005.

Mittelholtz, Erwin F., and Rose Graves. *Historical Review of the Red Lake Indian Reservation, Redlake, Minnesota: A History of Its People and Progress.* Bemidji, MN: Beltrami County Historical Society, 1957.

Montgomery, Florence M. *Textiles in America 1650–1870.* New York: W. W. Norton & Company, 1984.

Moss, Kathlyn, and Alice Scherer. *The New Beadwork.* New York: Harry N. Abrams, 1992.

Nichols, John D., and Earl Nyholm. *A Concise Dictionary of Minnesota Ojibwe.* Minneapolis: University of Minnesota Press, 1995.

Ojibwe People's Dictionary. http://ojibwe.lib.umn.edu/

Orchard, William C. *Beads and Beadwork of the American Indians: A Study Based on Specimens in the Museum of the American Indian, Heye Foundation.* New York: Museum of the American Indian Heye Foundation, 1929. Reprint: Libery, UT: Eagle's View Publishing, 1990.

Orlofsky, Patsy, and Myron Orlofsky. *Quilts in America.* New York: McGraw-Hill Book Company, 1974.

Palmquist, Peter E., and Thomas R. Kailbourn. *Pioneer Photographers from the Mississippi to the Continental Divide: A Biographical Dictionary 1839–1865.* Stanford, CA: Stanford University Press, 2005.

Peacock, Thomas D. *A Forever Story: The People and Community of the Fond du Lac Reservation.* Cloquet, MN: Fond du Lac Band of Lake Superior Chippewa, 1998.

Penney, David W. *Art of the American Indian Frontier: The Chandler-Pohrt Collection.* Seattle: Detroit Insititute of Arts/University of Washington Press, 1992.

Peterson, Jacqueline, and Jennifer S. H. Brown, eds. *The New Peoples: Being and Becoming Métis in North America.* Critical Studies in Native History. Winnipeg: University of Manitoba Press, 1985.

Petrulis, Alan. *Metropolitan Postcard Club of New York City, Guide to Real Photo Postcards.* http://www.metropostcard.com/guiderealphoto.html (accessed 2011).

Picken, Mary Brooks. *The Fashion Dictionary: Fabric, Sewing and Dress as Expressed in the Language of Fashion.* New York: Funk & Wagnalls Company, 1957.

Plains Art Museum. *Aazhoniingwa'igan: Ojibwe Bandolier Bag.* Video recording. Moorhead, MN: The Museum, 1992.

———. *On The Border: Native American Weaving Traditions of the Great Lakes and Prairie: Plains Art Museum.* Moorhead, MN: The Museum, 1990.

Pomedi, Michael. *Living with Animals: Visions and Sounds in Ojibwe Worlds.* Toronto: University of Toronto Press, 2013.

Porter, Duane F. "From the Reverend Duane F. Porter's Notebook." Typescript, c. 1934. Archive, Minnesota Annual Conference of the United Methodist Church, Minneapolis.

Purdham, Charles. *Fragile Starts: A History of United Methodist Ministries among Native American People in Minnesota.* Bloomington, MN: The Author, 1985.

Reagan, Albert B. "The Bois Fort Chippewa." *Wisconsin Archaeologist* 3 (September 1924): 101–32.

———. "Chief Moses Day Daybway-Waindung." *Proceedings of the Indiana Academy of Science* (1917): 519–22.

———. "Plants Used by the Bois Fort Chippewa (Ojibwa) Indians of Minnesota." *Wisconsin Archeologist* 7 (July 1925): 230–48.

Regan, Sheila. "Cheryl Minnema Beads Her Way to Preserving Her Culture." Native American Community Development Institute. April 28, 2010. http://www.nacdi.org/cheryl-minnema-beads-her-way-to-preserving-her-culture/ (accessed January 2, 2017).

Ryan, Carol Crawford. *Star Island: A Minnesota Community.* St. Paul: Pogo Press, 2000.

Safford, Carleton L., and Robert Bishop. *America's Quilts and Coverlets.* New York: Weathervane Books, 1974.

St. John's Abbey Archives. "Red Lake and White Earth Mission list." Finding aid. St. John's Abbey Archives. Collegeville, MN.

St. Mary's Industrial School, Odanah, Wisconsin. *Noble Lives of a Noble Race.* [Minneapolis: Books Press, 1909].

Sandweiss, Martha A. *Print the Legend: Photography and the American West.* New Haven, CT: Yale University Press, 2002.

Schoolcraft, Henry Rowe. *Narrative Journal of Travels Through the Northwestern Regions of the United States.* Albany, NY: E. & E. Hosford, 1821.

Severa, Joan L. *Dressed for the Photographer: Ordinary Americans and Fashion, 1840–1900.* Kent, OH: Kent State University Press, 1995.

Smith, John, and Thomas E. Smith. *Being the Life History of Chief John Smith: As Narrated by Himself and Interpreted by His Adopted Son, Thomas E. Smith.* Walker, MN: The Cass County Pioneer, [1921?].

Sybil Carter Indian Mission and Lace Industry Association. Annual Report, 2008. Copy in Cooper Hewitt, Smithsonian Design Museum, New York.

Tanner, John. *A Narrative of the Captivity and Adventures of John Tanner.* New York: G. & C. & H. Carvill, 1830. Reprint: Minneapolis: Ross & Haines, 1956.

Ten Thousand Lakes Greater Minnesota Association. *The Minnesota Book: Land of Pleasure, Land of Treasure.* St. Paul: The Association, 1929.

Thorstad, David. "The Sad Legacy of Moose Dung and Red Robe." Monthly Review Zine. September 11, 2012. http://mrzine.monthlyreview.org/2012/thorstad091112.html (accessed January 2, 2017).

Treuer, Anton. *Ojibwe in Minnesota.* St. Paul: Minnesota Historical Society Press, 2010.

———. *Warrior Nation: A History of the Red Lake Ojibwe.* St. Paul: Minnesota Historical Society Press, 2015.

Treuer, David R. "The Rhetoric of Reservoirs." *Minnesota History* 53 (Winter 1992): 157–60.

Tucker, Abigail. "Brave New World." *Smithsonian* (December 2008): 48–53.

Ulrich, Laurel Thatcher. *The Age of Homespun: Objects and Stories in the Creation of an American Myth.* New York: Alfred A. Knopf, 2001.

US Department of the Interior. "'Open House' Red Lake Reservation Commemorating a Century of Conservation, 1949." [Red Lake, 1949?]

US Office of Indian Affairs. Indian census rolls, 1885–1940. Microfilm at Minnesota Historical Society.

Vincent, Margaret. *The Ladies' Work Table: Domestic Needlework in Nineteenth-Century America.* Allentown, PA: Allentown Art Museum, 1988.

[Walco Bead Company.] *Indian Bead Craft.* New York: The Company, 1935.

Warner, Mary E. *A Big Hearted Paleface Man: Nathan Richardson and the History of Morrison County, Minnesota.* Little Falls, MN: Morrison County Historical Society, 2006.

Warren, William W. *History of the Ojibway People.* St. Paul: Minnesota Historical Society Press, 1984. Reprint of *History of the Ojibways,* Collections of the Minnesota Historical Society 5 (1885).

Whipple, Henry Benjamin. "The Indian Country." *Minnesota Missionary* (Faribault, MN) 3 (August 1880): 4.

———. *Lights and Shadows of a Long Episcopate: Being Reminiscences and Recollections of the Right Reverend Henry Benjamin Whipple, D.D., LL.D. Bishop of Minnesota.* New York: Macmillan Company, 1899.

White, Bruce. "The Power of Whiteness, or, The Life and Times of Joseph Rolette, Jr." *Minnesota History* 56 (Winter 1998–99): 180–97.

———. *We Are at Home: Pictures of the Ojibwe People.* St. Paul: Minnesota Historical Society Press, 2007.

White, Bruce, et al. "An Ethnographic Study of Indigenous Contributions to the City of Duluth." Duluth, MN: Duluth Indigenous Commission, 2015.

Wilcox, Alvin H., and Mrs. Jesse Campbell West. *A Pioneer History of Becker County, Minnesota.* St. Paul: Pioneer Press, 1907.

Wilmott, Cory. "Anishinaabe Regalia of the Reservation Era, 1870s–1930s." *American Indian Art Magazine* 37 (Summer 2012): 70–81.

Wilson, Bonnie G. "Working the Light: Nineteenth Century Professional Photographers in Minnesota." *Minnesota History* 52 (Summer 1990): 42–60.

Winchell, Newton H. *The Aborigines of Minnesota.* St. Paul: Minnesota Historical Society, 1911.

Index

Page numbers in *italics* indicate illustrations.